AF478006

art editions 1, 1995

Edition Schellmann
Alsdorfer Straße 1-3
D - 50933 Köln
Tel 0221 / 5461028
Fax 0221 / 5461030
**ab September 1995:*
Römer Straße 14
D - 80801 München
Tel. 089 / 331717
Fax 089 / 332800

Edition Schellmann
50 Greene Street
New York, N.Y. 10013
Tel 212 - 219 1821
Fax 212 - 941 9206

ISBN 3-921629-36-5
Printed in Germany

Artists Arakawa Artschwager Arman Armleder Baldessari Baselitz Baumgarten Becher Beuys Bickerton Brown Boltanski Buren Chamberlain Chia Christo Clegg + Guttmann Clemente Cragg Cucchi Darboven De Maria Fischl Flavin Fleury Förg Gilbert&George Gonzalez-Torres Gober Graham Grünfeld Halley Hamilton Haring Heizer Hirst Hockney Holzer Horn Hütte Immendorff Johns Jones Judd Kabakov Kelley Kelly Kienholz Kirkeby Knoebel Komar and Melamid Koons Kosuth Kounellis Lafontaine Lawler/McCollum LeWitt Lichtenstein Long Longo Lüpertz Mangold Mapplethorpe Marden McCollum Merz Merz Mucha Mullican Nauman Oldenburg Paik Paladino Palermo Paolini Penck Polke Prince Rainer Rauschenberg Reinhardt Richter Rollins and KOS Rosen Rosenquist Rückriem Ruff Ruthenbeck Salle Schnabel Serra Sherman Sieverding Simpson Steinbach Stella Tàpies Tuttle Twombly Ungers Vaisman Walther Warhol Weiner West Whiteread Winters Wool Zobernig

Editionen – Stirbt das Original aus?

Natürlich nicht. Aber: Das Kunstwerk hat "im Zeitalter seiner technischen Reproduzierbarkeit" neue Formen angenommen. Und: mehr Bildung und größere ökonomische Freiheit haben Kunst für mehr Menschen erreichbar gemacht, was nicht ohne Rückwirkungen auf die Produktionsmethoden geblieben ist.

Das Medium Druckgraphik bot die Möglichkeit, "Bilder" in Auflage herzustellen und zu verbreiten. Diese Kunstform hat in den sechziger Jahren durch den Wandel der ökonomisichen und soziologischen Bedingungen große Popularität erreicht und – zusammen mit dem Aufkommen des Multiple – einen neuen Markt für Kunst entstehen lassen.

Aber auch die Vorstellung davon, was ein Original ist, hatte sich verändert. Das traditionelle Kunstwerk, von der Hand des Künstlers individuell und einmalig

geschaffen, ist nur noch **eine** Form der Kunstproduktion. Daneben entwickelten sich Arbeitsmethoden, bei denen der Künstler einen Entwurf erarbeitet, dem dann die Ausführung, meist von anderer Hand, etwa einem Handwerks- oder Industriebetrieb, folgt. Die Entstehung solcher Kunstwerke folgt den Schritten: Entwurf, Prototyp, Produktion – Prinzip der industriellen Produktion.
Es lag nahe, anstatt nur einer Ausführung eines Entwurfs mehrere oder viele herzustellen. So existieren Werke zahlreicher Künstler seit den sechziger Jahren in mehreren Exemplaren. Jedes Exemplar ist eine gleichrangige Ausführung des Entwurfs; ein höherrangiges Original gibt es nicht.

Auf den hier erfolgten Untergang des Originals hat die Terminologie des Kunstbetriebes noch nicht reagiert. Nach Entwurf mehrmals hergestellte Werke werden zum Teil als "Bildhauerauflagen", meistens aber einfach als "Originale" bezeichnet. Es wurde daher von uns ein neuer Begriff vorgeschlagen: Werke, die durch Entwurf (des Künstlers) und Ausführung (von anderer Hand) entstehen, sind Unikate, wenn sie einmal ausgeführt werden, es sind **Multikate**, wenn sie mehrmals hergestellt werden.

Editionen heutiger Kunst sind also Druckgraphik, Multiple und Multikat, wobei das Multiple eine Variante des Multikats – vereinfacht, preiswert und in größerer Auflage produziert – darstellt.

Die Edition Schellmann hat neben der Herausgabe von Druckgraphik und Multiples ihr Interesse auf die Herstellung auch von Multikaten gerichtet. Die Ausstellung *Wall Works* 1993/94 in unserer Ausstellungshalle in Köln stellte einen neuen Editionstypus vor: Wandinstallationen in Auflage. Die Entwürfe der Künstler sind am Ort des Käufers von Handwerkern zu realisieren, wobei die unterschiedlichen Orte der Ausführung zu vom Künstler beabsichtigten Varianten der Arbeit führen.

Der vorliegende Angebotskatalog *art editions,* Fortführung der Reihe *graphics 1–5* erschienen von 1980–1991, zeigt neben Druckgraphik und Multiples interessante Beispiele von Multikaten der aktuellen Kunst. Der neue Titel dieser Publikation folgt dem erweiterten Inhalt.

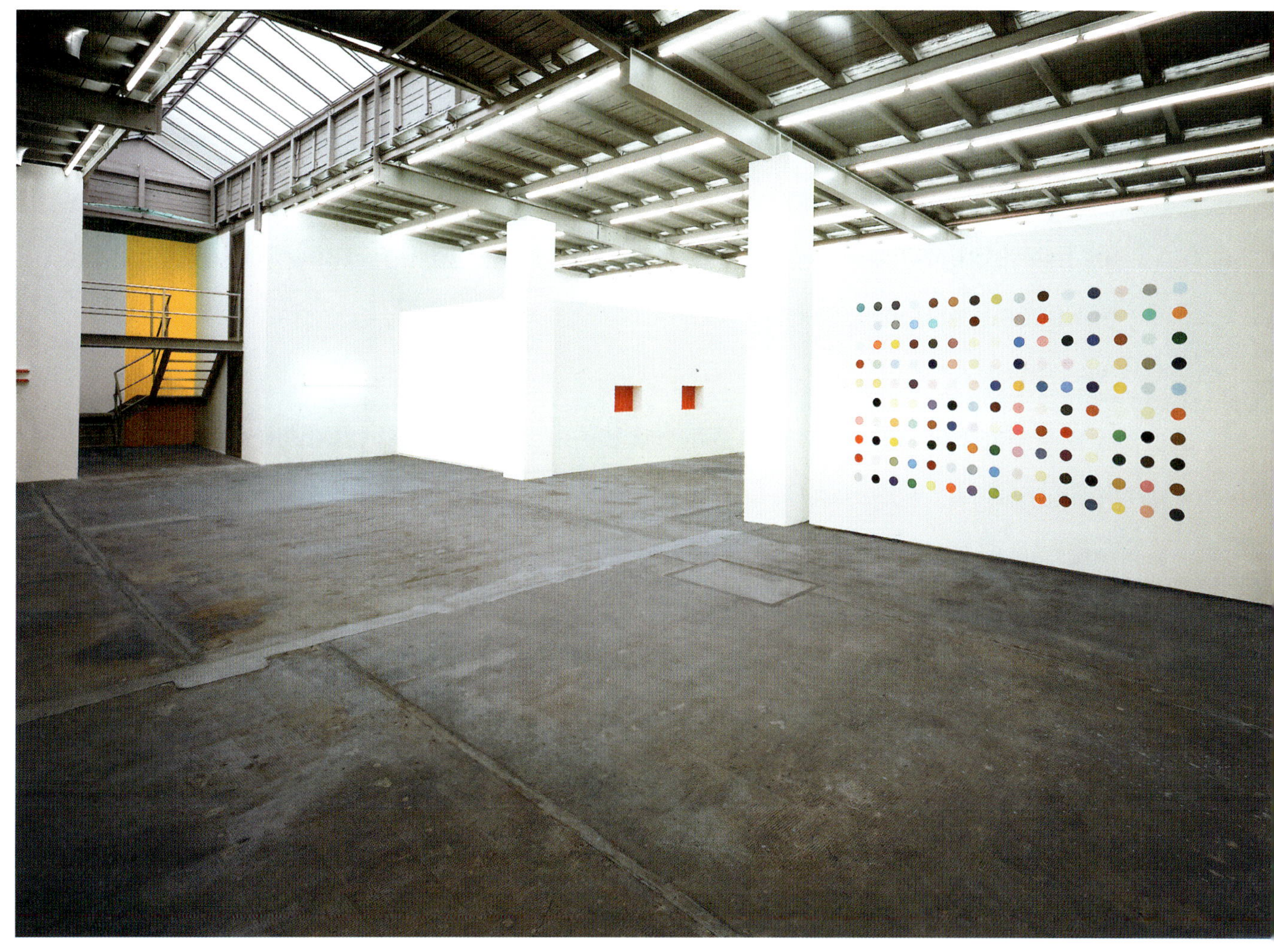

Ausstellung Wall Works *mit Arbeiten von 20 Künstlern (Abb.: Förg, Flavin, Judd, Hirst), Ausstellungshalle Edition Schellmann, Köln 1993*

Editions – Is the Original Endangered?

Of course not. But: In the age of its "mechanical reproduction" the work of art has assumed new shape. And: Due to better education and economical freedom art has become more accessable to a broader public, a fact that has effected the production of contemporary art.

It was the fine art print that offered the opportunity to produce and distribute "pictures" in editions. This medium -- along with the up and coming multiple -- became very popular during the 60ies and has conquered a steadily growing market.

Beyond that, the idea of what an original work of art was, had changed with the art and the market of the sixties. The traditional work of art, created individually by the artist's hand has been only **one** way of producing art. Since then, many artists work outside these parameters. Their art consists of the development of a design or concept whose execution they delegate to other hands: to assistants, or to a workshop or commercial operation. The genesis of work of this type follows the basic paradigm of twentieth-century industrial manufacture -- design, prototype, and production.

This working method offered the option to produce more than one piece from a given concept. Consequently, works of many artist of the 60ies through the 90ies come in more than one example. Each example represents a version of the concept equal in form and value to the next. An original of higher quality does not exist.

The terminology of the art world has not yet responded to the fall of the original in contemporary art of the minimal or conceptual type, or recent movements. As the works concerned are generally and incorrectly marketed as "originals", we would like to suggest new terminology:

Works characterized by the method of conceptional design (by the artist) and execution (by another hand) would be called unique works, if only one version is made, and **multique** works if several examples are made. Thus, prints, multiples, and multique works all represent contemporary art editions.

Besides publishing prints and multiples, Edition Schellmann has also directed its interest in the production of multique works. In the exhibition *Wall Works,* held at our exhibition hall in Cologne in 1993/94, we presented a new type of edition: Wall installations in editions. The concepts of the artists are to be executed on the buyers' walls by professional craftsmen according to the artist's instructions. In the specific case of these wall works, most artists' projects had offered variations to respond to the given architectural setting of the owner of the work.

This new catalogue, *art editions* -- successor of *graphics 1–5*, published from 1980 through 1991 -- features not only prints and multiples, but also interesting examples of multique works in today's art. The new title results from the new contents.

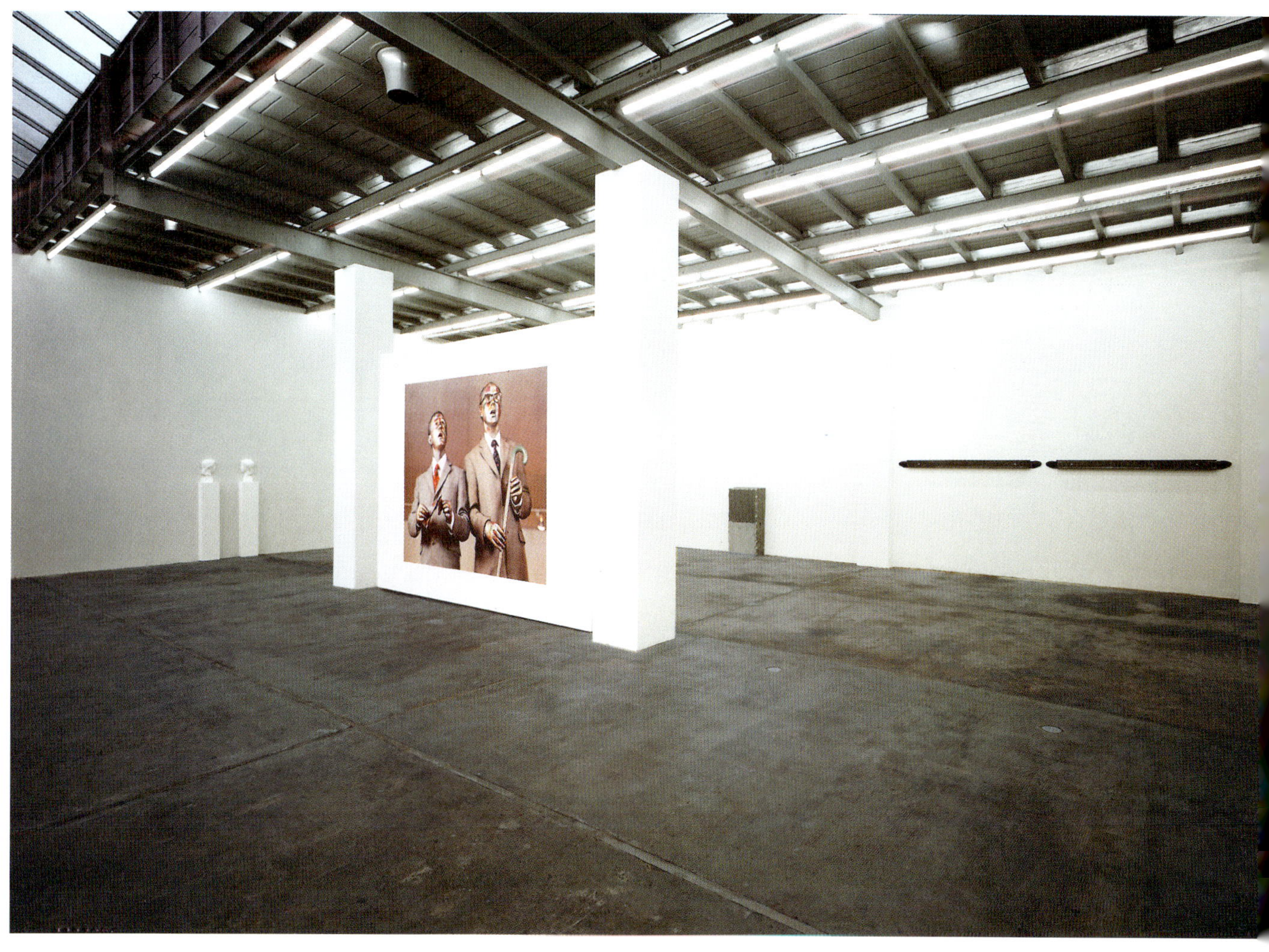

Exhibition Wall Works *with works by 20 artists (ill. Paolini, Gilbert & George, Rückriem, Kounellis), exhibition hall Edition Schellmann, Cologne 1993*

Alle Graphikblätter und Objekte
sind handsigniert und numeriert,
falls nicht anders vermerkt.
Katalognummern gekennzeichnet mit
■ = Eigeneditionen
□ = Vertrieb Edition Schellmann

*All works of art are handsigned
and numbered unless otherwise noted.
Catalog numbers marked with*
■ = *Edition Schellmann publications,*
□ = *distributed by Edition Schellmann*

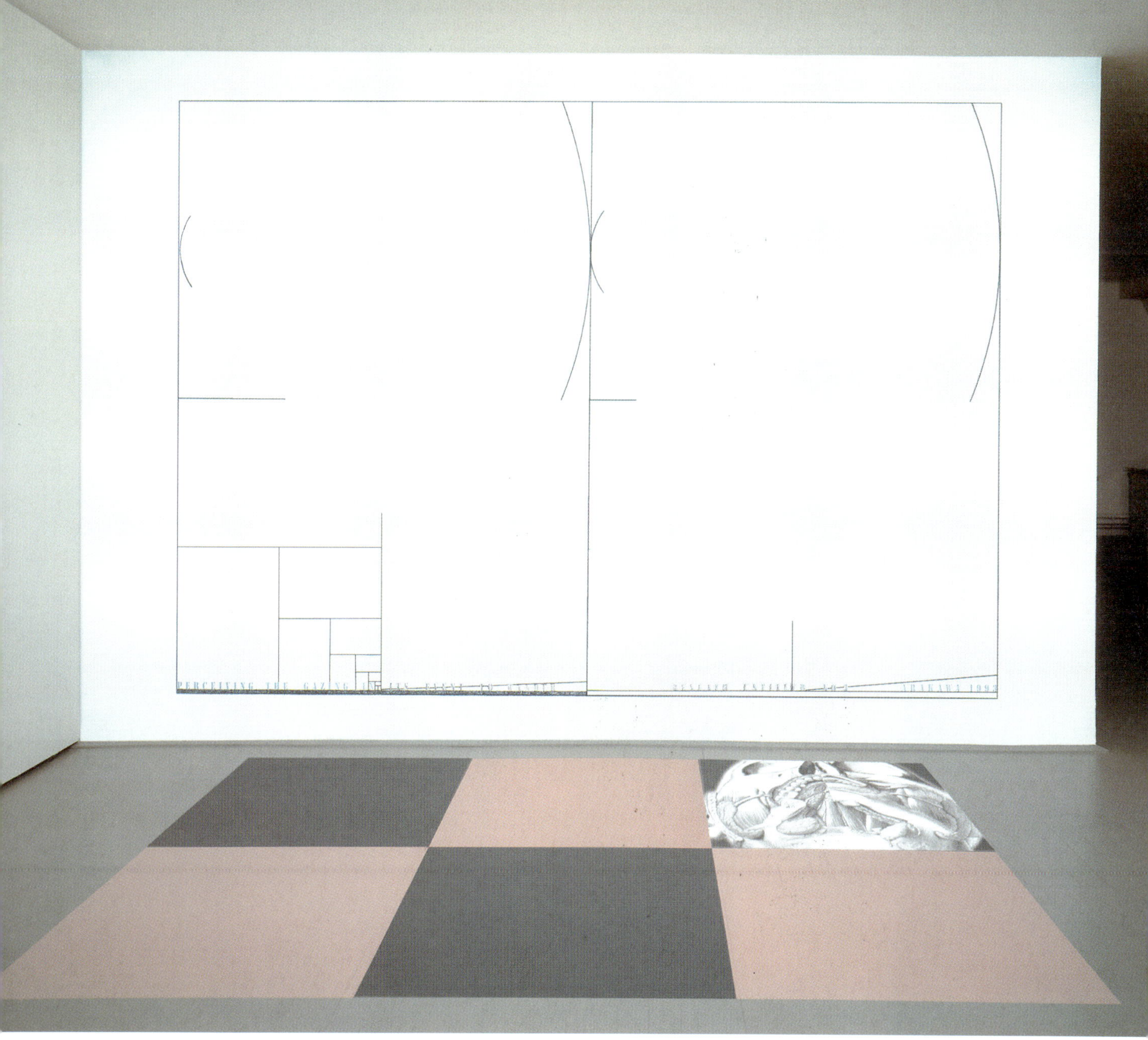

1 Shusaku Arakawa ■
Perceiving the gazing in its event to wander: Beneath Untitled No.3, 1988/93
Wandzeichnung (Graphit); Dispersion und Siebdruck auf Fußboden. Maße variabel. Zu installieren nach den Anweisungen des Künstlers, siehe Appendix. Auflage: 10, mit sign. und num. Zertifikat.
Wall drawing in graphite, floor painting in latex with silkscreen, size of the work variable. To be installed according to the artist's instructions, see appendix. Edition: 10, with a signed and numbered certificate.

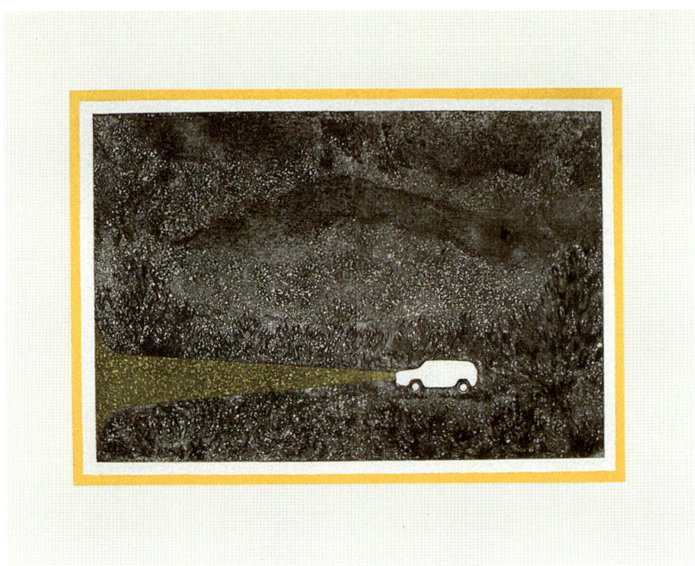

2 Richard Artschwager
Cherokee, 1991
Aquatinta-, Kaltnadel- und
Weichgrundradierung, 100 x 130 cm
Auflage: 60
Aquatint, drypoint and softground etching, 39¼ x 51 in. Edition: 60

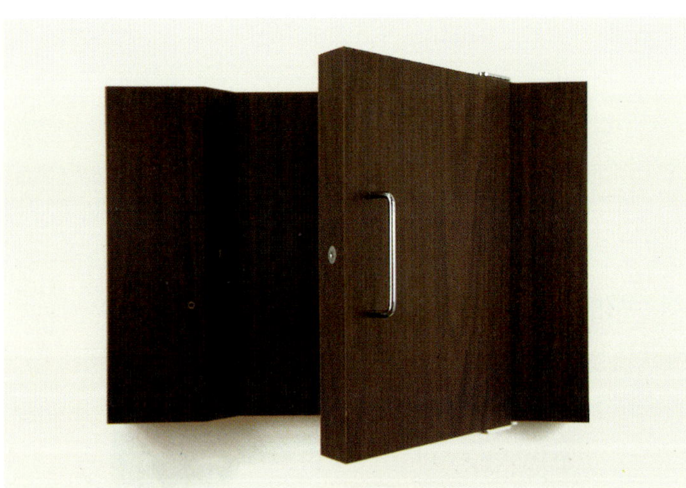

3 Richard Artschwager
Door, 1987
Holz, Resopal-beschichtet,
Metallbeschläge, 45 x 64 x 13 cm
Auflage: 25
Formica, hardware and wood, 17½ x 25 x 5 in. Edition: 25

4 Richard Artschwager ■ →
Corner Splat, 1993
Malerei (Acryl) auf Folie, verschiedene Maße, an einer Wandecke anzubringen.
Auflage: 20 unterschiedliche Varianten. Siehe Appendix.
Painting in acrylic on mylar, different sizes, to be mounted on the wall in or at a corner. See appendix. Edition: 20, each work unique in configuration

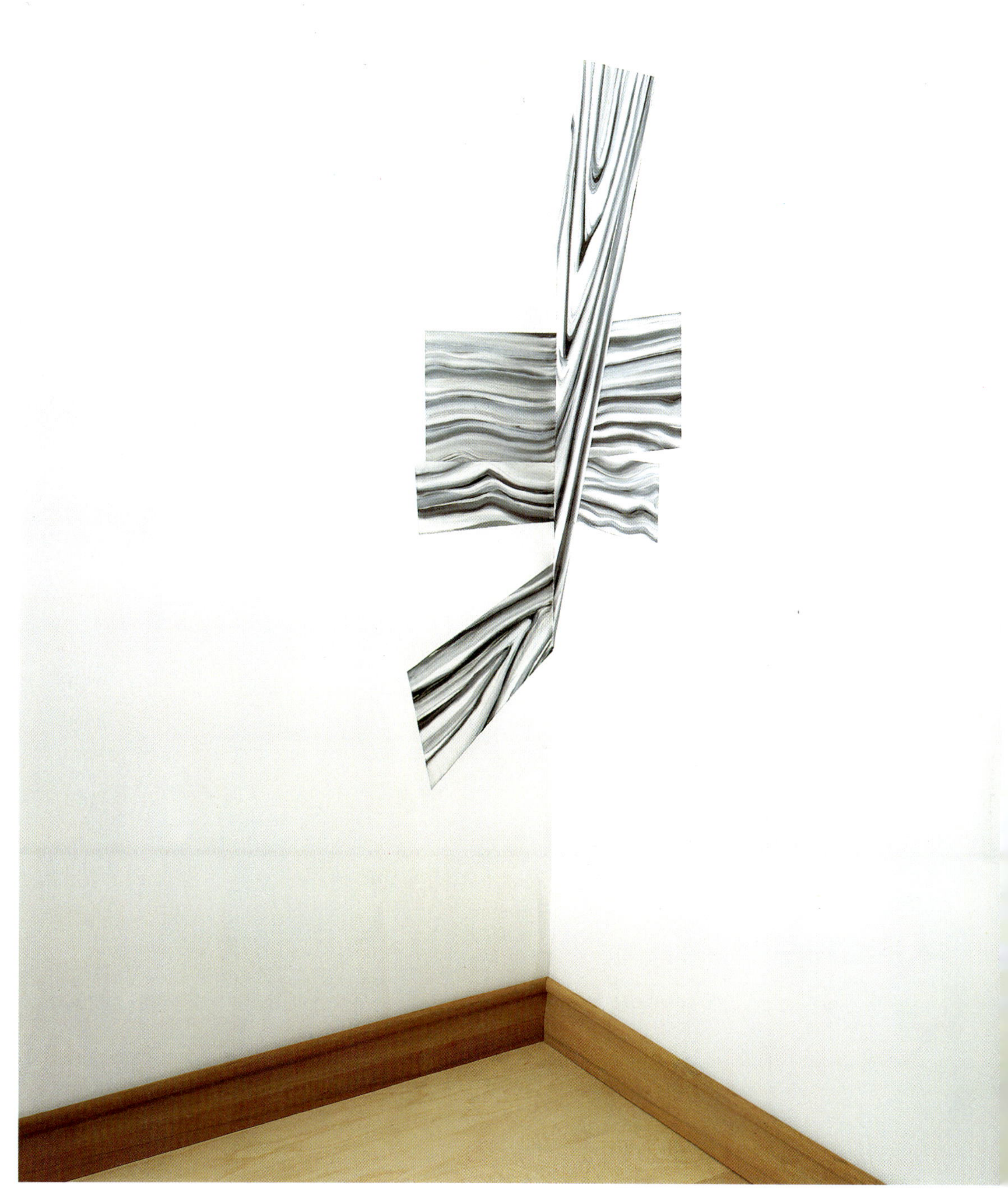

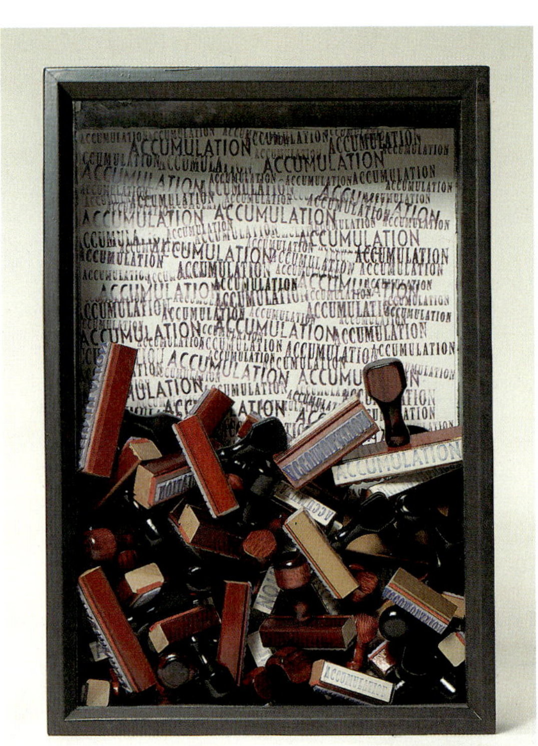

5 Arman ■
Accumulation, 1973
Stempelgraphik und Stempel in Holzkasten,
43 x 30 x 8 cm. Variante (3 Exemplare) einer
Auflage von 100
Stamped print and rubber stamps in wooden box,
17¾ x 11¾ x 3¼ in. Variation (3 copies) of an
edition of 100

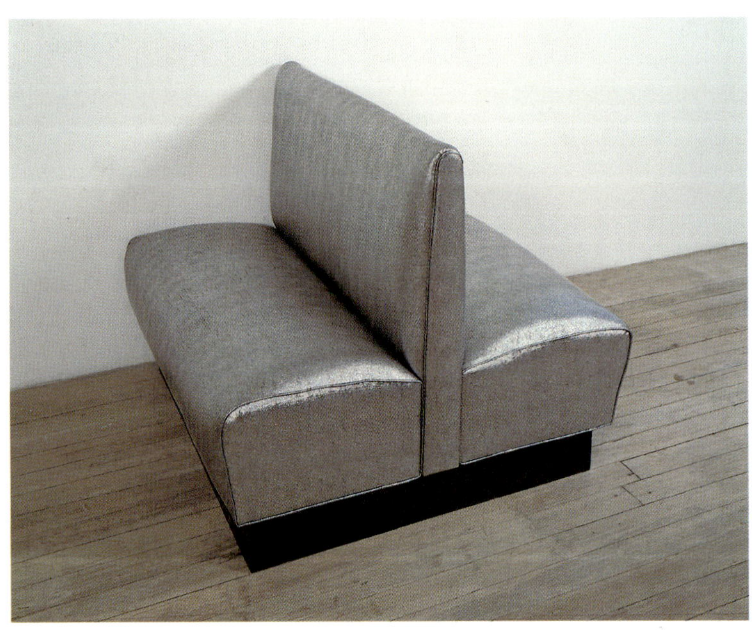

6 John Armleder
Diner Booth, 1988
Diner-Bank, bezogen mit
Kunstsoff (Haifisch-Imitat),
81 x 112 x 117 cm. Auflage: 12
Sharkskin vinyl on double
sided banquette, 32 x 44 x 46 in.
Edition: 12

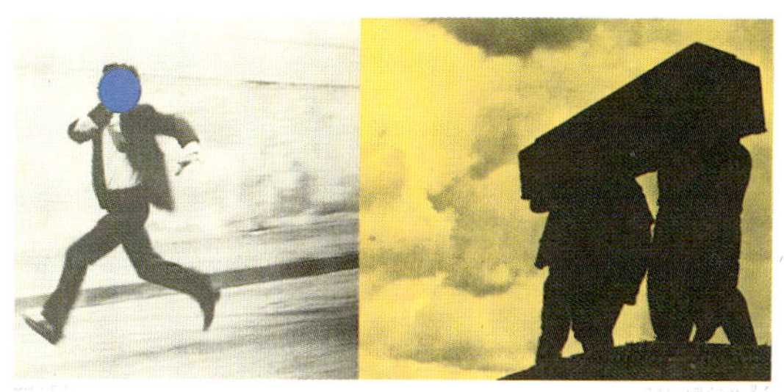

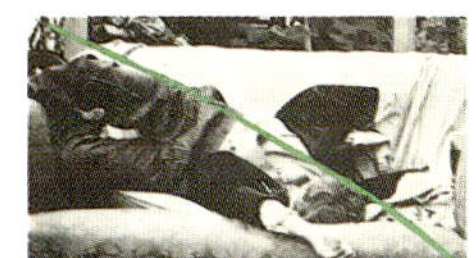

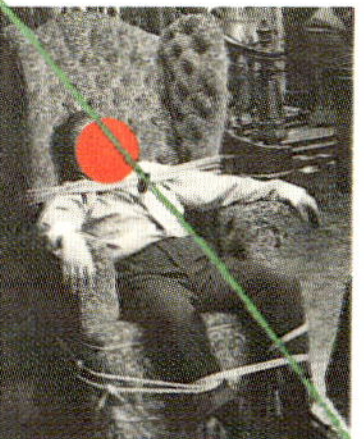

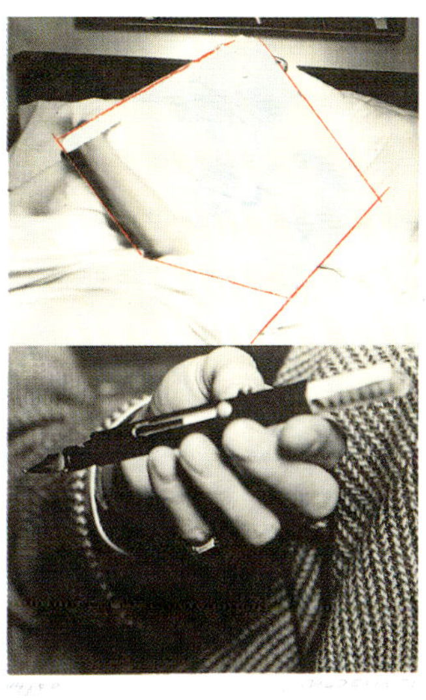

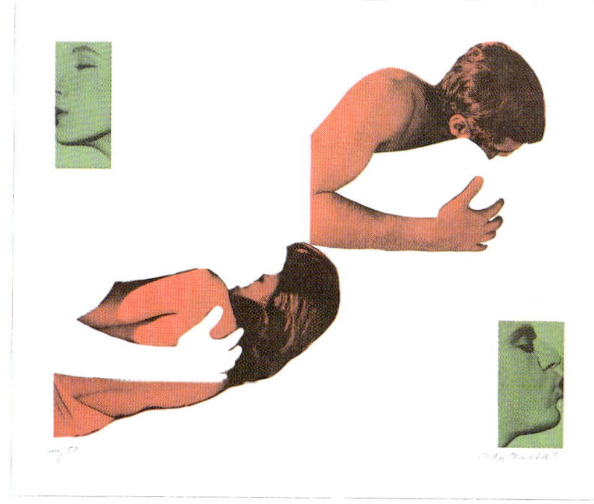

7 John Baldessari
Tristam Shandy, 1988
5 Lithographien und Buch von Laurence Sterne, verschiedene Maße, max. 75 x 58 cm. Auflage: 50
5 lithographs and a book by Laurence Sterne, different sizes, 29½ x 23 in. max. Edition: 50

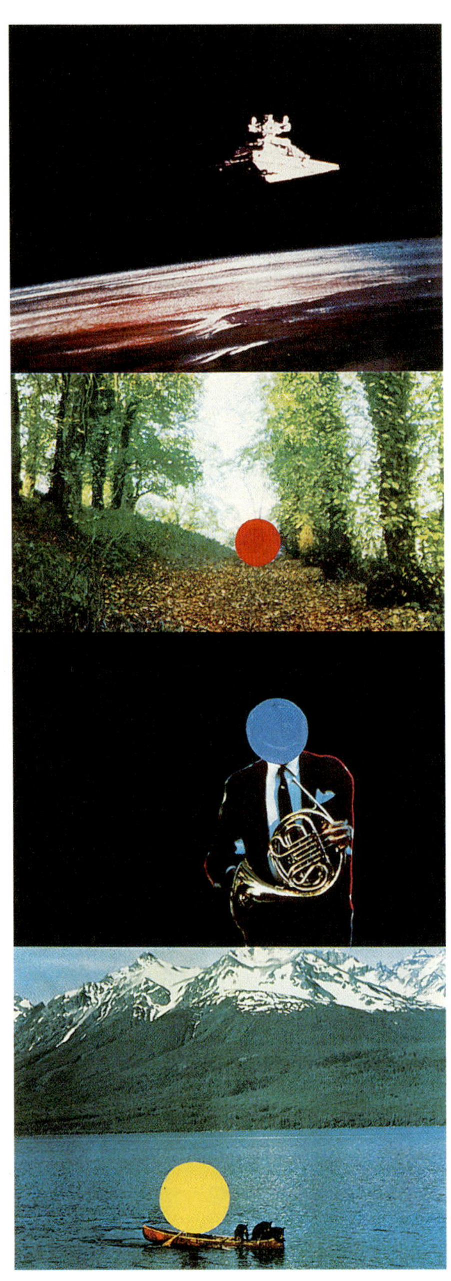

8 John Baldessari
French Horn Player, 1994
Lithographie/Serigraphie, 152 x 56 cm. Auflage: 45
Lithograph/silkscreen, 60 x 22 in. Edition: 45

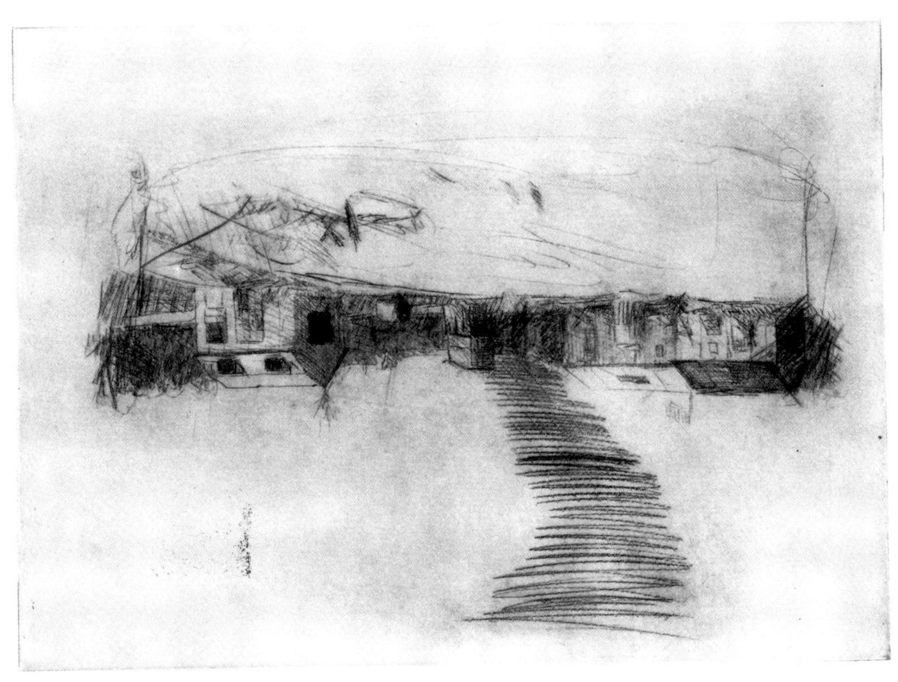

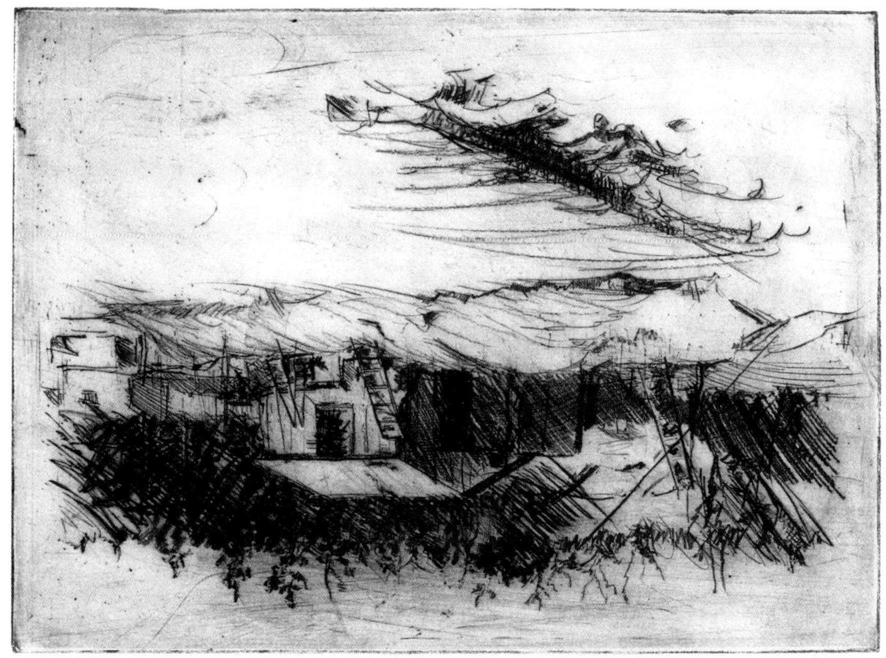

9 Georg Baselitz
Eine Woche, 1972
Mappe mit 7 Kaltnadelradierungen, 36 x 49 cm, auf Bütten 50 x 70 cm. Auflage: 52
Portfolio with 7 drypoints, 14 x 19 in. on BFK Rives 19¾ x 27½ in. Edition: 52

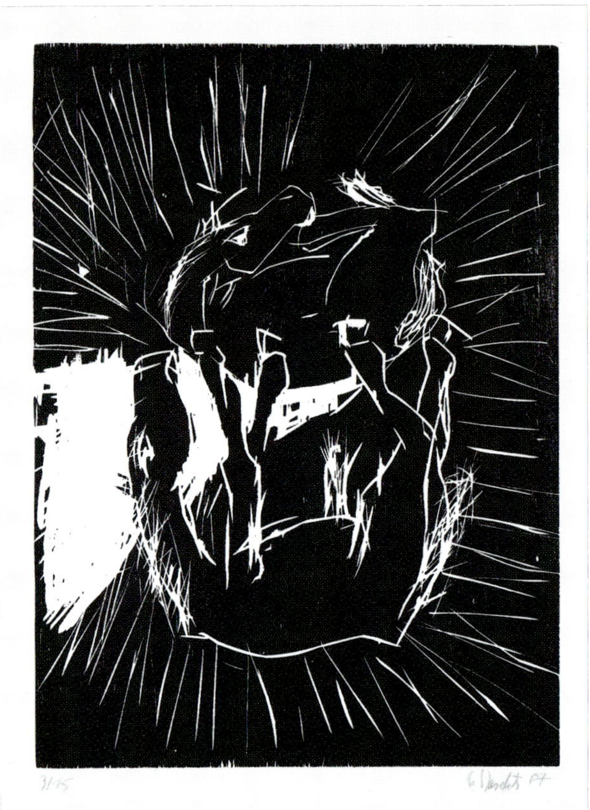

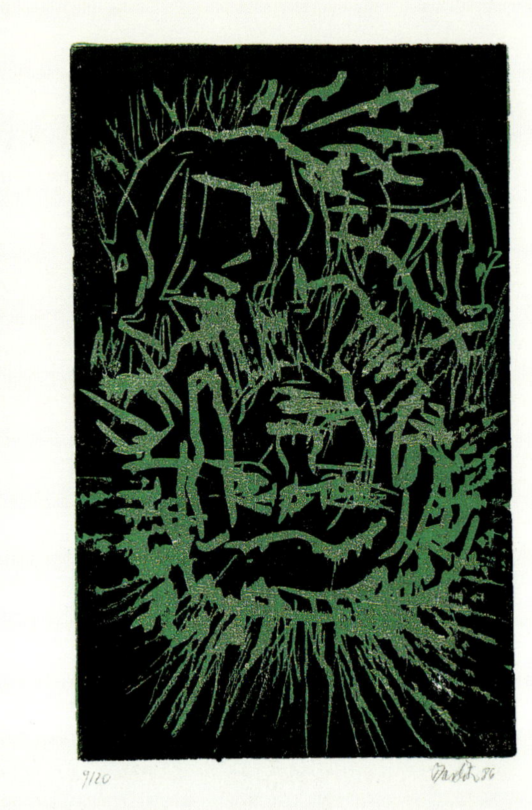

10 Georg Baselitz
Zwei Pferde, 1987
Holzschnitt, 75 x 55 cm. Auflage: 15
Woodcut, 29½ x 21½ in. Edition: 15

11 Georg Baselitz
Richard Wagner als Frau, 1986/87
Holzschnitt auf Japanpapier, 75 x 53 cm. Aufl.: 20
Woodcut on Japanese paper, 29½ x 21 in. Ed.: 20

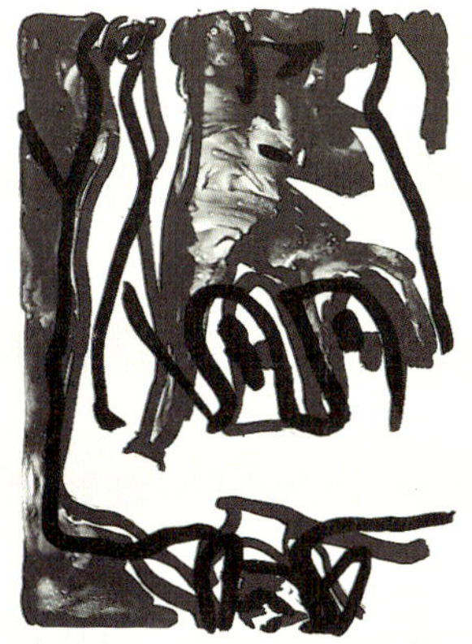

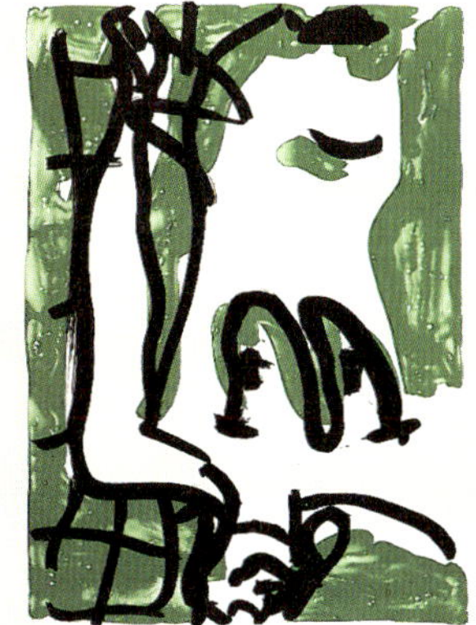

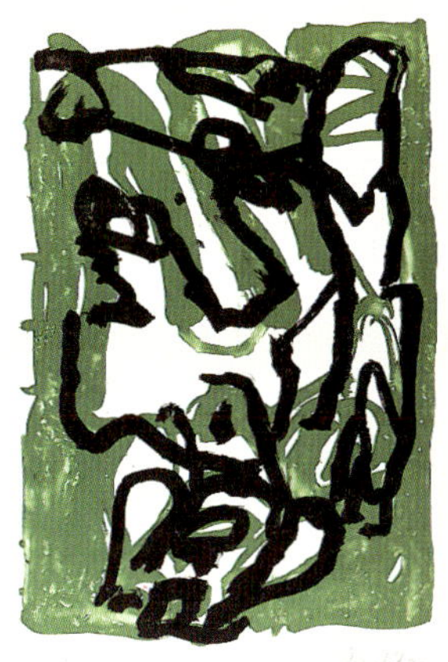

12 Georg Baselitz
3 Lithographien auf Bütten, 1993
a. Rose, 76,5 x 57 cm; *30 x 28½ in.*
b. Lebe, 76,5 x 57 cm; *30 x 28½ in.*
c. Else, 70 x 50 cm; *27½ x 19¾ in.*
Auflage: 15
3 lithographs on rag paper. Edition: 15

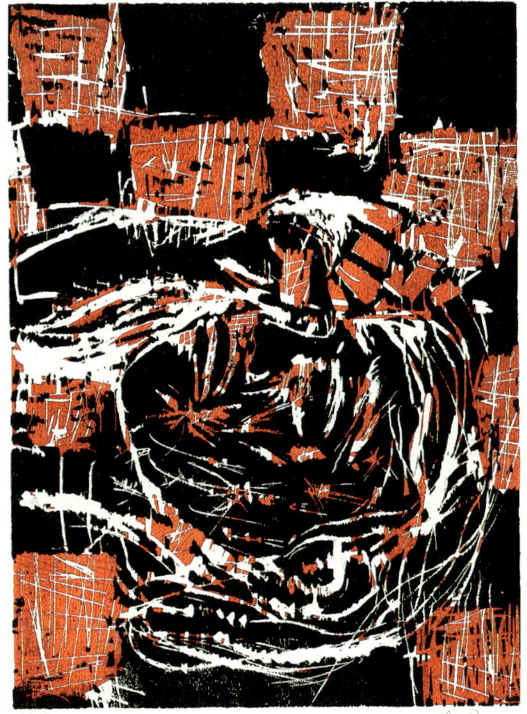

13 Georg Baselitz
Liegender Kopf, 1985/88
Farbholzschnitt, 86 x 61 cm. Auflage: 15
Woodcut, 34 x 24 in. Edition: 15

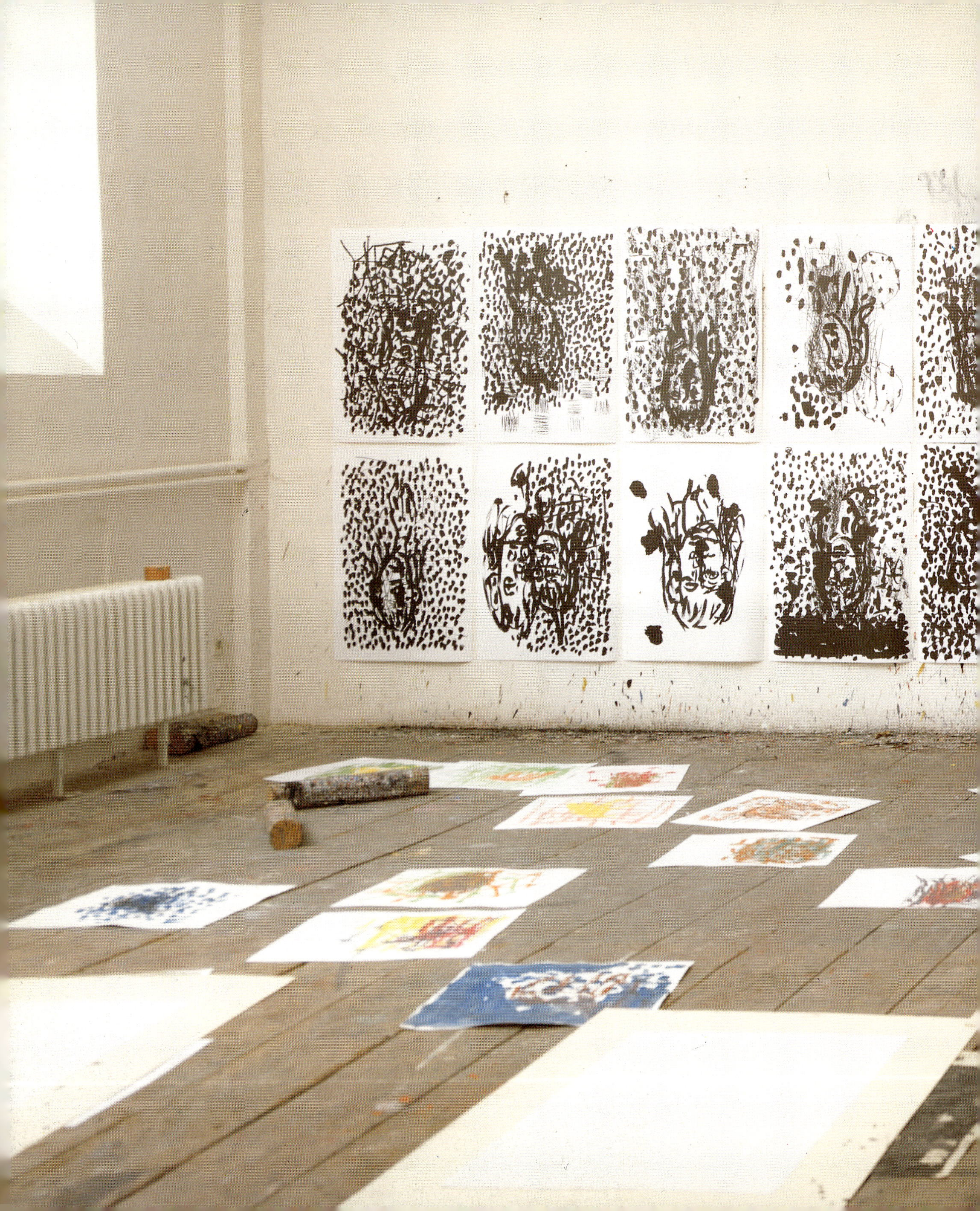

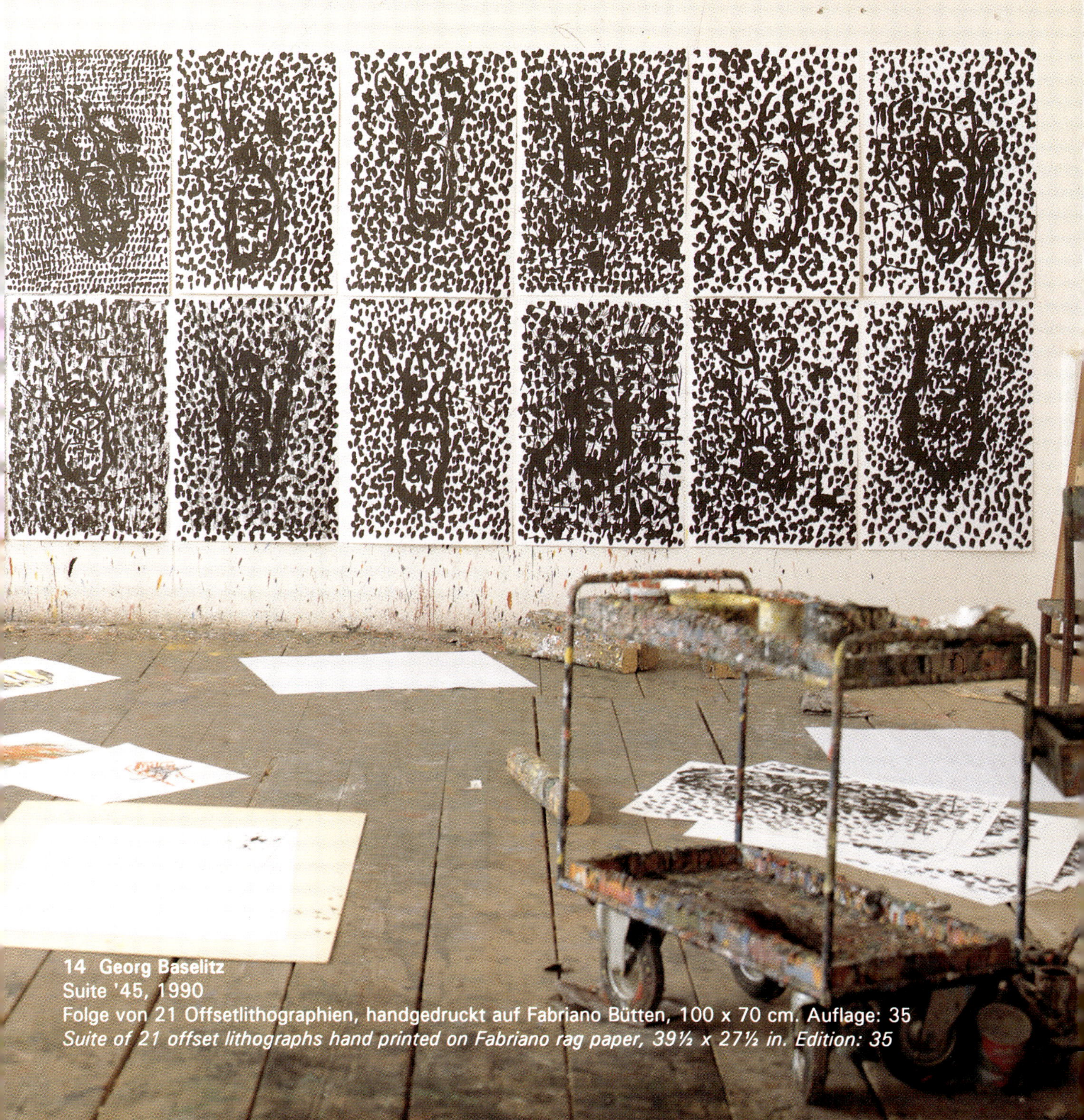

14 Georg Baselitz
Suite '45, 1990
Folge von 21 Offsetlithographien, handgedruckt auf Fabriano Bütten, 100 x 70 cm. Auflage: 35
Suite of 21 offset lithographs hand printed on Fabriano rag paper, 39½ x 27½ in. Edition: 35

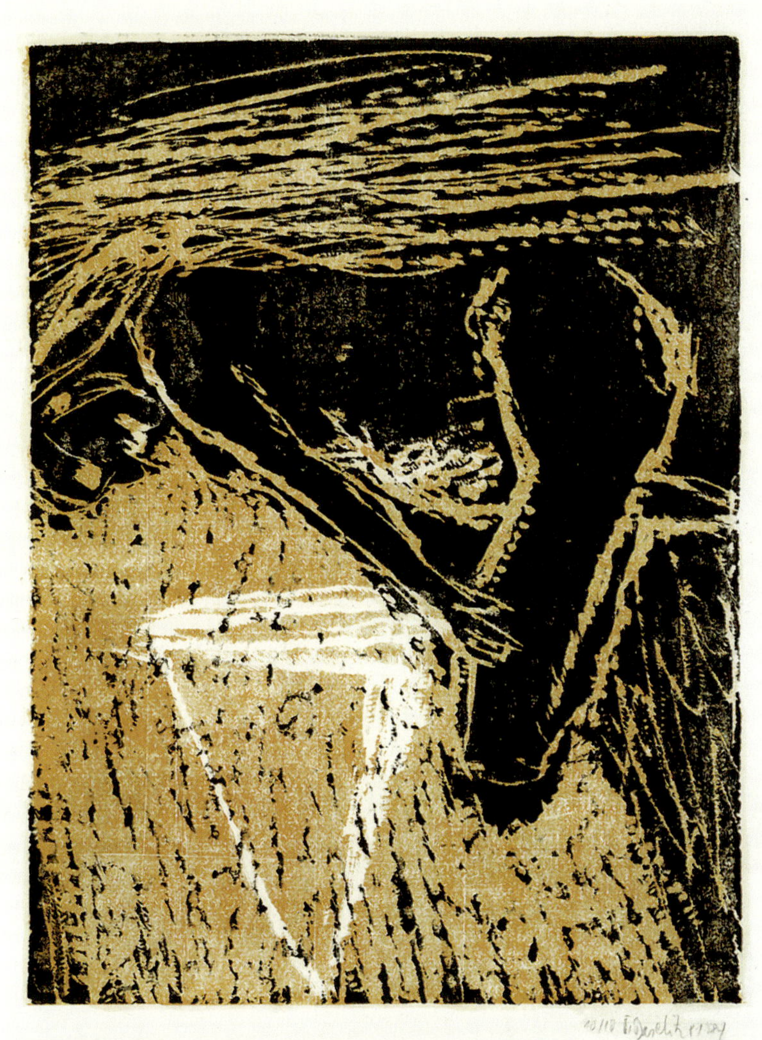

15 Georg Baselitz
Frau am Strand, 1981/84
Farbholzschnitt, 124 x 88 cm. Auflage: 10
Woodcut, 48¾ x 34½ in. Edition: 10

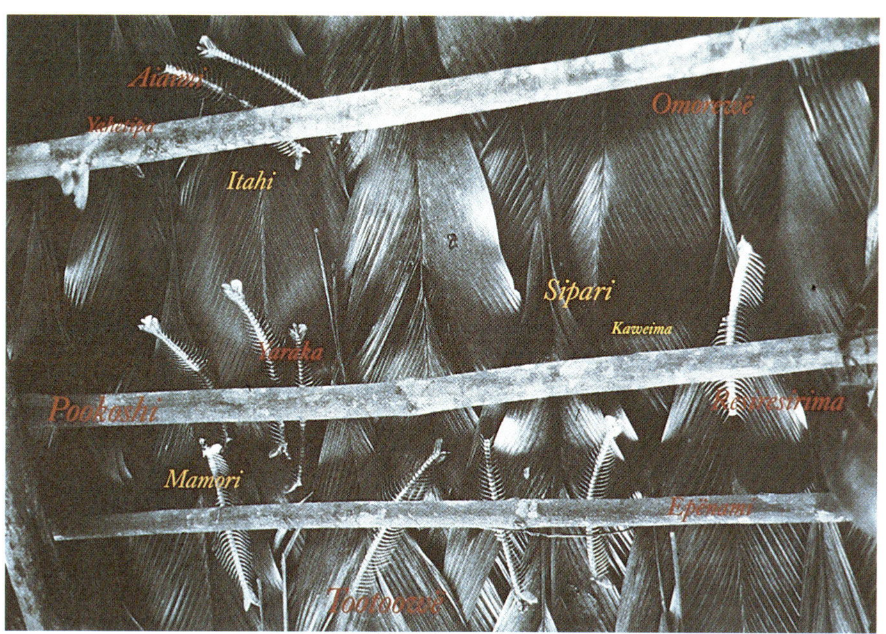

16 Lothar Baumgarten
Fish, 1985
Serigraphie, 80 x 115 cm.
Auflage: 35
Silkscreen, 31 x 45 in.
Edition: 35

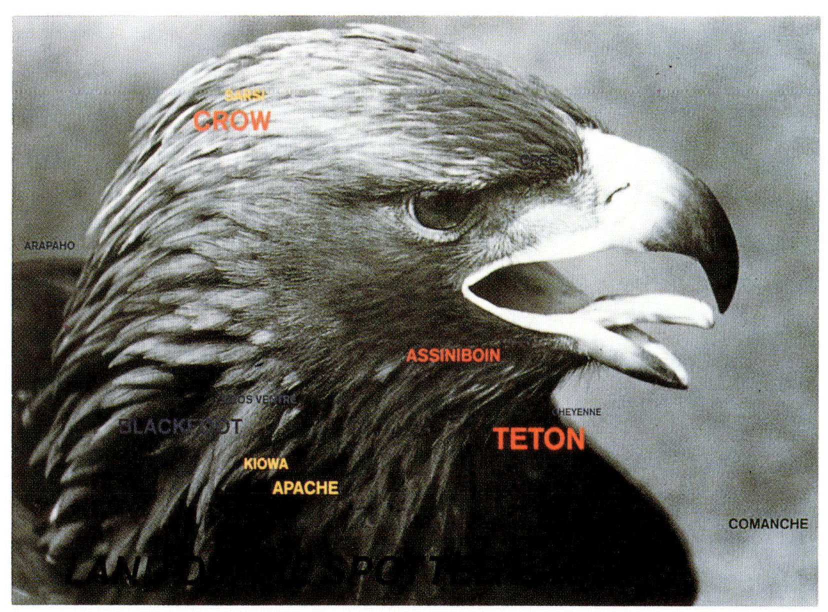

17 Lothar Baumgarten
Land of the Spotted Eagle, 1983
Offset/Serigraphie, 60 x 83 cm,
Auflage: 80
Offset/silkscreen, 23½ x 32½ in.
Edition: 80

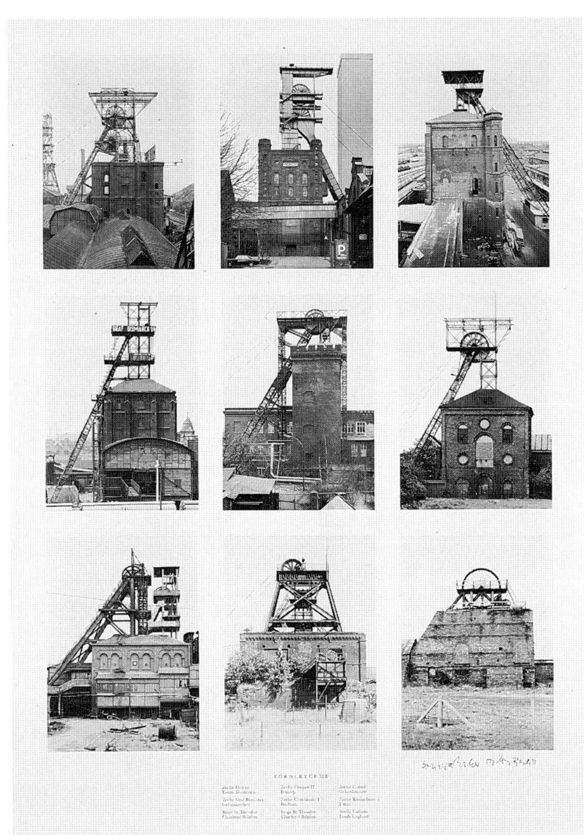

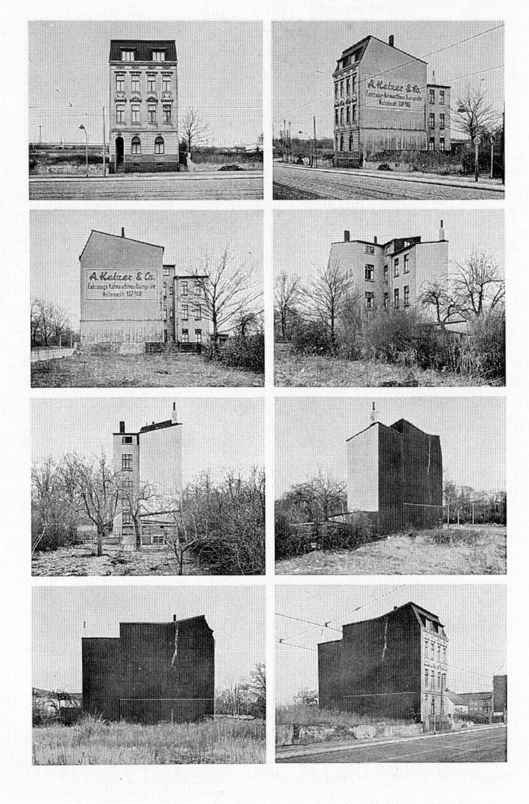

18 Bernd und Hilla Becher
Fördertürme, ca 1975
Offsetdruck, 65 x 47 cm. Auflage: ca. 100
Offset print, 25½ x 18½ in. Edition: 100 approx.

19 Bernd und Hilla Becher
Acht Ansichten des Hauses Sternbuschweg 362,
Duisburg, 1978
Buchdruck, 80 x 55,5 cm. Künstlerexemplar (Aufl. 100)
Letterpress, 31½ x 22 in. Artist's proof (ed. 100)

20 Bernd und Hilla Becher →
Sechs Doppelwassertürme, 1972
Mappe mit 6 Offsetdrucken, 42 x 52 cm. Künstlerexemplar (Aufl. 100) sign. und num. auf Titelblatt
Portfolio with 6 offset prints 16½ x 20½ in. Artist's proof (ed. 100), signed and numbered on frontispiece

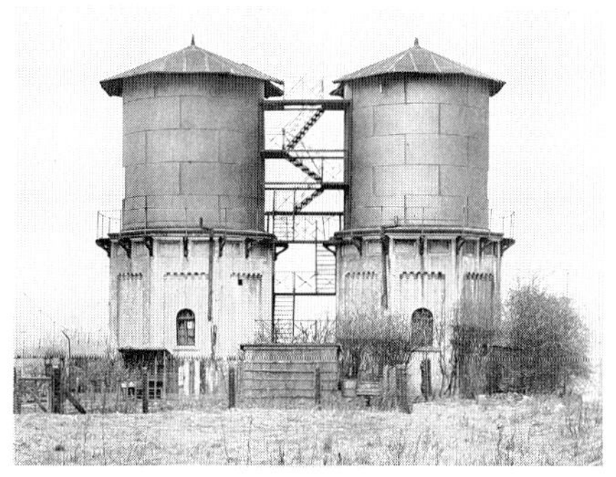
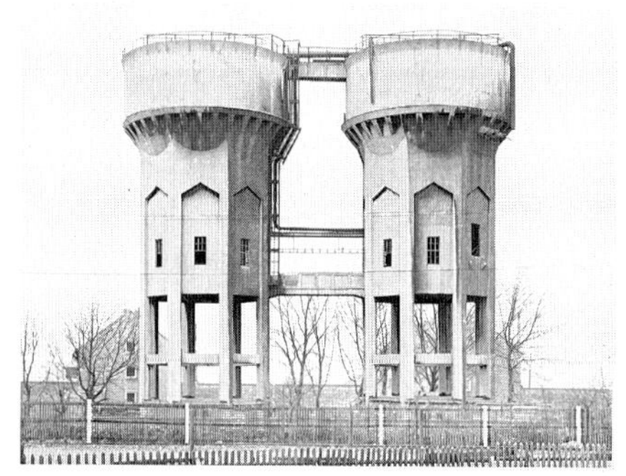
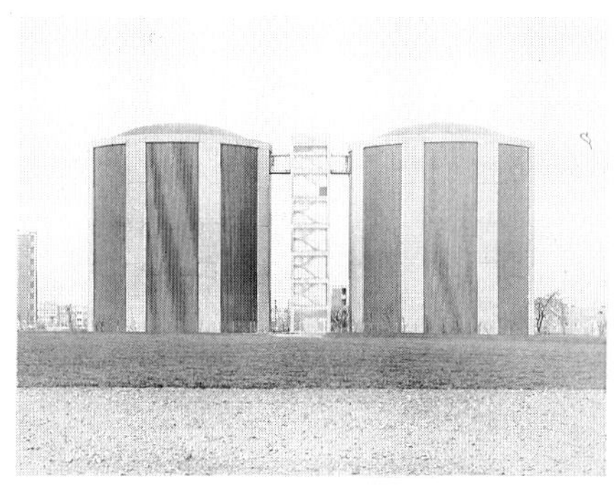
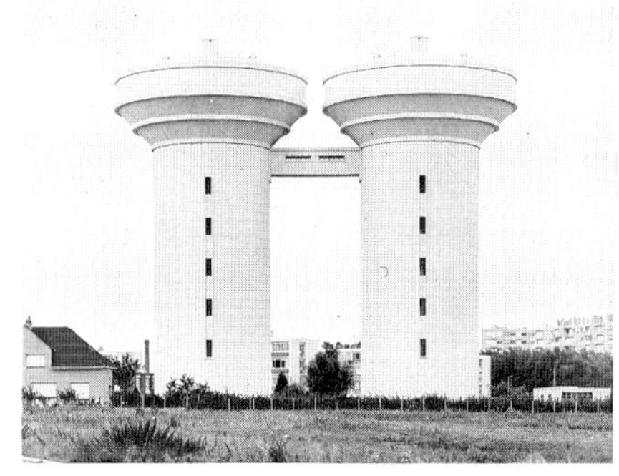
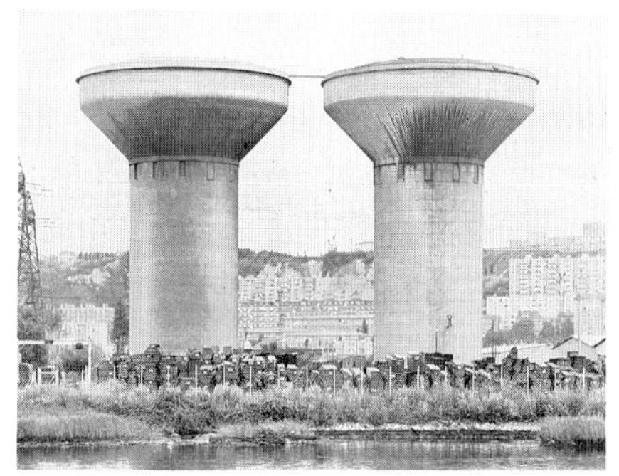
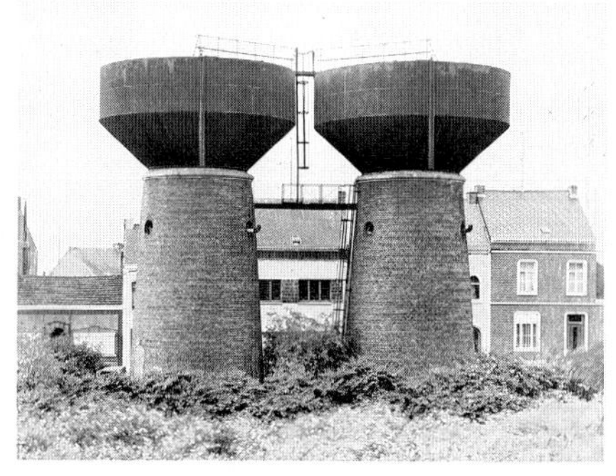

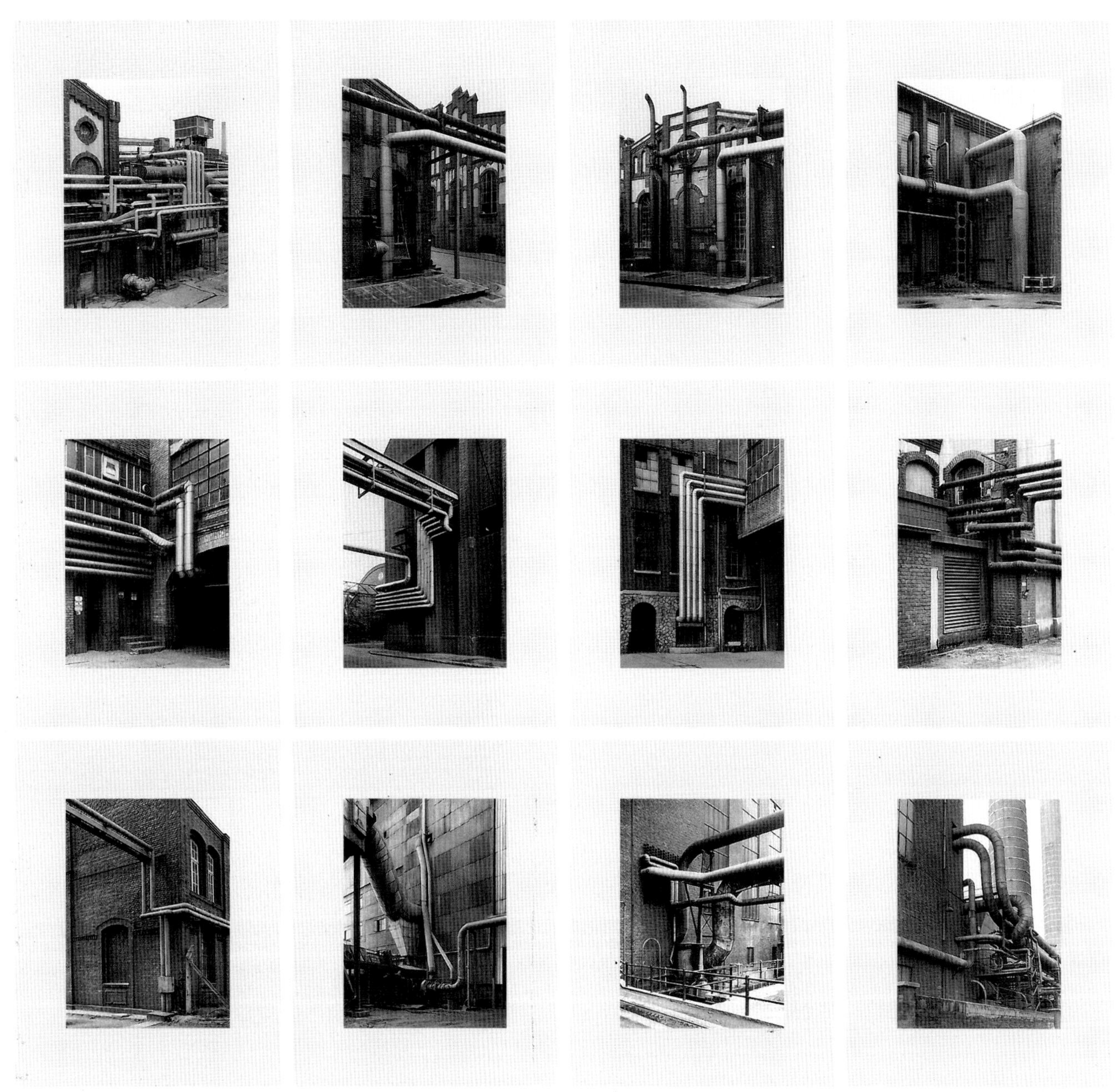

21 Bernd und Hilla Becher □
Walls and Conduits, 1991
Mappe mit 12 Offsetdrucken (Duotone), 63 x 50 cm. Auflage: 100
Portfolio with 12 duotone offset prints, 24¾ x 19¾ in. Edition: 100

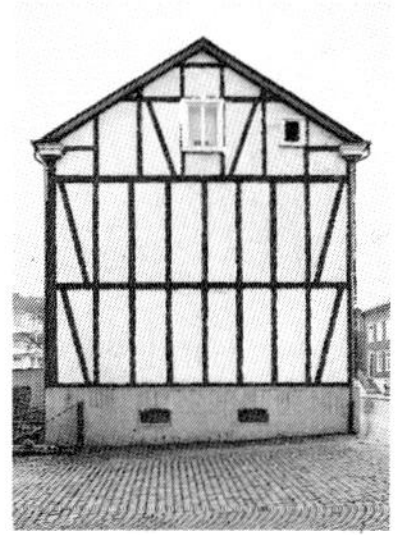
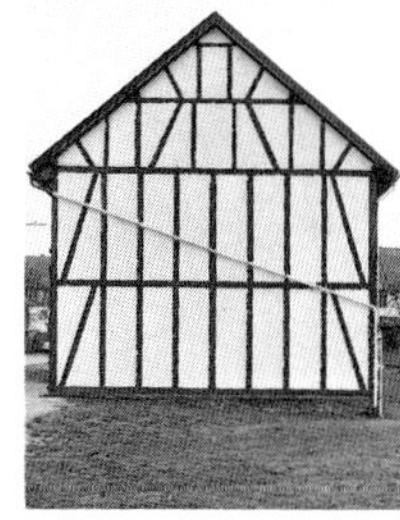
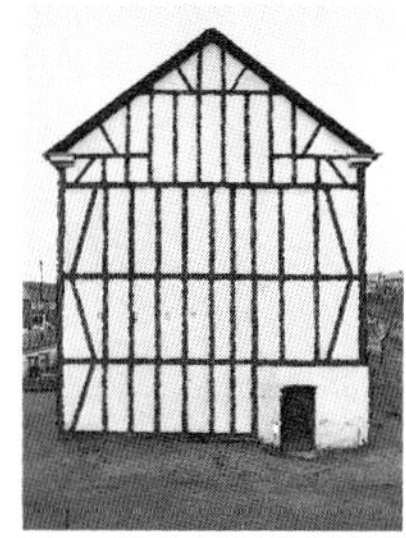
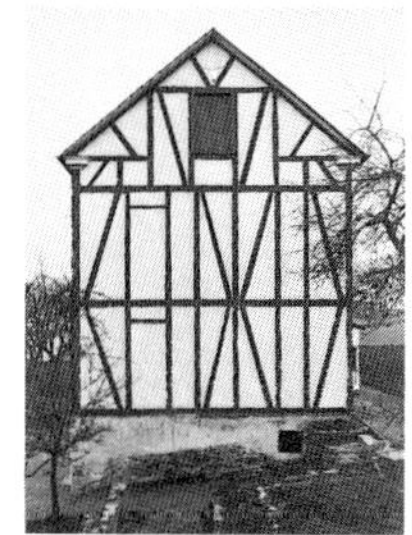
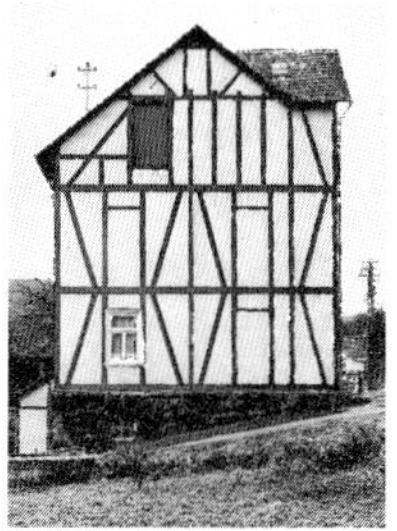
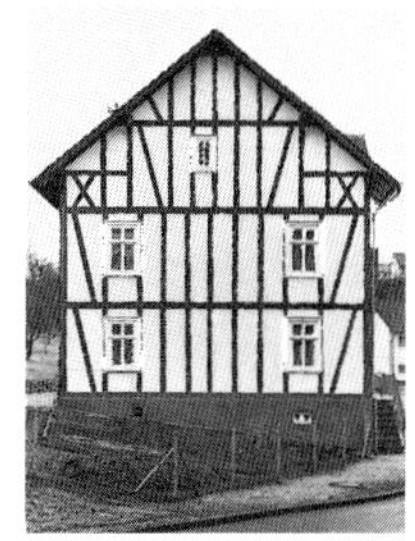
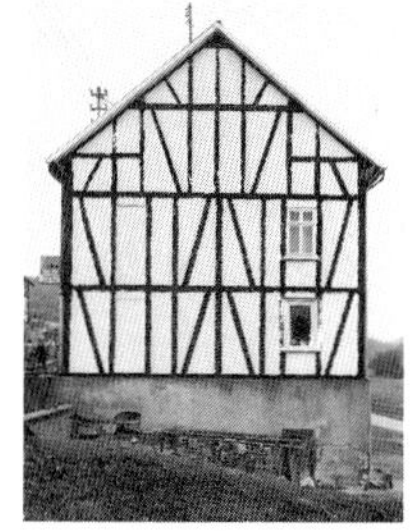
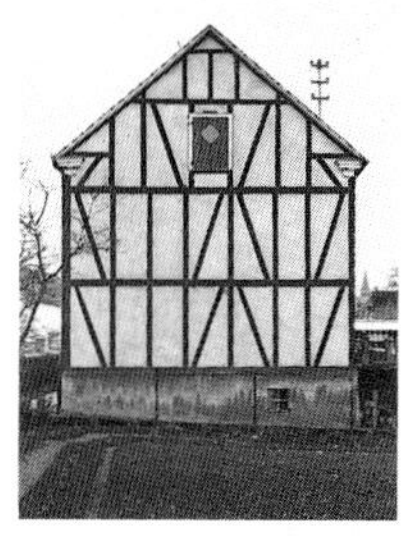
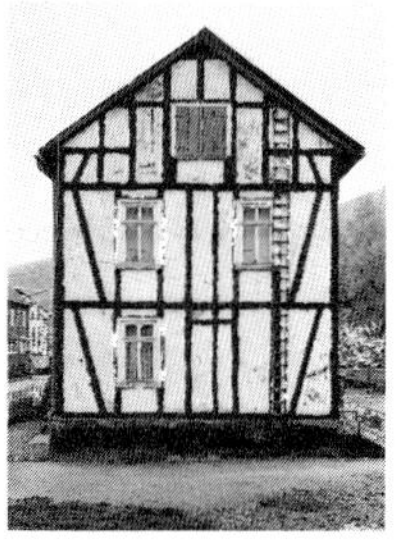
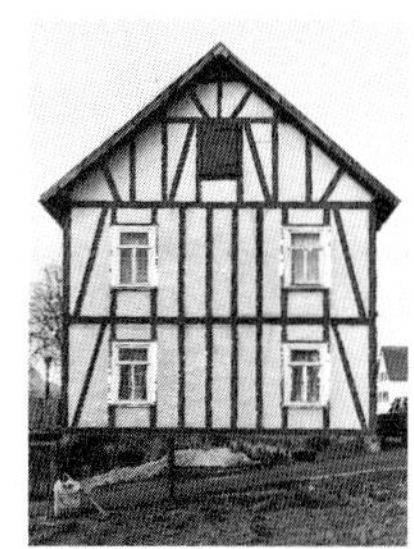
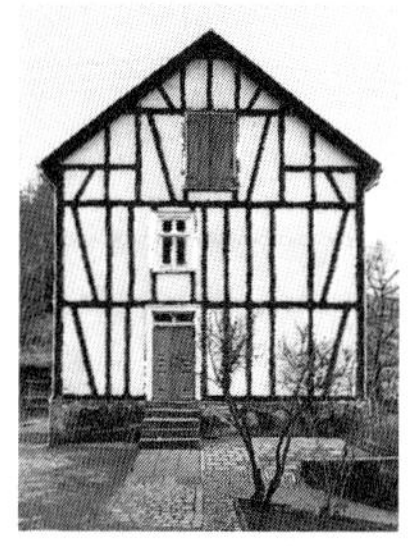
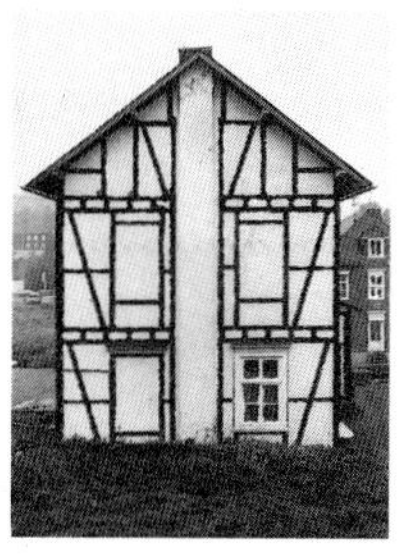

22 **Bernd und Hilla Becher** ■
Fachwerkhäuser, Siegener Industriegebiet, 1993
Mappe mit 12 Offsetdrucken (Duotone), 63 x 50 cm. Auflage: 50
Portfolio with 12 duotone offset prints, 24¾ x 19¾ in. Edition: 50

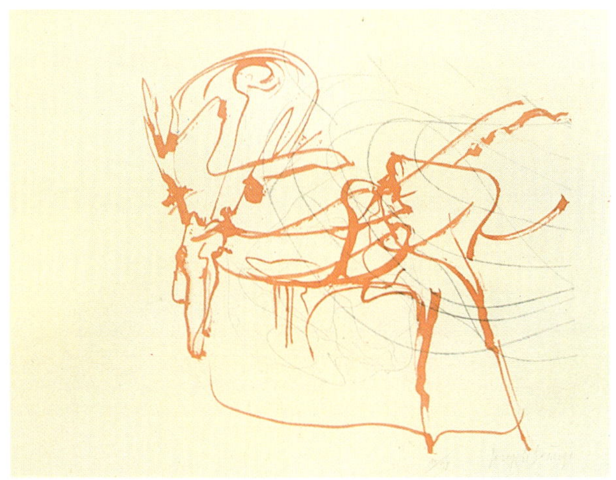

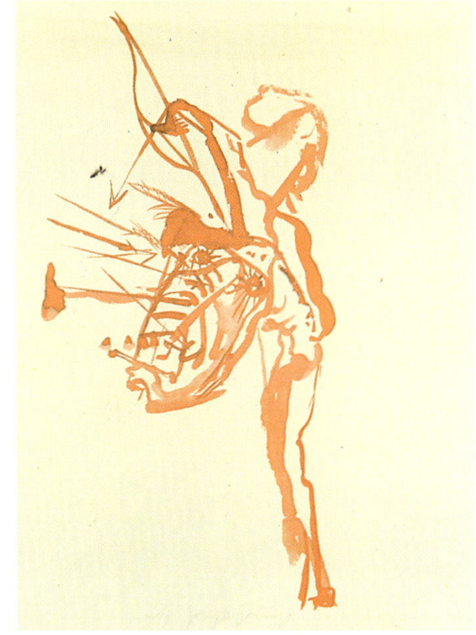

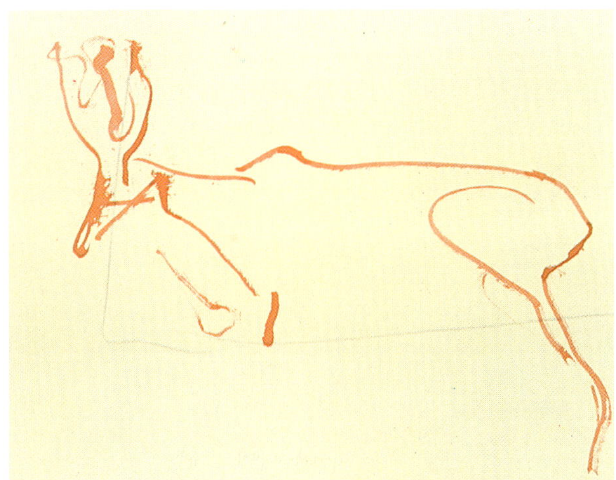

23 Joseph Beuys
Blätter aus Mappe: Spur I, 1974
a. o.T. (Hirsch und Sonne)
b. o.T. (Hirsch)
c. o.T. (Indianer mit Pfeilen beschossen)
Lithographien, 52 x 72 cm. Auflage: 98
Lithographs, 20 x 28 in. Edition: 98

24 Joseph Beuys □ →
Zeichnungen zu: Leonardo 'Codices Madrid', 1975
Buch mit 81 Granolithographien und 1 lose eingelegtem Granolitho, 23 x 32 cm.
Insges. 9 verschiedene Motive, Auflage: je 100
Book with 81 granolithographs and one loose granolithograph, 9 x 12 in.
Altogether 9 different images, edition: 100 ea.

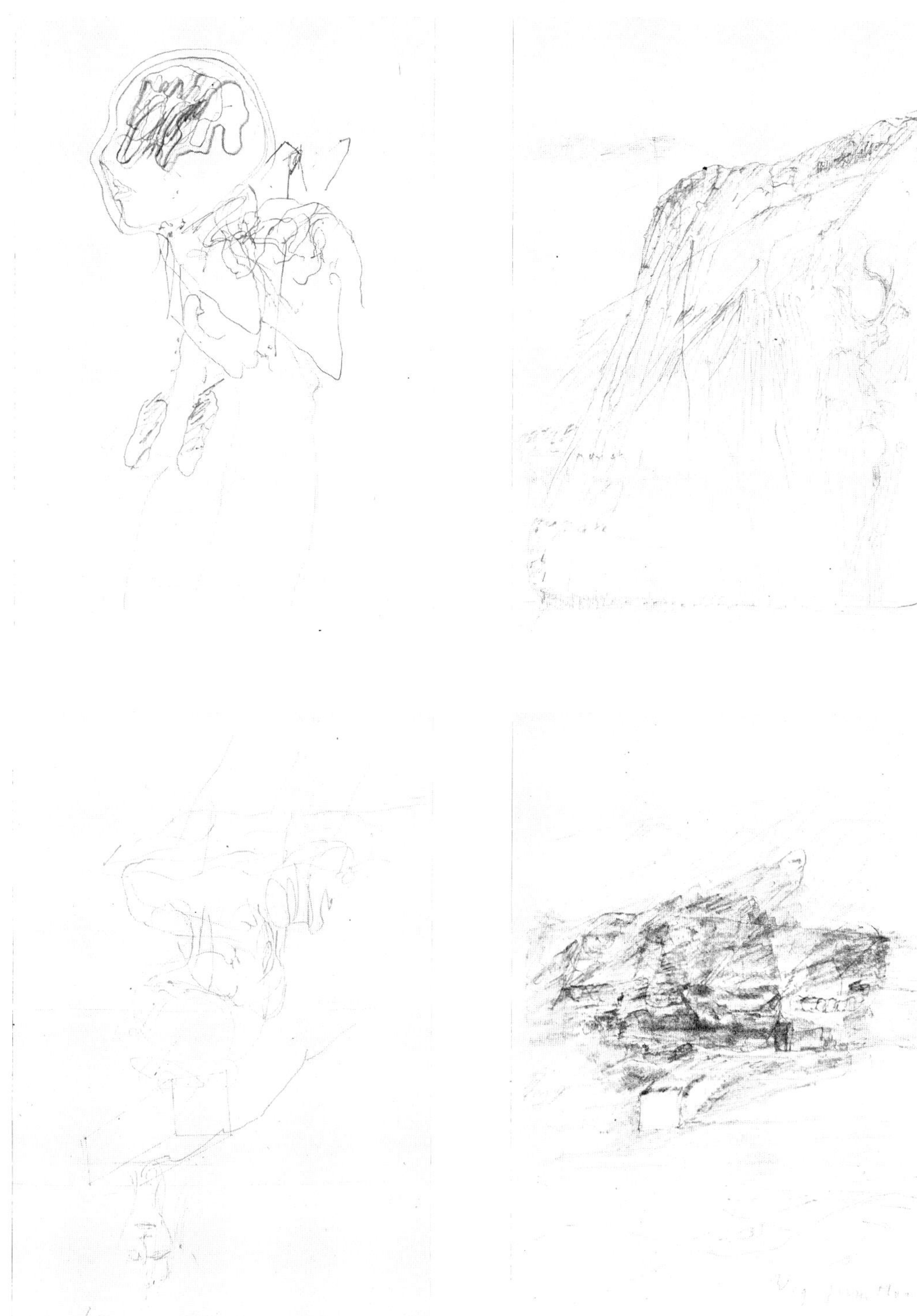

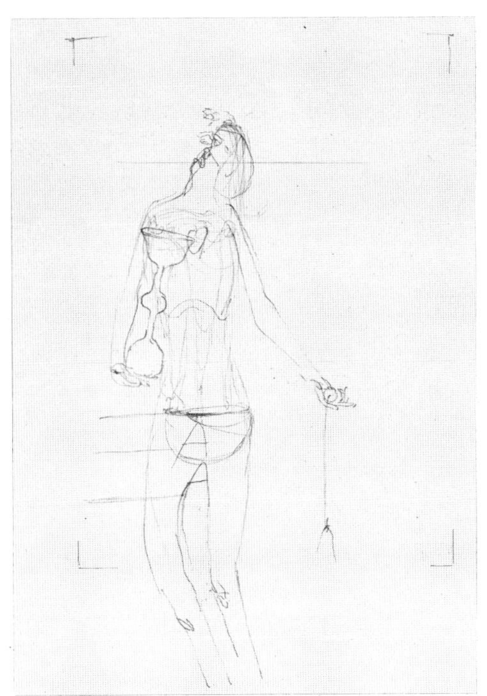

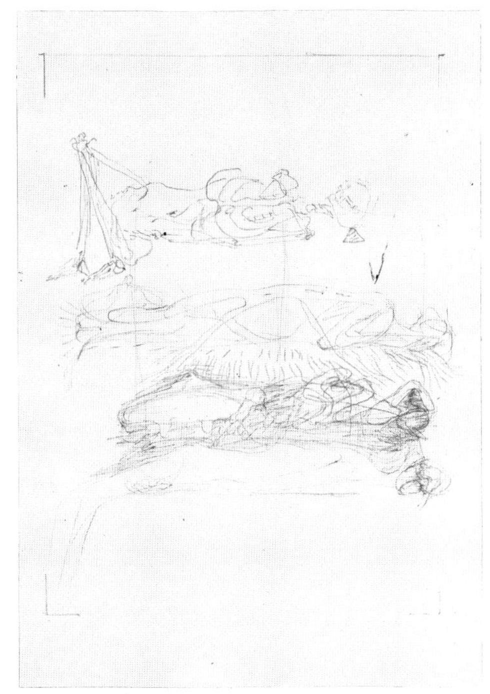

25 Joseph Beuys □
Zeichnungen zu: Leonardo 'Codices Madrid', 1975
Buch wie Nr. 24, aber mit Graphikmappe mit 12 Granolithographien, eingelegt in Passepartouts 36 x 30 cm. Auflage: 100
Book, same as No. 24, but with portfolio of 12 grano lithographs, 14 x 12 in. Edition: 100

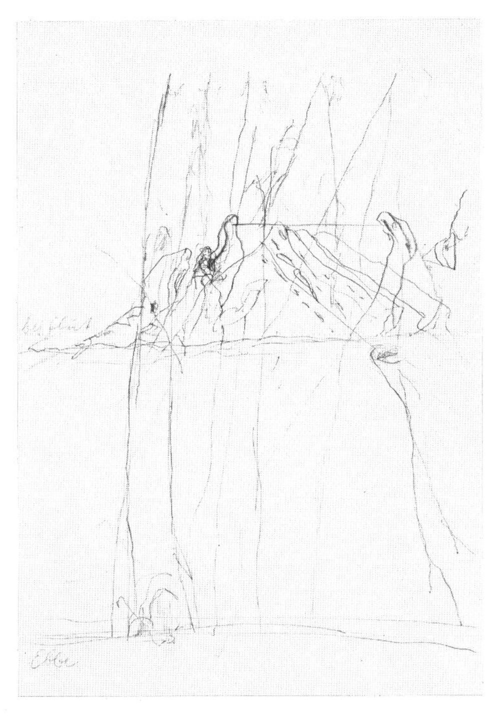

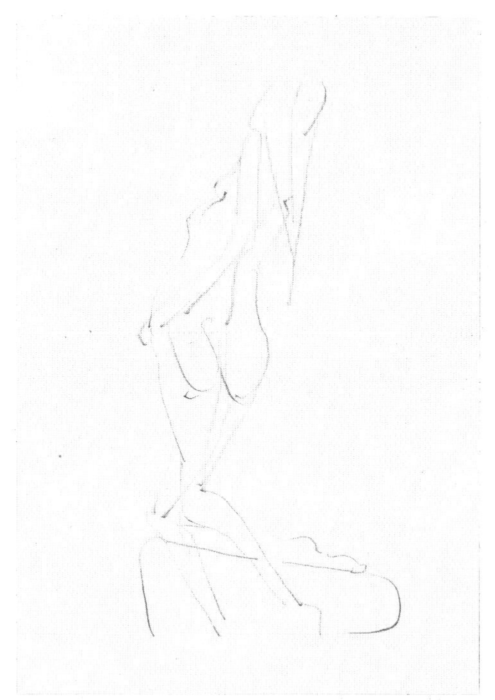

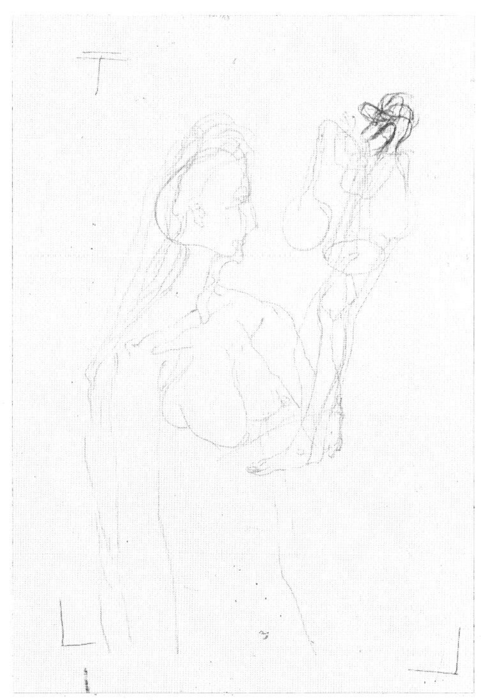

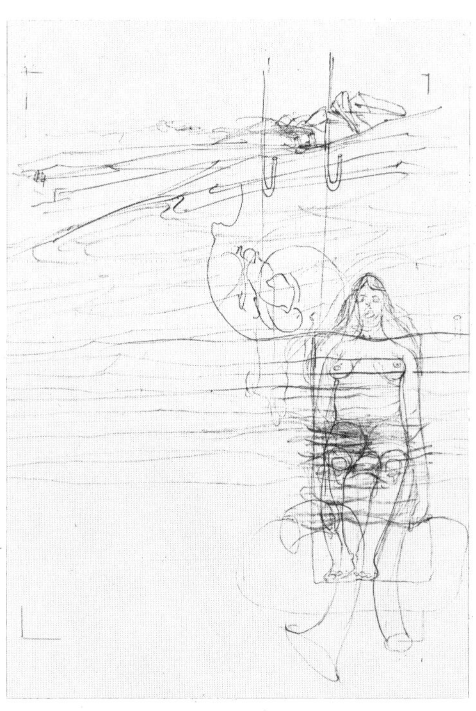

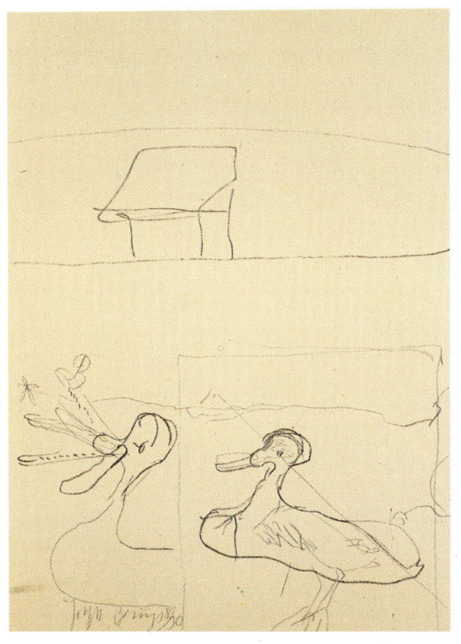

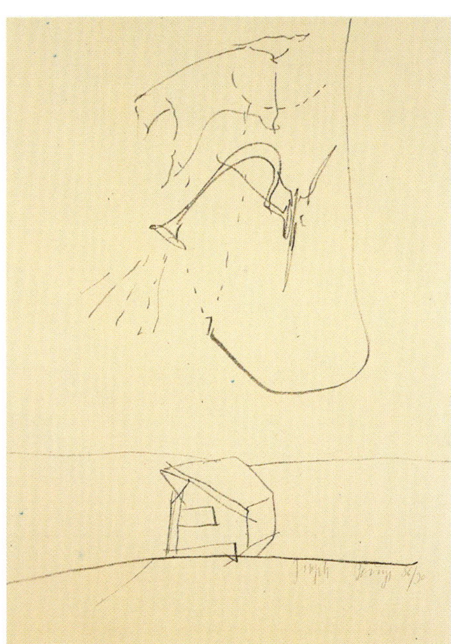

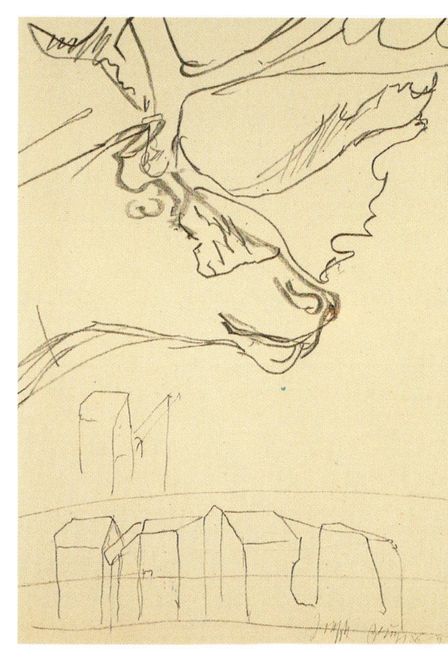

26 Joseph Beuys ■
Triptychon, 1981
a. Geschnatter unterhalb der Hütte **b.** Sternbild des Bären **c.** Junger Elch über dem Haus des alten Müllers
3 Lithographien, 76 x 56 cm. Auflage: 90. *Set of 3 lithographs, 30 x 22 in. Edition: 90*

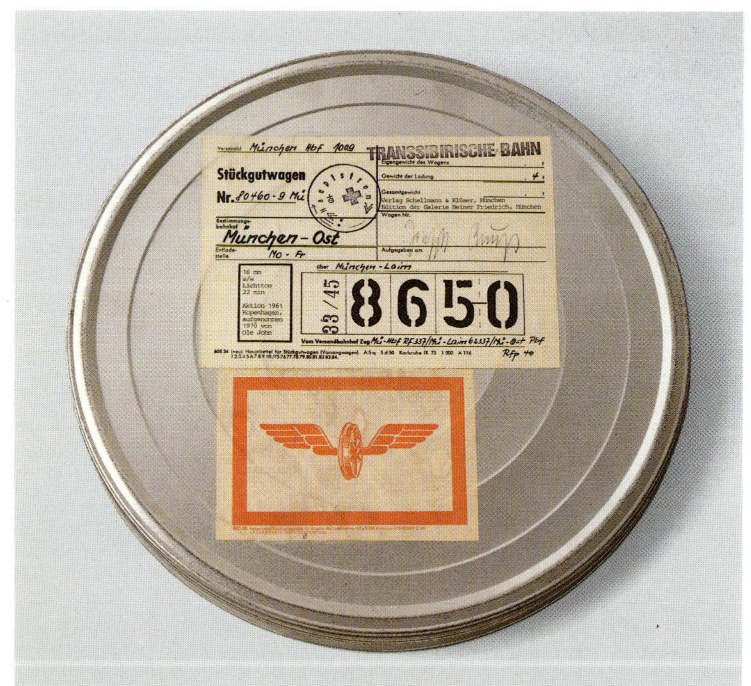

27 Joseph Beuys ■
Transsibirische Bahn, 1980
Film, 16mm, in bearbeiteter Metalldose,
2,5 x 37 cm ∅. Auflage: 45
Film, 16mm, in tin with railway labels,
1 in. x 15 in. diam. Edition: 45

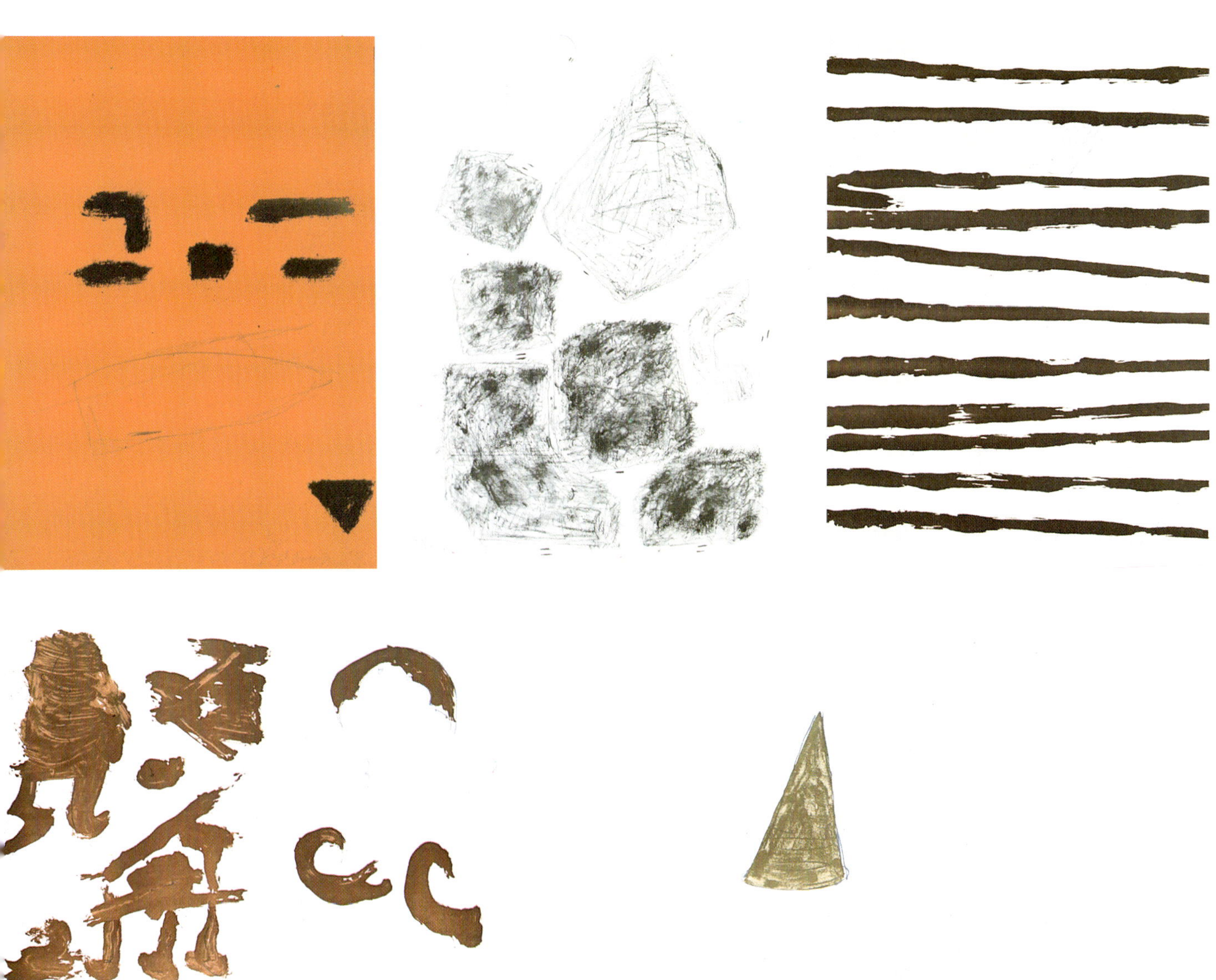

28 Joseph Beuys
Blätter aus Mappe: Spur II , 1977
a. o.T. **b.** o.T. (Filzblöcke) **c.** o.T. (Stinktier) **d.** o.T. **e.** o.T. (Goldkuchen)
Lithographien, 76 x 56 cm. Auflage: 98. *Lithographs, 30 x 22 in. Edition: 98*

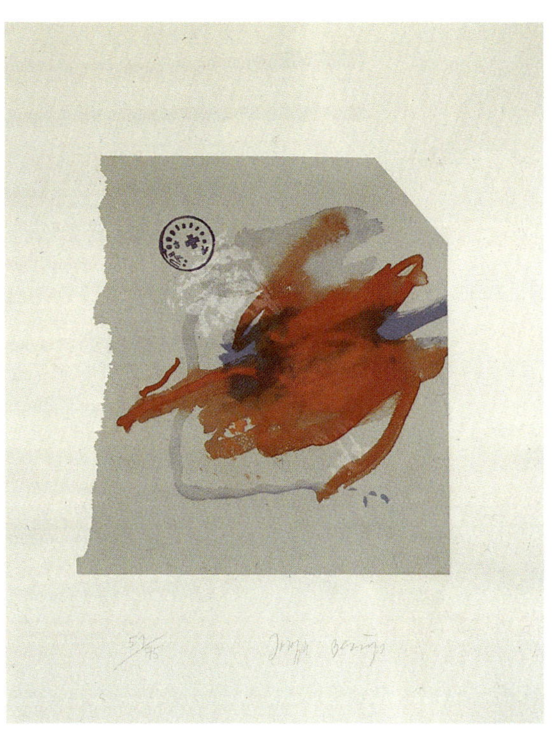

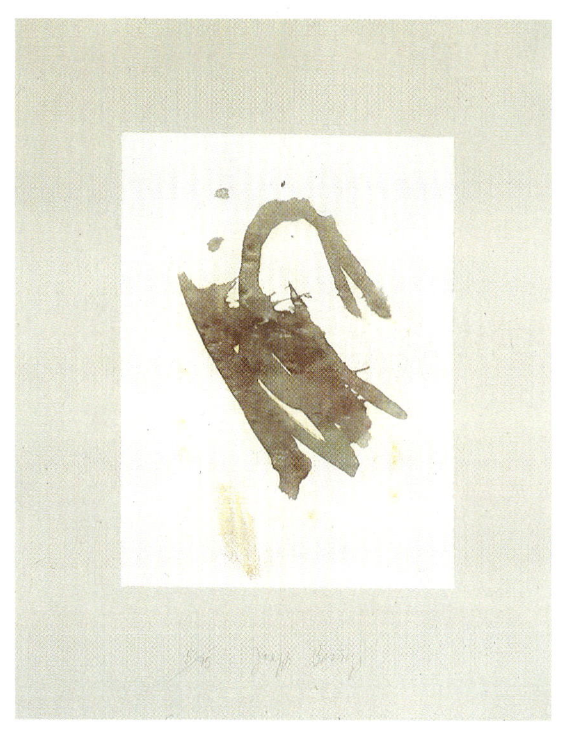

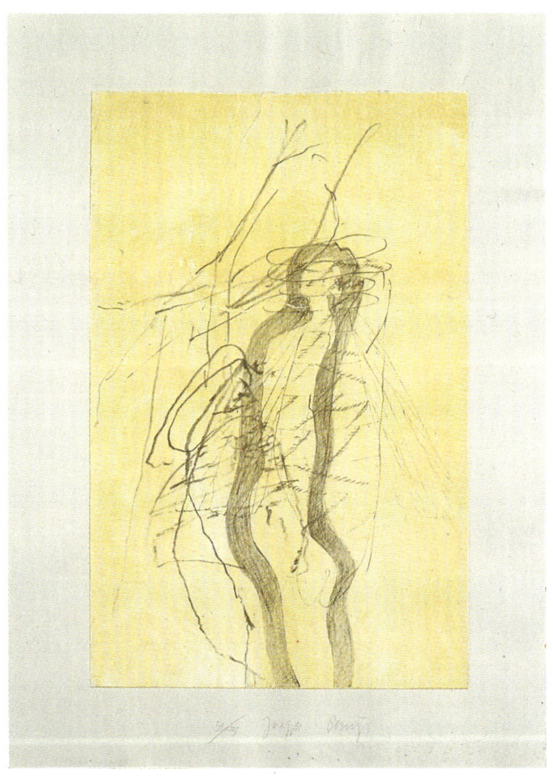

29 Joseph Beuys
Blätter aus: Suite Schwurhand, 1980
a. Hirsch. Aquatinta und Lithographie, 57 x 45 cm. Auflage: 75
Stag. Aquatint and lithograph, 22½ x 17¾ in. Edition: 75
b. Schwan. Radierung, Aquatinta und Lithographie, 56,5 x 45 cm. Auflage: 75
Swan. Etching, aquatint and lithograph, 22¼ x 17¾ in. Edition: 75
c. Blitz und Bienenkönigin. Aquatinta und Lithographie, 76 x 56,5 c Auflage: 75
Lightning and Queen Bee. Aquatint and lithograph, 30 x 22¼ in. Edition: 75

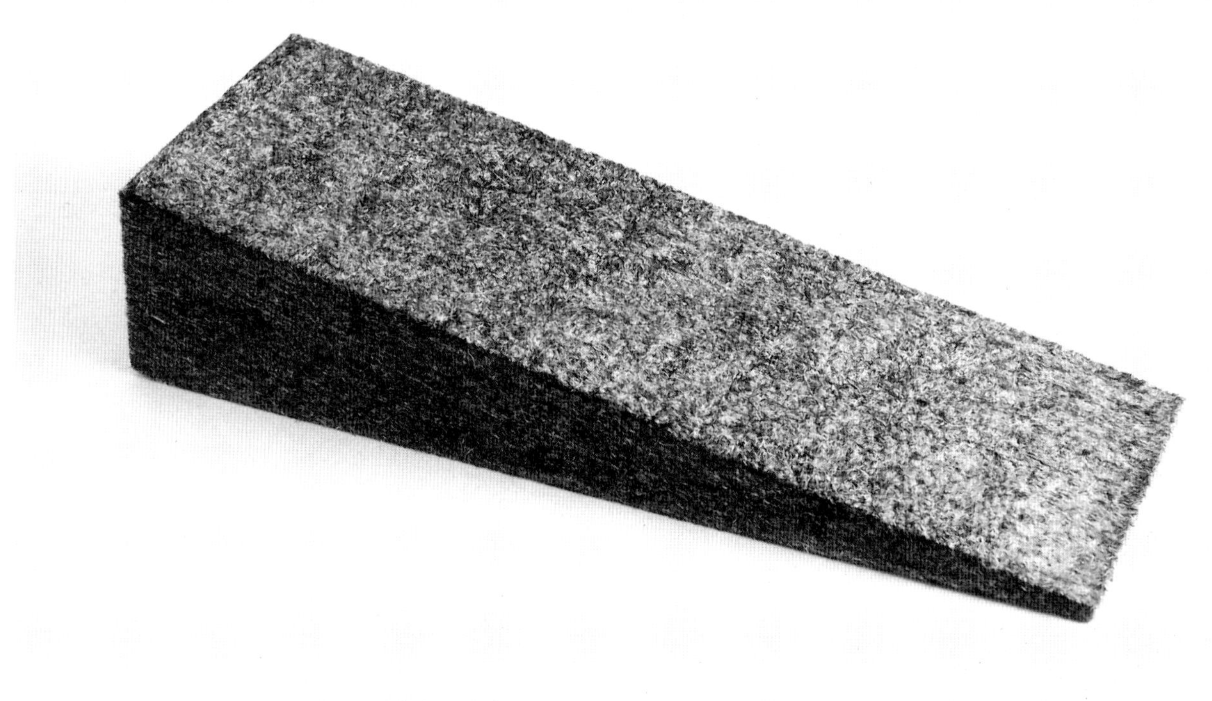

30 Joseph Beuys
Filzkeil, 1984-86
Gepreßter Filz, 5,5 x 8,5 x 25 cm. Auflage: 47, mit Nachlaßzertifikat.
Compressed felt, 2¼ x 3¼ x 9¾ in. Edition: 47, with the Estate's certificate.

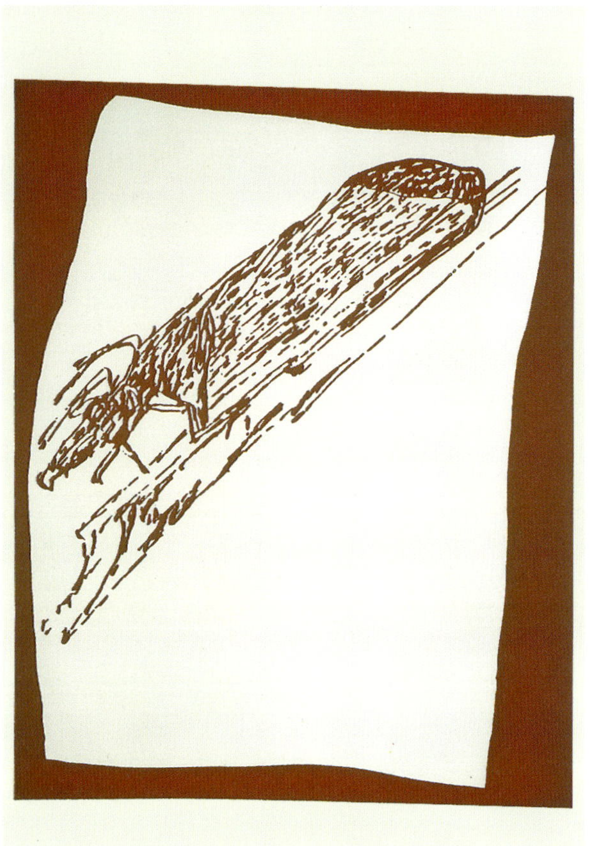

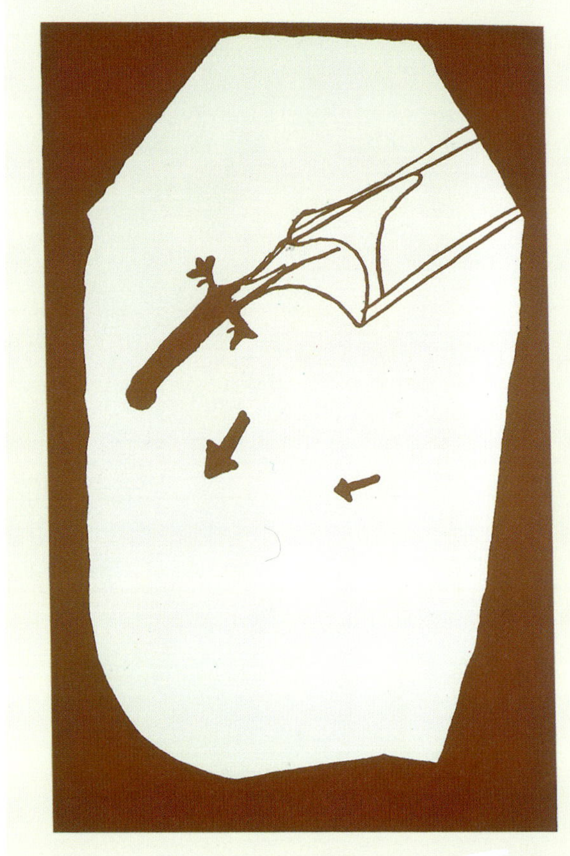

31 Joseph Beuys
A. Hirsch auf Urschlitten, **B.** Elch in der Strömung, 1985
Siebdrucke auf Karton, 90 x 63 cm. Auflage: 180,
Silkscreens on cardstock, 35½ x 24¾ in. Edition: 180

32 Joseph Beuys →
Blätter aus: Suite Zirkulationszeit, 1982
a. Honiggefäß. Radierung und Aquatinta auf Bütten grau, 56,5 x 45 cm. Auflage: 75
Honey Vessel. Etching and aquatint on grey rag paper, 22¼ x 17¾ in. Edition: 75
b. Bär. Lithographie auf Bütten weiß, 76,5 x 40 cm. Auflage: 75
Bear. Lithograph on white rag paper, 30 x 15¾ in. Edition: 75
c. o.T., (Mädchen). Radierung auf Bütten weiß, 65,5 x 50 cm. Auflage: 75
Untitled (Girl). Etching on white rag paper, 25½ x 19¾ in. Edition: 75

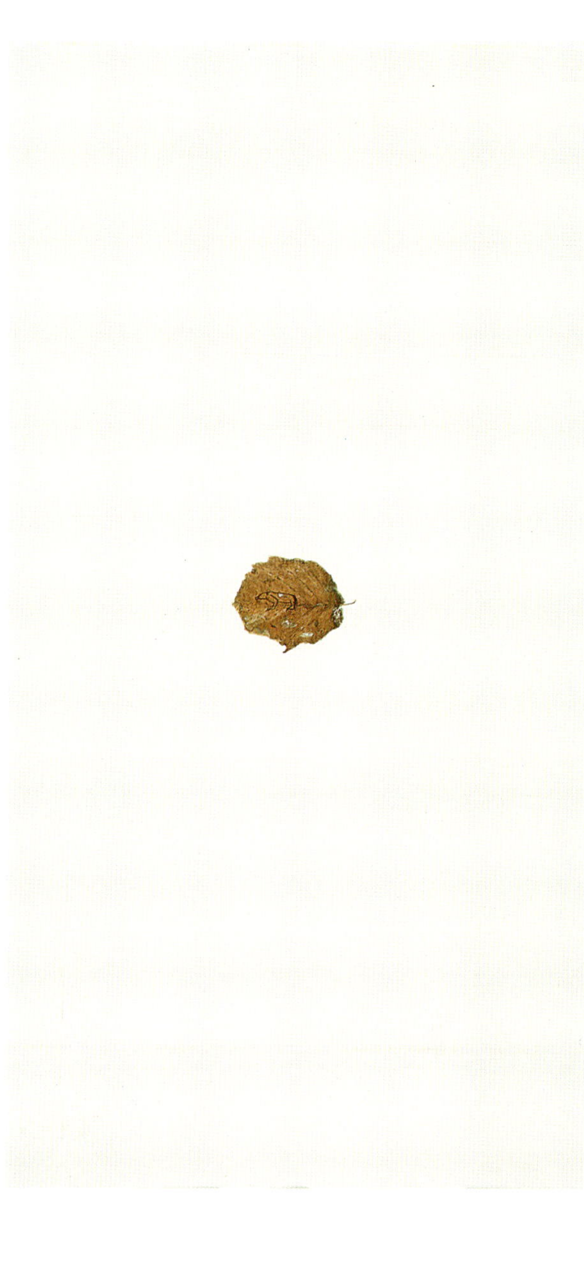

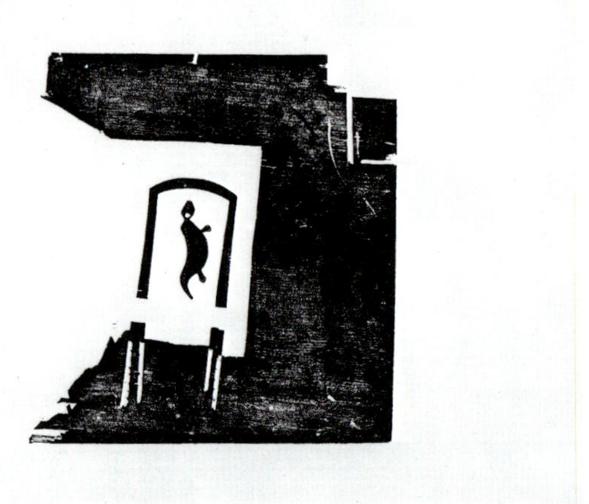

33 Joseph Beuys
Esse, 1973/74
Holzschnitt, 50 x 65 cm. Auflage: 50
Woodcut, 20 x 25 in. Edition: 50

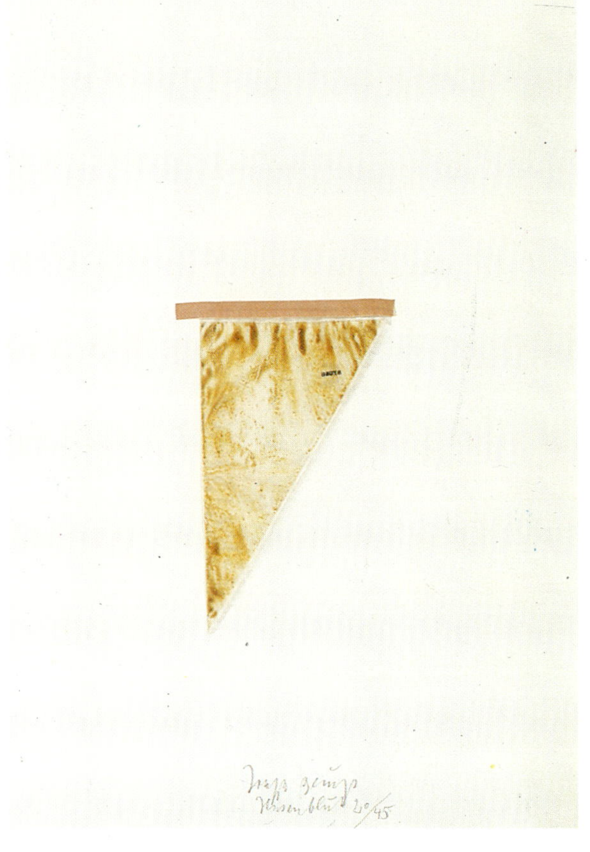

35 Joseph Beuys
Schiefertafel, 1972
Schiefertafel mit Siebdruck, beidseitig,
17 x 25 cm. Auflage: 200
Slate blackboard with silkscreen on both sides, 6¾ x 9¾ in. Edition: 200

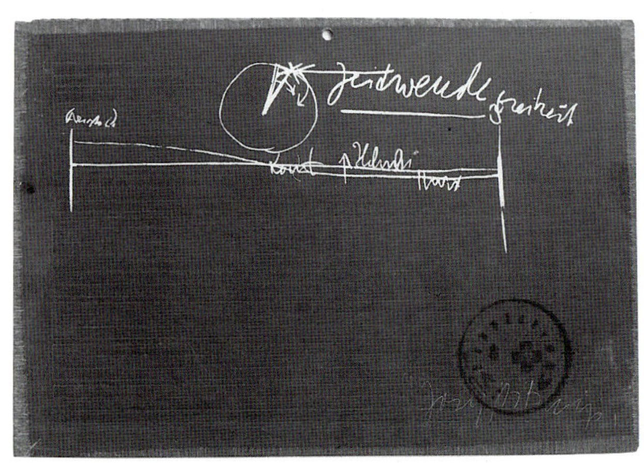

34 Joseph Beuys →
Hasenblut, 1971/79
Plastiktasche mit Hasenblut, mit Heftpflaster
auf Papier montiert, 62 x 45 cm. Auflage: 45
Plastic bag with hare's blood, mounted on paper with sticking plaster, 24 x 17 in. Edition: 45

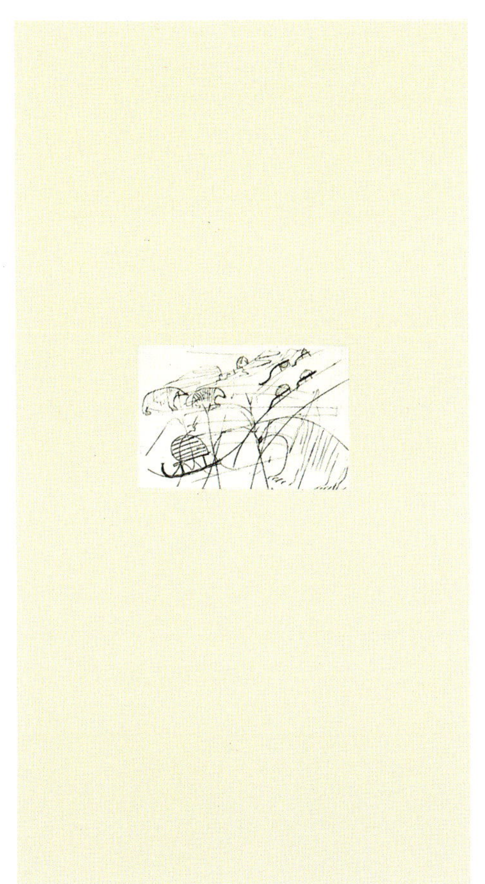

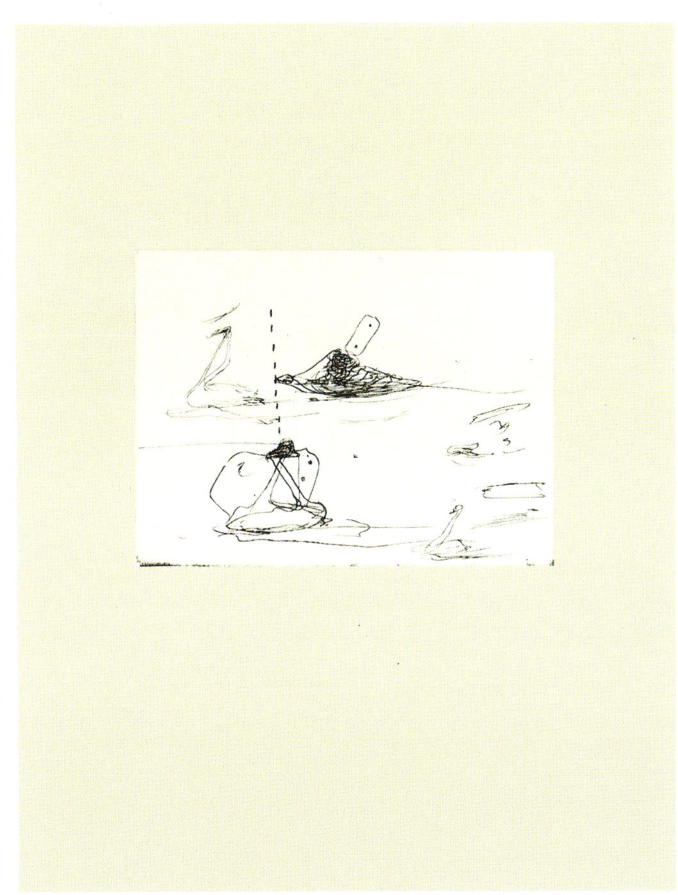

36 Joseph Beuys
Blätter aus: Suite Tränen, 1985
a. Nordpol. Radierung auf Bütten grau, 57 x 31,5 cm. Auflage: 75
North Pole. Etching on grey rag paper, 22½ x 12½ in. Edition: 75
b. Intelligenz der Schwäne. Radierung auf Bütten grau, 57 x 45 cm. Auflage: 75
Intelligence of Swans. Etching on grey rag paper, 22½ x 17¾ in. Edition: 75

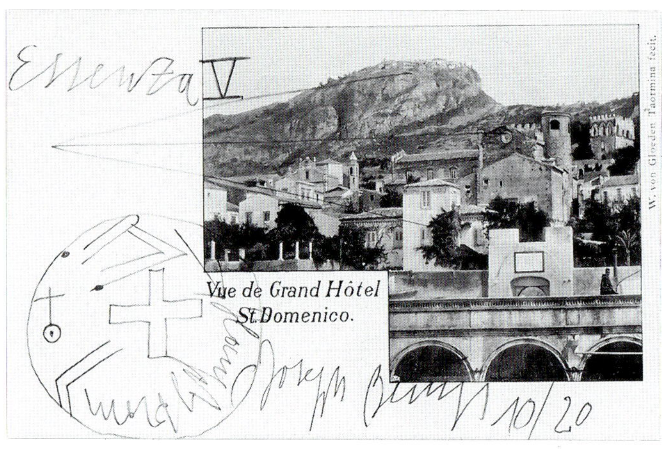

37 Joseph Beuys
von Gloeden-Postkarte, 1978
Postkarte mit Bleistiftzeichnung,
14 x 9 bzw. 9 x 14 cm. Auflage: 20
Postcard with pencil drawing,
5½ x 3½ in. Edition: 20

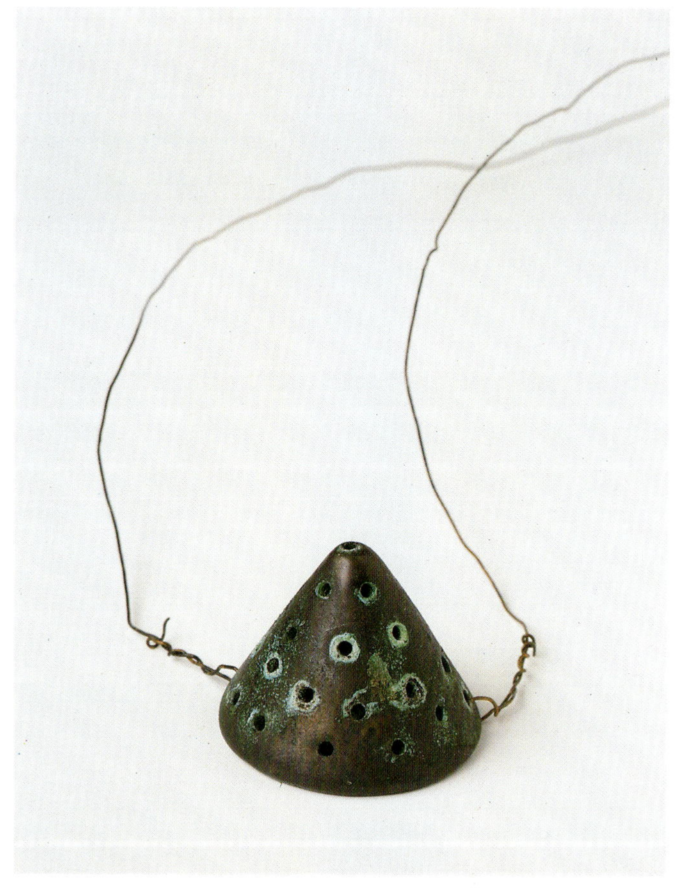

38 Joseph Beuys ■
Brustwarze, 1984
Bronzeguß, 2,5 x 2,8 cm,
Messingdraht. Auflage: 40
Bronze, 1 x 1 in., brass wire.
Edition: 40

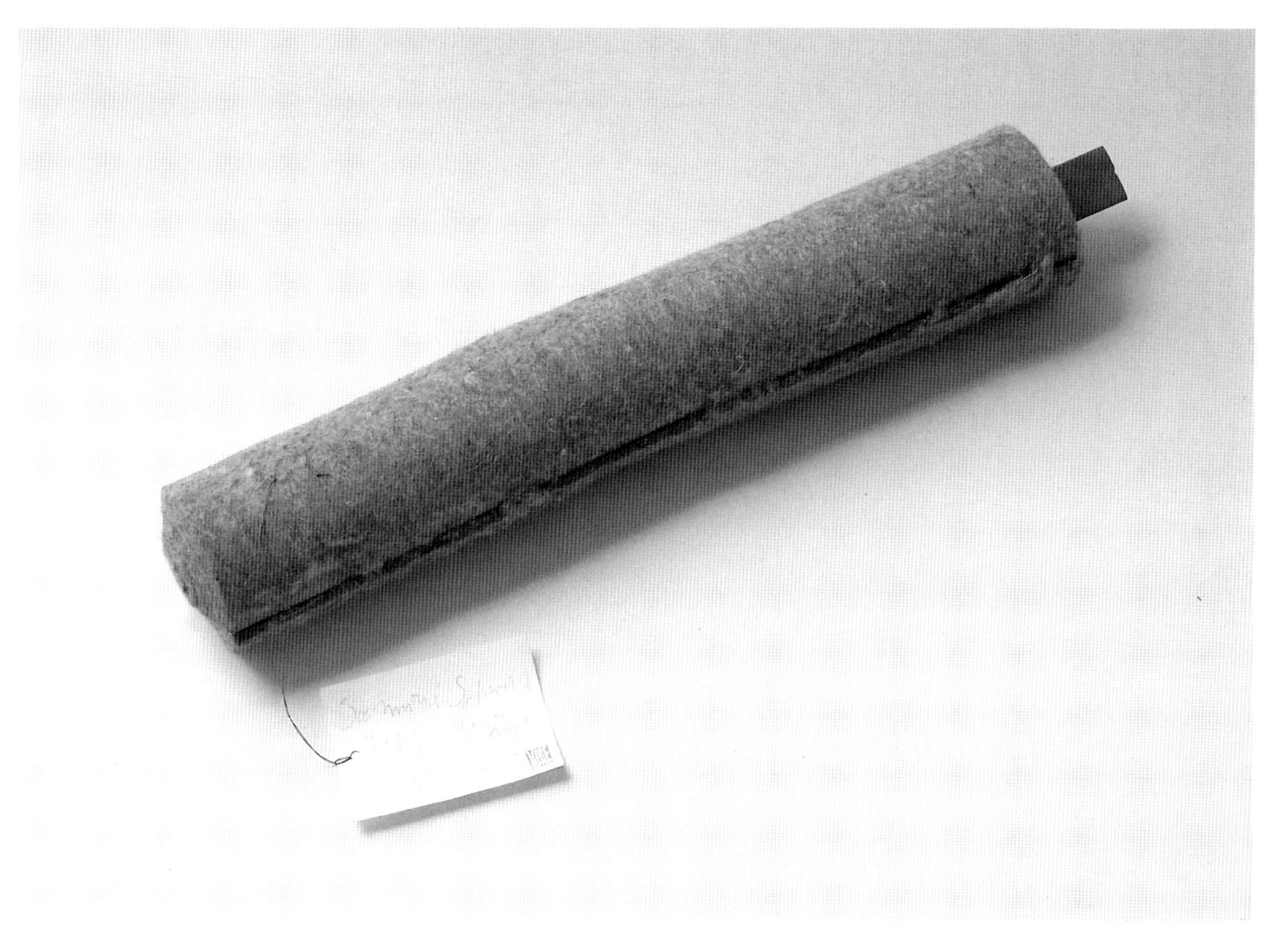

39 Joseph Beuys
Samurai-Schwert, 1983
Filzrolle um Stahlklinge, 54 x 9 cm. Auflage: 30
Roll of felt with steel blade, 21¼ x 3½ in. Edition: 30

40 Joseph Beuys
Filzwinkel, 1985
Filzobjekt, 36 x 10,5 x 1 cm. Auflage: 80 *Felt object, 14 x 4 x ½ in. Edition:.80*

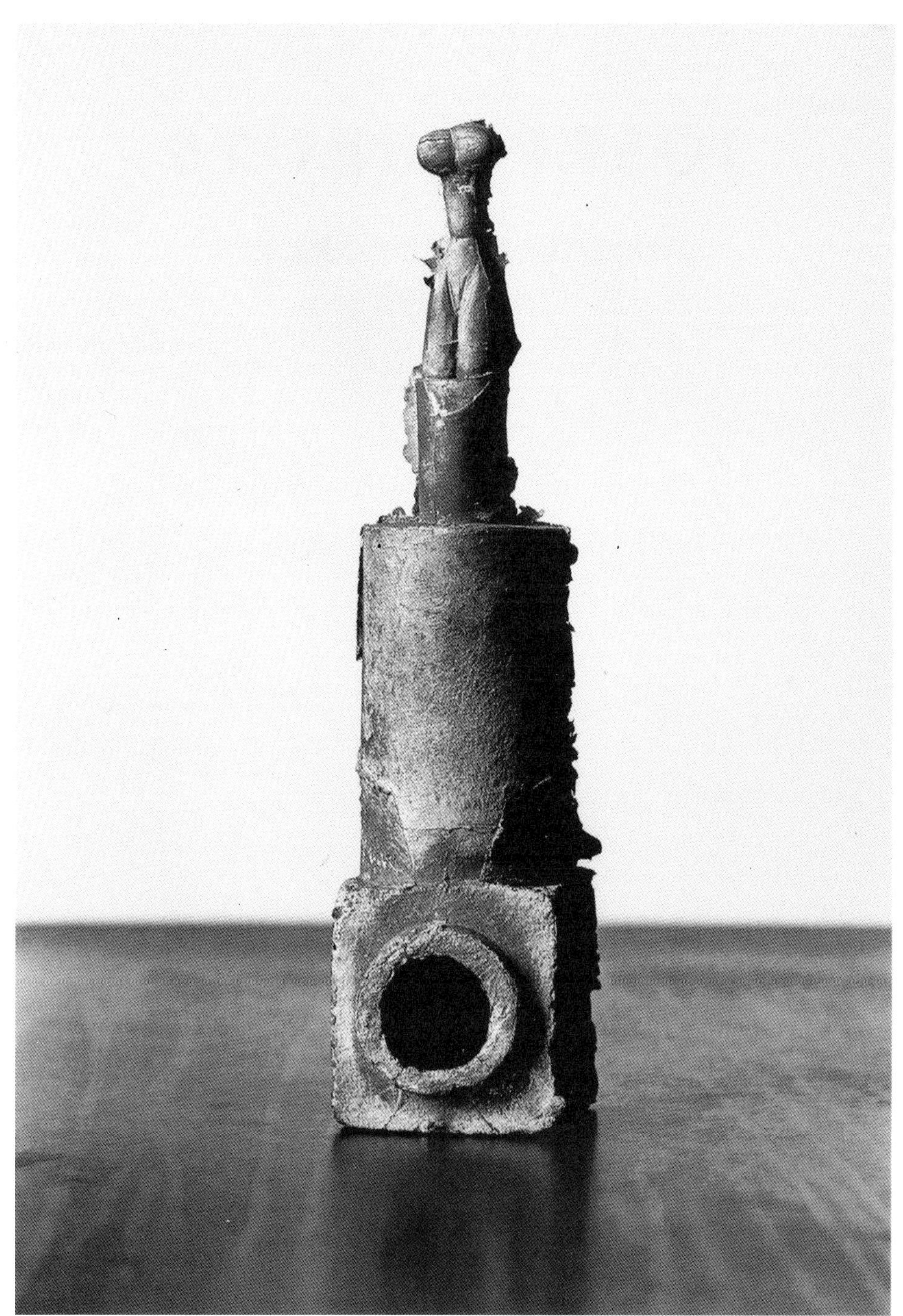

41 Joseph Beuys ■
Ofen, 1950
Bronzeguß, 31 x 7 x 7,5 cm. Insgesamt 9 Güsse, davon 2 wie hier, 7 mit "Badewanne für eine Heldin"
Bronze, 12¼ x 3 x 2¾ in. Altogether 9 casts made, out of which 2 as ill. here, 7 with "Bathtub for a Heroine"

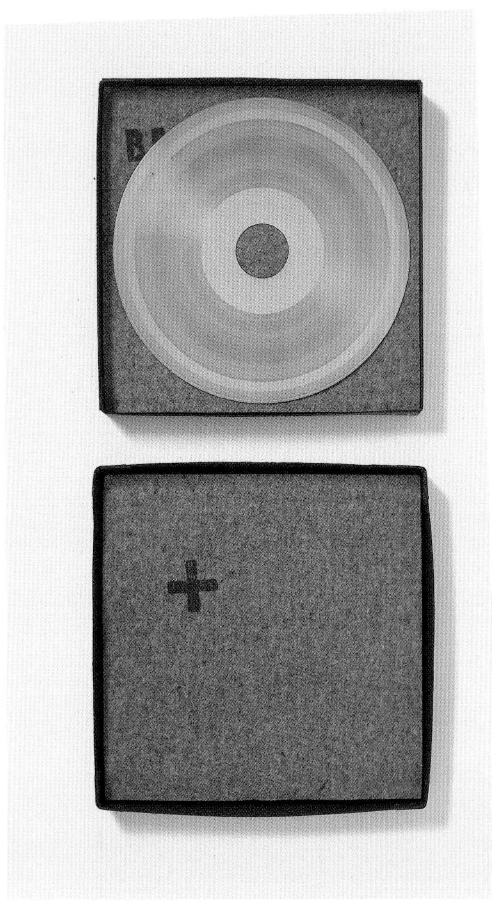

42 Joseph Beuys ■
Sonnenscheibe, 1973
Schallplattenmater mit zwei braun gestempelten Filzplatten,
in Karton, 38 x 38 x 4 cm.
Auflage: 77
Record master-mold with two pieces of felt stamped with brown paint, in box 15 x 15 x 1 in.
Edition: 77

43 Joseph Beuys ■ →
Joseph Beuys, 4 Bücher aus: "Projekt Westmensch" 1958, 1992
4 Bände, Halbleinen, gedruckt in Granolithographie (4-12 Farben).
Insges. 1168 Seiten, davon 454 bedruckt, 30 x 22 x 1,8 cm. Auflage: 365, numeriert.
4 volume book, printed in grano lithography (4-12 colors), altogether 1168 pages, 454 of which bear imagery and notations, 11¾ x 8½ x ¾ in. Edition: 365, numbered.

Faksimile-Edition von vier Skizzenbüchern, die in den Jahren 1958 bis 1965 entstanden, und in denen Joseph Beuys in Form von Zeichnungen, Texten, Aquarellen und zum Teil verschlüsselten Notationen für zukünftige Projekte nahezu sein gesamtes künstlerisches Vokabular niedergelegt hat.
Bitte gesonderte Broschüre anfordern!
Facsimile edition of four notebooks by Joseph Beuys, done in the years 1958-1965 in which the artist mapped out almost his complete artistic vocabulary in the form of drawings, texts, watercolors and notations for future projects. Brochure available!

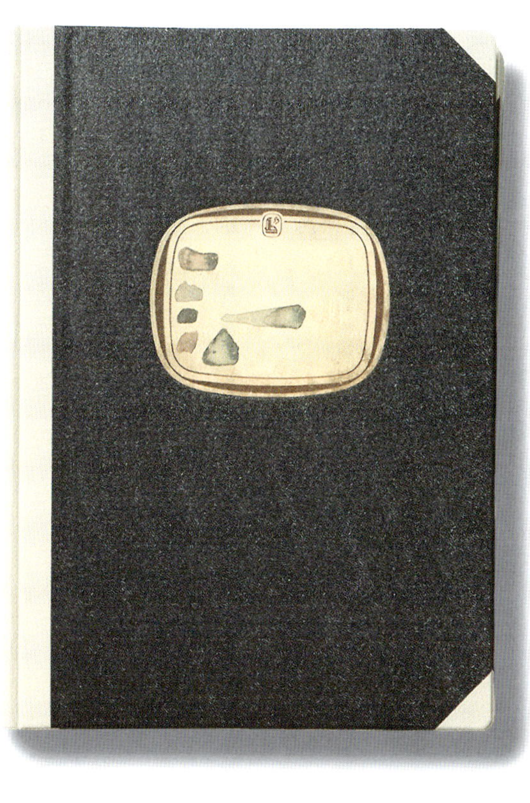
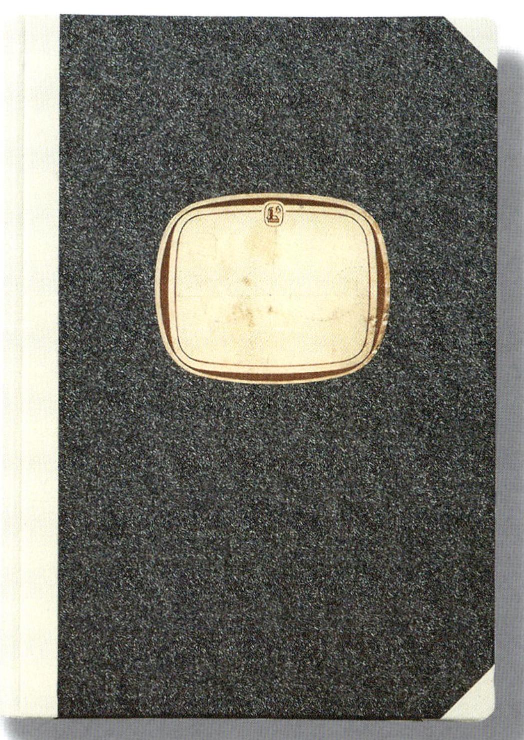
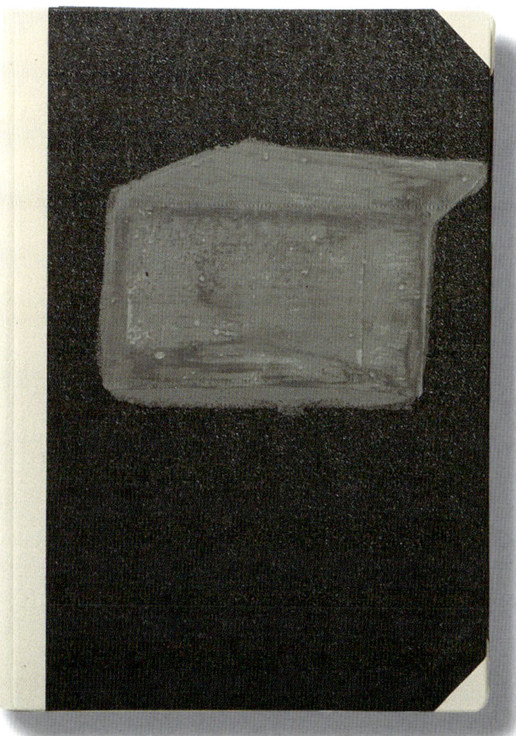

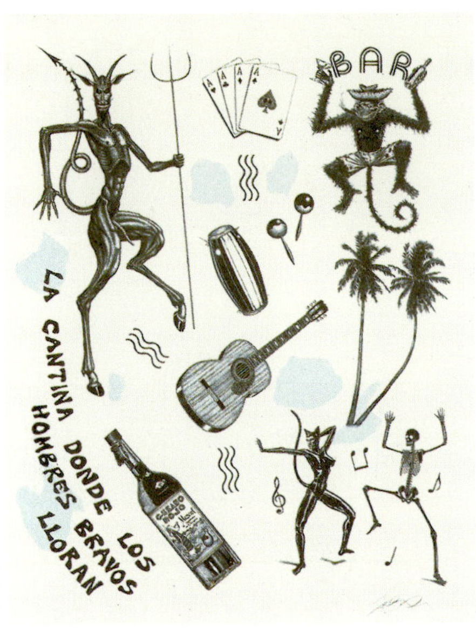

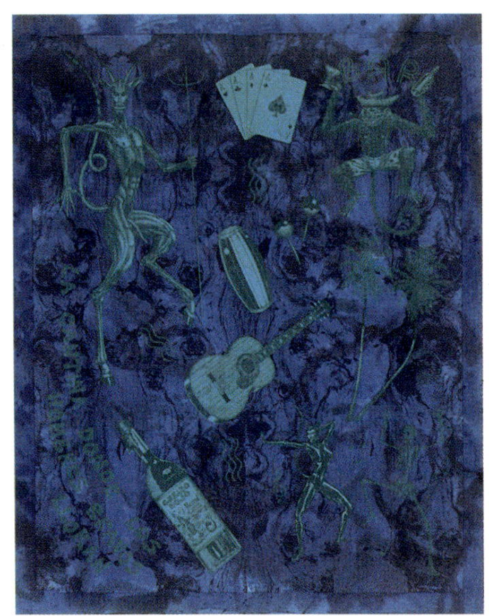

44 Ashley Bickerton
a Cantina, 1992 Lithographie und Siebdruck, handkoloriert, 103 x 83 cm. Auflage: 35
Lithograph, silkscreen and hand coloring, 40½ x 32¾ in. Edition: 35
b Blue Cantina, 1992 Lithographie, handkoloriert, 105 x 86 cm. Auflage: 40
Lithograph with handcoloring, 41½ x 33¾ in. Edition: 40

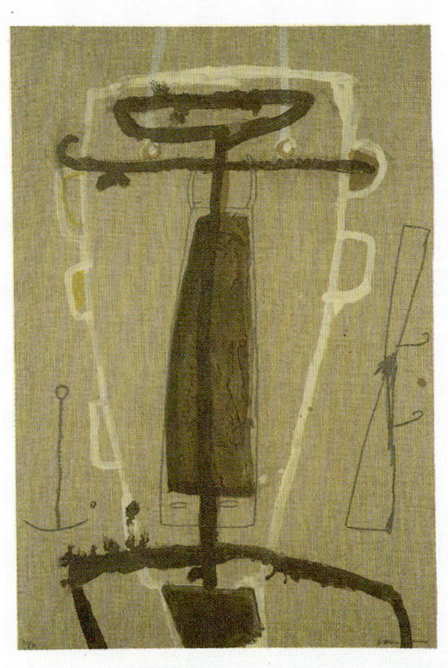

45 James Brown ■
The Whitewater, aus Mappe:
Für Joseph Beuys, 1986
Lithographie auf Leinen, aufgezogen
auf Bütten, 81,3 x 61 cm. Auflage: 90
Lithograph on linen, mounted on rag paper, 32½ x 24 in. Edition: 90

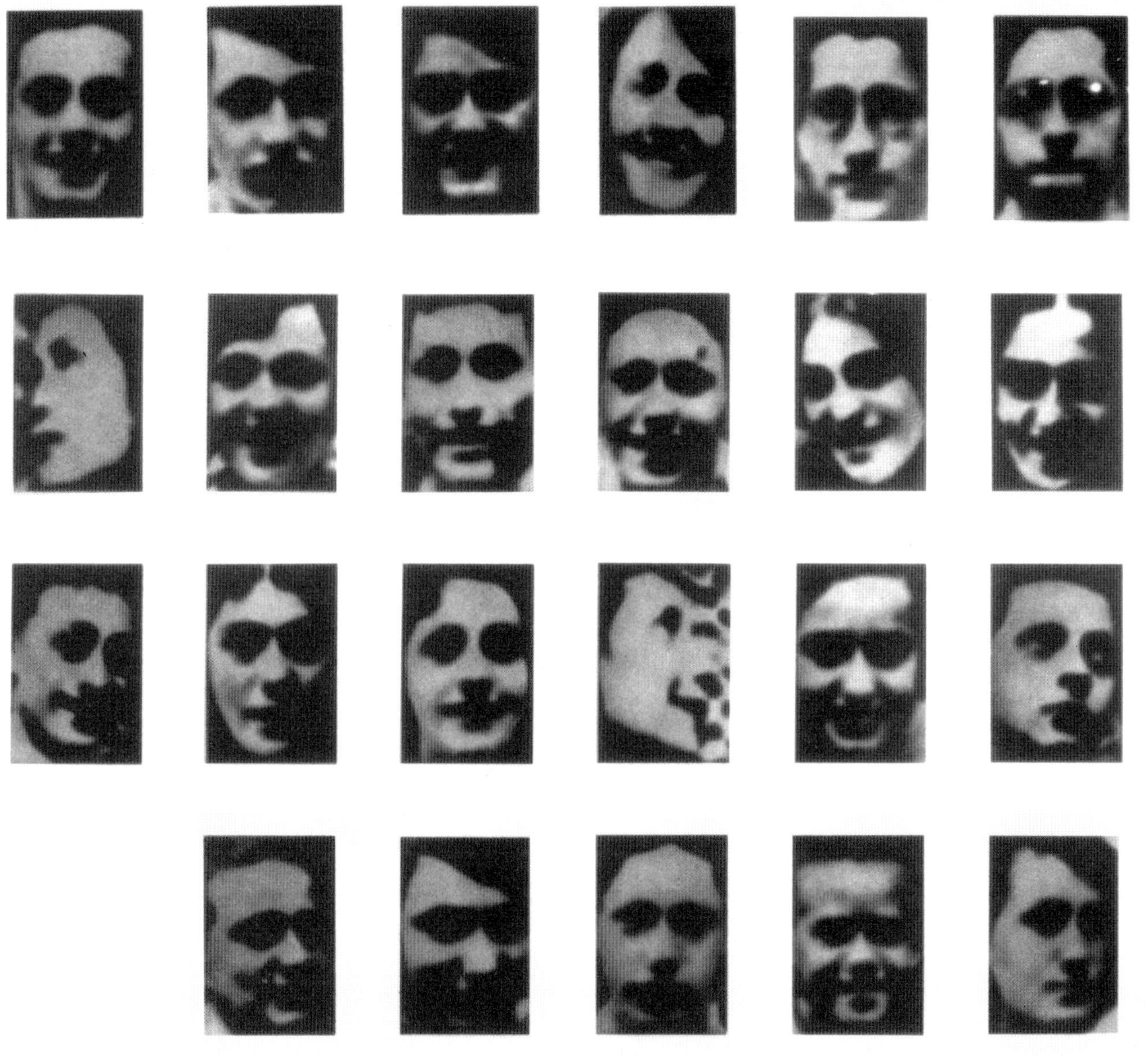

46 Christian Boltanski
Gymnasium Chases, 1991
Mappe mit 24 Heliogravuren, in Metallkassette, 59 x 42 cm. Auflage: 15
Portfolio of 24 photogravures in metal box, 23¼ x 16½ in. Edition: 15

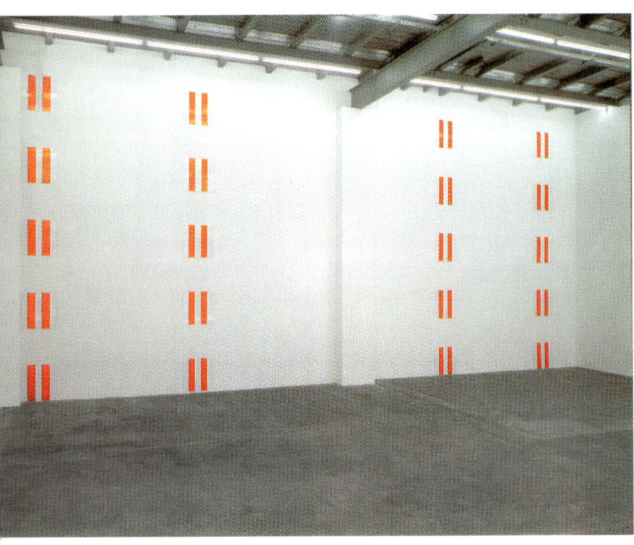

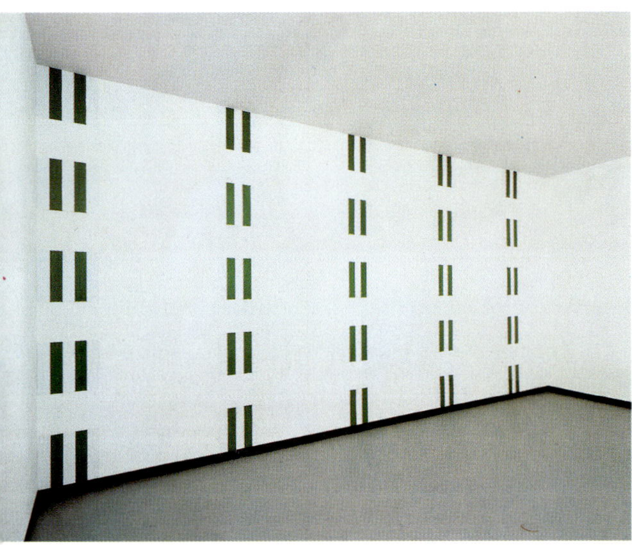

47 Daniel Buren ■

25 Enamel Plates, 1993

Emaillierte Metallplatten, je 43,5 x 43,5 cm, nach den Anweisungen des Künstlers auf einer Wand zu installieren, siehe Appendix. Gesamtmaße variabel. Auflage: 15, jede Arbeit in einer anderen Farbe, mit sign. und num. Zertifikat.

25 pieces of steel with baked enamel, 17¼ x 17¼ in. ea., to be installed on a wall according to the artist's instructions, see appendix. Edition: 15, each work unique in color, with a signed and numbered certificate.

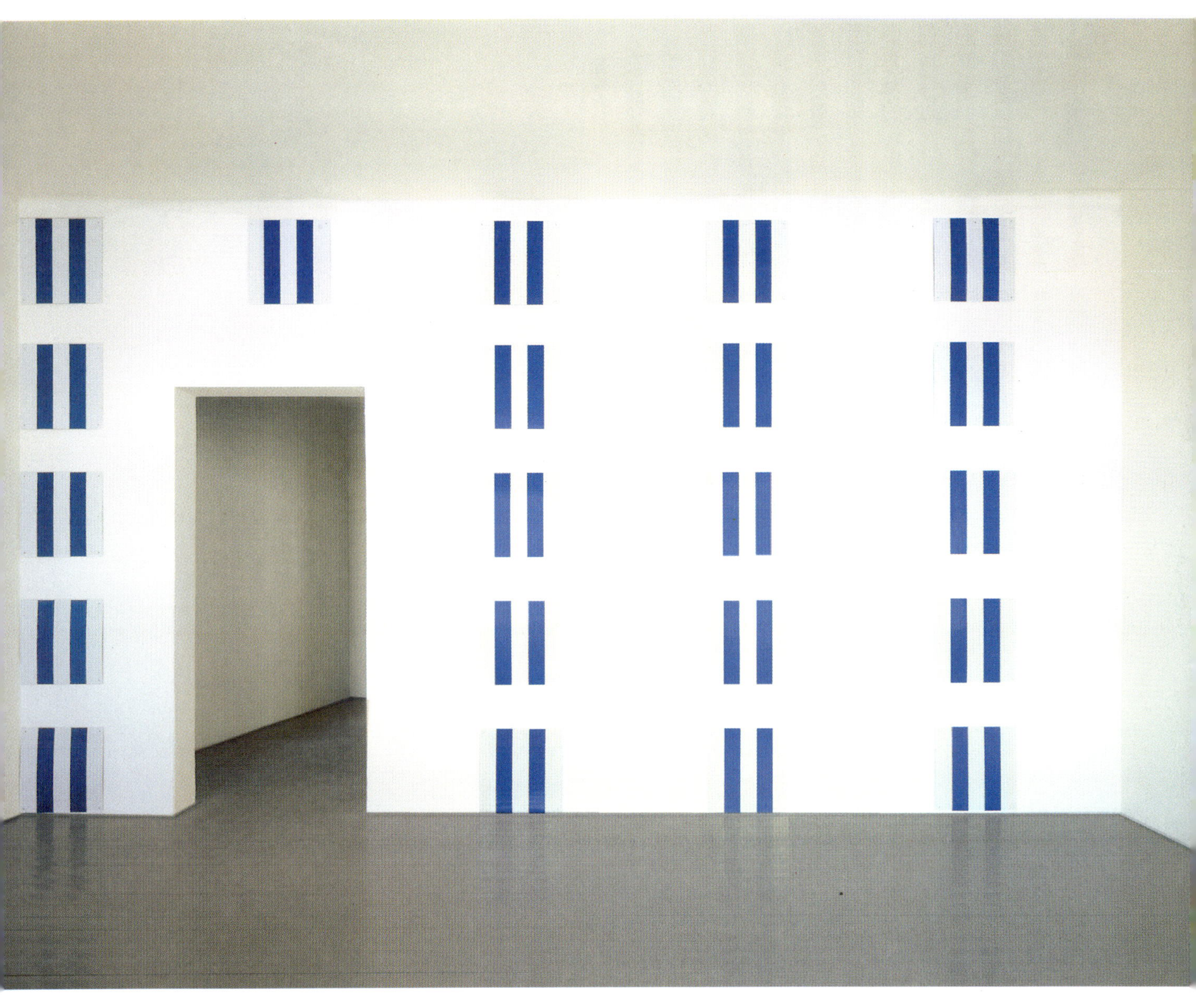

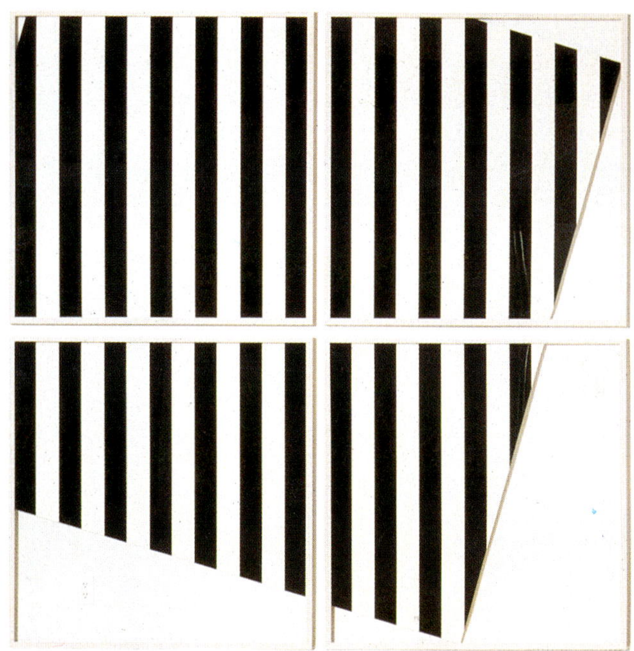

48 Daniel Buren
The Rotating Square In and Out of the Frame, 1989
4-teilige Lithographie, 242,5 x 242,5 cm.
Auflage: 36, jede in einer anderen Position
Series of situated lithographs in 4 panels, 96½ x 96½ in.
Edition: 36, each unique in position

49 Daniel Buren ■ →
Three Light Boxes for One Wall, 1989
Wandobjekt bestehend aus 3 Leuchtkästen, Plexiglas mit Siebdruck, 60 x 80, 80 x 80 und 100 x 80 cm, je 8,5 cm tief. Auflage: 15, jede Arbeit in einer anderen Farbe
Wall object consisting of 3 electrical light boxes with silkscreen on plexi, 23½ x 31½, 31½ x 31½, and 39 x 31½ in. Edition: 15, each work unique in color

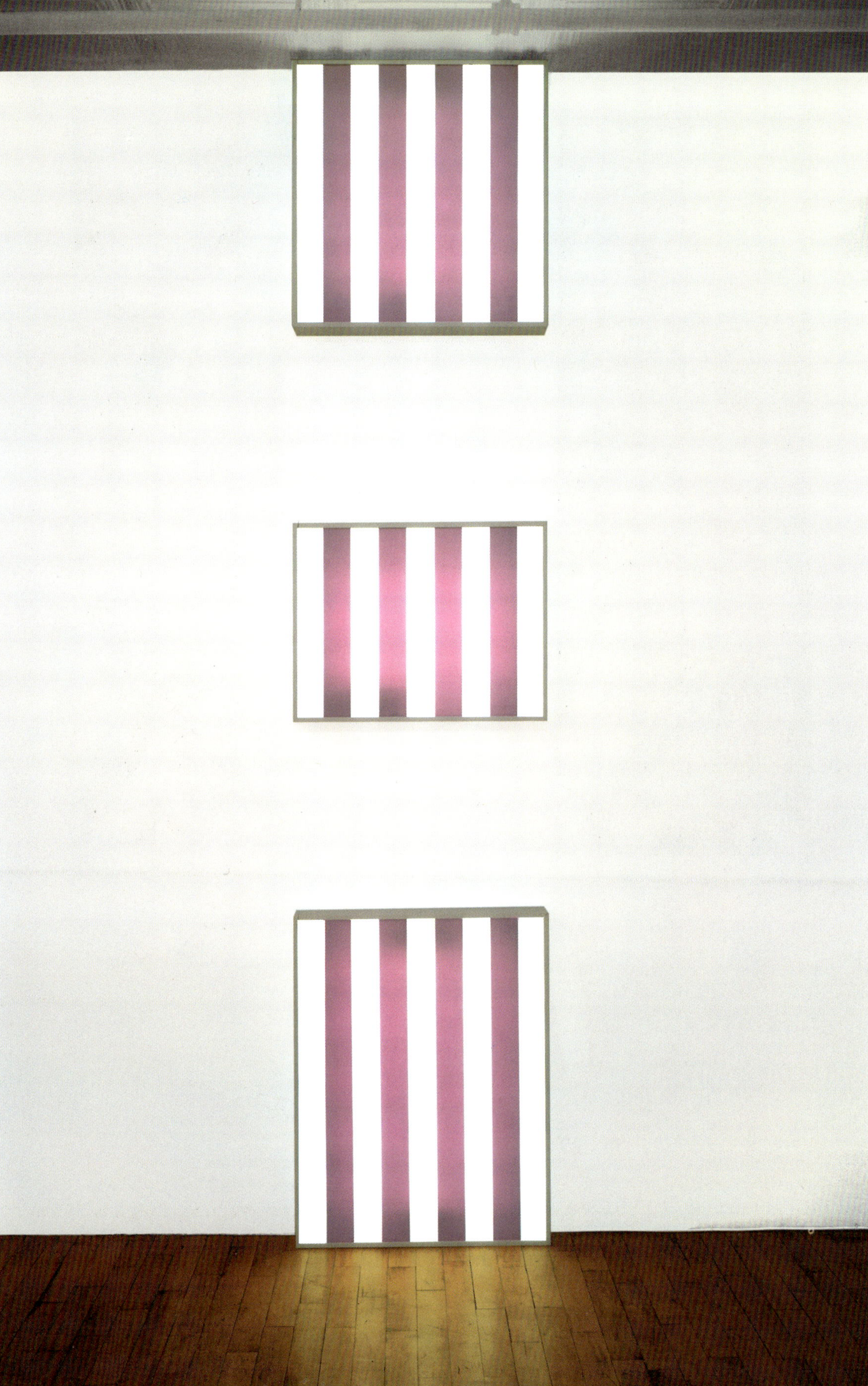

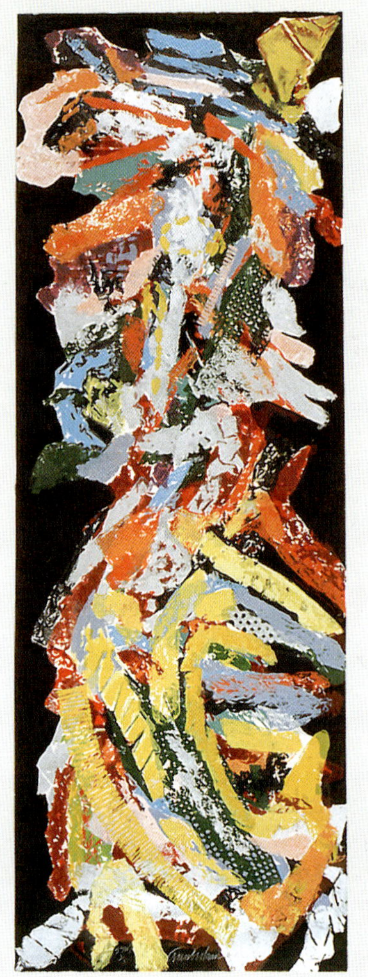

50 John Chamberlain
Untitled (Spurtlux), 1993
Serigraphie und Prägung, 209,5 x 75 cm.
Auflage: 27
Silkscreen and relief print, 82½ x 29½ in.
Edition: 27

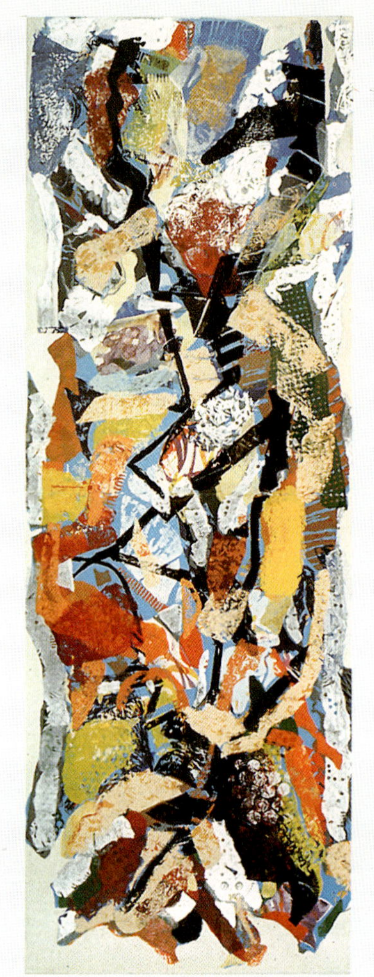

51 John Chamberlain
After Dogberry, 1993
Serigraphie und Prägung, 209,5 x 75 cm.
Auflage: 33
Silkscreen and relief print, 82½ x 29½ in.
Edition: 33

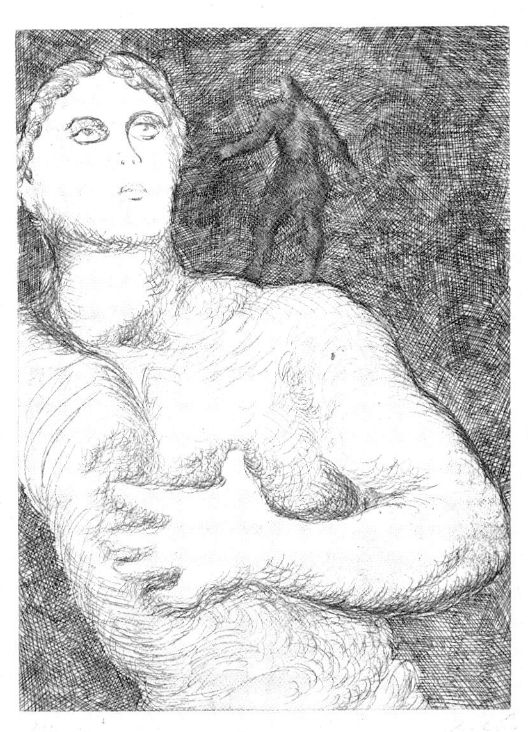

52 Sandro Chia ■
Boy and his Double, 1983
Radierung, 122 x 80 cm. Auflage: 25. *Etching, 48 x 31 in. Edition: 25*

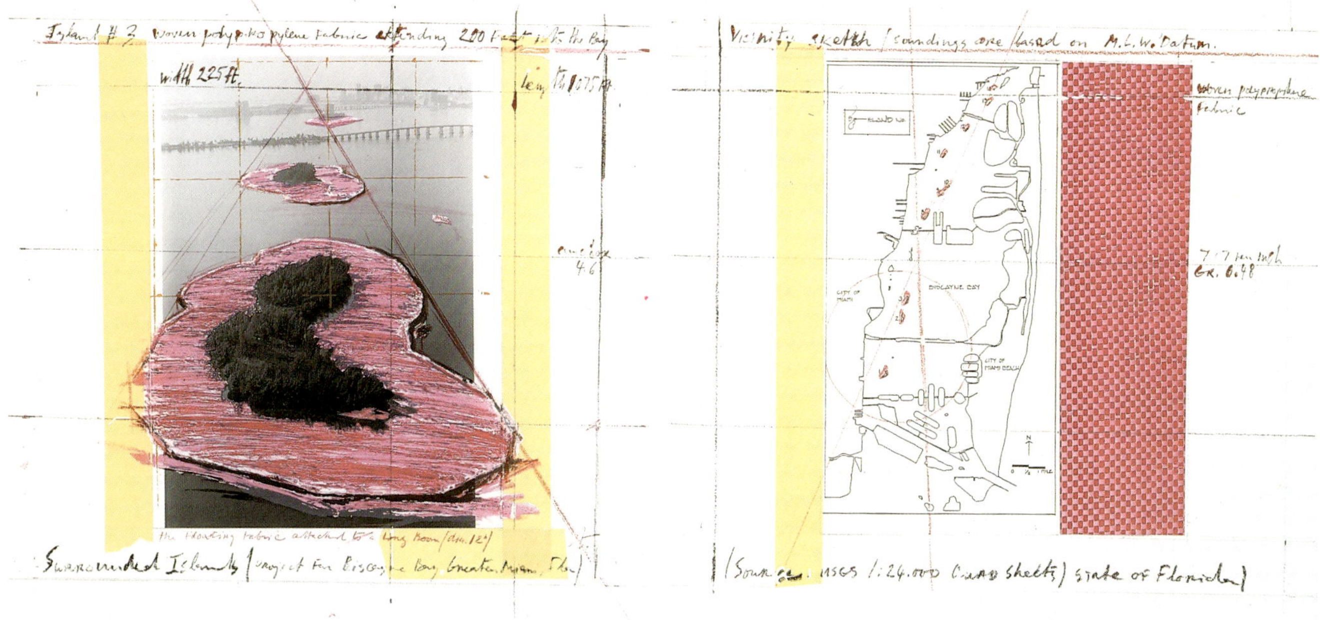

53 Christo ■

Surrounded Islands, 1987

Photo, Siebdruck, Lichtdruck, Klebeband; zweiteilig, je 38 x 40 cm. Auflage: 125

Photograph with silkscreen, collotype and masking tape; two parts, 15 x 15¾ in. ea. Edition: 125

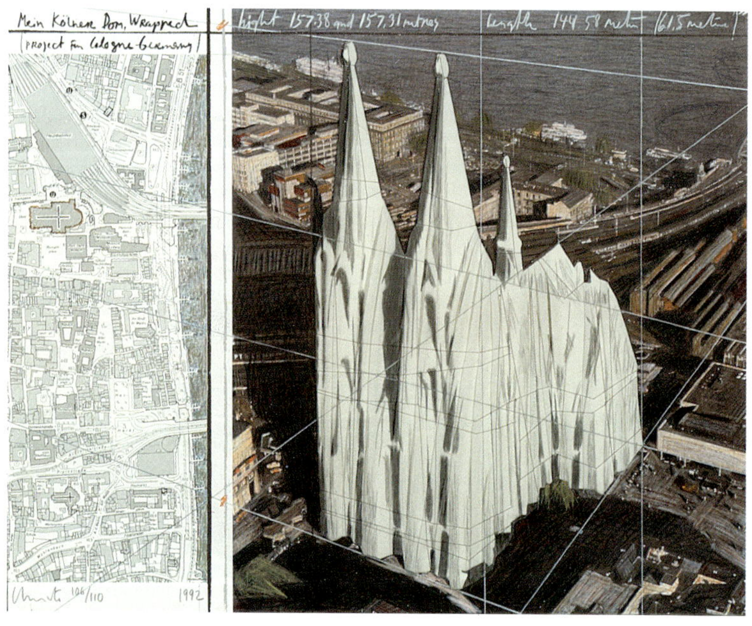

54 Christo

Mein Kölner Dom, Wrapped, Project for Cologne, 1992

Lithographie mit Collage (Stoff, Bindfaden, mit Kohle- und Bleistift überarbeitet), 71 x 56 cm. Auflage: 110

Lithograph with collage of fabric and twine, with charcoal and pencil additions, 28 x 22 in. Edition: 110

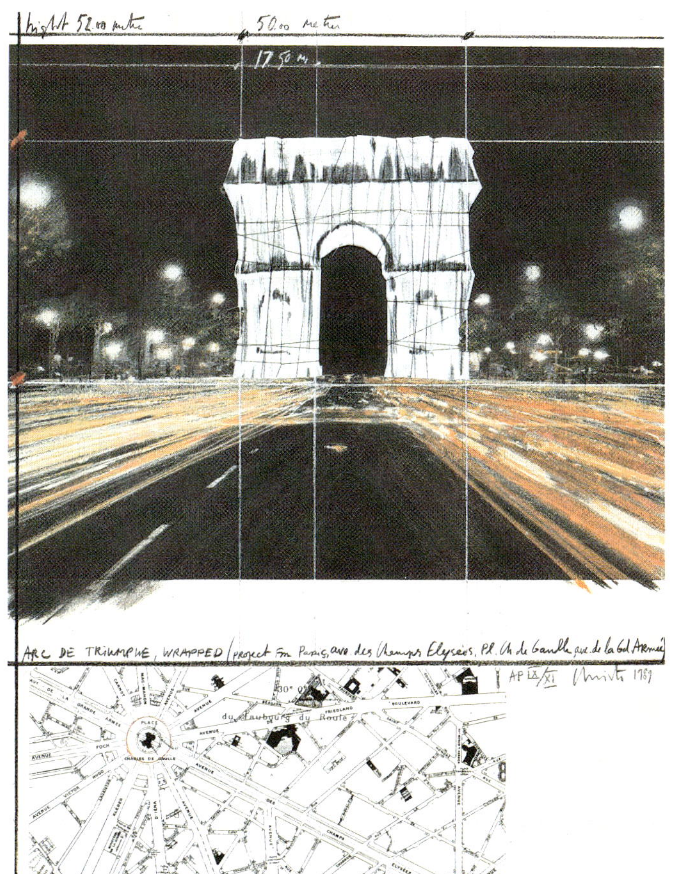

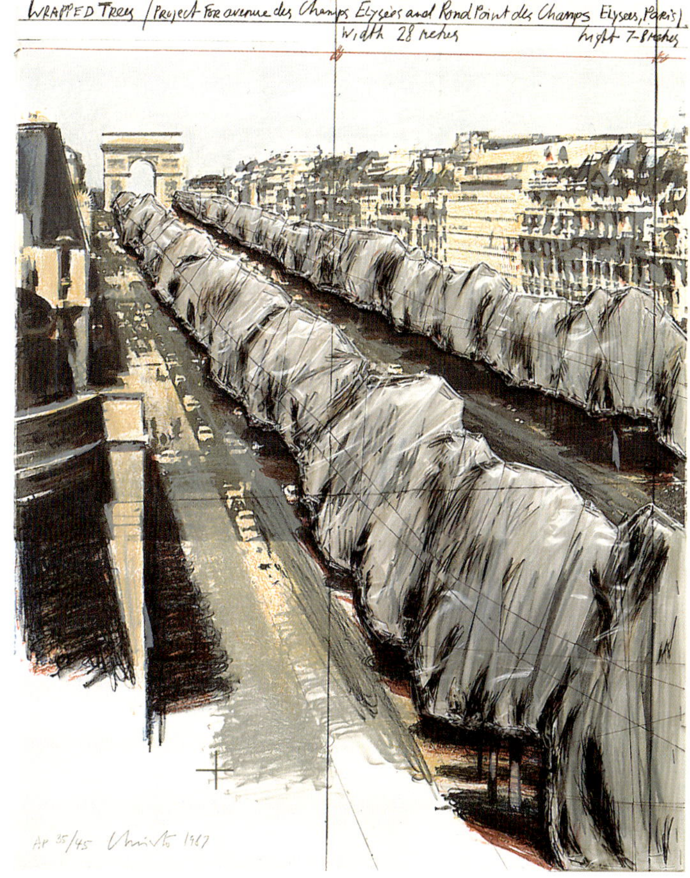

55 Christo
Arc de Triomphe, Wrapped, Project for Paris, 1989
Lithographie mit Collage (Stoff, Zwirn und Stadtplan, mit Farb- und Kohlestift überarbeitet), 71 x 56 cm.
Auflage: 150
Lithograph with collage of cloth, thread, and city map, with additions of charcoal and crayon, 28 x 22 in.
Edition: 150

56 Christo
Wrapped Trees, Project for the Champs Elysées, Paris, 1987
Lithographie mit Collage (transparente Folie, Zwirn, Heftklammern, mit Filzstift bearbeitet), 71 x 56,5 cm.
Auflage: 200
Lithograph with collage of transparent polyethylene, thread, and staples, with felt marker additions, 28 x 22¼ in. Edition: 200

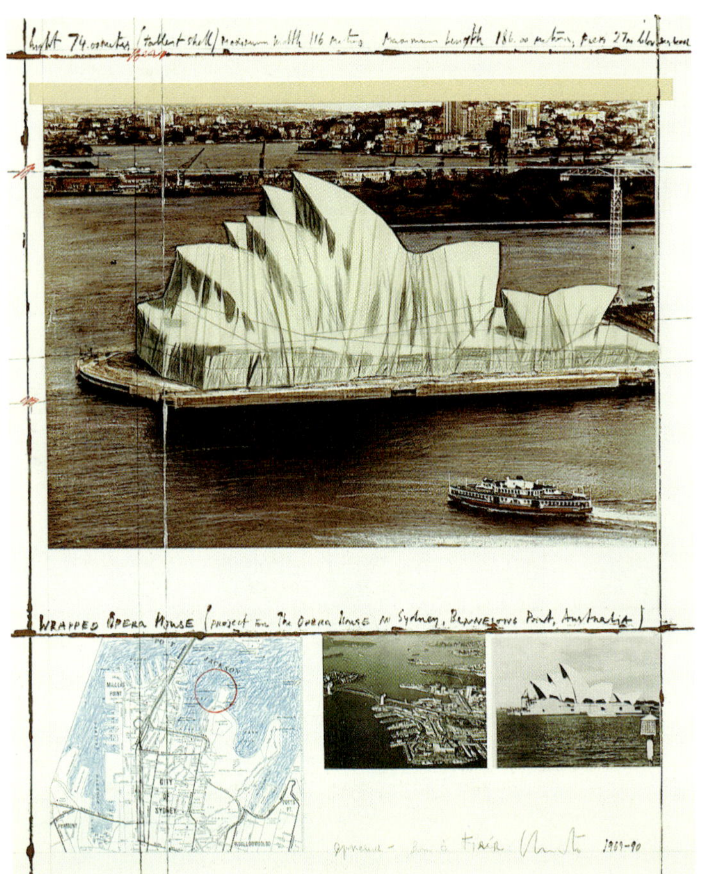

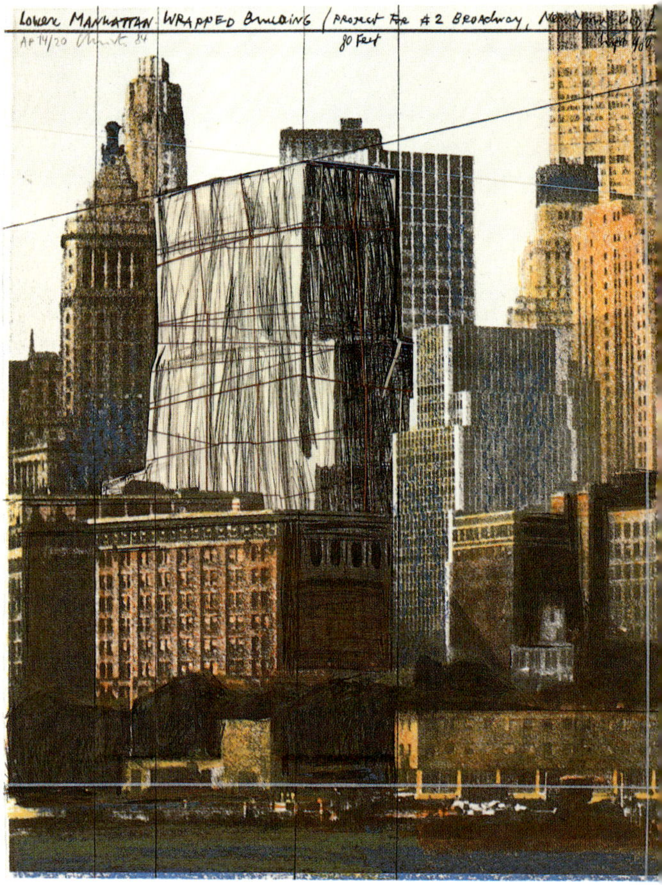

57 Christo
Wrapped Opera House, Sydney, 1991
Lithographie mit Collage (Stoff, Bindfaden, Photos und Klebstreifen), 77 x 63 cm. Auflage: 120
Lithograph with collage of fabric, thread, photographs and masking tape, 30¼ 24¾ in. Edition: 120

58 Christo
Lower Manhattan Wrapped Building, New York, 1984
Lithographie mit Collage (Stoff, Bindfaden, Zwirn), 71 x 56 cm. Auflage: 110
Lithograph with collage of fabric, twine, and thread, 28 x 22 in. Edition: 110

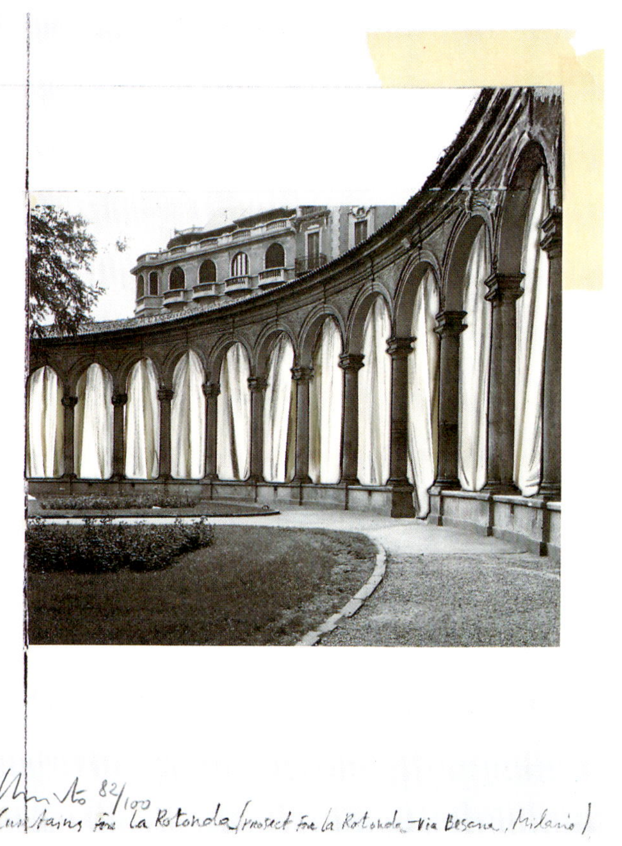

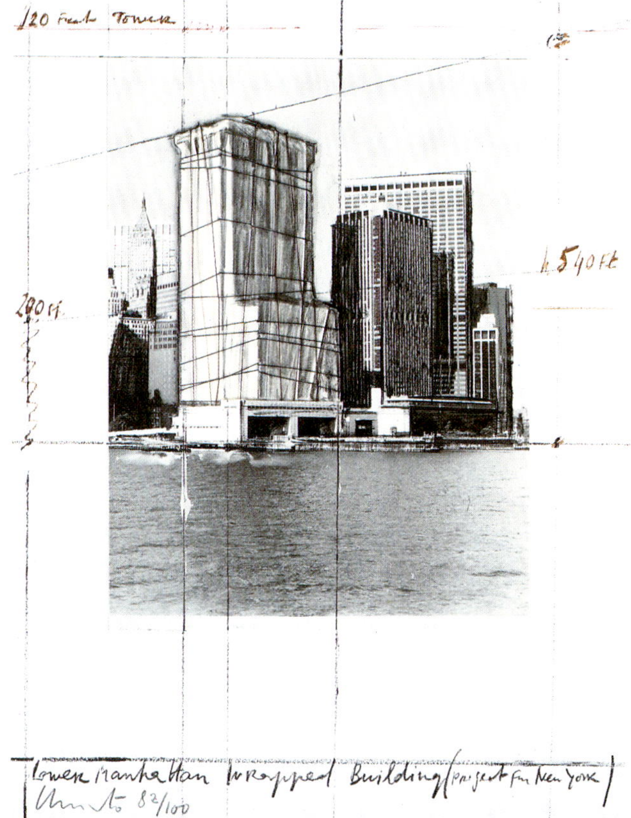

59 Christo ■
Five Urban Projects, 1985
Mappe mit 5 Collagen (Photo, Lichtdruck, Siebdruck, Stoff, Polyäthylenfolie, Faden, Bleistift), 35,5 x 28 cm. Auflage: 100
Portfolio with 5 collage prints (Photograph, collotype, silkscreen, fabric, polyethylene, twine; pencil and felt marker additions). 14 x 11 in. Edition: 100

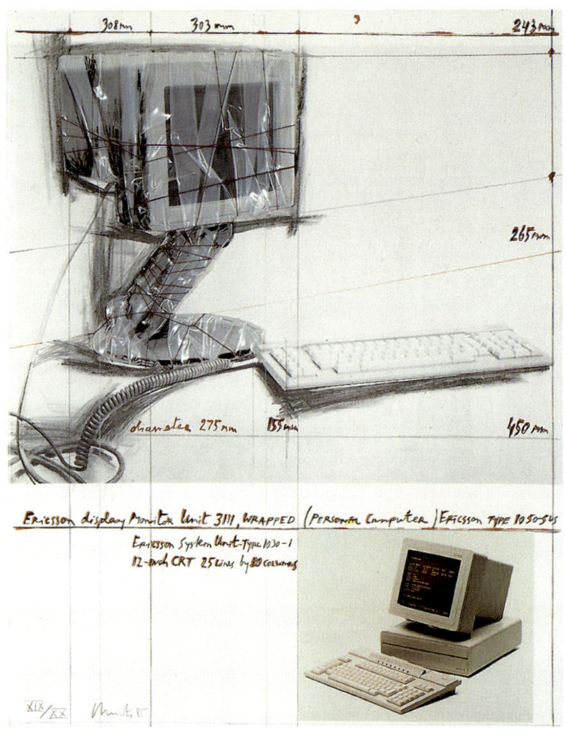

60 Christo
Ericsson Display Monitor, Wrapped, 1985
Lithographie mit Collage (Polyäthylenfolie, Bindfaden und Photo), 71 x 57 cm. Auflage: 100 + XX
Lithograph with collage of polyethylene, twine, and photograph, 28 x 22 in. Edition: 100 + XX

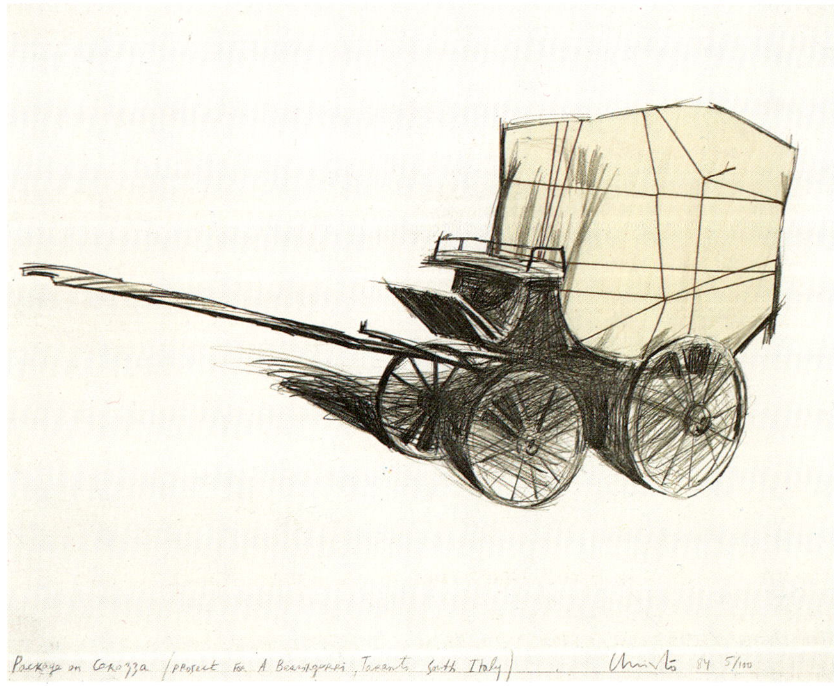

61 Christo ■
Package on Carozza, 1984
Lithographie mit Collage (Stoff und Schnur), 56 x 71 cm.
Auflage: 100
Lithograph with collage of fabric and twine, 22 x 38 in.
Edition: 100

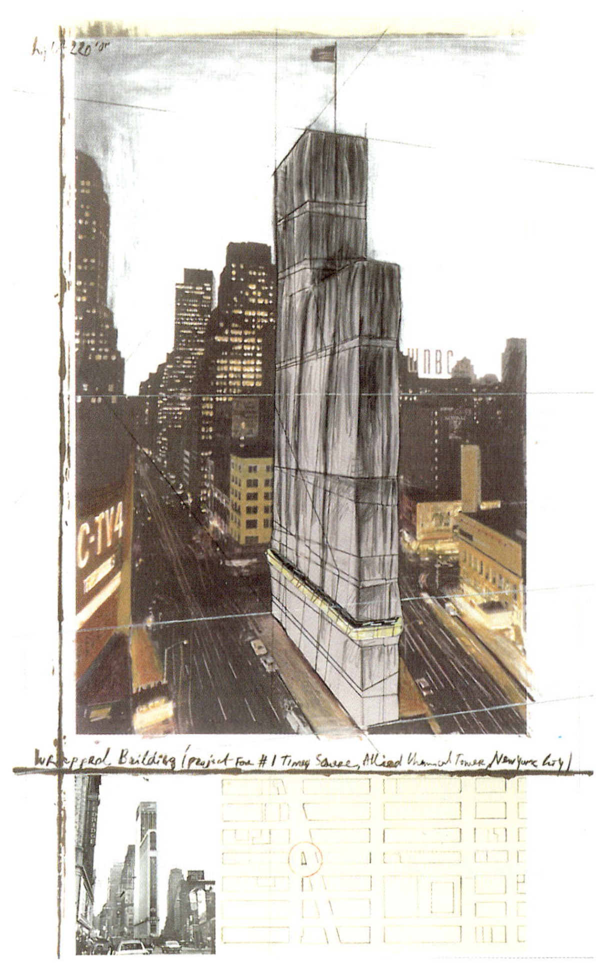

62 Christo

Wrapped Building, 1 Times Square, New York, 1991

Lithogaphie mit Collage (Stoff, Zwirn, Polyäthylen, Heftklammern, Photo, Plan und Klebstreifen, mit Kohle- und Farbstift bearbeitet), 100 x 63,5 cm. Auflage: 125

Lithograph with collage of fabric, thread, polyethylene, staples, map, masking tape, and crayon additions, 39½ x 25 in. Edition: 125

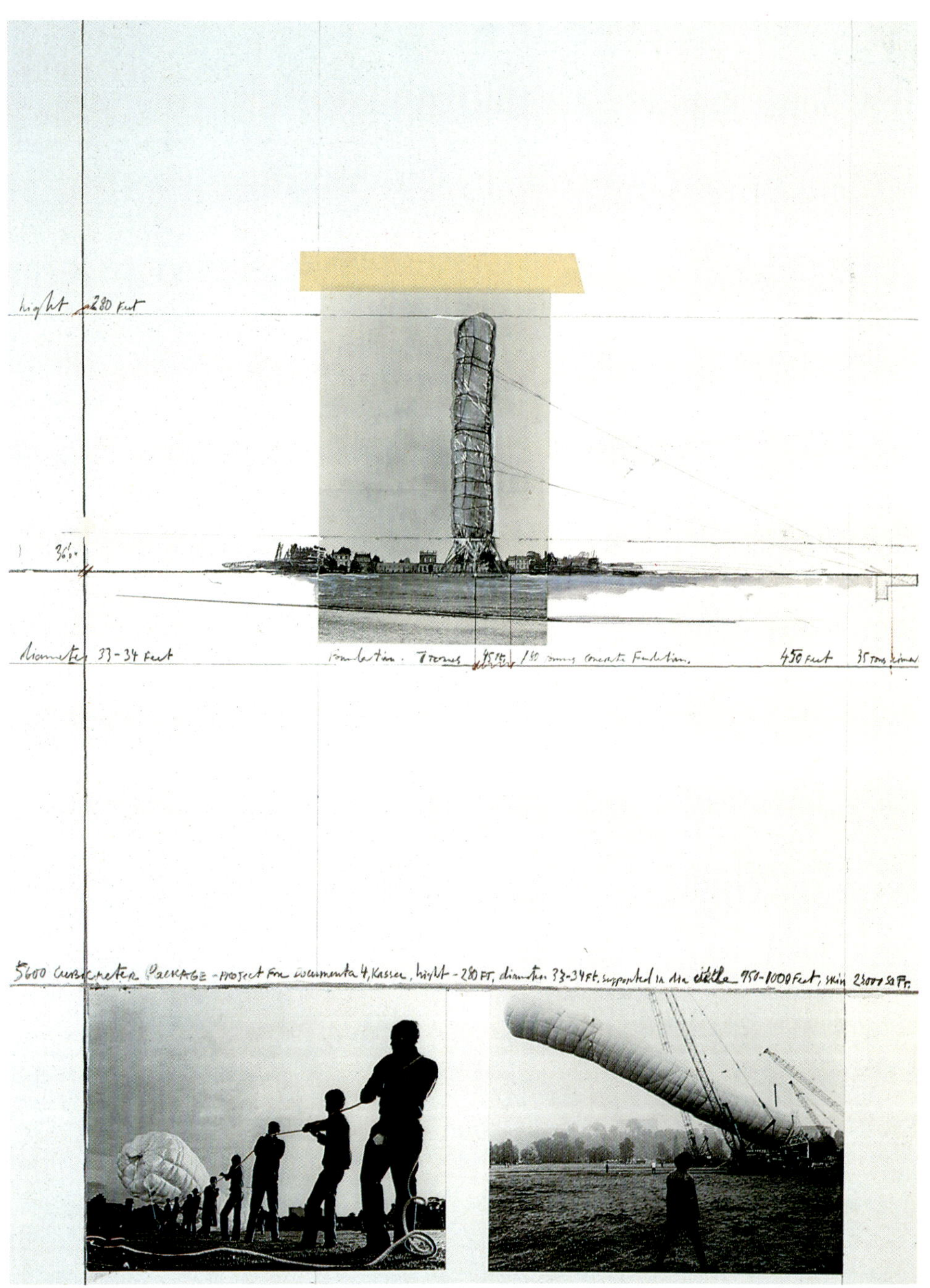

63 Christo ■

5,600 Cubic Meter Package, Kassel, 1986

Lichtdruck und Serigraphie mit Collage (Photos, Klebeband, Plastikfolie, Faden), 80 x 60 cm. Auflage: 90

Collotype and silkscreen with collage of photographs, masking tape, polyethylene and twine, 31½ x 23½ i
Edition: 90

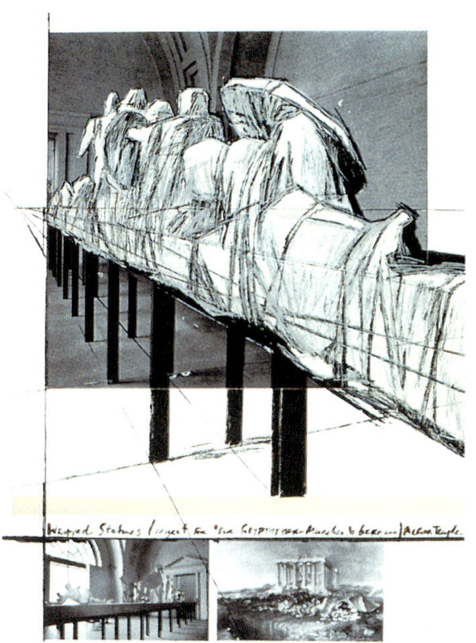

64 Christo
Wrapped Statues, Glyptothek München, 1988
Siebdruck und Collage, 89 x 68,5 cm.
Auflage: 300
Silkscreen and collage, 35 x 27 in.
Edition: 300

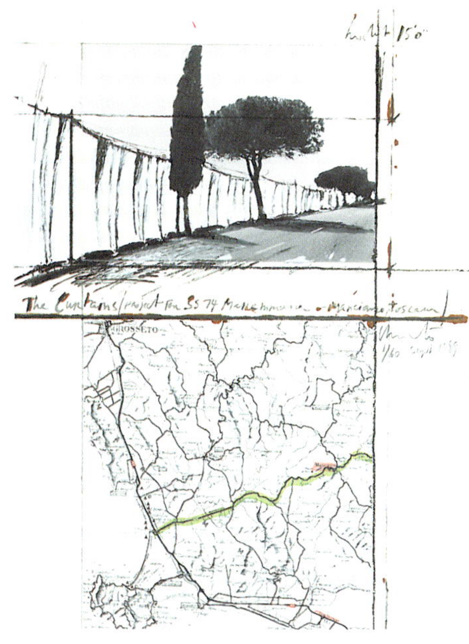

65 Christo ■
The Curtains, Project for Tuscany, 1989
Siebdruck und Collage, 38,5 x 28 cm.
Auflage: 60
Silkscreen and collage, 15 ¼ x 11 in.
Edition: 60

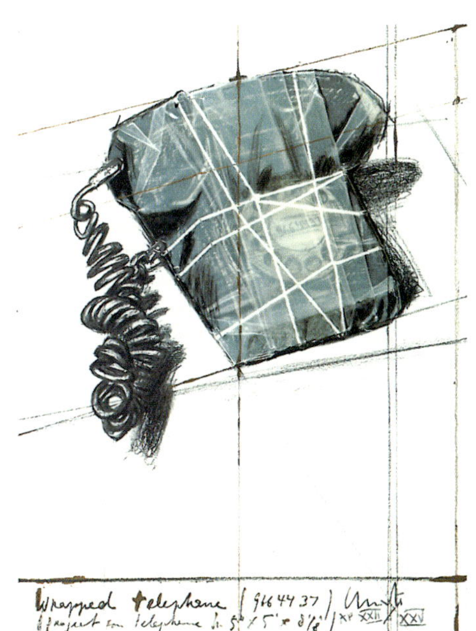

66 Christo
Wrapped Telephone, 1988
Lithographie mit Collage (Polyäthylen, Schnur,
mit Wachsstift bearbeitet), 56 x 38 cm. Auflage: 100
Lithograph with collage of polyethylene and twine,
with grease pencil additions, 22 ¼ x 15 in. Edition: 100

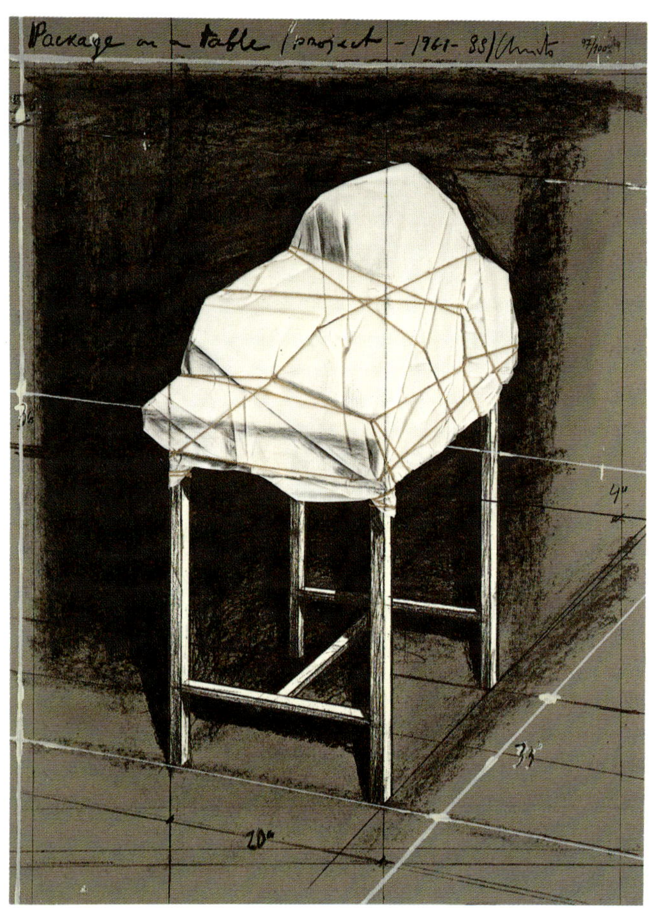

67 Christo
Package on a Table, 1988
Lithographie und Bleistift auf Pappe mit Collage (Stoff und Schnur), 81 x 61 cm. Auflage: 100
Lithograph and pencil on cardboard with collage of fabric and twine, 32 x 24 in. Edition: 100

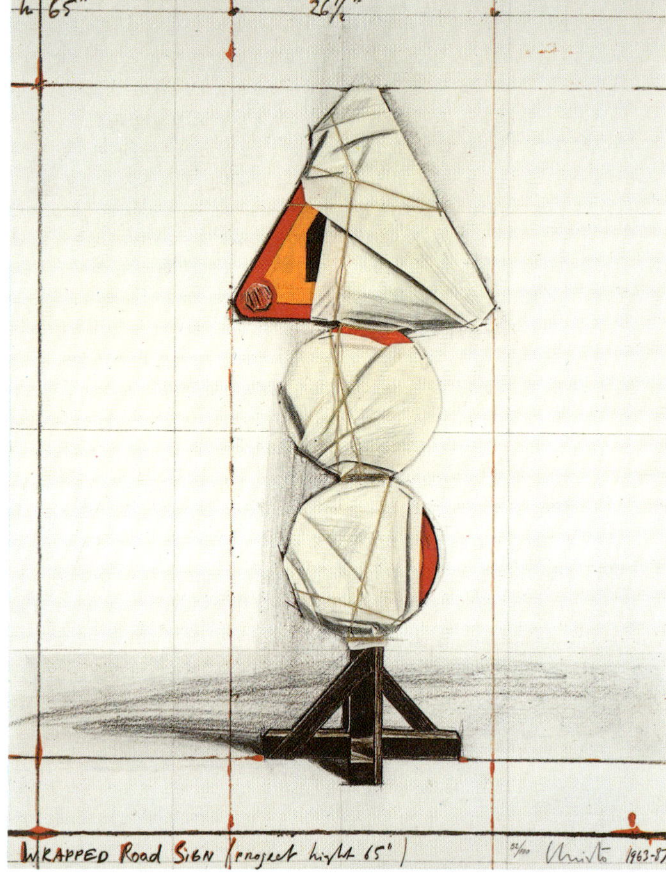

68 Christo
Wrapped Road Sign, 1988
Lithographie mit Collage (Stoff und Schnur), 70,5 x 55,5 cm. Auflage: 100
Lithograph with collage of fabric and twine, 28 x 22 in. Edition: 100

69 Christo ■ →
Wrapped Roman Sculptures, 1990
Collage aus Stoff, Polyäthylen und Schnur, mit Lichtdruck und Serigraphie, mit Bleistift bearbeitet, 100 x 70 cm
Auflage: 111
Handmade collage of fabric, polyethylene, twine with collotype, silkscreen and pencil additions, 39½ x 28½ in. Edition: 111

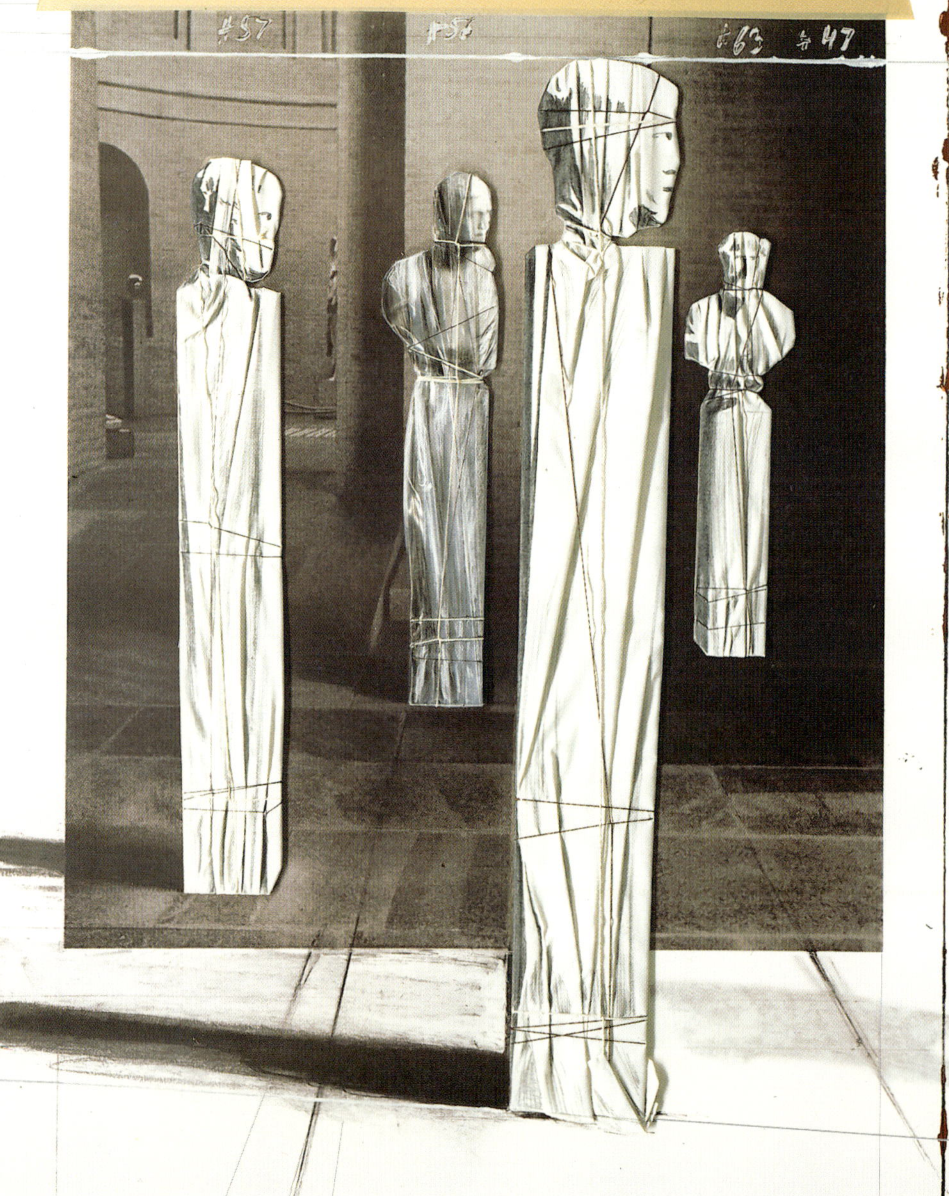
#57 #56 #63 #47
#57 - head of a man 260 A.D.
#63 - Large head of a man early 4th century A.D.
#47 - Bust of a man - 200 A.D.
WRAPPED Roman Sculptures (PROJECT FOR DIE GLYPTOTHEK - München) Christo 71/III

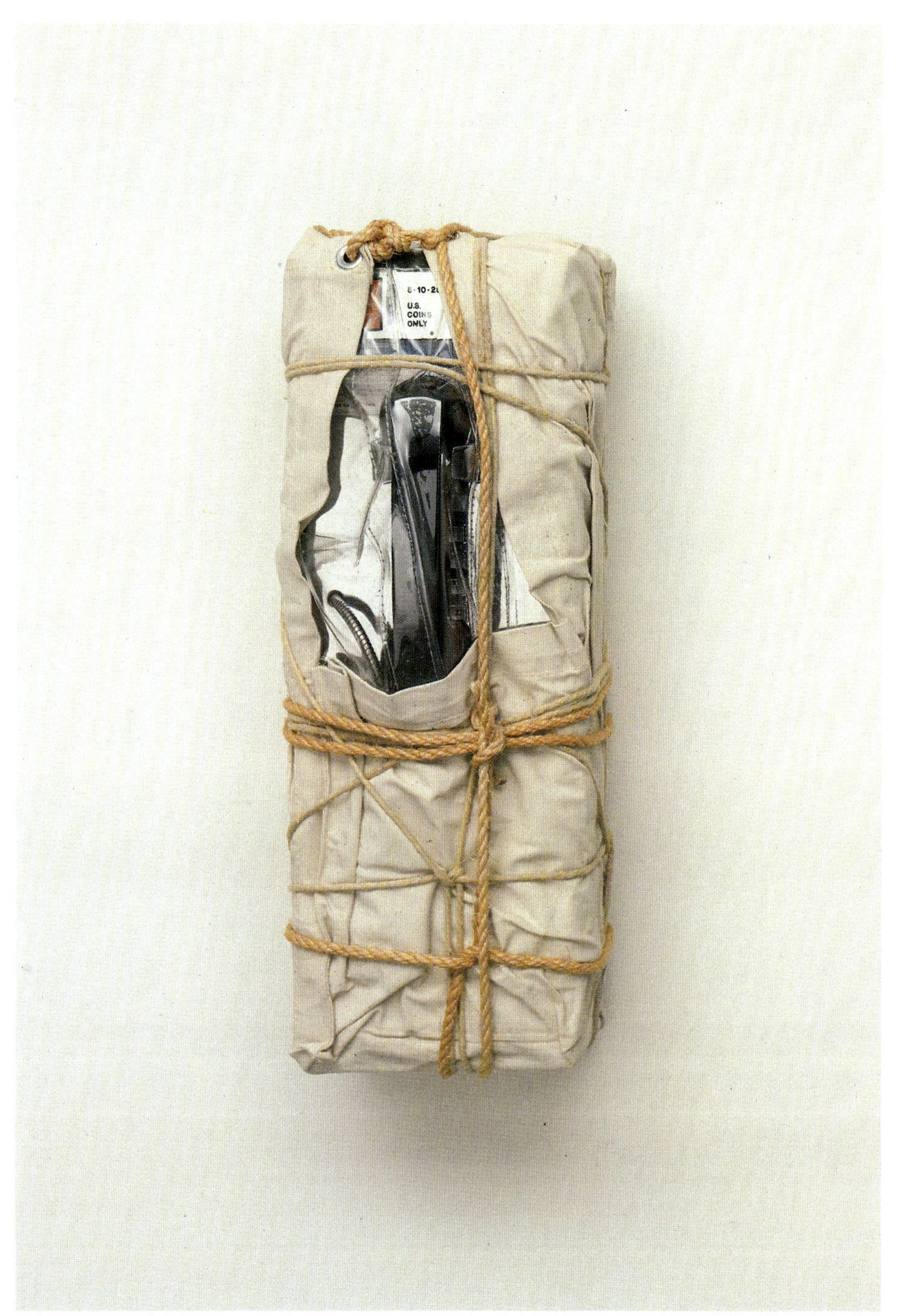

70 Christo ■

Wrapped Payphone, 1988

New Yorker Münztelephon verpackt mit Stoff, Polyäthylen und Schnur, 58 x 24,5 x 23,5 cm. Auflage: 30

New York payphone wrapped in canvas, polyethylene and rope, 23 x 10 x 9 in. Edition: 30

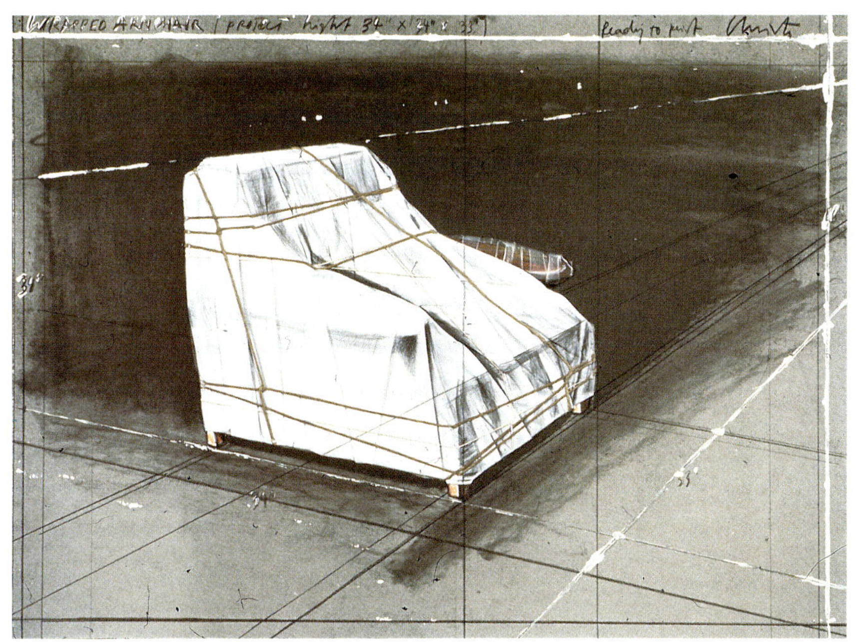

71 Christo
Wrapped Armchair, 1990
Lithographie und Serigraphie mit Collage (Stoff, Polyäthylen, Bindfaden und Heftklammern, mit Bleistift bearbeitet),
64 x 88 cm. Auflage: 100
Lithograph and silkscreen with collage of cloth, polyethylene, string, twine, staples, and crayon additions, 25 x 35 in.
Edition: 100

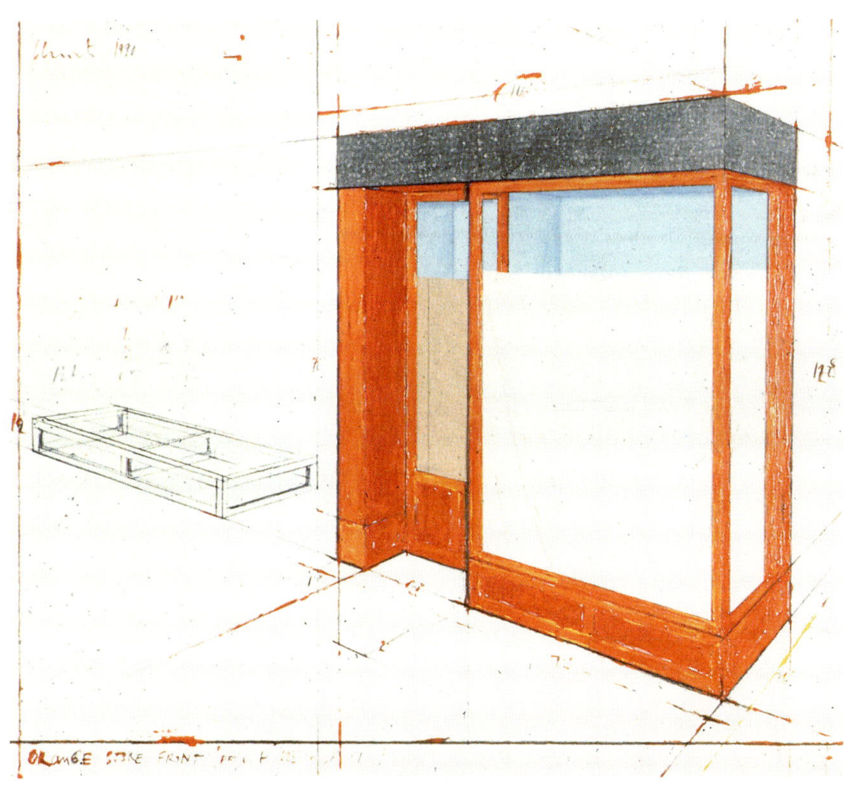

72 Christo
Orange Store Front, 1991
Lithographie, drucklackiert, mit Collage (Packpapier, Stoff, Heftklammern, Klarsichtfolie und verzinktes Eisenblech),
68,5 x 80 cm. Auflage: 100
Lithograph, varnished, with collage of brown wrapping paper, broadcloth, staples, acetate, and galvanized iron sheet,
27 x 31½ in. Edition: 100

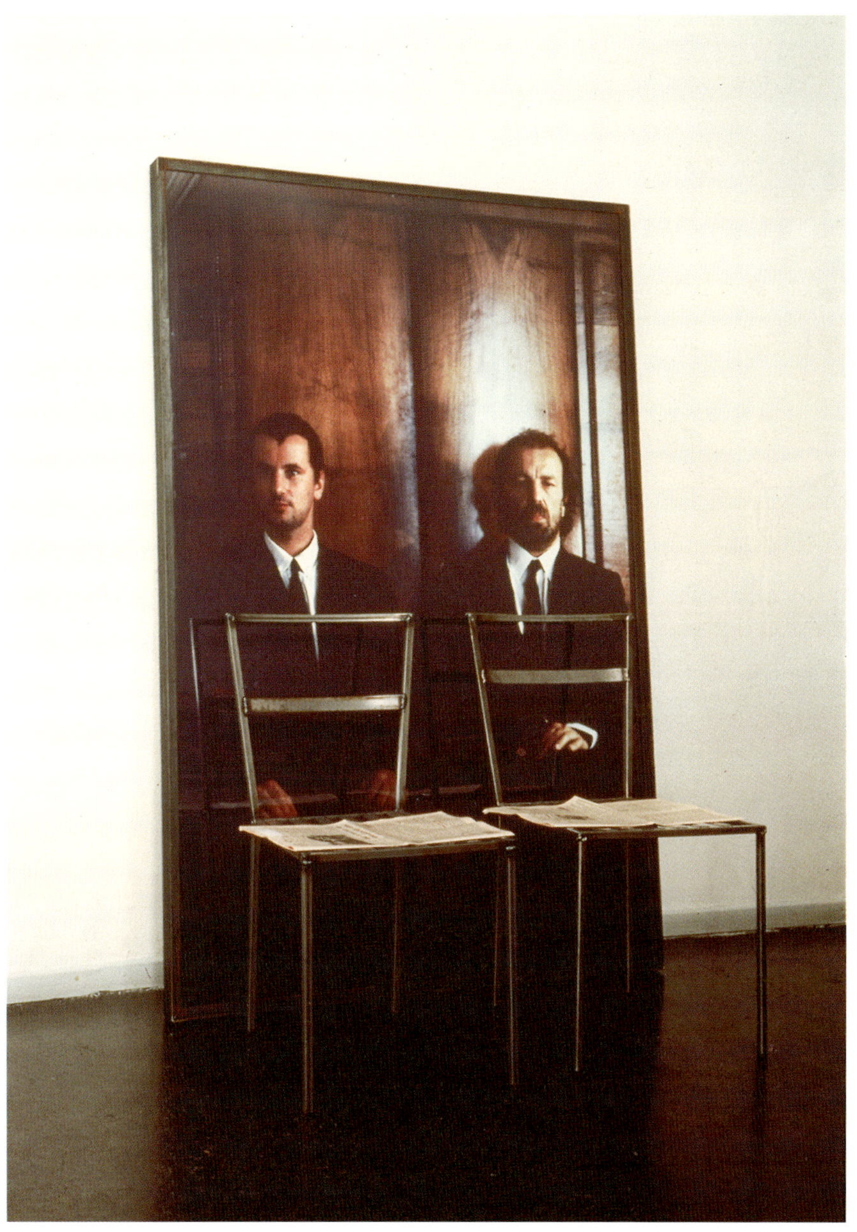

73 Clegg and Guttmann
Two and Four, 1990
Gemeinschaftsarbeit mit Franz West und Mathis Esterhazy.
Cibachrom-Photo in Stahlrahmen und zwei Stühle entworfen von Mathis Esterhazy;
Photo 183 x 125 cm, Stühle je 84 x 38 x 42 cm. Auflage: 9
Collaborative work with Fanz West and Mathis Esterhazy.
Cibachrome print with steel frame and two steel chairs designed by Mathis Esterhazy.
Print size: 72 x 49 in., size of each chair: 33 x 15 x 16½ in. Edition: 9

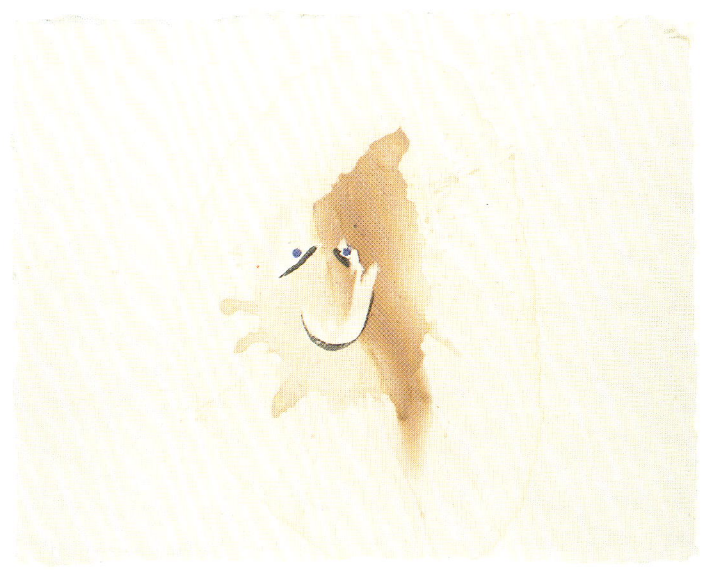

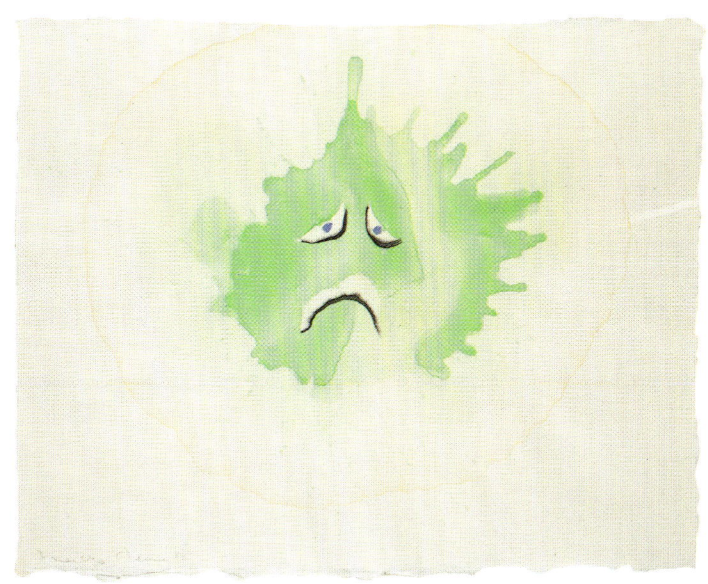

74 Francesco Clemente
'Riso' und 'Pianto', 1981
Tempera auf Reispapier, 51 x 66. Auflage: 50 verschiedene Originale
Drawing with tempera on rice paper, 20 x 26 in. Edition: 50 different originals

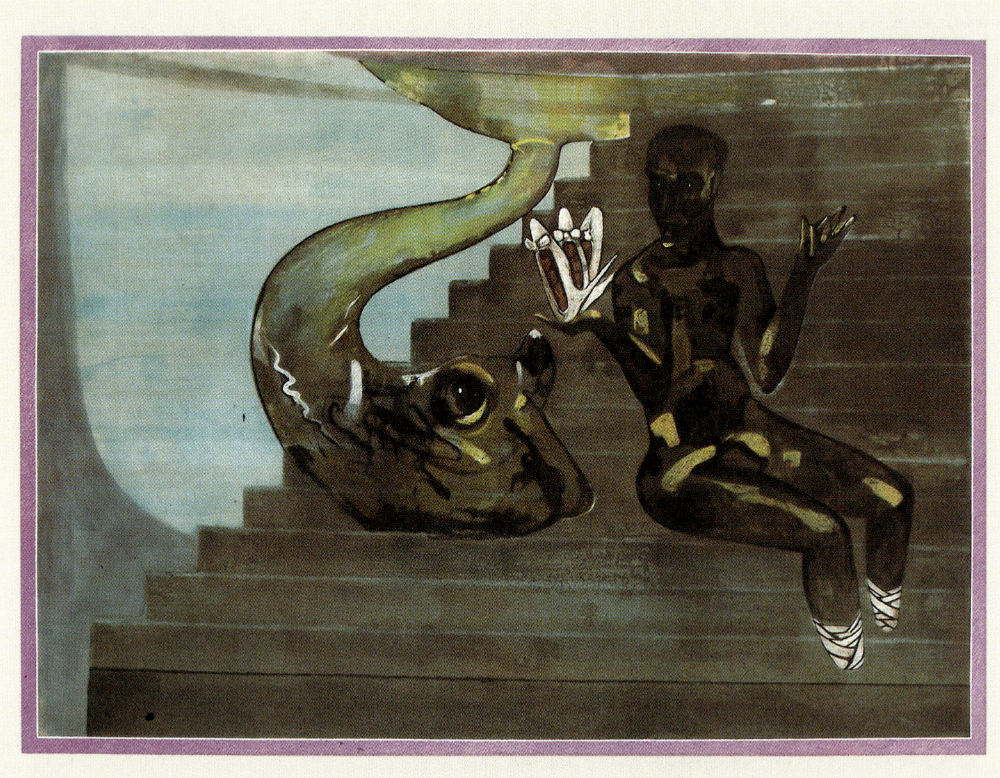

75 Francesco Clemente
Friendship, 1989
Aquatinta- und Kaltnadelradierug, 131 x 205 cm. Auflage: 70
Aquatint and drypoint, 51½ x 80¾ in. Edition: 70

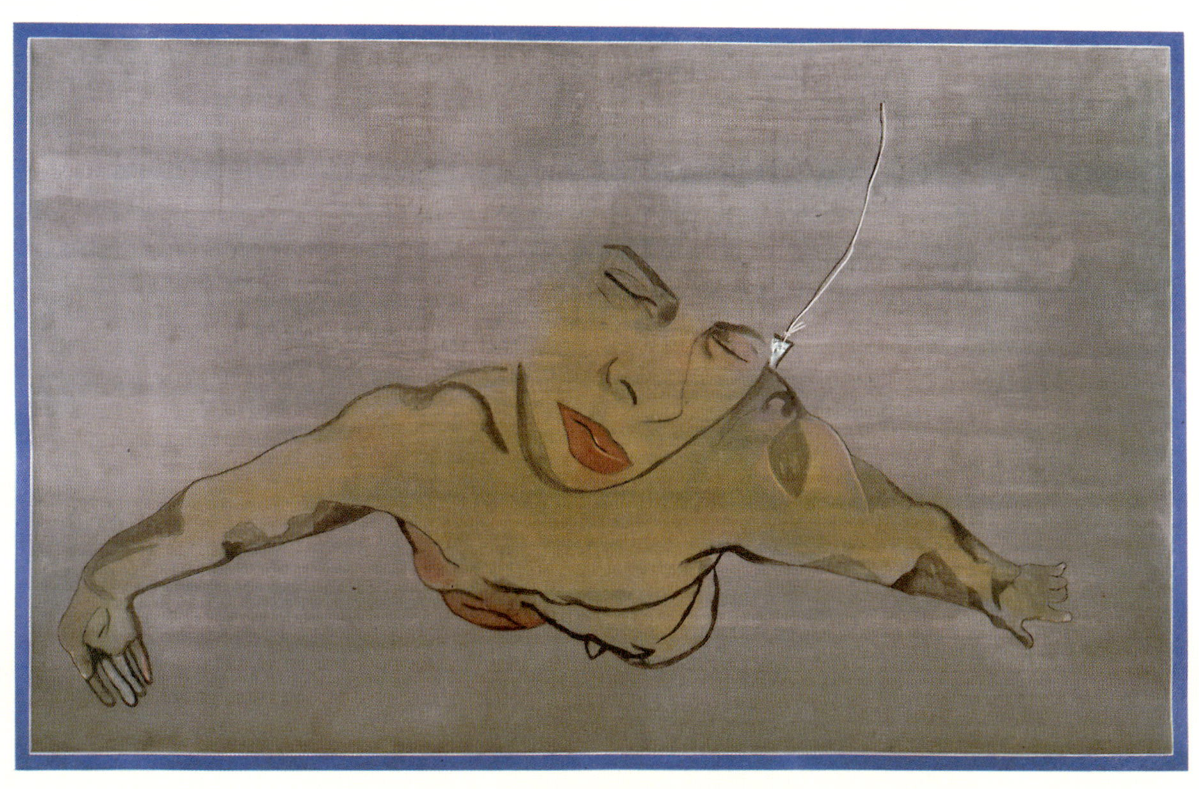

76 Francesco Clemente
Semen, 1987
Aquatinta- und Weichgrundradierung, 136 x 230 cm. Auflage: 55
Aquatint and softground, 53½ x 90½ in. Edition: 55

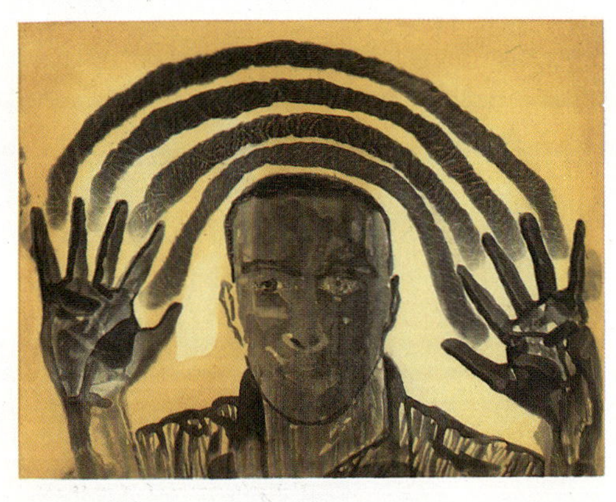

77 Francesco Clemente ■
'Faith' und 'Hope', 1986
2 Aquatinta- und Weichgrundradierungen, 45 x 62 cm. Auflage: 40
2 aquatints with softground, 18 x 24 in. Edition: 40

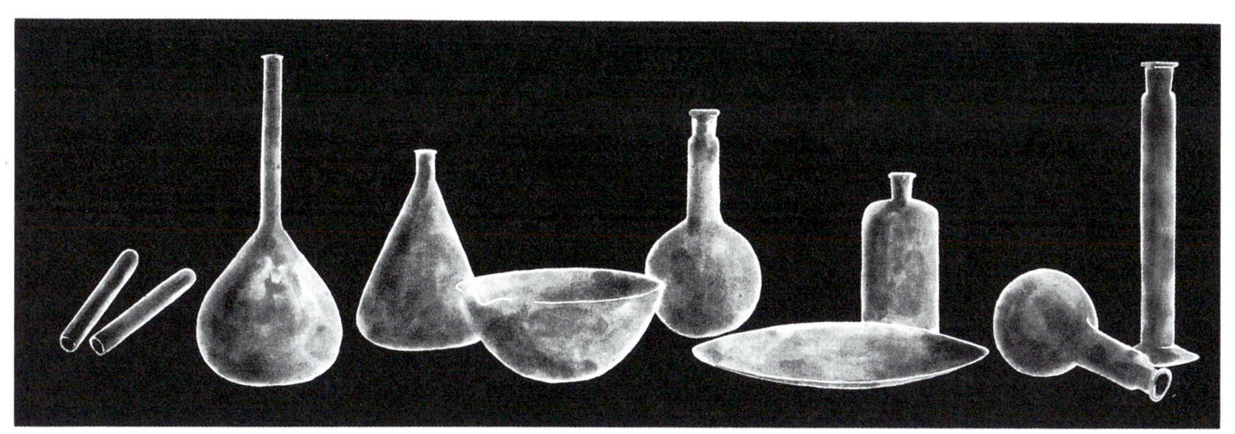

78 Tony Cragg
Laboratory Still Life No. 2, State 1, 1988
Aquatintaradierung, 53,5 x 112 cm. Auflage: 30
Aquatint, 21 x 44 in. Edition: 30

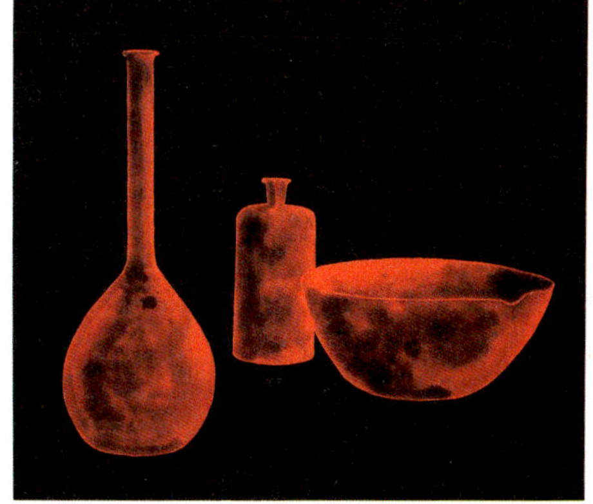

79 Tony Cragg
Laboratory Still Life No. 1, State 2, 1988
Aquatintaradierung, 58 x 59 cm. Auflage: 30
Aquatint, 23 x 23 in. Edition: 30

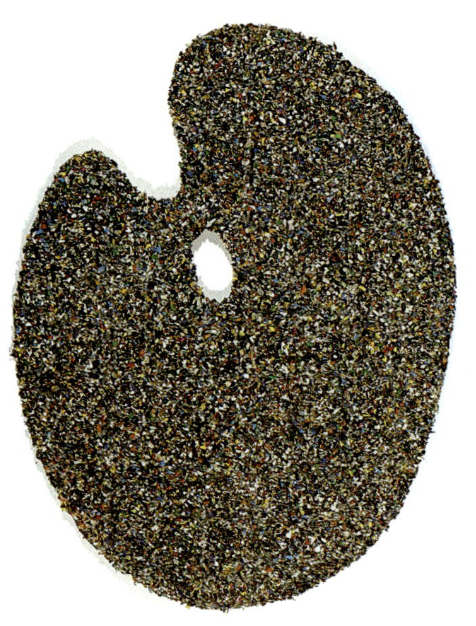

80 **Tony Cragg** ■
Palette, aus Mappe: Für Joseph Beuys, 1986
Plastikgranulat auf Holz, 74 x 57 x 1,5 cm. Auflage: 90
Wood covered with plastic granules, 29 x 22½ x ½ in.
Edition: 90

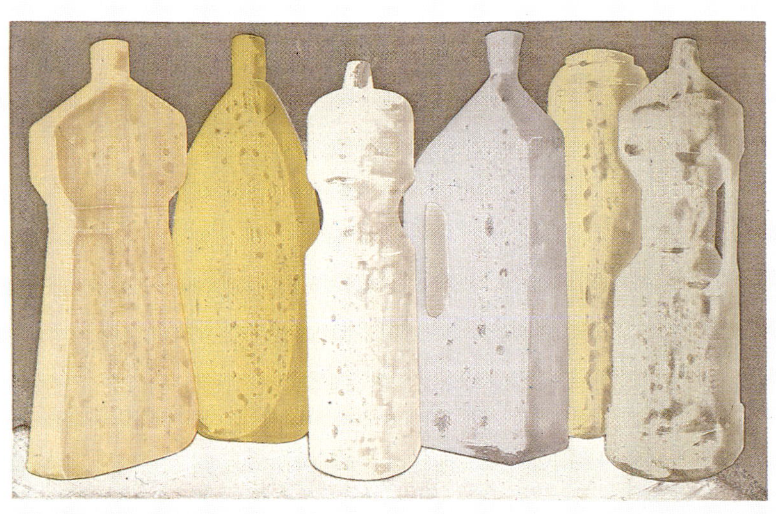

81 **Tony Cragg**
Six Bottles Large, State 2, 1988
Aquatintaradierung, 77 x 98 cm. Auflage: 25
Aquatint, 30 x 38½ in. Edition: 25

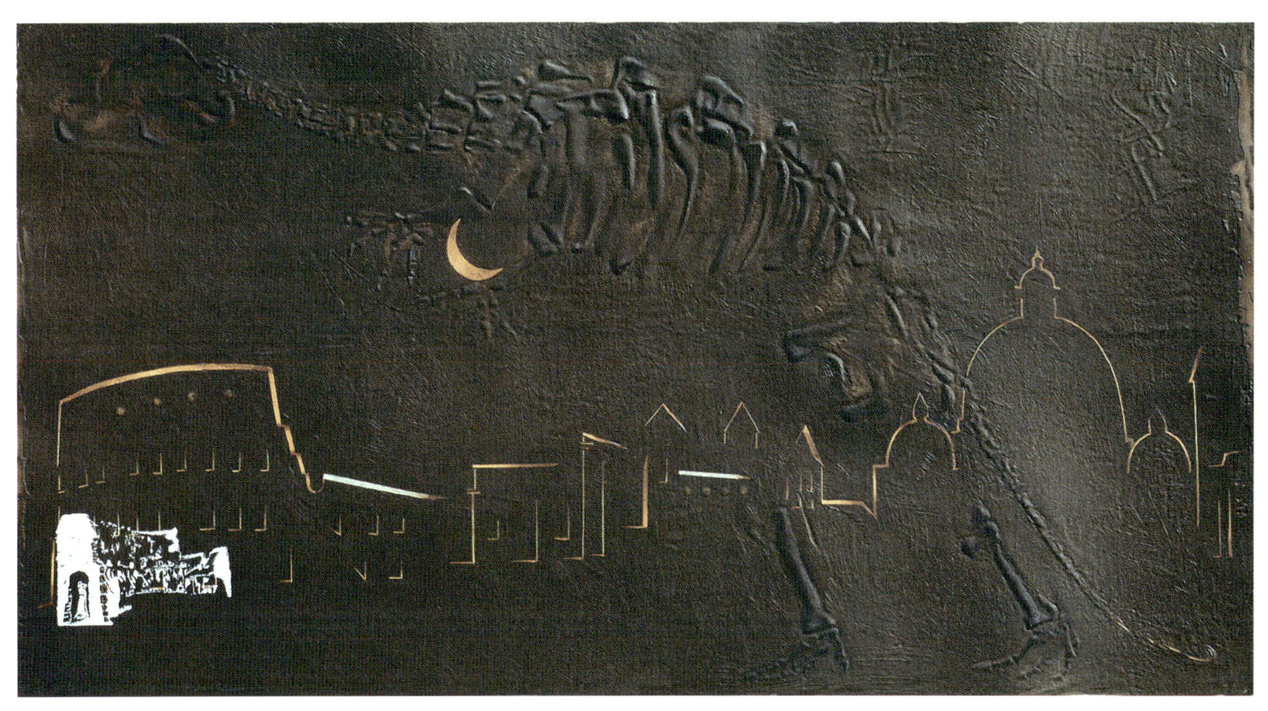

82 Enzo Cucchi
Roma, 1991
Radierung und Aquatinta, 146 x 270 cm. Auflage: 60
Etching and aquatint, 57½ x 106¼ in. Edition: 60

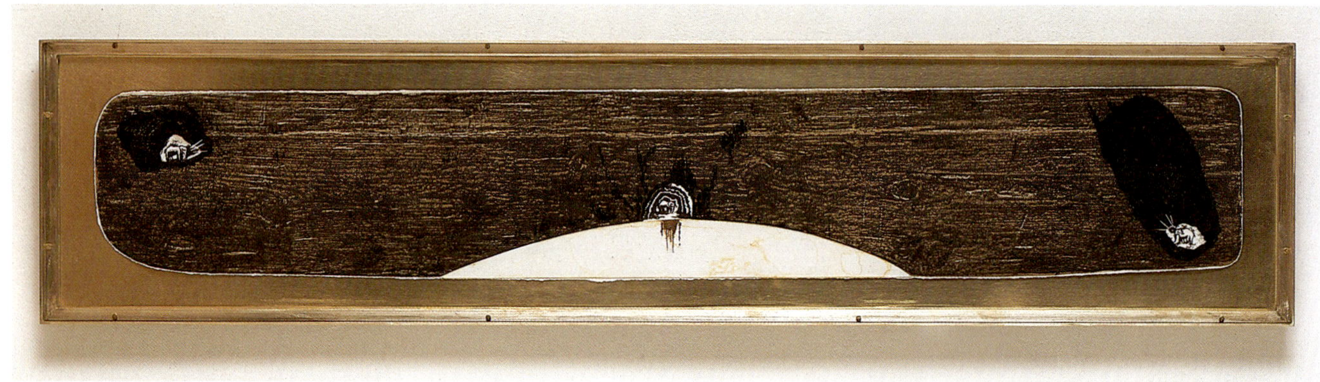

83 Enzò Cucchi ■
L' Elefante di Giotto, 1986
Lithographie und bemaltes Eisenblech, in Messingrahmen, 28 x 128 cm. Auflage: 60
Painted iron mounted on a lithograph, in brass frame, 11 x 50 in. Edition: 60

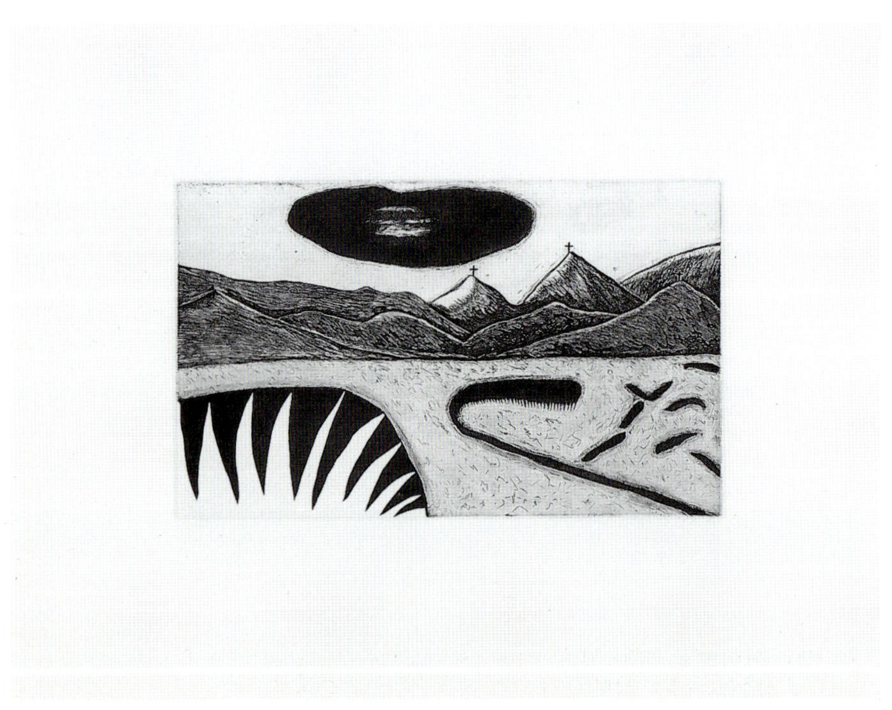

84 Enzo Cucchi
Le montagne in guerra, 1981
Aquatintaradierung, 60 x 79 cm.
Auflage: 50
Aquatint, 23½ x 31 in.
Edition: 50

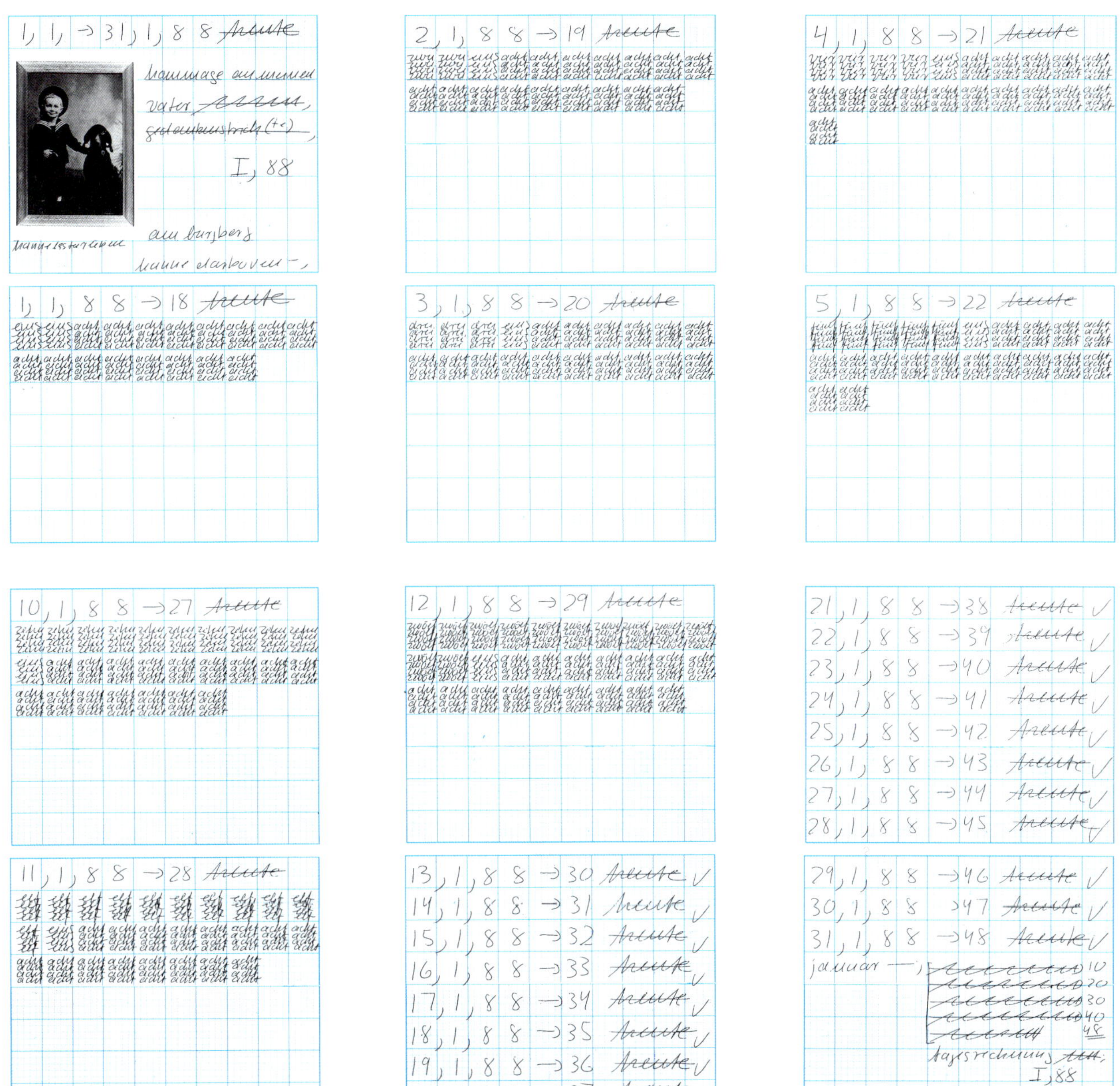

85 Hanne Darboven ■
Hommage an meinen Vater, 1989
96 Offsetlithographien, davon 12 mit collagiertem Photo, in Kassette, 29,5 x 42 cm. Auflage: 50
96 offset lithographs, 12 with photograph attached, in portfolio box, 23 x 17 in. Edition: 50

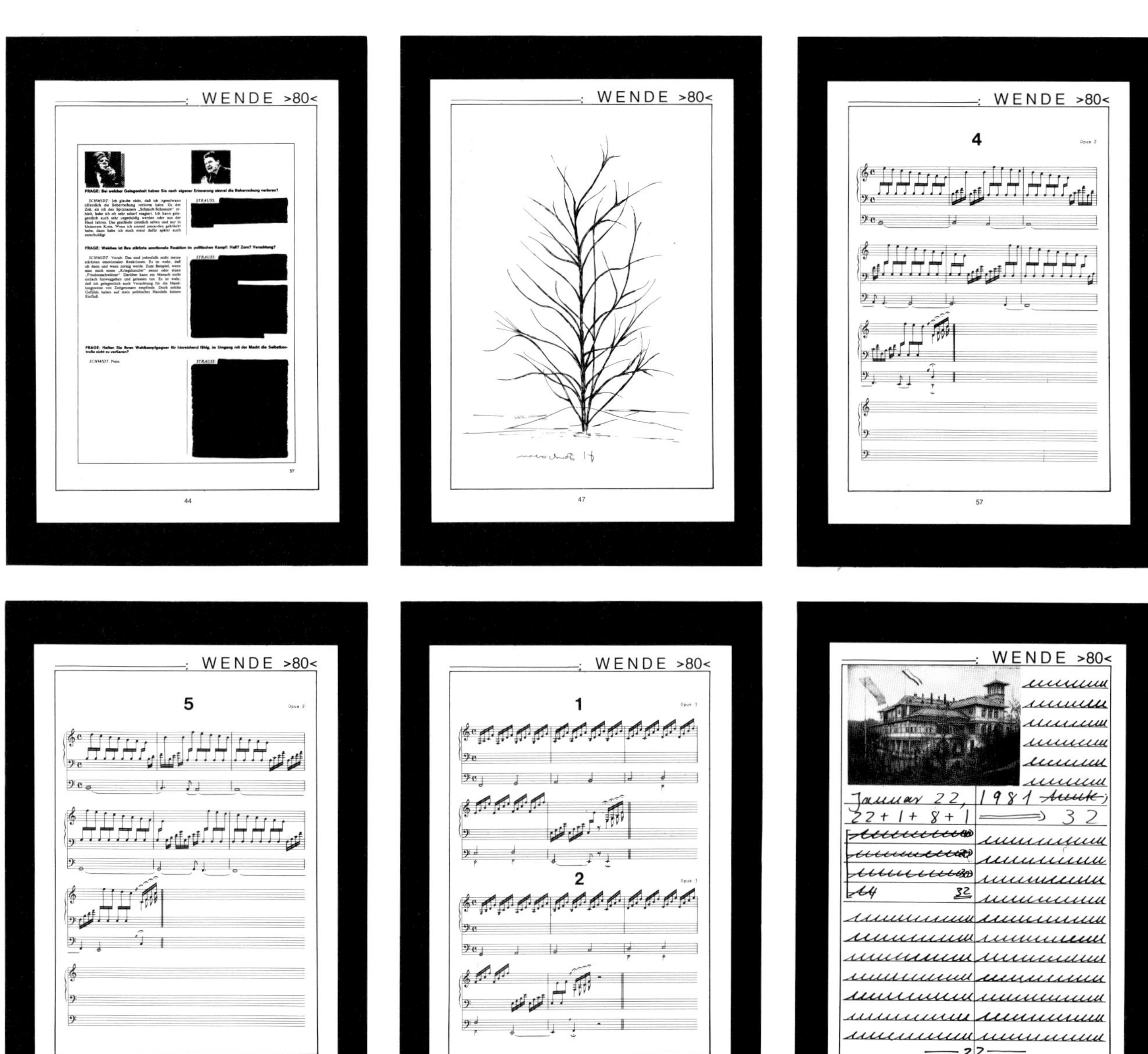

86 Hanne Darboven ☐
Wende >80<, 1980
416 Offsetlithographien DIN A3, in Kassette, und 6 Langspielplatten. Auflage: 250
416 offset lithographs in portfolio box, 23 x 17 in., with 6 records. Edition: 250

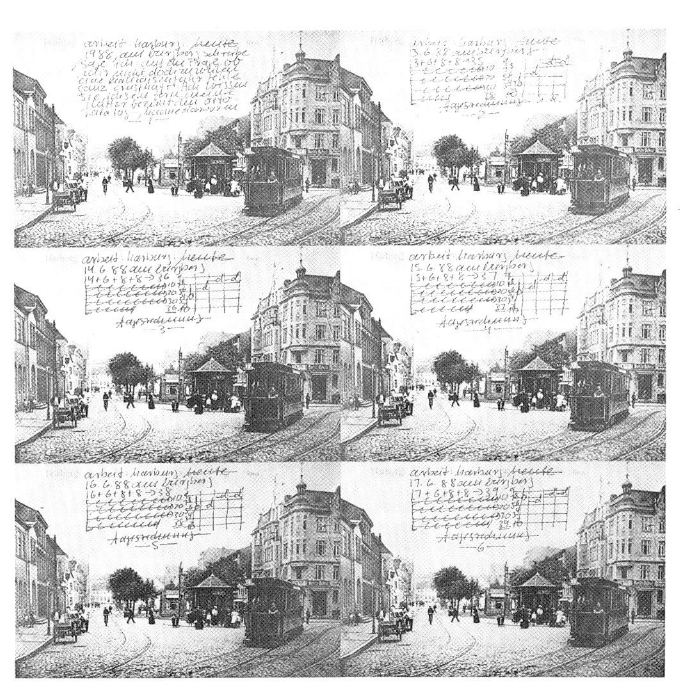

87 Hanne Darboven ■
Harburg Sand, 1988
Lichtdruck/Serigraphie, 97 x 80 cm. Auflage: 75
Collotype/silkscreen, 38 x 31½ in. Edition: 75

1 3 5 7 9 11

1 3 5 7 9 11

2 4 6 8 10 12

2 4 6 8 10 12

13 15 17 19 21 23

13 15 17 19 21 23

14 16 18 20 22 24

14 16 18 20 22 24

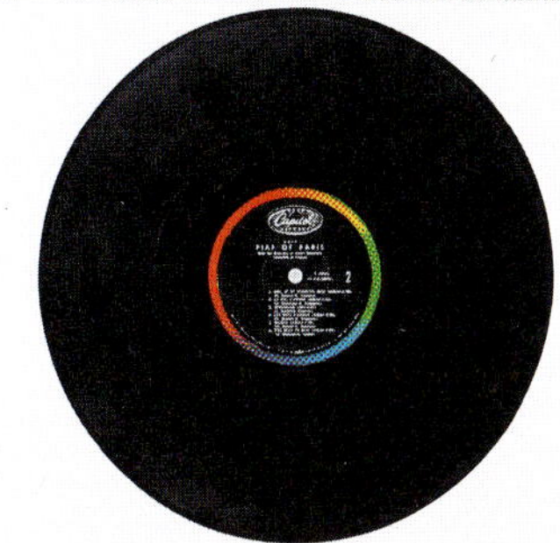

←

88 Hanne Darboven ■

a. 24 Gesänge, 1990 [abgebildet]

Zweiteilige Serigraphie, eine mit Collage, und Tonbandkassetten: "24 Gesänge, Opus 14a" (Orgel, Akkorde). Blätter zusammen 155 x 266 cm. Auflage: 33

[illustrated] Two-part silkscreen print, one with collage, and music cassettes: "24 Chants, Opus 14a" (Organ, chords). Overall size 61 x 105 in. Edition: 33

b. 24 Gesänge, 1990 [nicht abgebildet]

Vierteilige Serigraphie, eine mit Collage, und Tonbandkassetten: "24 Gesänge, Opus 14a" (Orgel, Melodie). Blätter zusammen 155 x 532 cm. Auflage: 33

[not illustrated] Four-part silkscreen print, one with collage, and music cassettes: "24 Chants, Opus 14a" (Organ, melody). Overall size 61 x 210 in. Edition: 33

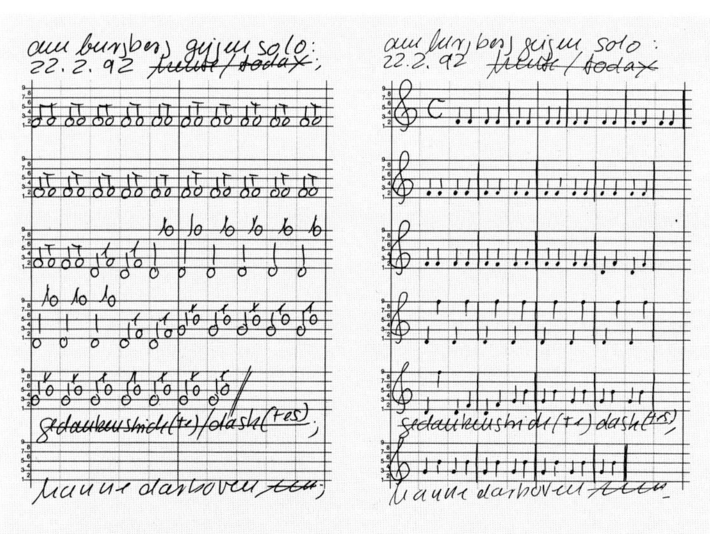

89 Hanne Darboven ■

Geigensolo, 1992

Miniatur-Violine mit Karte "Polis: Burg, Berg, Staat" auf lackiertem Holzsockel, 102 x 33 x 33 cm. Auflage: 28

Miniature violin with card "Polis: Burg, Berg, Staat" on laquered wooden column, 40 x 13 x 13 in. Edition: 28

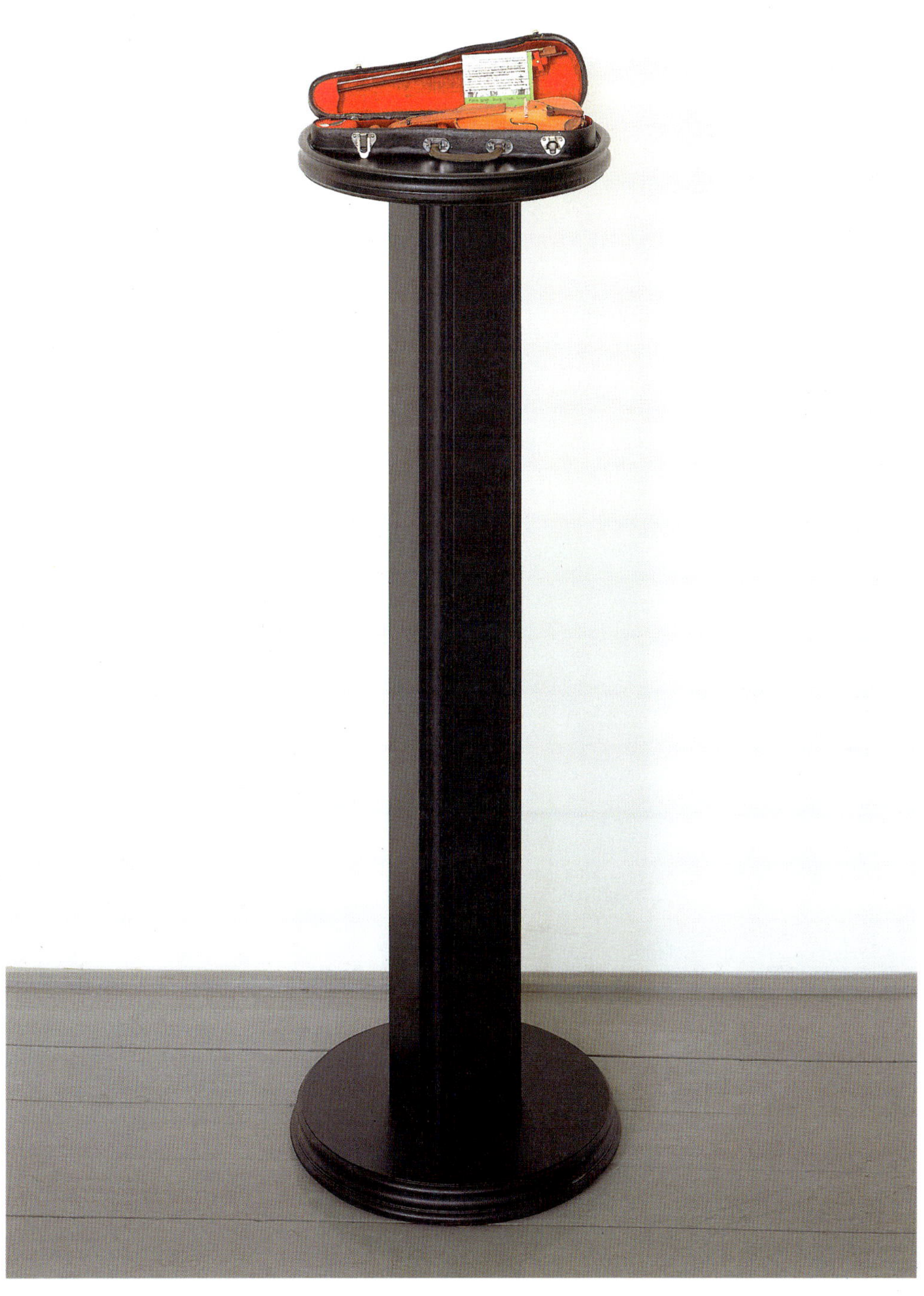

90 Walter De Maria
Untitled, 1971
Collage auf Karton, 80 x 120 cm. Auflage: 9
Collage on white board, 31½ x 47¼ in. Edition: 9

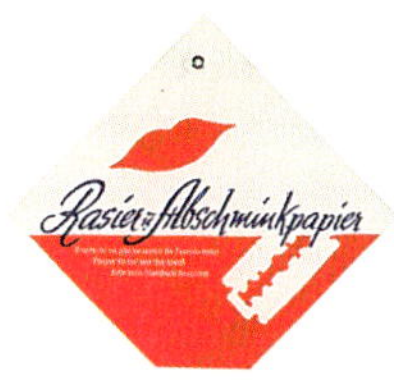

91 Walter De Maria
Untitled (Razor Piece), 1971
Collage auf Karton, 120 x 80 cm. Auflage: 9
Collage on white board, 47¼ x 31½ in. Edition: 9

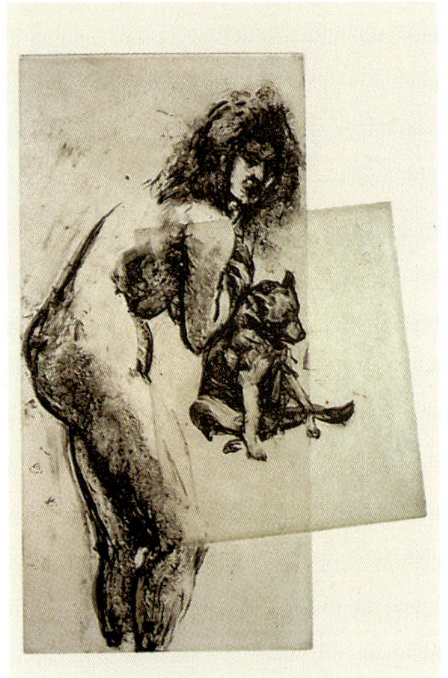
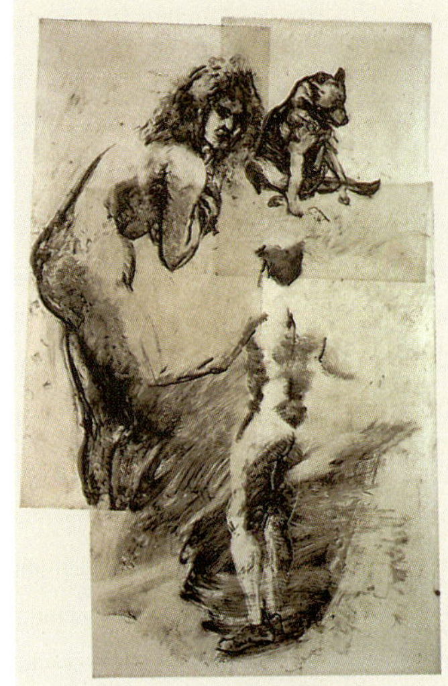
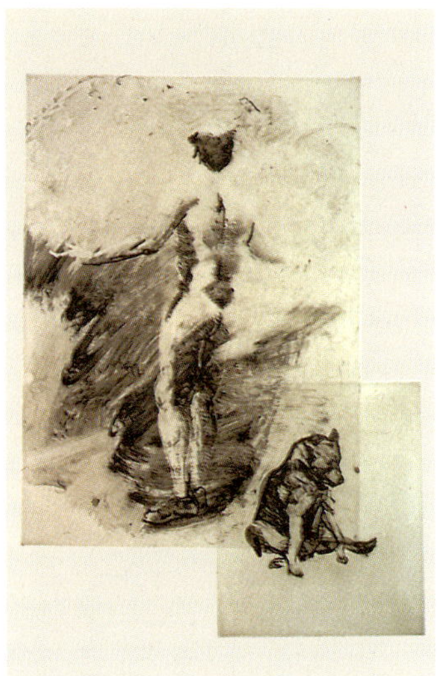
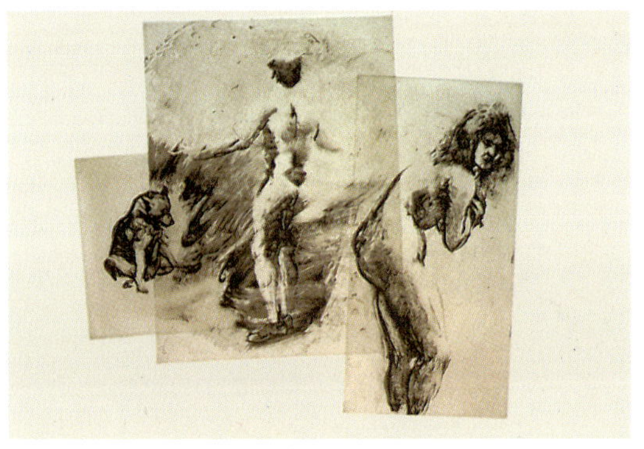
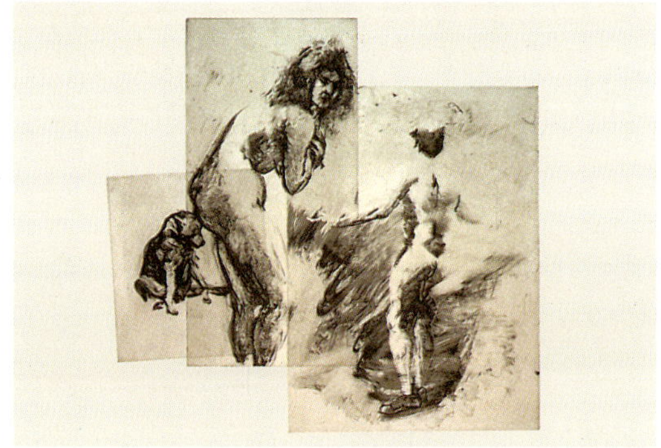

92 Eric Fischl
Dog, Boy and Woman, 1992
Suite von 5 Radierungen (gedruckt von sonnenbelichteten Platten), 56,5 x 76 cm. Auflage: 25
Series of 5 solar intaglio prints, 22¼ x 30 in. Edition: 25

93 Dan Flavin →
Untitled (for Rento), 1986
2 Serigraphien, 75 x 105 cm. Auflage: 40
2 silkscreens, 29½ x 41½ in. Edition: 40

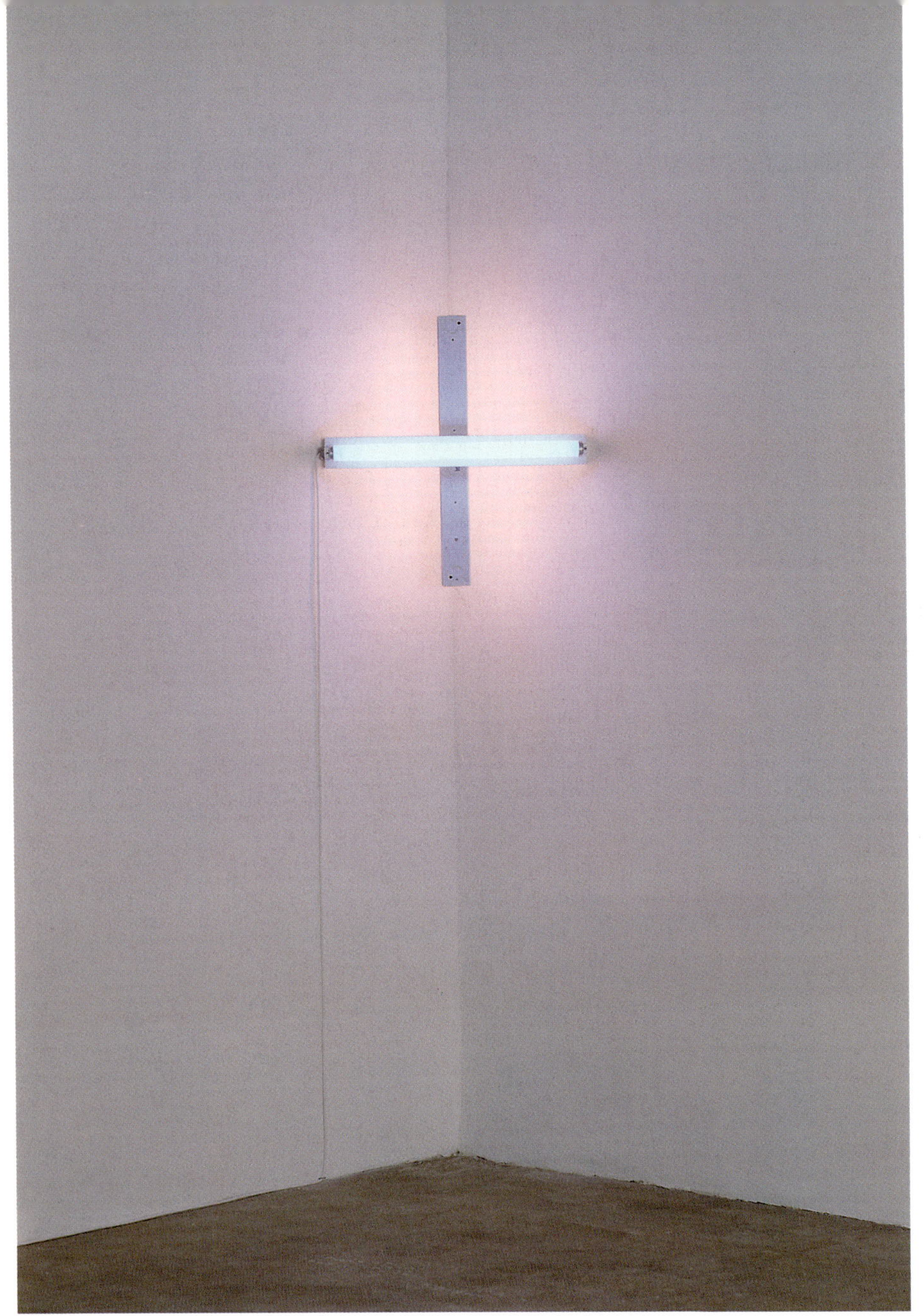

94 Dan Flavin
Untitled (to Barbara Nüsse), 1971
Leuchtstoffröhren blau und pink, 60 x 60 x 5 cm. Auflage: 50, davon nur 16 ausgeführt, sign. und num. auf einem Zertifikat.
Blue and pink fluorescent light, 24 x 24 x 2 in. Edition: 50 planned, only 16 made, signed and numbered on a certificate.

95 Dan Flavin
Untitled (to Don Judd, colorist), 1986
Farblithographien auf grauem Bütten, 73,5 x 104 cm. Auflage: 30
Color lithographs on grey rag paper, 29 x 41 in. Edition: 30

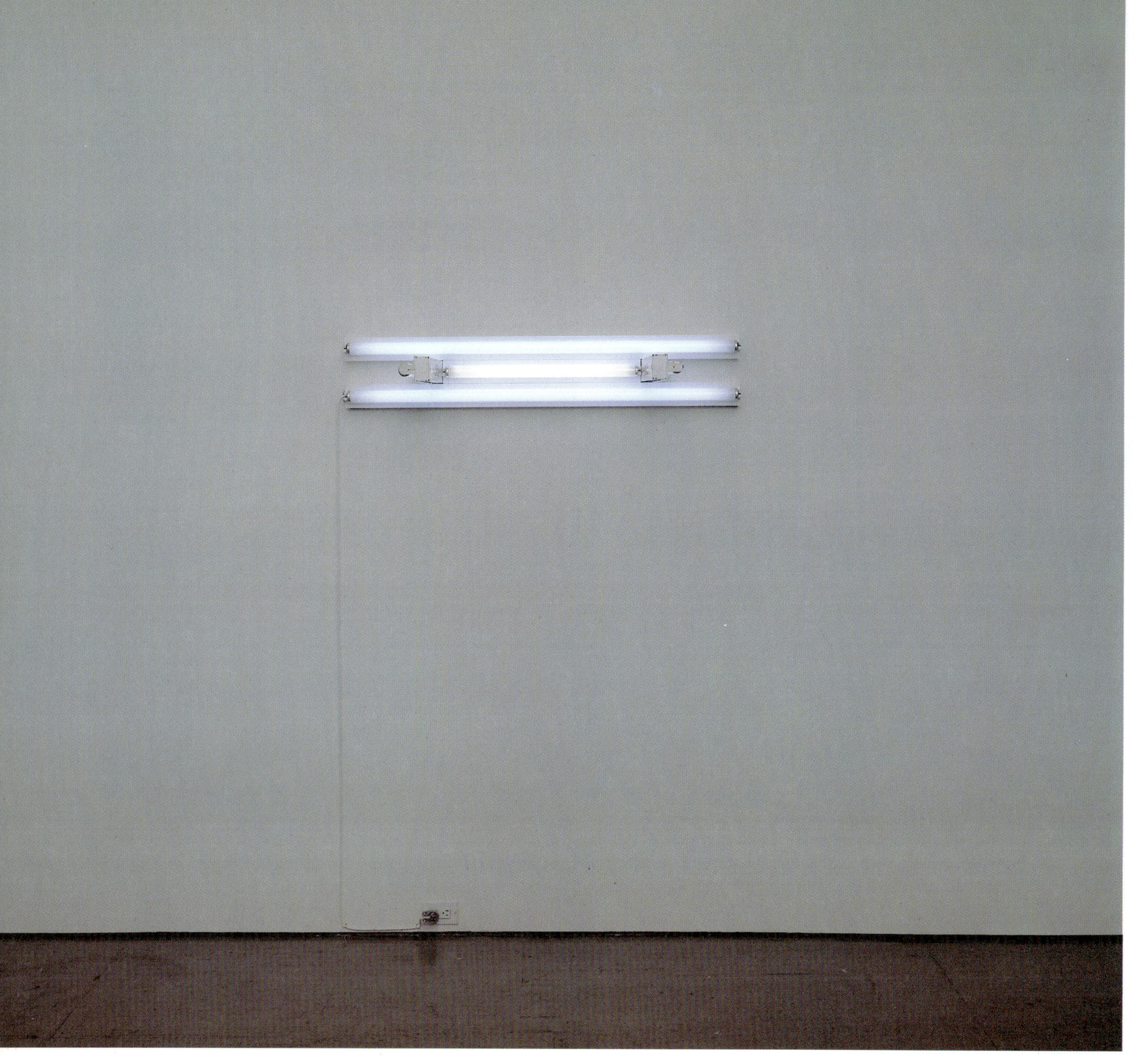

96 Dan Flavin ■
Untitled (to Mary Elizabeth), 1992
Leuchtstoffröhren tageslichtweiß und warmtonweiß, 21 x 122 x 61 cm.
Auflage: 5, mit sign. und num. Zertifikat, siehe Appendix.
Daylight and warm white fluorescent light, 8 x 48 x 24 in.
Edition: 5, with a signed and numbered certificate, see appendix.

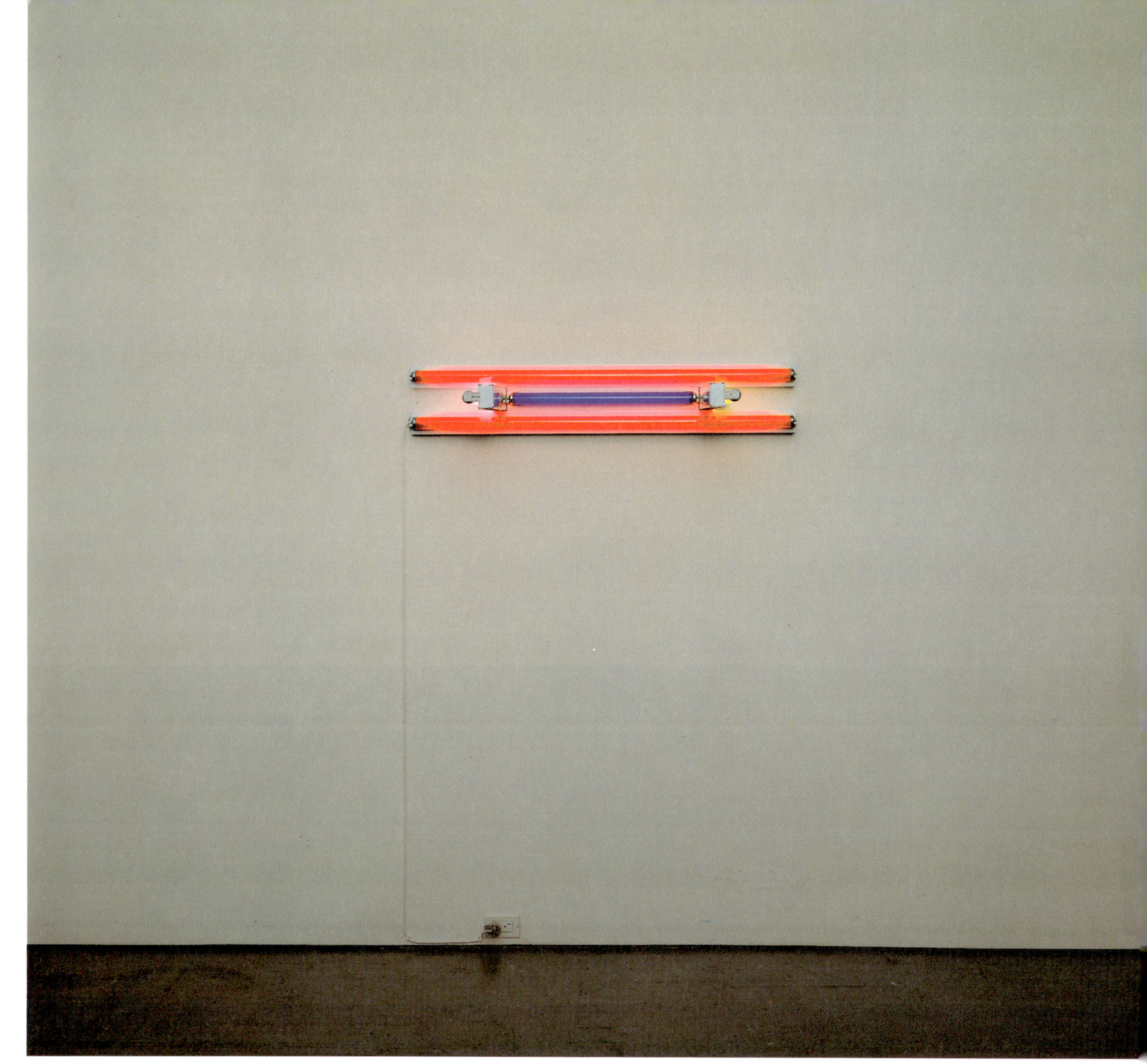

97 Dan Flavin ■
Untitled (to Madeline and Eric Kraft), 1992
Leuchtstoffröhren rot, rosa, gelb, ultraviolett, 21 x 122 x 61 cm.
Auflage: 5, mit sign. und num. Zertifikat. Siehe Appendix.
Red, pink, yellow, and ultra violet fluorescent light, 8 x 48 x 24 in.
Edition: 5, with a signed and numbered certificate. See appendix.

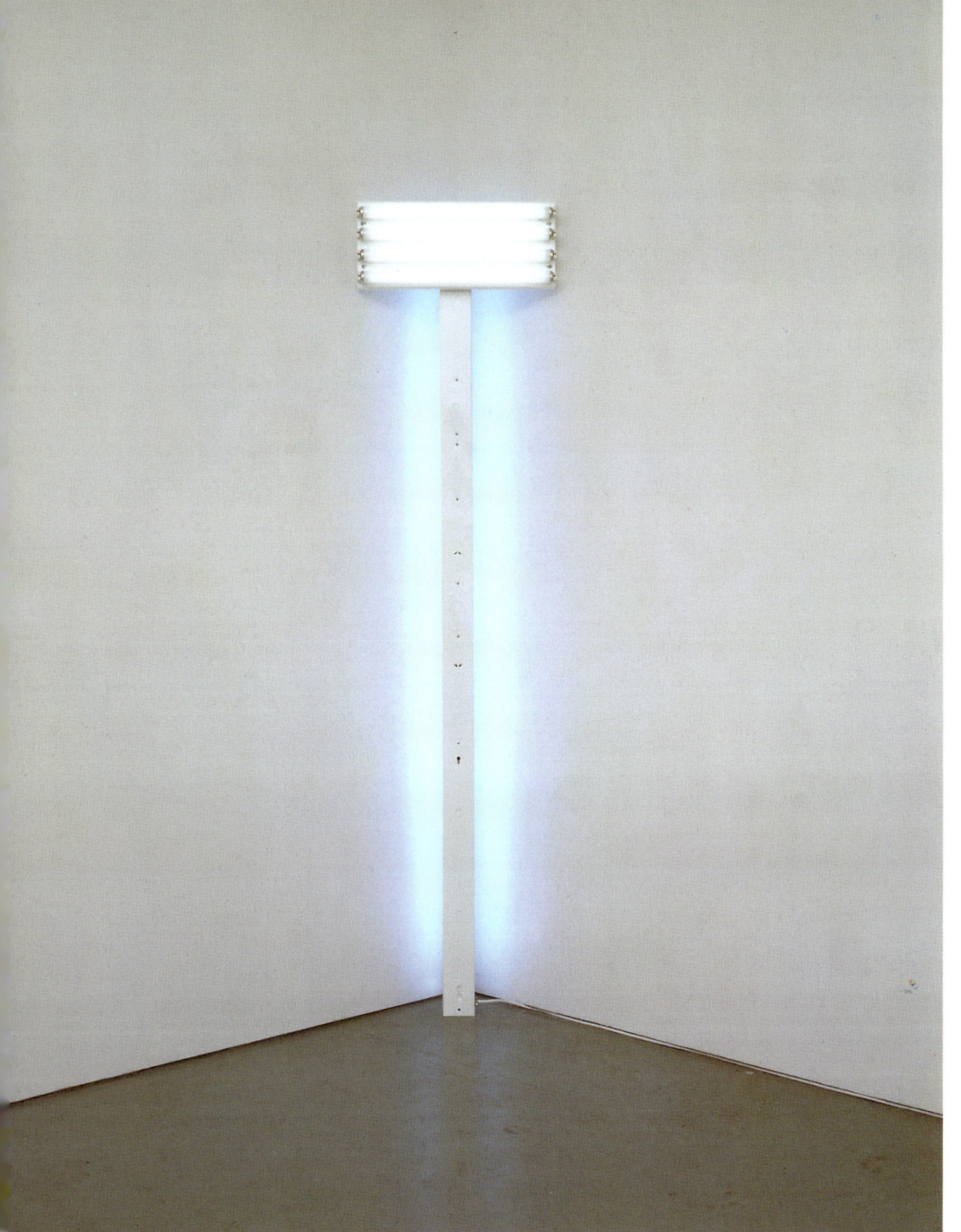

98 Dan Flavin ■

Untitled (to Jörg Schellmann), 1994

Leuchtstoffröhren tageslichtweiß und warmtonweiß, 234 x 61 x 20 cm. Auflage: 5, mit sign. und num. Zertifika

Daylight and warm white fluorescent light, 92 x 24 x 8 in. Edition: 5, with a signed and numbered certificate.

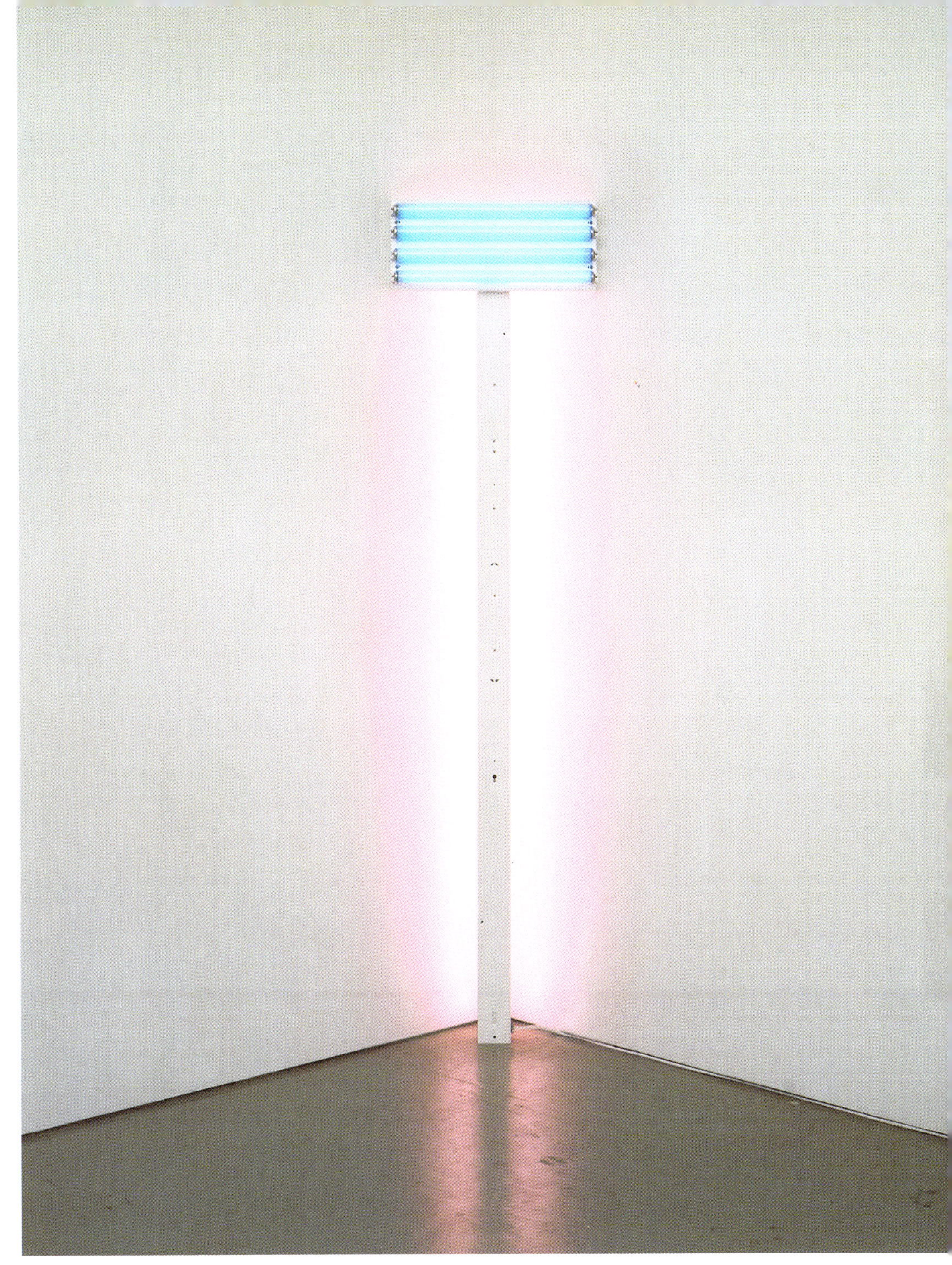

99 Dan Flavin ■
Untitled (to Jörg Schellmann), 1994
Leuchtstoffröhren blau und pink, 234 x 61 x 20 cm. Auflage: 5, mit sign. und num. Zertifikat.
Blue and pink fluorescent light, 92 x 24 x 8 in. Edition: 5, with a signed and numbered certificate.

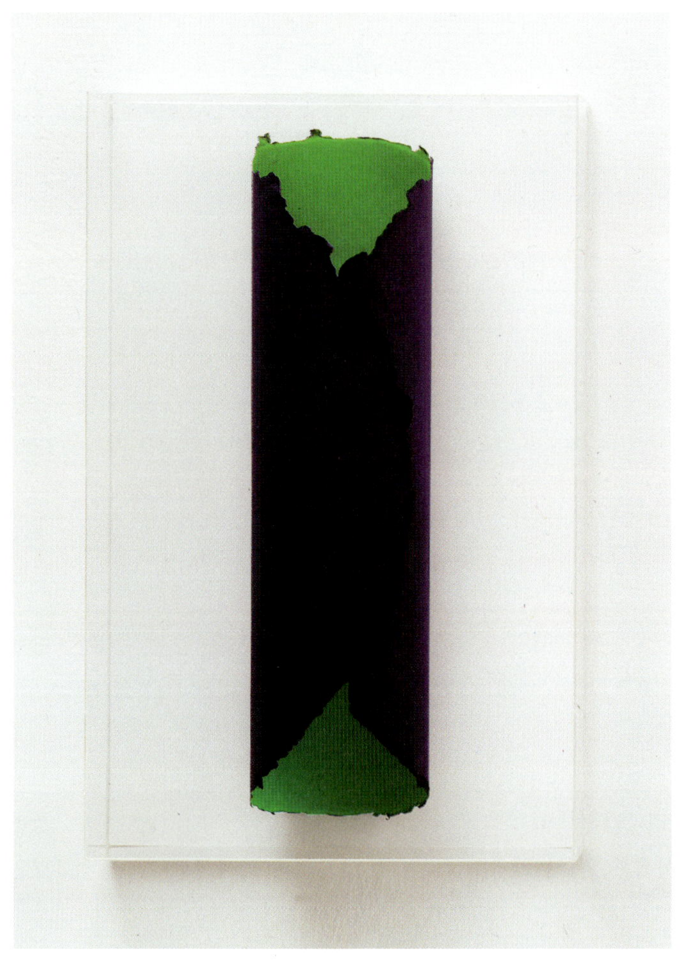

100 Dan Flavin ■
Untitled, 1994
Folge von 3 Aquatintaradierungen, beidseitig gedruckt auf handgeschöpftes Bütten, 71 x 20 cm,
in Plexiglaskasten 82 x 54 x 23,5 cm. Auflage: je 15
a. violett/grün **b**. rot/orange **c**. violett/gelb
Suite of 3 aquatints printed on both sides of handmade Twinrocker paper, 28 x 8 in., mounted in plexi box 32 x 21 x 9 in. Edition: 15 ea.
***a**. violet/green **b**. red/orange **c**. violet/yellow*

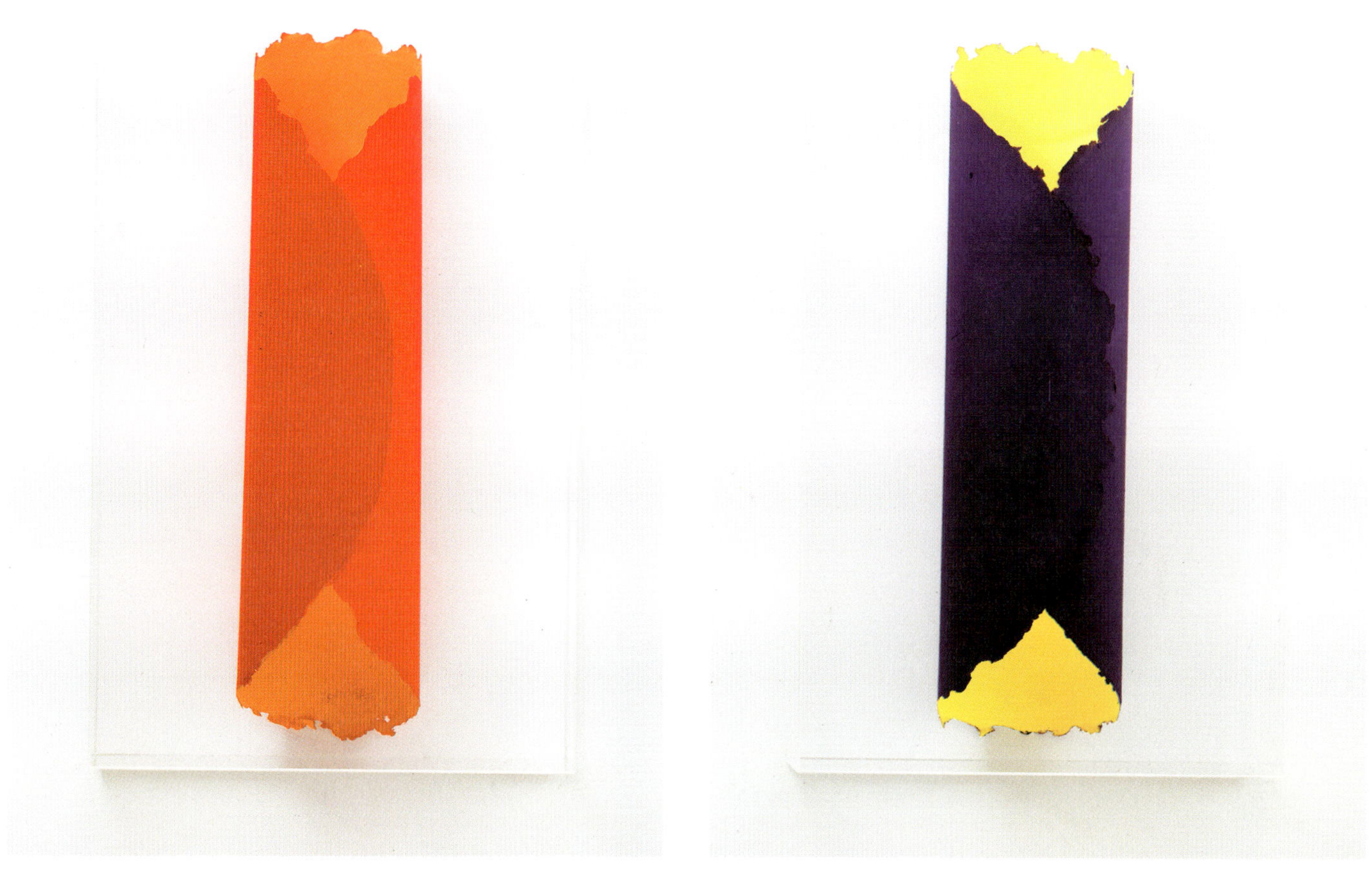

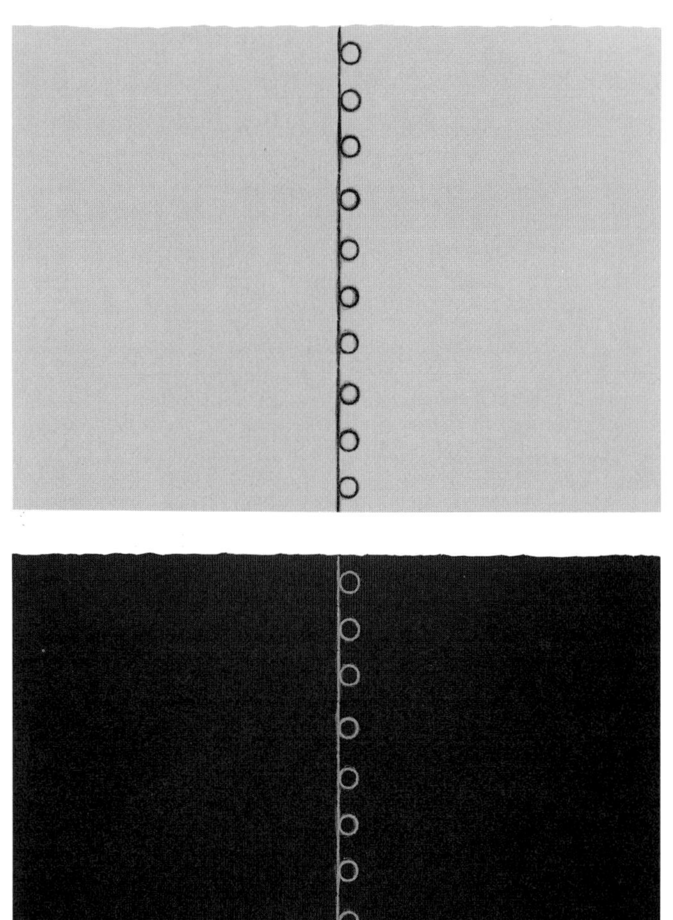

101 Dan Flavin
Untitled, 1986
3 Lithographien (**a**. grau, **b**. schwarz, **c**. weiß [nicht abgebildet]), 54,5 x 76 cm. Auflage: 25
*3 lithographs (**a**. grey, **b**. black, **c**. white [not ilustrated]), 21½ x 30 in. Edition: 25*

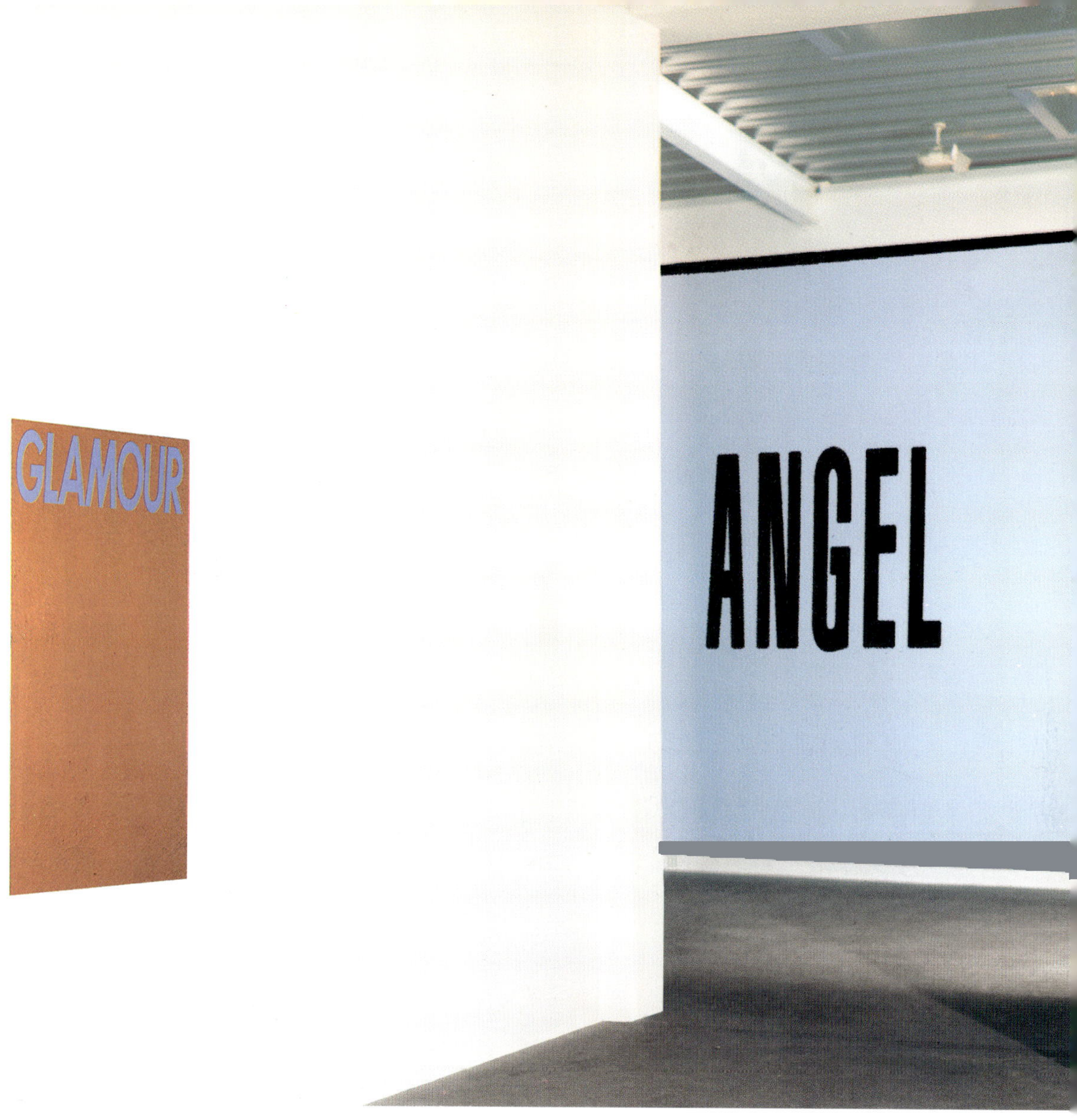

102-103 Sylvie Fleury

102 Glamour, 1994
Acrylfarbe auf Wand, 41,5 x 30 cm. Auflage: 24
Acrylic paint on a wall, 16¼ x 11¾ in. Edition: 24

103 Framed Angel, 1994
Acrylfarbe auf Wand, Maße variabel. Auflage: 3
Acrylic paint on a wall, dimsions variable. Edition: 3

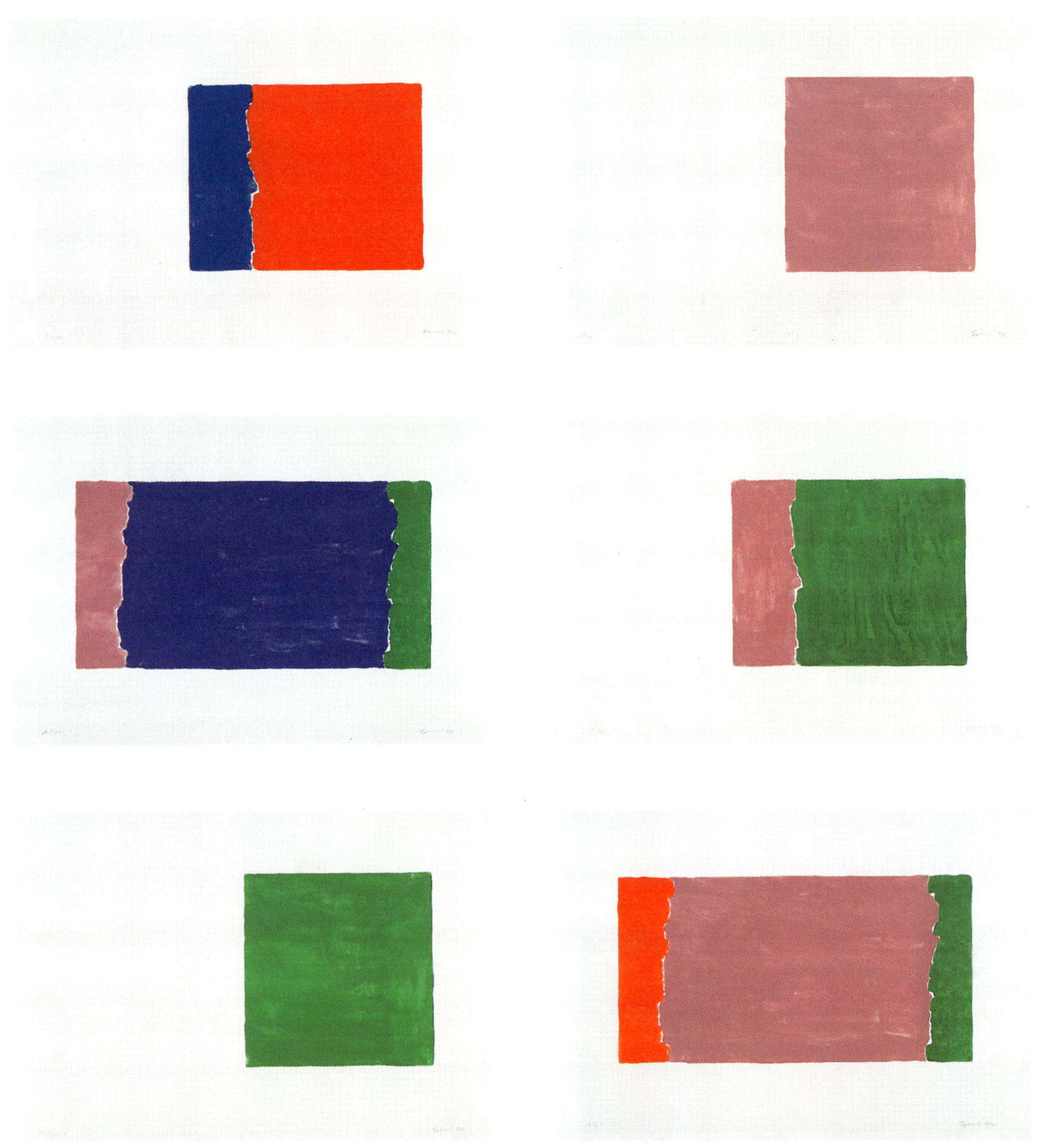

104 Günther Förg
Capri, 6 Cantos, 1994
Folge von 6 Farblithographien auf Bütten, 54 x 80 cm. Auflage: 40 + X
Suite of 6 lithographs on rag paper, 21¼ x 31½ in. Edition: 40 + 10 Roman numerals

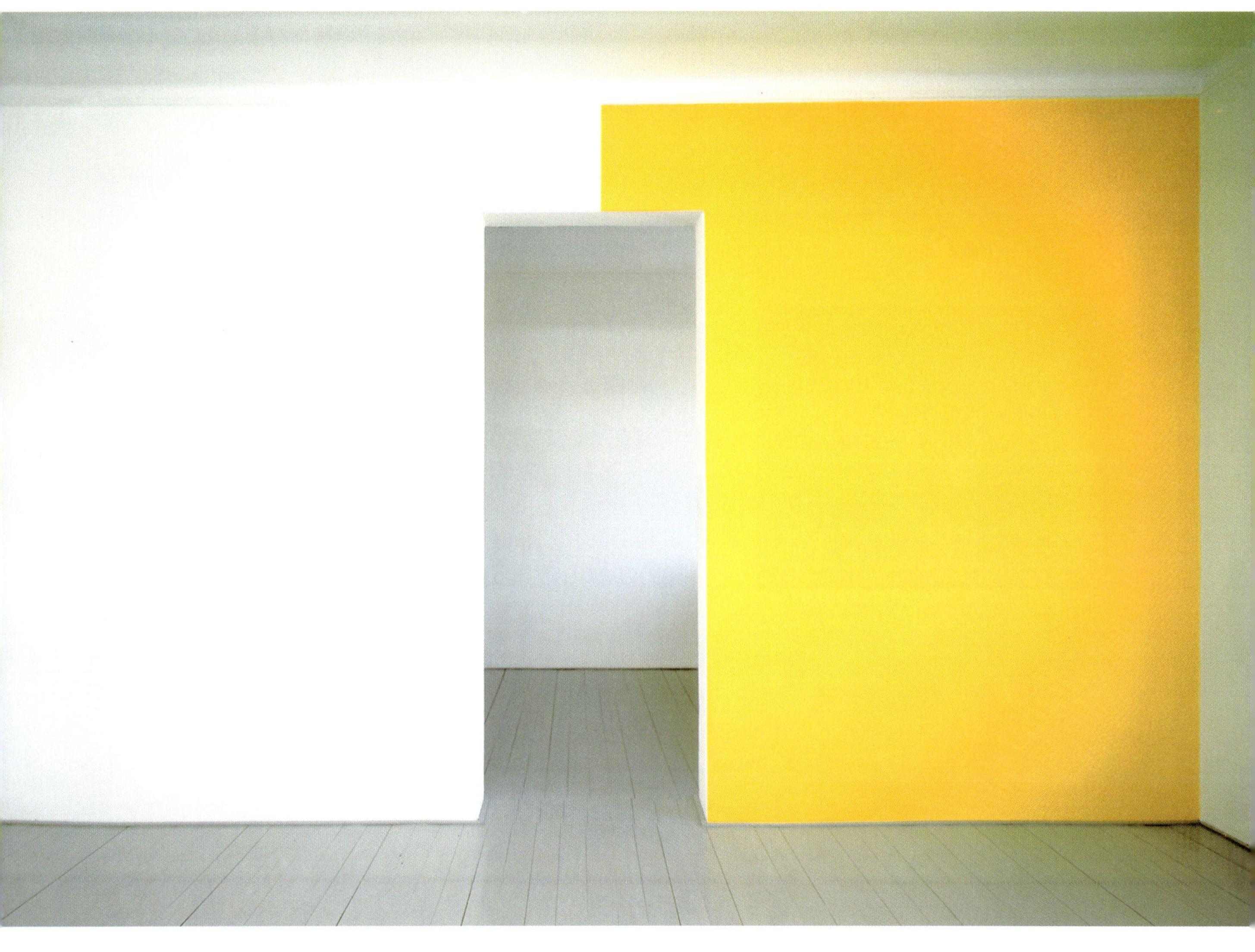

105 Günther Förg ■
Wandteilung, 1986-93
Wandmalerei, auszuführen nach den Anweisungen des Künstlers, siehe Appendix. Maße variabel.
Auflage: 12, mit Gouache und sign. und num. Zertifikat
Wall painting, to be executed according to the artist's instructions, see appendix. Size of the work variable.
Edition: 12, with a gouache and a signed and numbered certificate

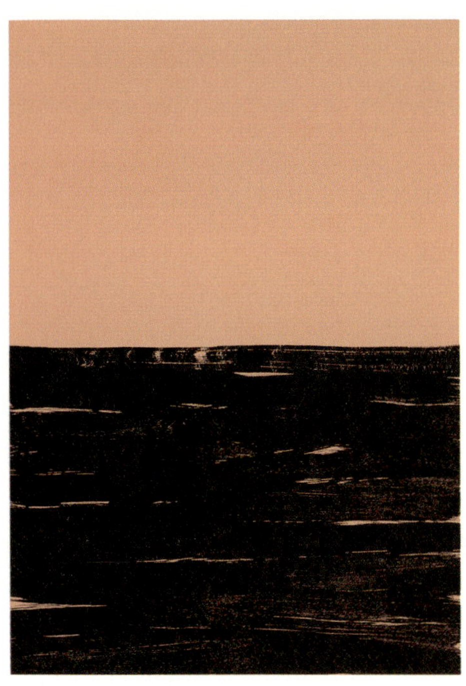

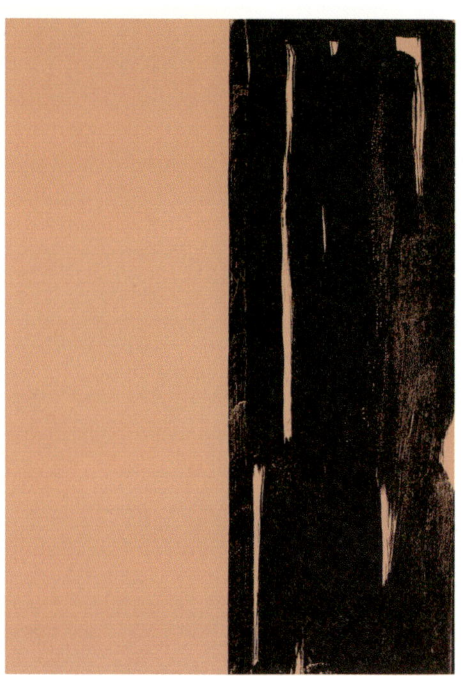

106 Günther Förg
Ohne Titel, 1993
2 Siebdrucke, 96 x 69 cm.
Auflage: 50
2 silkscreens, 38 x 27 in.
Edition: 50

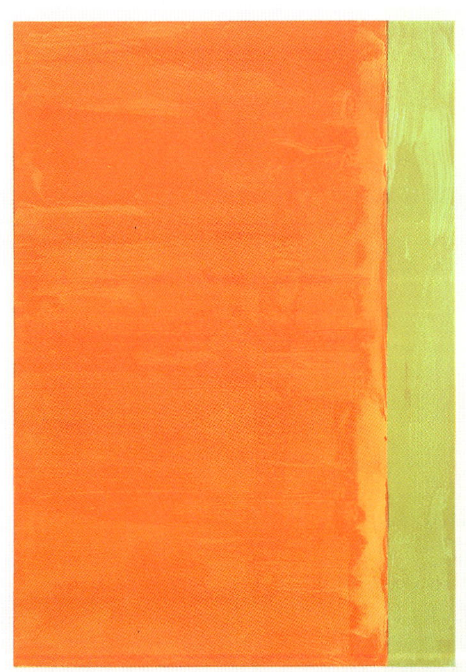

107 Günther Förg
Architektur I, 1993
Folge von 5 Heliogravuren auf Bütten, 96 x 69 cm.
Auflage: 60
Suite of 5 photo etchings on rag paper, 37¾ x 27¼ in.
Edition: 60

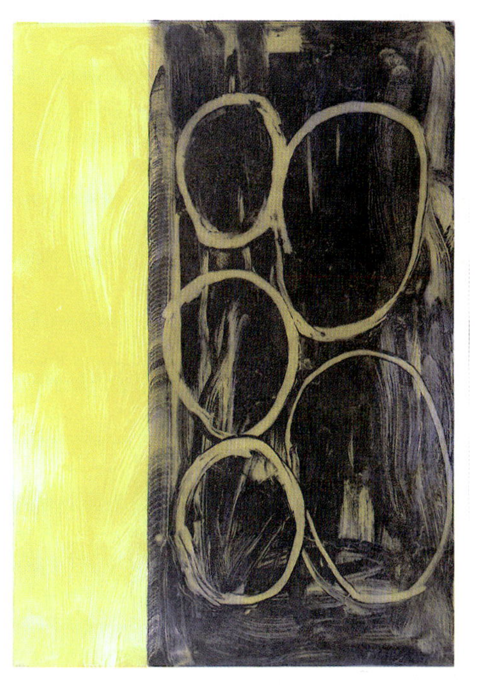
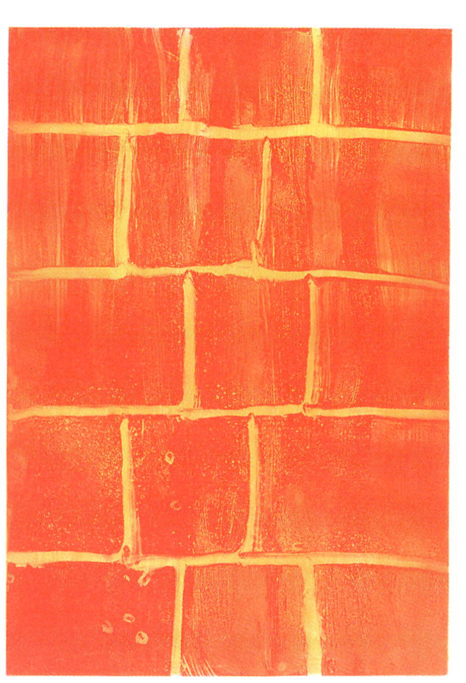
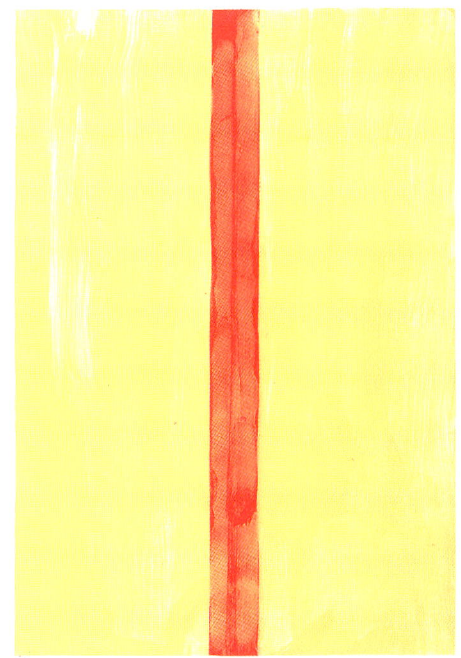
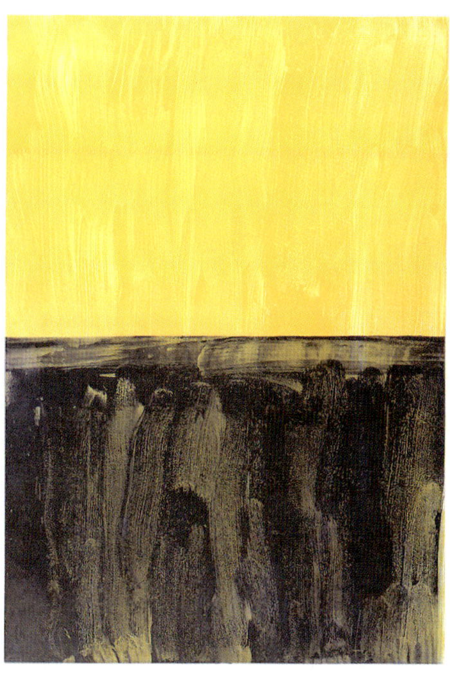

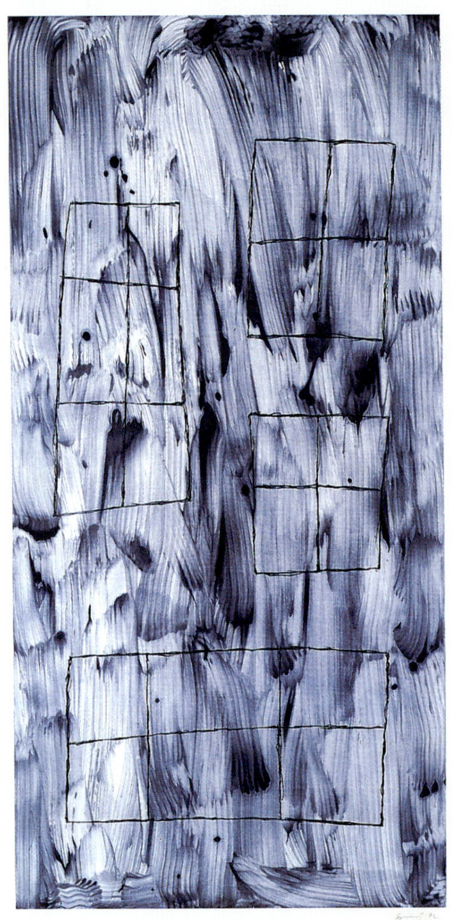

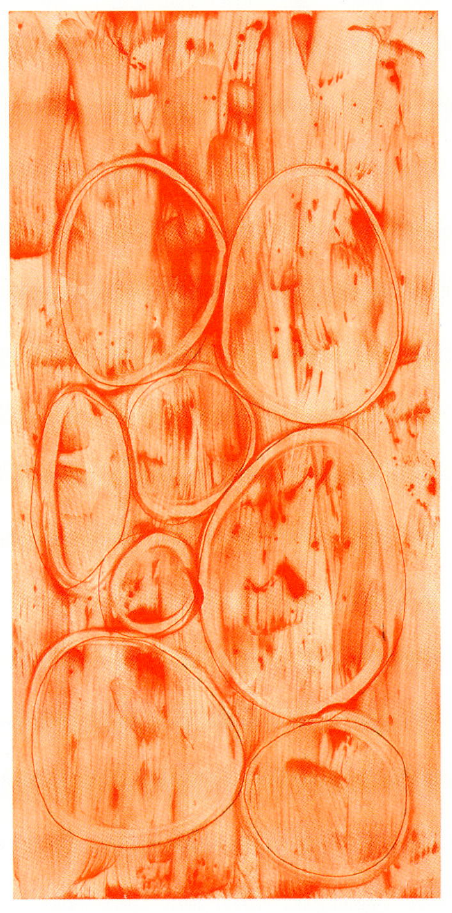

108 Günther Förg
Ohne Titel, 1992
6 Aquatintaradierungen auf Somerset Bütten, 219 x 118 cm. Auflage: 10
6 aquatints on Somerset rag paper, 86 x 46½ in. Edition: 10

109 Günther Förg →
Bronzerelief, 1991
Bronzeguß, patiniert, 49 x 39 cm. Auflage: 14
Bronze cast patined, 19¼ x 15½ in. Edition: 14

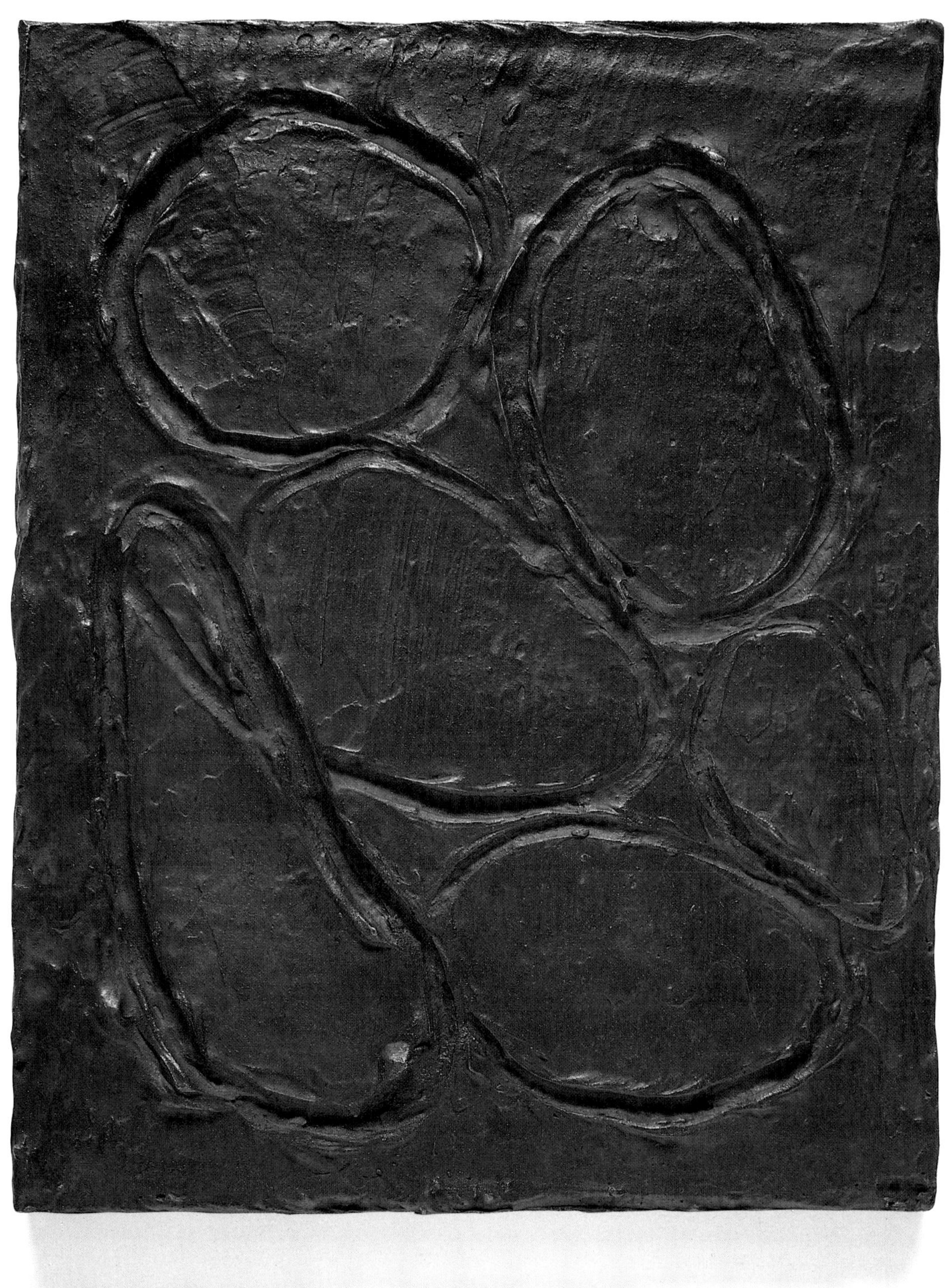

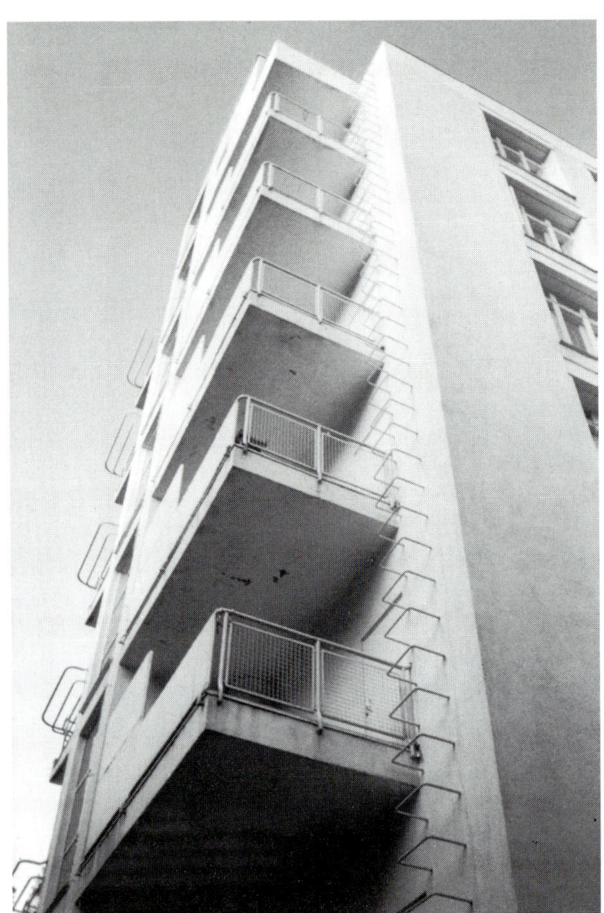

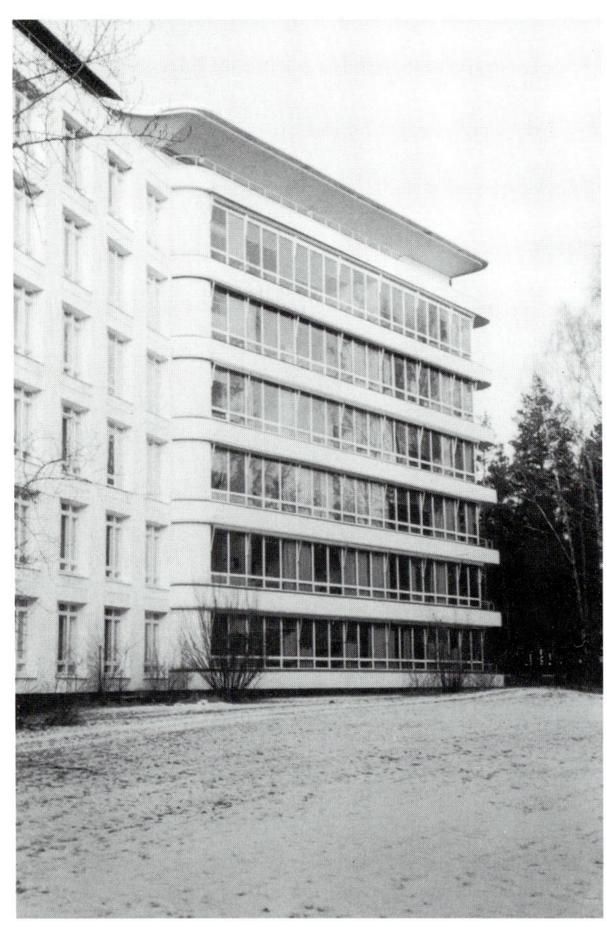

110 Günther Förg
Architektur II, 1993
Folge von 5 Photographien s/w, 96 x 69 cm. Auflage: 60
Suite of 5 black and white photographs, 37¾ x 27¼ in. Edition: 60

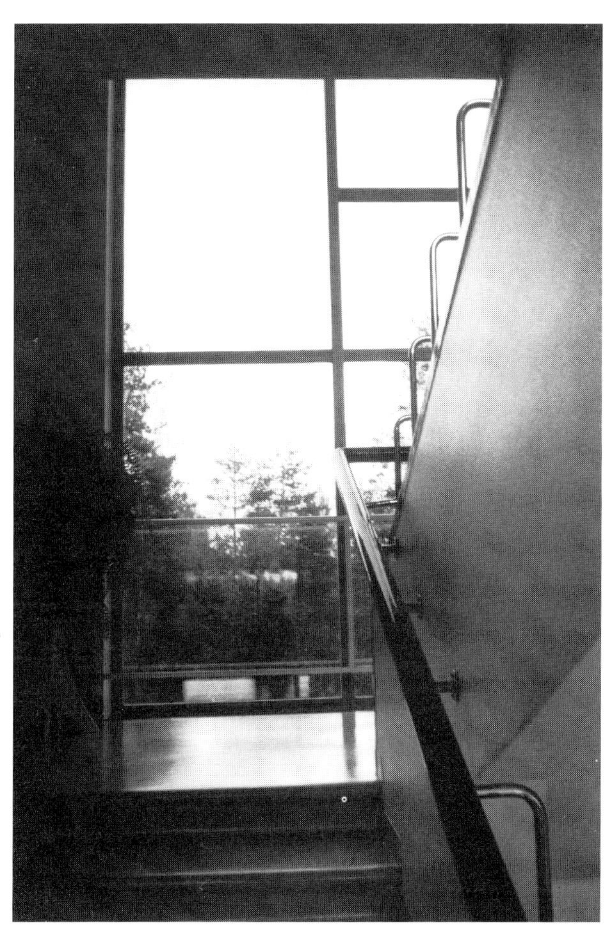

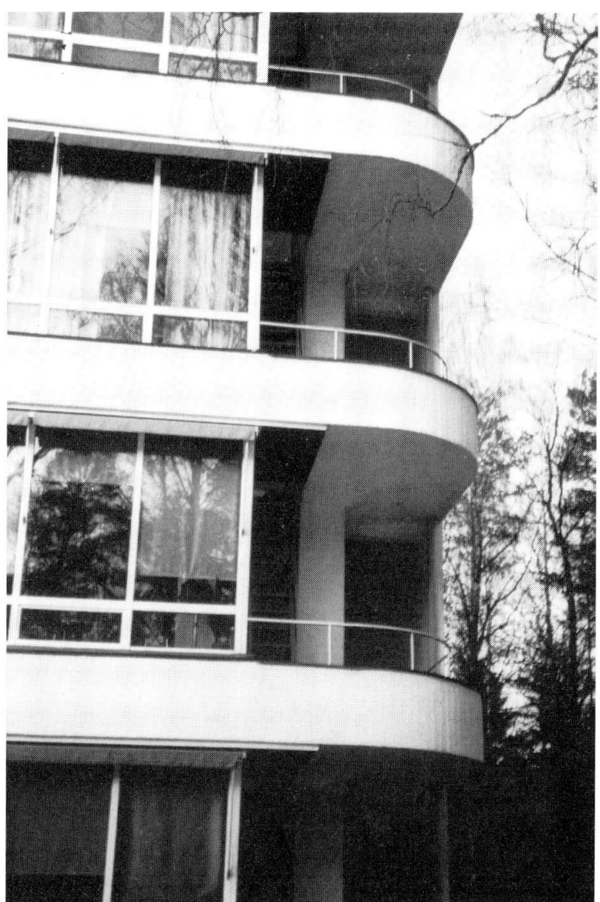

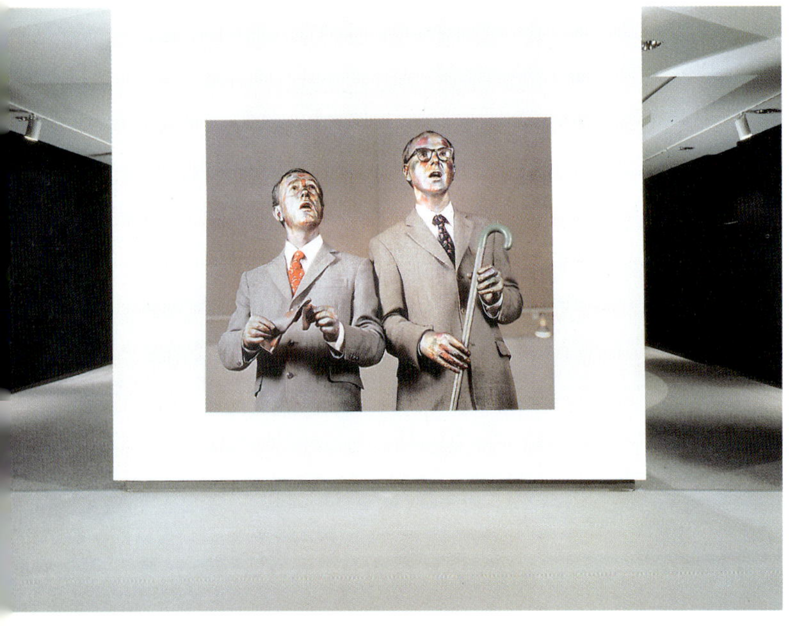

111 Gilbert & George ■
The Singing Sculpture 1969-91, 1993
Wandplakat, Offset vierteilig, direkt auf eine Wand zu kleben, siehe Appendix.
Gesamtmaße: 220 x 270 cm. Auflage: 20, mit sign. und num. Exemplar als Zertifikat
Wall poster, offset in four parts, to be pasted directly on a wall, see appendix.
Overall size: 86 ½ x 106 ¼ in. Edition: 20, signed and numbered on a second set

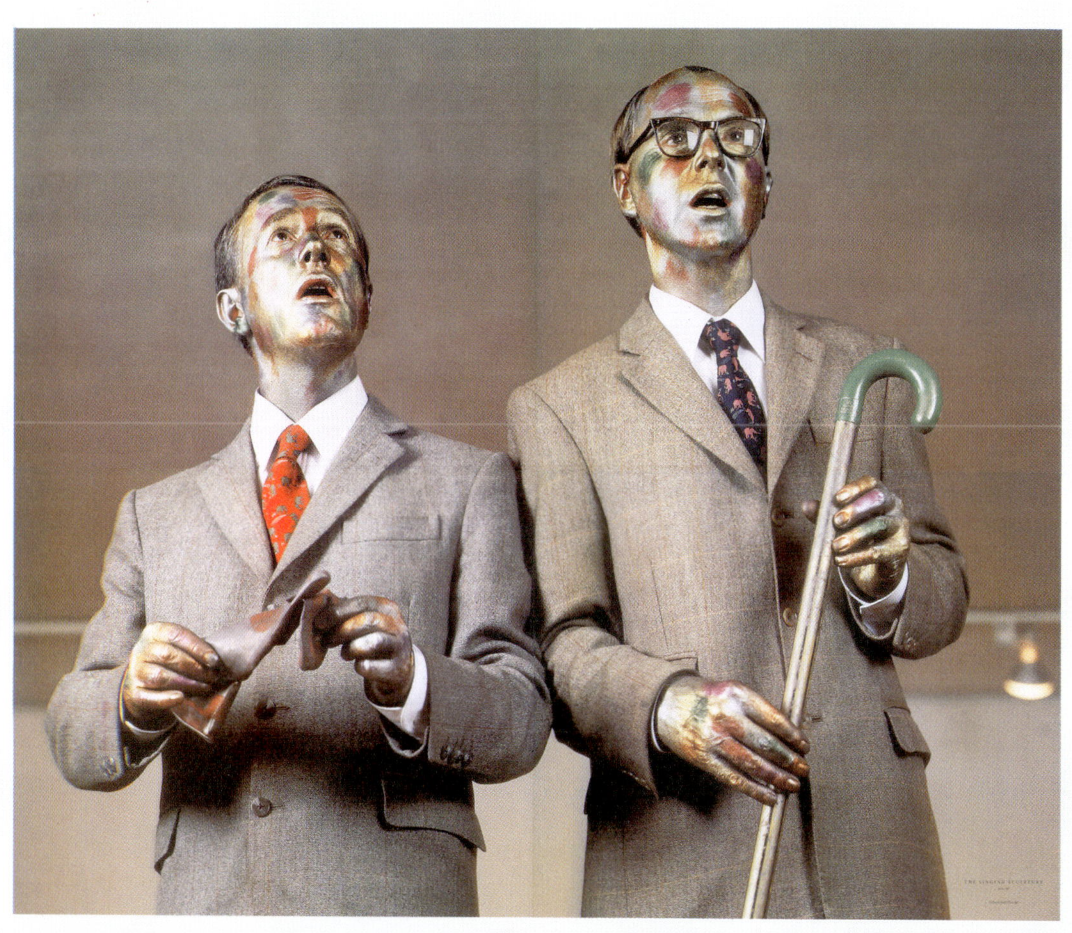

THE SINGING SCULPTURE

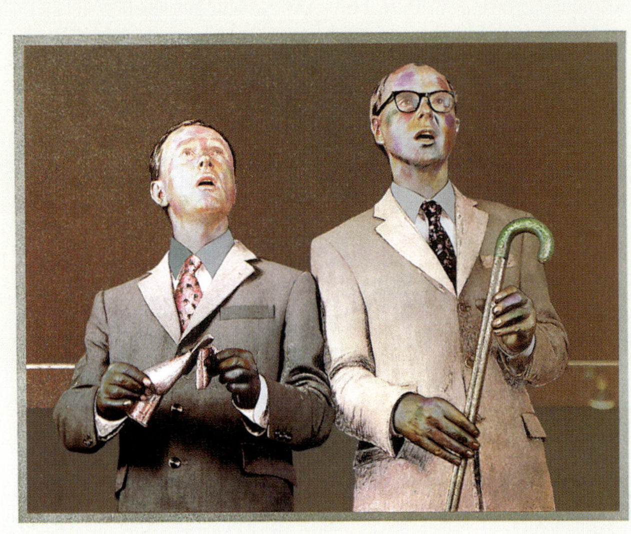

112 Gilbert & George ■
The Singing Sculpture 1969-91, 1993
Aluminium-Reliefdruck (Dufex), aufgezogen auf Karton
mit Siebdruck, 78,5 x 86 cm. Auflage: 100
Aluminum foil relief print (Dufex), mounted on cardboard
with silkscreen, 31 x 34 in. Edition: 100

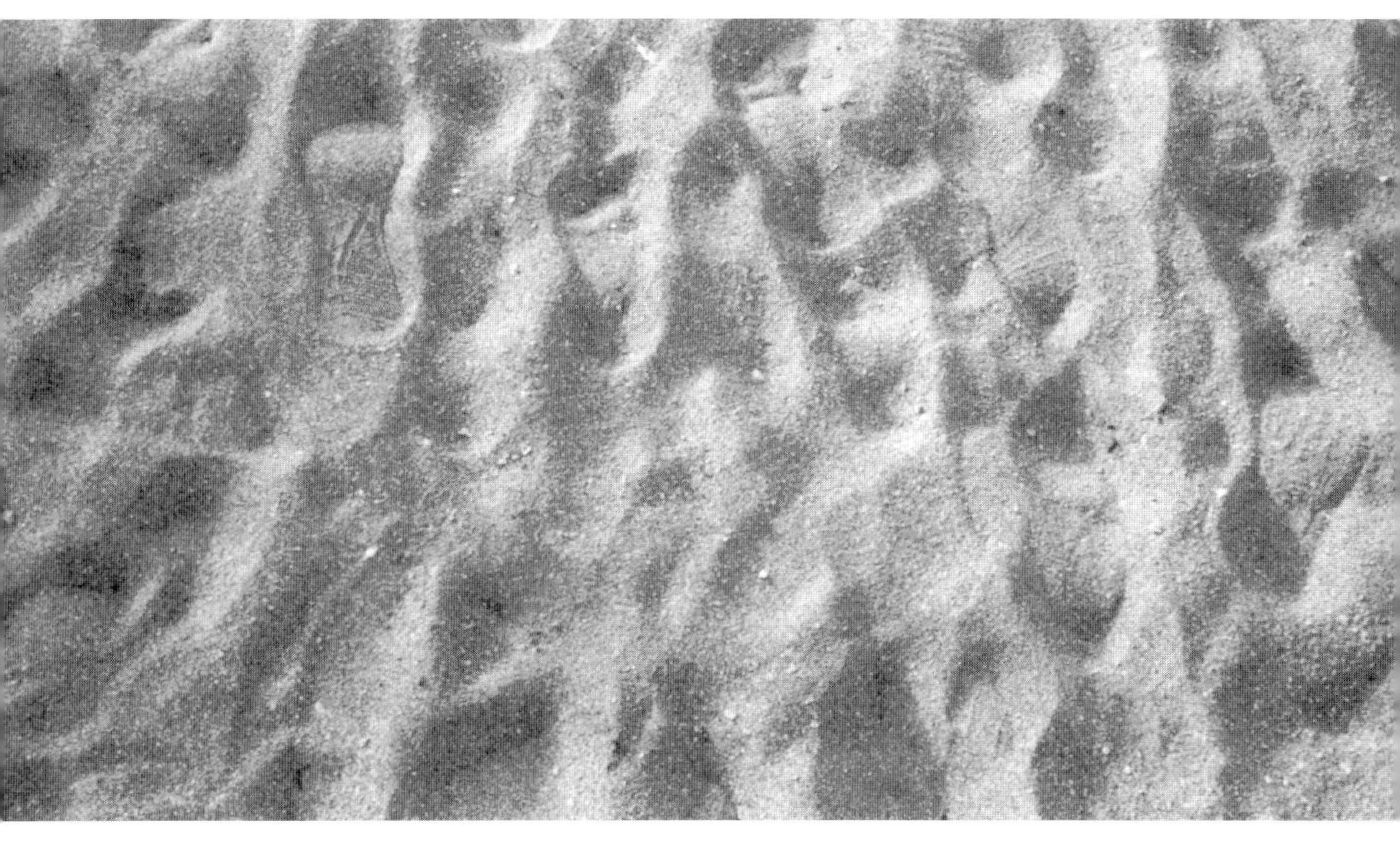

113 Felix Gonzalez-Torres
Untitled (for Parkett), 1994
Plakat (8 Blatt), Siebdruck auf Appleton-Plakatpapier, alle acht oder weniger Blatt an eine Wand zu kleben, je nach Größe der Wand. Maximale Größe: 317,5 x 691 cm. Auflage: 84, mit sign. und num. Zertifikat.
8-sheet billboard (silkscreen on Appleton coated stock), to be installed on a wall in its entirety or in fragments, according to available space. Maximum size: 125 x 272 in. Edition: 84, with a signed and numbered certificate.

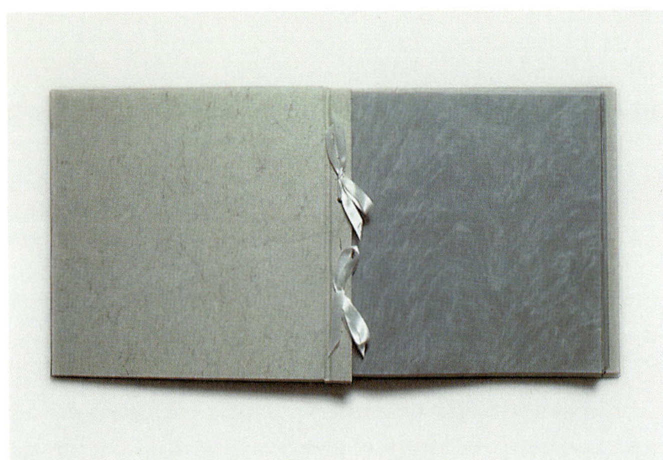

114 Felix Gonzalez-Torres
Untitled (Album), 1992
Photoalbum, gebunden in Leder, vom Besitzer "fertigzustellen". 36 x 36 cm. Auflage: 12
Leather bound photograph album to be "completed" by individual owners. 14 x 14 in. Edition: 12

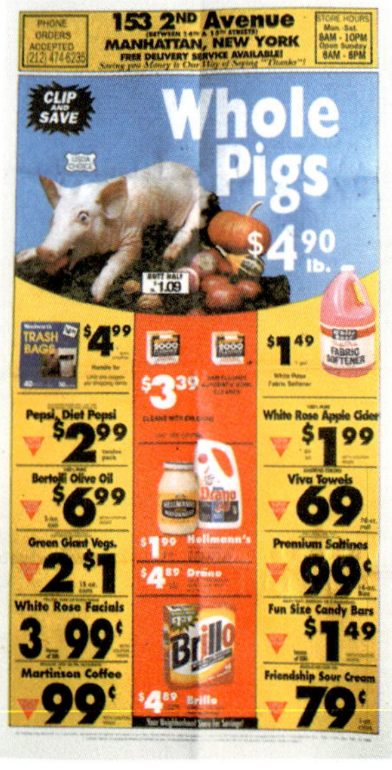

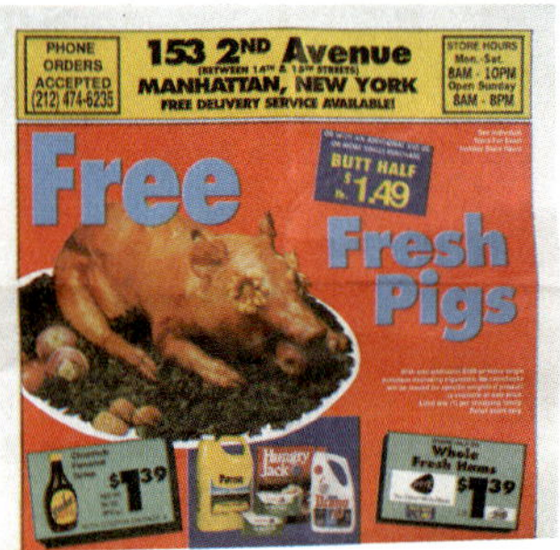

115 Robert Gober
Untitled, 1993-94
Zwei Blätter, Photolitho auf Bütten, 57 x 30,5 und 28,5 x 30,5 cm. Auflage: 75
Two prints. Photolithography on archival paper, 22½ x 12 and 11¼ x 12 in. Edition: 75

116 Dan Graham →
Detumescence, 1966
Schwarze Farbe auf Wand, Maße variabel (Proportionen: 5:4). Auflage: 10
Black paint on a wall, dimensions variable (5:4 proportions). Edition: 10

Involuntary body contractions ensue bringing a steep drop in excitation. The most obvious indication of this is the rapid loss of penile erection and the return of the scrotum and testes to an unstimulated state. This action occurs in two stages. The first leaves the penis enlarged while a continued shrinkage takes place concurrently at a slower rate. The body slackens its tension. There is a loosening of physical tautness, and a simultaneous sense of release and relaxation. Sensations of orgasm or desire are extinguished; emotions recede; and ego is again bounded. Psychologically, there may be feelings of anxiety, relief, pleasurable satiation, disappointment, lassitude, leaden exhaustion, disgust, repulsion, or indifference, and occasionally hatred depending on the partner and the gratification achieved in the orgasm state.

117 Dan Graham
View Interieur, New Highway Restaurant, Jersey City, N.J., 1967
Zwei Farbphotographien, aufgezogen auf Karton, 132,5 x 101,5 cm. Auflage: 30
Two ektacolor photographs mounted on museum board, 52¼ x 40 in. Edition: 30

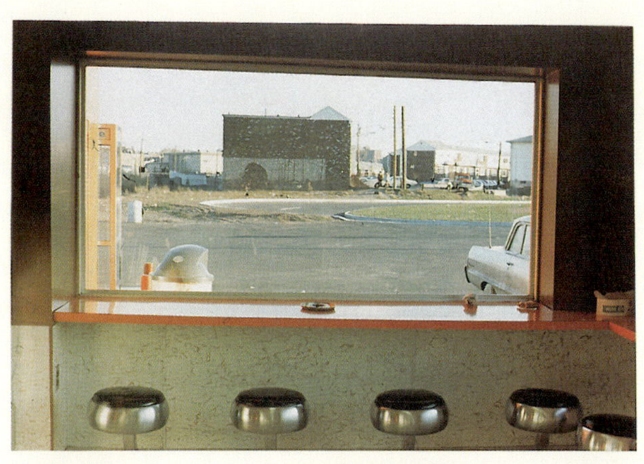

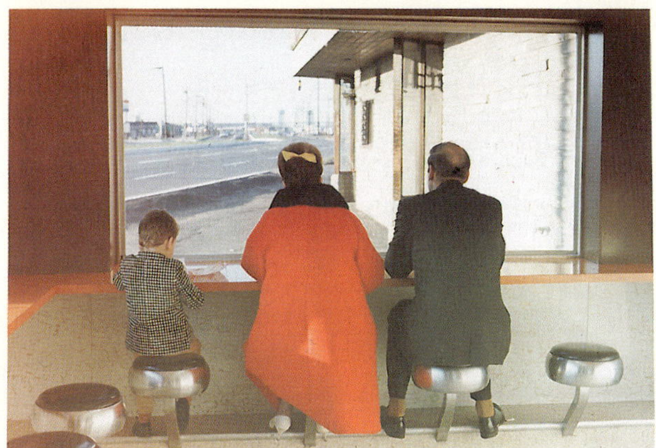

118 Thomas Grünfeld ■ →
Ohne Titel, 1992
Holz, Schaumstoff, Leder, 97,5 x 210 x 35 cm; Wandmalerei (Dispersion), auszuführen nach den Anweisungen des Künstlers, siehe Appendix. Gesamtmaße variabel.
Auflage: 11, jede Arbeit in anderen Farben, mit einem sign. und num. Zertifikat.
Wood, foam, leather, 38½ x 82½ x 13¾ in.; to be executed according to the artist's instructions, see appendix. Overall size of the work variable.
Edition: 11, each work unique in colors, with a signed and numbered certificate.

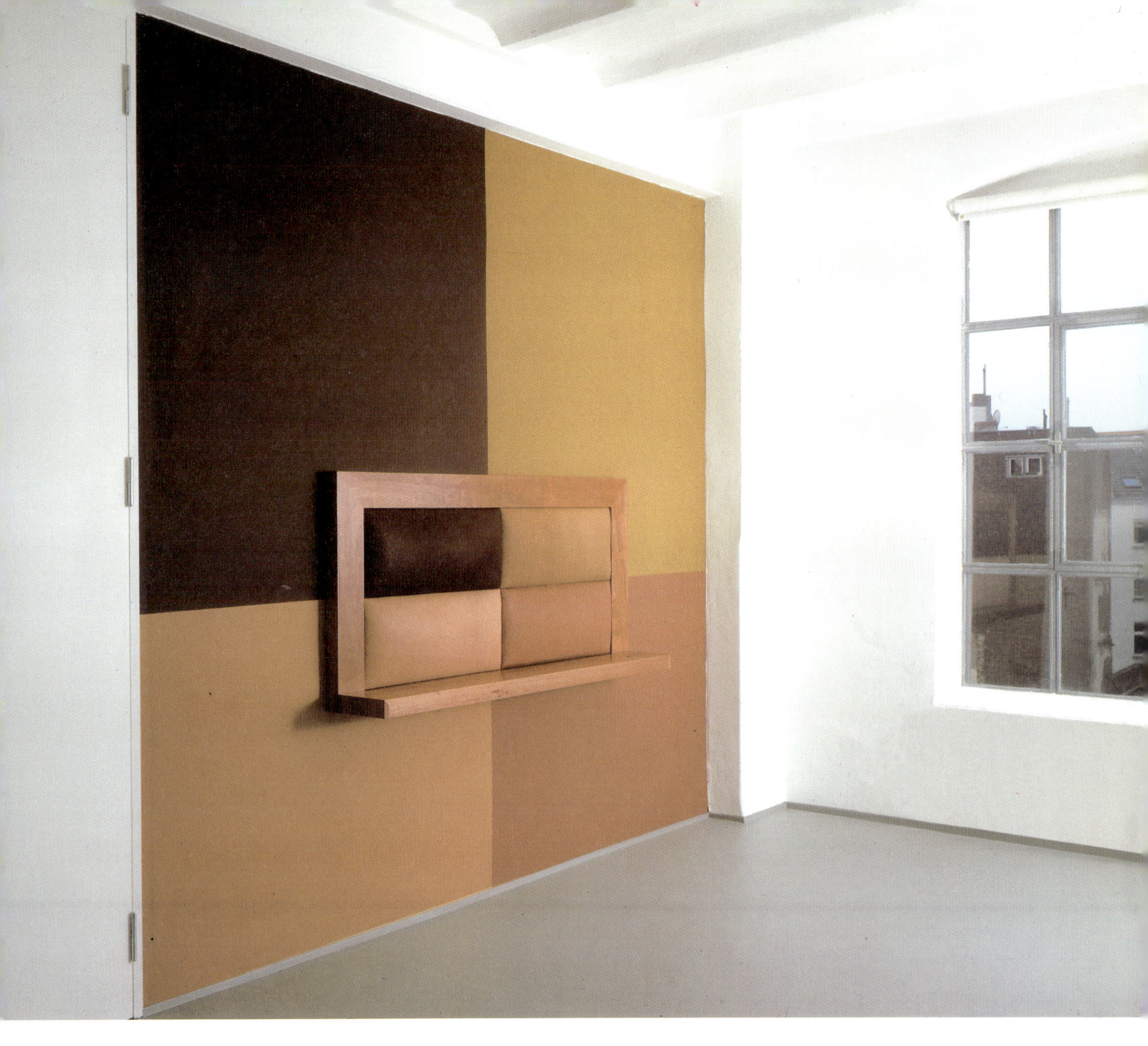

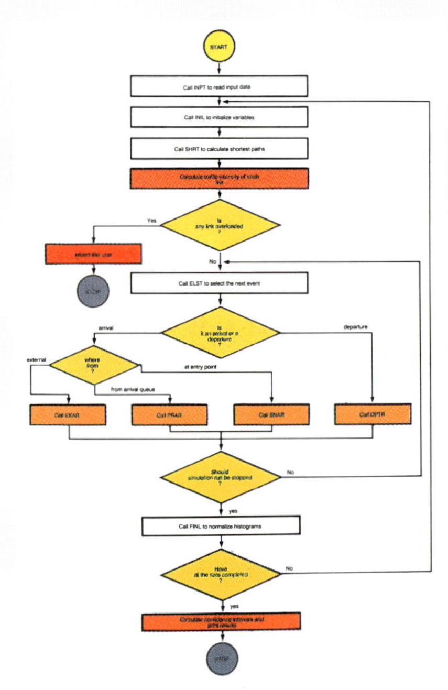

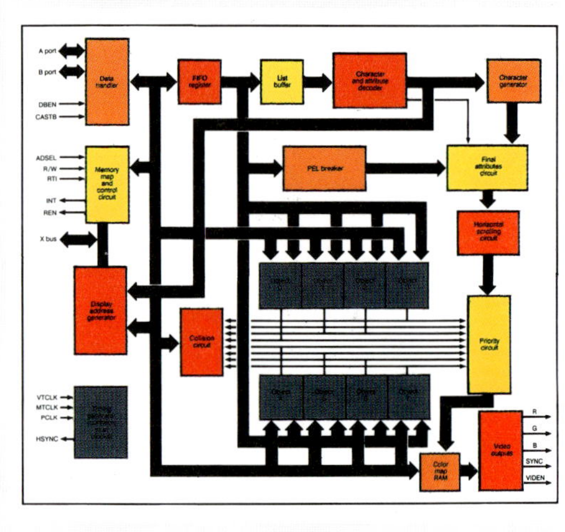

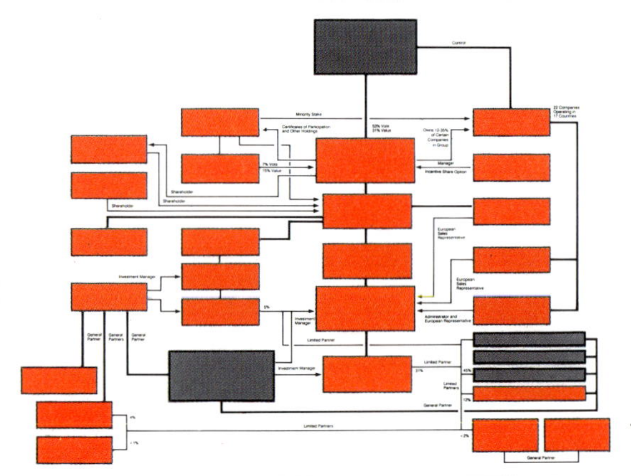

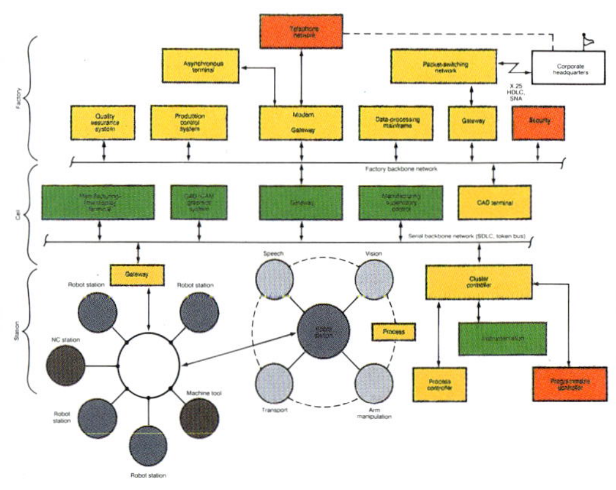

119 Peter Halley ■

Untitled, 1990

a. Is it an Arrival or a Departure? **b.** Final Attributes **c.** Limited Partners **d.** Station, Cell, Factory

Mappe mit 4 Serigraphien auf transparenter Folie, Maße unterschiedlich, ca. 60 x 80 cm. Auflage: 50

Portfolio of 4 silkscreens on mylar, different sizes, approx. 24 x 32 in. Edition: 50

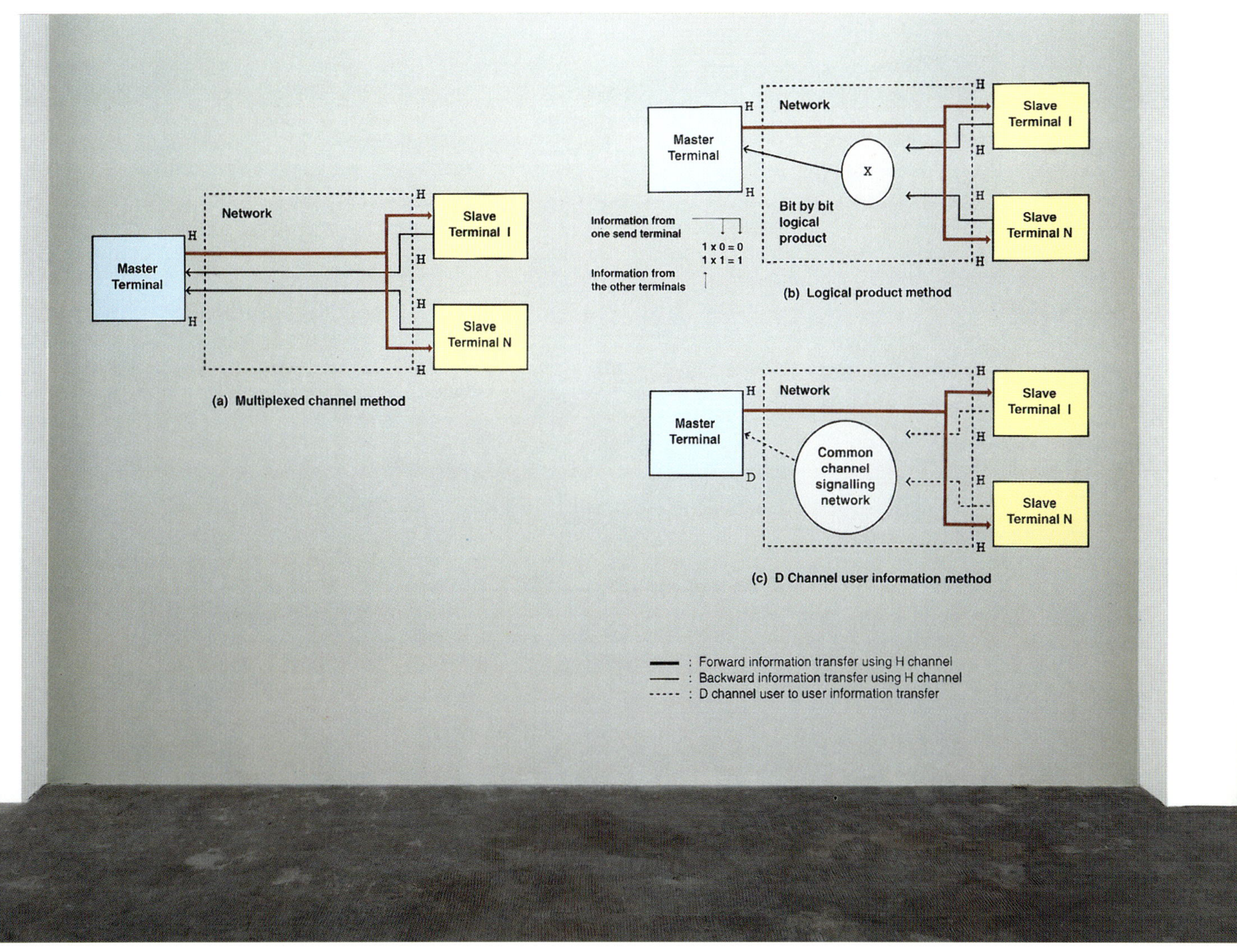

120 Peter Halley ■
Master Terminal / Slave Terminal, 1993
Wandzeichnung (Wandfarbe und Siebdruck), auszuführen nach den Anweisungen des Künstlers, siehe Appendix.
Gesamtmaße variabel. Auflage: 10, mit einem sign. und num. Zertifikat
Wall drawing in latex paint, with silkscreen, to be executed according to the artist's instructions, see appendix.
Overall size of the work variable. Edition: 10, with a signed and numbered certificate

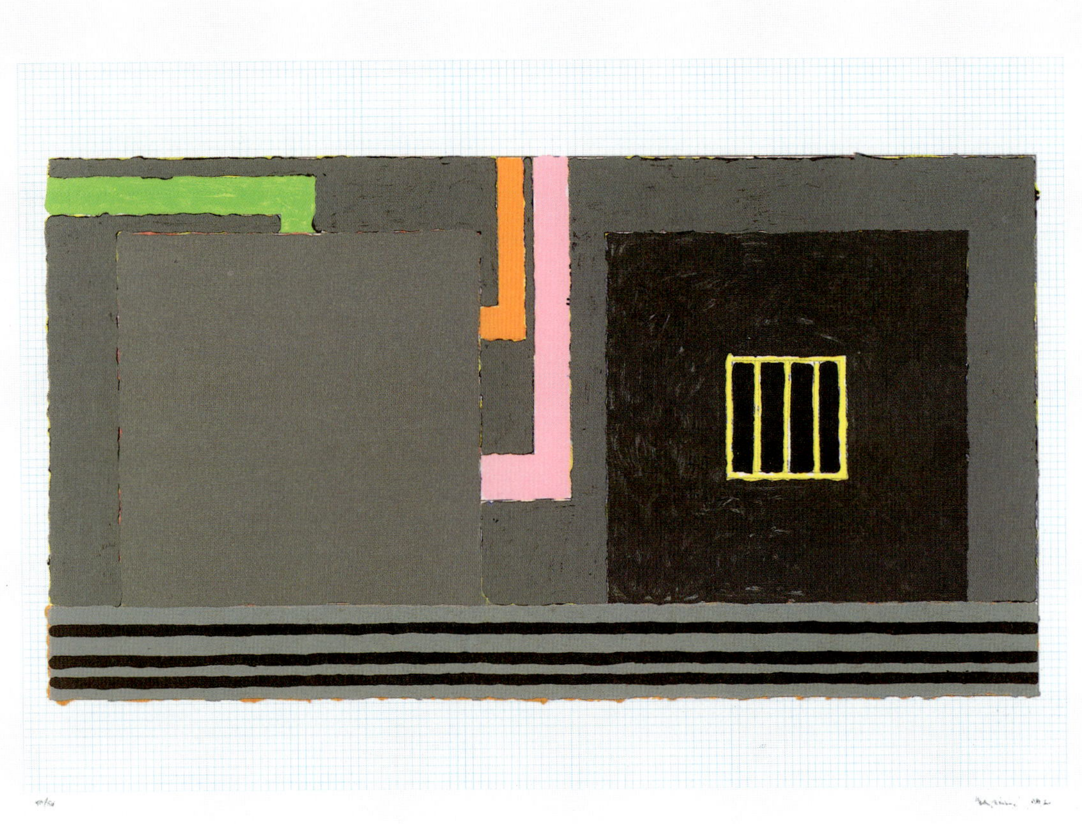

121 Peter Halley ■
Nowhere, 1993
Serigraphie auf Bütten, 101,5 x 140,3 cm. Auflage 50
Silkscreen on rag paper, 40 x 55¼ in. Edition: 50

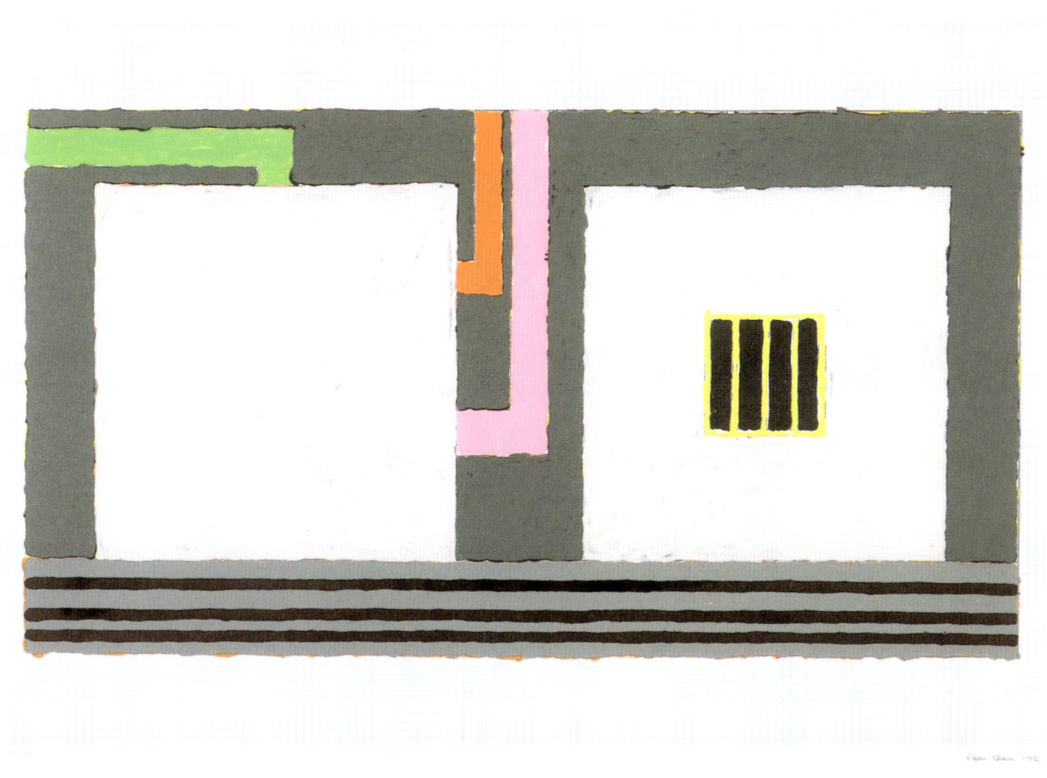

122 Peter Halley ■
Elsewhere, 1993
Serigraphie auf Bütten, 101,5 x 140,3 cm. Auflage 50
Silkscreen on rag paper, 40 x 55¼ in. Edition: 50

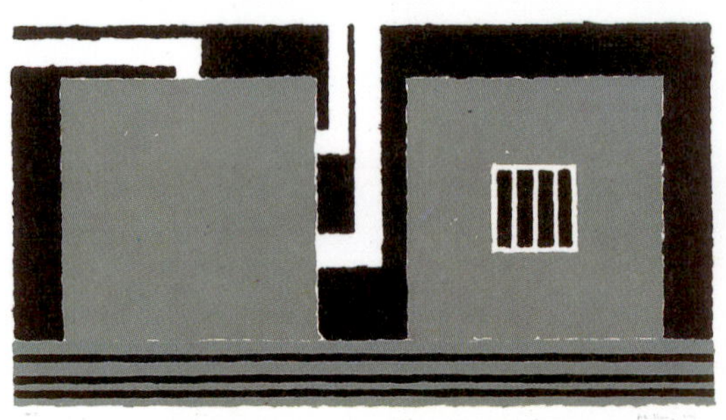

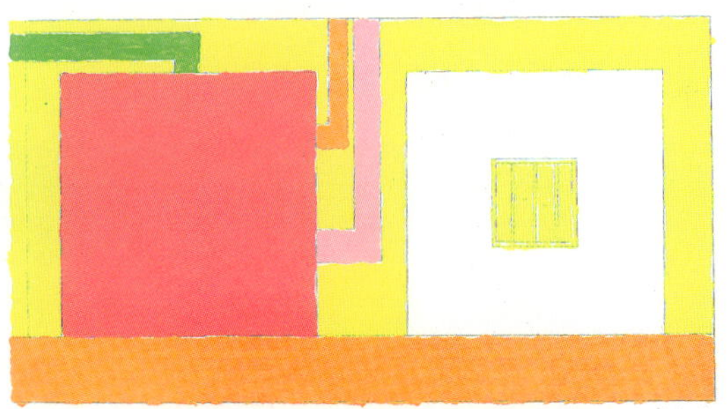

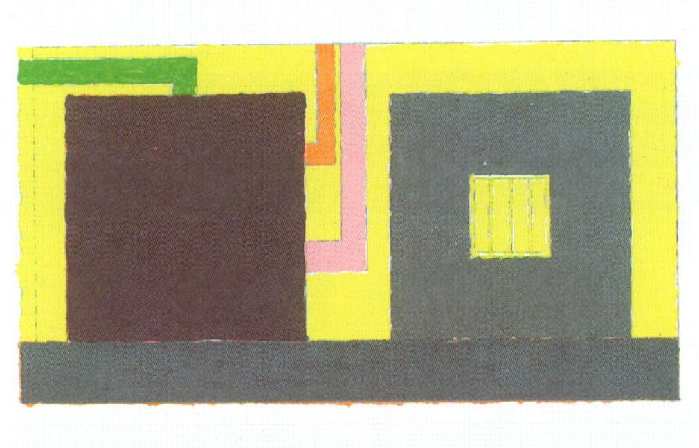

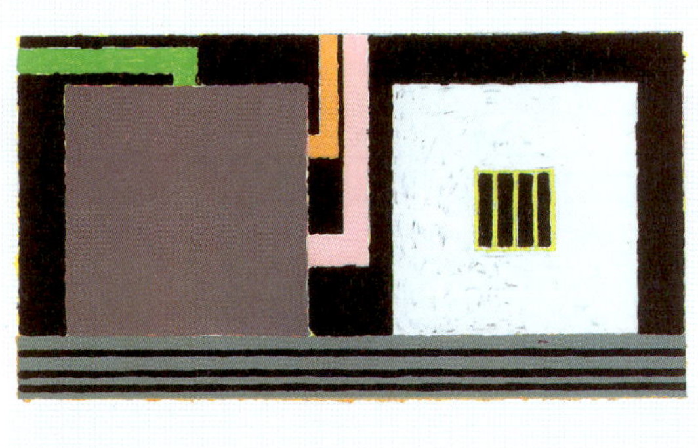

123 Peter Halley ■
Nowhere / Elsewhere, States I - IV, 1993
Serigraphien (Progressive Proofs) auf Bütten, 101,5 x 140,3 cm. Auflage: 12
Silkscreens (progressive proofs) on rag paper, 40 x 55½ in. Edition: 12

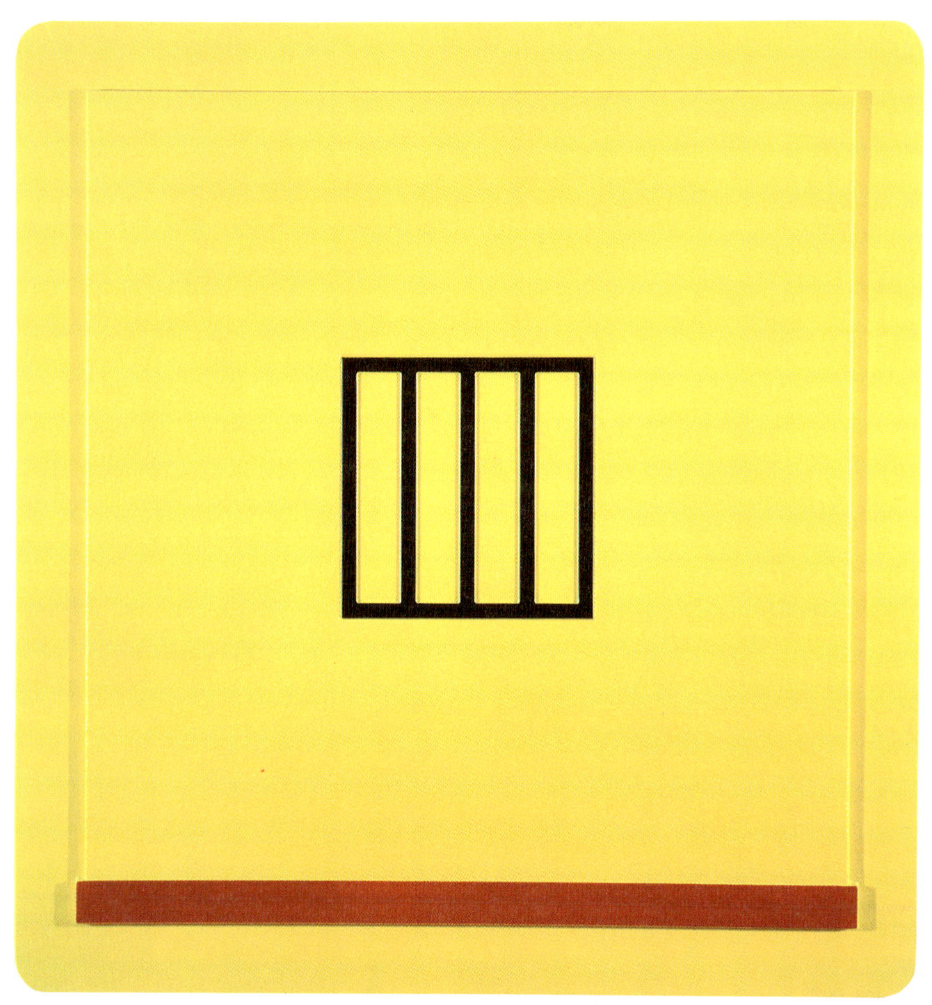

124 Peter Halley
Prison, 1987
Tiefgezogenes Kunstoffrelief mit Siebdruck, 112 x 93,5 x 2,5 cm. Auflage: 18
Vacuum formed plastic relief with silkscreen, 44 ¼ x 36 ¾ x 1 in. Edition: 18

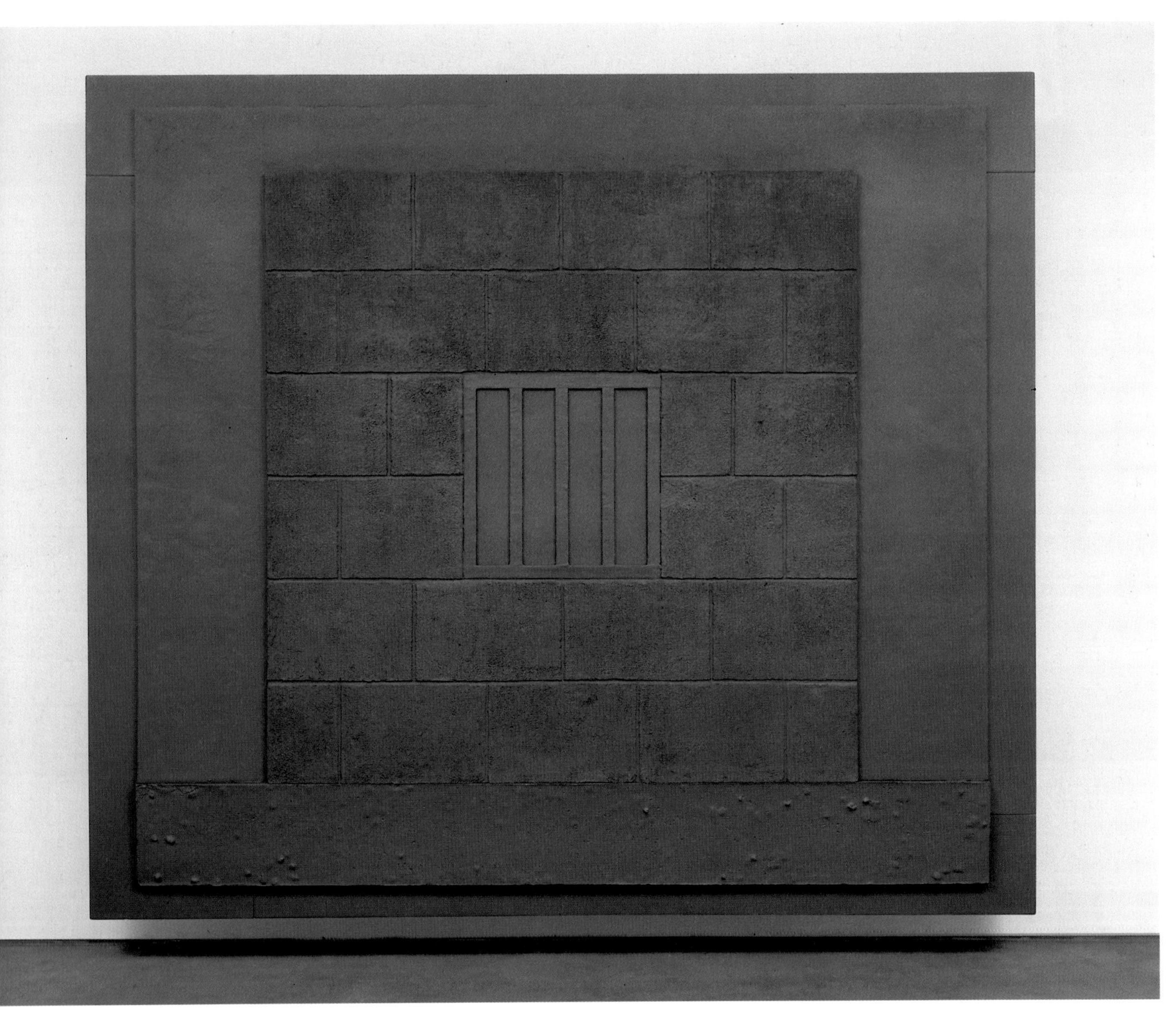

125 Peter Halley
Cinder Block Prison, 1990
Fiberglasrelief, 254 x 295 x 33 cm. Auflage: 3
Fiberglass relief, 100 x 116 x 13 in. Edition: 3

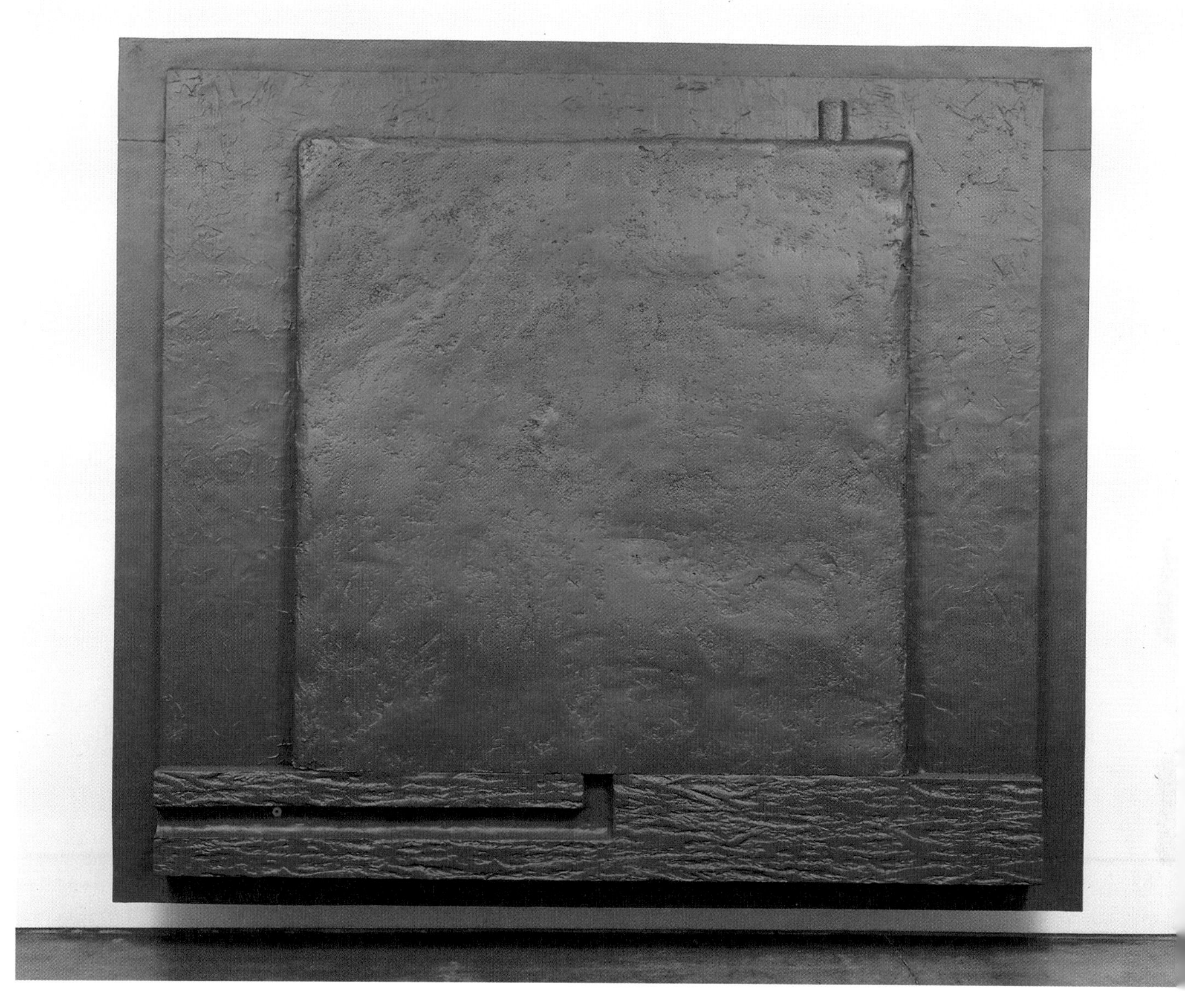

126 Peter Halley
Cell With Smoke Stack and Conduit, 1990
Fiberglasrelief, 253 x 295 x 38 cm. Auflage: 3
Fiberglass relief, 99½ x 116 x 15 in. Edition: 3

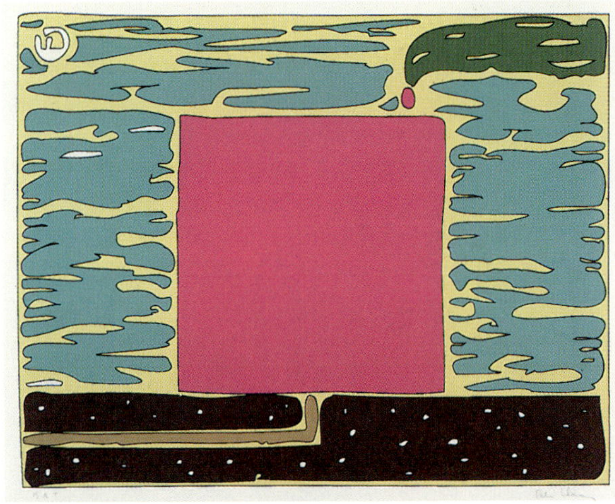

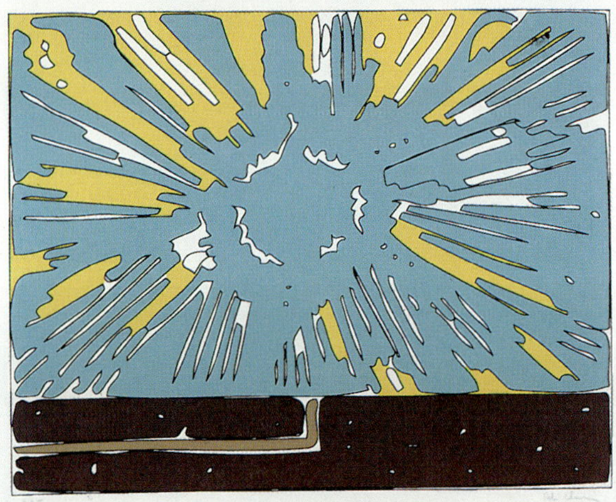

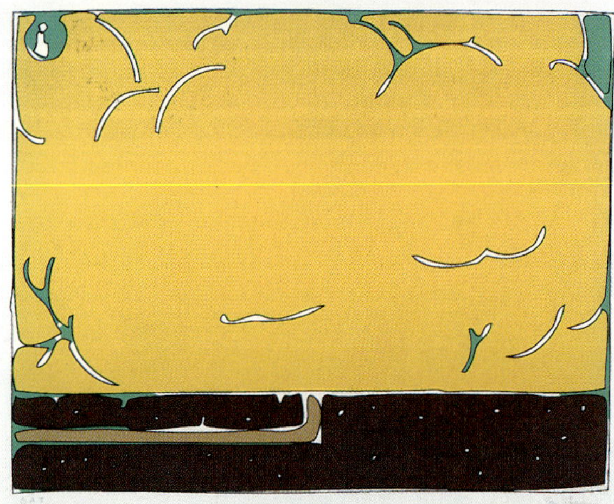

127 Peter Halley ■
Exploding Cell, 1994
Mappe mit 9 Serigraphien auf Museumskarton,
94 x 122 cm. Auflage: 32
Set of 9 silkscreens on 2-ply museum board,
37 x 48 in. Edition: 32

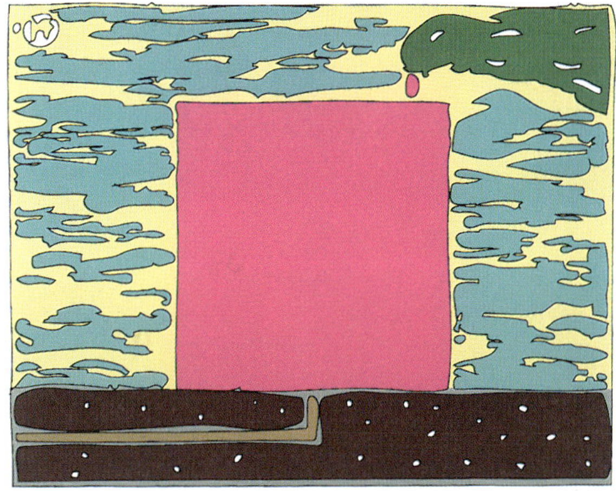
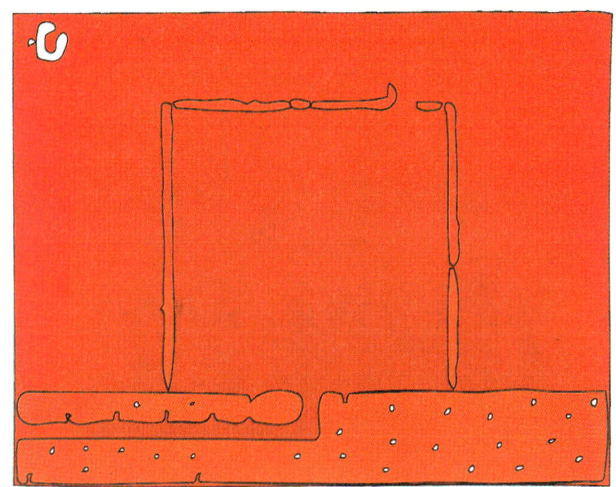
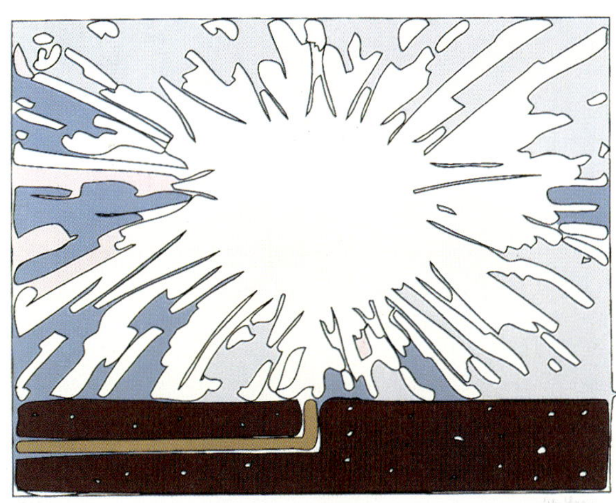
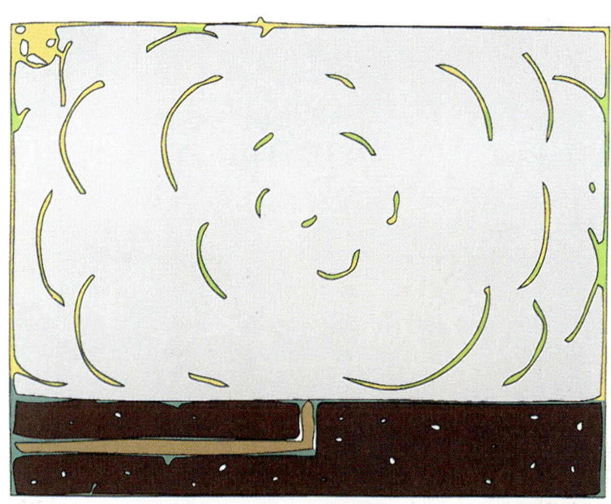
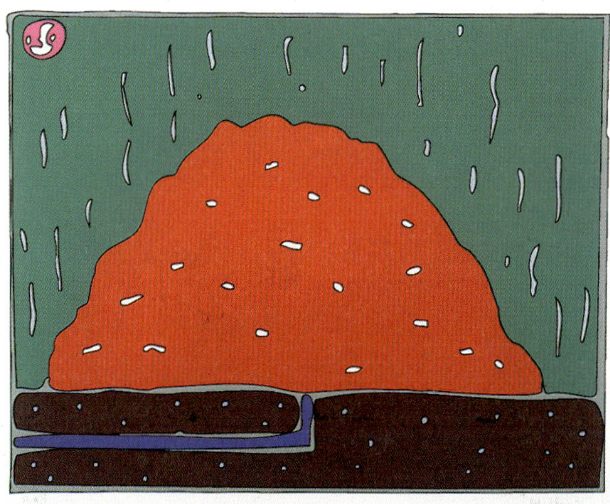
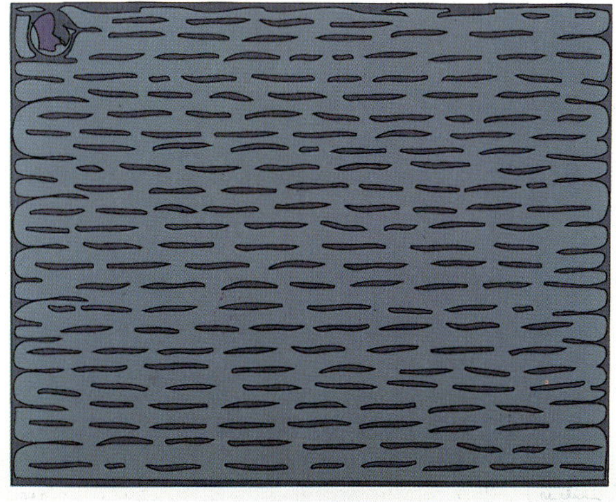

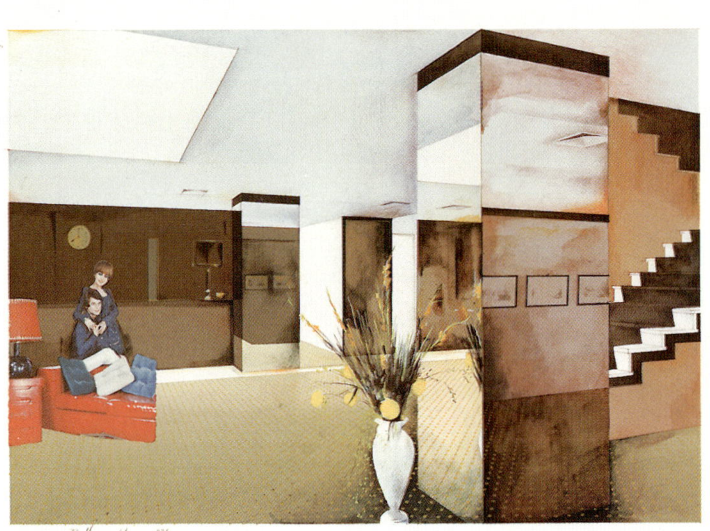

128 Richard Hamilton
Lobby, 1984
Lichtdruck und Siebdruck,
43 x 58,3 cm. Auflage: 88
Collotype and screenprint,
17 x 23 in. Edition: 88

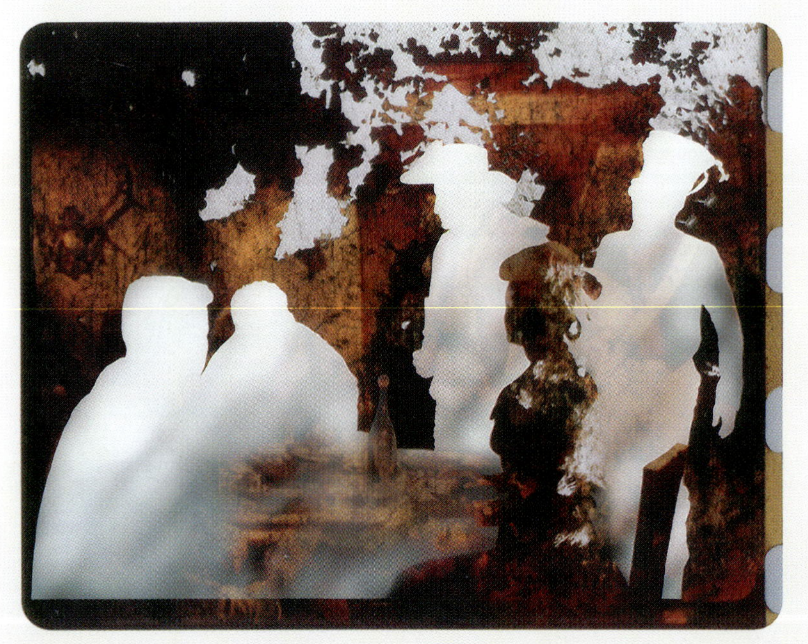

129 Richard Hamilton
Ghosts of Ufa, 1994
Offsetlithographie von einer computer-
erzeugten Vorlage, 63 x 88 cm.
Auflage: 120
Offset lithograph from a computer
generated film, 24¾ x 34½ in.
Edition: 120

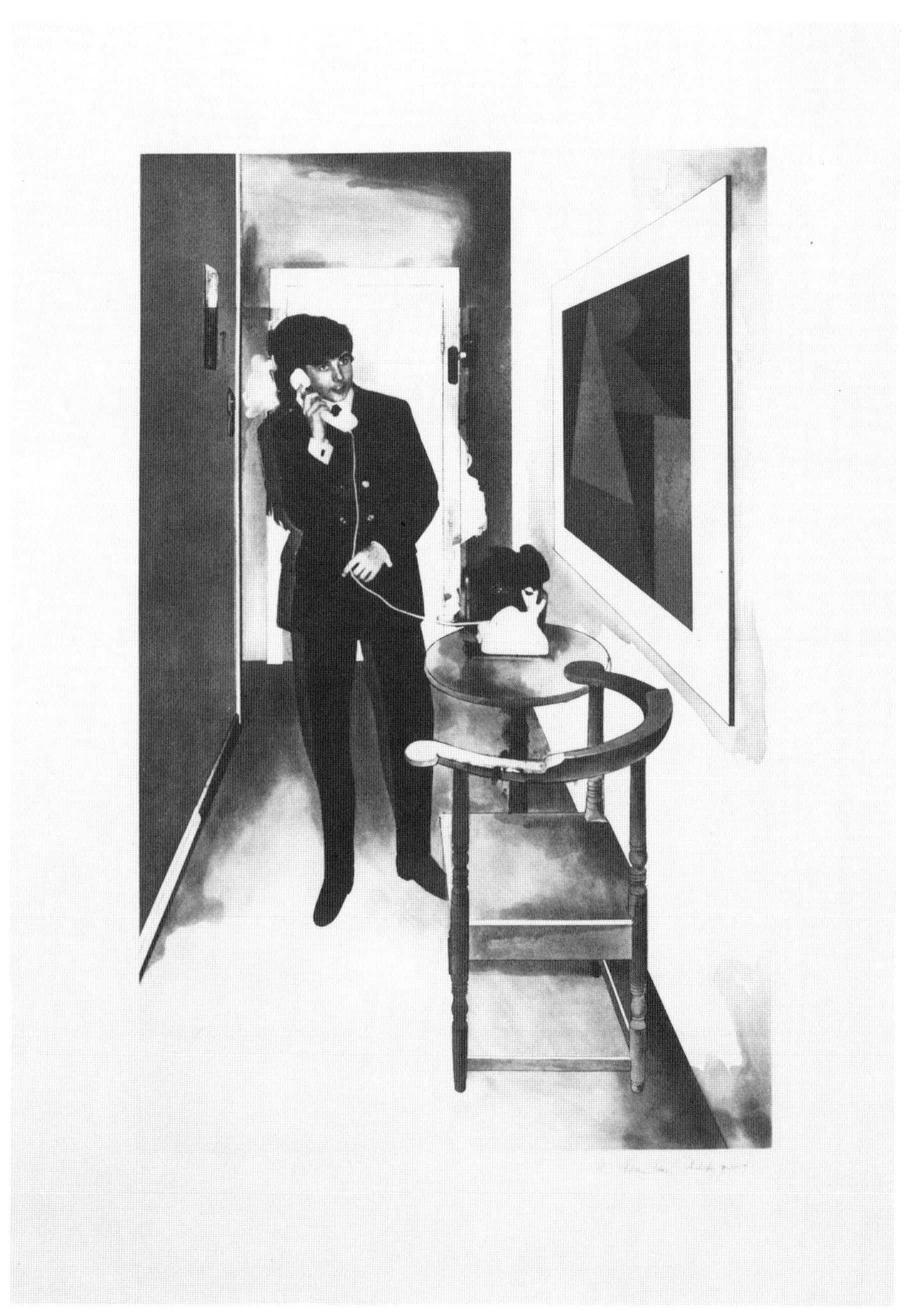

130 Richard Hamilton
Dedicated Follower of Fashion, 1980
Aquatintaradierung auf Bütten, 75 x 57 cm. Auflage: 100
Etching and aquatint, 30 x 22 in. Edition: 100

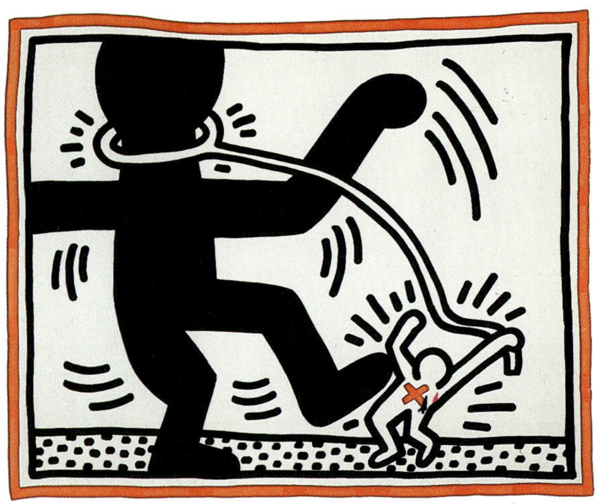

131 Keith Haring ■
Free South Africa, 1985
Folge von 3 Lithographien, 81 x 100 cm. Auflage: 60
Suite of 3 lithographs, 32 x 40 in. Edition: 60

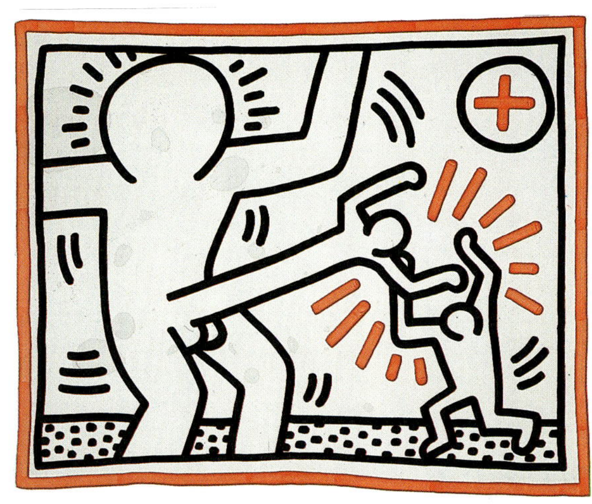

132 Keith Haring ■
Untitled, 1985
Folge von 3 Lithographien, 81 x 100 cm. Auflage: 80
Suite of 3 lithographs, 32 x 40 in. Edition: 80

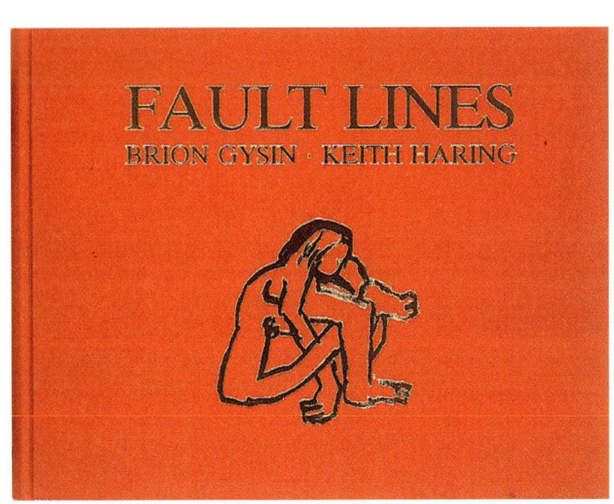

133 Keith Haring ■
Fault Lines, 1986
Buch von Brion Gysin mit Zeichnungen (Lichtdruck) von K.H. Leinen, Bütten, in Schuber 23 x 29 x 3 cm. Auflage 200, signiert und numeriert.
Book by Brion Gysin with collotype illustrations by K.H. Cloth bound, rag paper, in slipcase, 9 x 11 x 1 in. Edition: 200, signed and numbered

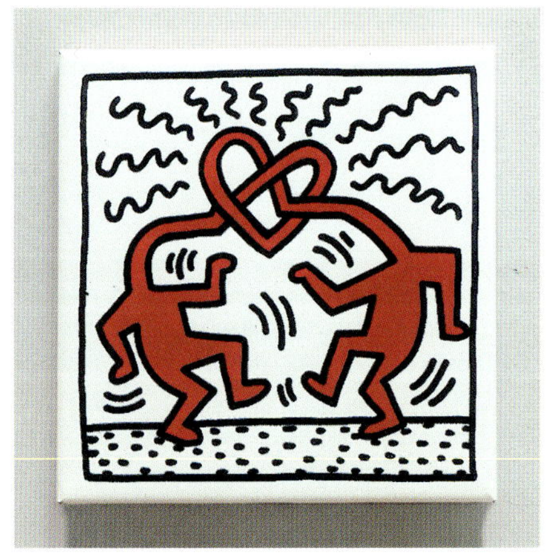

134 Keith Haring ■
Untitled, 1989
Siebdruck auf Leinwand, auf Keilrahmen, 20,5 x 20,5 x 2 cm. Auflage: 60
Silkscreen on stretched canvas, 8 x 8 x ¾ in. Edition: 60

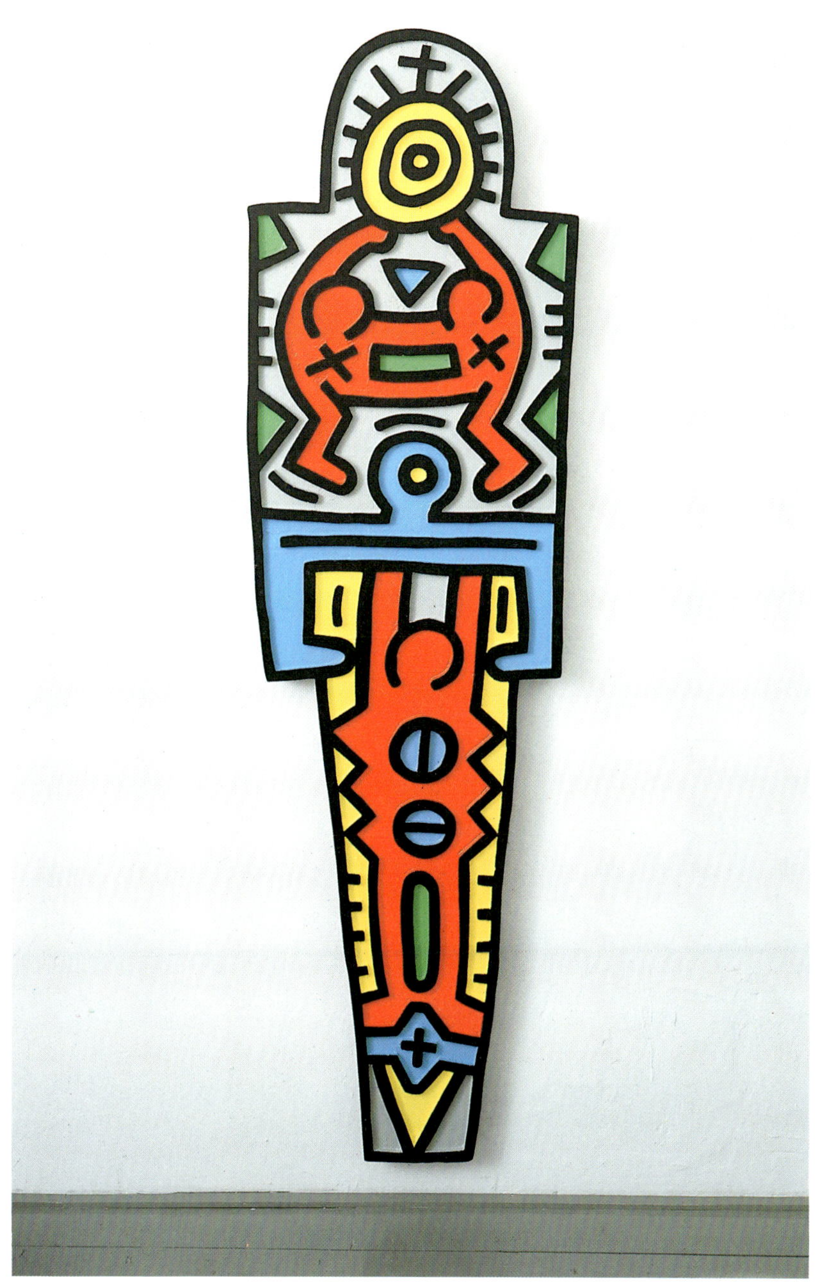

135 Keith Haring ■
Totem, 1988
Sperrholzrelief, farbig lackiert, 184 x 56 x 5 cm. Auflage: 35
Carved plywood, painted in colors, 72 x 22 x 2½ in. Edition: 35

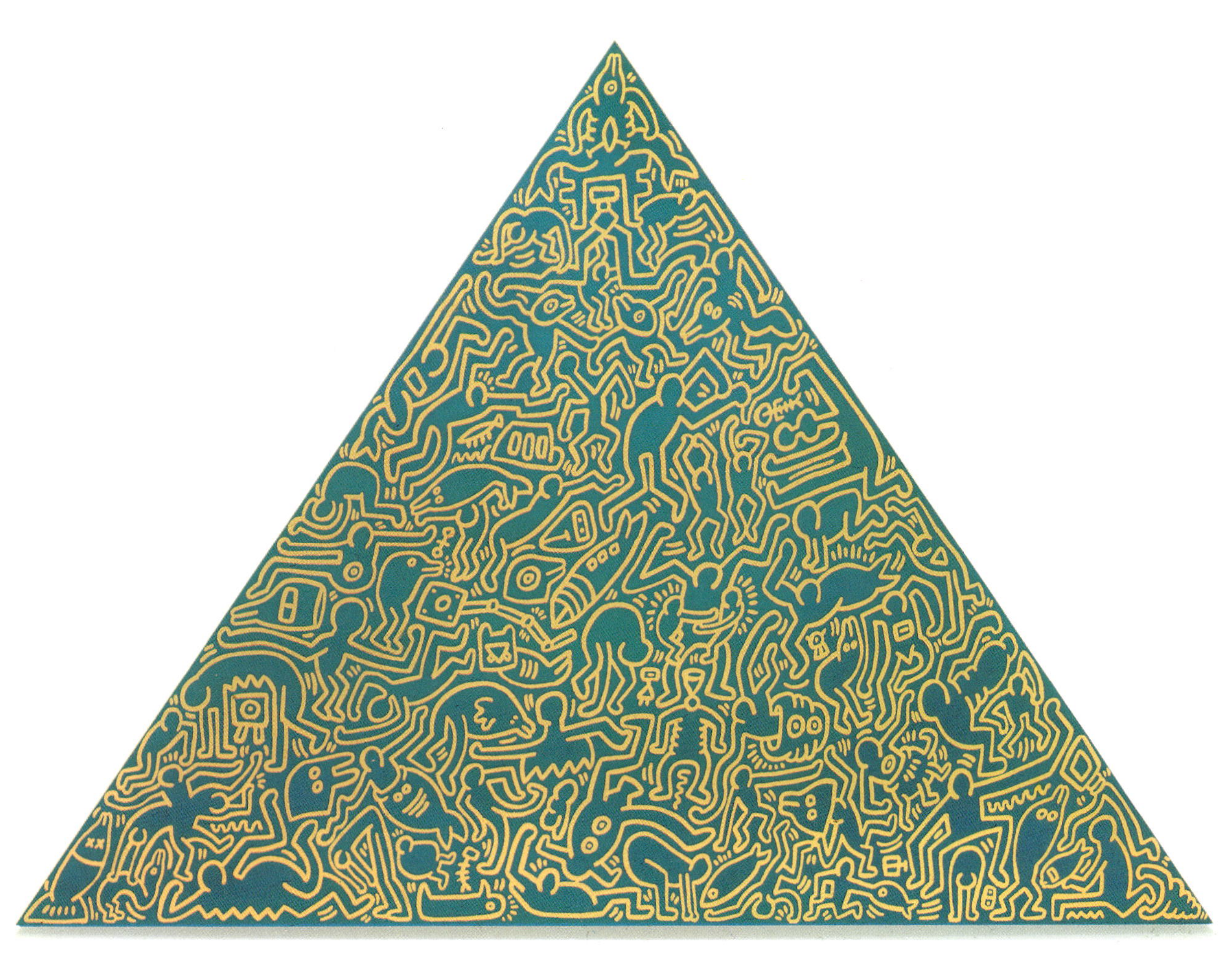

136 Keith Haring ■
Pyramid, 1989
4 eloxierte Aluminiumplatten (2 abgebildet), 104 x 144 x 3 cm. Auflage: 30
4 anodized aluminum plates (2 of them ill.), 41 x 56½ x 1 in. Edition: 30

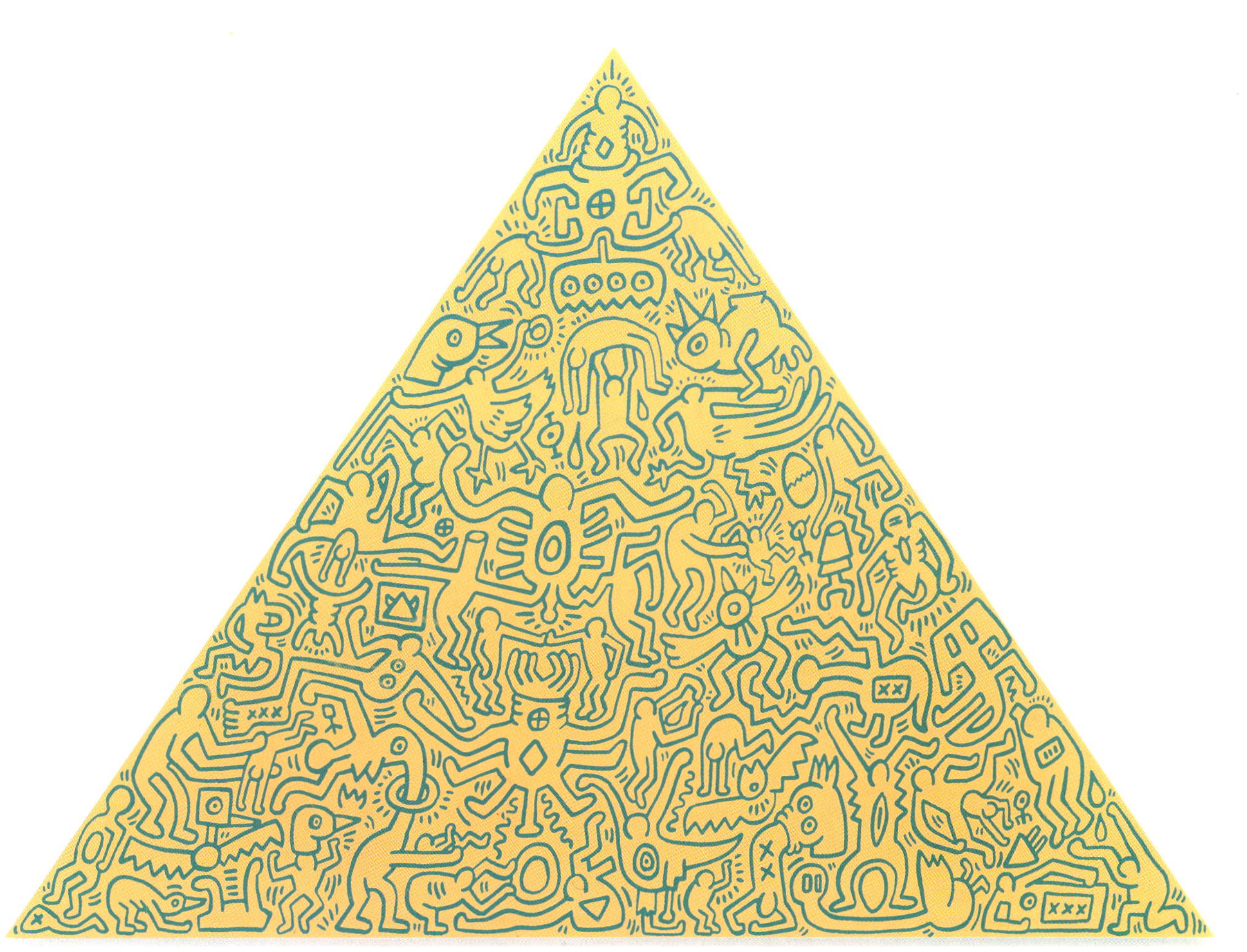

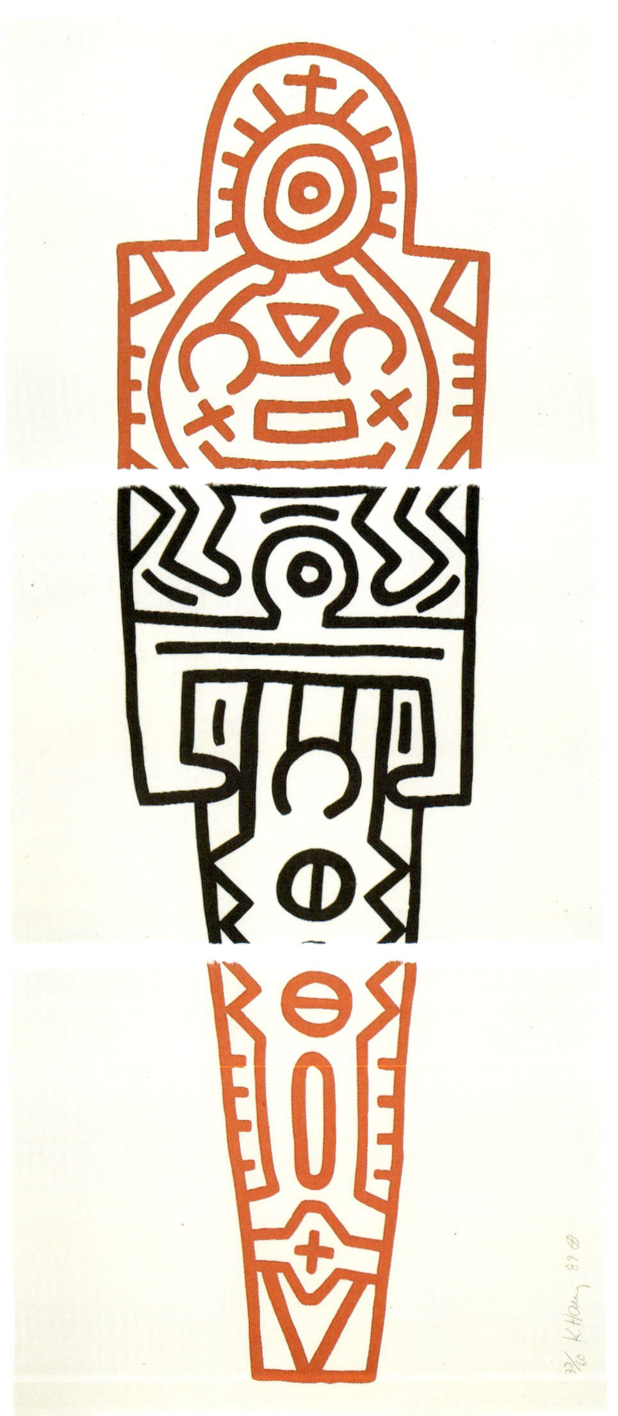

137 Keith Haring ■
Totem, 1989
3-teiliger Holzschnitt auf Japanpapier,
191,5 x 89 cm. Auflage: 60
Three-part woodcut on Japanese paper,
75½ x 35 in. Edition: 60

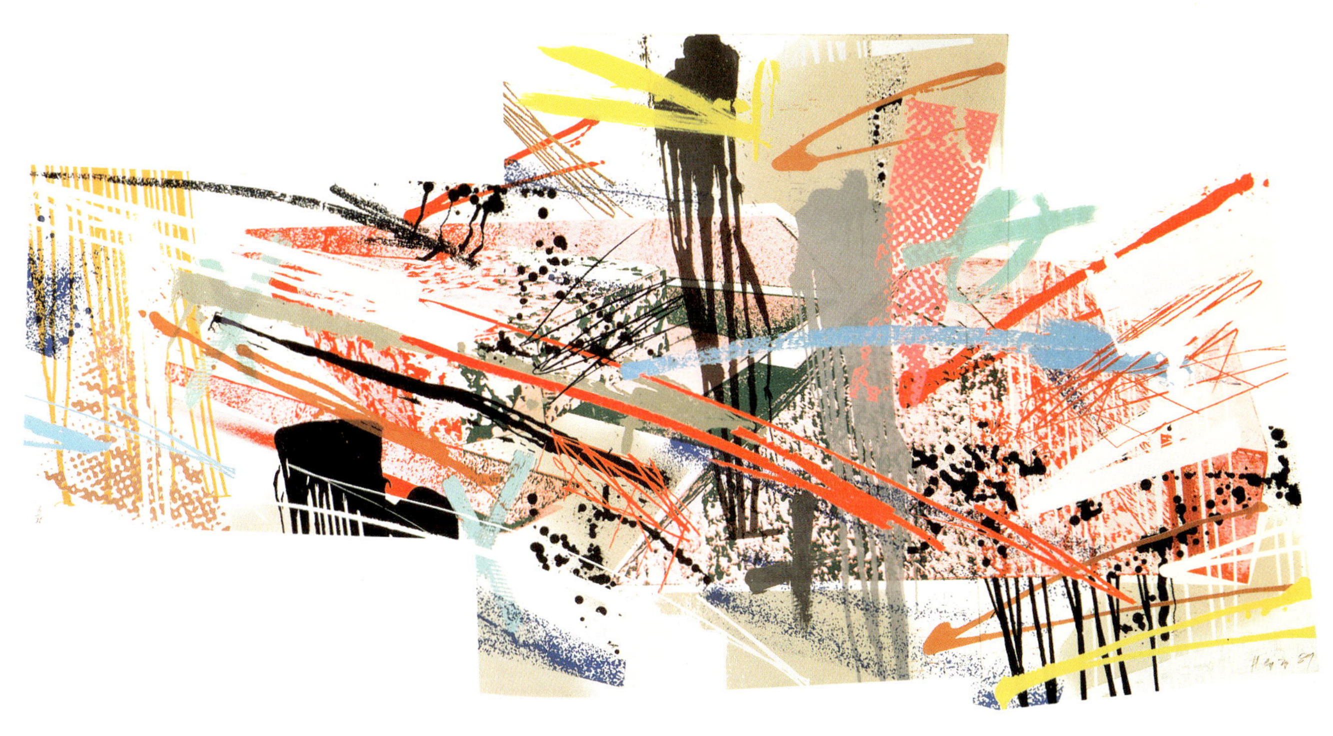

138 Michael Heizer □
Dragged Mass Diametric, 1989
4-teilige Farbserigraphie, Gesamtmaß 140 x 257 cm. Auflage: 36
4-part silkscreen in colors, overall size 55 x 101 in. Edition: 36

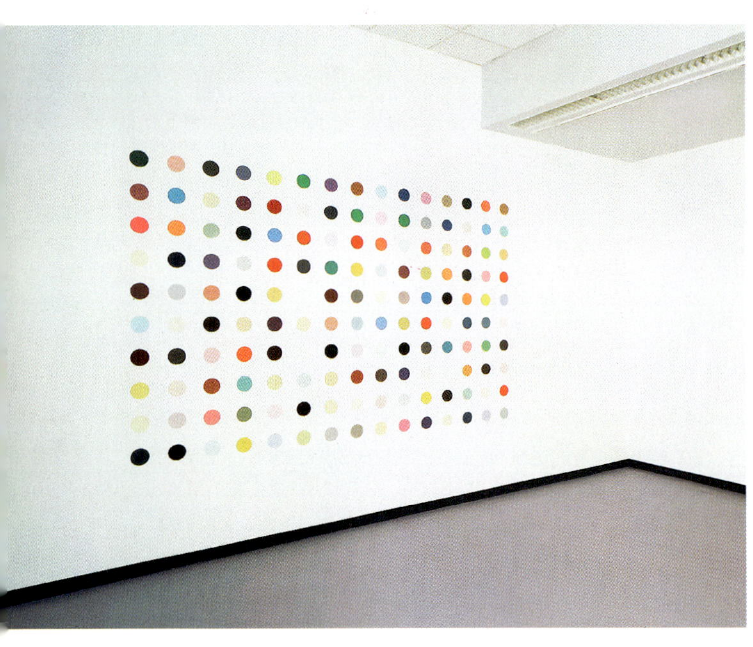

139 Damien Hirst ■
Pharmaceutic Wall Painting, Five Blacks, 1993
Wandmalerei (Lackfarbe), auszuführen nach den Anweisungen des Künstlers, siehe Appendix. Maße variabel.
Auflage: 10, jede Arbeit in einer anderen Farbkombination, mit einem sign. und num. Zertifikat.
Wall painting in enamel paint, to be executed according to the artist's instructions, see appendix. Size variable.
Edition: 10, each work unique in color combination, with a signed and numbered certificate.

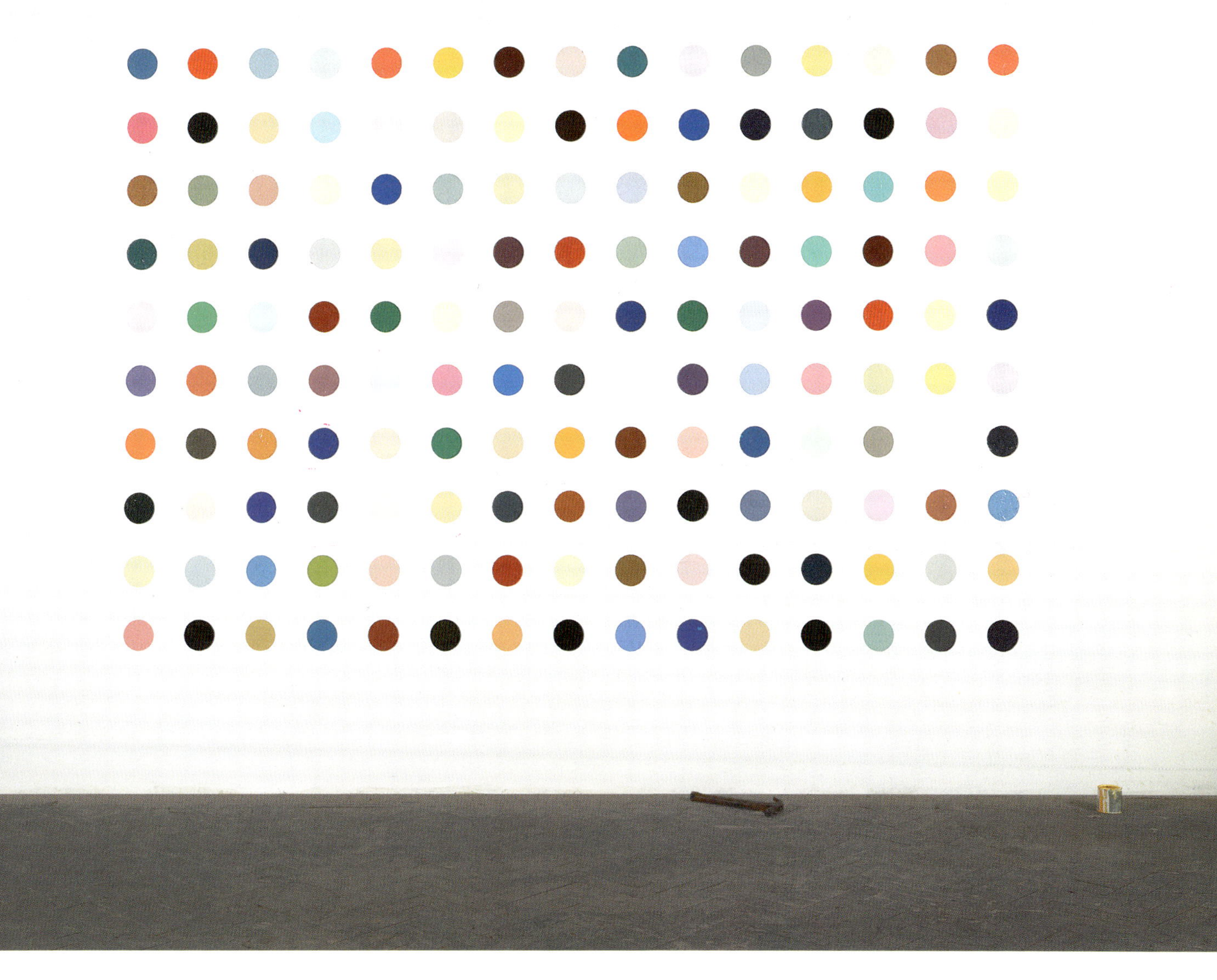

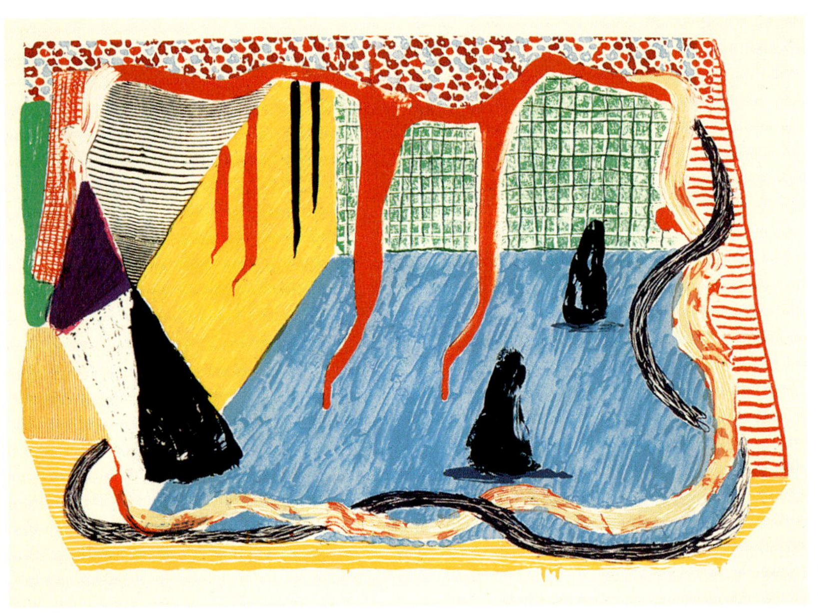

140 David Hockney
Ink in The Room, 1993
Lithographie/Serigraphie, 65 x 90 cm. Auflage: 68
Lithograph/screenprint, 25½ x 35½ in. Edition: 68

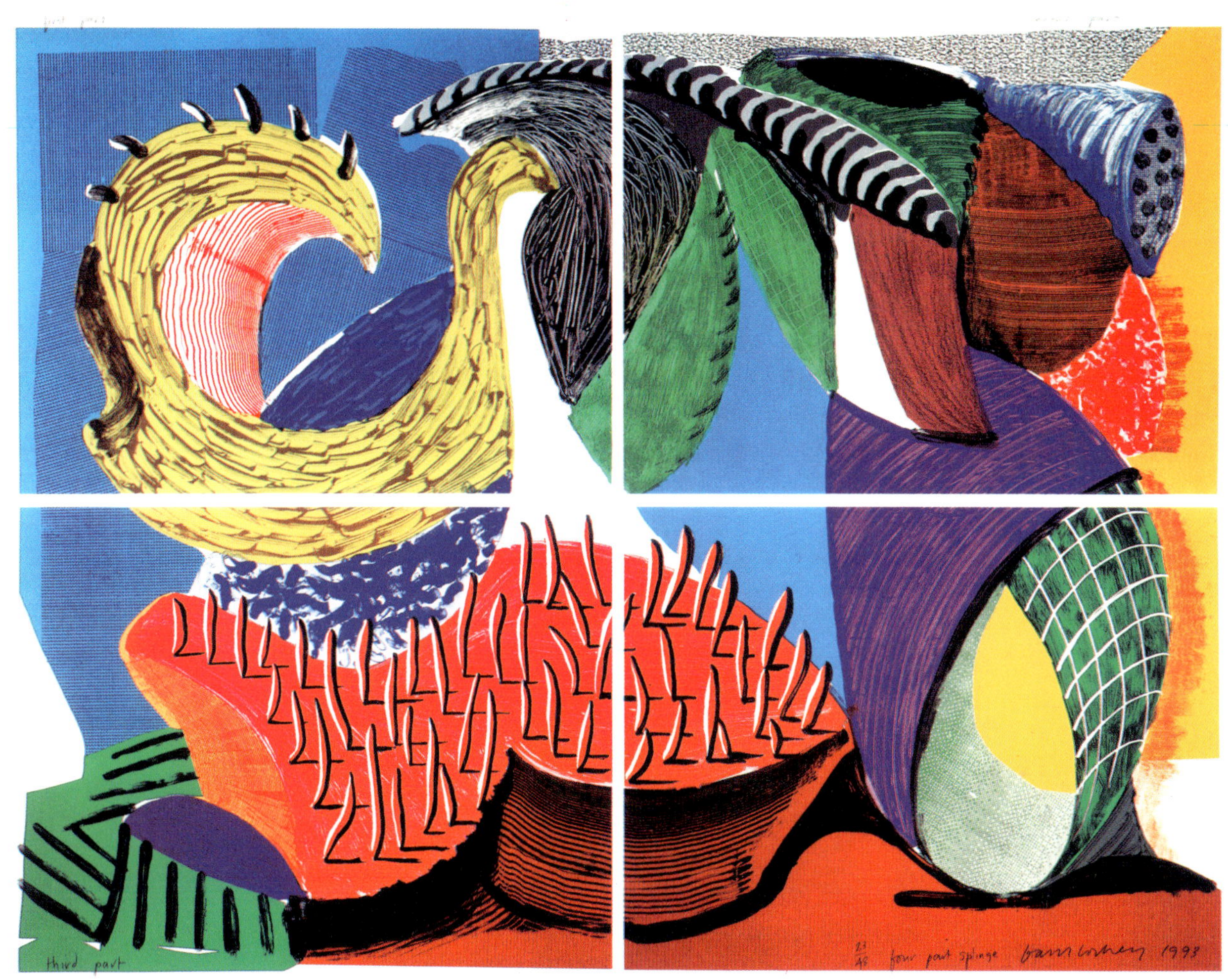

141 David Hockney
Four Part Splinge, 1994
Lithographie/Serigraphie in vier Teilen, 124 x 168 cm. Auflage: 48
Lithograph/screenprint in four parts, 49 x 66 in. Edition: 48

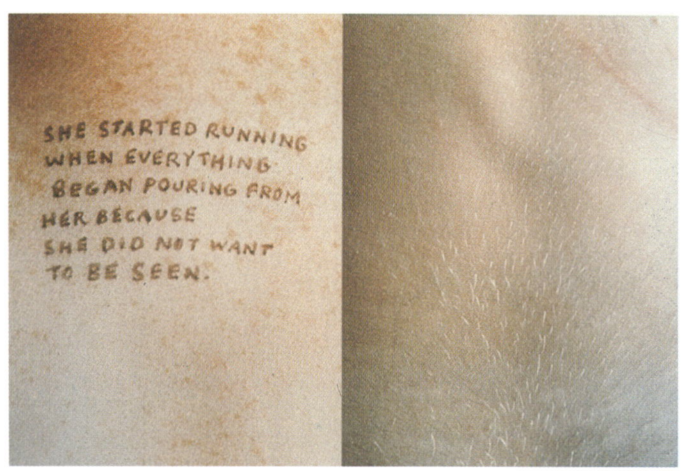

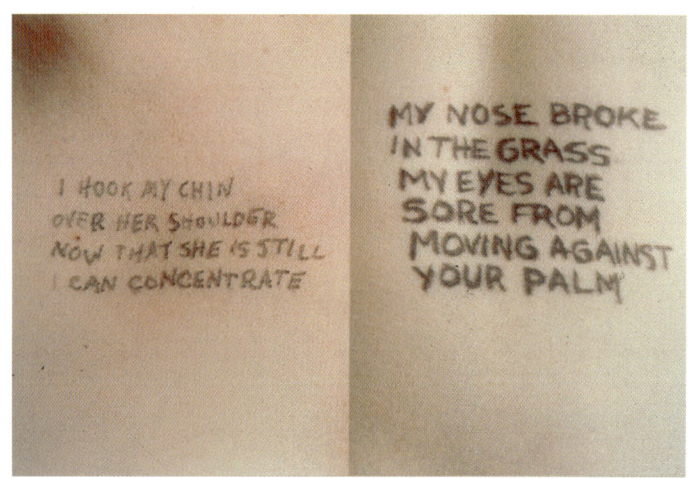

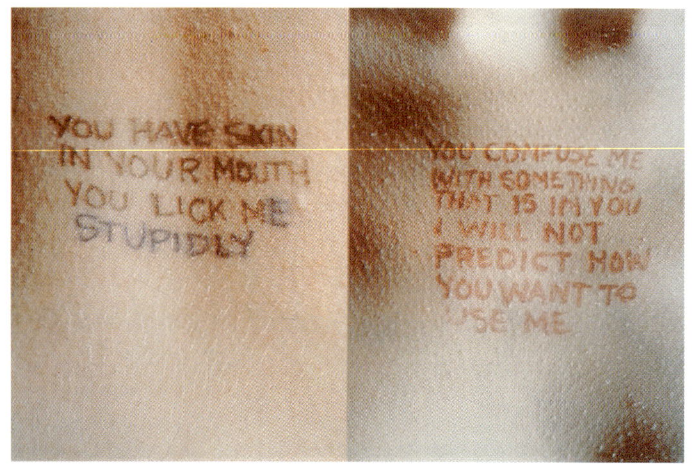

142 Jenny Holzer
Untitled (Selections from LUSTMORD),
1993-94
Folge von 14 Farbphotographien,
33 x 51 cm. Auflage: 20
Series of 14 Cibachromes,
13 x 20 in. Edition: 20

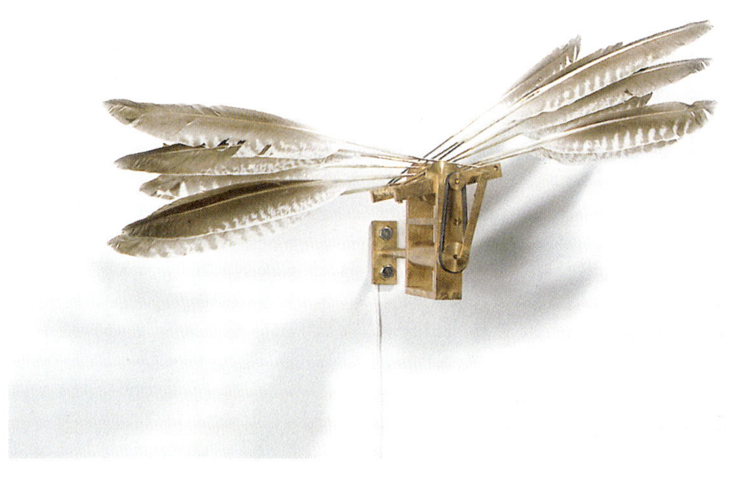

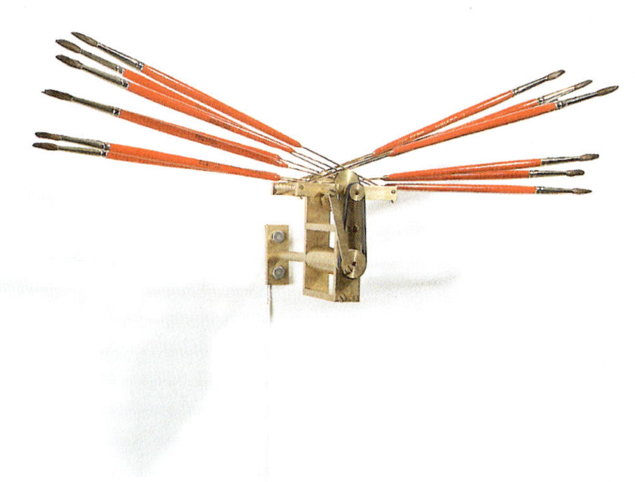

143 Rebecca Horn
a The Bird Wings, 1993
Federn, Elektromotor, 18 x 38 x 19 cm, an die Wand zu montieren. Auflage: 10
Feathers, motor, 7 x 15 x 7½ in., to be mounted on a wall. Edition: 10

b The Brush Wings, 1993
Pinsel, Elektromotor, 18 x 44,5 x 19 cm, an die Wand zu montieren. Auflage: 10
Brushes, motor, 7 x 17½ x 7½ in., to be mounted on a wall. Edition: 10

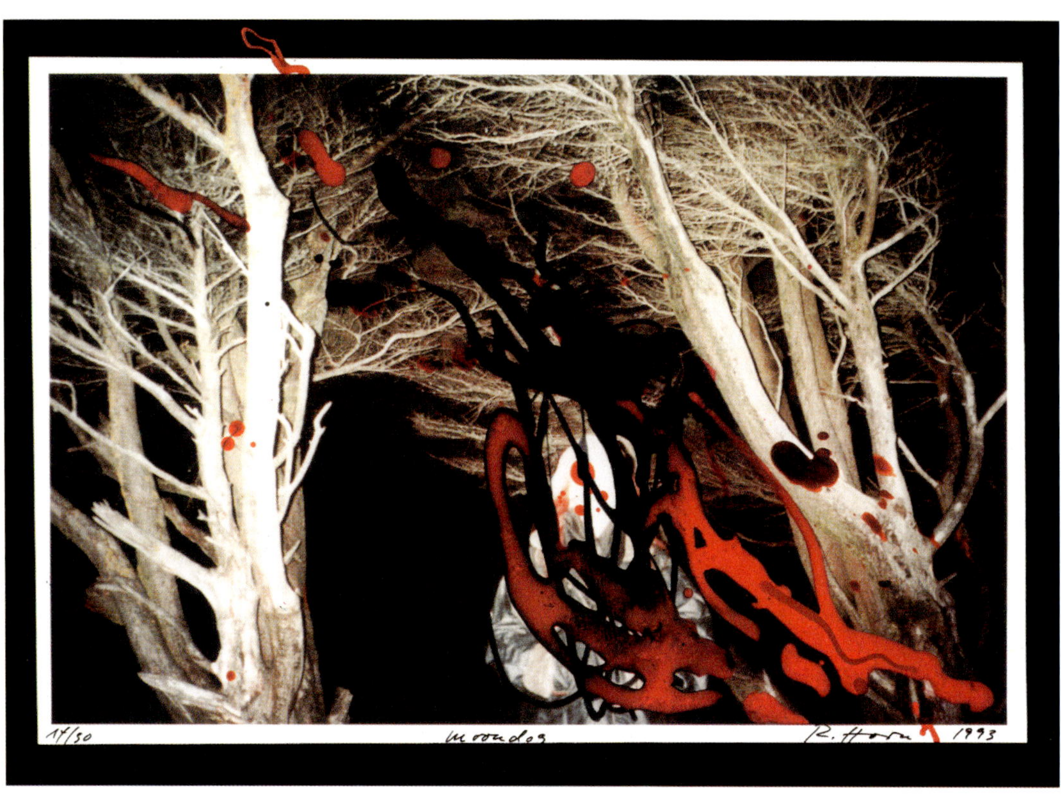

144 Rebecca Horn
Aran Moon, 1993
Zeichnung (Tinte) auf Foto, 68,5 x 99 cm. Auflage: 20, Zeichnungen unterschiedlich
Ink drawing on photograph, 27 x 39 in. Edition: 20, all drawings different within the edition

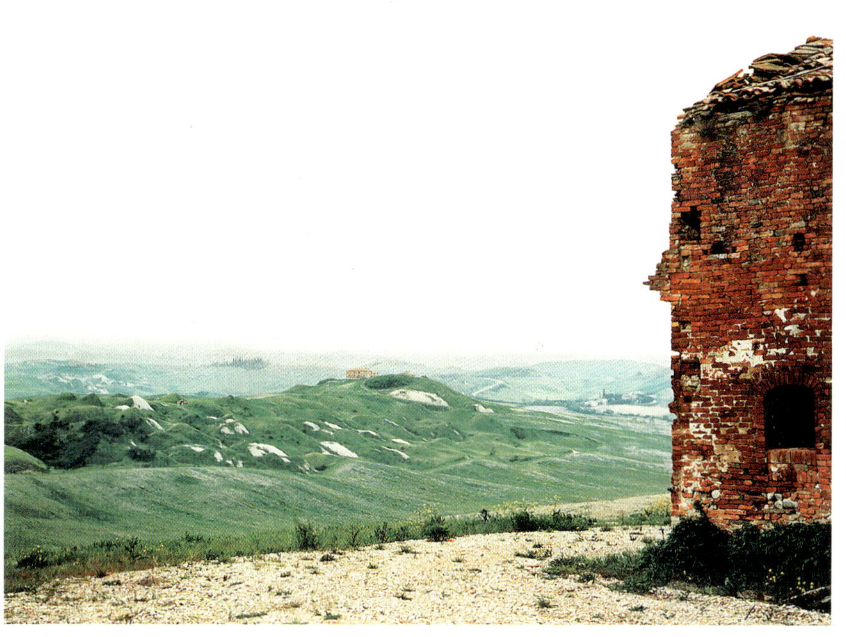

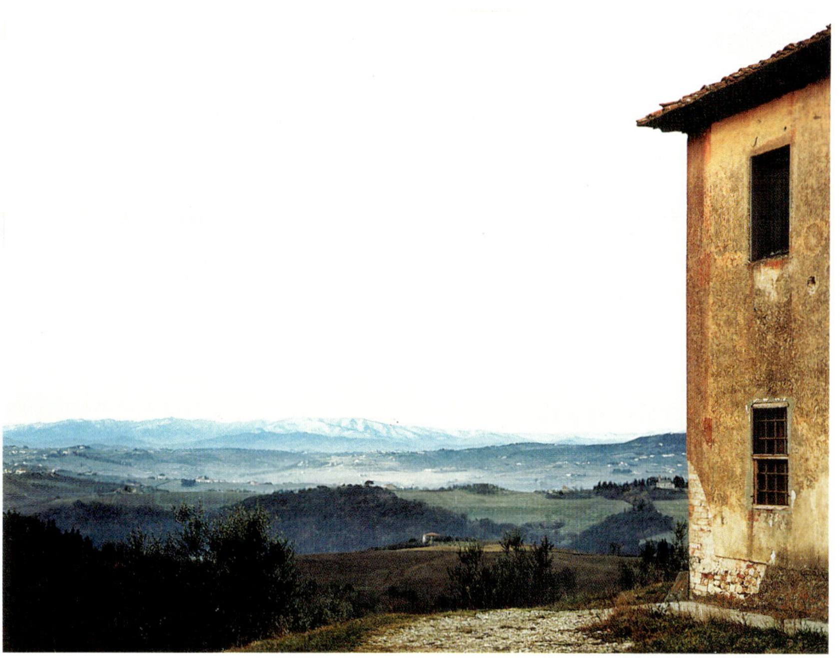

145 Axel Hütte
Italien, 1991-92
6 Photographien, 65 x 87,5 cm. Auflage: 10
6 photographs, 25¾ x 34½ in. Edition: 10

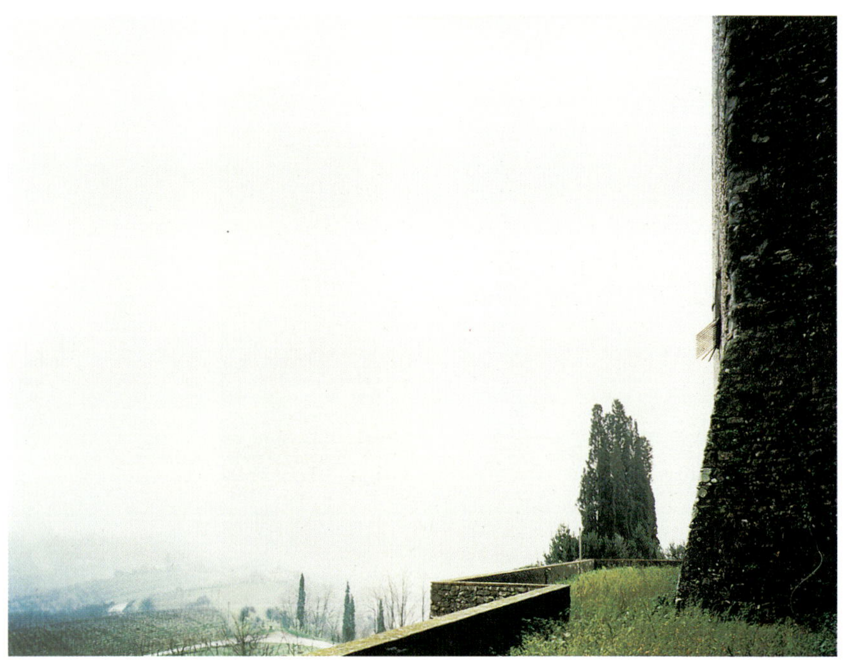

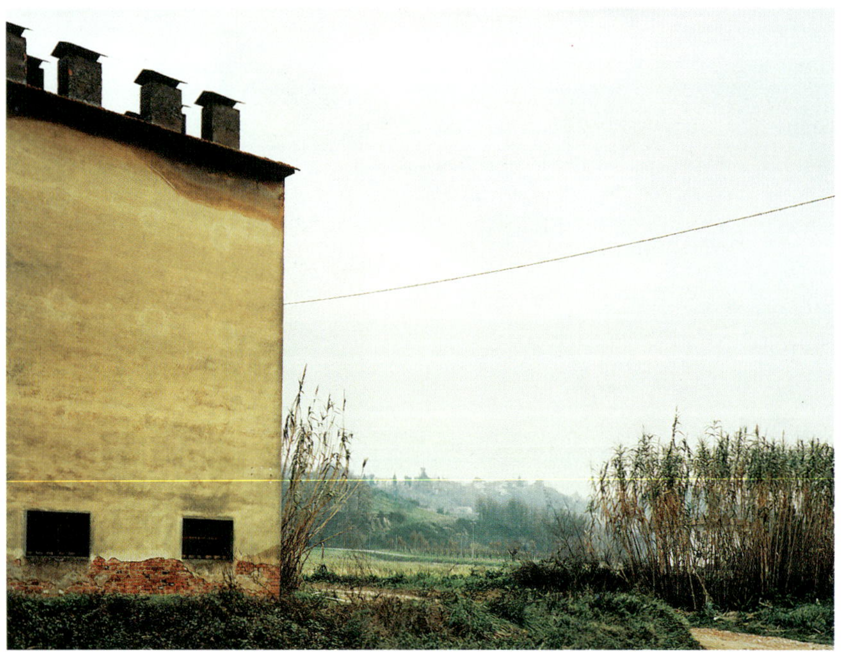

145 Axel Hütte
←

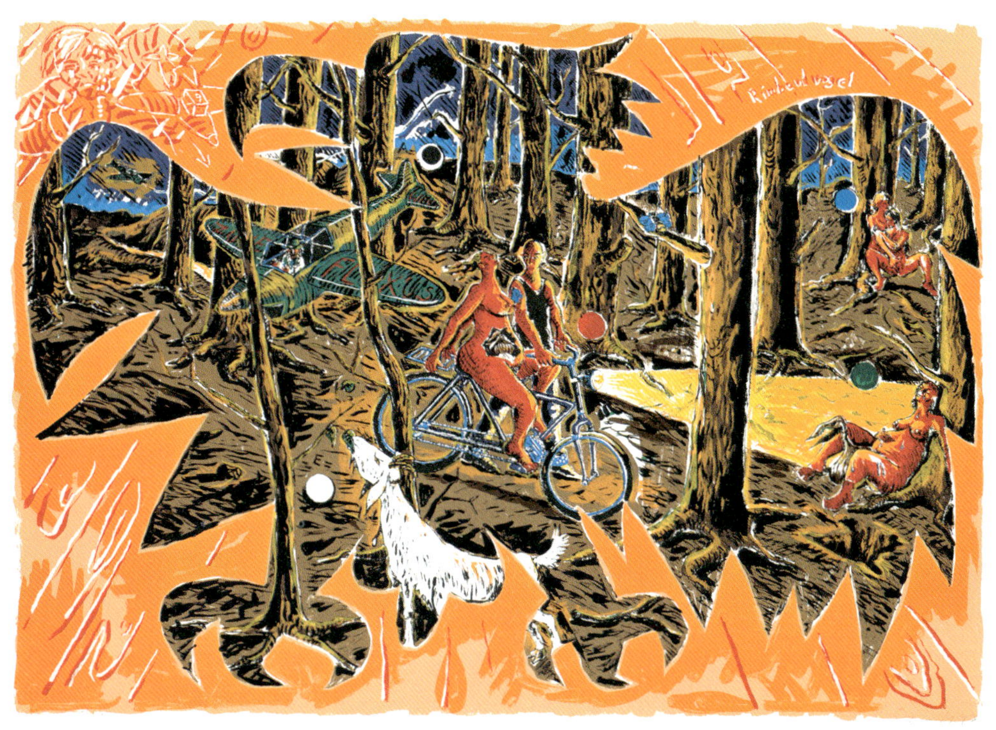

146 Jörg Immendorff
Rimbaudvogel, 1993
Farbsiebdruck, 90 x 130 cm. Auflage: 60
Color silkscreen, 35½ x 51 in. Edition: 60

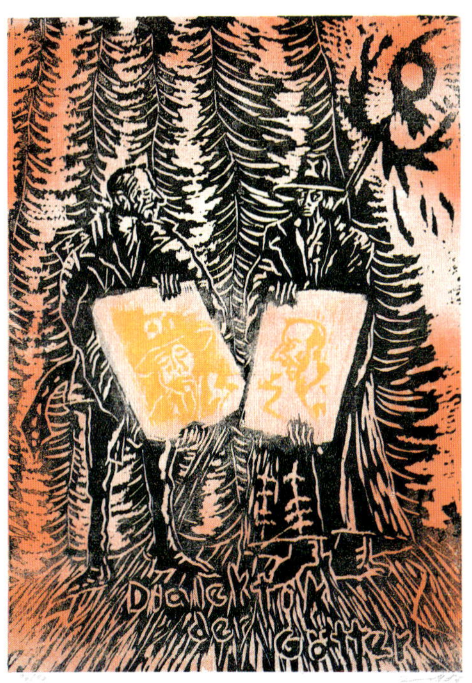

147 Jörg Immendorff ■
Dialektik der Götter, aus Mappe: Für Joseph Beuys, 1986
Holzschnitt auf Bütten, 80 x 60 cm. Auflage: 90
Woodcut on Japanese paper, 31½ x 23½ in. Edition: 90

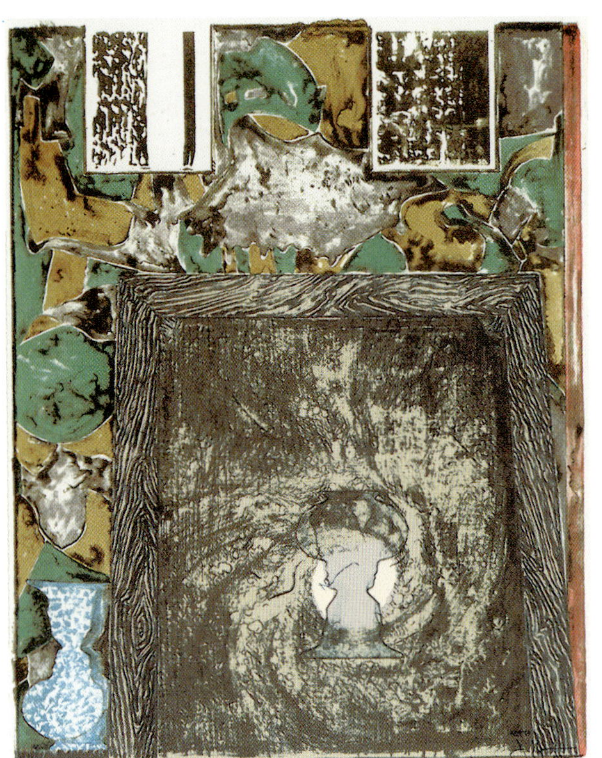

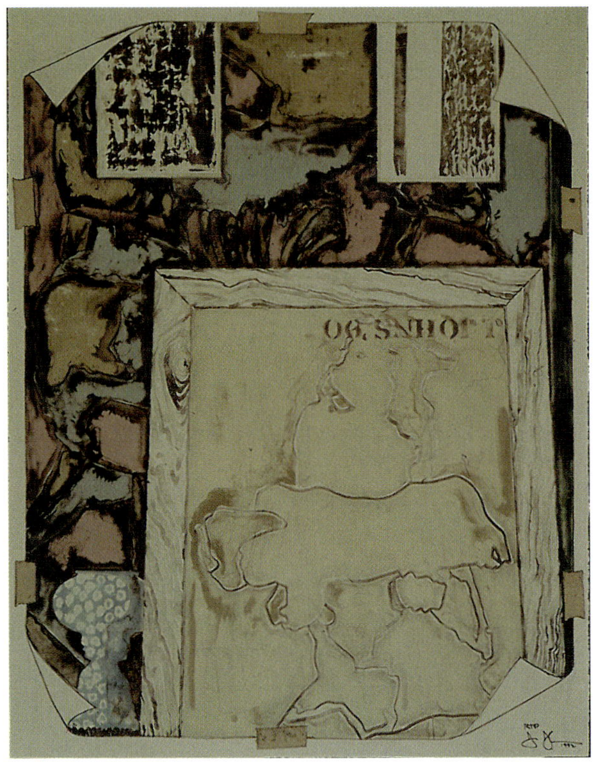

148 Jasper Johns
Untitled, 1992
Lithographie, 98,5 x 79,5 cm. Auflage: 72
Lithograph, 38¾ x 31¼ in. Edition: 72

149 Jasper Johns
Untitled, 1992
Lithographie, 98,5 x 79,5 cm. Auflage: 74
Lithograph, 38¾ x 31¼ in. Edition: 74

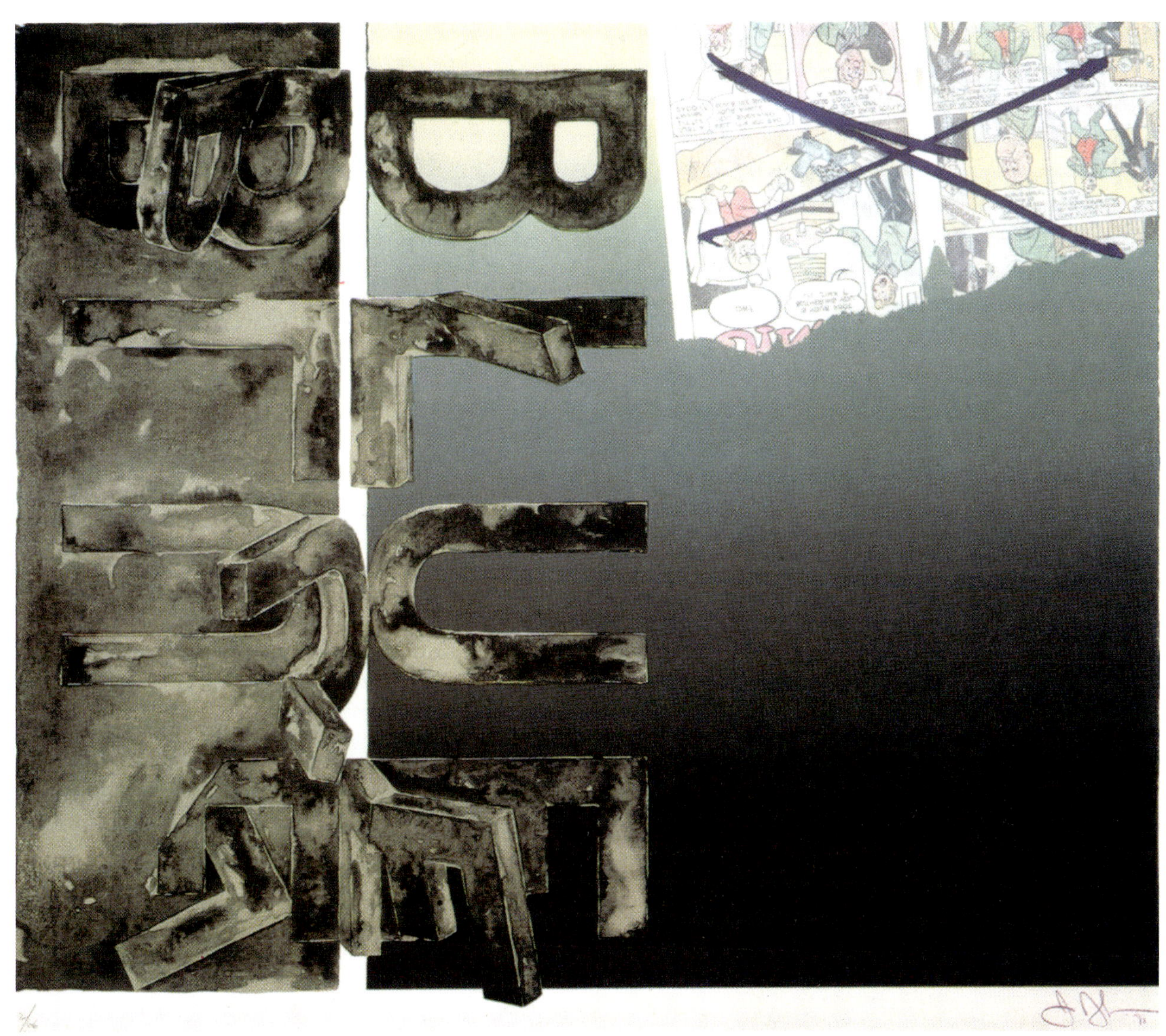

150 Jasper Johns
Fragment - According to What - Bent "Blue", 1971
Lithographie, collagiert, 65 x 73 cm. Auflage: 66
Lithograph with newspaper monotype, 25½ x 28¾ in. Edition: 66

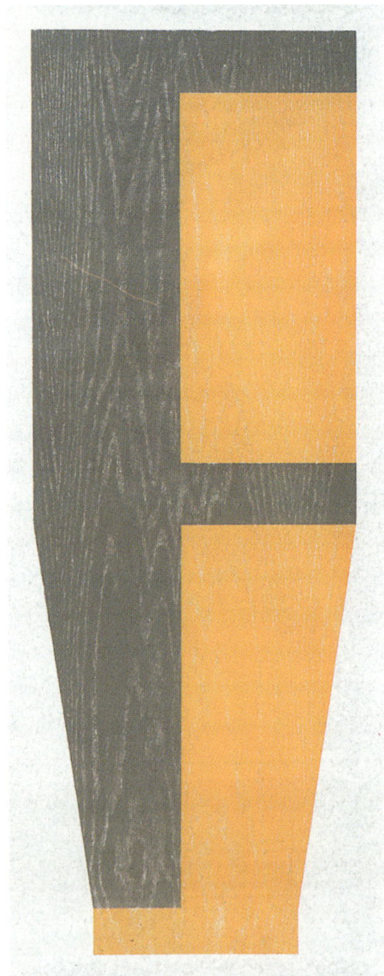

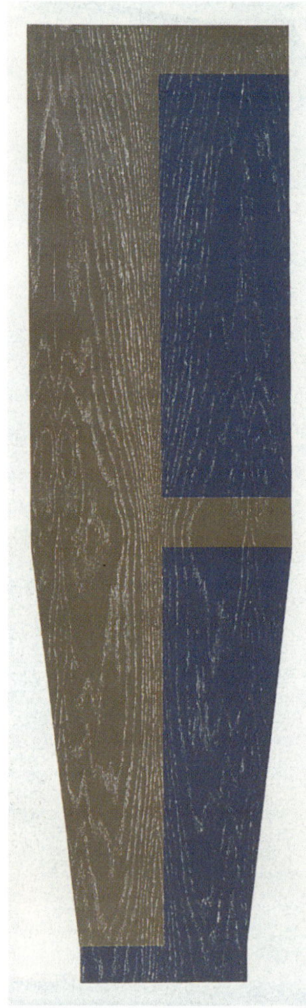

151 Ronald Jones
Untitled (Male and Female), 1990
2 Holzschnitte auf Bütten, 206 x 66 cm und 163 x 66 cm. Auflage: 10
2 woodcuts on rag paper, 81 x 26 in. and 64 x 26 in. Edition: 10

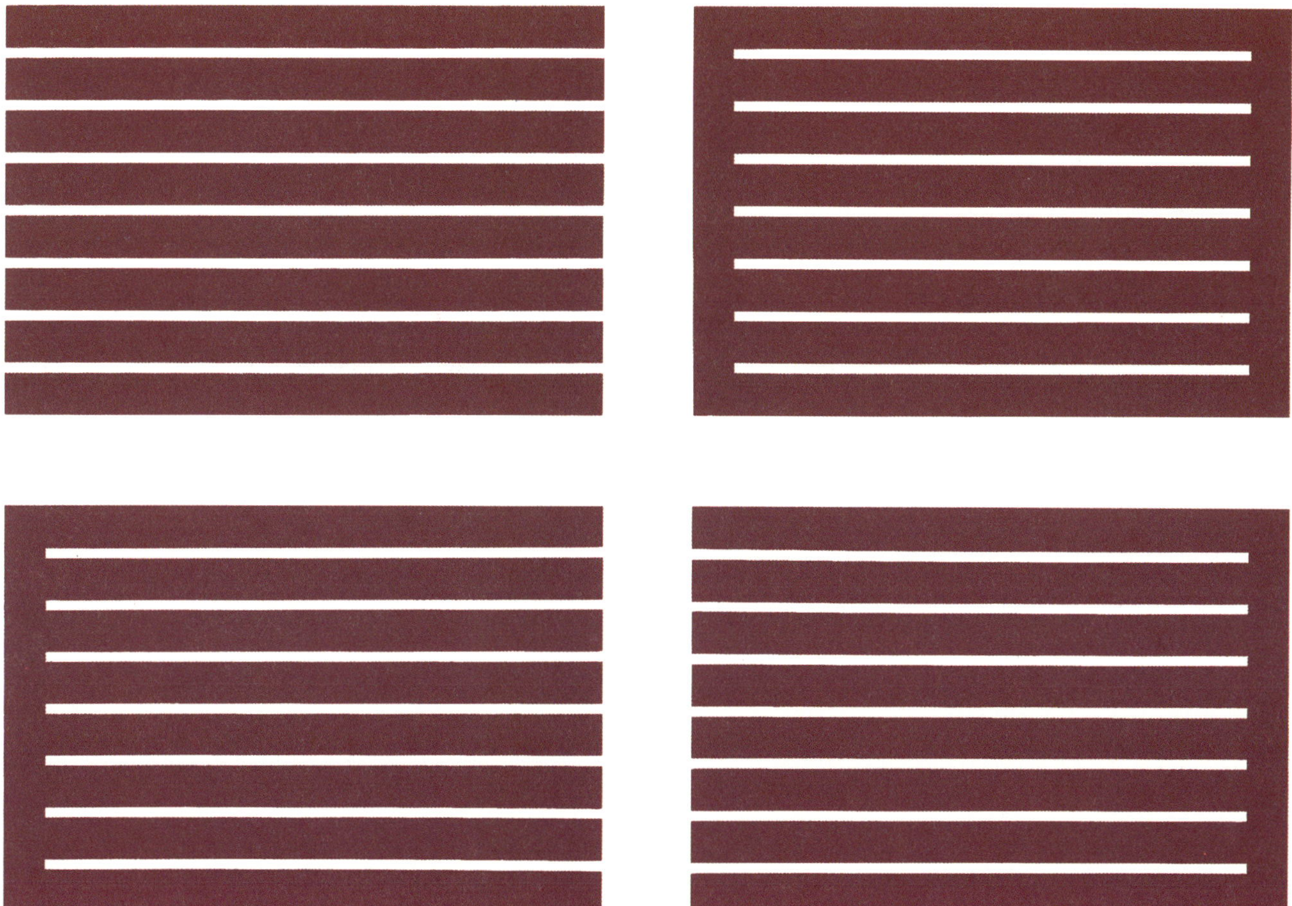

152 Don Judd
Untitled, 1992-94
Suite von 4 Holzschnitten, 67 x 99 cm.
Set of 4 woodcuts, 26½ x 38½ in.
a. erdgrün, Auflage: 25 *earth green, edition: 25*
b. venezianisch rot, Auflage: 25 *venetian red, edition: 25*
c. cadmiumgelb, Auflage: 15 *cadmium yellow, edition: 15*
d. cadmiumrot, Auflage: 15 *cadmium red, edition: 15*
e. elfenbeinschwarz, Auflage: 15 *ivory black, edition: 15*
f. ultramarinblau, Auflage: 15 *ultramarine blue, edition: 15*

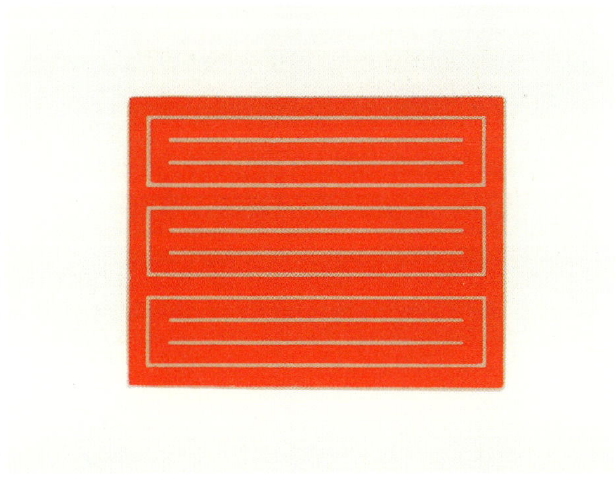

153 Donald Judd
Untitled, 1962-79
Holzschnitt cadmium rot, 52,5 x 77,7 cm. Auflage: 25
Woodcut in cadmium red, 20½ x 30¼ in. Edition: 25

154 Donald Judd □ →
Untitled, 1980
6 Aquatintaradierungen auf Bütten, 74 x 86,5 cm. Auflage: 150
6 aquatints on rag paper, 29 x 34 in. Edition: 150

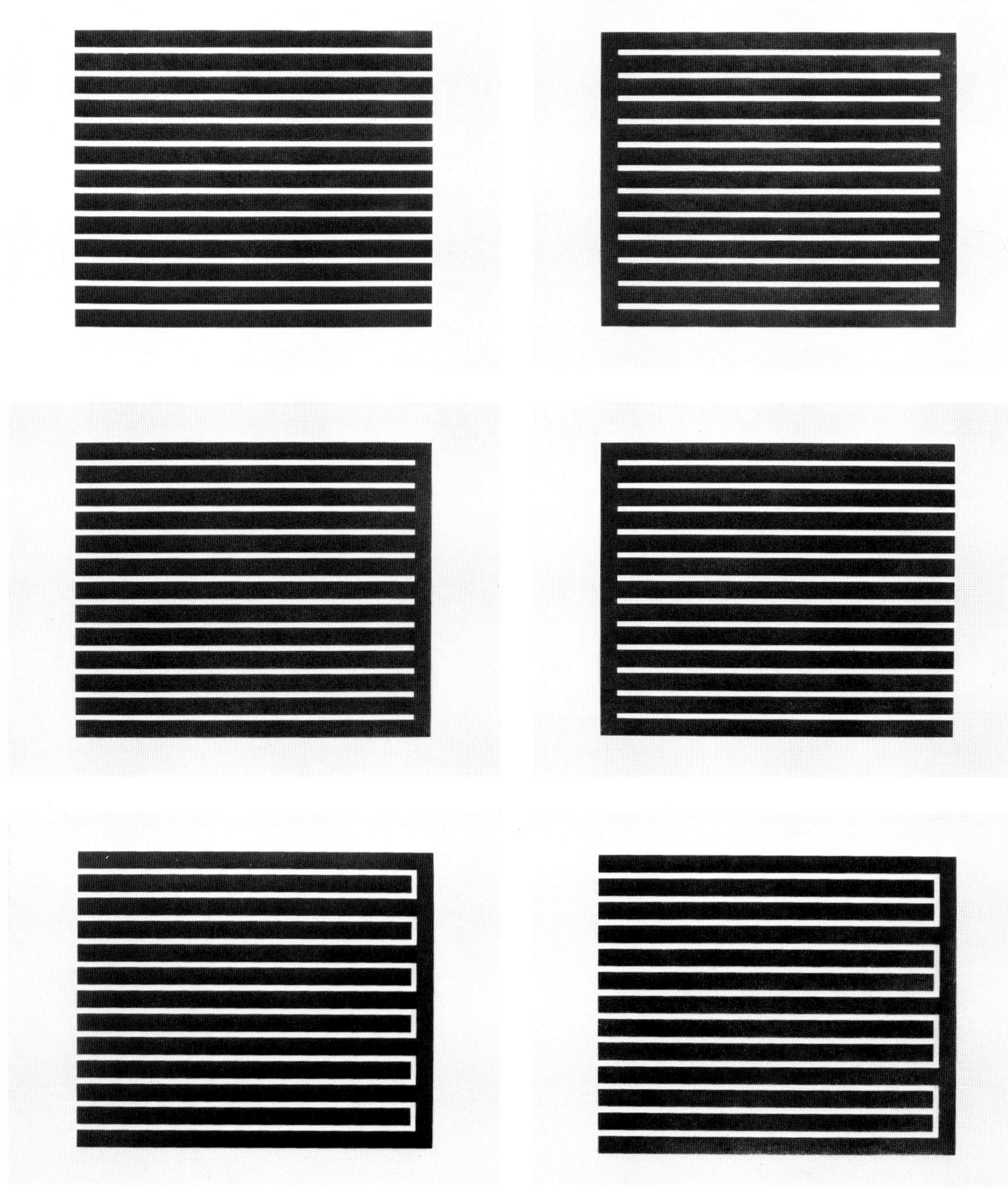

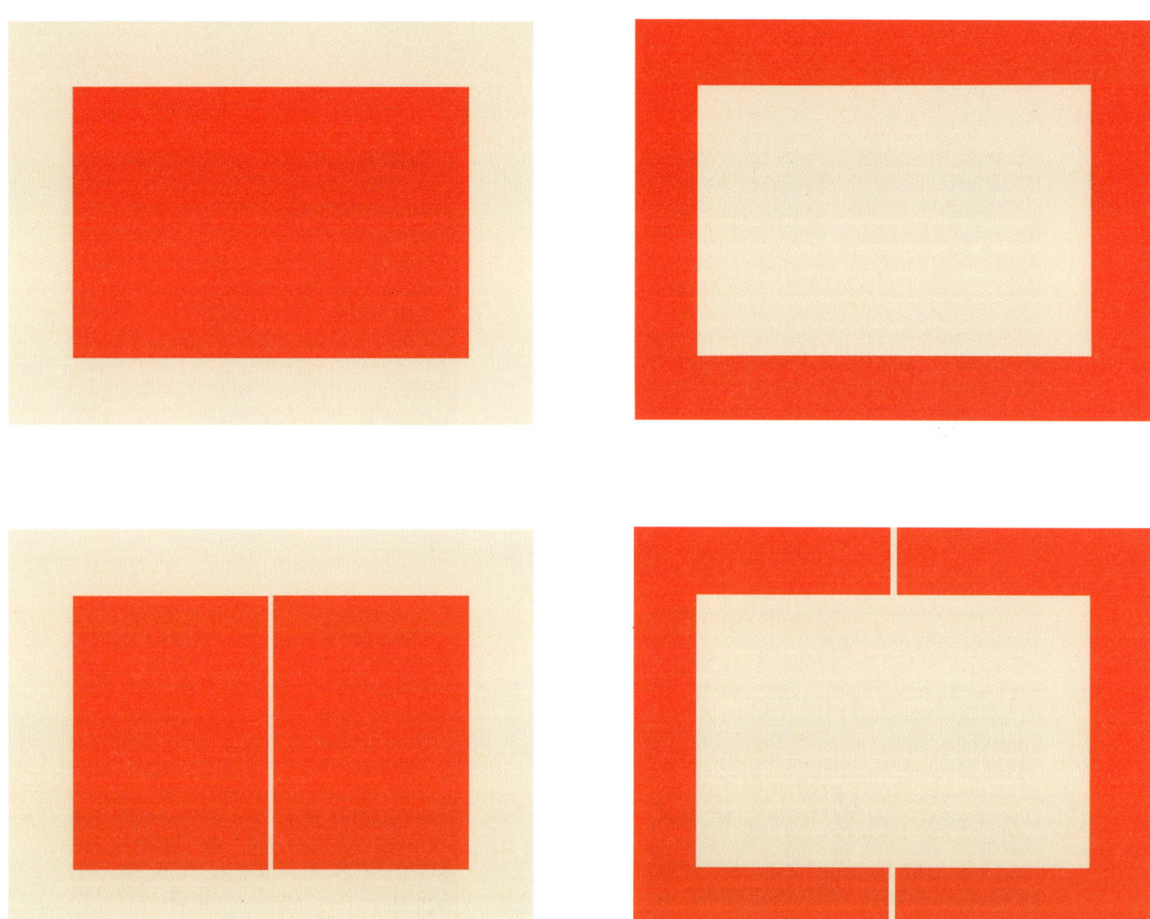

155 Donald Judd
Untitled, 1988
Serie von 10 Holzschnitten auf Japanpapier, 60 x 80 cm
Series of 10 woodcuts on Okawara paper, 23½ x 31½ in.
A gedruckt in kadmiumrot. Auflage: 25
printed in cadmium red. Edition: 25
B gedruckt in elfenbeinschwarz. Auflage: 25
printed in ivory black. Edition: 25

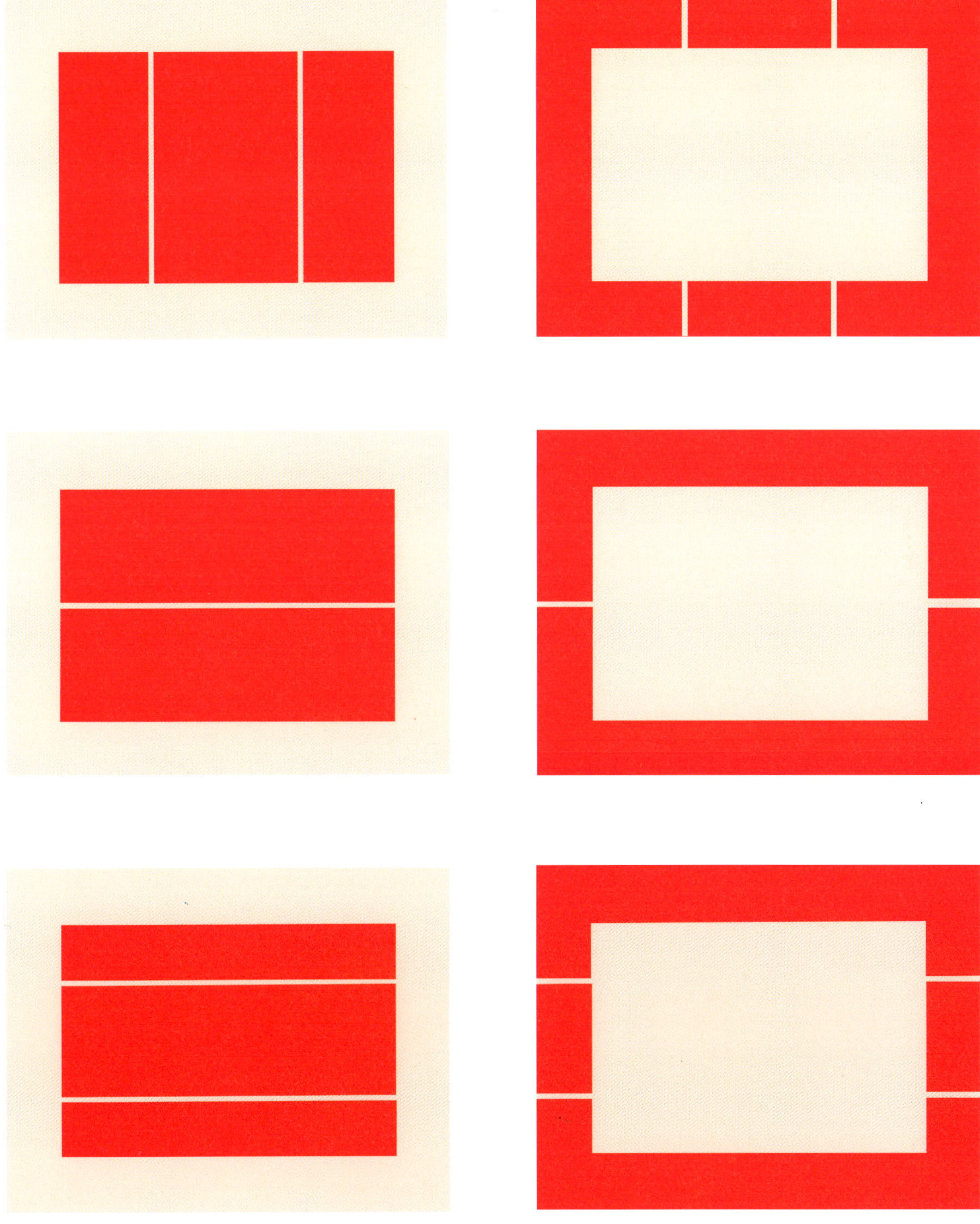

156 Donald Judd ■
Untitled, 1991
Serie von Wandobjekten, Aluminium, eloxiert in zwölf verschiedenen Farben, 15 x 105 x 15 cm.
Auflage: 12
Series of wall objects, extruded aluminum, anodized in 12 different colors, 6 x 41¼ x 6 in. Edition: 12

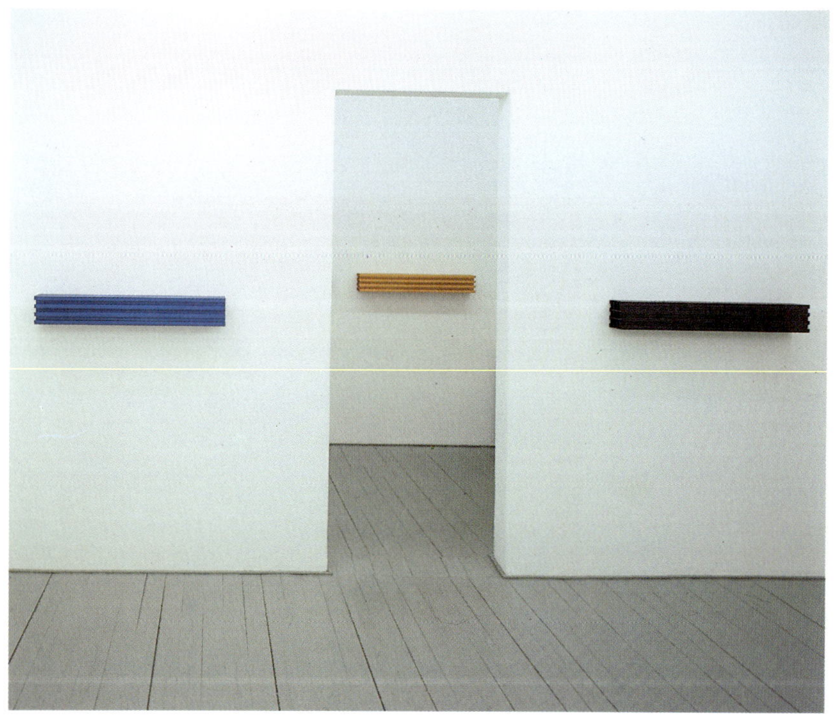

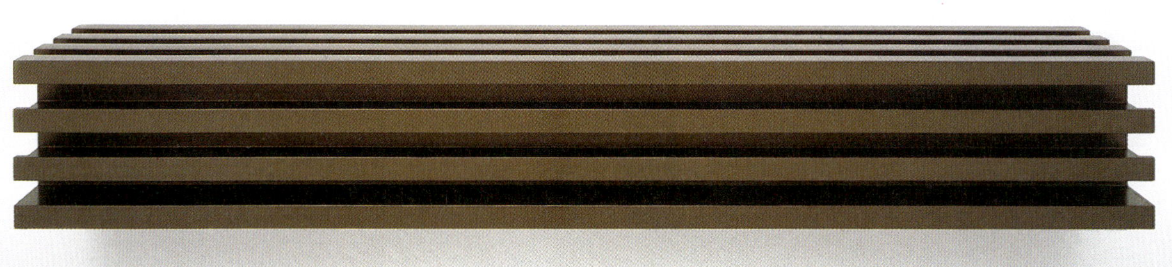

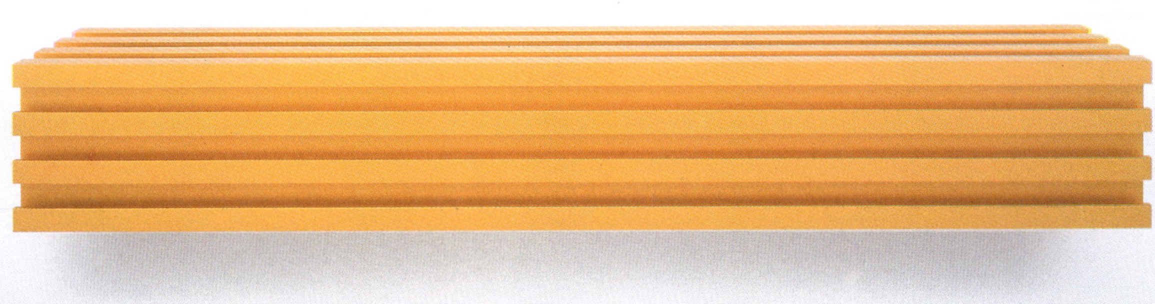

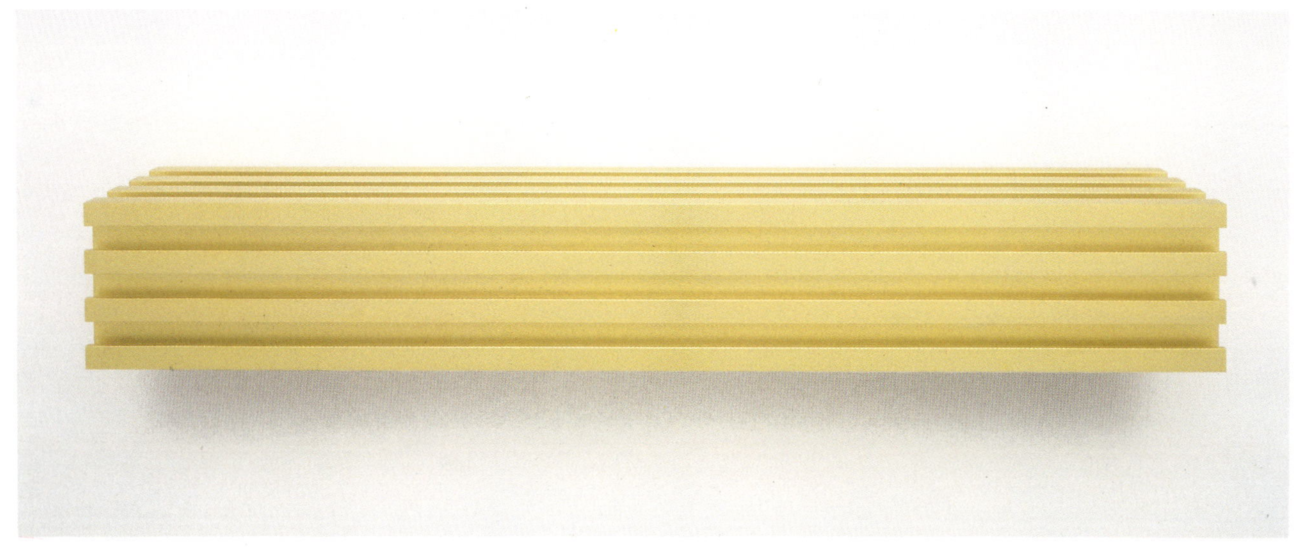

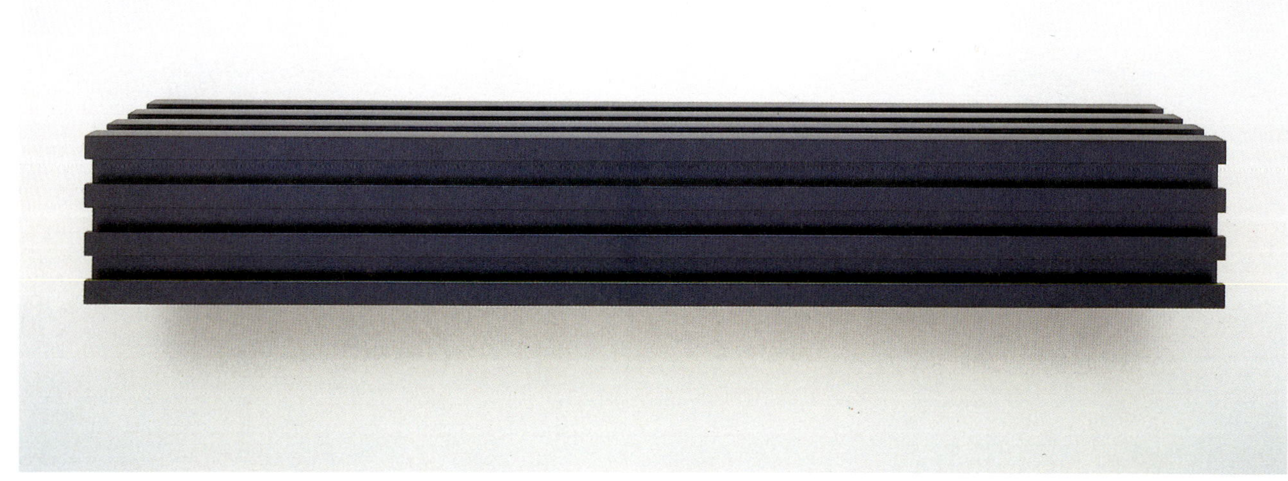

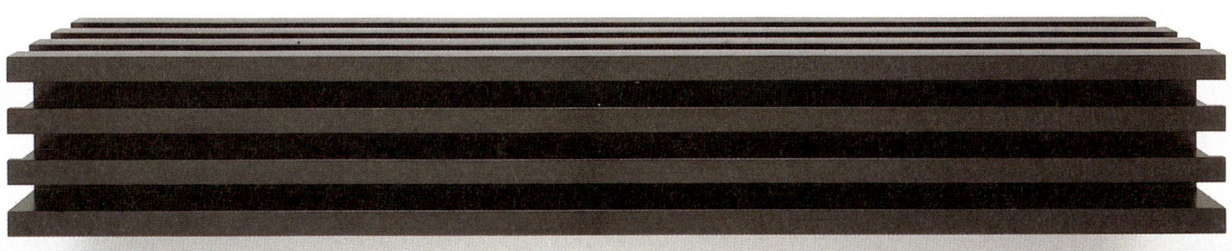

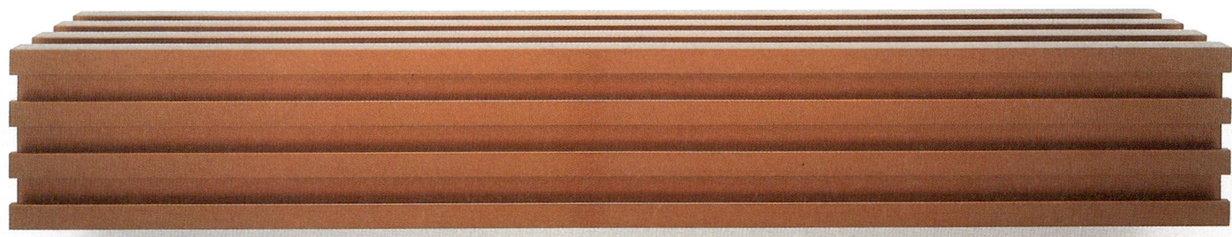

157 Donald Judd ■
Untitled, aus Mappe: Für Joseph Beuys, 1986
Holzschnitt auf Japanpapier, 60 x 80 cm.
Auflage: 90 + XXX, davon 30 gedruckt in braun
Woodcut on handmade Japanese paper, 23½ x 31½ in.
Edition: 90 + 30 Roman numerals, 30 printed in brown

158 Donald Judd ■ →
Untitled, 1993
Folge von 4 Holzschnitten, in Rahmen aus verzinktem Eisenblech,
Glas mit Ölfarbe bemalt; 61 x 81 x 2,5 cm. Auflage: 25
a. elfenbeinschwarz/dunkelrot b. gelb/schwarz
c. ultramarinblau/schwarz c. orange/dunkelrot
Suite of 4 woodcuts with an oil painted stripe on the glass of a galvanized iron frame, 24 x 32 x 1 in. Edition: 25
***a.** ivory black/dark red **b.** yellow/black*
***c.** ultramarine blue/black **c.** orange/dark red*

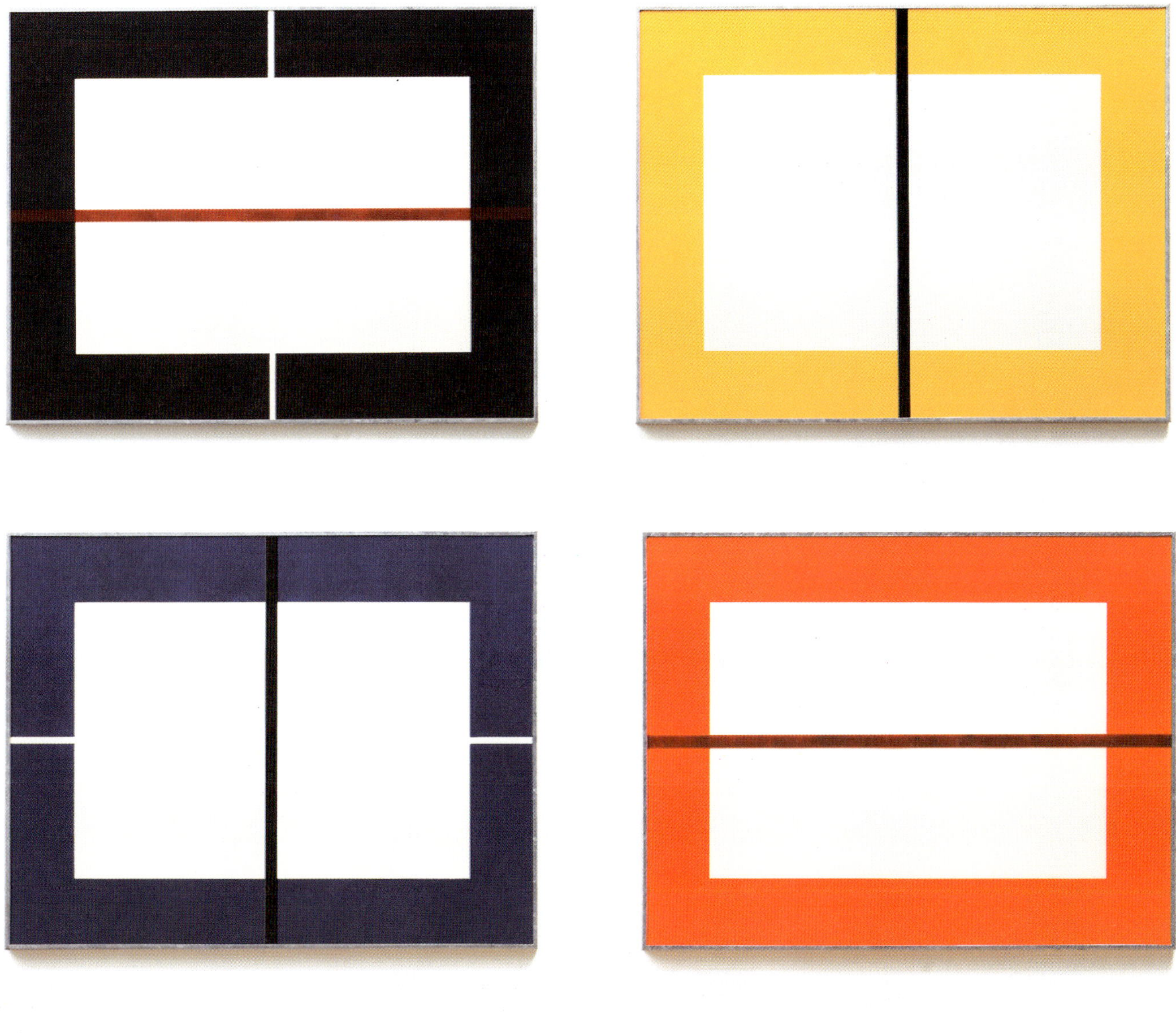

159 Donald Judd ■ →

Untitled, 1992

Zwei Vertiefungen (je 75 x 50 x 25 cm) in einer Wand, mit Plexiglas rot, blau oder grün oder verzinktem Eisenblech, zu installieren nach den Anweisungen des Künstlers, siehe Appendix. Gesamtmaße variabel. Auflage: 12 insgesamt, mit Zertifikat, sign. und num. vom Nachlaß.

Two recesses (29½ x 19¾ x 10 in. ea.) on a wall, with red, blue or green plexiglass or galvanized iron, to be installed according to the artist's instructions, see appendix. Overall size of the work variable. Edition: 12 in total, with a certificate signed and numbered by the estate.

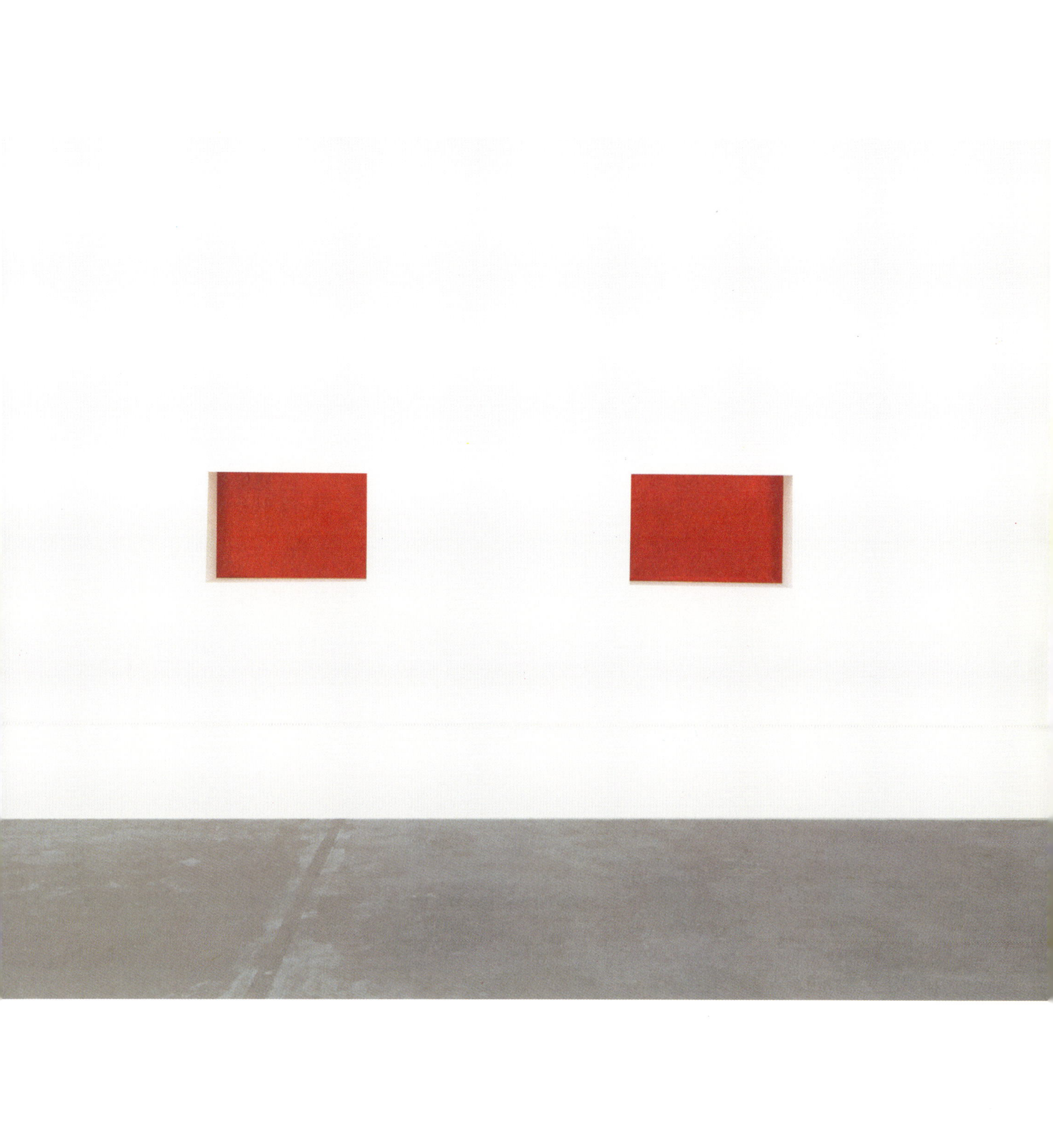

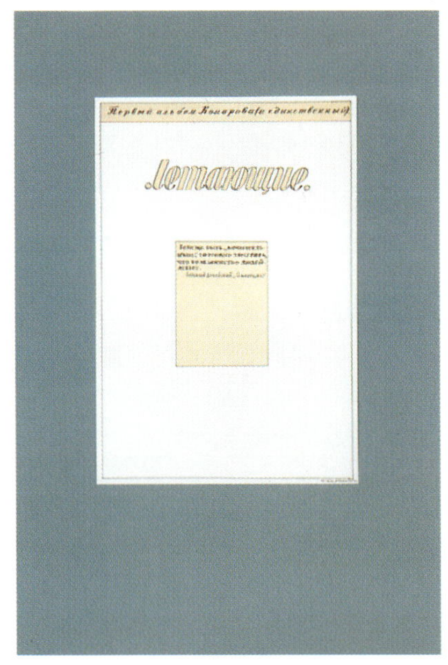

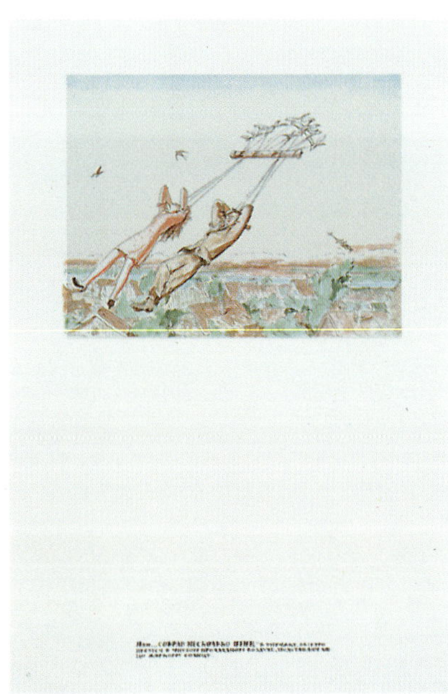

160 Ilya Kabakov
The Flying Komarov (from The Ten Characters), 1994
32 Offsetlithographien, auf weißen bzw. grauen Karton aufgezogen, 51 x 35 cm. Auflage: 200, dazu 20 mit je einer Originalzeichnung.
32 offset lithographs mounted on white or grey board, 20 x 13¾ in. Edition: 200 regular, plus 20 each set with an original drawing

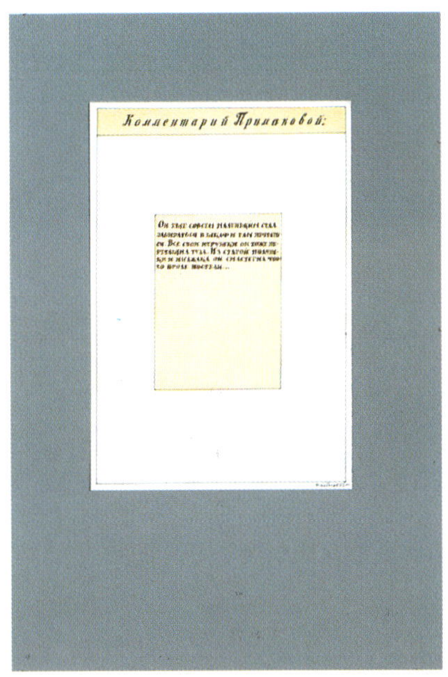

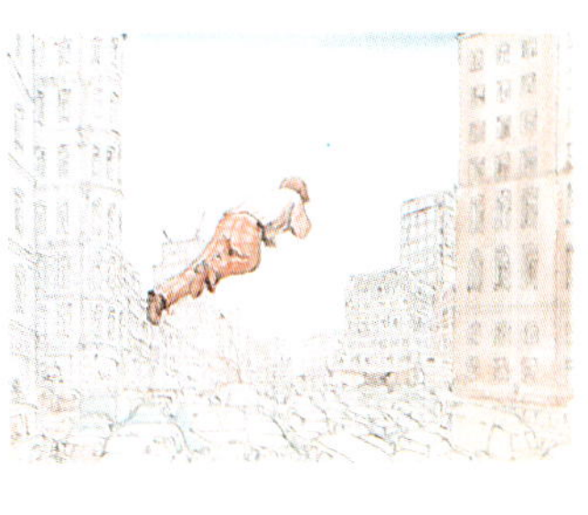

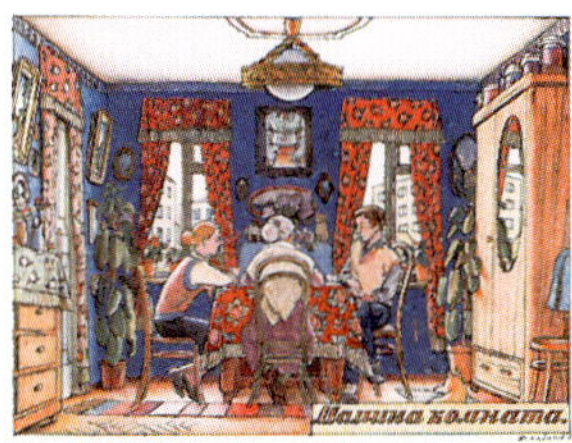

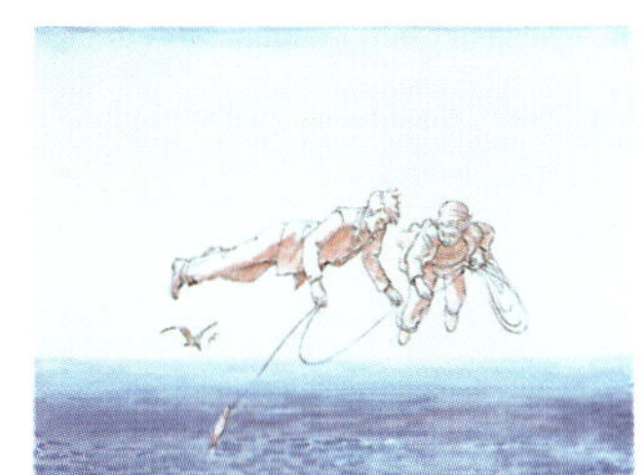

161 Ilya Kabakov
Sitting in the Closet Primakov, 1994
47 Offsetlithographien, auf weißen bzw. grauen Karton aufgezogen, 51 x 35 cm. Auflage: 200, dazu 20 mit je einer Originalzeichnung.
47 offset lithographs mounted on white or grey board, 20 x 13¾ in. Edition: 200 regular, plus 20 each set with an original drawing

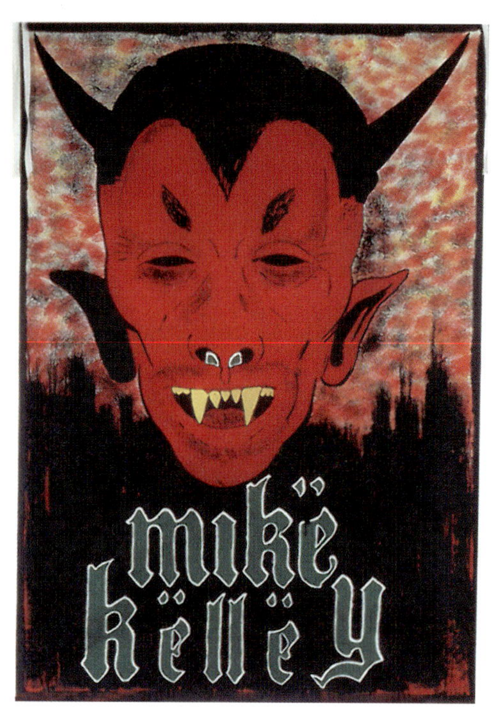

162 Mike Kelley
Pansy Metal / Clovered Hoof, 1989
Serie von Siebdrucken auf China-Seide,
134,5 x 96,5 cm. Auflage: 40
Oversized silk scarves, silkscreen on
Habotai China Silk, 53 x 38 in. Edition: 40

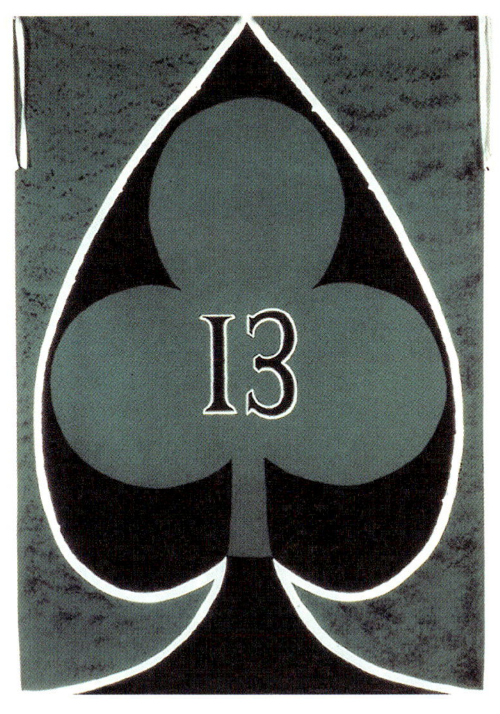
13

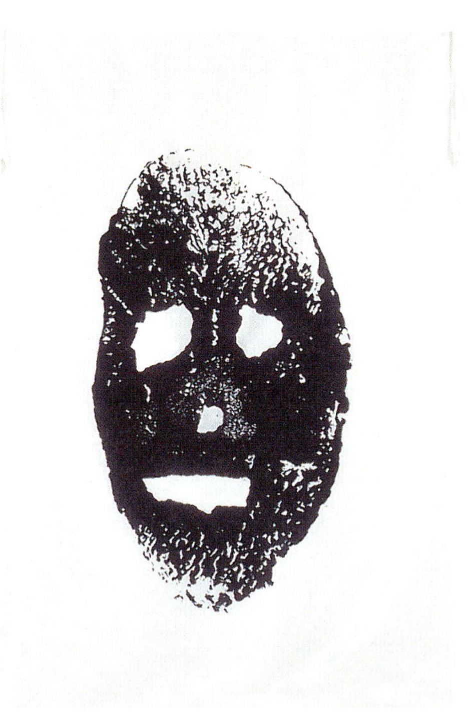

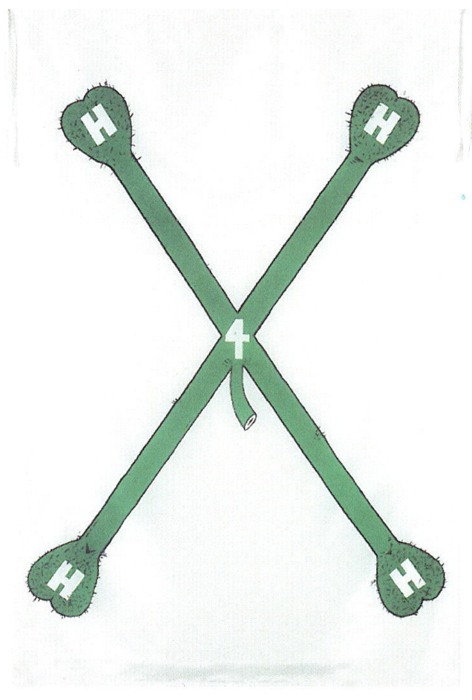
H
H
4
H
H

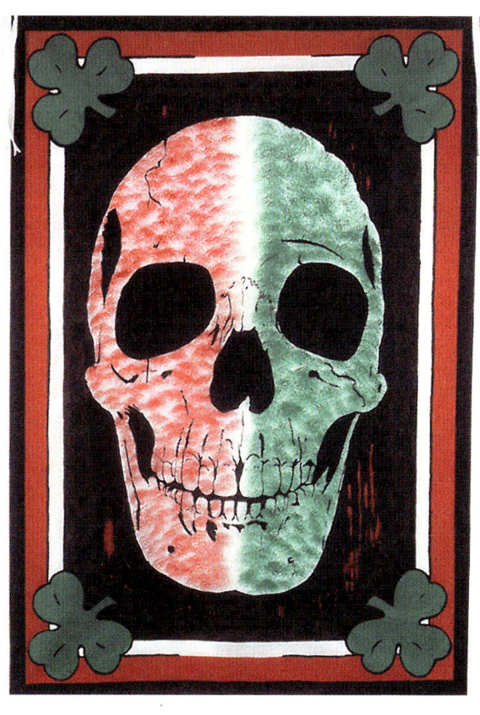

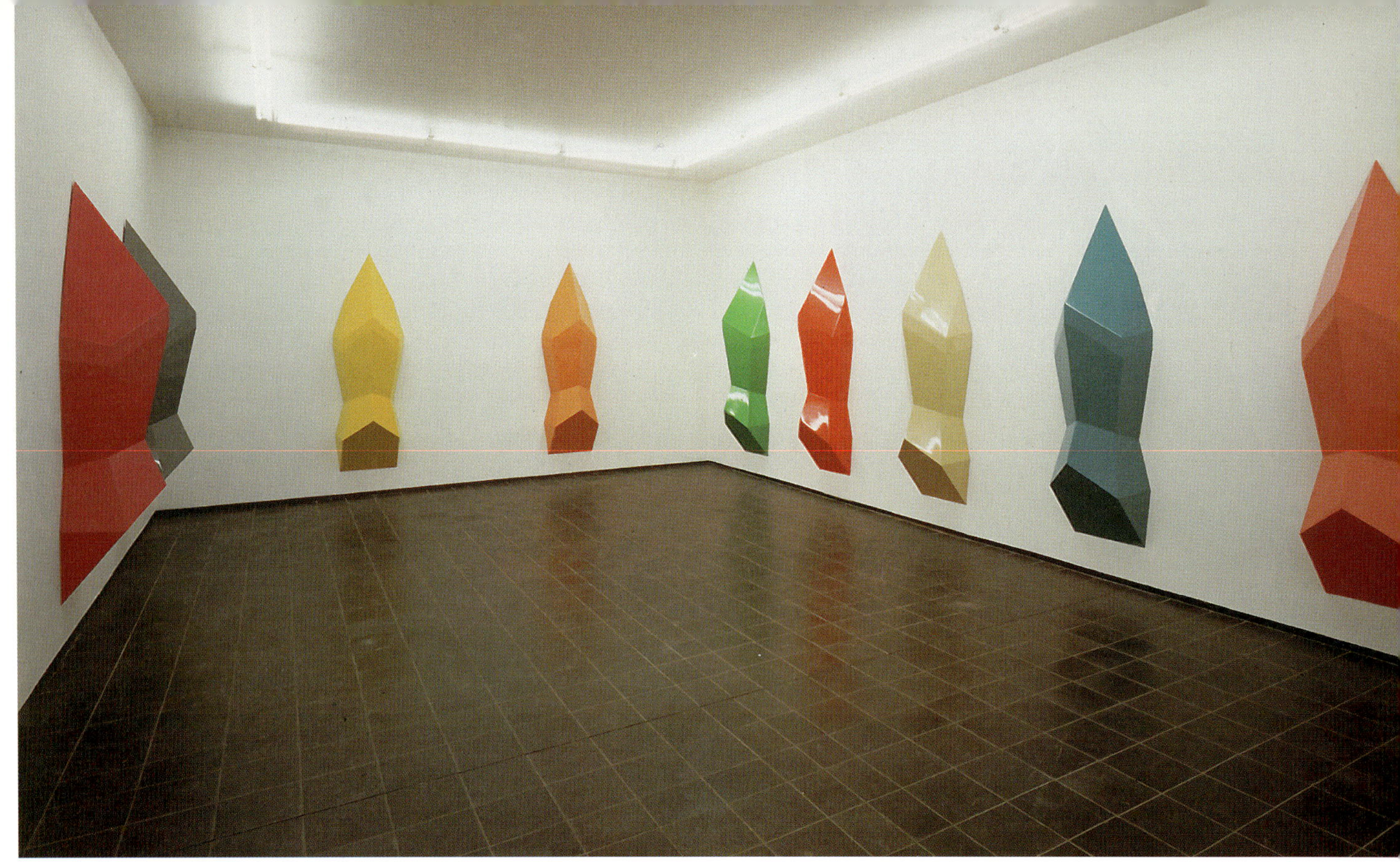

163 Mike Kelley
Deodorizers, 1991
Fiberglas, Autolack, Elektromaschine, destill. Wasser, Fichtennadelöl, 215 x 60 x 43 cm. Auflage: 13, jedes Exemplar in einer anderen Farbe
Fiberglass, enamel, electric machine, distilled water, spruce-needle oil, 84½ x 23½ x 17 in. Edition: 13, each different in color

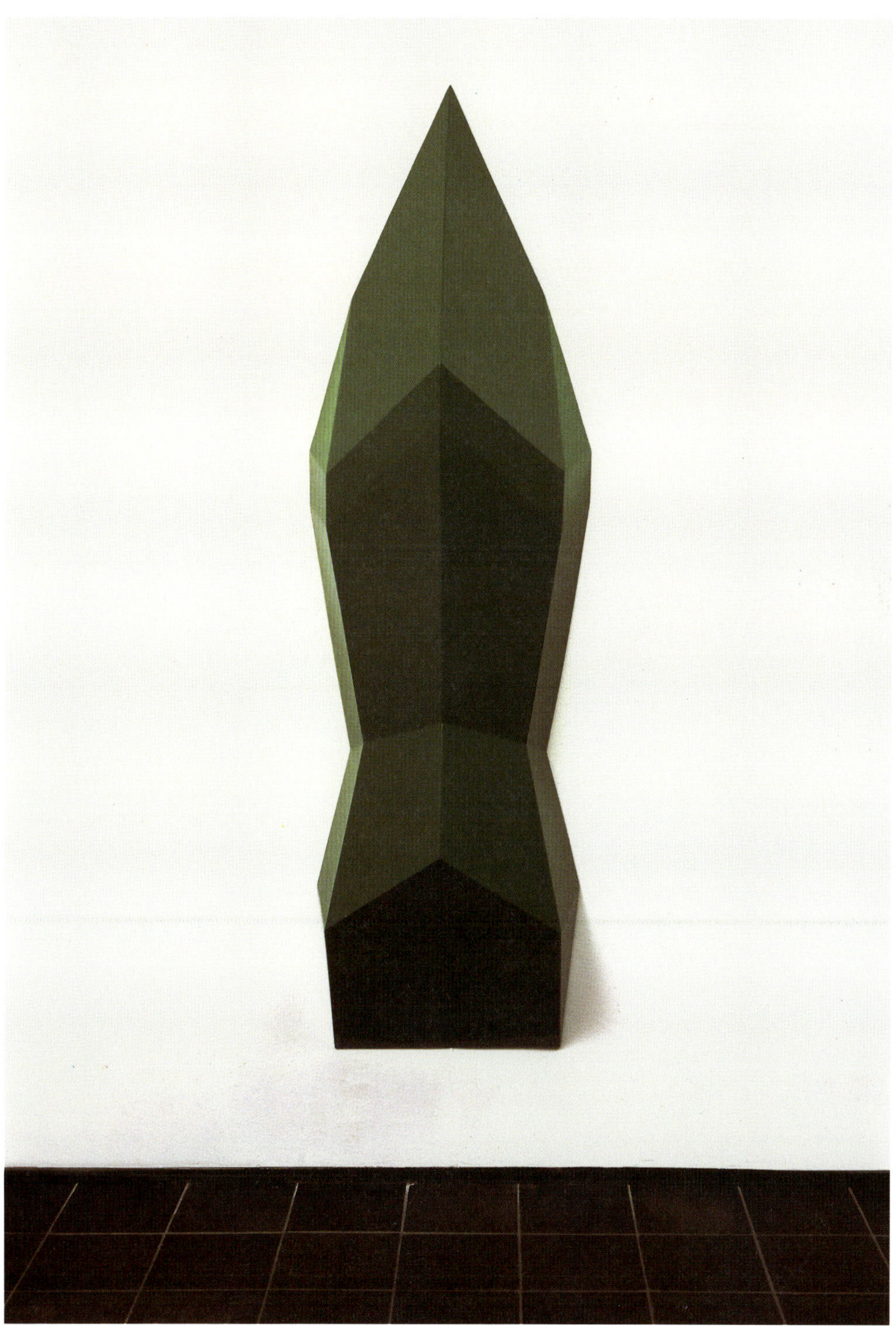

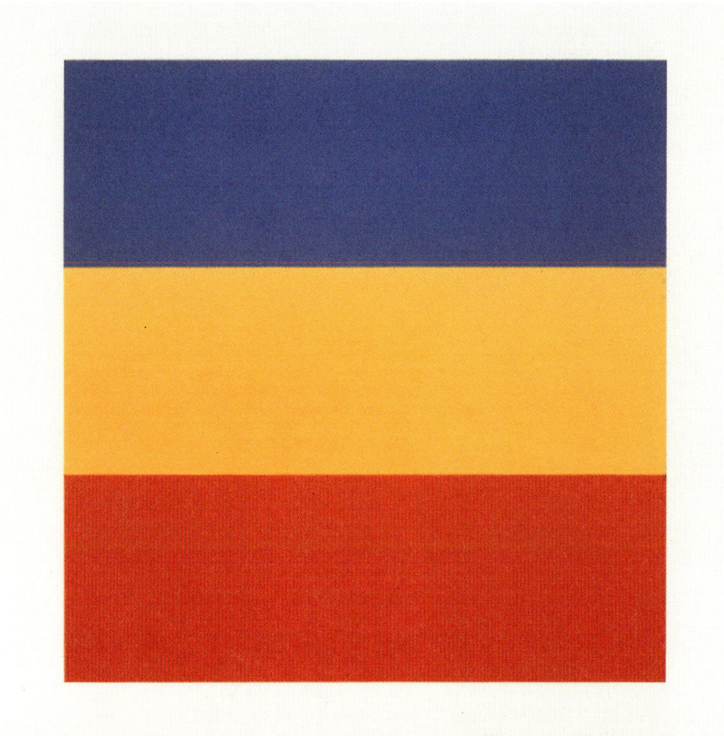

164 Ellsworth Kelly
Blue/Yellow/Red, 1991
Lithographie, 94 x 91½ cm. Auflage: 80
Lithograph, 37 x 36 in. Edition: 80

165 Ellsworth Kelly →
a. Blue Curve, 1988
Lithographie, 95 x 231,5 cm. Auflage: 15 *Lithograph, 37½ x 84 in. Edition: 15*
b. Dark Grey Curve, 1988
Lithographie, 66 x 231,5 cm. Auflage: 15 *Lithograph, 26 x 84 in. Edition: 15*
c. Green Curve (State I), 1988
Lithographie, 95 x 231,5 cm. Auflage: 15 *Lithograph, 37½ x 84 in. Edition: 15*

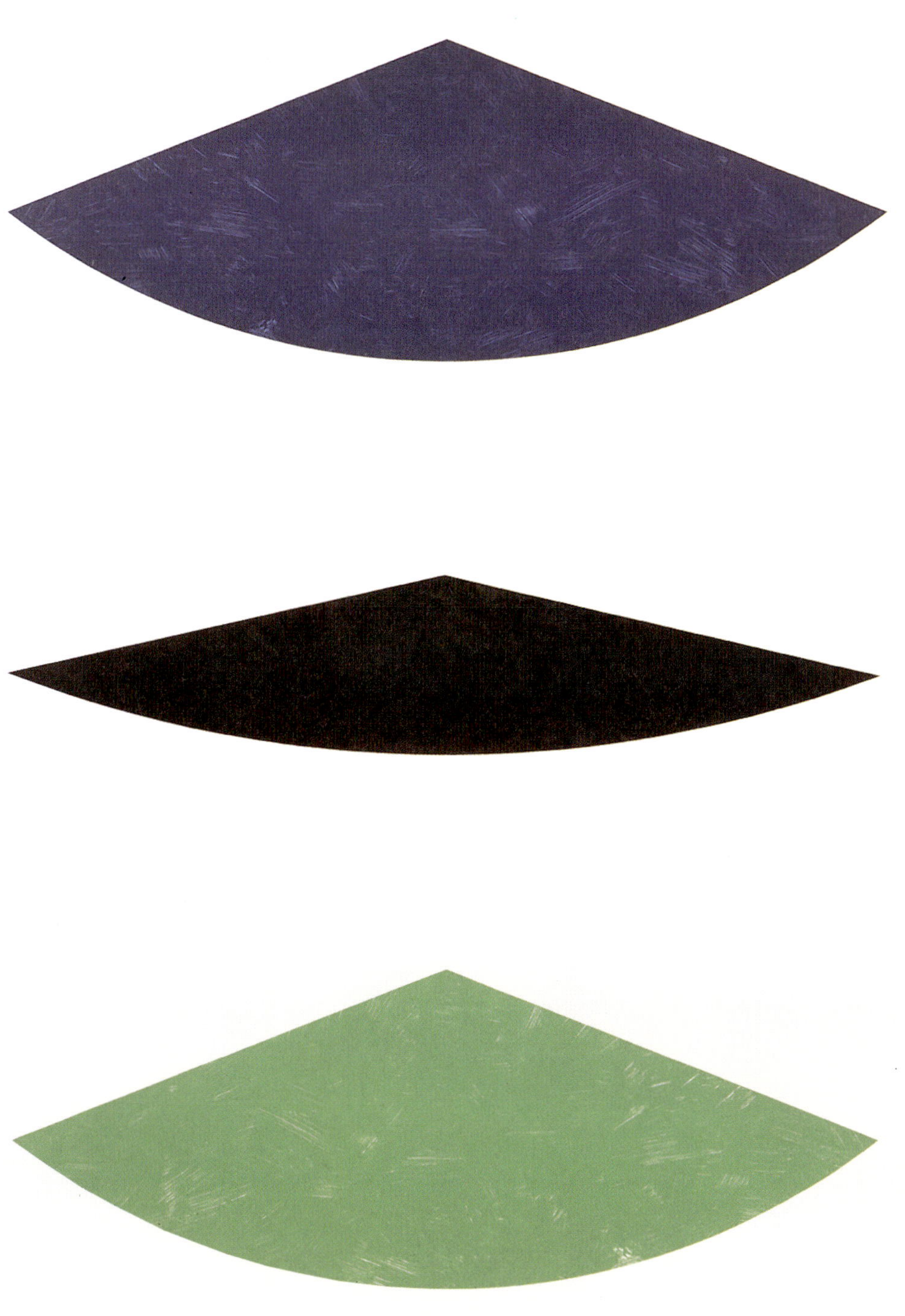

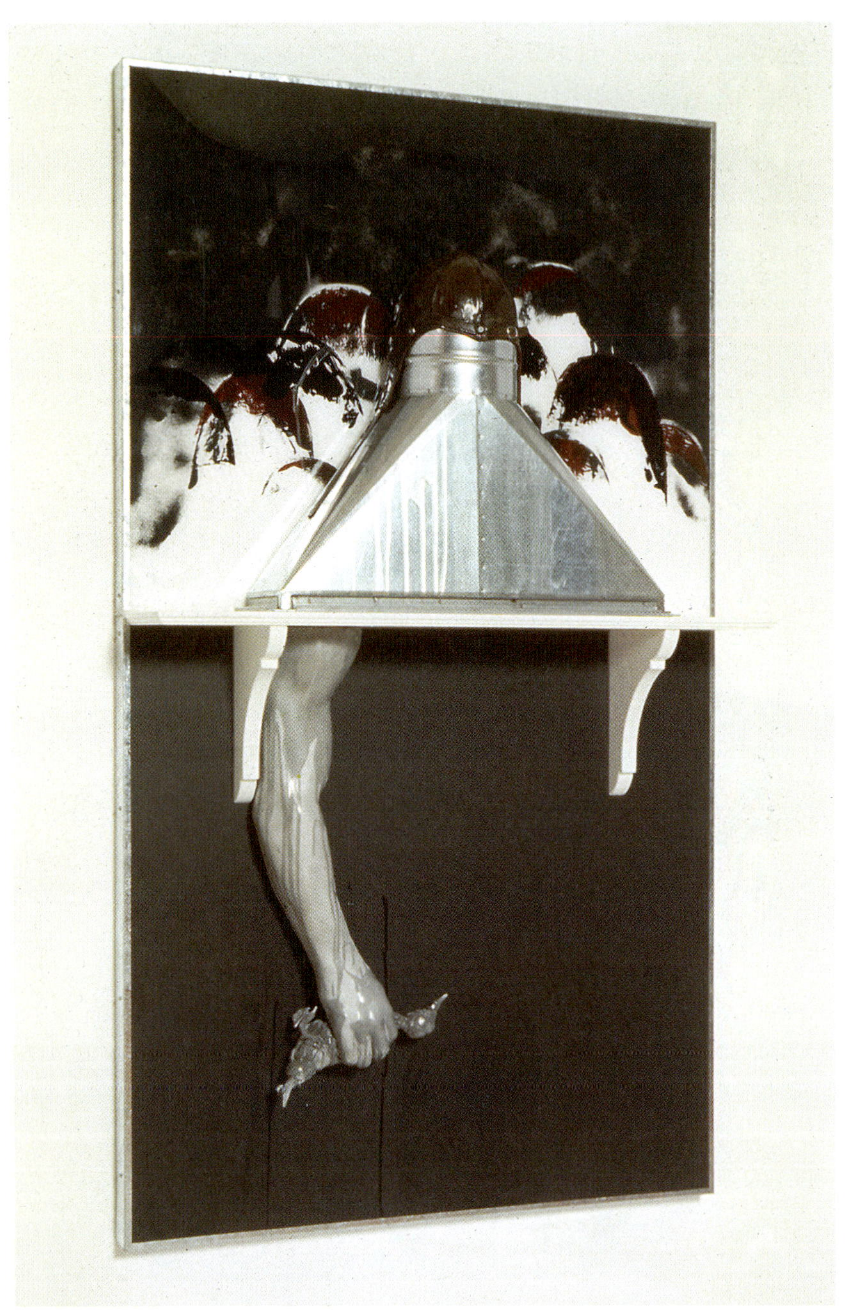

166 Edward Kienholz & Nancy Reddin Kienholz
Bound Duck - Black, 1991
Holz, Metall, Siebdruck, Kunstharz und Aluminiumguß, 170 x 100 x 25 cm. Auflage: 25
Wood, metal, screenprinting, resin, and cast aluminum, 67 x 39½ x 10 in. Edition: 25

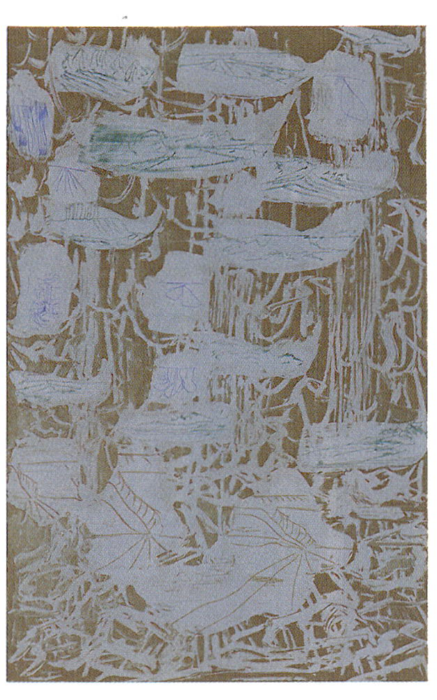

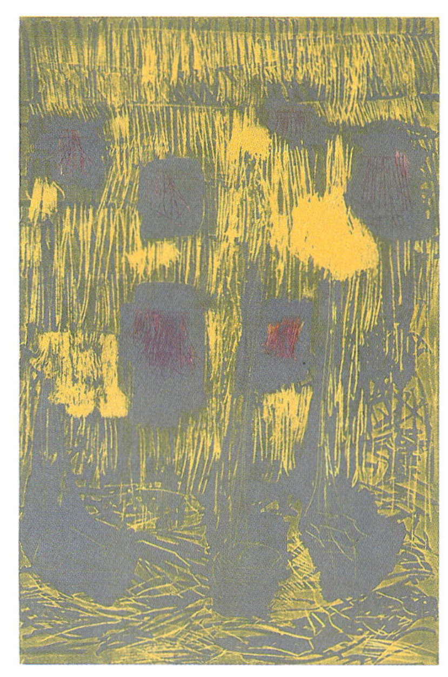

167 Per Kirkeby
O.T., 1993
Radierungen, 88 x 66,5 cm. Auflage 25 (Abb. links) bzw. 15 (Abb. rechts)
Etchings, 34¾ x 26¼ in. Edition: 25 (ill. left) and 15 (ill. right)

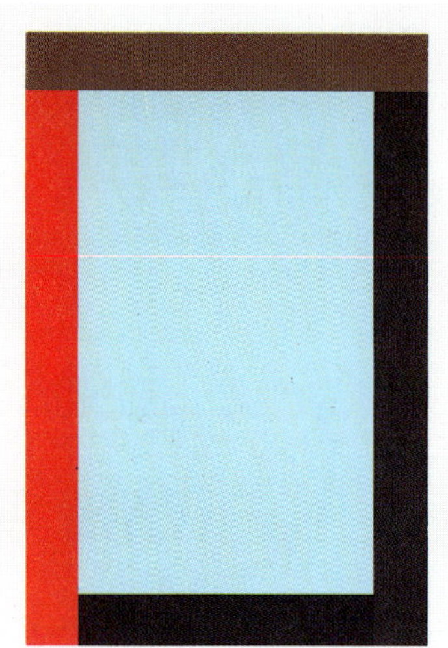

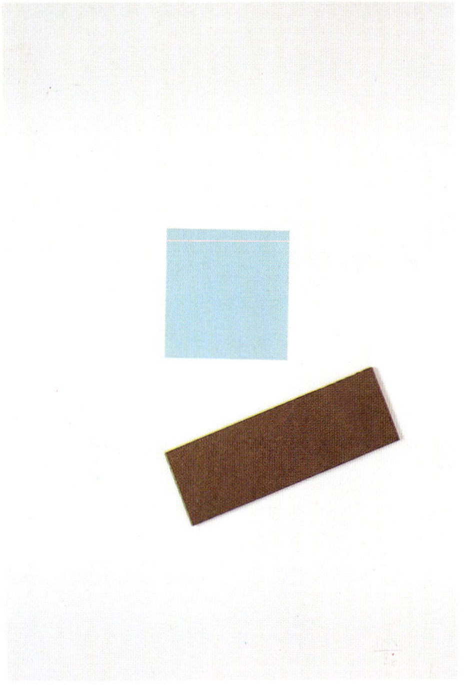

168 IMI Knoebel
Grace Kelly I, 1990
Mappe mit 5 Serigraphien, 102 x 73 cm.
Auflage: 90, auf einem Blatt sign. und num.
Portfolio with 5 silkscreens, 40 x 29 in.
Edition: 90, signed and numbered on one print

169 IMI Knoebel ■
o.T., aus Mappe: Für Joseph Beuys, 1986
Lithographie und Hartfaserplatte, 80 x 60 cm.
Auflage: 90
Lithograph and hardboard, 31½ x 23½ in.
Edition: 90

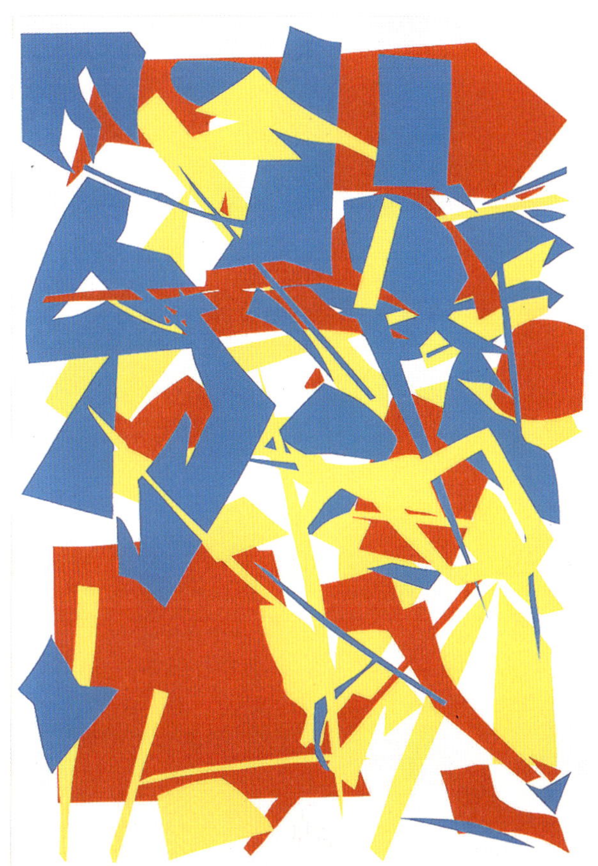

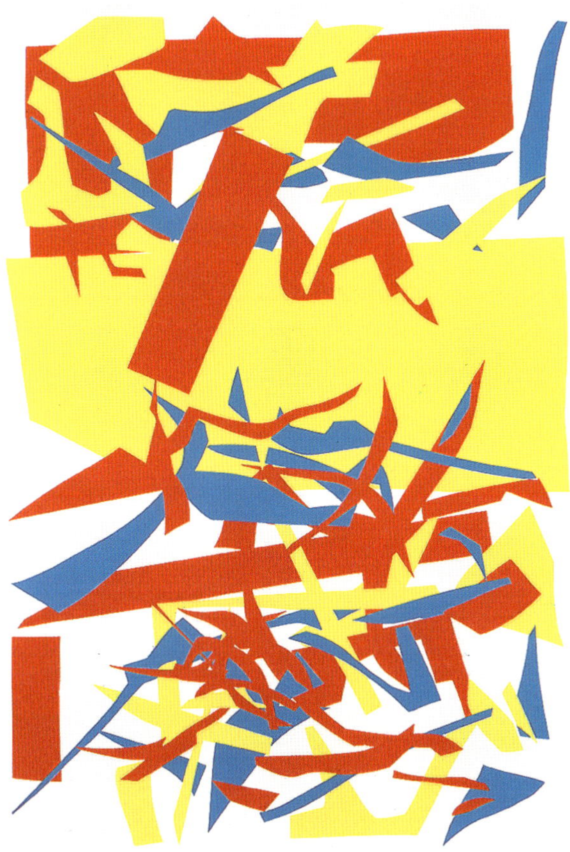

170 IMI Knoebel
Rot Gelb Blau, 1977/93
Siebdruck, 93 x 65 cm. Insges. 54 verschiedene Varianten
Silkscreen, 36½ x 25½ in. Altogether 54 different variations

171 IMI Knoebel
Stab - weiß, gelb, rot, blau, 1994
Aluminium und Acrylfarbe,
264 x 8 x 8 cm. Auflage: 12
Aluminum painted with acrylic,
104 x 3¼ x 3¼ in. Edition: 12

172 IMI Knoebel ■ →
Mennige (Fünfeck), 1992
Wandmalerei (Bleimennige), auszuführen nach den Anweisungen des Künstlers, siehe Appendix.
164,5 x 197,7 cm. Auflage: 12, mit einer sign. und num. Gouache
Wall painting in red lead, to be executed according to the artist's instructions, see appendix,
61 x 68 in. Edition: 12, with a signed and numbered gouache

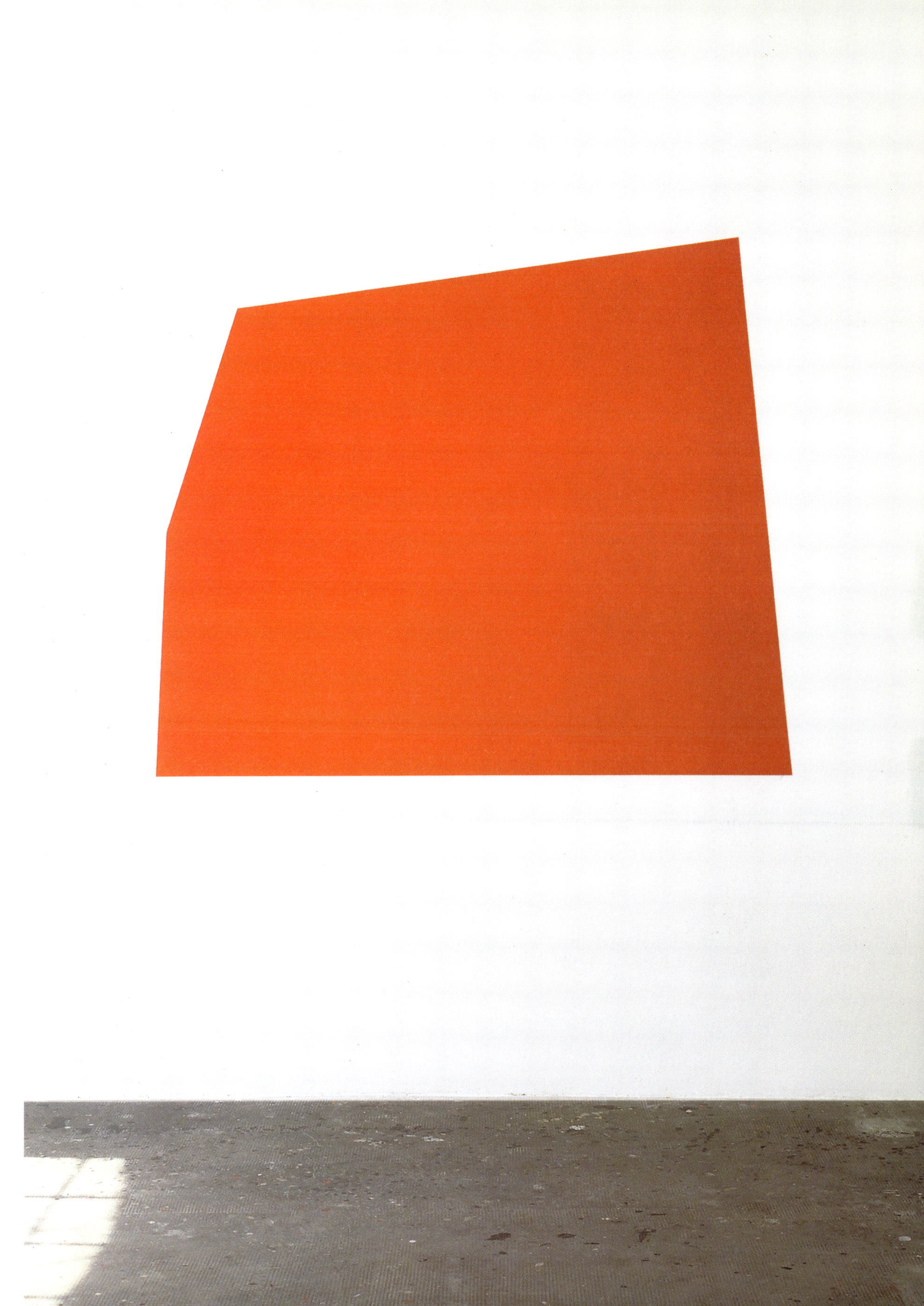

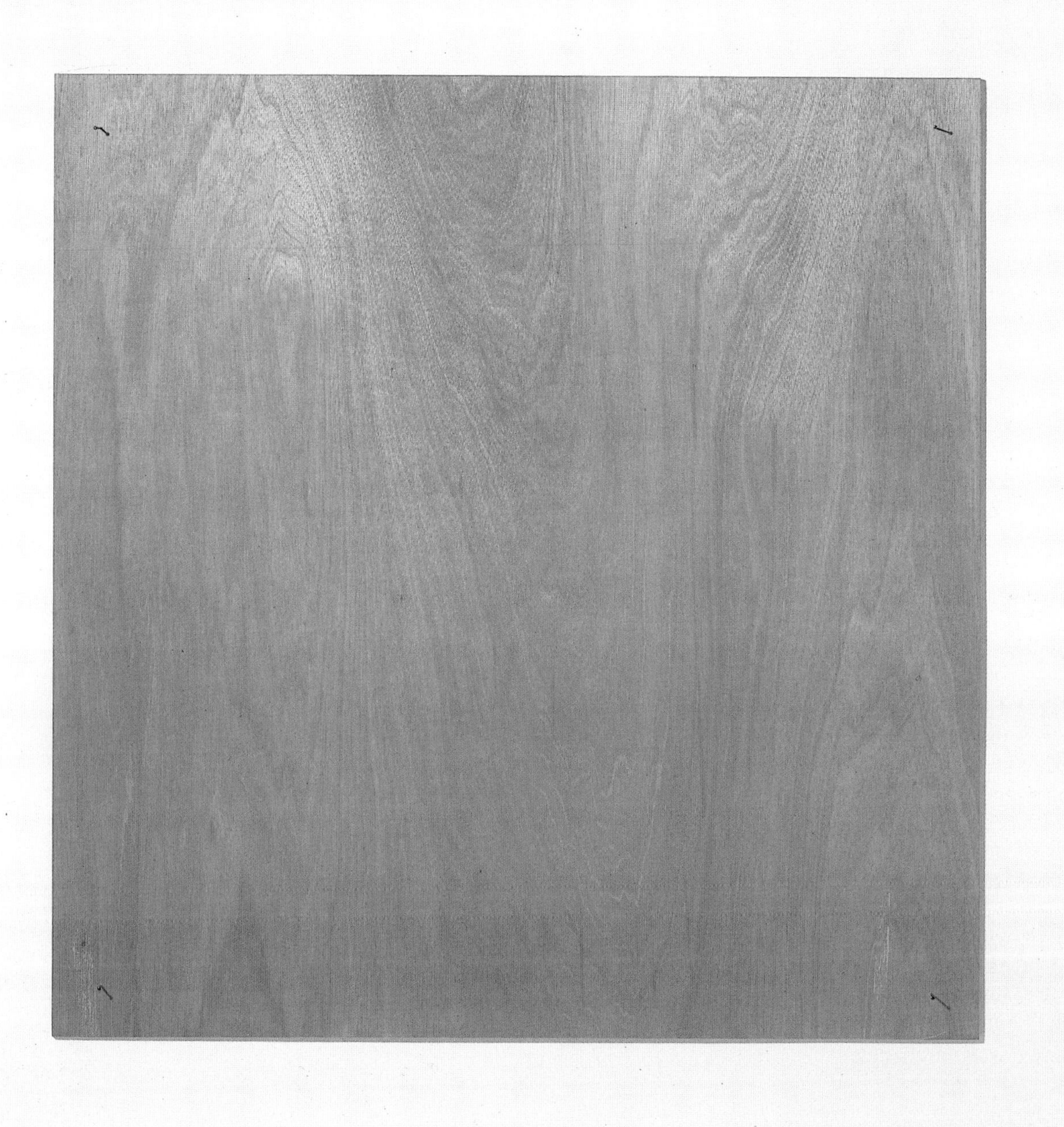

173 IMI Knoebel ■
Mennige, 1988
Zwei Sperrholzplatten, innen mit Mennige bemalt, außen lackiert, Nägel. 100 x 100 x 1 cm. Aufl.: 21
Two sheets of plywood, doubled and painted with red primer on the inside, varnished on the outside, four nails. 40 x 40 x ½ in. Edition: 21

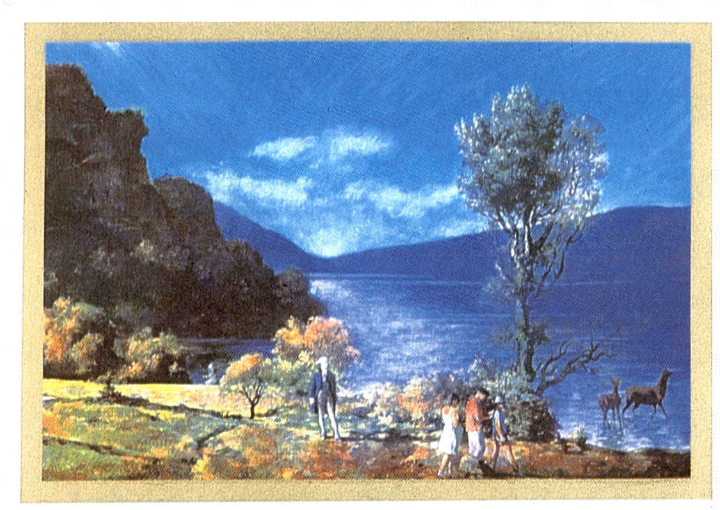

Die Blätter entstanden nach einer repräsentativen Umfrage über die Einstellung der Amerikaner zur bildenden Kunst. Die Folge enthält 2 Siebdrucke, die die Künstler nach den Ergebnissen der Umfrage als "schönstes" bzw. "häßlichstes" Bild nach dem Geschmack des amerikanischen Publikums gestaltet haben. Dazu 3 Blätter mit den Umfrageergebnissen.
The prints result from a scientifically valid poll of American attitudes towards the visual arts. The portfolio contains two prints created by the artists utilizing the findings of the poll to make the American public's most and least preferred art works. The portfolio also contains three prints that visually detail additional results of the poll.

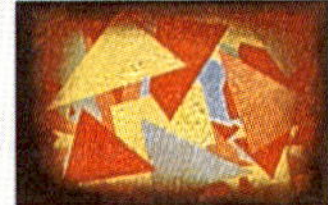

174 Komar & Melamid
The People's Choice Portfolio, 1994
Folge von 5 Siebdrucken, 56 x 75 cm. Auflage: 50
Suite of 5 silkscreen prints, 22 x 29½ in. Edition: 50

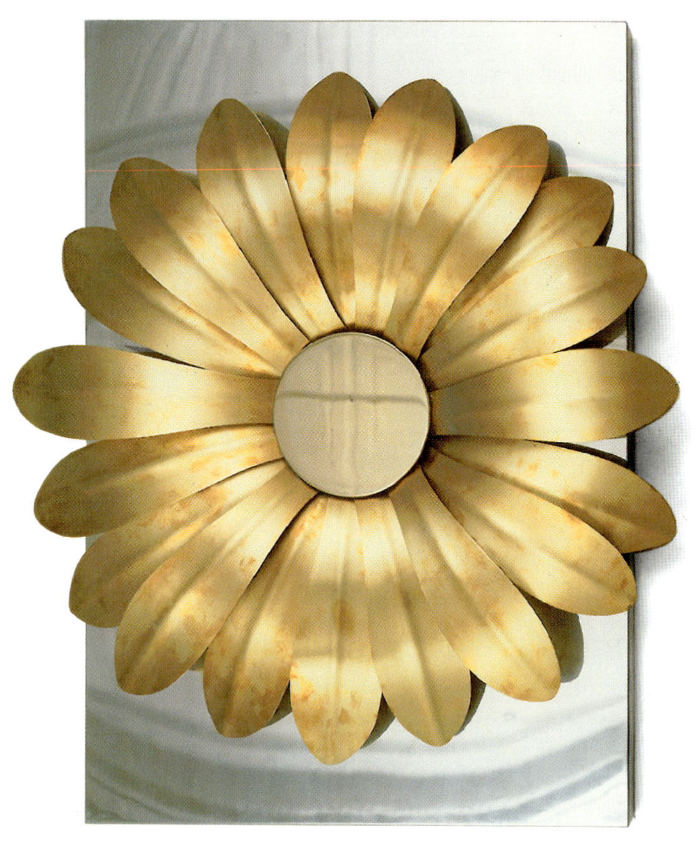

175 Jeff Koons ■
Jeff Koons, 1995
Wandobjekt. Messing/Bronze-Skulptur auf Kassette aus poliertem Aluminium, 101 x 86 x 15 cm, darin Mappe mit 7 Offsetlithographien, 100 x 70 cm.
Wall object. Brass/bronze sculpture on a polished aluminum box, 40 x 34 x 6 in., containing a portfolio with 7 offset lithographs, 39½ x 27½ in. Edition: 50

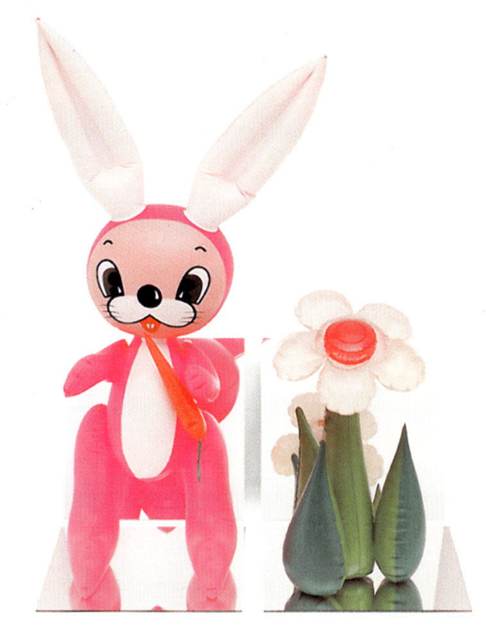

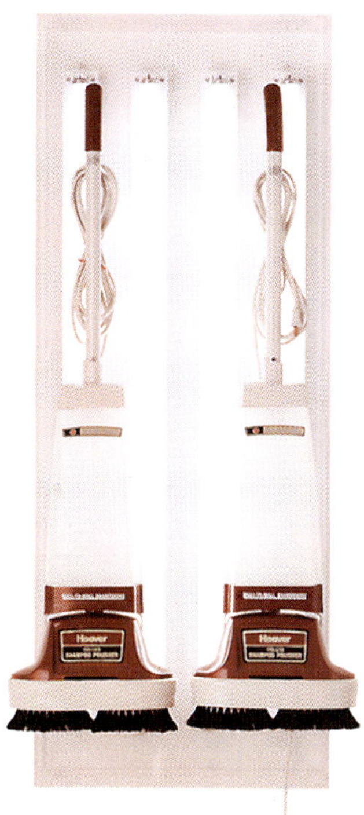

1. Inflatable Flower (Tall white, Pink Bunny), 1979
2. New Hoover Deluxe Shampoo Polishers, 1980

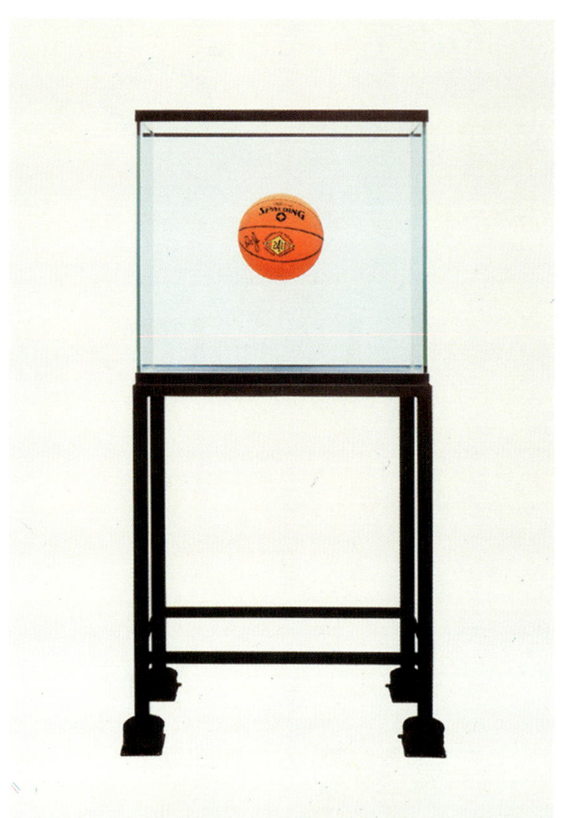

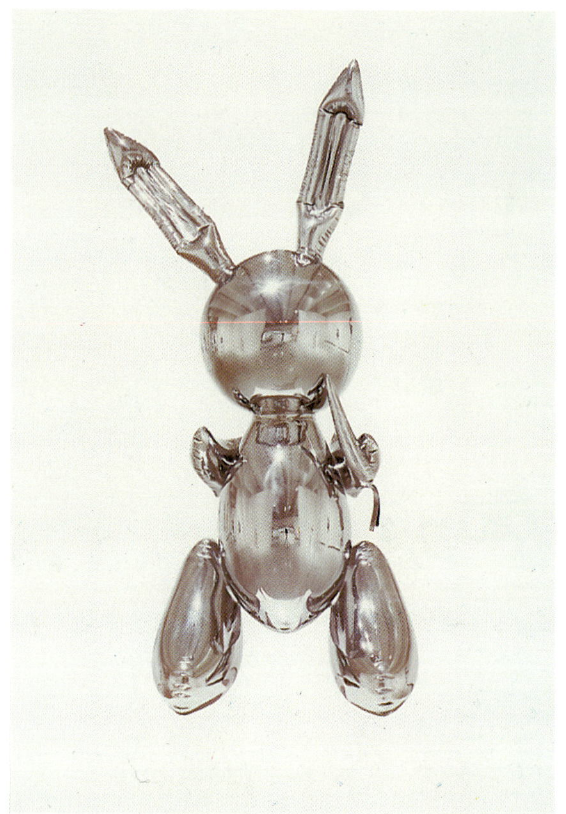

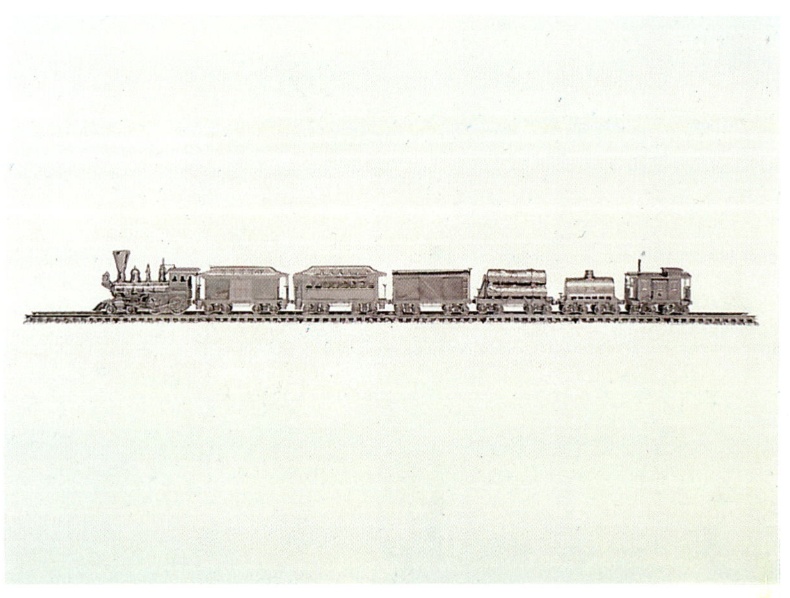

3. One Ball Total Equilibrium Tank (Spalding Dr. J. 241 Series), 1985
4. Rabbit, 1986
5. Jim Beam - J.B. Turner Train, 1986

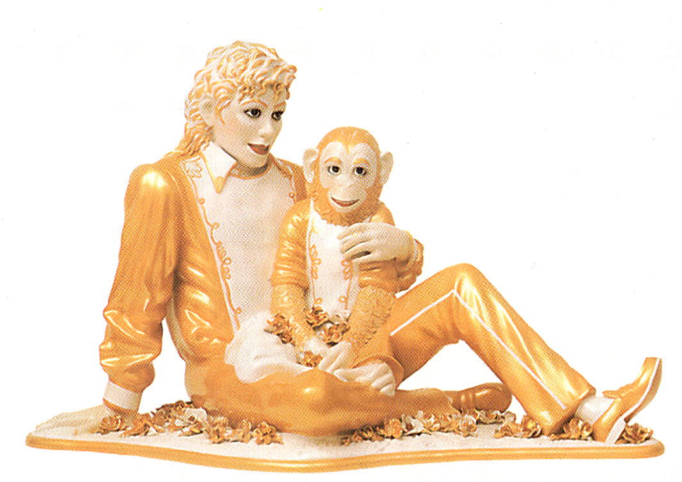

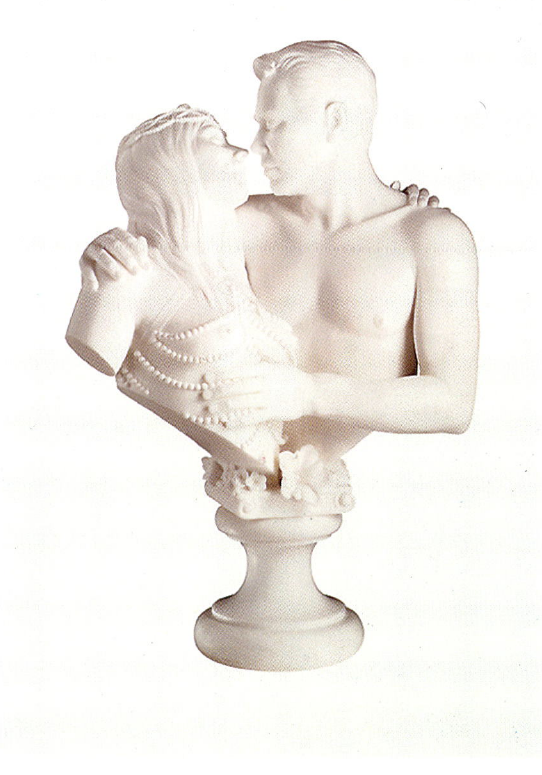

6. Michael Jackson and Bubbles, 1988
7. Bourgeois Bust, 1991

176 Joseph Kosuth
'Zero and Not', für Berggasse 19, Wien, aus Anlaß des 50. Todestages
von Sigmund Freud, 23.9.1989
Siebdruck auf Fabriano Bütten, 14-teilig, 320 x 756 cm. Auflage: 12
Published on the occasion of the 50th anniversary of Sigmund Freud's death.
Silkscreen on Fabriano rag paper, 14 parts, overall 126 x 297½ in. Edition: 12

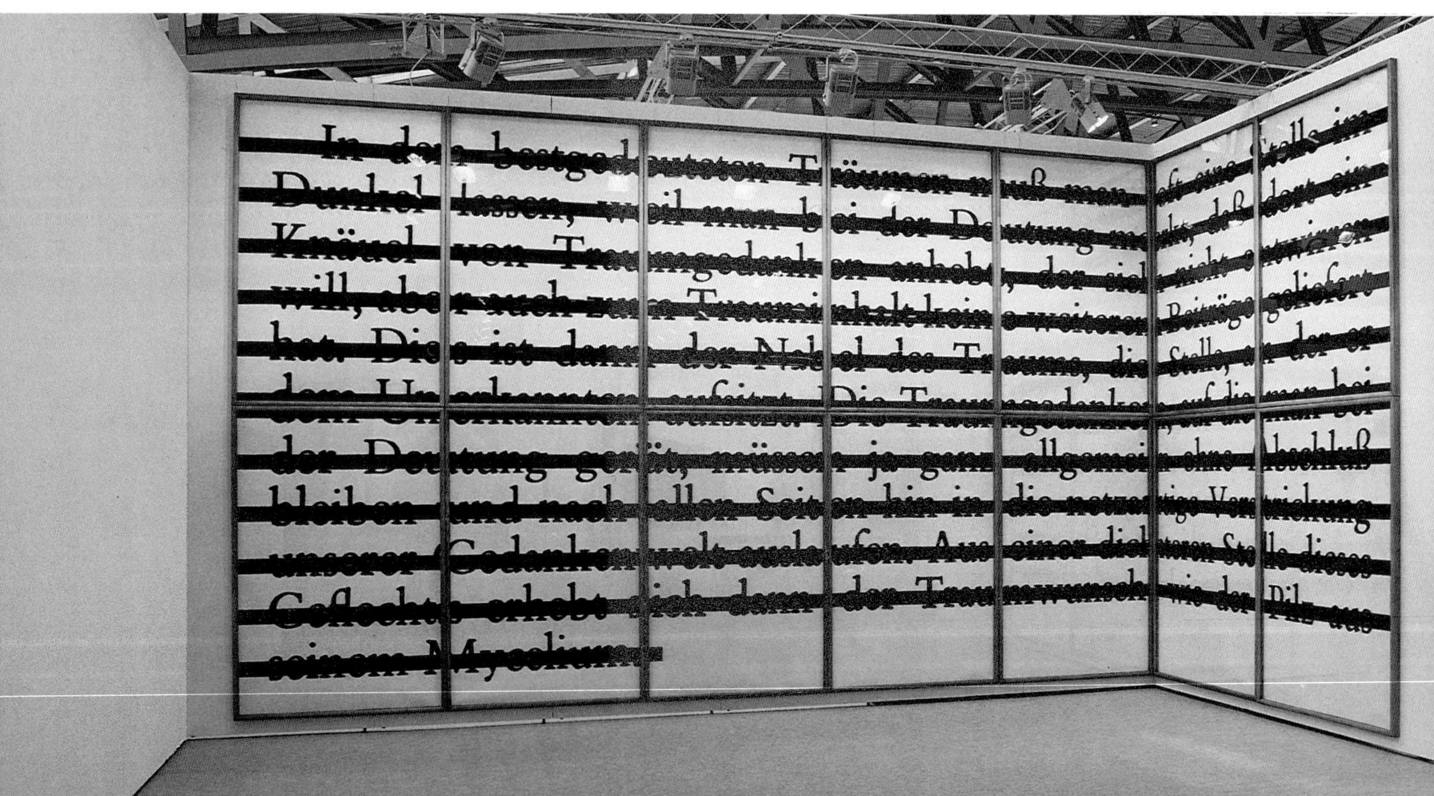

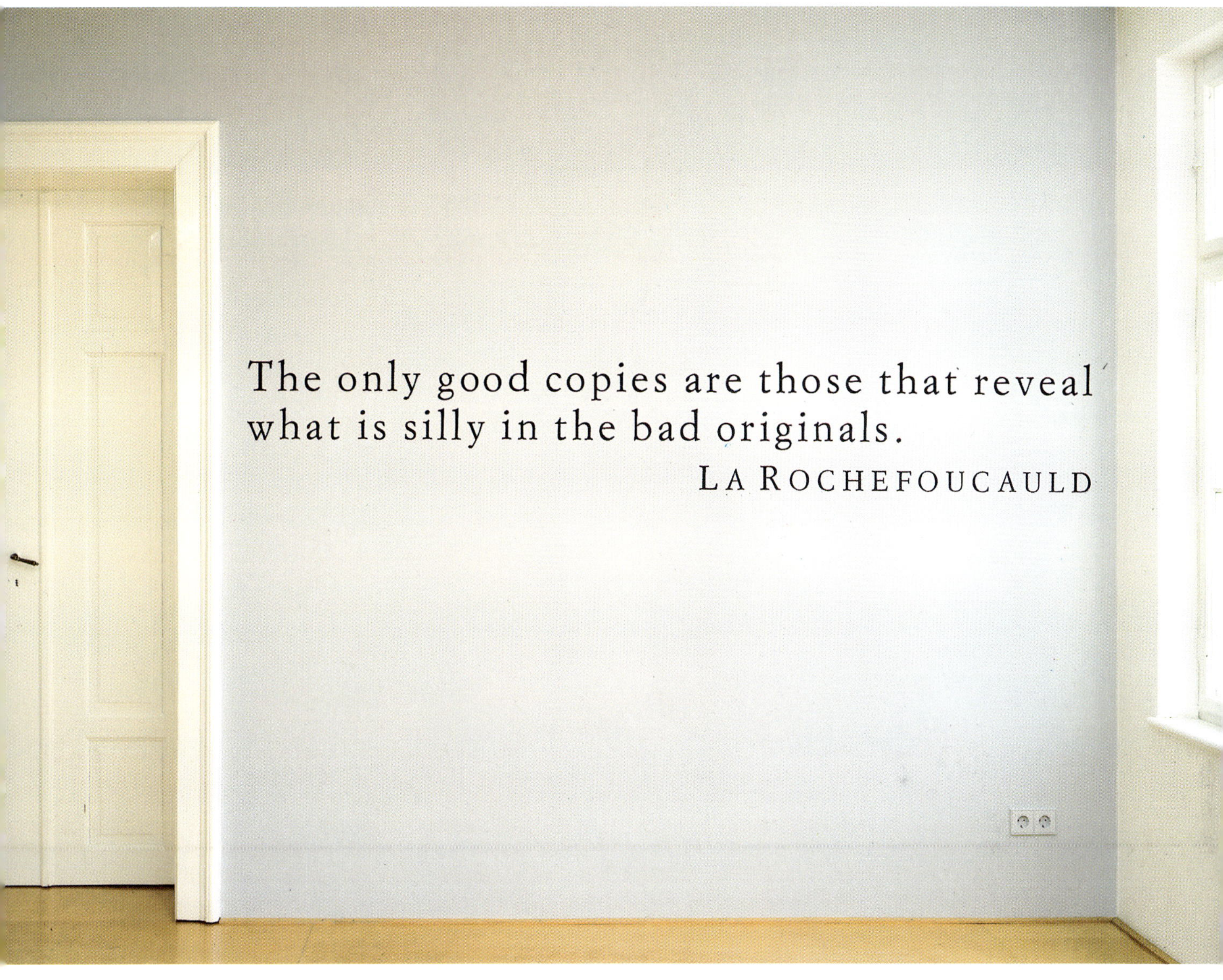

177 Joseph Kosuth ■
Copied Authentic, 1993
Text auf einer Wand (Wandfarbe schwarz, weiß oder grau), auszuführen nach den Anweisungen des Künstlers, siehe Appendix, 44 x 275 cm.
Auflage: 12, mit einem sign. und num. Zertifikat
Text on a wall, in black, white or grey paint, to be executed according to the artist's instructions, see appendix, 17¼ x 108¼ in.
Edition: 12, with a signed and numbered certificate

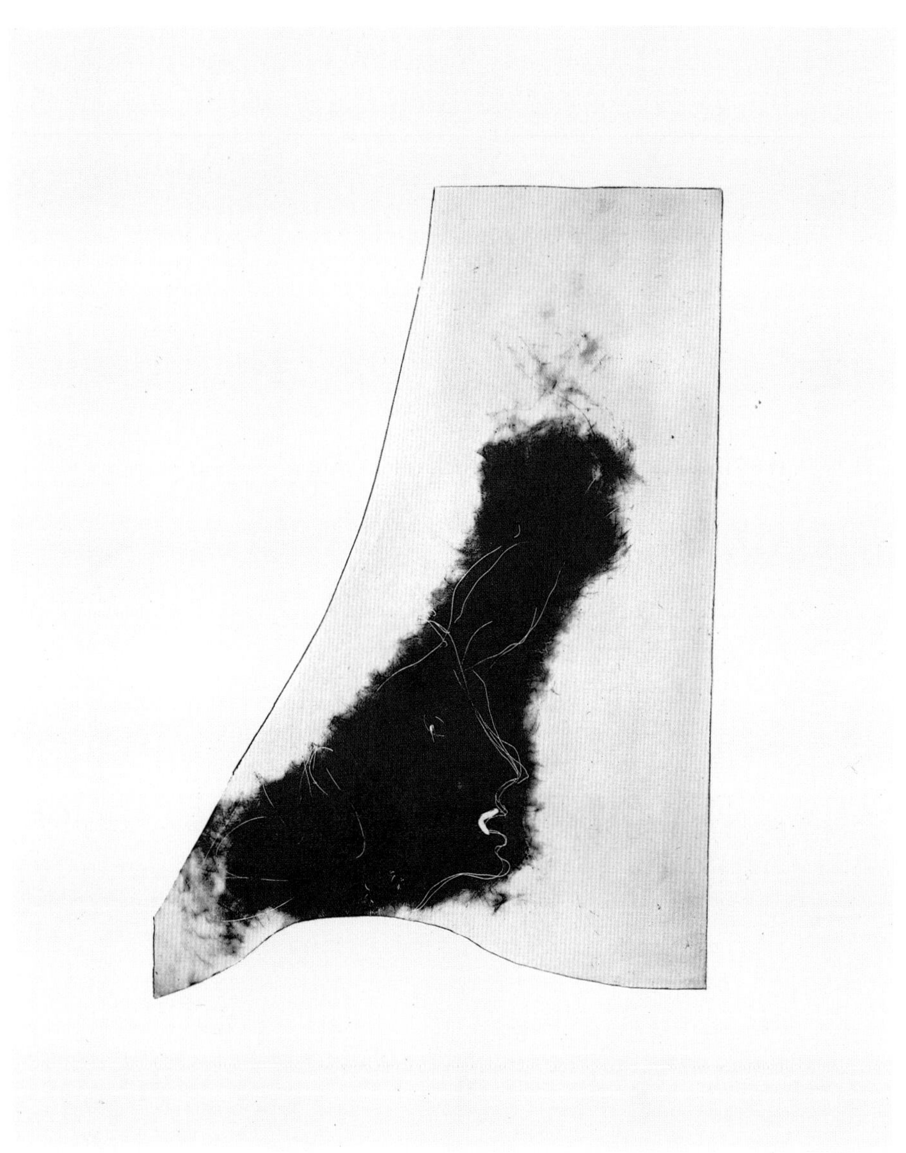

178 Jannis Kounellis ■
Frammenti di Danza, 1982
Mappe mit 7 Heliogravuren/Kaltnadelradierung, 93 x 76 cm. Auflage: 55
Portfolio with 7 photo etchings/drypoint, 36 x 30 in. Edition: 55

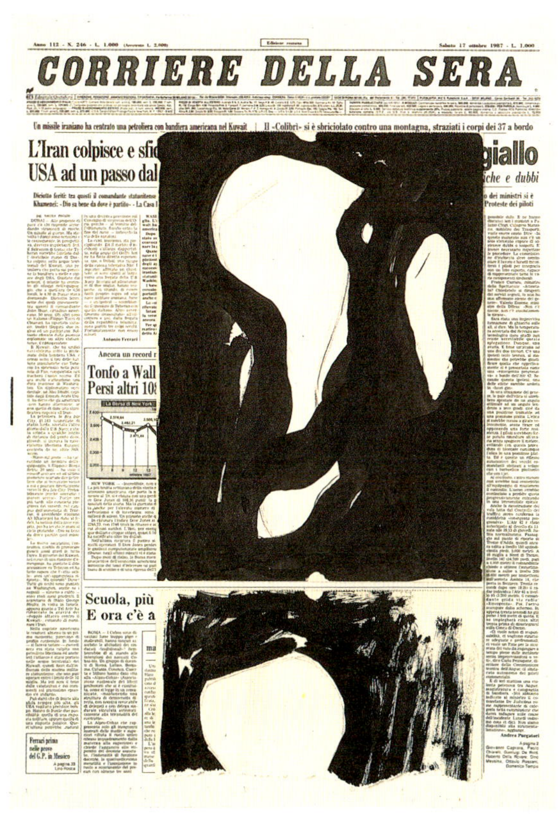

179 Jannis Kounellis ■
Edizione notturna, aus Mappe: Für Joseph Beuys, 1987
Zeitung, aufgezogen auf Bütten, collagiert mit zwei Blatt Lichtdruck, 76 x 57 cm. Auflage: 90
Newspaper with collage of two collotype prints, mounted on rag paper, 30 x 22½ in. Edition: 90

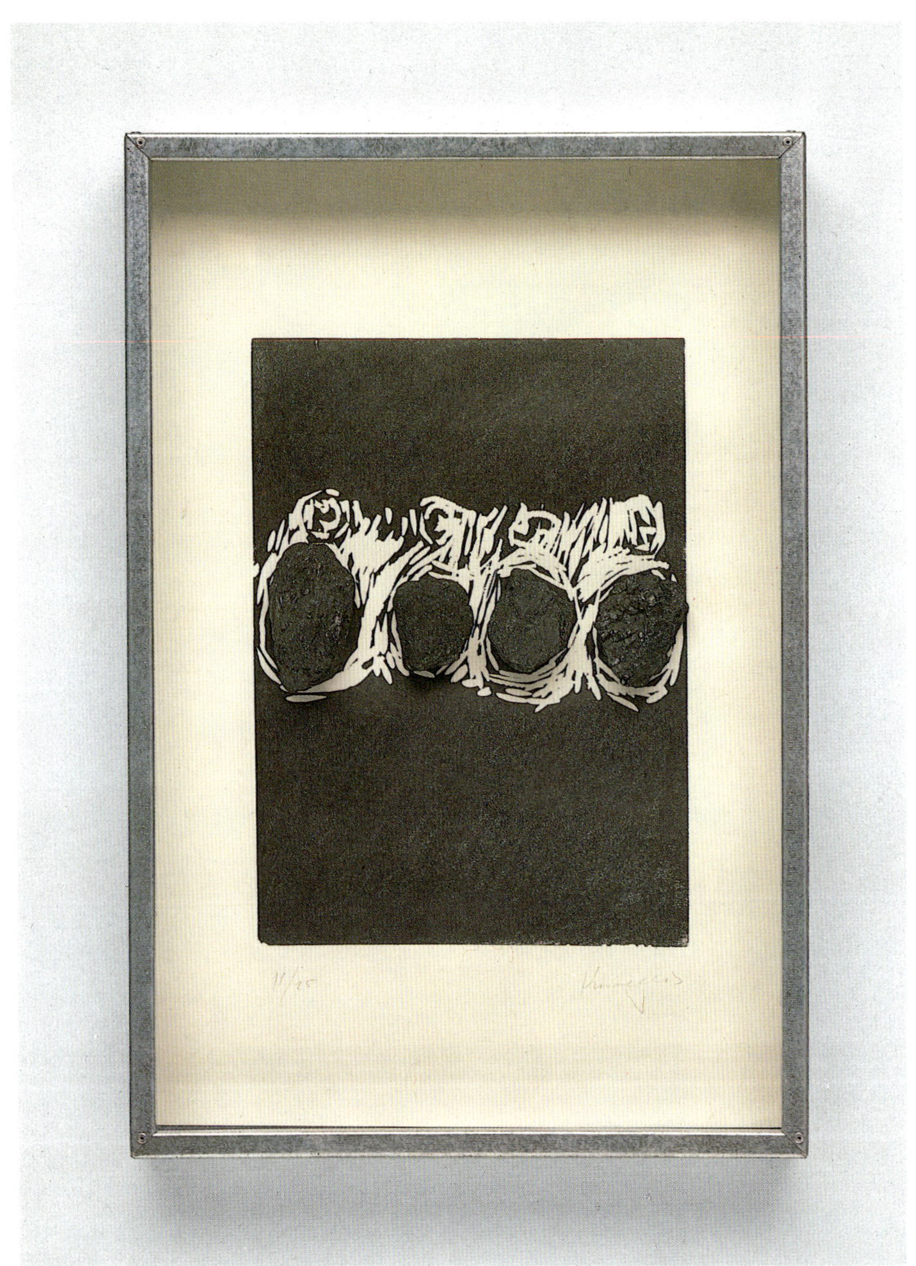

180 Jannis Kounellis
Untitled, 1989
Linolschnitt auf Japanpapier, Kohle; in Kasten aus verzinktem Eisenblech,
66 x 45,5 x 7,5 cm. Auflage: 25
Linocut on Japanese paper and mineral coal, mounted in galvanized iron box,
26 x 18 x 3 in. Edition: 25

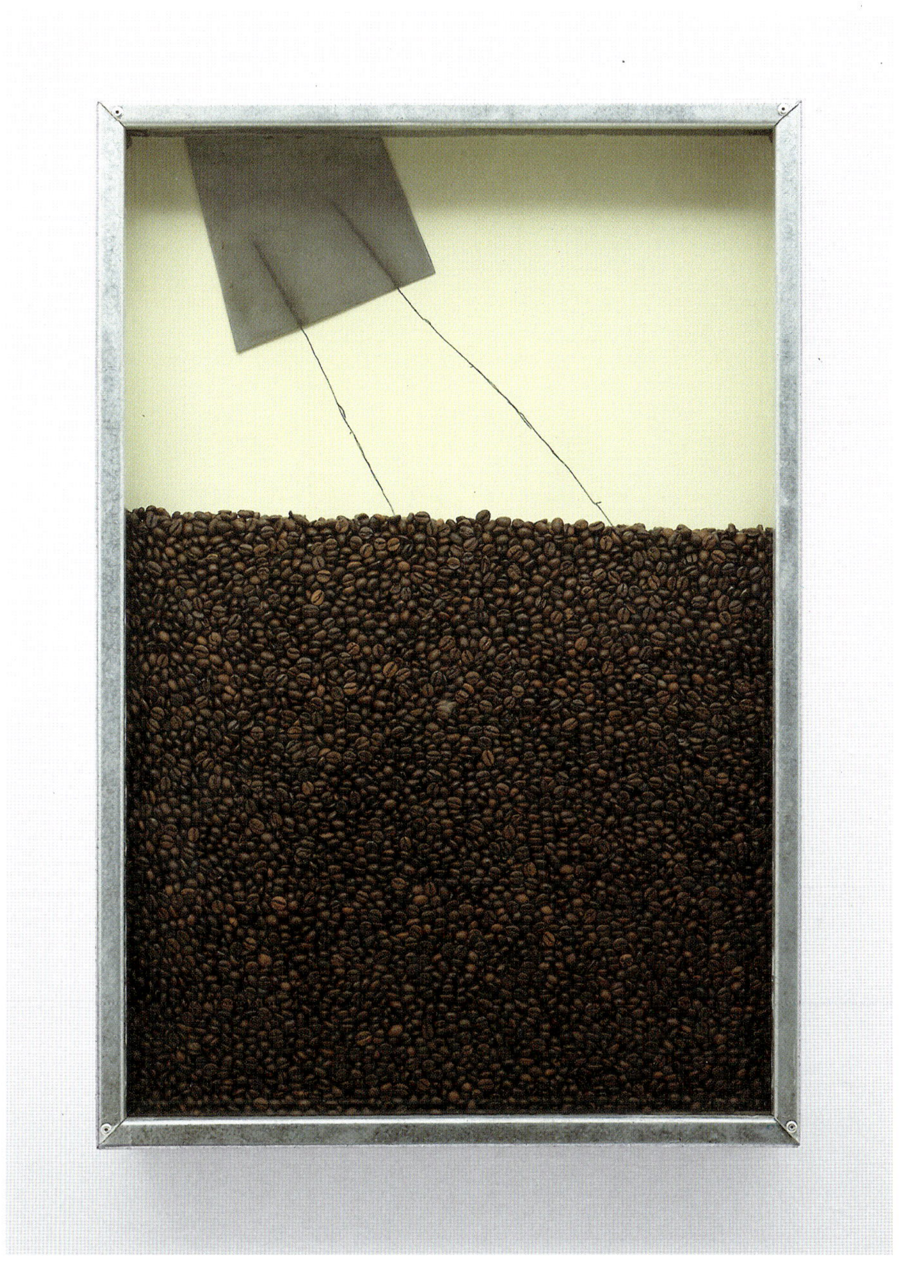

181 Jannis Kounellis
Untitled, 1991
Radierung auf Bütten, Blei, Kaffeebohnen zwischen zwei Glasplatten,
in Kasten aus verzinktem Eisenblech, 65,5 x 45,5 x 7,5 cm. Auflage: 25
Etching on rag paper, etched lead, and coffee beans between two glass plates,
mounted in galvanized iron box, 26 x 18 x 3 in. Edition: 25

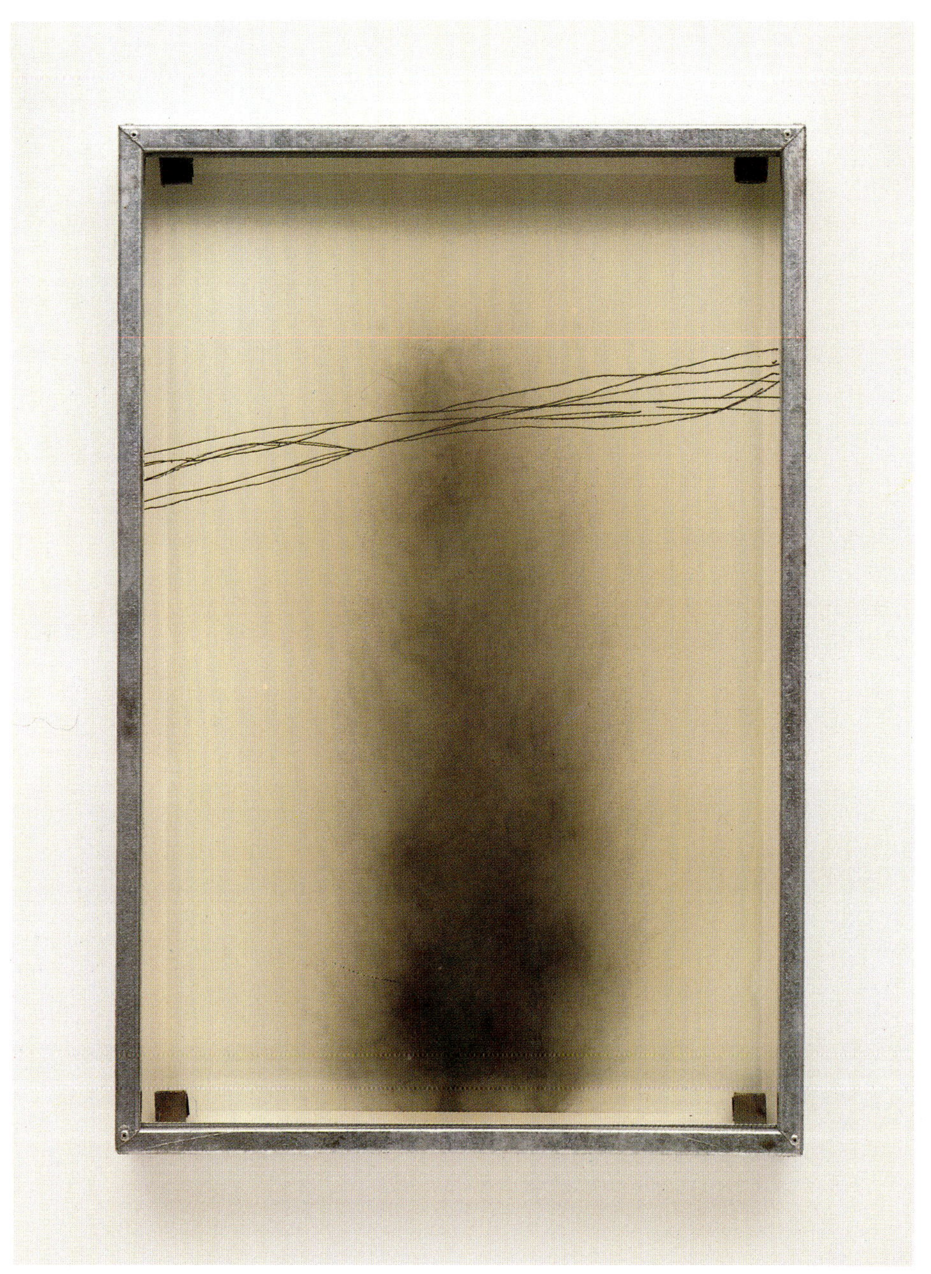

182 Jannis Kounellis ■
Untitled, 1990
Radierung und Glasplatte mit Rauch, in Kasten aus verzinktem Eisenblech, 60 x 45 x 7,5 cm. Auflage: 25
Etching and sheet of smoked glass, in galvanized iron box, 23½ x 18 x 3 in. Edition: 25

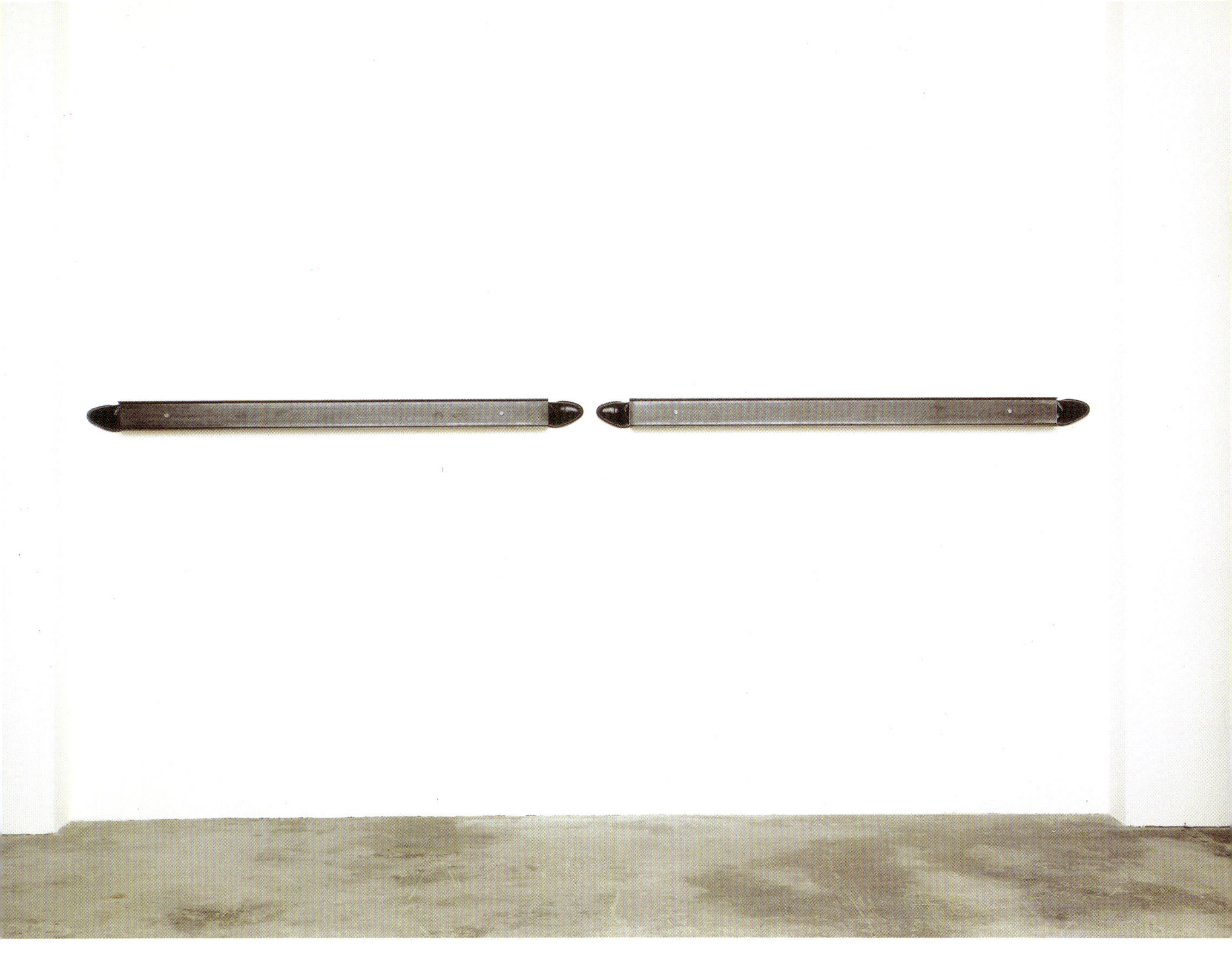

183 Jannis Kounellis ■
Untitled, 1993
Zwei Eisenträger, zwei Paar Schuhe, montiert an einer Wand,
siehe Appendix. Träger 12 x 6 cm Querschnitt, Länge variabel.
Auflage: 10, mit einem sign. und num. Zertifikat
Two steel girders, two pairs of shoes, mounted on a wall, see appendix.
I-Beam cross section 5 x 2½ in., length variable.
Edition: 10, with a signed and numbered certificate

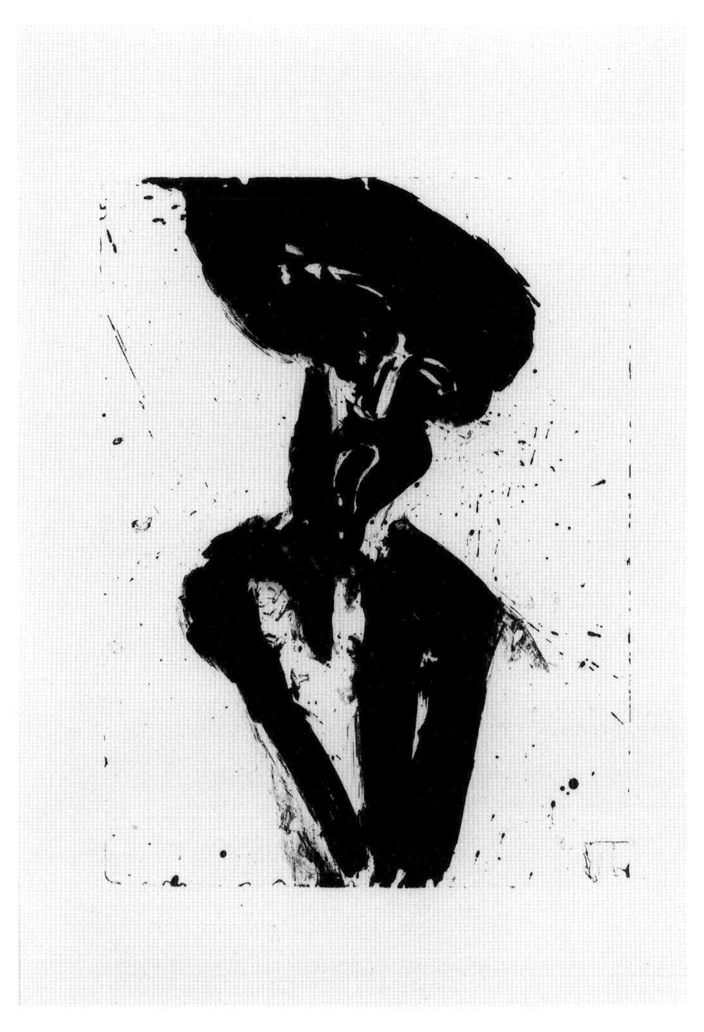

184 Jannis Kounellis
Fumo di Pietra, 1992
Folge von 10 Lithographien, Formate zwischen
60 x 80 und 90 x 130 cm. Auflage: 21
Suite of 10 lithographs, sizes between 24 x 32
and 35 x 51 in. Edition: 21

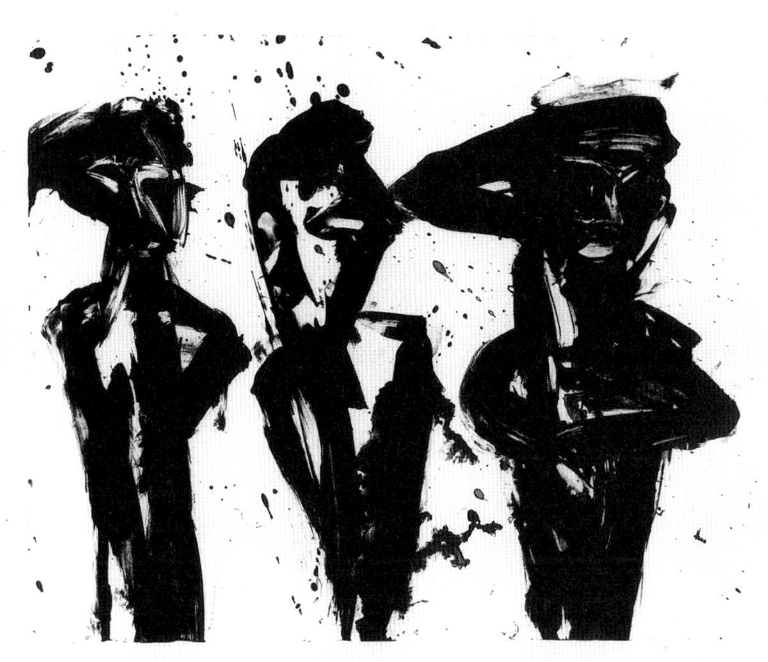

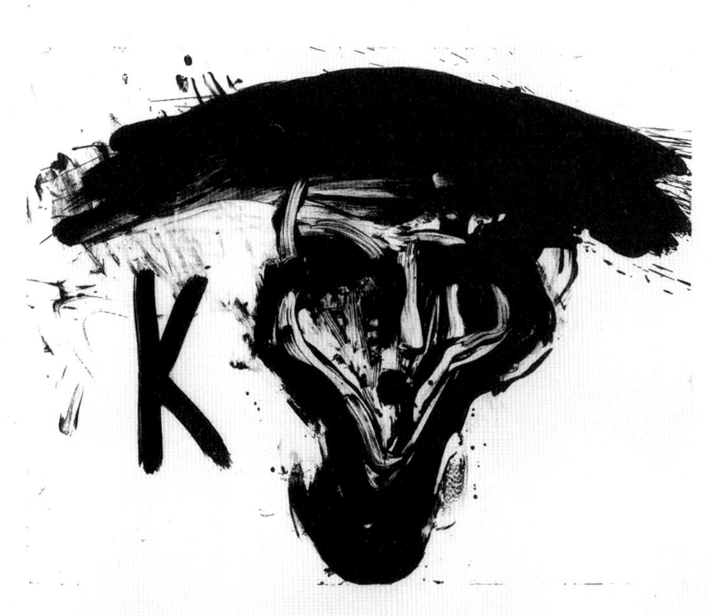
K

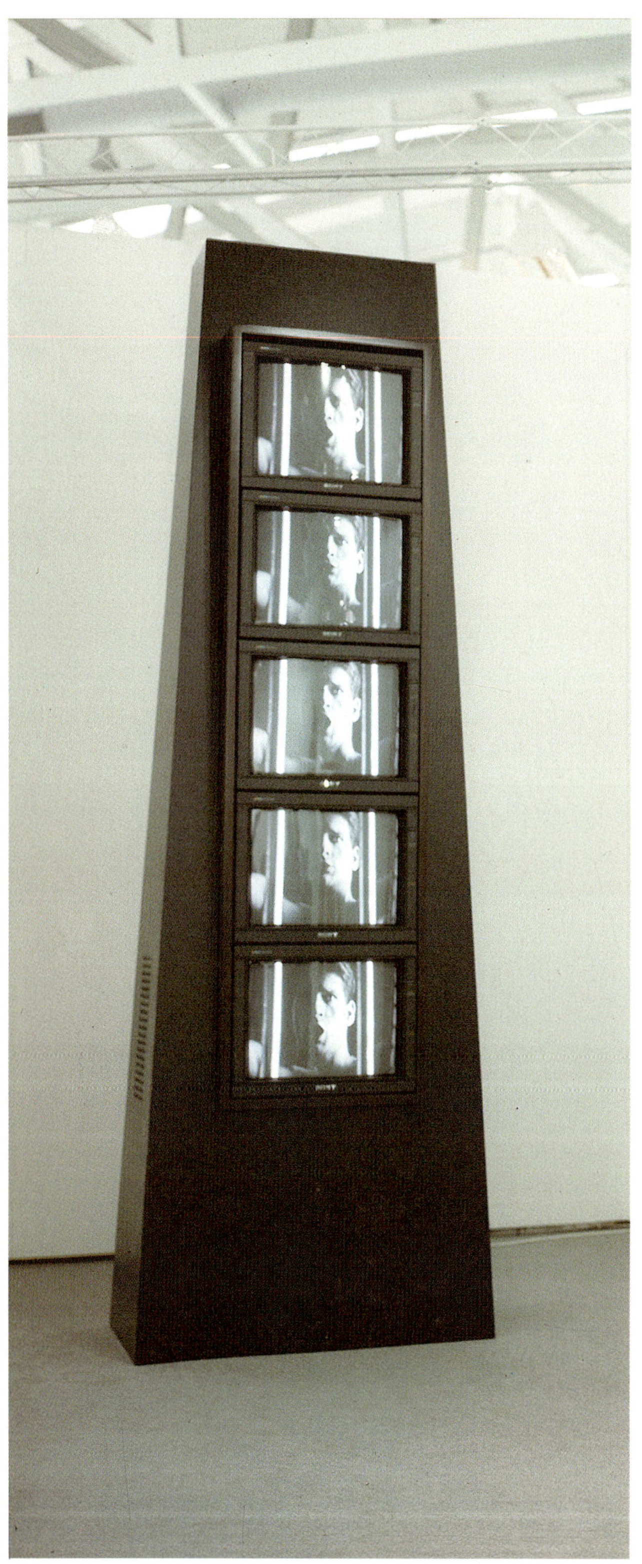

185 Marie-Jo Lafontaine
Les larmes d'acier, 1988/89
Sony-Monitore, U-matic-Player,
Computer, Holzschassis;
303 x 100 x 65 cm.
Auflage: 7
Sony monitors, U-matic player,
computer, wooden casing;
119¼ x 39½ x 25½ in.
Edition: 7

186 Louise Lawler / Allan McCollum →
Fixed Intervals, 1988-92
Folge von 5 Messingobjekten,
Maße unterschiedlich.
Auflage: 25
Set of 5 brass objects,
dimensions variable.
Edition: 25

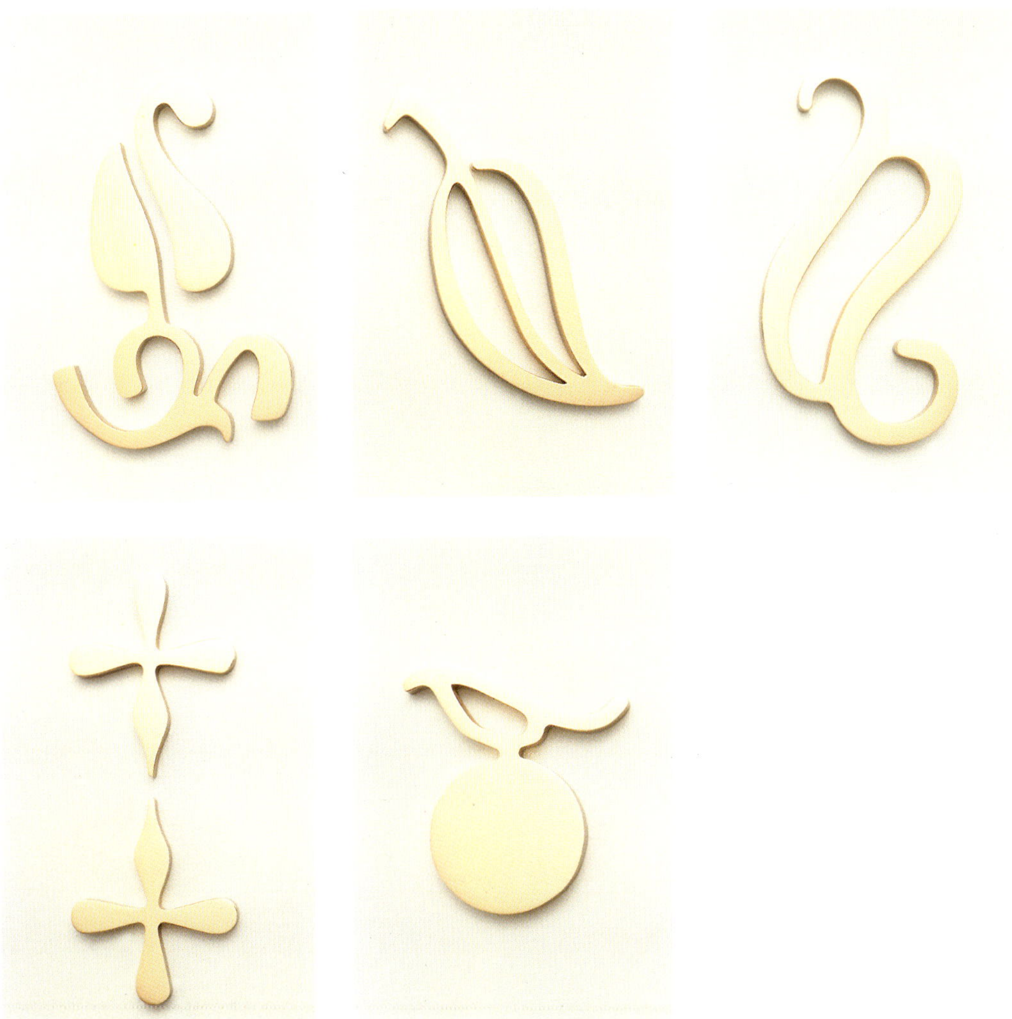

"Fixed Intervals sollen 'spielerisch' als kunstgeschichtlicher Kniff auf einer Wand eingesetzt werden." Sie können zwischen ähnlichen oder verschiedenen Kunstwerken plaziert werden, vor und nach einem einzelnen Kunstwerk, oder sie können paarweise zu einem mit der Ansicht zur Wand gedrehten Werk angeordnet werden. Ein einzelner Fixed Interval kann den Platz eines abgehängten Kunstwerkes einnehmen. Aber ein Paar von Fixed Intervals kann nicht ohne Kunstwerke zwischen ihnen plaziert werden." Ein Fixed Interval als solches ist kein eigenständiges Kunstwerk."

"Fixed Intervals are to be used 'facetiously' as an art historical device on a wall". The objects may be placed between similar or different works, before and after an isolated work or paired with its reverse. If a work is absent, a single interval may take its place. But two fixed intervals are never to be placed without works between." A fixed interval is not a work in itself."

188 Sol LeWitt ■
Red, Yellow, Blue and Gray Squares, Bordered by a Black Band, 1989
4 Aquatintaradierungen, 46 x 46 cm. Auflage: 25
Set of 4 aquatints, 18 x 18 in. Edition: 25

← **187 Sol LeWitt** ■
Wall Piece (16 modules high), 1988
Holzkonstruktion, schwarz gestrichen, 191 x 13 x 13 cm. Auflage: 20
Painted pinewood construction, 76 x 5 x 5 in. Edition: 20

189 Sol LeWitt ■
Two Cubes with Colors Superimposed, 1988
2 Serigraphien (25 Farben), 76 x 241 cm. Auflage: 30
2 silkscreens in 25 colors, 30 x 95 in. Edition: 30

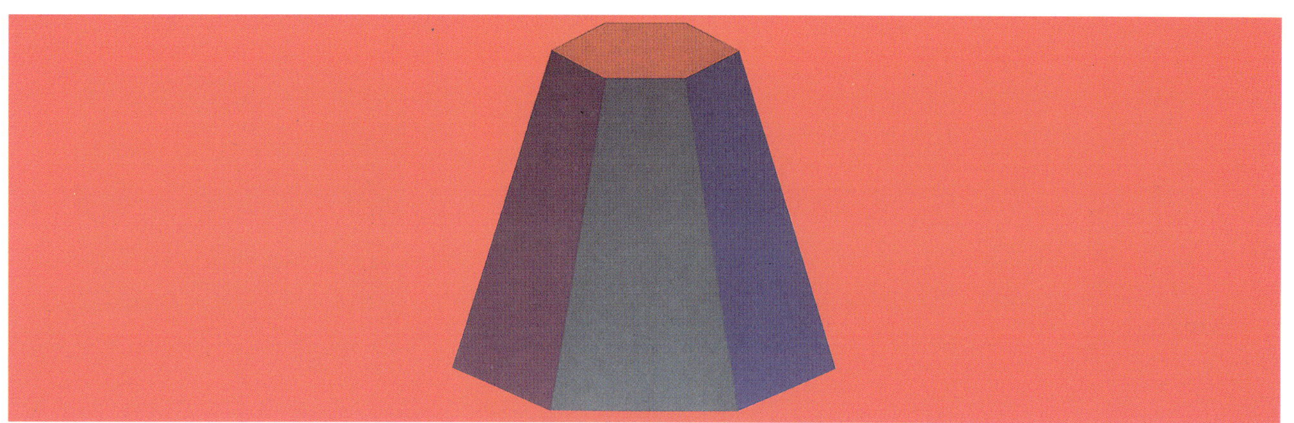

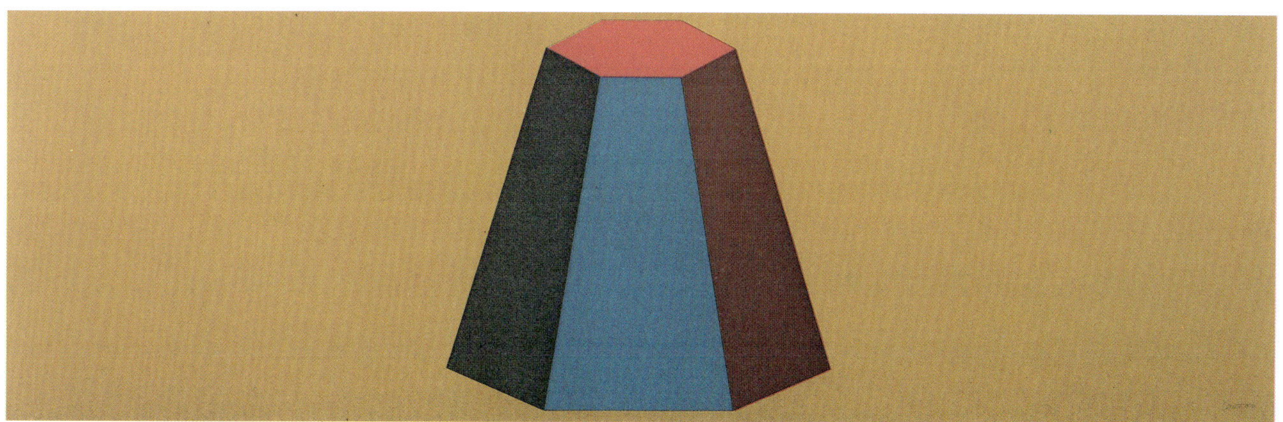

190 Sol LeWitt ■
Flat Top Pyramid with Colors Superimposed, 1988
2 Serigraphien (20-23 Farben), 76 x 241 cm. Auflage: 30
2 silkscreens in 20-23 colors, 30 x 95 in. Edition: 30

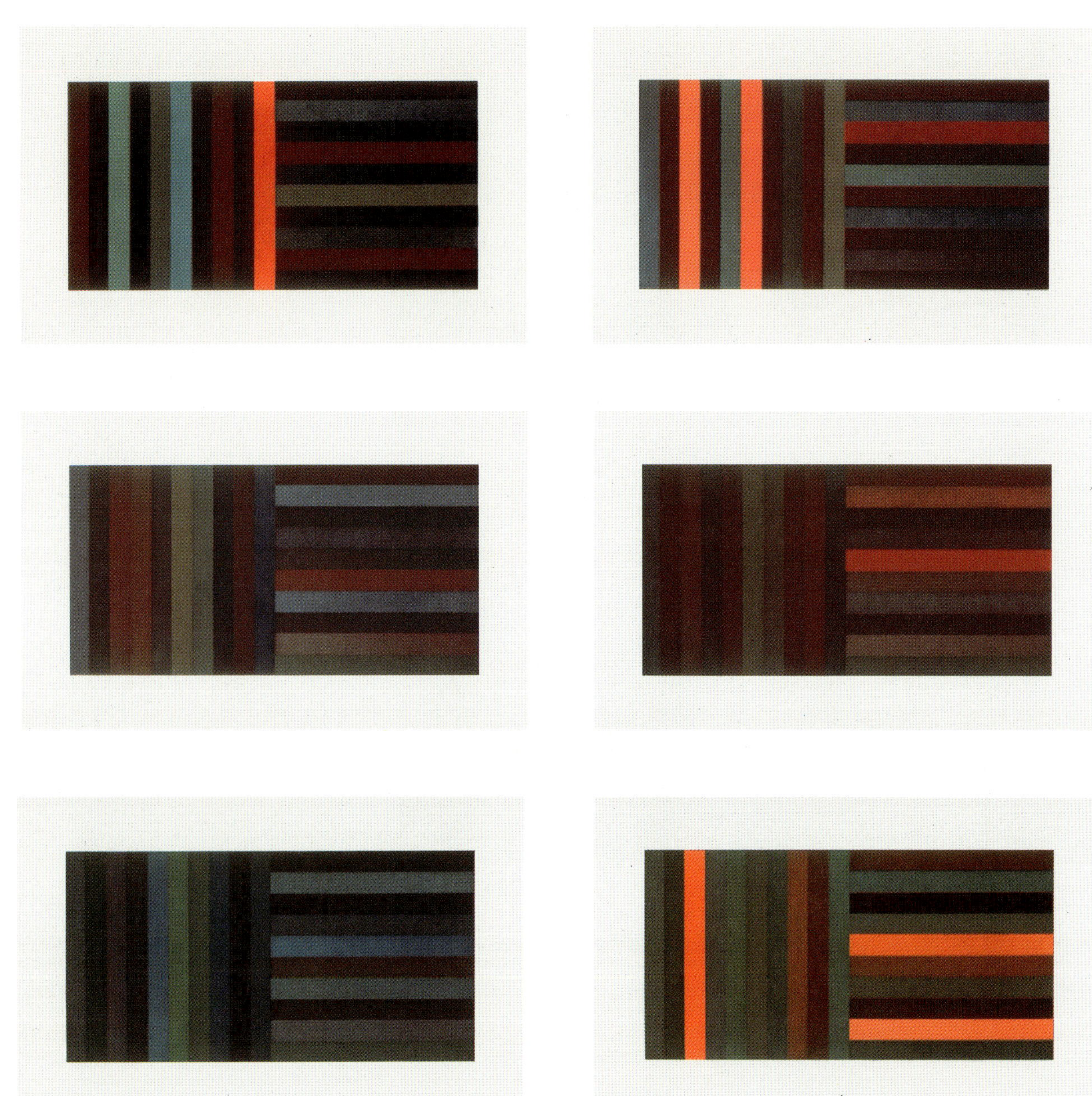

191 Sol LeWitt
Horizontal Color Bands and Vertical Color Bands, 1991
Folge von 7 Aquatintaradierungen, 61 x 105,5 cm. Auflage: 30
Suite of 7 aquatints, 24 x 41½ in. Edition: 30

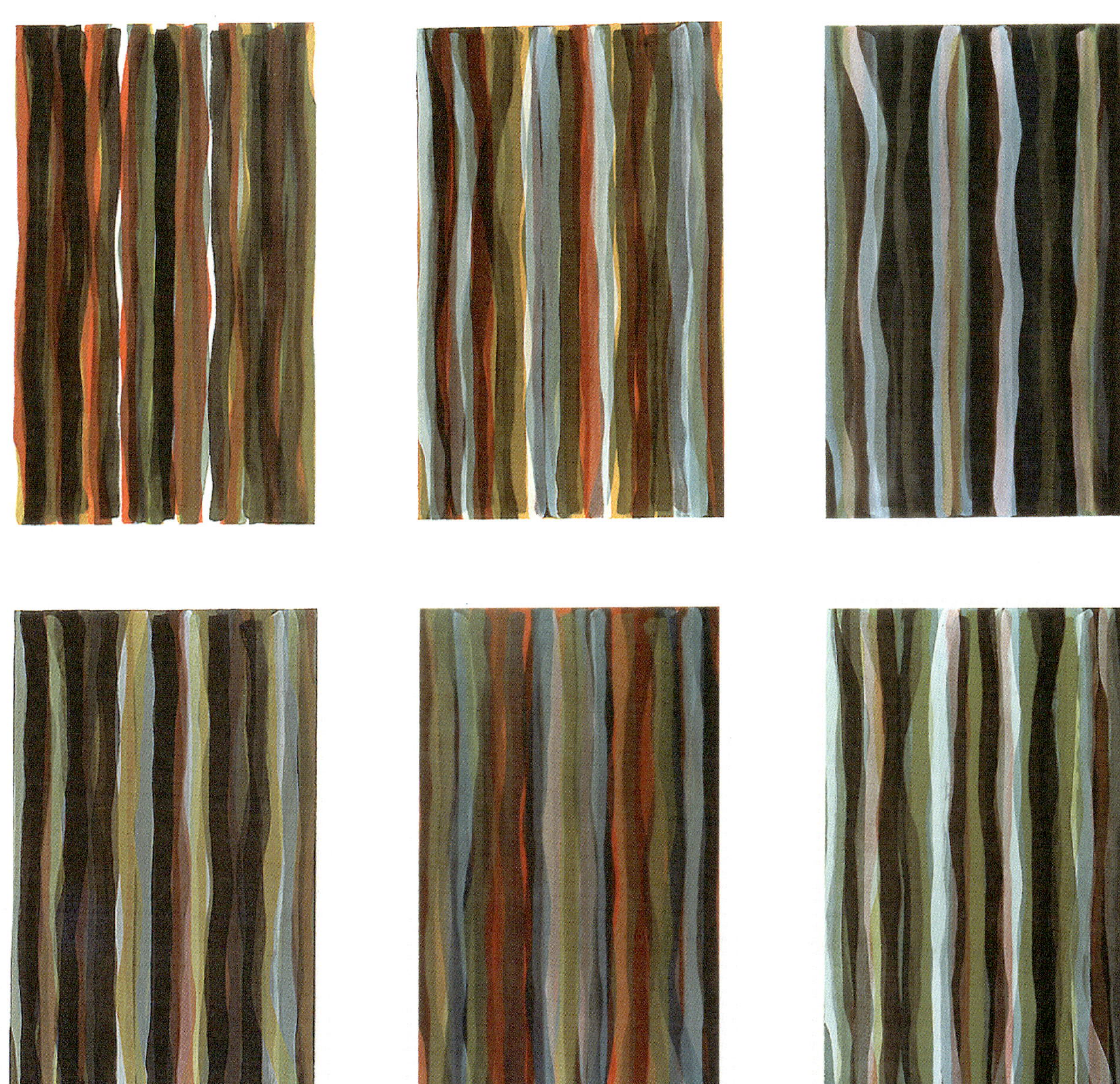

192 Sol LeWitt
Brushstrokes in Different Colors in Two Directions, 1993
Folge von sechs Radierungen, 119 x 74 cm. Auflage: 35
Suite of six etchings, 46¾ x 29¼ in. Edition: 35

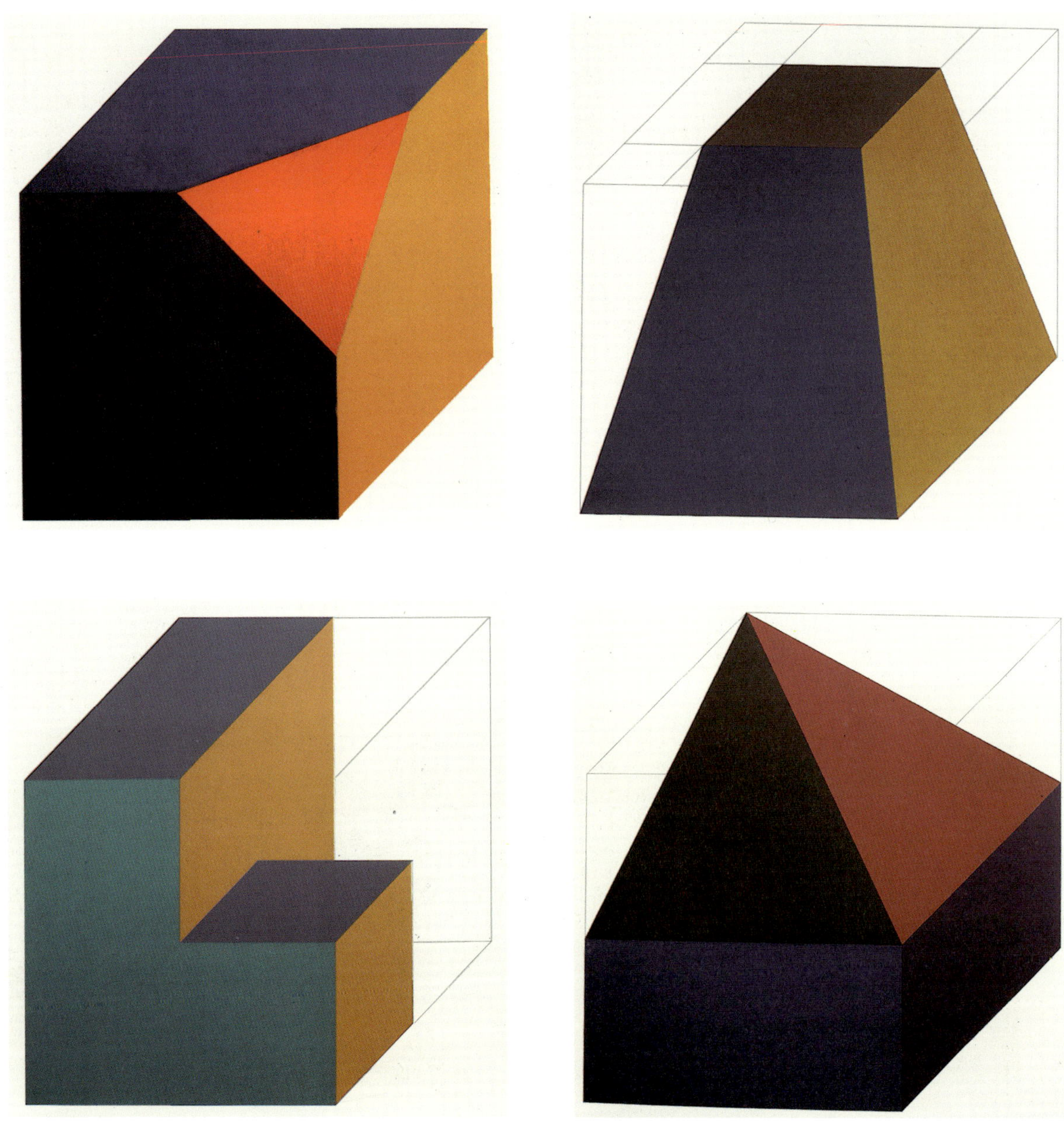

193 Sol LeWitt
Forms Derived from a Cube (Color), 1991
Folge von 12 Serigraphien auf Somerset Karton, 81 x 81 cm. Auflage: 35
Set of 12 silkscreens, printed on Somerset board, 32 x 32 in. Edition: 35

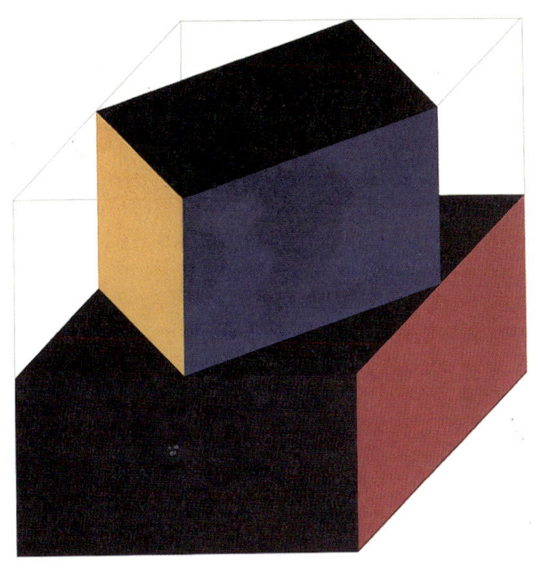
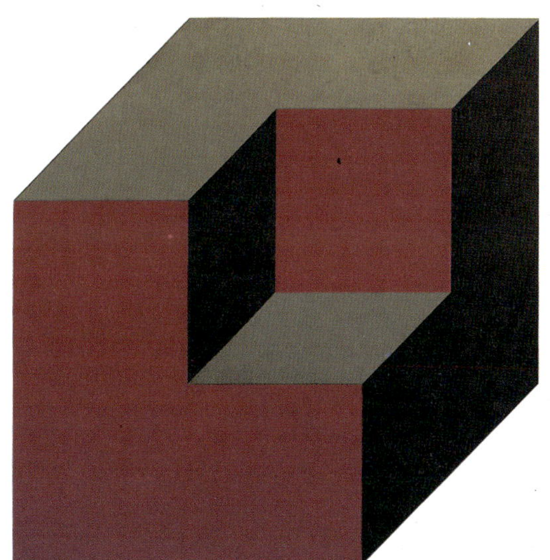
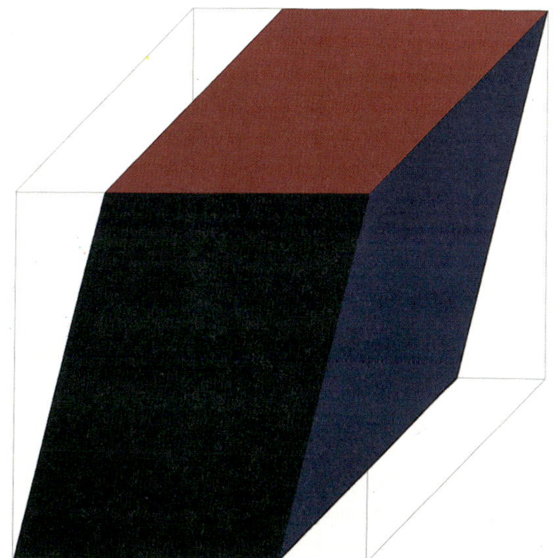
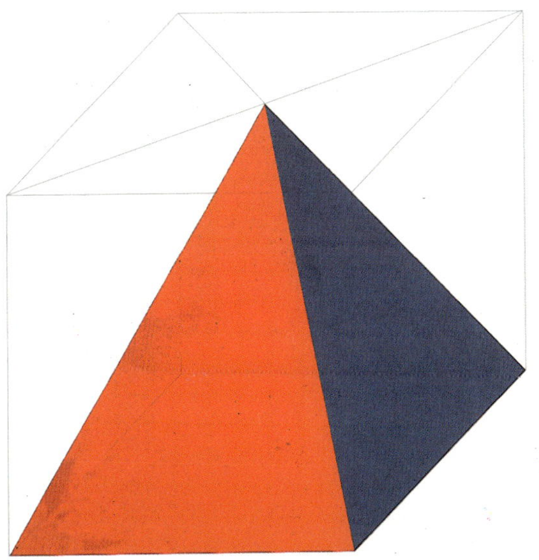

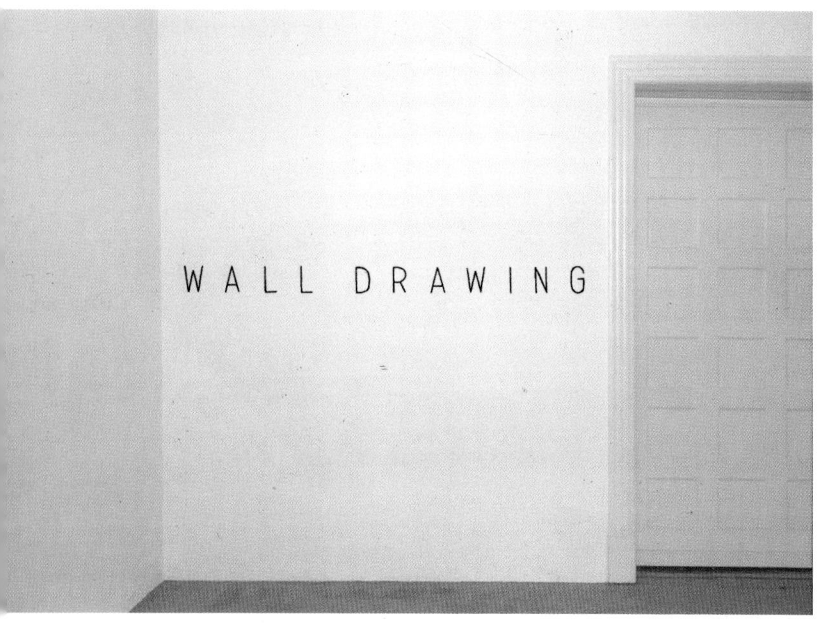

194 Sol LeWitt ■
Wall Drawing, 1992
"Wall Drawing" vom Besitzer der Arbeit an eine Wand zu schreiben, Techik und Größe frei zu bestimmen, siehe Appendix. Auflage: 10, signiert und numeriert auf einem Photo-Zertifikat
"Wall Drawing" to be written on a wall in the hand of the owner, medium and size to be chosen by the owner, see appendix. Edition: 10, with a signed and numbered certificate photo

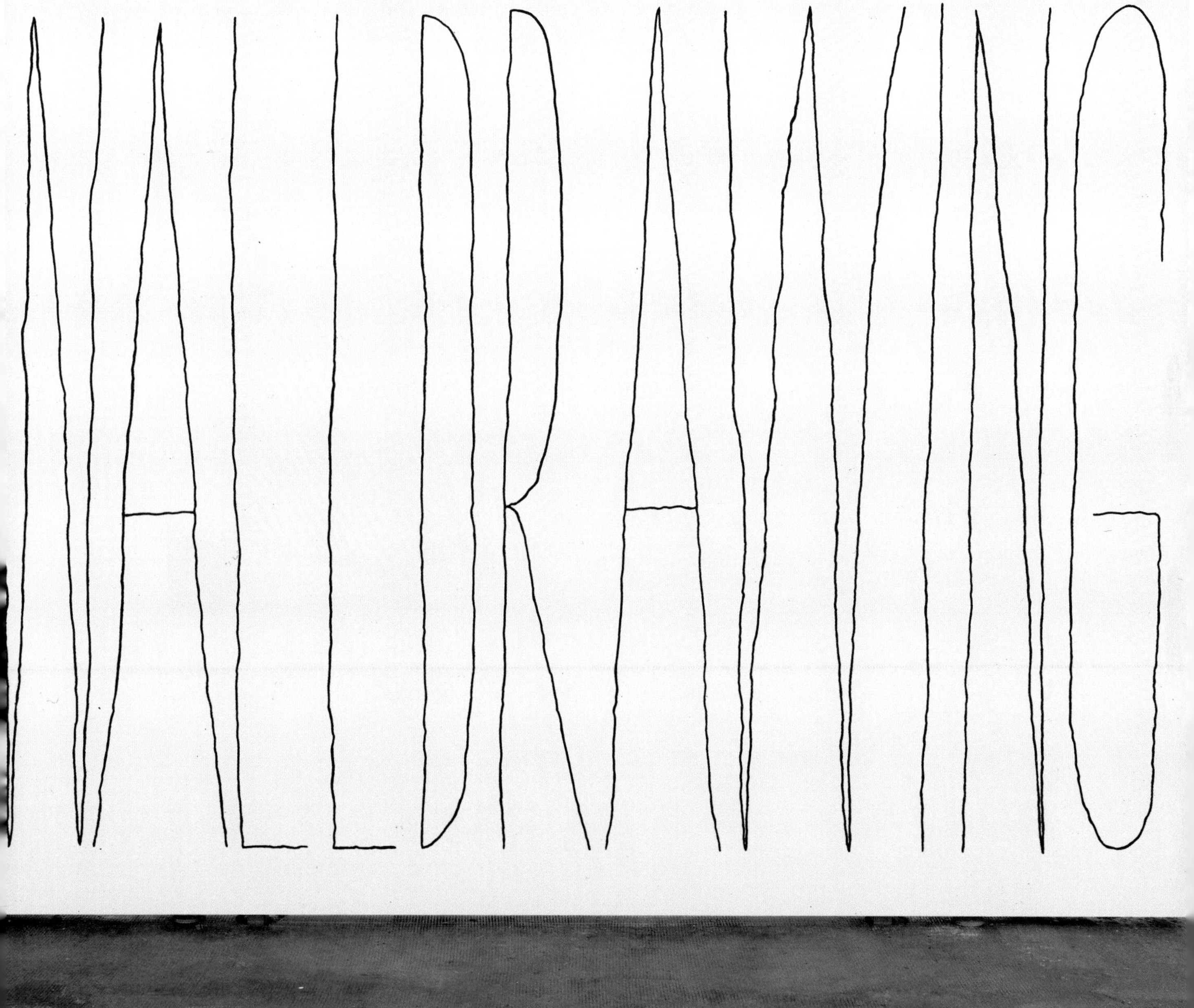

WALLDRAWING

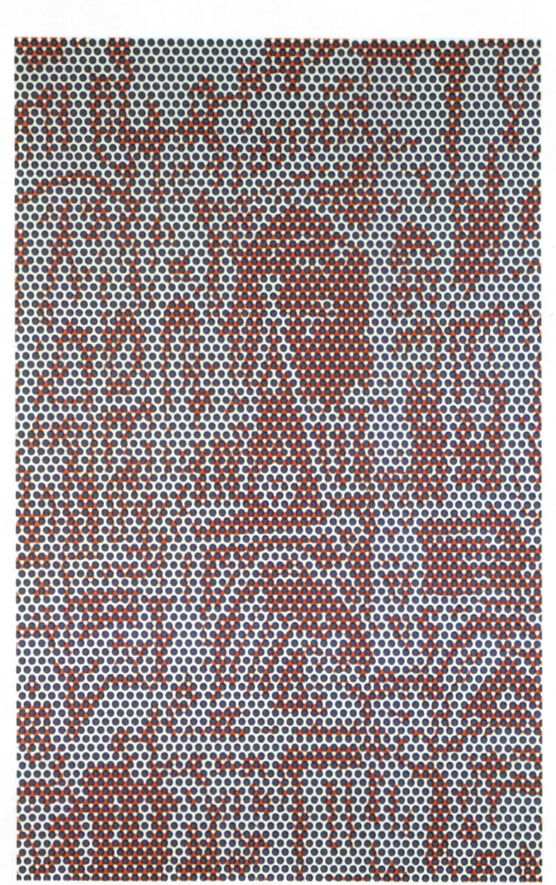

195 Roy Lichtenstein
Rouen Cathedral #4, 1969
Lithographie, 122,5 x 82 cm. Auflage: 75
Lithograph, 48 x 32 in. Edition: 75

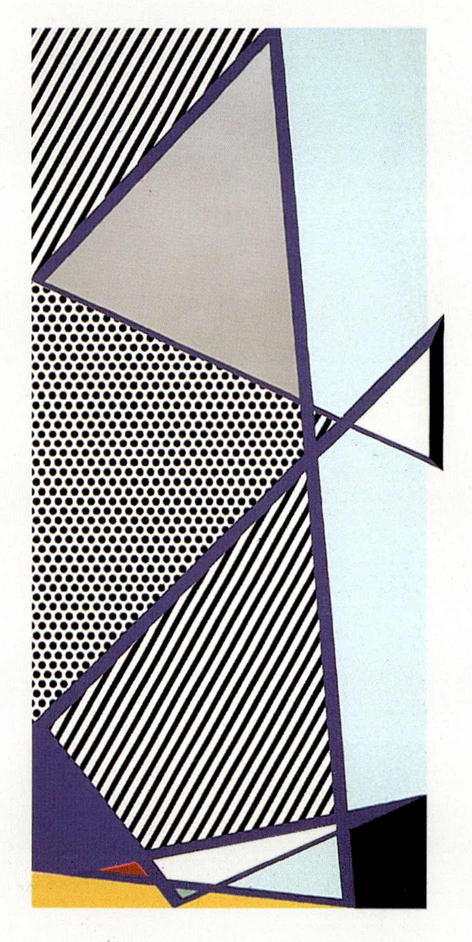

196 Roy Lichtenstein
Imperfect for B.A.M., 1988
Holzschnitt und Siebdruck, 150 x 79 cm. Aufl.: 75
Woodcut and screenprint, 59 x 31 in. Edition: 75

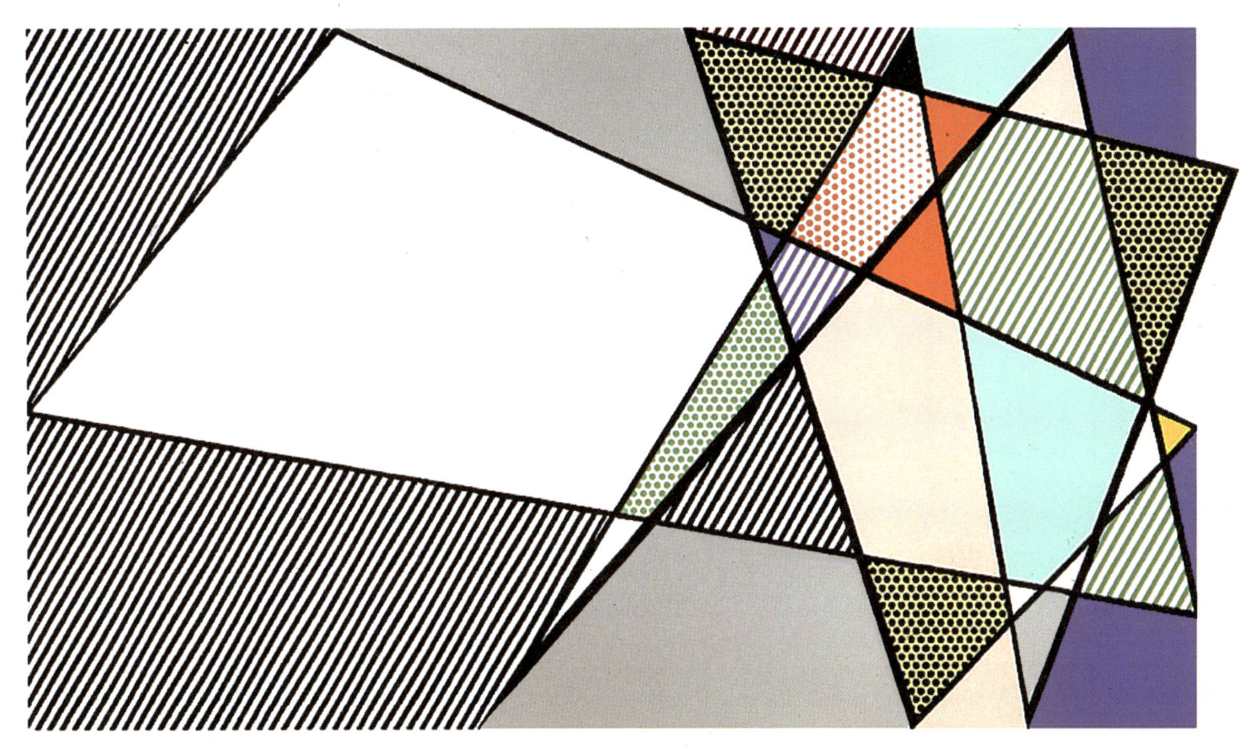

197 Roy Lichtenstein
Imperfect, 1988
Holzschnitt, Siebdruck, Collage, 147,5 x 245 cm. Auflage: 45
Woodcut, screenprint, collage, 58 x 92½ in. Edition: 45

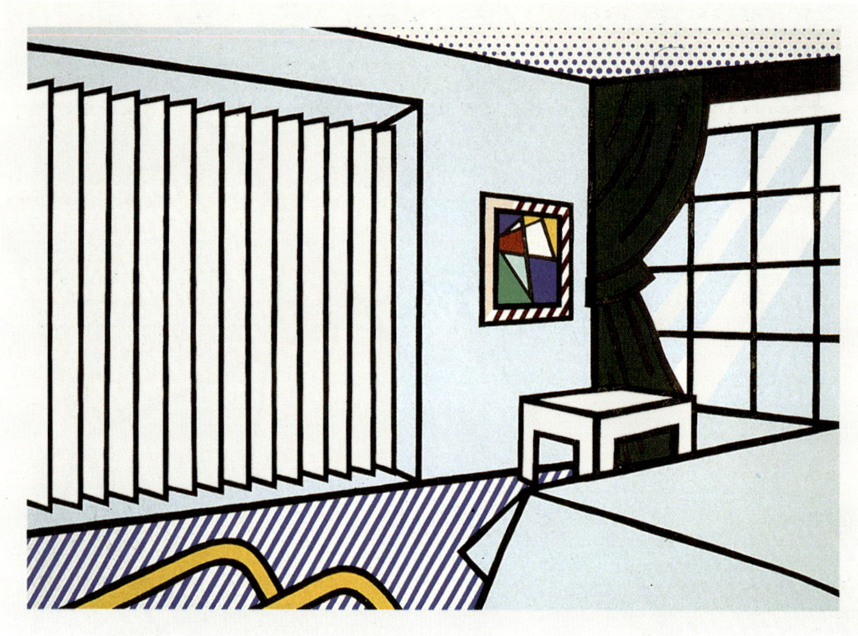

198 Roy Lichtenstein
Bedroom, 1991
Lithographie, Holzschnitt und Siebdruck,
145 x 201 cm. Auflage: 60
Woodcut and screenprint, 57 x 79 in.
Edition: 60

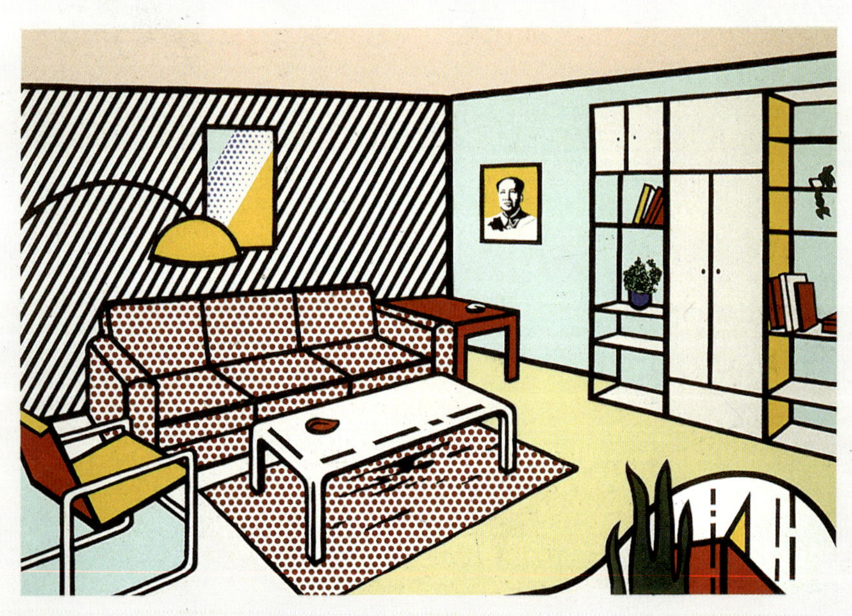

199 Roy Lichtenstein
Modern Room, 1991
Lithographie, Holzschnitt und Siebdruck,
142 x 206 cm. Auflage: 60
Woodcut and screenprint, 56 x 81 in.
Edition: 60

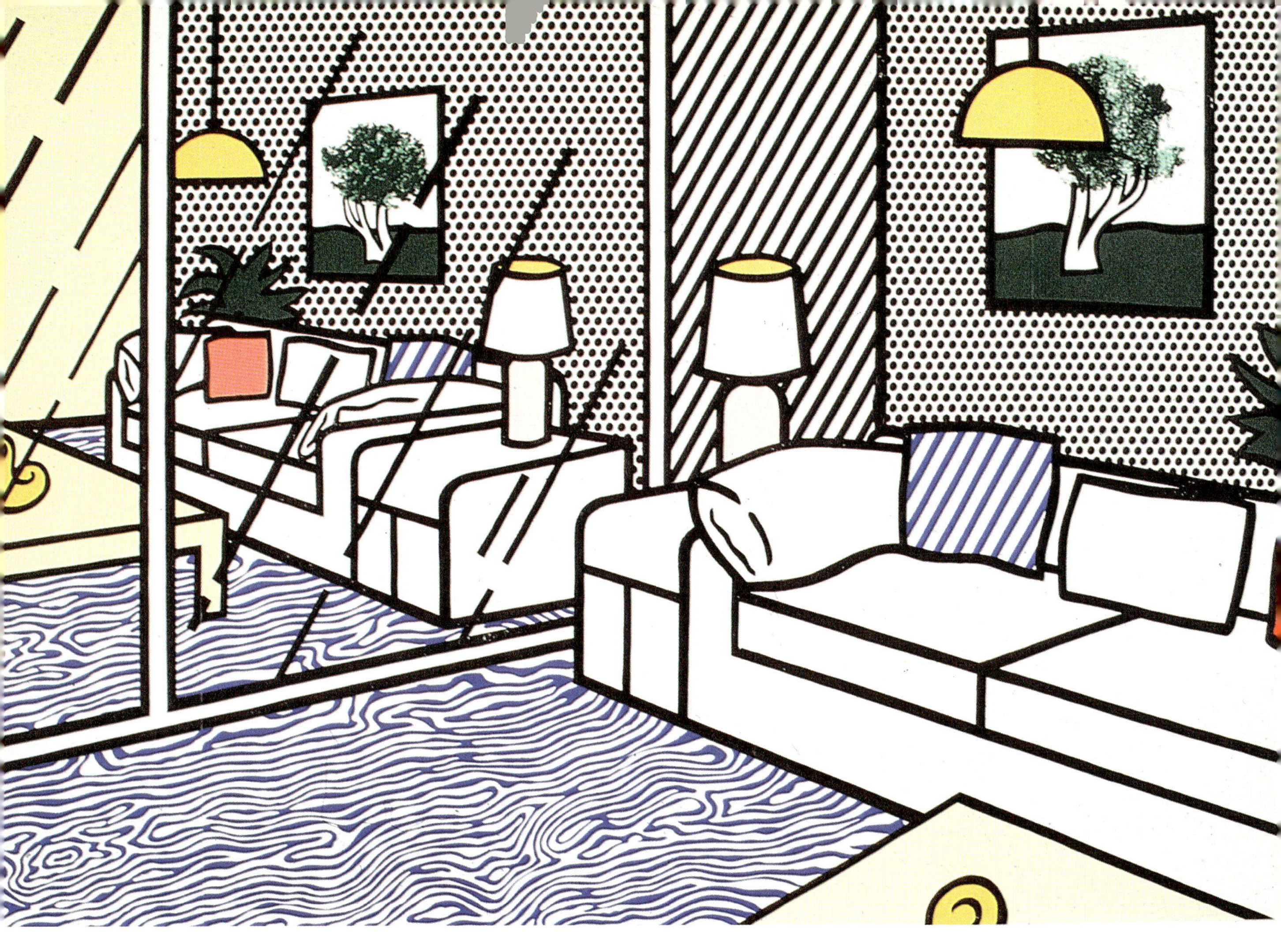

200 Roy Lichtenstein
Wallpaper With Blue Floor Interior, 1992
Serigraphie, 5-teilig, auf Folie, zum Aufziehen auf eine Wand. 259 x 387 cm. Auflage: 300
Screenprint on Waterleaf paper, in 5 panels, to be mounted on a wall. 102 x 152½ in. Edition: 300

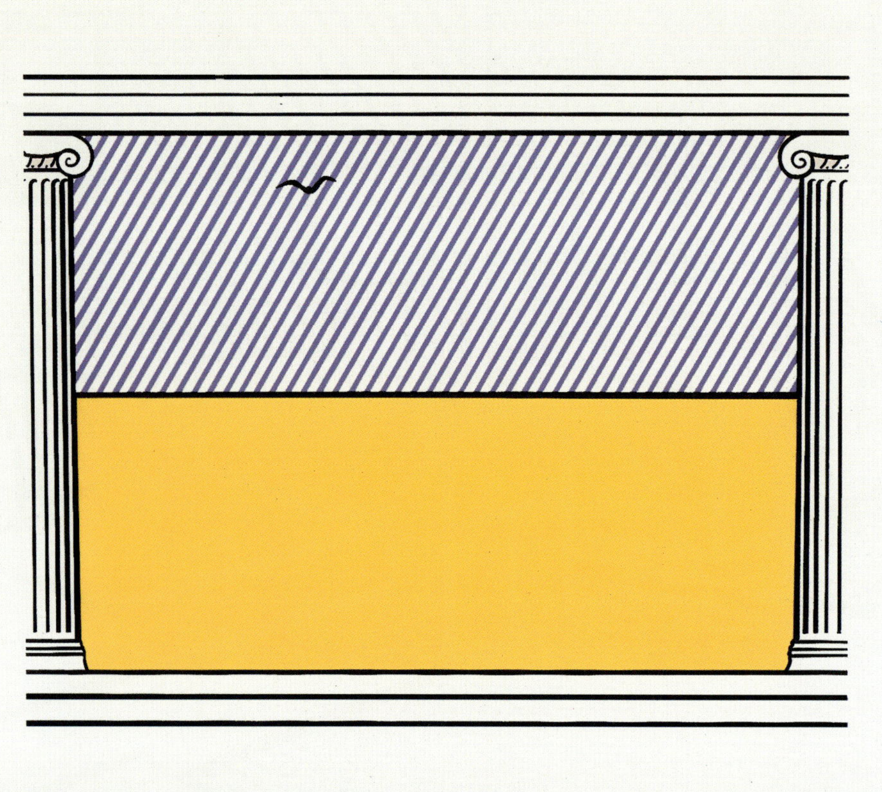

201 Roy Lichtenstein
Liberté, 1991
Serigraphie auf Bütten, 100 x 120 cm. Auflage: 75 + 25 E.A. + 5 H.C.
Silkscreen on rag paper, 39½ x 47½ in. Edition: 75 + 25 E.A. + 5 H.C.

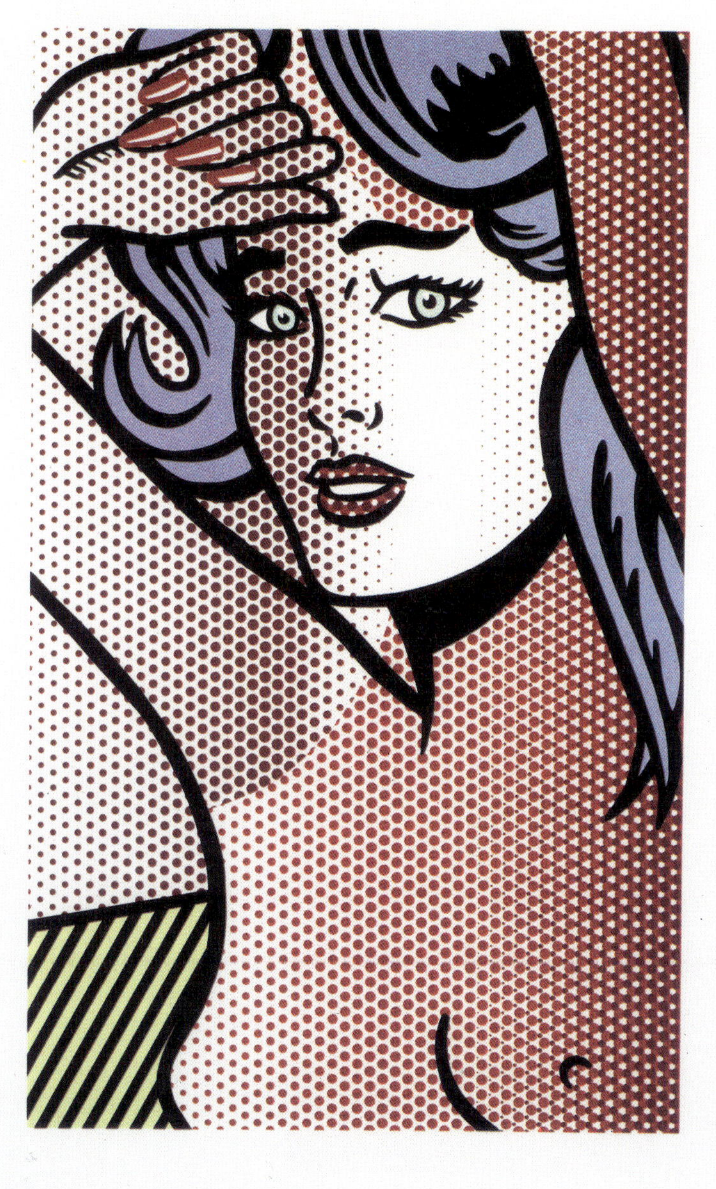

202 Roy Lichtenstein
Nude with Blue Hair, 1994
Reliefdruck auf Rives Bütten, 147 x 95 cm. Auflage: 40
Relief print on Rives rag paper, 58 x 37½ in. Edition: 40

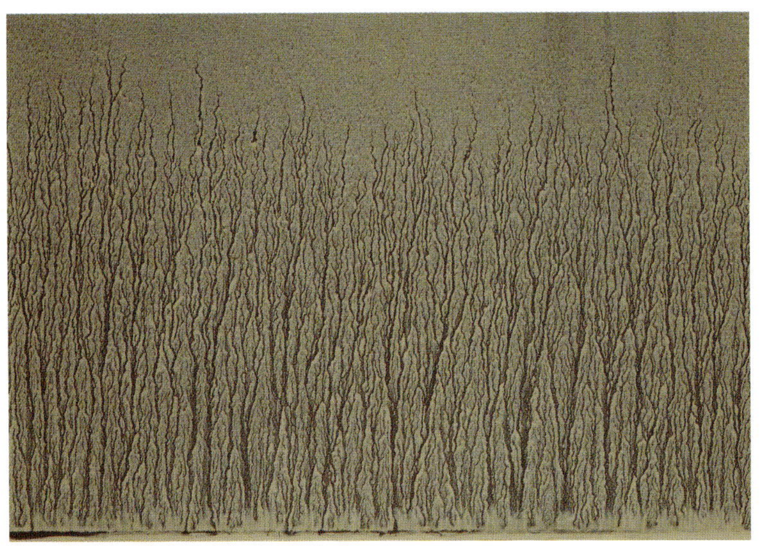

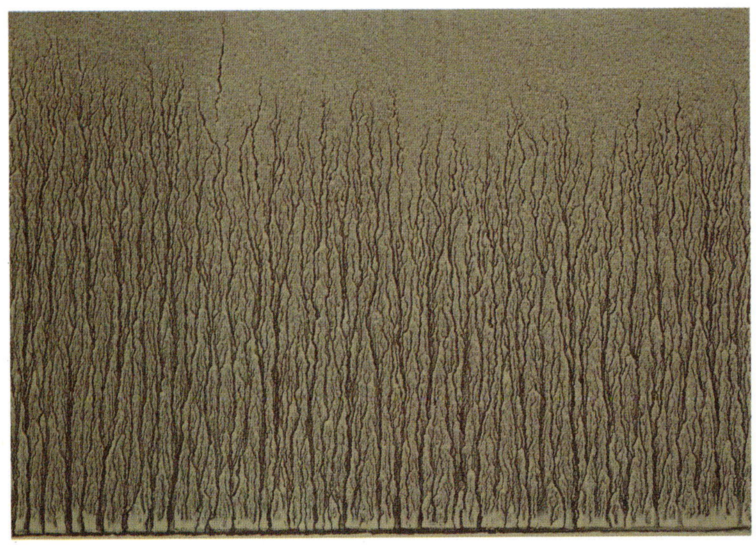

203 Richard Long ■
River Avon Mud Drawings, 1989
Mappe mit 1 Serigraphie (Titelblatt) und 3 Granolithographien, 65 x 96 cm. Auflage: 60
Set of 1 silkscreen (title page) and 3 grano lithographs, 25½ x 37½ in. Edition: 60

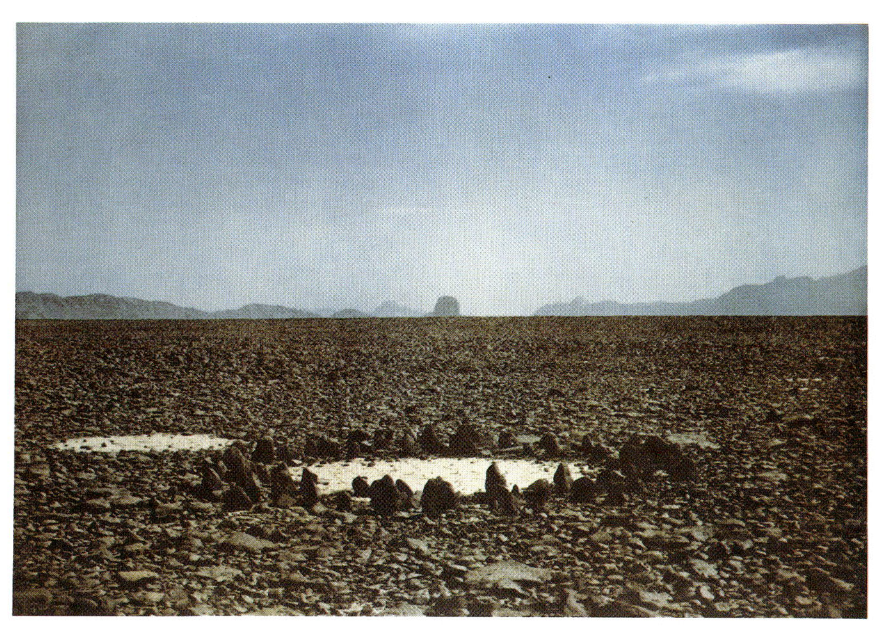

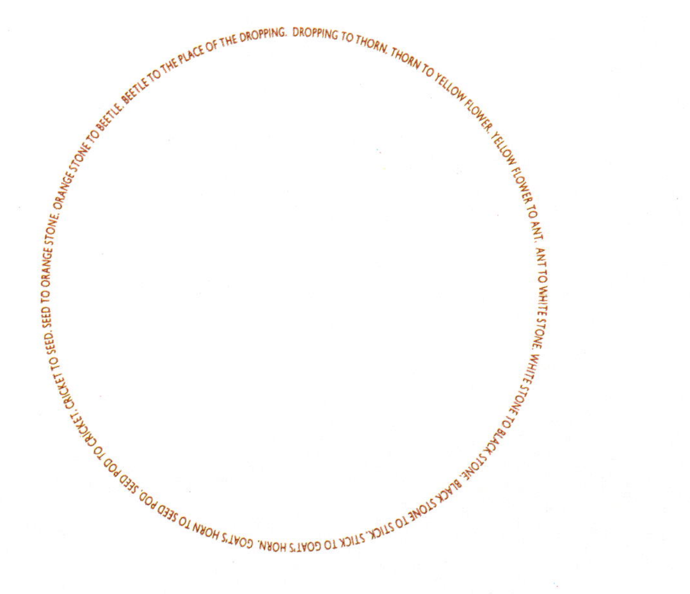

204 Richard Long □
Two Sahara Works, 1988
1 Granolithographie und 1 Serigraphie, 63 x 93 cm. Auflage: 75
Set of 1 grano lithograph and 1 silkscreen. 24¾ x 36½ in. Edition: 75

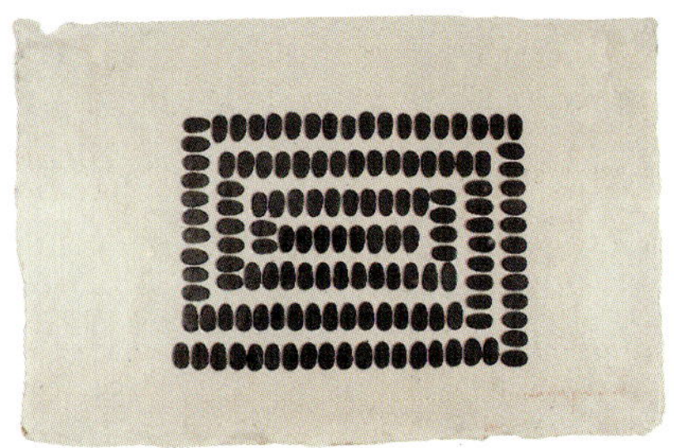
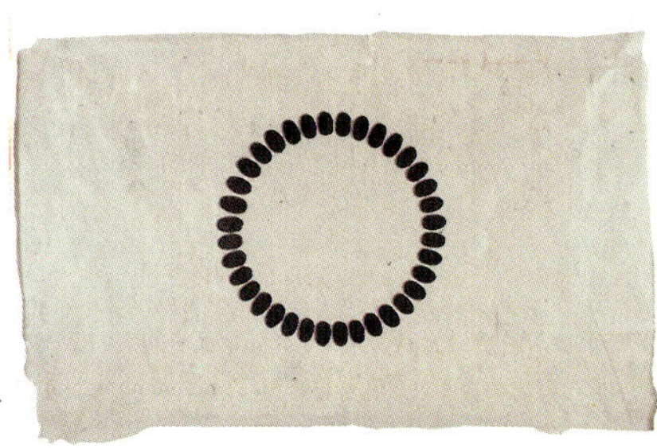
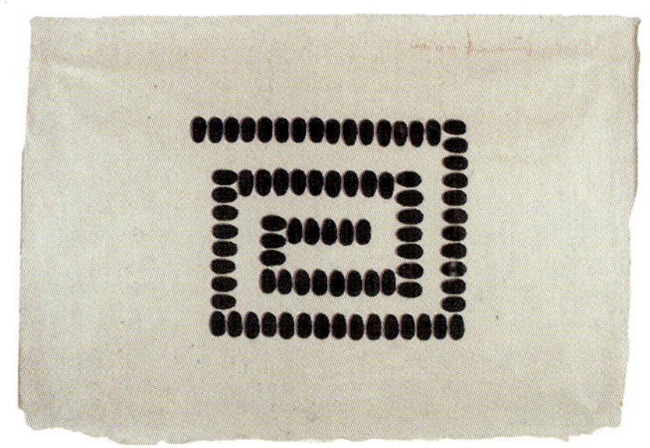
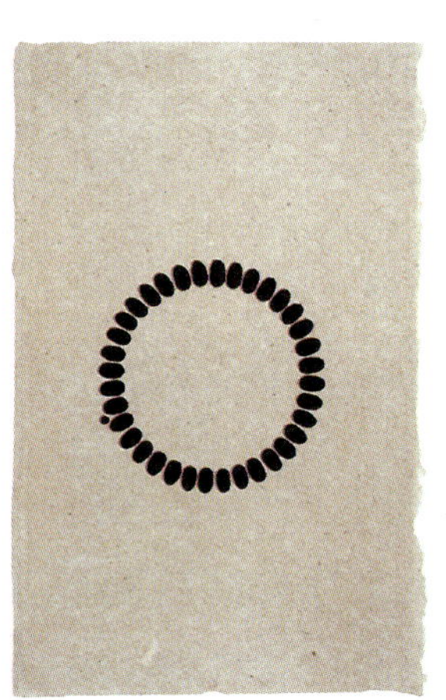
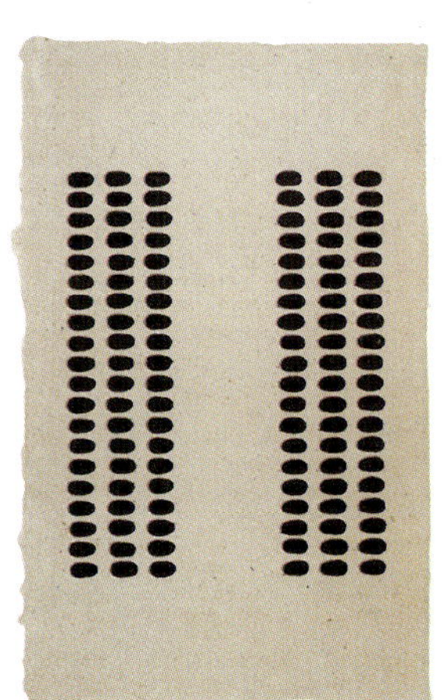
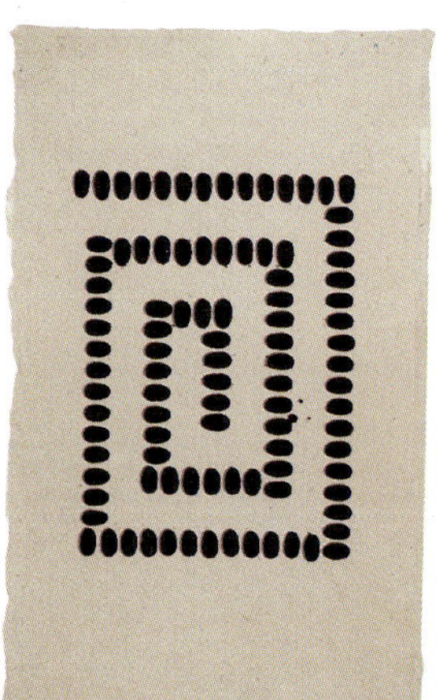

205 Richard Long
Untitled, 1994
a. Drei Lithographien auf handgeshöpftes Papier, 56 x 83 cm. Auflage: 40
Suite of three lithographs printed on handmade paper, 22 x 32½ in. Edition: 40
b. Drei Lithographien auf handgeshöpftes Papier, 84 x 55 cm. Auflage: 40
Suite of three lithographs printed on handmade paper, 33 x 21½ in. Edition: 40

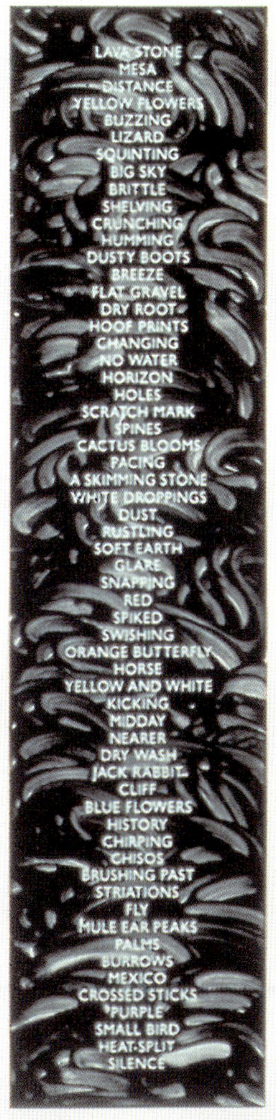

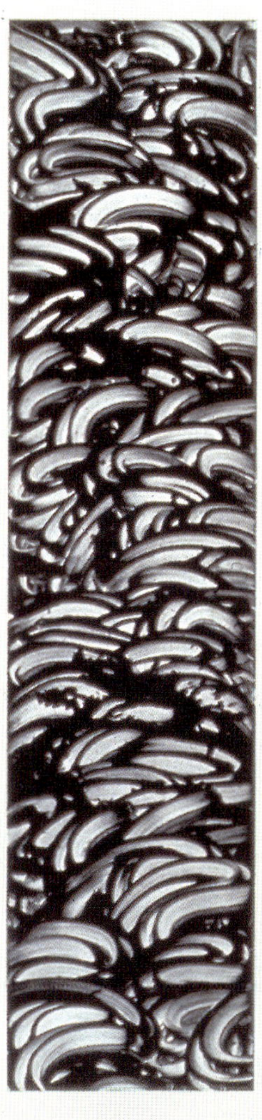

206 Richard Long
60 Minute Walk, 1990
Lithographie und Siebdruck, 188,5 x 92 cm.
Auflage: 60
Lithograph with silkscreen, 74¼ x 36¼ in.
Edition: 60

207 Richard Long
Black Dust Hand Line, 1990
Lithographie und Siebdruck, 190 x 92 cm.
Auflage: 60
Lithograph with silkscreen, 74¾ x 36¼ in.
Edition: 60

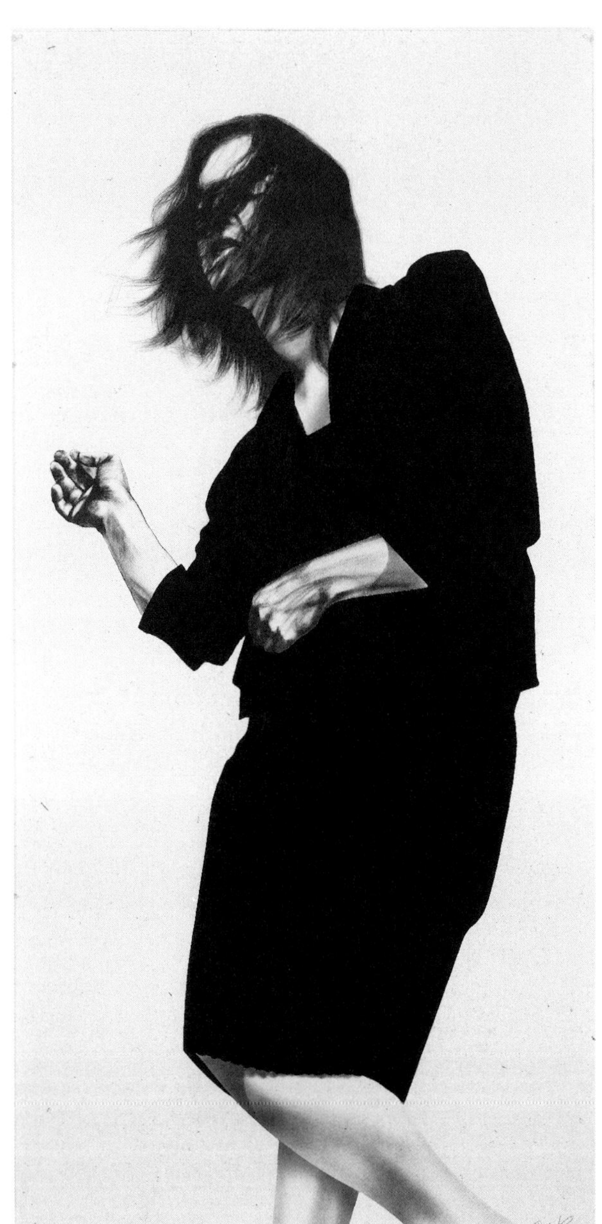

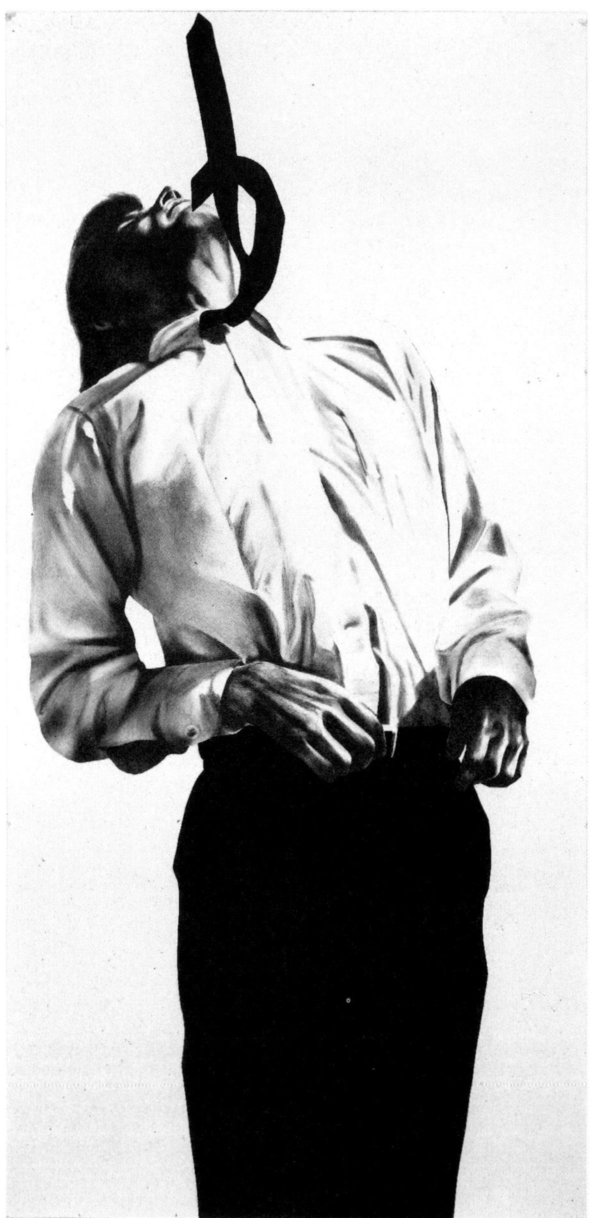

208 Robert Longo ■
Gretchen and Eric, 1985
2 Lithographien, 182 x 98 cm. Auflage: 48
2 lithographs, 72 x 38½ in. Edition: 48

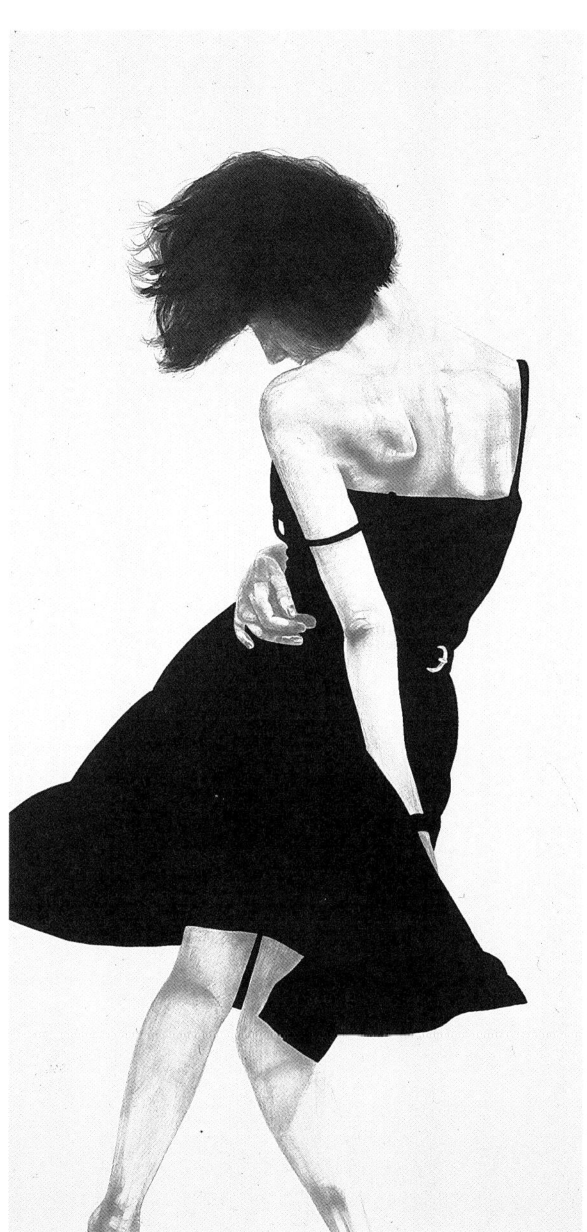

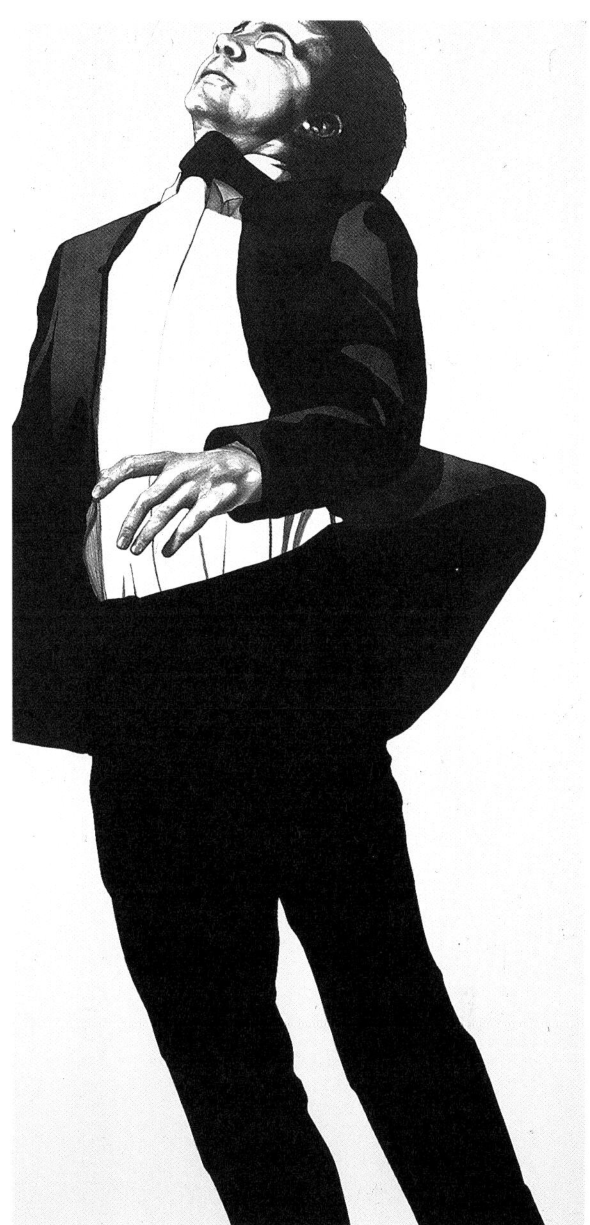

209 Robert Longo ■
Meryl and Jonathan, 1988
2 Lithographien, 182 x 98 cm. Auflage: 48
2 lithographs, 72 x 38½ in. Edition: 48

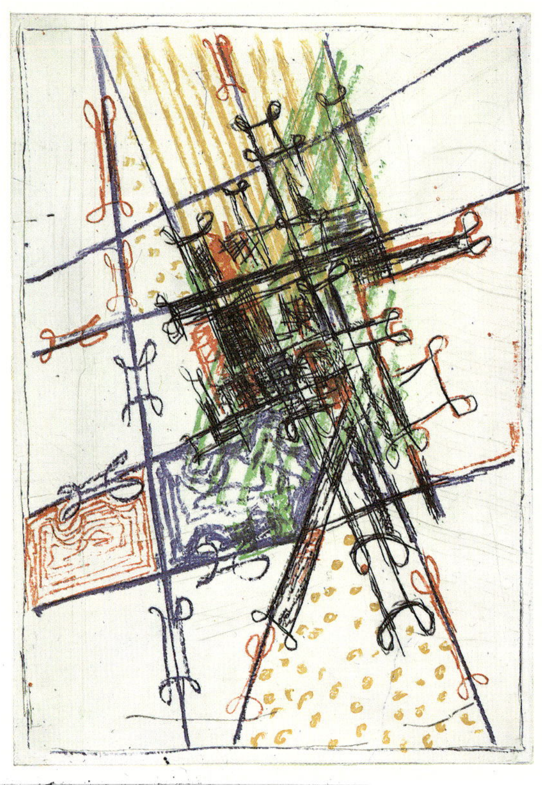

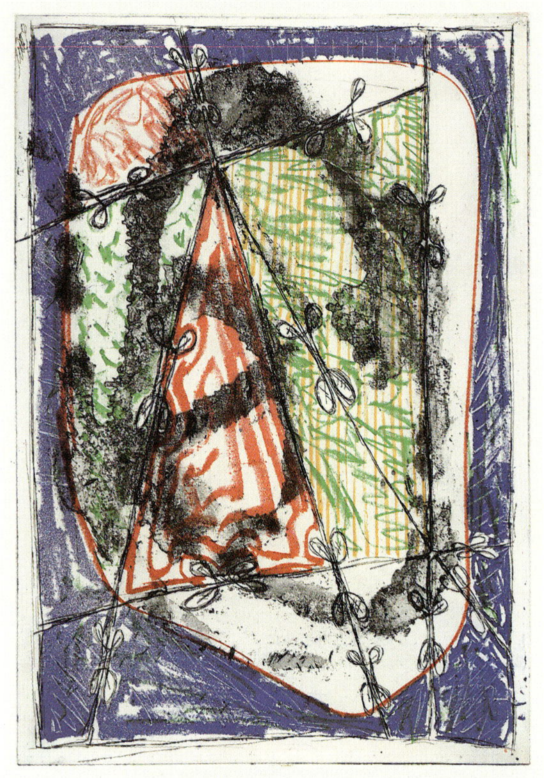

210 Markus Lüpertz
Fenster, 1993
Radierungen 90 x 68 cm. Auflage: 20
Etchings, 35½ x 26¾ in. Edition: 20

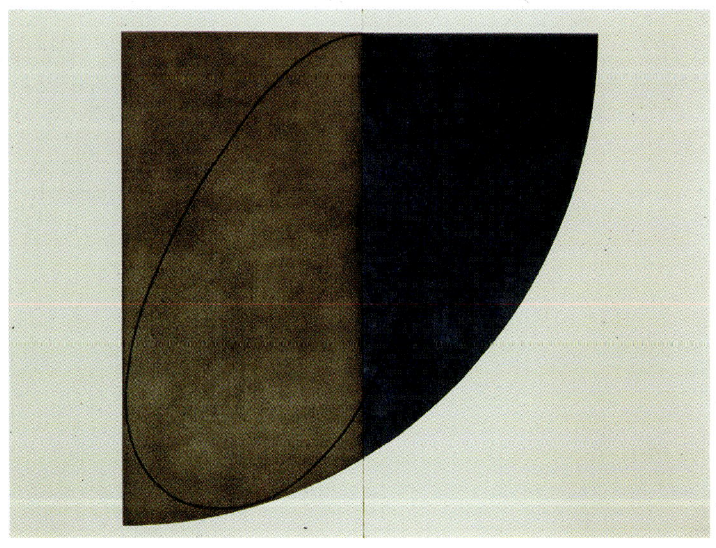

211 Robert Mangold
Curved Plane / Figure I, 1994
Radierung und Aquatinta,
108,5 x 147,5 cm. Auflage: 50
*Etching and aquatint, 42¾ x 58 in.
Edition: 50*

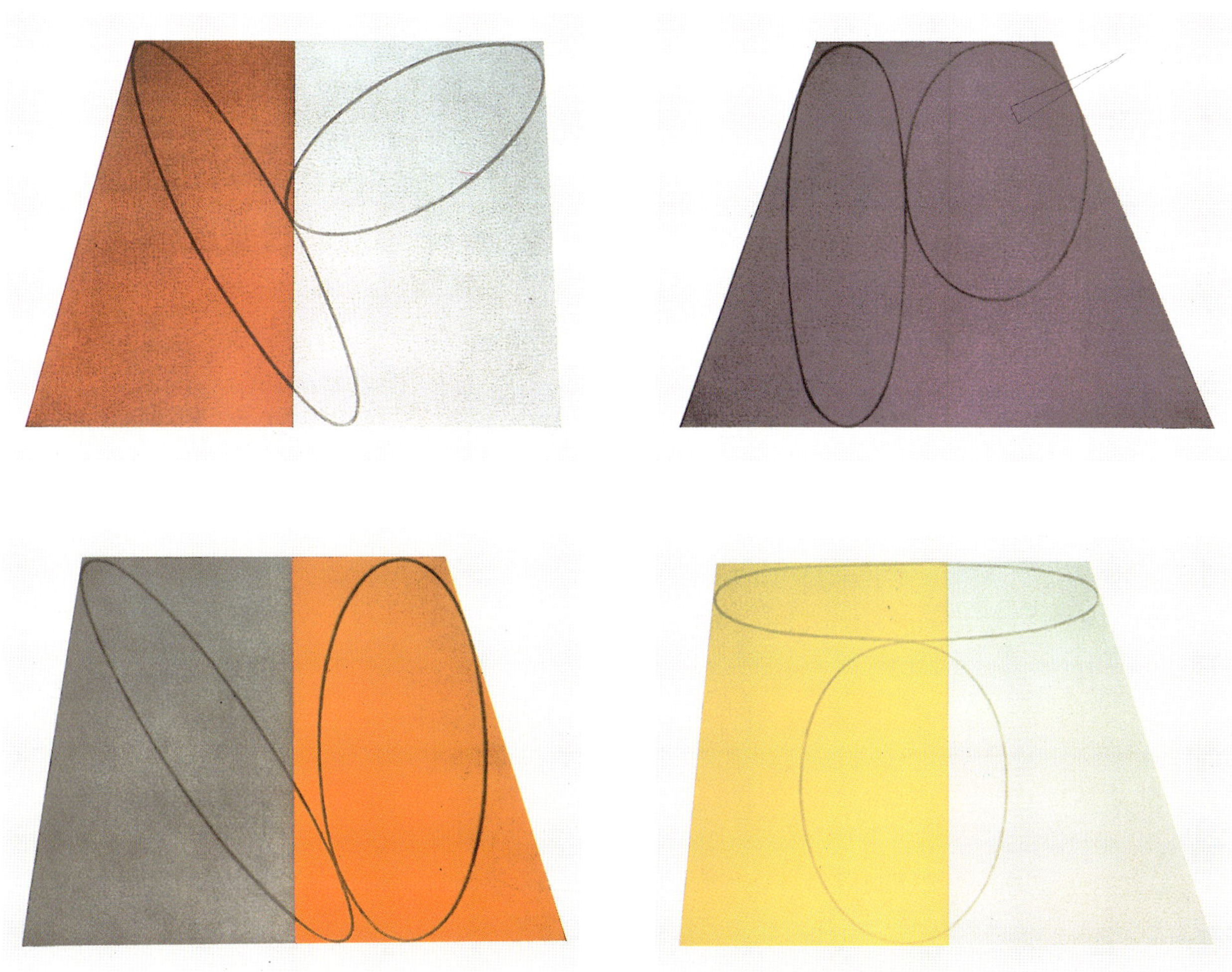

212 Robert Mangold
Plane/Figure Series, 1993
Folge von 4 Weichgrund-Radierungen mit Aquatinta, 57 x 76 cm. Auflage: 60
Suite of 4 etchings with softground and aquatint, 22½ x 30 in. Edition: 60

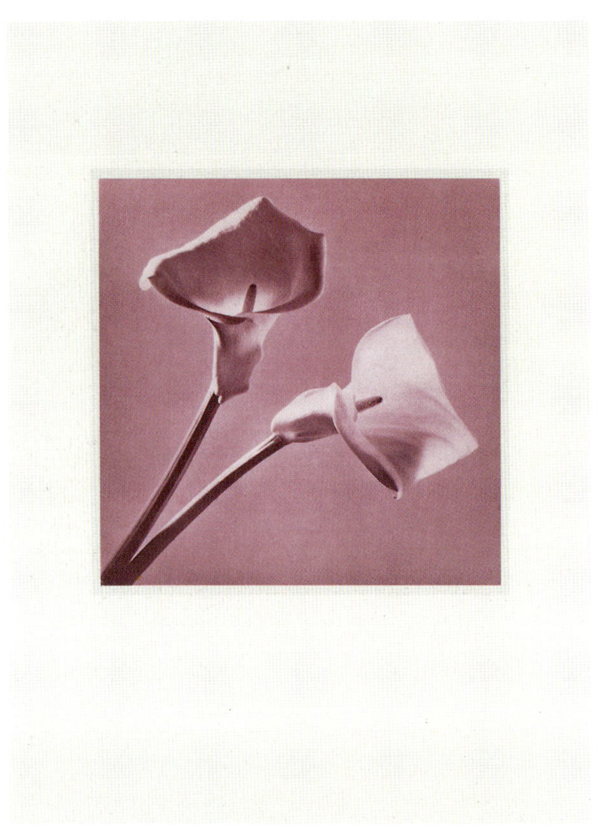

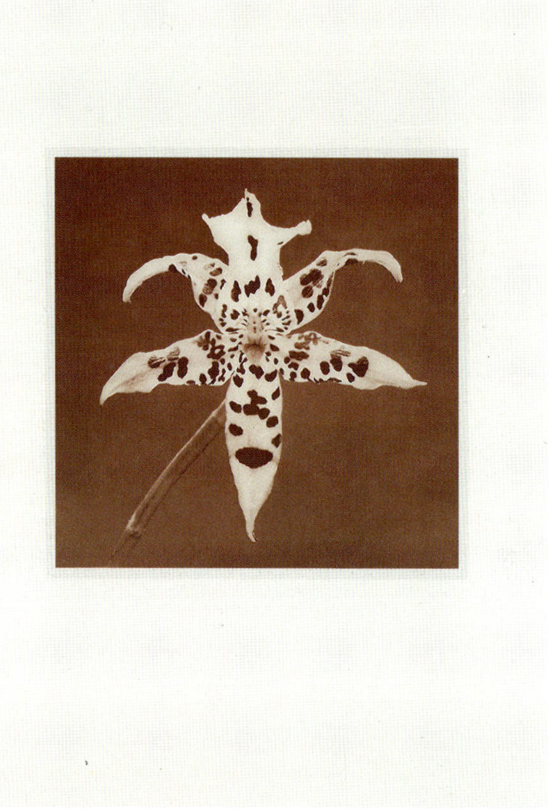

213 Robert Mapplethorpe
Flowers, 1988
Farbheliogravuren, 91 x 63 cm. Auflage: 25
Photo etchings, 36 x 25 in. Edition: 25

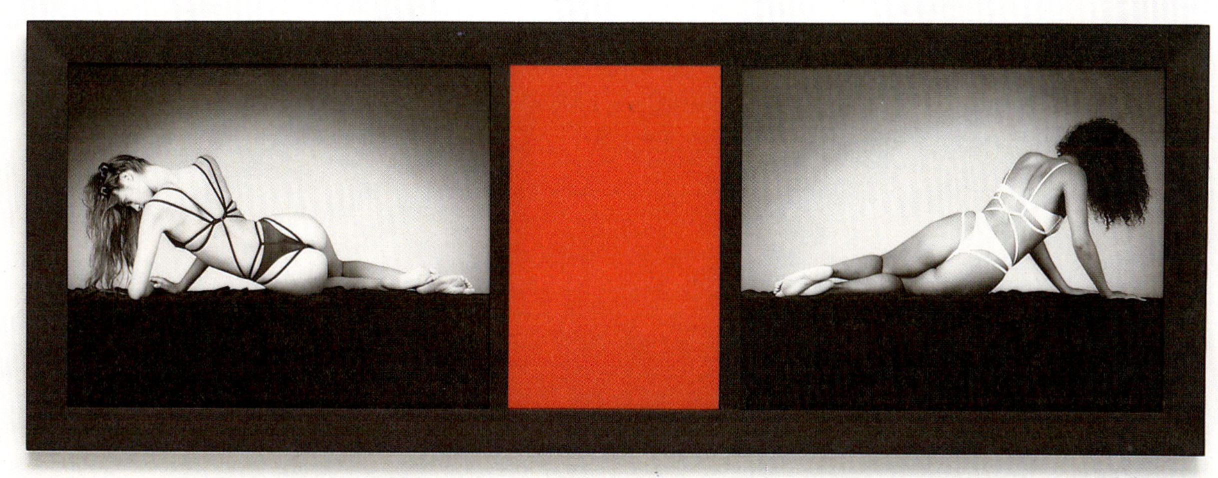

214 Robert Mapplethorpe ■
Mirror Image, 1988
2 Photographien (gelatine silver print), Plexiglas-Spiegel, in schwarz lackiertem Holzrahmen, 48,3 x 134,6 x 2,5 cm. Auflage: 18
Two laminated silver prints surrounding mirrored plexi, in a black wooden frame, 19 x 53 x 1 in. Edition: 18

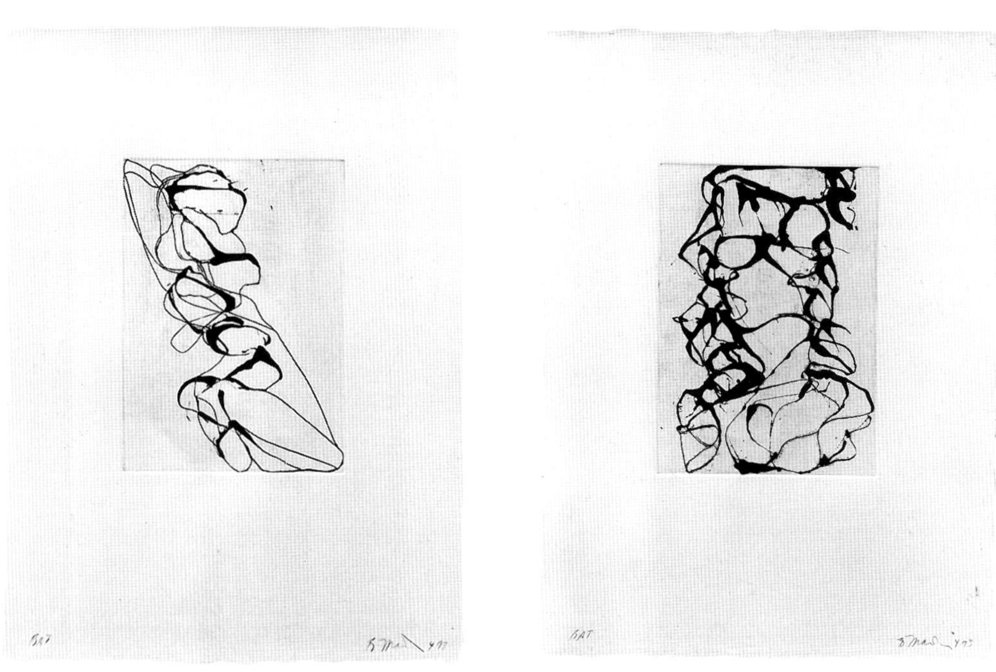

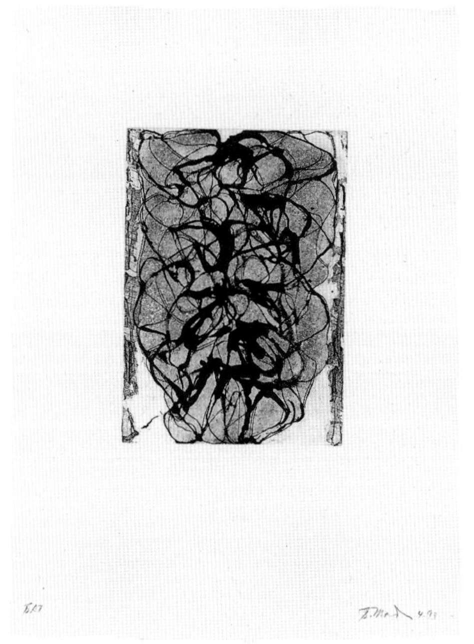

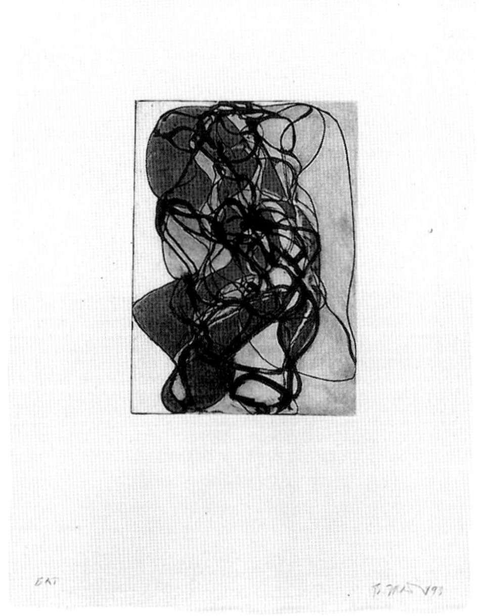

215 Brice Marden
Han Shan Exit 1-6, 1992-93
Mappe mit 6 Radierungen/Aquatinta, 38 x 28,5 cm. Auflage: 45
Suite of 6 etchings with aquatint, 15 x 11¼ in. Edition: 45

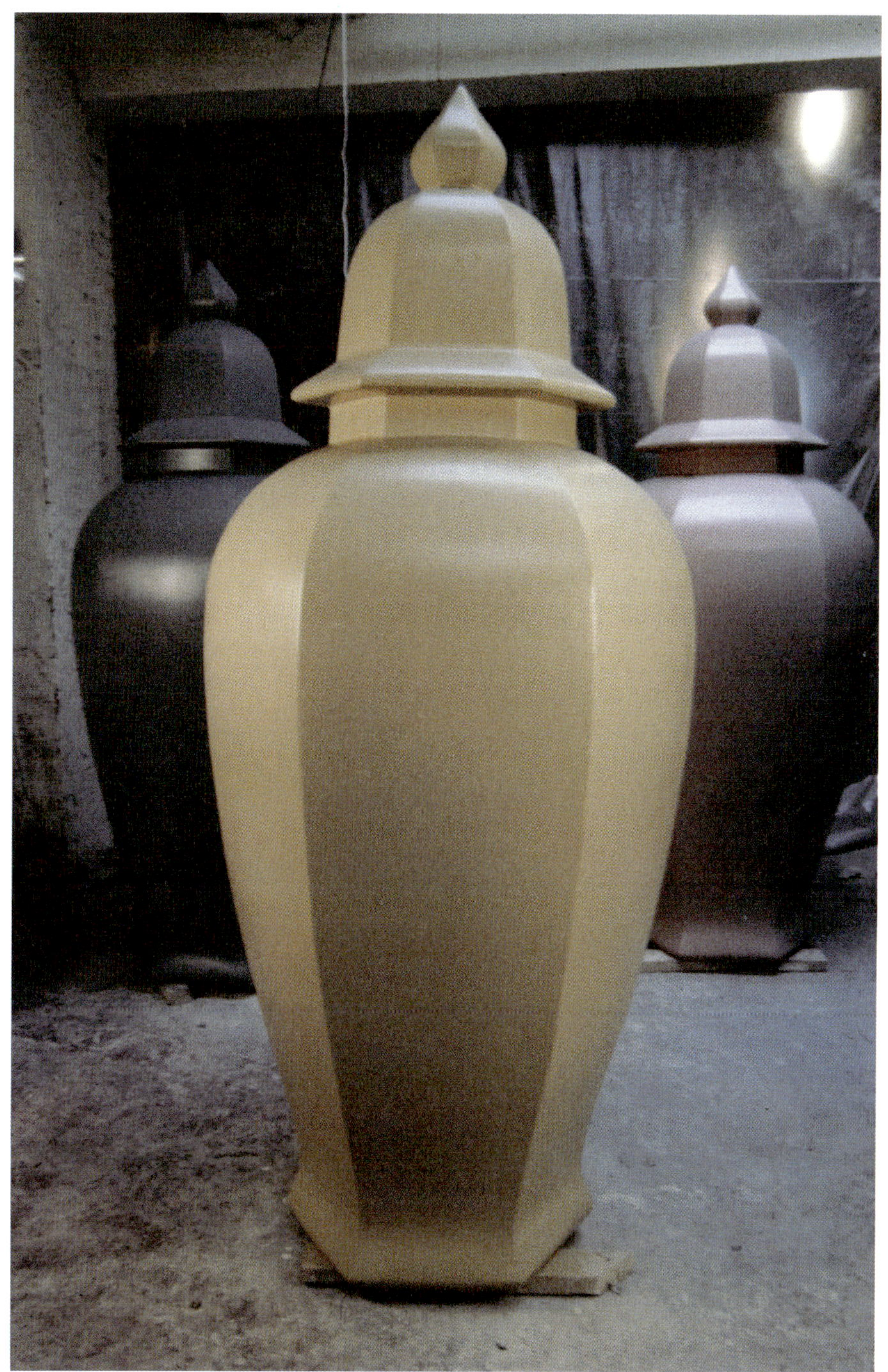

216 Allan McCollum
Perfect Vehicle, 1989-90
Acryl auf Zement, 198 x 91,5 cm. Unlimitierte Auflage, jedes Exemplar in einer anderen Farbe.
Acrylic on cement, 78 x 36 in. Unlimited edition, each piece comes in a different color.

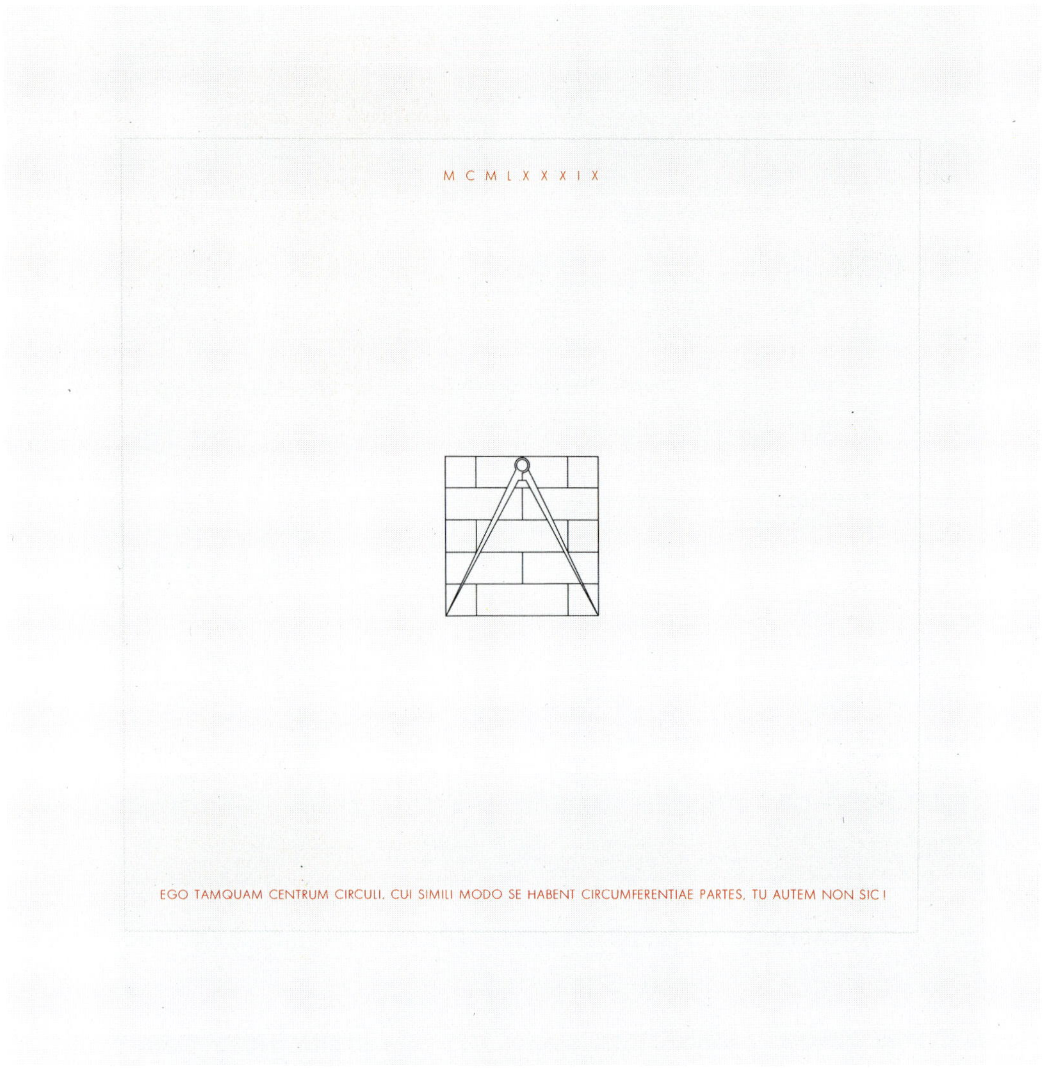

217 Gerhard Merz ■
Costruire, 1990
Zinkätzung, 82 x 83 cm. Auflage: 60
Etching, 32 x 32½ in. Edition: 60

218 Gerhard Merz ■ →
Architekturen, 1992
Mappe mit 3 Serigraphien und 3 Duotone Offsetlithographien, 48 x 65 cm. Auflage: 40
Portfolio of 3 silkscreens and 3 duotone offset prints, 19 x 25½ in. Edition: 40

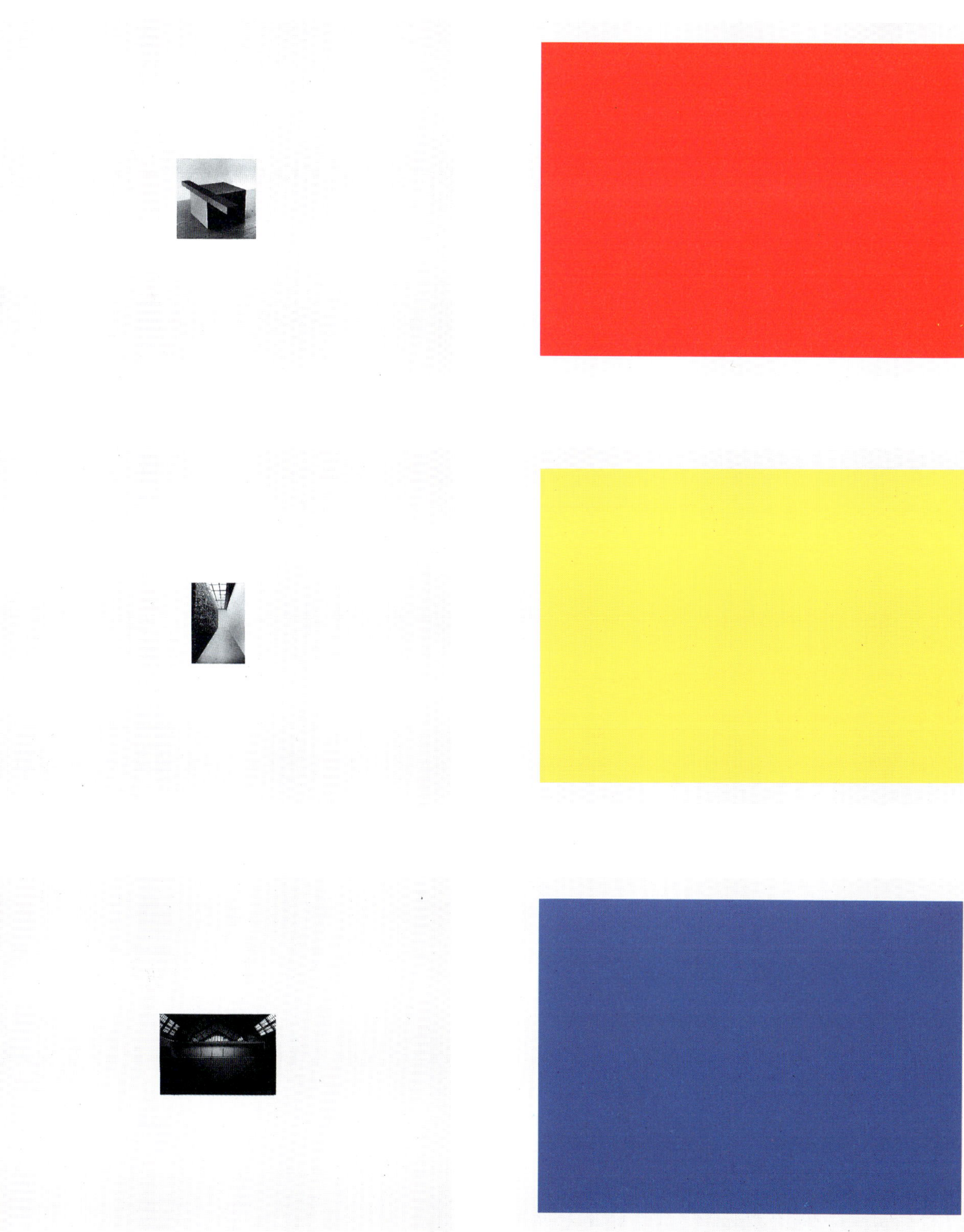

R E V O L U T I O N Ä R

■

K L A S S I S C H

■

R A T I O N A L

■

Ü B E R L E G E N

■

A R I S T O K R A T I S C H

■

R E A K T I O N Ä R

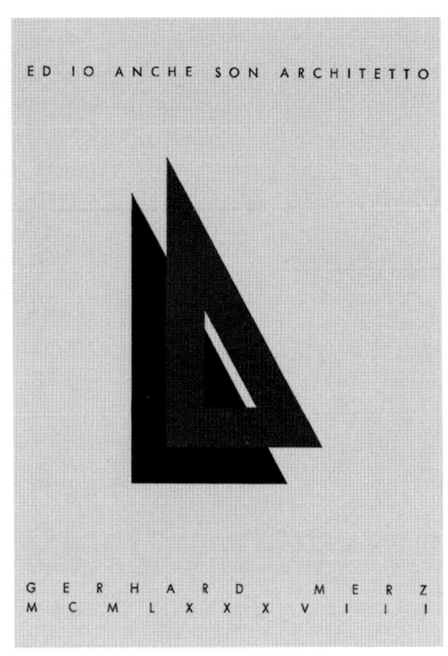

219 Gerhard Merz □
Revolutionär klassisch rational ... ,
1988
Offsetlithographie auf Bütten,
70 x 50 cm. Auflage: 50.
Offset lithograph on rag paper,
27½ x 19¾ in. Edition: 50

220 Gerhard Merz □
Ed io anche son architetto,
1988
Siebdruck auf Transparentpapier,
70 x 50 cm. Auflage: 75
Silkscreen on transparent paper,
27½ x 19¾ in. Edition: 75

221 Gerhard Merz ■ →
Costruire, 1991
Aluminium eloxiert, 90 x 90 x 6 cm und 180 x 6 x 6 cm. Auflage: 5 schwarz, 5 blau, 5 rot
Anodized aluminum, 35½ x 35½ x 2½ in. 71 x 2½ x 2½ in. Edition: 5 in black, 5 in blue, 5 in red

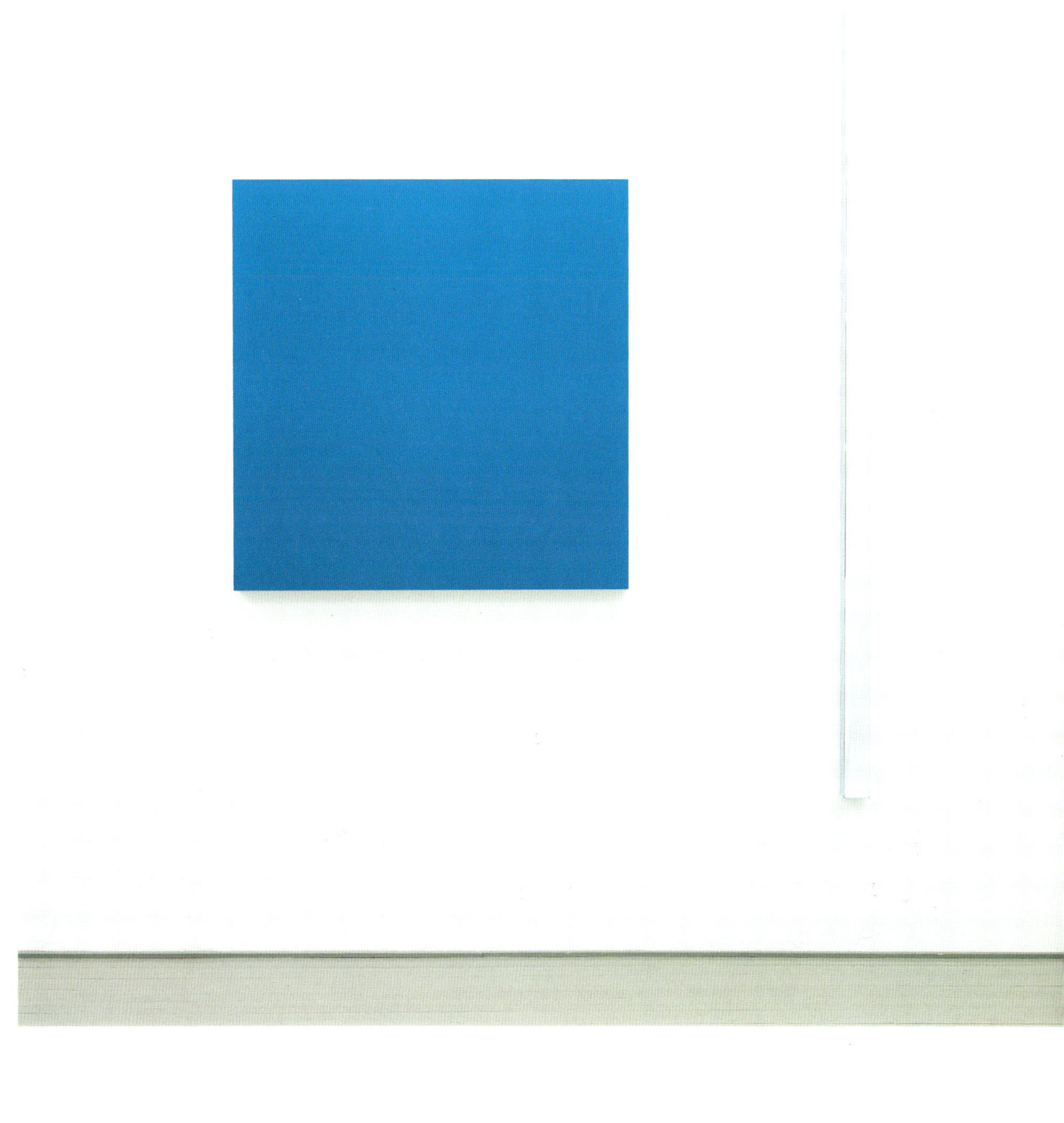

COSTRUIRE

MCMLXXXIX

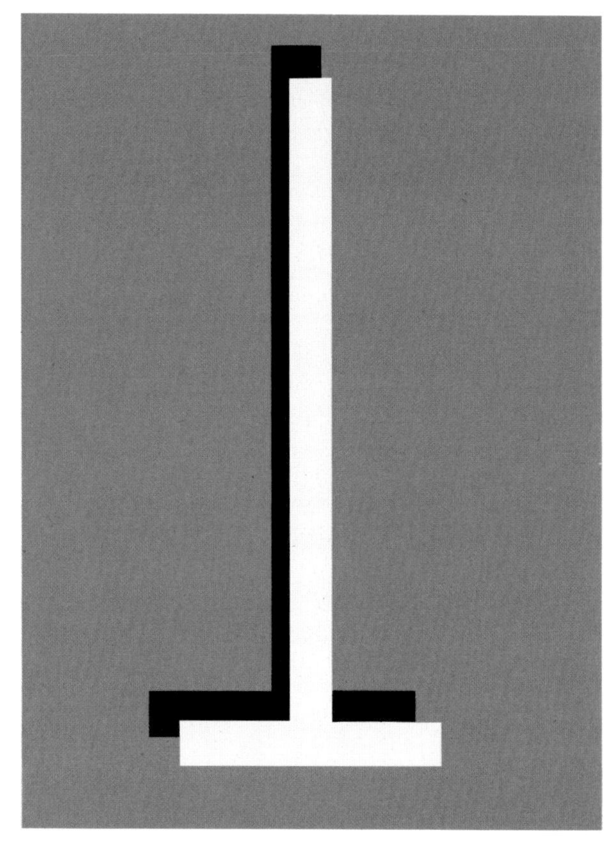

222 Gerhard Merz ■
Ed io anche son architetto, 1989
Mappe mit 3 Aquatintaradierungen, 1 Heliogravur und 1 Offsetlithographie, 108 x 81 cm.
Auflage: 30 gedruckt in Caput mortuum, 30 gedruckt in Veronese (abgebildet)
Portfolio of 3 aquatints in colors, 1 photoetching and 1 offset print, 42½ x 32 in.
Edition: 30 printed in caput mortuum and 30 printed in veronese (ill.)

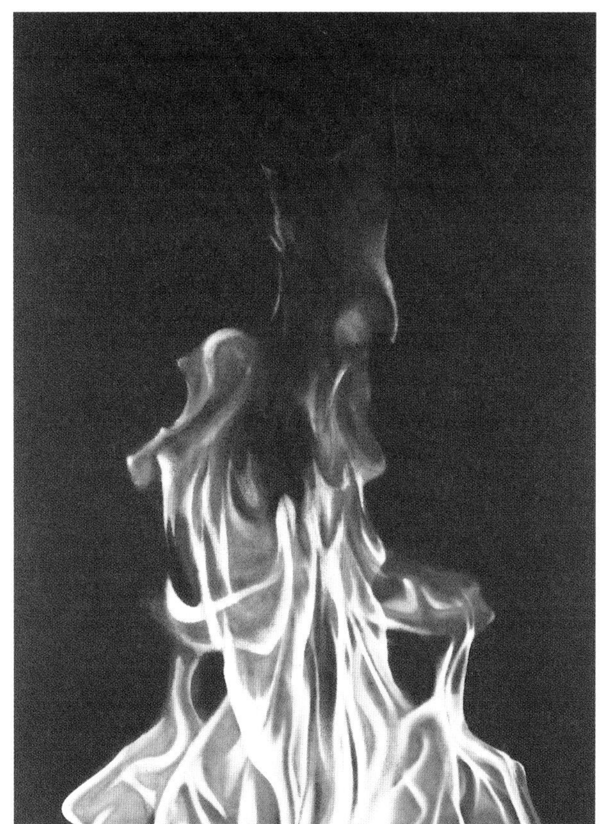

DEN MENSCHEN DER ZUKUNFT

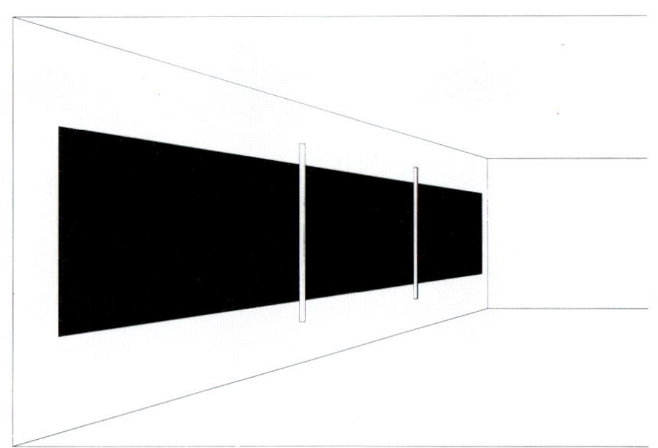

223 Gerhard Merz ■
Den Menschen der Zukunft, 1990
Mappe mit 4 Lithographien, 1 Offsetlithographie
und 1 Blatt Pigment auf Bütten, 56 x 80 cm. Auflage: 45
Portfolio with 4 lithographs, 1 offset lithograph
and 1 handpainted gouache, 22 x 31 ½ in. Edition: 45

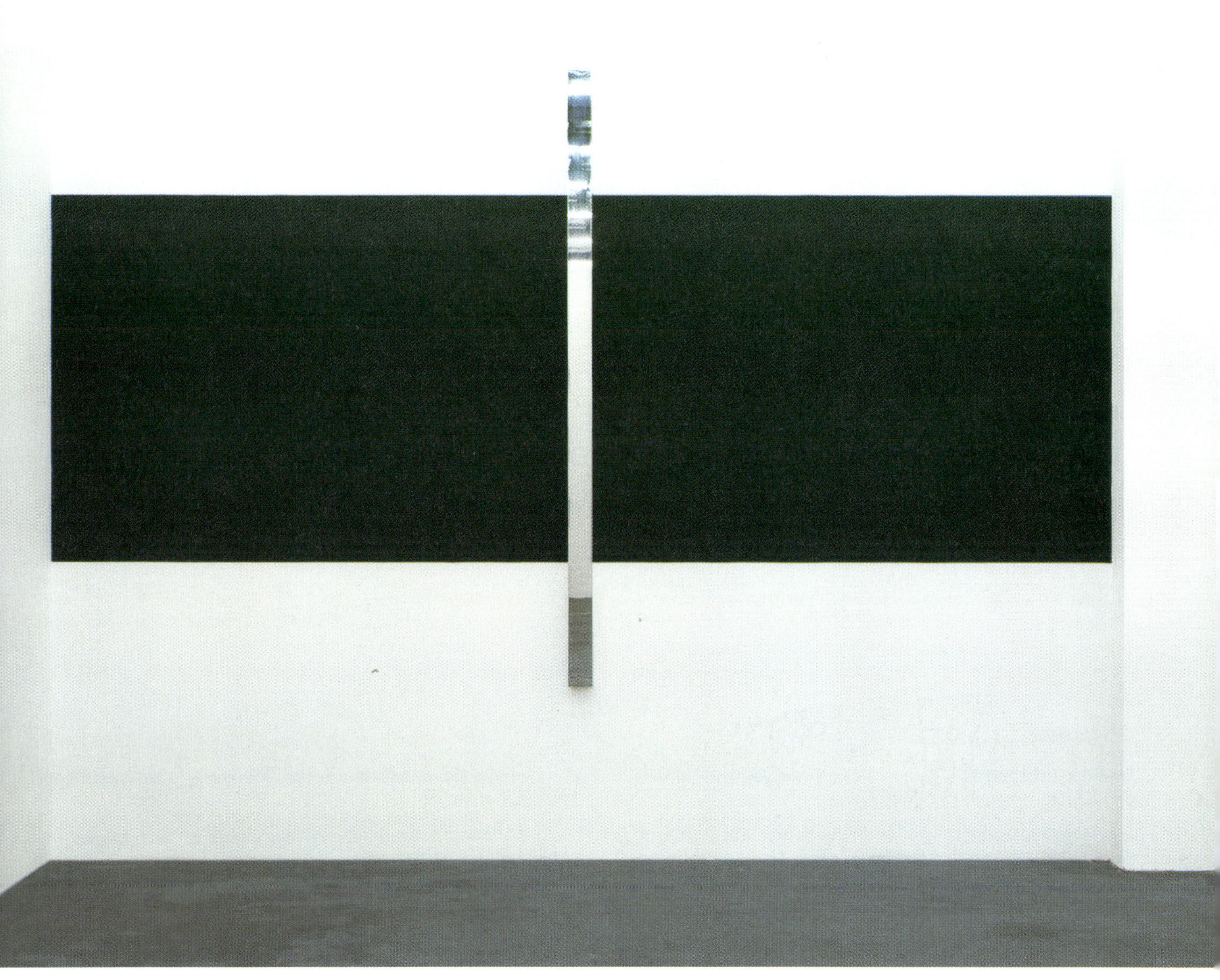

224 Gerhard Merz ■
Ohne Titel, 1993
Wandmalerei (Pigment kobaltgrün), Edelstahl poliert 250 x 10 x 10 cm, zu installieren nach den Anweisungen des Künstlers, siehe Appendix. Gesamtmaße variabel. Auflage: 10, mit sign. und num. Zertifikat
Wall painting in cobalt green pigment, polished stainless steel, 98 ½ x 4 x 4 in. to be installed according to the artist's instructions, see appendix. Overall size of the work variable. Edition: 10, with a signed and numbered certificate

225 Gerhard Merz ■
Ohne Titel, 1994
Leuchtstoffröhren Lumilux 11, weiß, 60 cm, auf die Länge einer Wand (Maß variabel);
MDF, grau lackiert, 204 x 54 x 3 cm, auf Mitte einer anderen Wand. Auflage: 4
Lumilux 11 white fluorescent lights, 24 in. high, width of one given wall (variable);
and hardboard, painted grey, 80 x 21 x 1 in. centered on another wall. Edition: 4

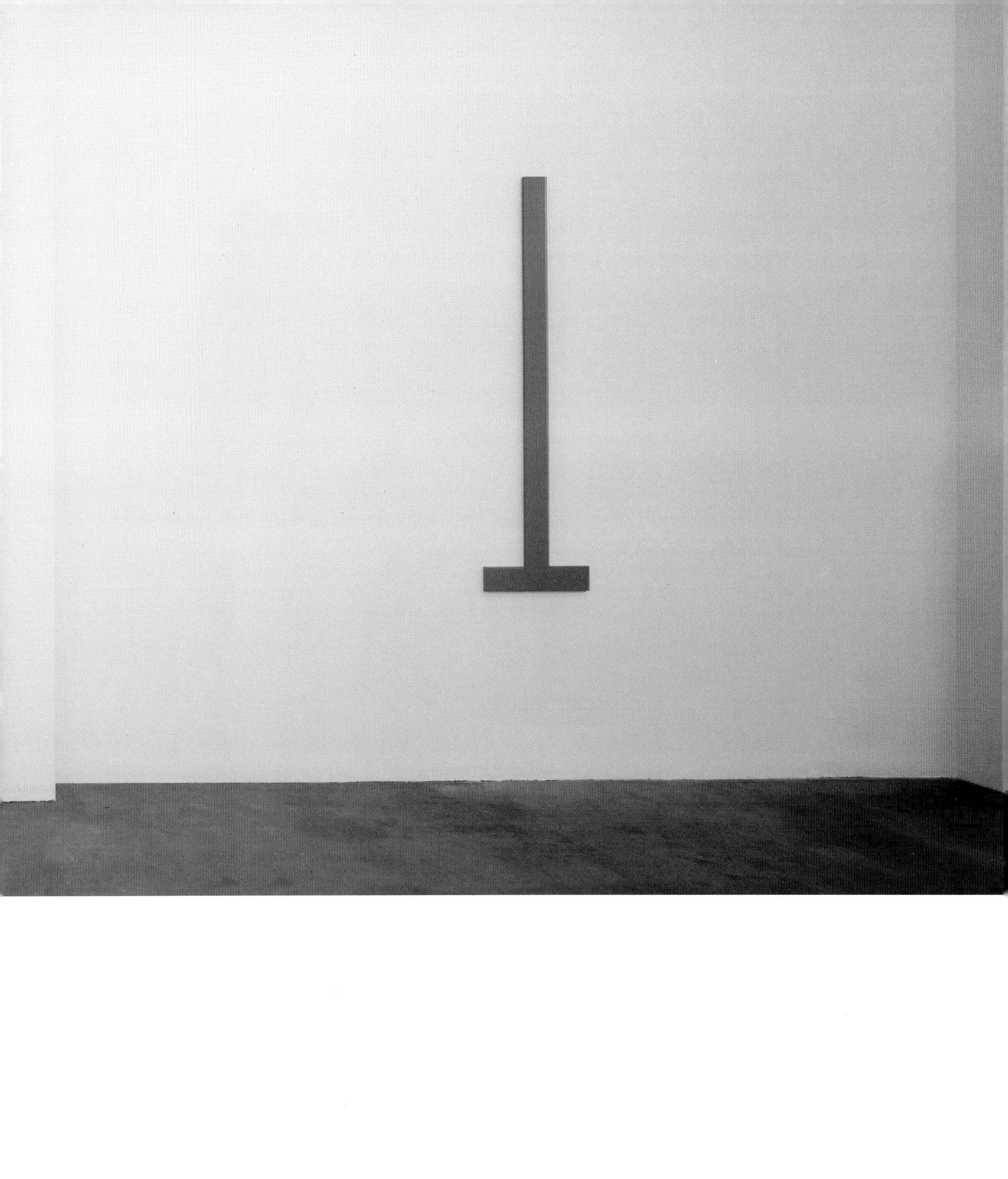

226 Gerhard Merz ■
Ohne Titel, 1994
Wandobjekt. MDF, grau lackiert, 204 x 54 x 2 cm. Auflage: 10
Wall object. Hardboard, painted grey, 80¼ x 21¼ x ¾ in. Edition: 10

227 Mario Merz
Macerata, 1974
Mappe mit 4 Lithographien, 70 x 90 cm. Auflage: 125
Portfolio with 4 lithographs, 27½ x 35½ in. Edition: 125

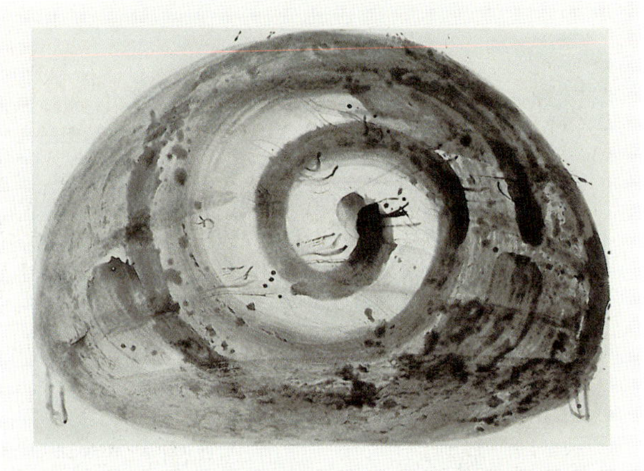
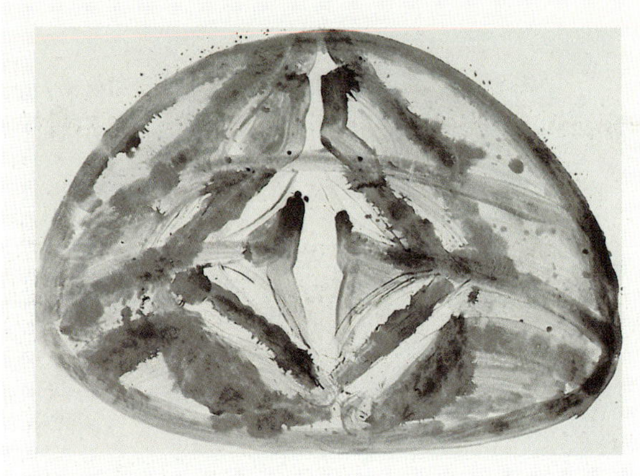
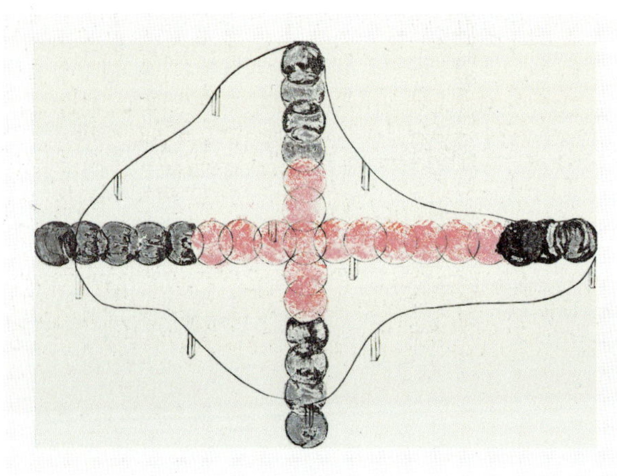

228 Mario Merz
O.T., 1993
Radierungen, 81 x 110 cm. Auflage: 20
Etchings, 32 x 43¼ in. Edition: 20

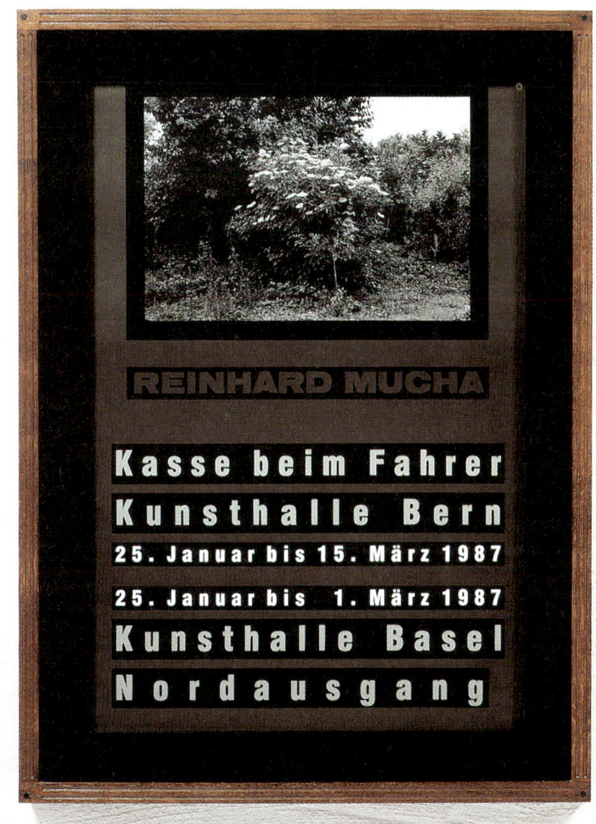

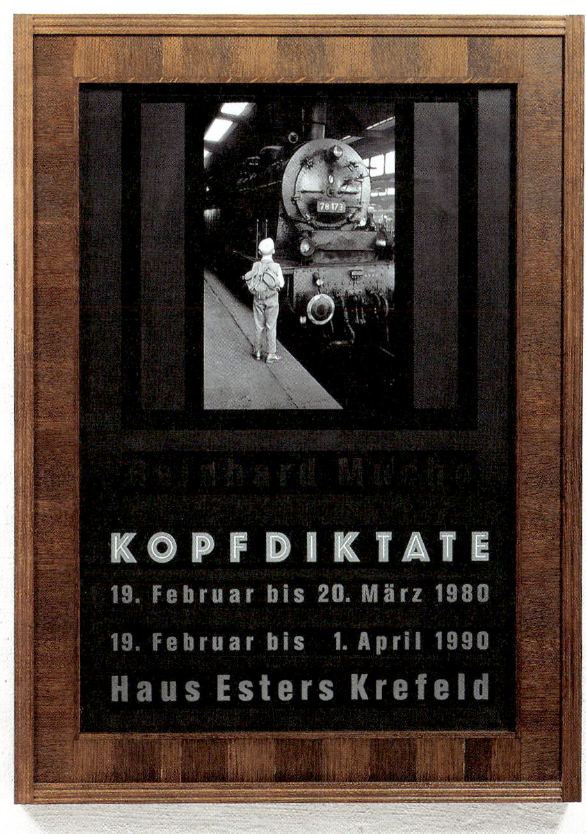

229A Reinhard Mucha
BBK Edition, 1990
2 Plakatdrucke in Vitrinen (Holz gebeizt, Glas), je115 x 87 x 6 cm. Auflage:25
2 posters in vitrines (stained wood, glass), 45¼ x 34½ x 2½ in. ea. Edition: 25

229B Reinhard Mucha [nicht abgebildet / *not illustrated*] ■
SL Edition, 1995
2 Offsetdrucke in Vitrinen (Eiche gebeizt, Glas), je115 x 87 x 6 cm. Auflage: 27
[bitte Abbildung anfordern!]
2 offset prints, in vitrines (stained oak, glass), 45¼ x 34½ x 2½ in. ea. Edition: 27
[please ask for visuals!]

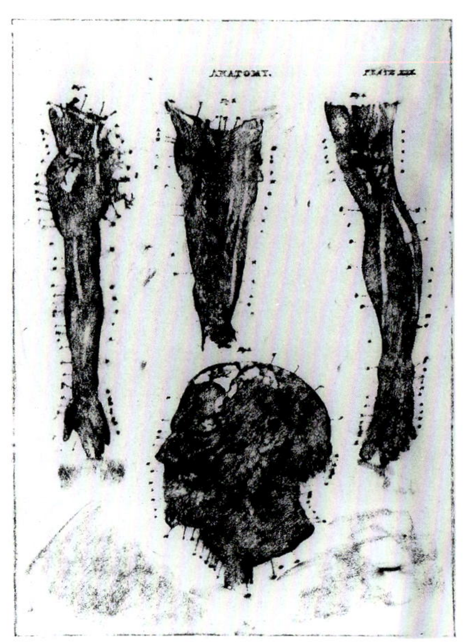

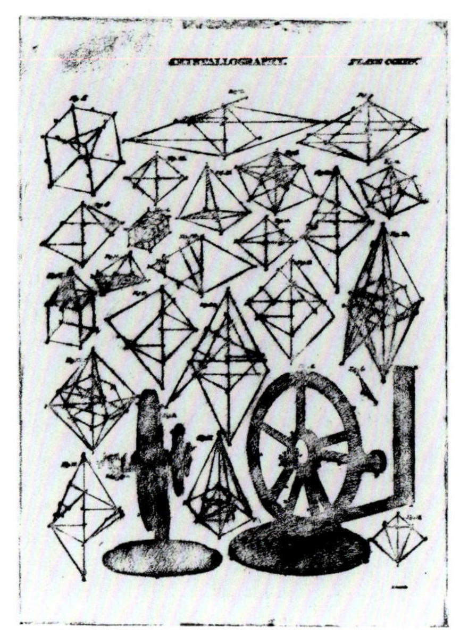

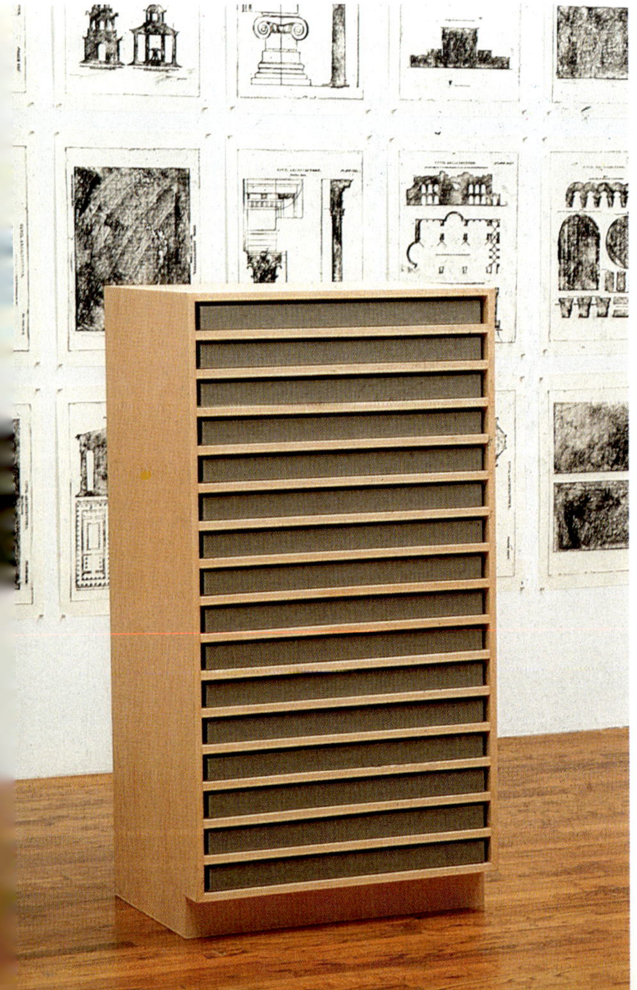

230 Matt Mullican
Untitled, 1990-91
449 Ölkreide-Frottagen, in 16 Kästen,
in Holzschrank, 144 x 77,5 x 65 cm.
Auflage: 16
449 black oilstick on paper rubbings in 16 boxes in wood cabinet, 56¾ x 30½ x 22 in. Edition: 16

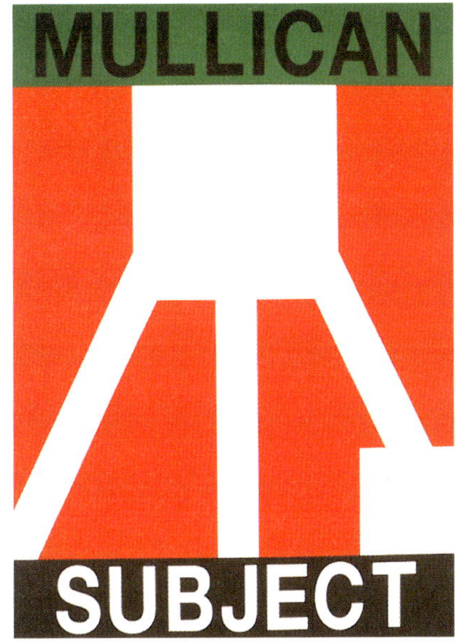

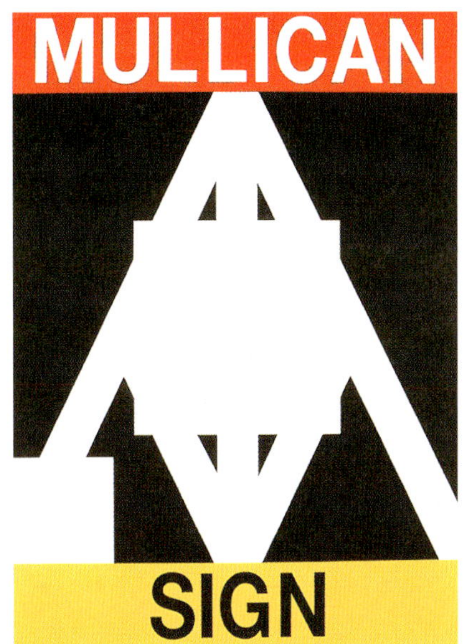

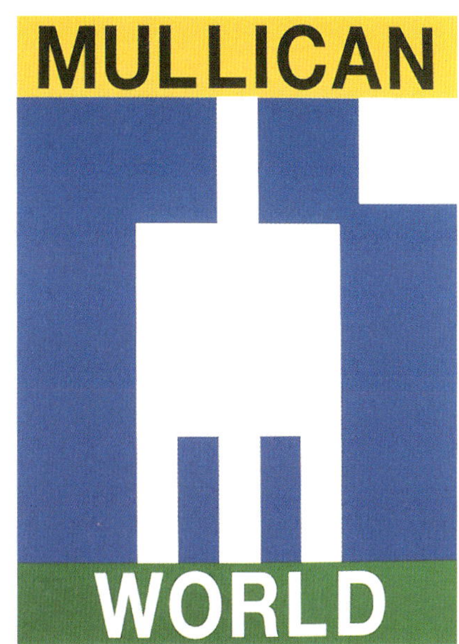

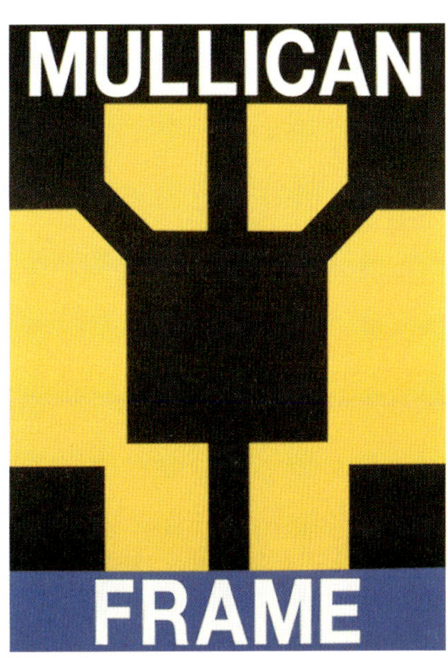

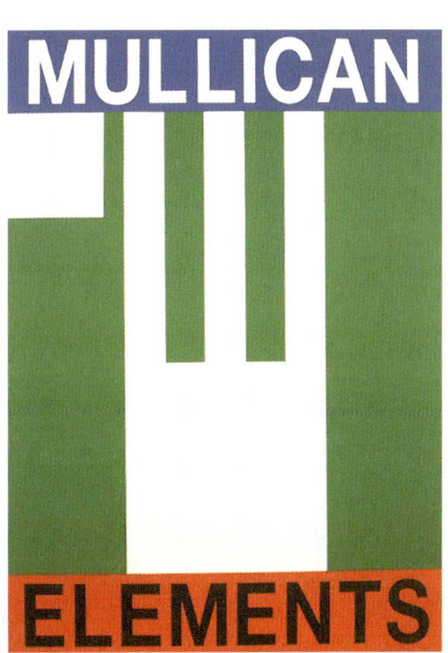

231 Matt Mullican
Subject, Sign, World, Frame, Elements, 1992
Suite von 5 Serigraphien auf Rives Bütten, 94 x 69 cm. Auflage: 15
Suite of 5 screenprints on Rives BFK, 37 x 27¼ in. Edition: 15

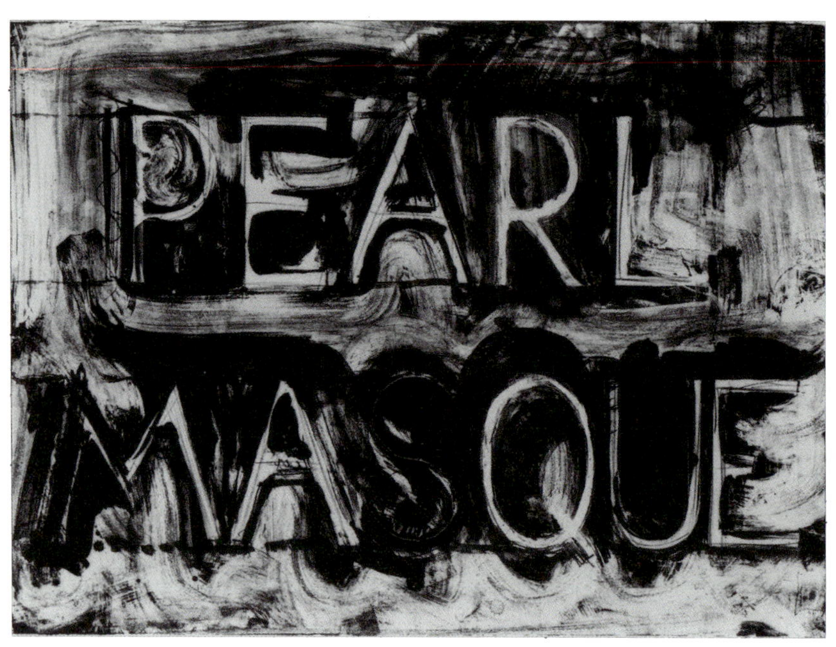

232 Bruce Nauman
Pearl Masque, 1981
Lithographie auf Bütten,
72,5 x 95,5 cm. Auflage: 50
Lithograph on rag paper,
28½ x 37½ in. Edition: 50

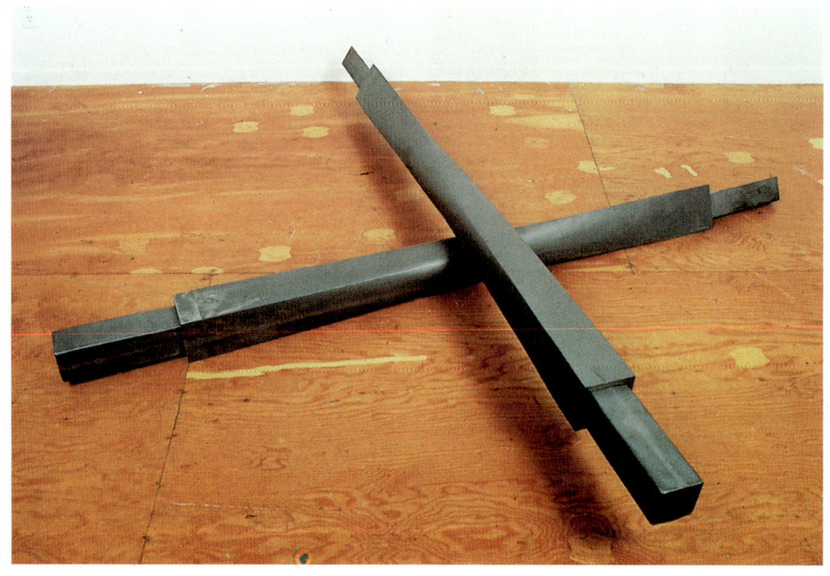

233 Bruce Nauman
Untitled, 1983
Gußeisen, 13 x 219 x 12,5 cm.
Auflage: 25
Cast iron bars, 5¼ x 86¼ x 5 in.
Edition: 25

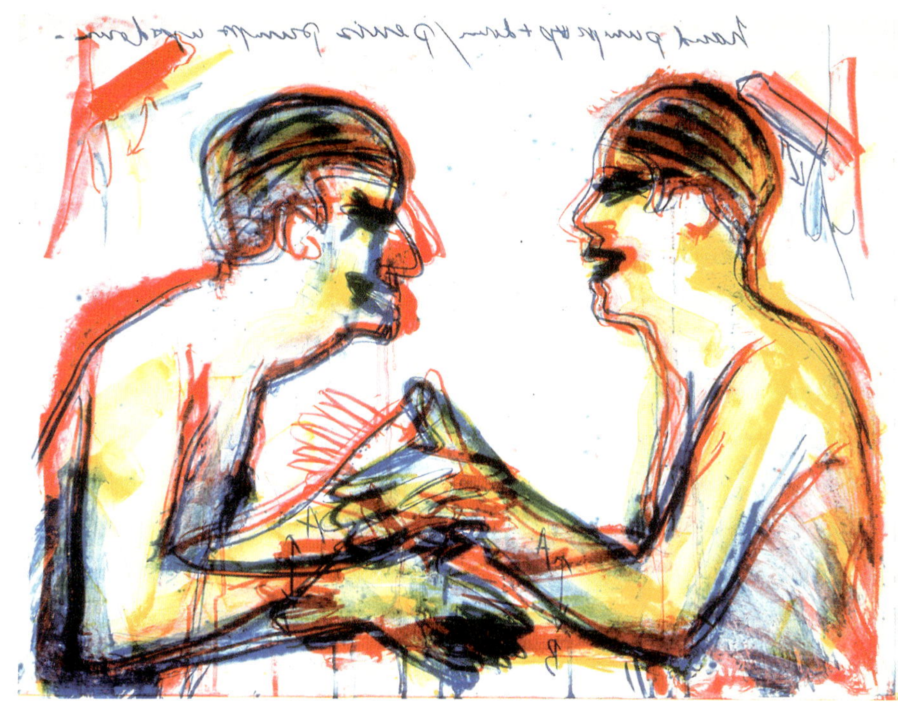

234 Bruce Nauman
Untitled, 1994
Lithographie, 76 x 102 cm.
Auflage: 50
Lithograph, 40 x 30 in.
Edition: 50

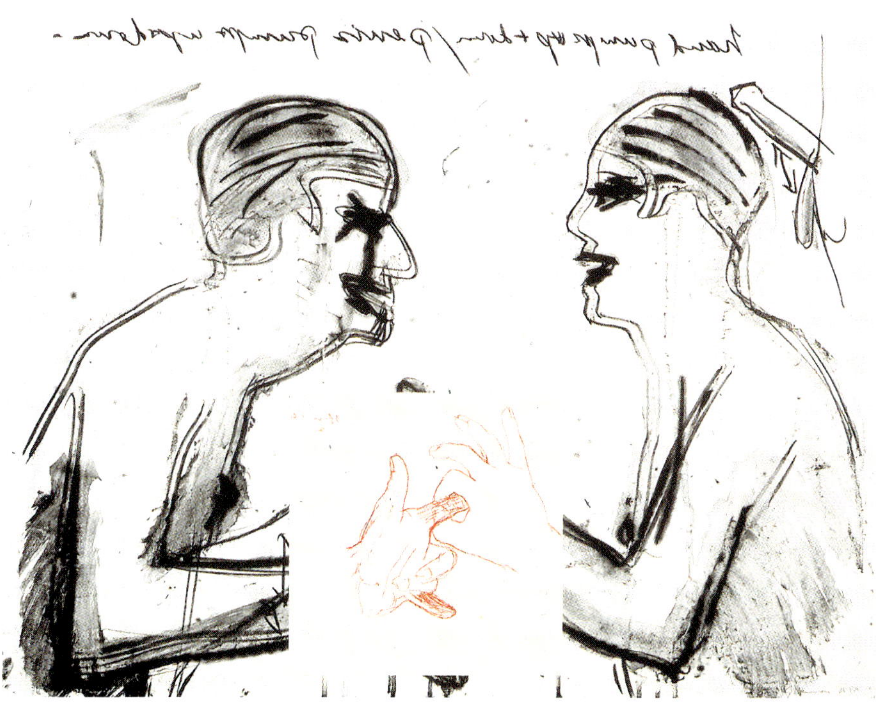

235 Bruce Nauman
Untitled, 1994
Lithographie/Siebdruck, 76 x 102 cm.
Auflage: 50
Lithograph/silkscreen, 40 x 30 in.
Edition: 50

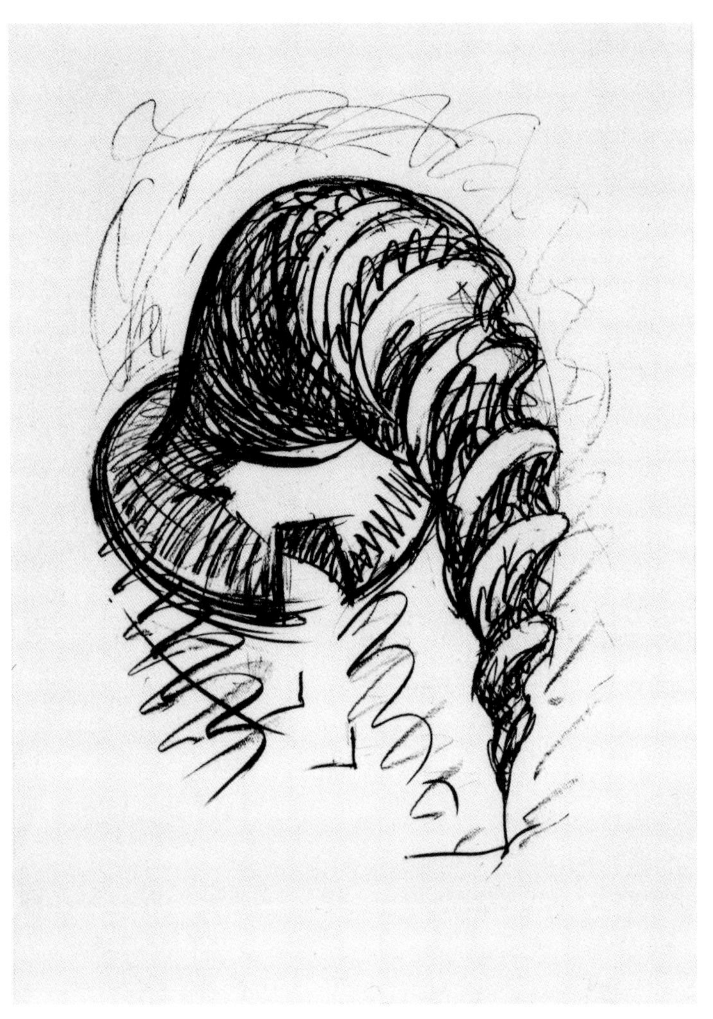

236 Claes Oldenburg
Arched Soft Screw as Building, 1976
Lithographie, 171,5 x 114 cm. Auflage: 35
Lithograph, 67½ x 45 in. Edition: 35

237 Claes Oldenburg
Miniature Soft Drum Set, 1970
Leinwand mit Siebdruck,
Wäscheleine, Holz, Sprühlack,
Holz mit Papier überzogen,
25 x 48 x 35 cm. Auflage: 200
Serigraph on canvas, washline, wood, spray enamel, wood covered with serigraphed paper, 10 x 19 x 14 in. Edition: 200

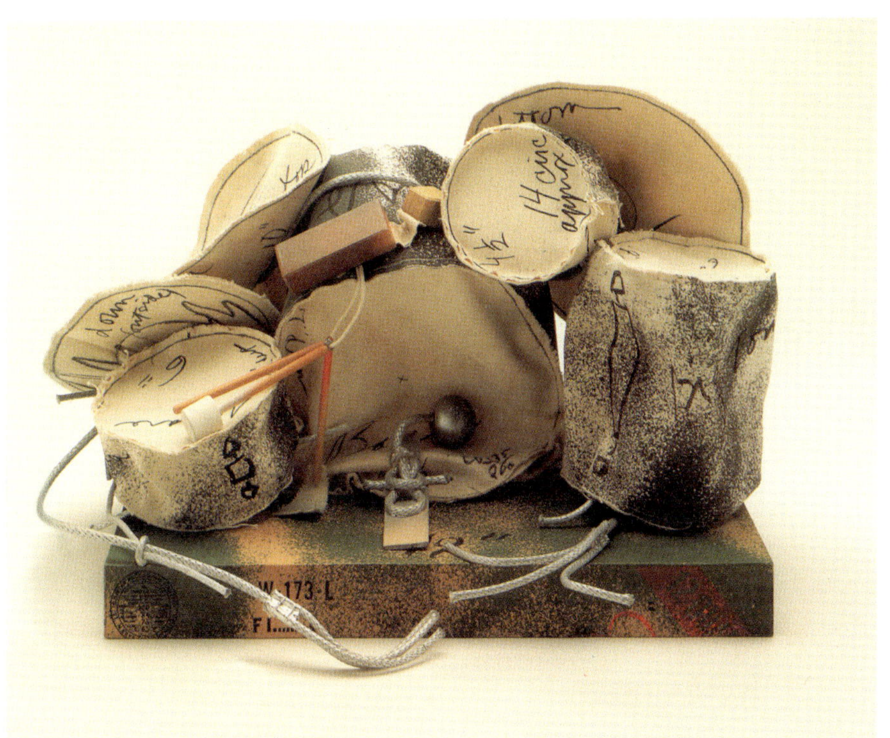

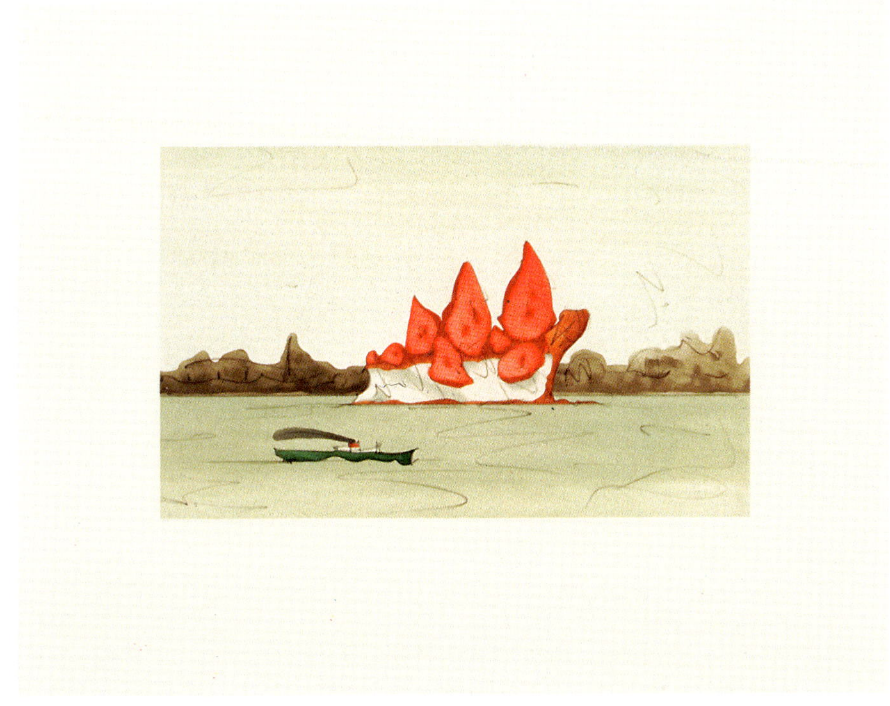

238 Claes Oldenburg
Proposed ... Strawberry Shortcake, 1992
Radierung auf Bütten, 58,5 x 75 cm.
Auflage: 60
Etching on rag paper, 23 x 29½ in. Edition: 60

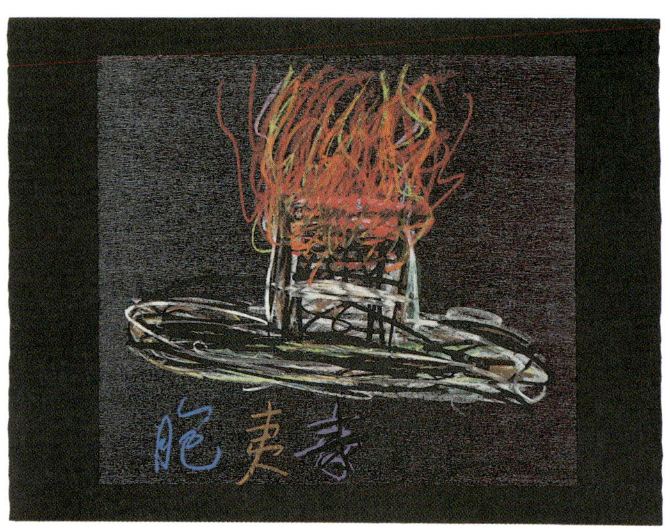

239 Nam June Paik
Burning Hat, 1986
Serigraphie auf schwarzem Bütten, 60 x 80 cm. Auflage 90
Silkscreen on black rag paper, 23½ x 31½ in. Edition: 90

240 Nam June Paik ■ →
Born Again, 1991
Bronzeguss, patiniert, mit 3 Fernsehmonitoren, Antennen, Elektrokabel, 48 x 59 x 15 cm. Auflage: 24
Bronze, patined, with TV monitors, antennas, plug, 19 x 23 x 6 in. Edition: 24

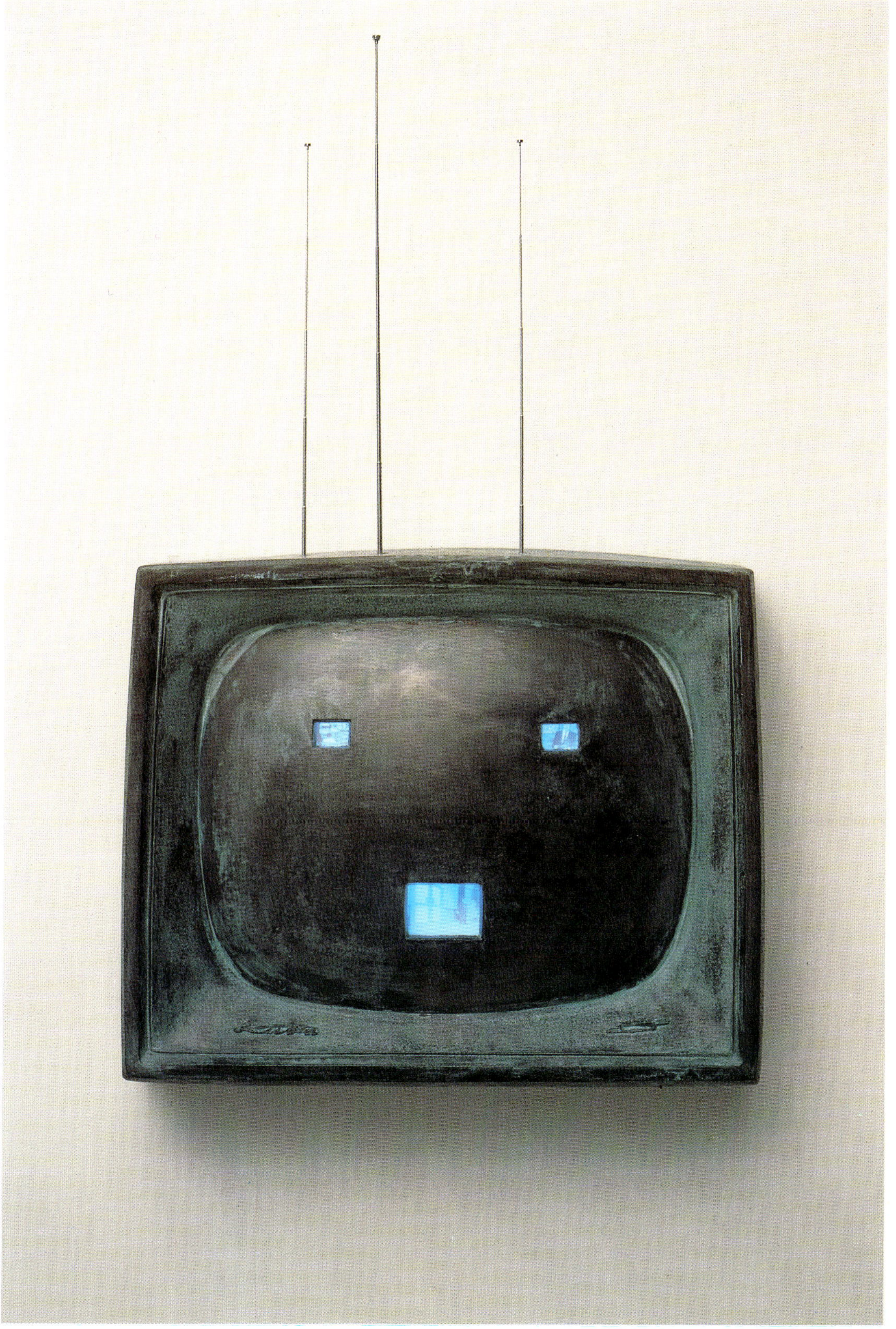

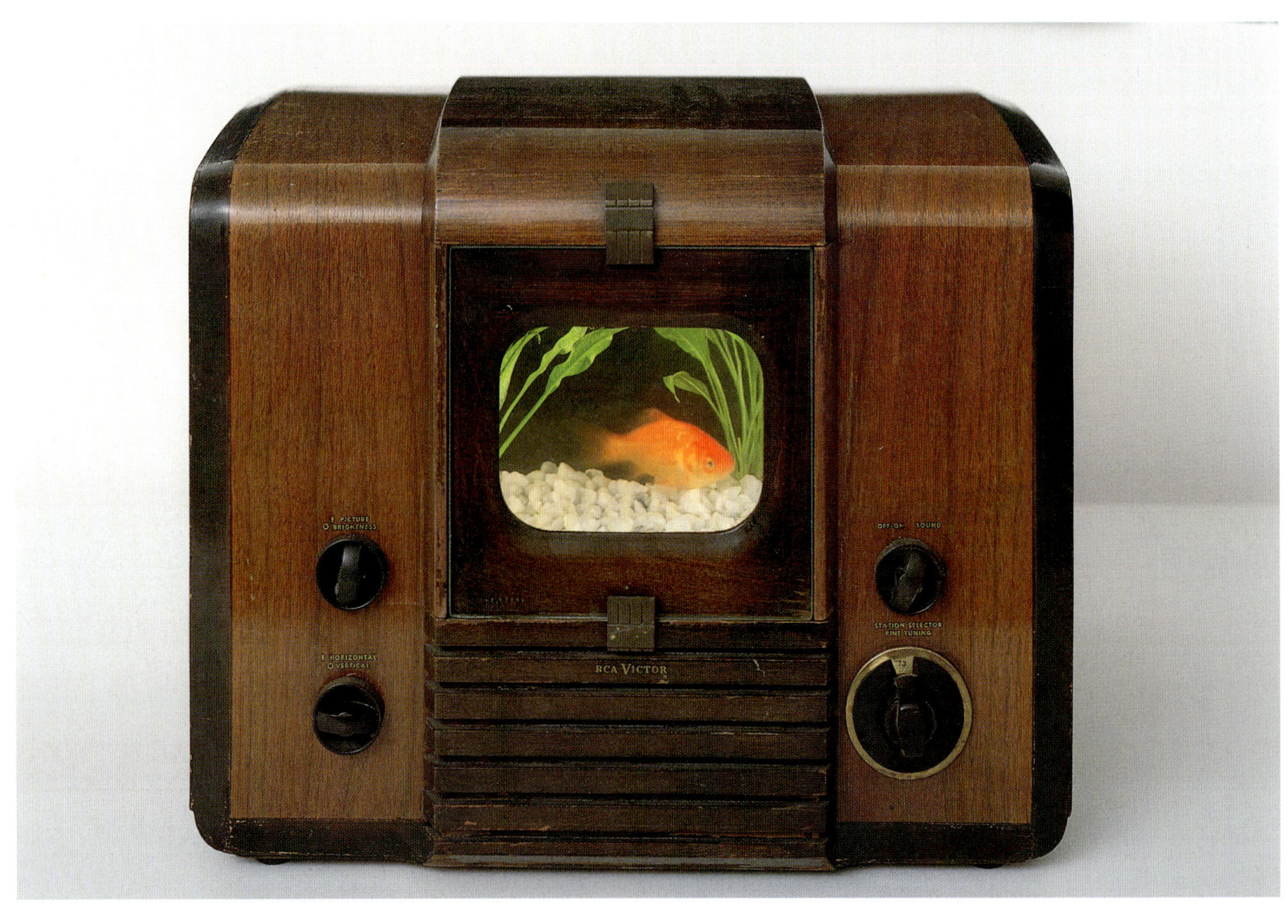

241 Nam June Paik ■
Sonatine for Goldfish, 1992
Fernsehgehäuse (RCA Victor, 1946), mit Aquarium, 40 x 49 x 41 cm. Auflage: 12
TV casing (RCA Victor, 1946), with aquarium, 15¼ x 19½ x 16½ in. Edition: 12

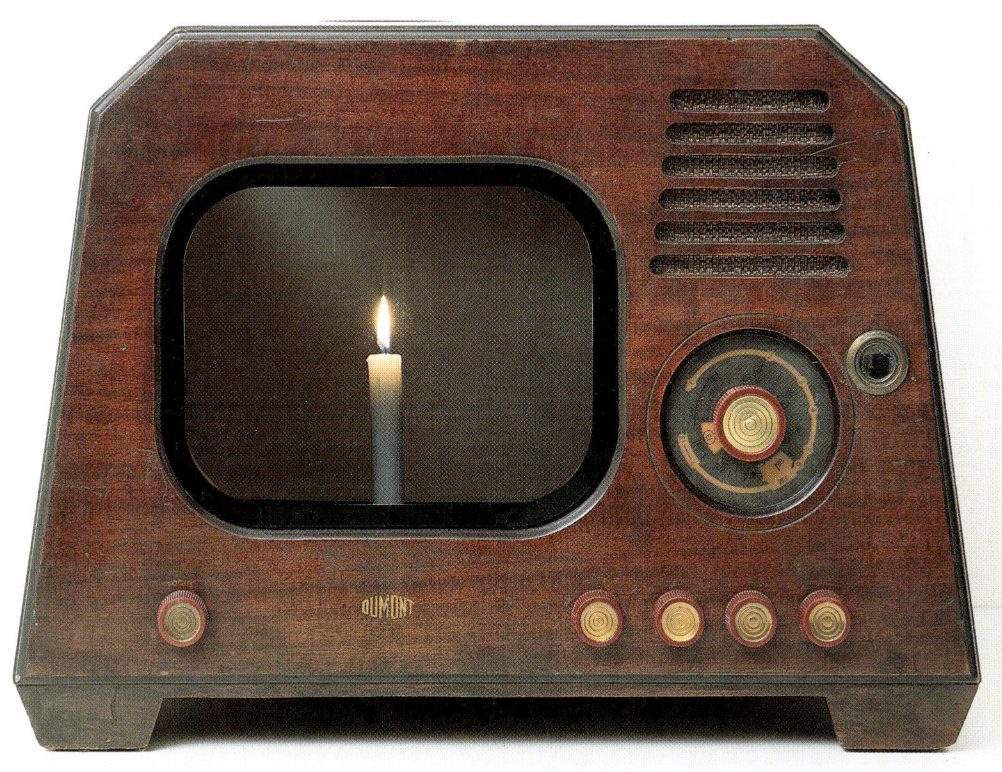

242 Nam June Paik ■
Before the word there was light, after the word there will be light, 1992
Fernsehgehäuse (Dumont, 1948), mit Kerze, 44 x 60 x 50 cm. Auflage: 18
TV casing (Dumont, 1948), with candle, 17 x 23½ x 20 in. Edition: 18

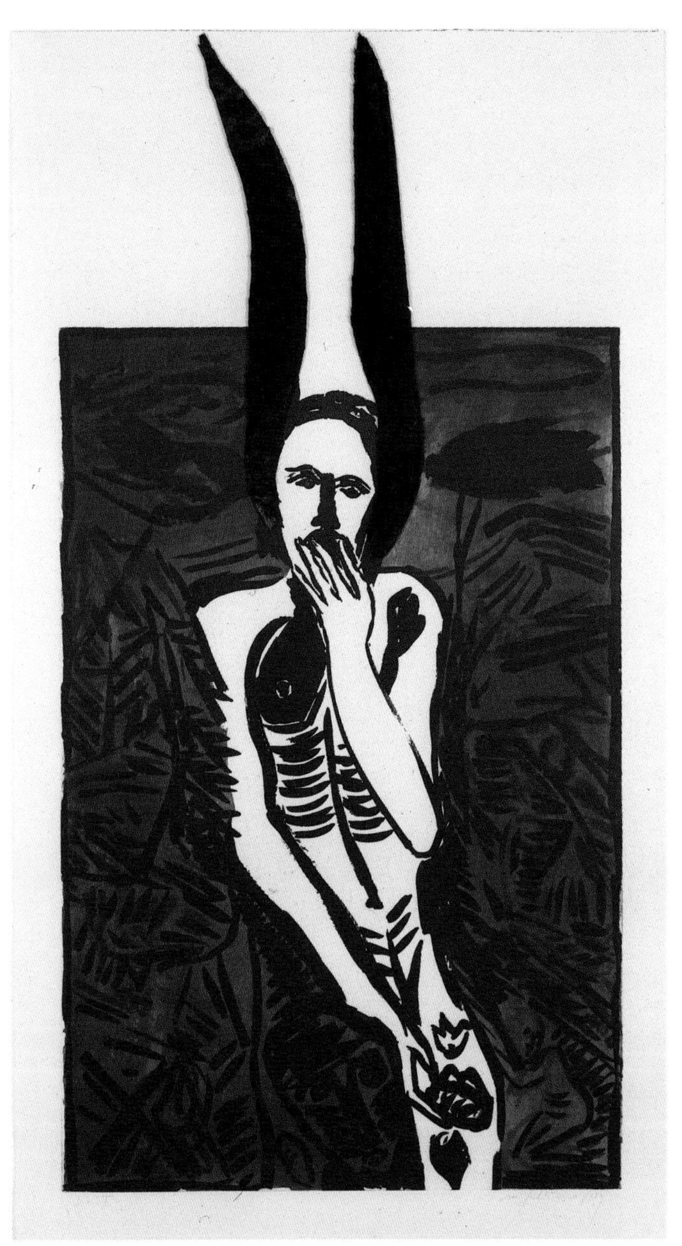

243 Mimmo Paladino ■
Muto, 1985
Aquatinta und Sugarlift, collagiert mit Fell,
155 x 87 cm. Auflage: 35
Etching with aquatint and sugarlift, with collage of fur,
61 x 34 in. Edition: 35

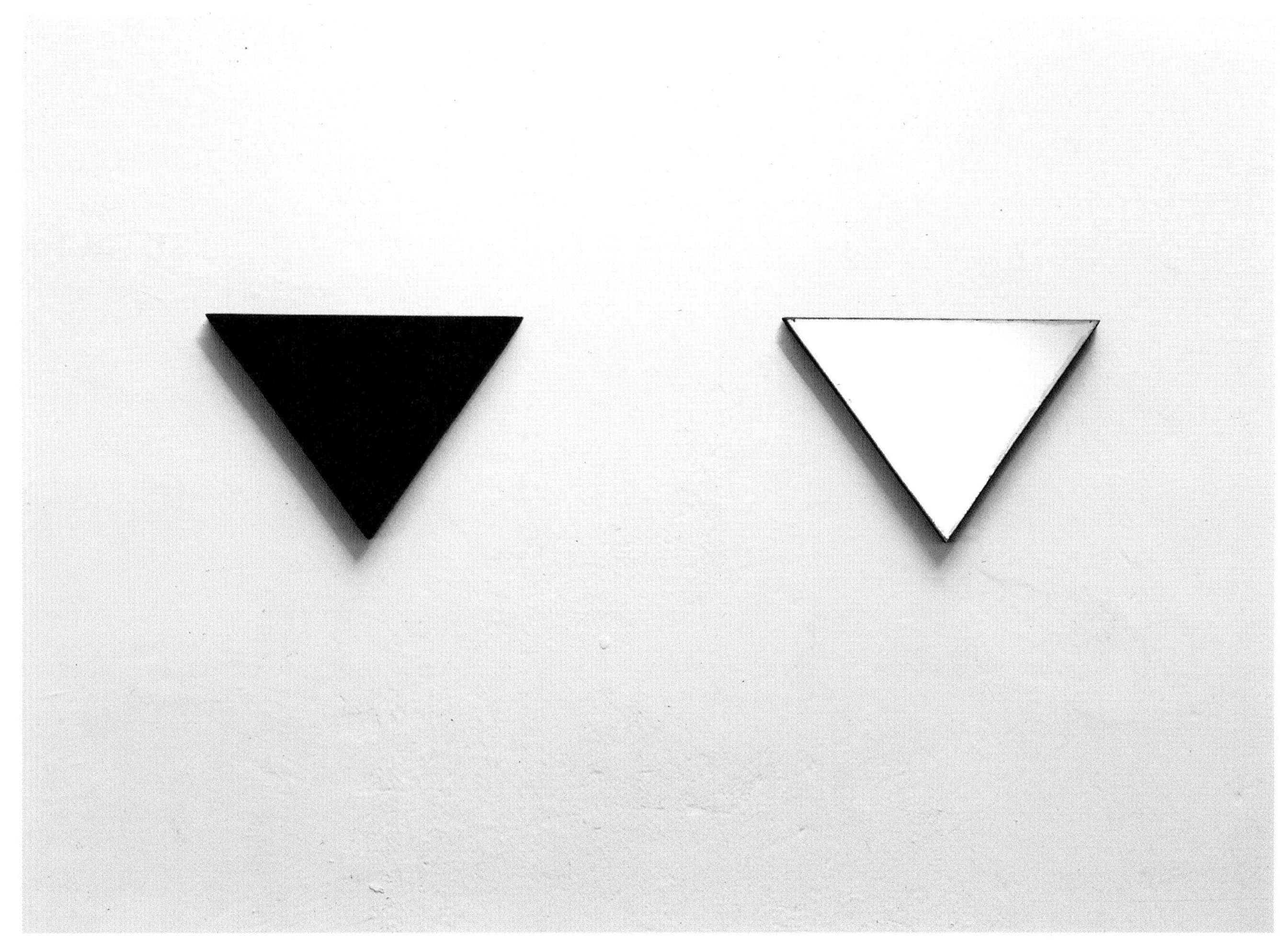

244 Blinky Palermo
Ohne Titel, gewidmet: Thelonius Monk, 1973
Sperrholz schwarz bemalt, Sperrholz mit Spiegel, je 32 x 22 x 3 cm. Auflage: 30
Plywood painted black, and plywood with mirror, 12½ x 8¾ x 1¼ in. Edition: 30

245 Giulio Paolini ■
Vis-à-vis (Hera), 1992
Zwei halbe Gipsabgüsse auf Sockel, an eine Wand plaziert, 169 x 90 x 15 cm.
Siehe Appendix. Auflage: 10, mit sign. und num. Zertifikat.
Two halves of a plaster cast on pedestals, installed against a wall, 66½ x 35½ x 6 in.
See appendix. Edition: 10, with a signed and numbered certificate.

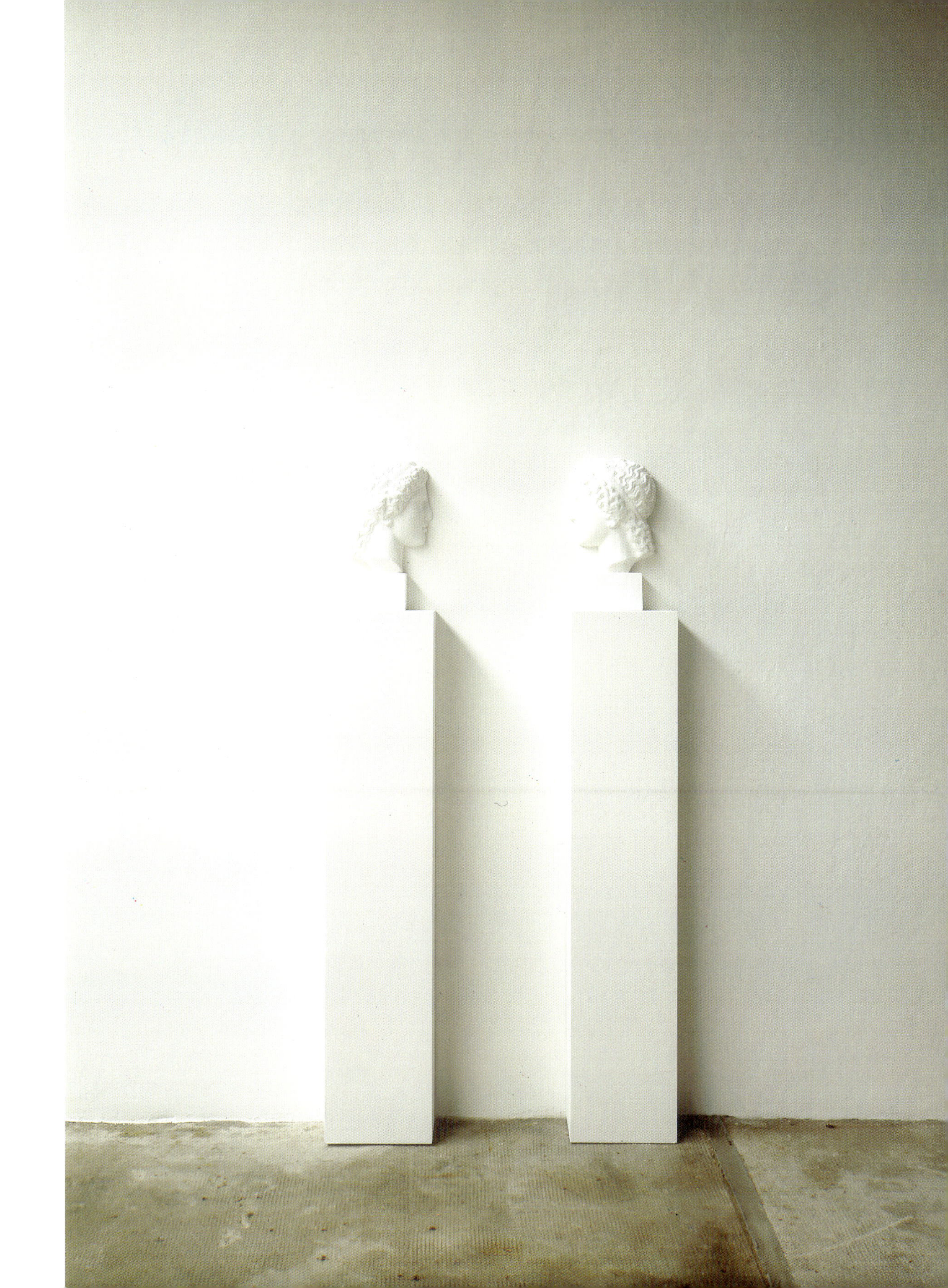

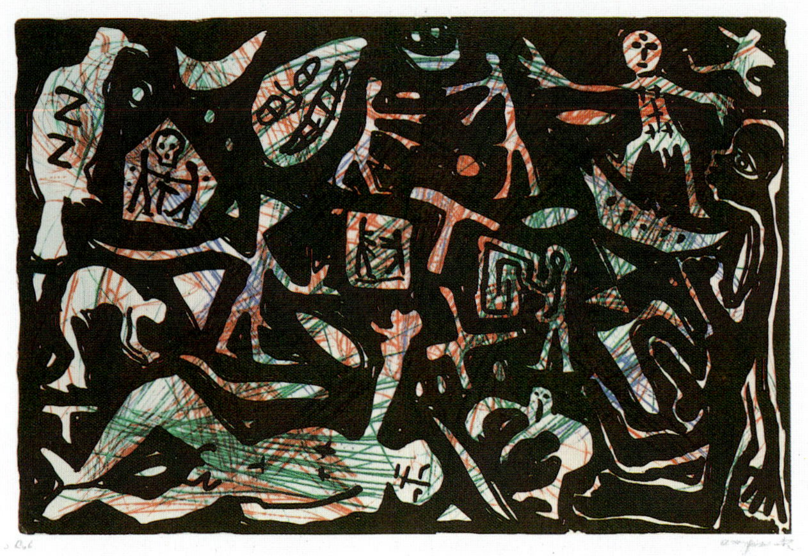

246 A. R. Penck
Loch in der Mauer, 1989
Aquatinta/Kaltnadelradierung,
98 x 123 cm. Auflage: 35
Aquatint/drypoint, 38½ x 48½ in.
Edition: 35

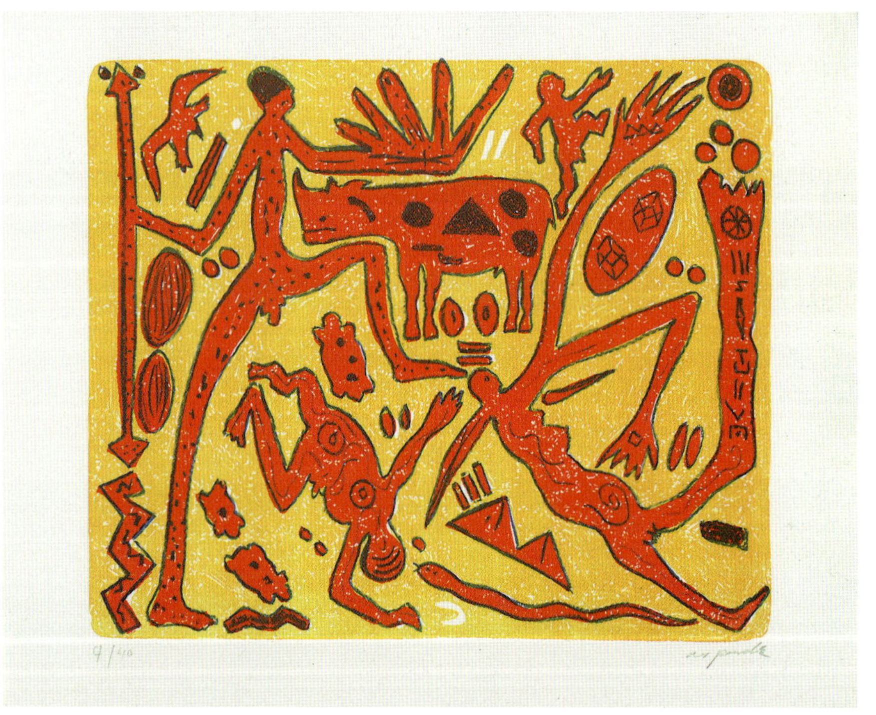

247 A. R. Penck
Das rote Flugzeug, 1985
Lithographie, 58 x 74 cm.
Auflage: 40
Lithograph, 23 x 29 in.
Edition: 40

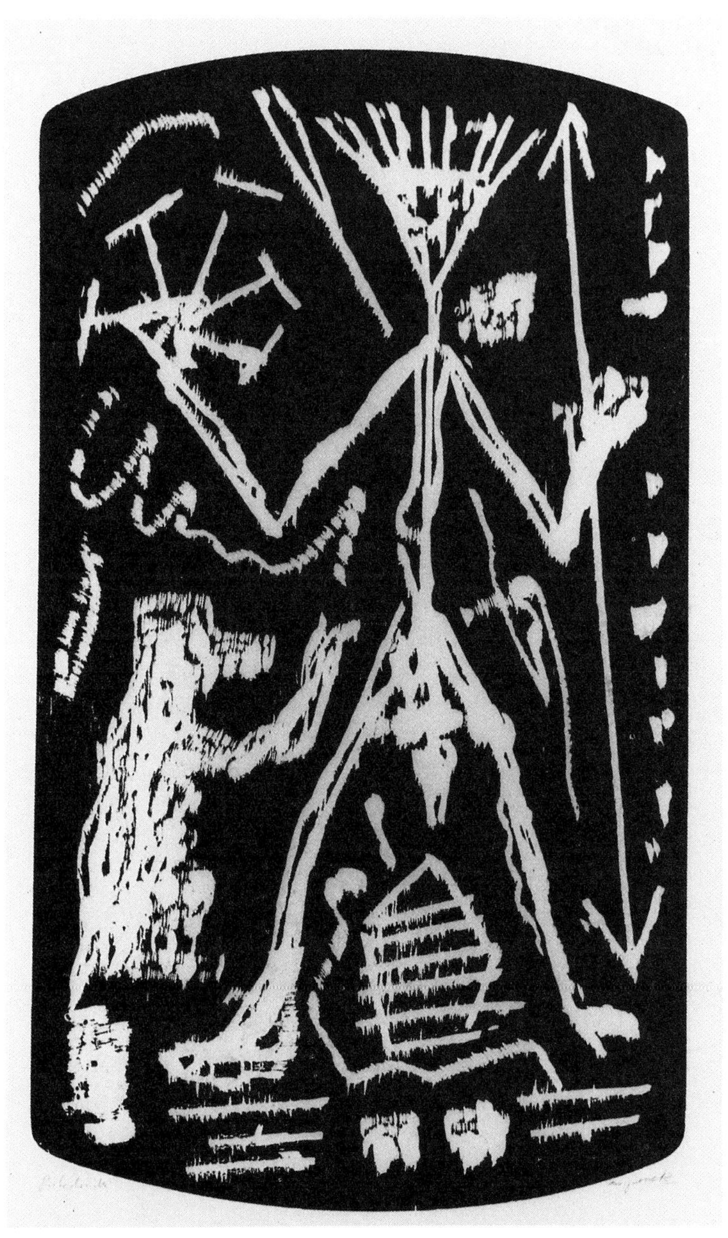

248 A.R. Penck
Jäger (Standardkonzept West), 1985
Holzschnitt, 124 x 84 cm. Auflage: 30
Woodcut, 49 x 33 in. Edition: 30

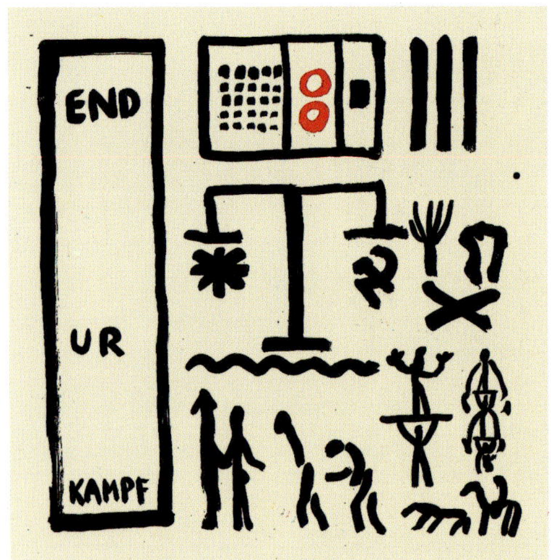

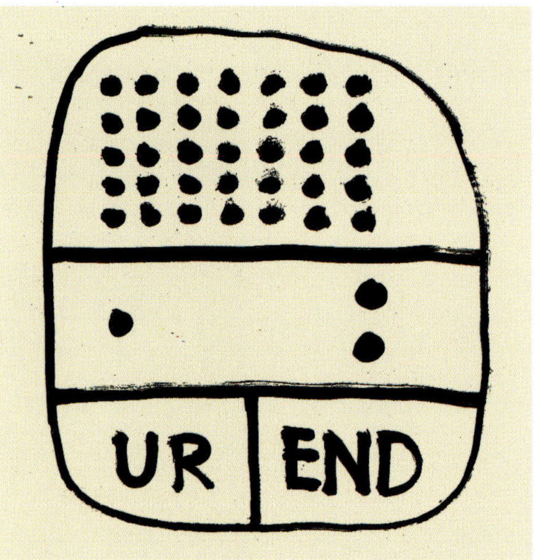

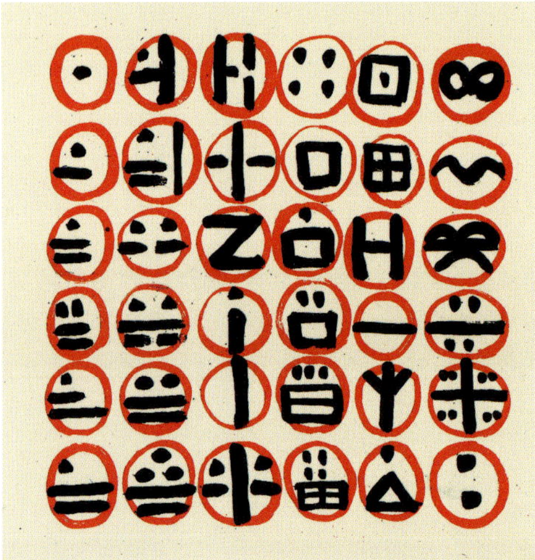

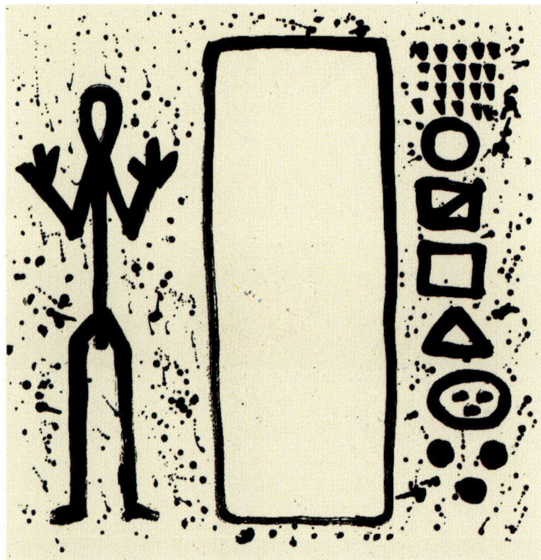

249 A.R. Penck
UR END STANDART, 1972
Mappe mit 11 Siebdrucken, 70 x 70 cm. Auflage: 75
Portfolio with 11 silkscreens, 27½ x 27½ in. Edition: 75

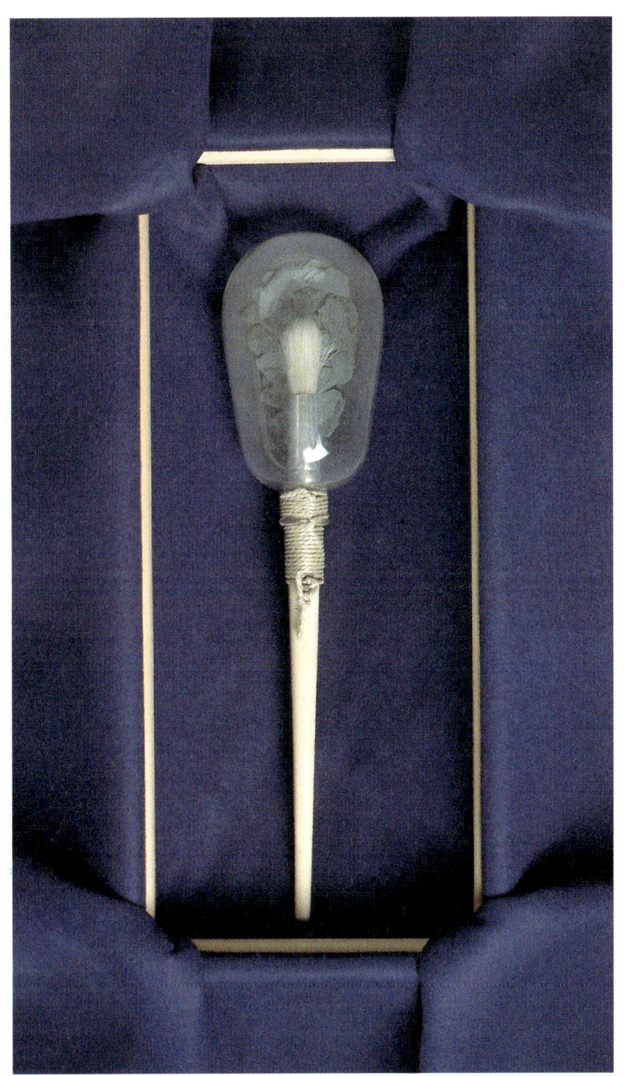

250 Sigmar Polke
Schieferpinselrassel (Rasselpinselschieferstaub), 1994
Objekt bestehend aus Künstlerpinsel, handgeblasenem Glas, Schieferstücken, Bindfaden, 41 x 9 x 9 cm, in Kasten ausgeschlagen mit Filz, 23,5 x 48,5 x 16,5 cm. Auflage: 20
Object consisting of paint brush, handblown glass, chips of slate, twine, 16 x 3½ x 3½ in., in wooden box, inside covered with felt, 9¼ x 19 x 6½ in. Edition: 20

251 Sigmar Polke
Dr Pabscht het ...., 1980/91
Computer-Reproduktion auf Vinyl, aufgezogen auf Keilrahmen, 50 x 40 cm. Auflage: 100
Computer reproduction on vinyl, mounted on stretcher, 19¾ x 15¾ in. Edition: 100

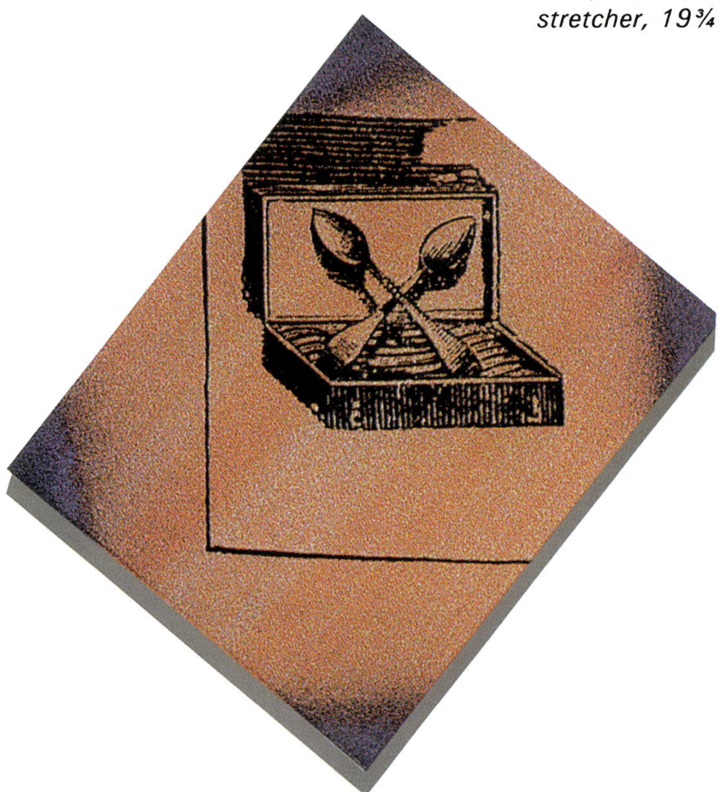

252 Richard Prince →
Cowboys and Girlfriends, 1992
Mappe mit 14 Farbphotographien, 51 x 61 cm. Auflage: 26
Portfolio with 14 ektacolor photographs, 20 x 24 in. Edition: 26

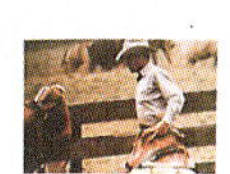
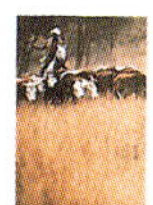
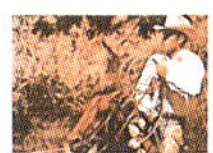
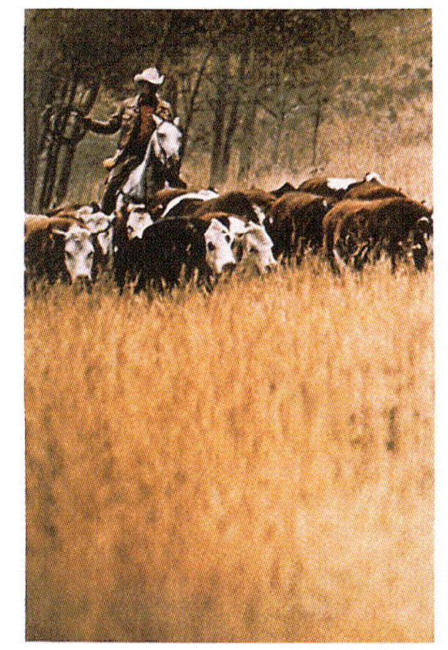
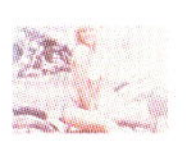
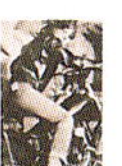
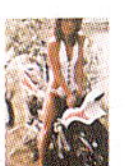

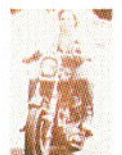
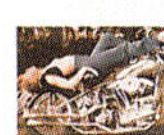

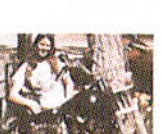
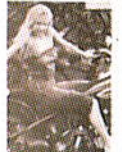
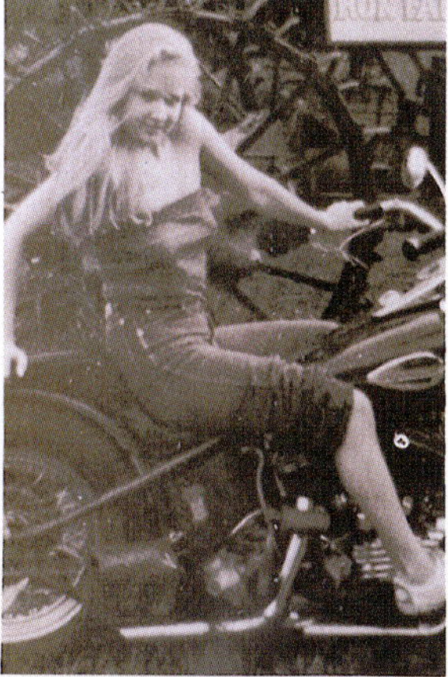
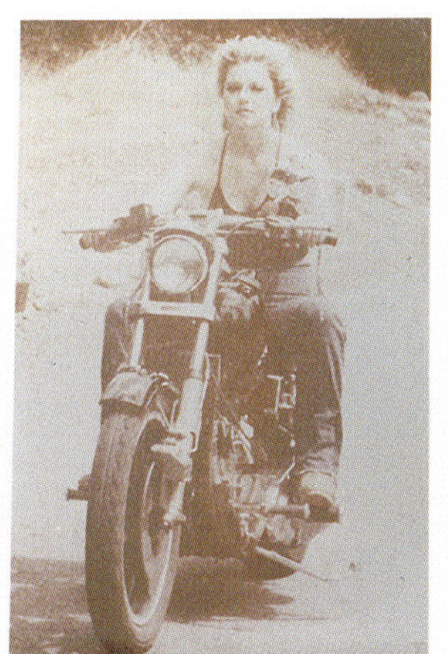
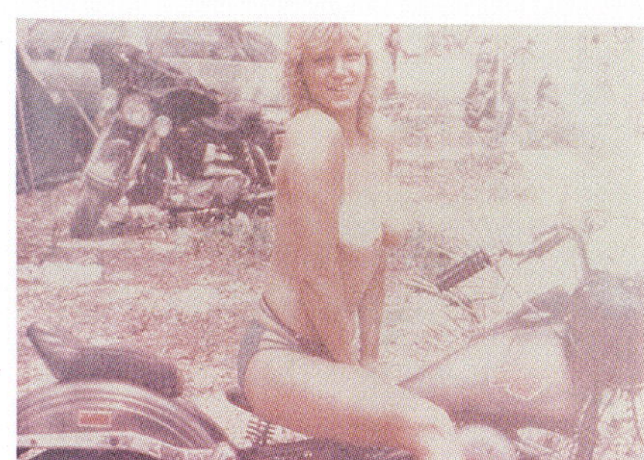
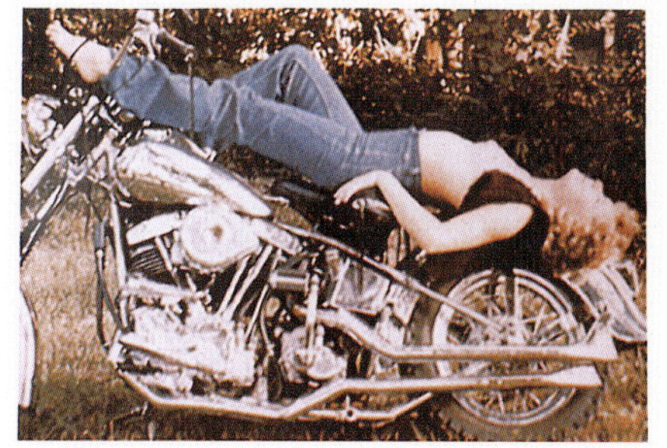

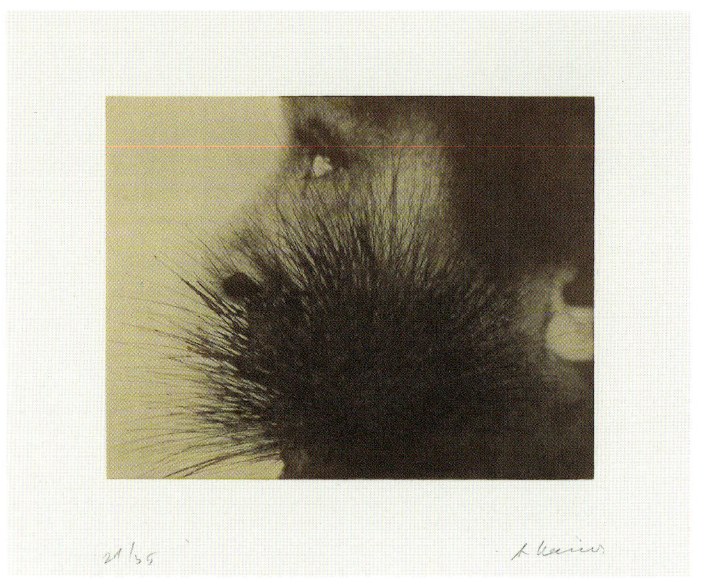

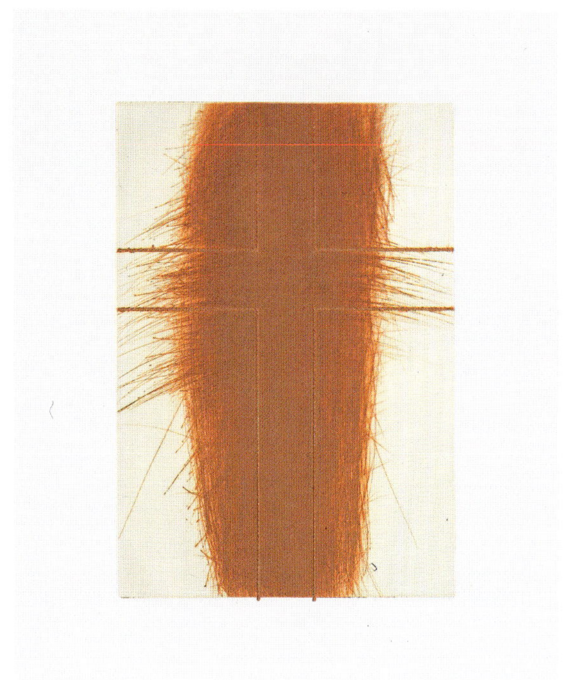

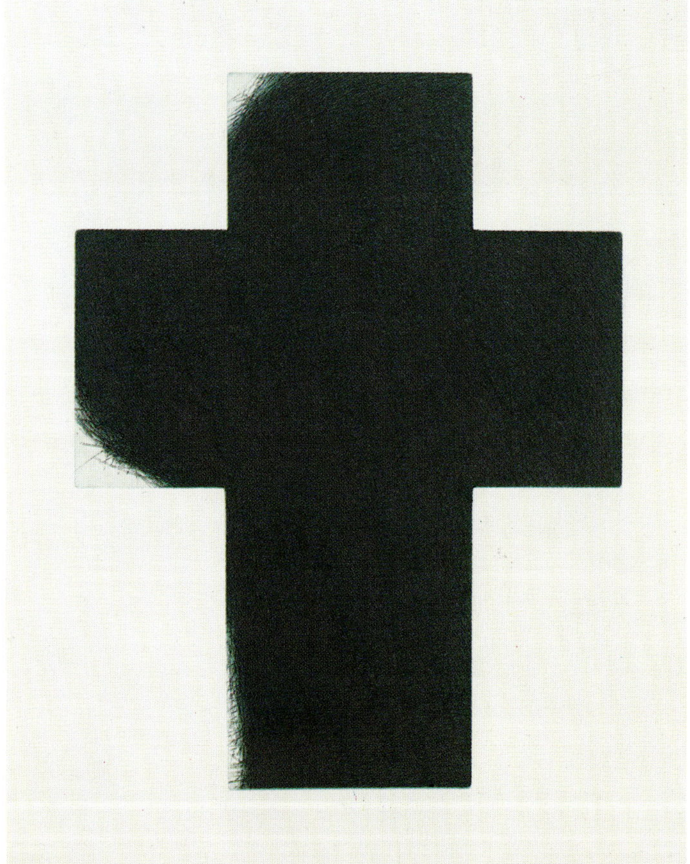

↖ **253 Arnulf Rainer**
Bartbrand, 1993
Kaltnadel und Heliogravure, 58,5 x 53,5 cm. Aufl.: 35
Drypoint and photo etching, 23 x 21 cm. Edition: 35

254 Arnulf Rainer ↑
Kreuz, 1990
Kaltnadelradierung, 65 x 50 cm. Auflage: 35
Drypoint, 25½ x 19½ in. Edition: 35

← **255 Arnulf Rainer**
Tannenkreuz, 1989
Kaltnadelradierung, 78 x 68 cm. Auflage: 50
Drypoint, 30½ x 27 in. Edition: 50

256 Arnulf Rainer
Ohne Titel, 1989
5 Kaltnadelradierungen (abgebildet: "Grüner Schild", "Violettes Tuch"),
65 x 50 cm. Auflage: 35
5 drypoint etchings (2 ill.), 25½ x 19¾ in. Edition: 35

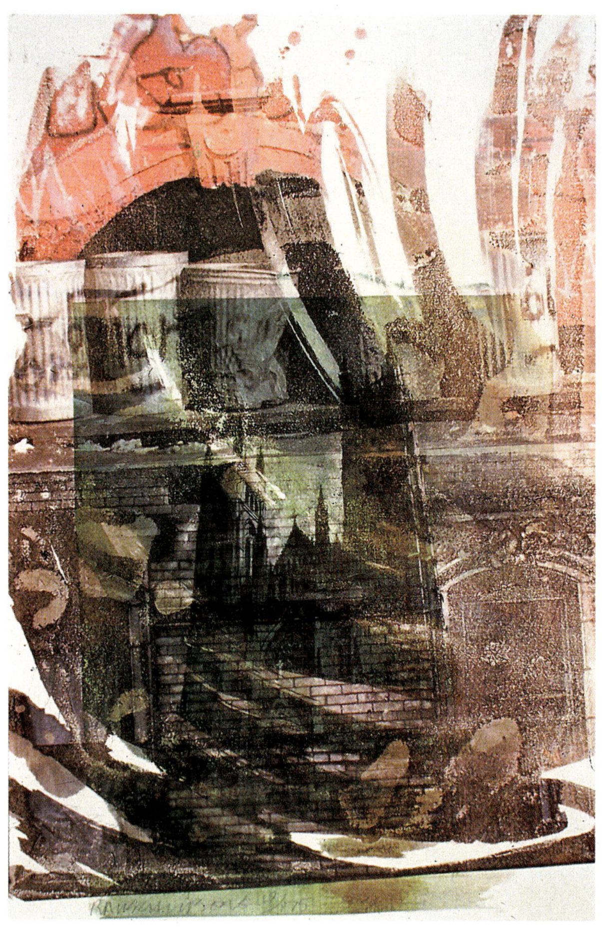

257 Robert Rauschenberg
St. John the Divine ("Cathedral Print"), 1993
Lithographie auf Bütten, 91 x 64,5 cm. Auflage: 175
Lithograph on rag paper, 35¾ x 25½ in. Edition: 175

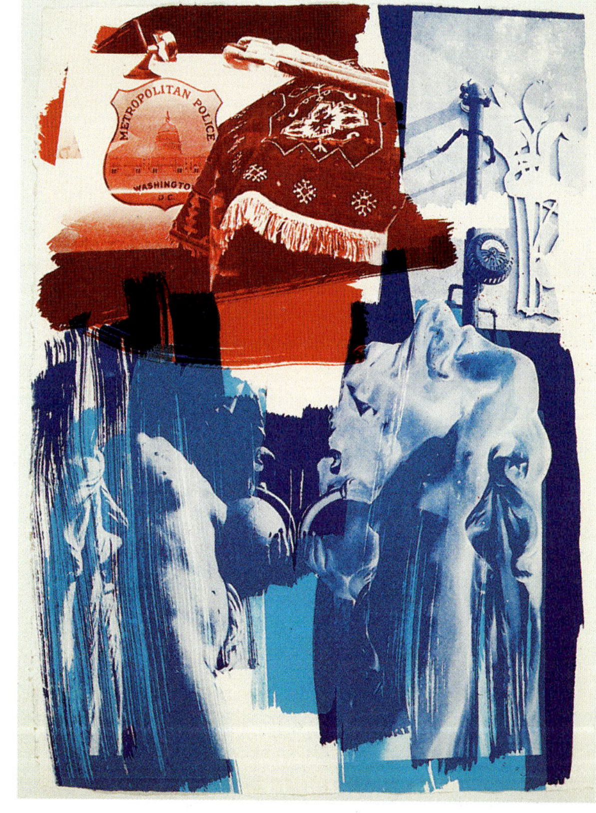

258 Robert Rauschenberg
Blues, 1992
Lithographie auf Bütten, 104 x 79 cm. Auflage: 57
Lithograph on rag paper, 41 x 31 in. Edition: 57

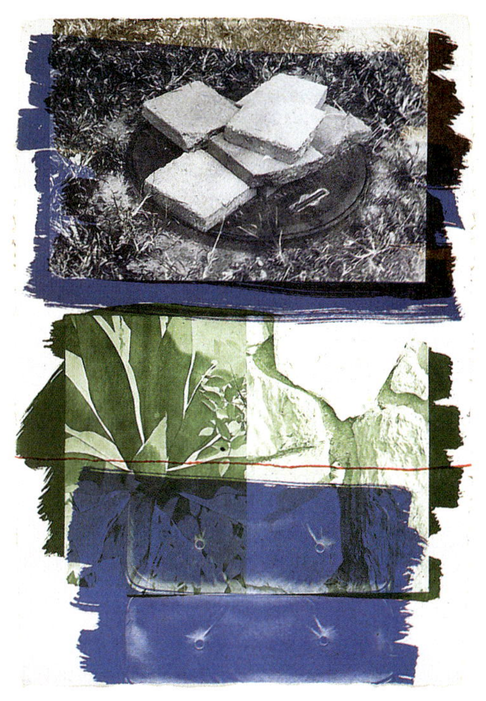

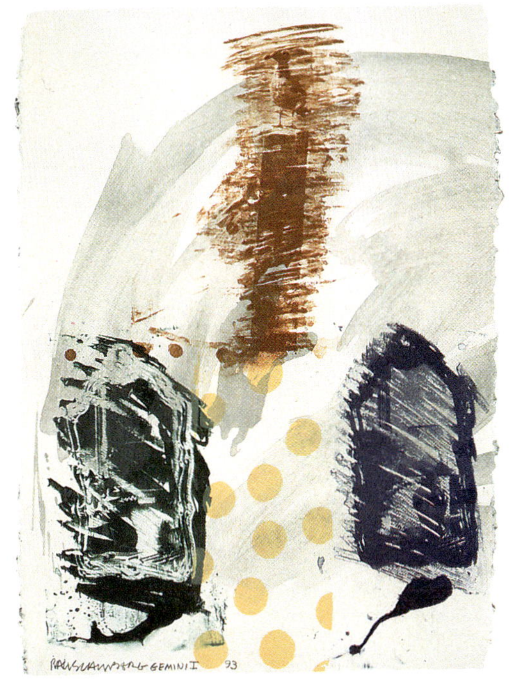

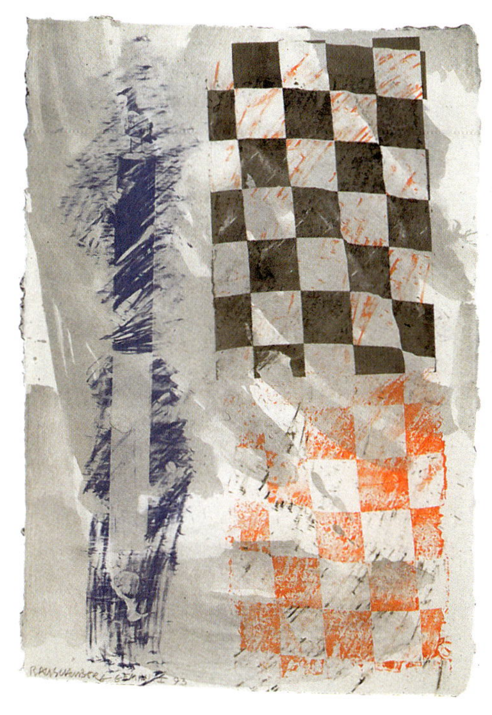

259 Robert Rauschenberg
a. Viaduct, 1992
Lithographie, 103 x 74 cm. Auflage: 54
Lithograph, 40½ x 29 in. Edition: 54

b. Bird Dock, 1993
Lithographie, 81 x 61,5 cm. Auflage: 43
Lithograph, 32 x 24¼ in. Edition: 43

c. Grid Gull, 1993
Lithographie, 94,5 x 68,5 cm. Auflage: 50
Lithograph, 37¼ x 27 in. Edition: 50

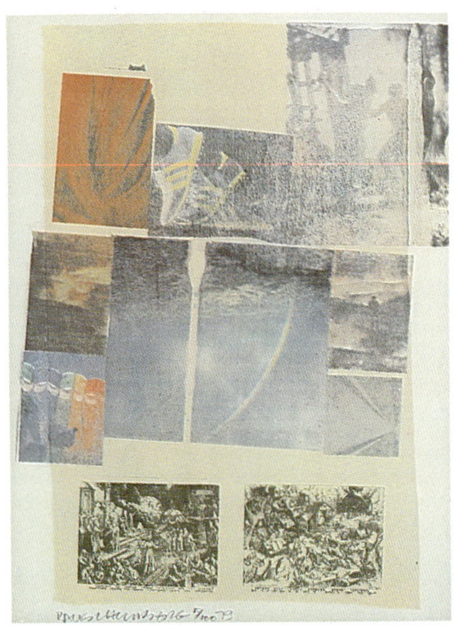
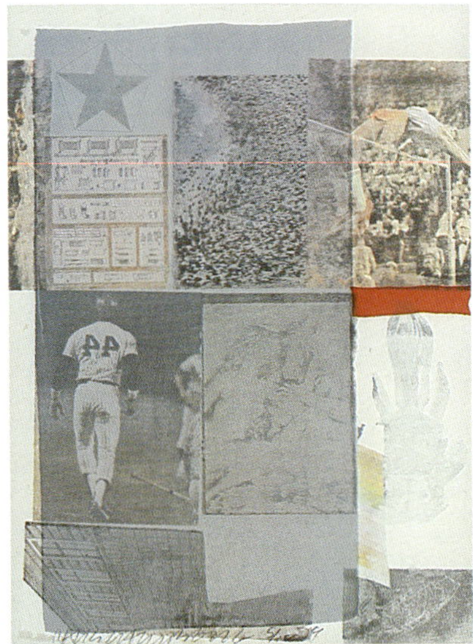
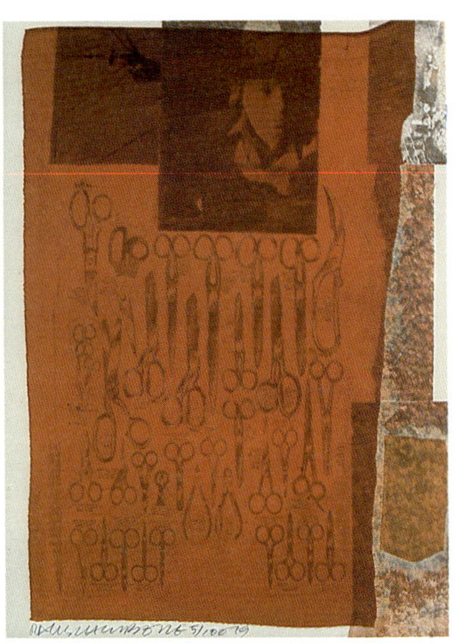

260 Robert Rauschenberg
Farbserigraphien auf Bütten, 1979
78 x 59 cm. Auflage: 100
Silkscreens on rag paper, 30 x 23 in. Edition: 100

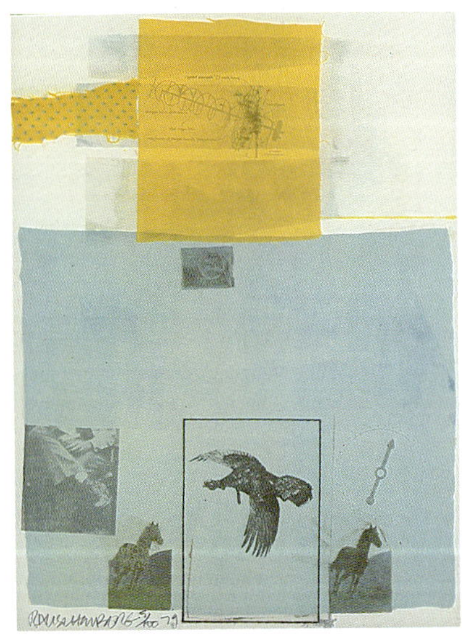
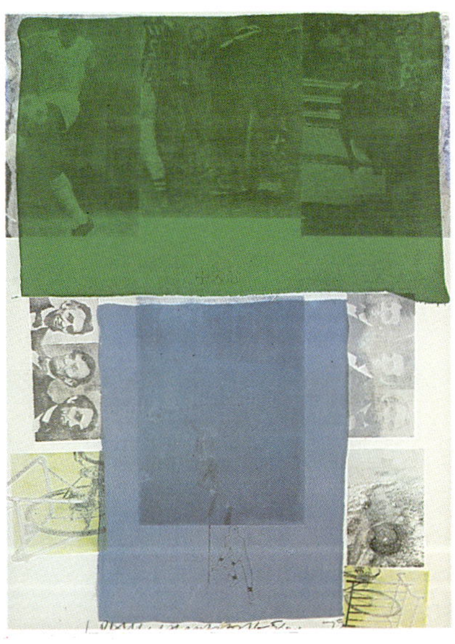
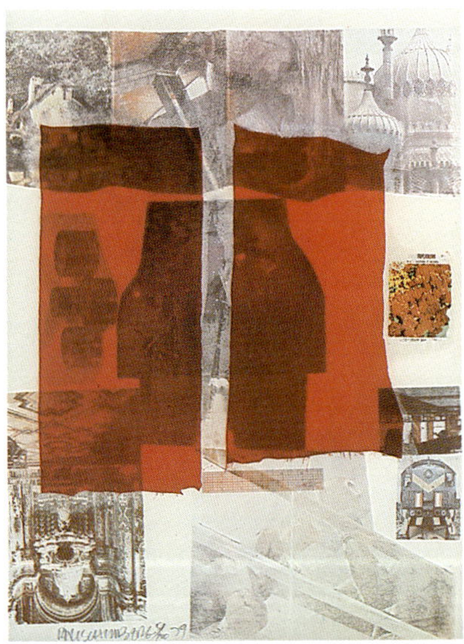

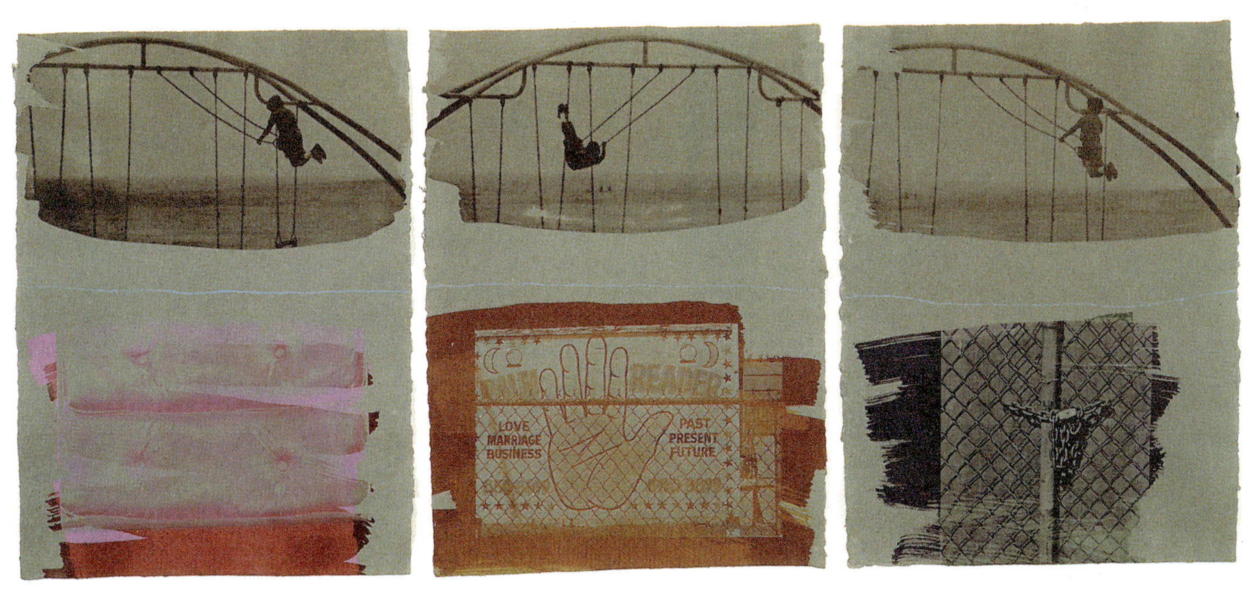

261 Robert Rauschenberg
Blue Line Swinger, 1992
Lithographie, dreiteilig, insges. 76 x 170 cm. Auflage: 68
Three panel lithograph, overall 30 x 67 in. Edition: 68

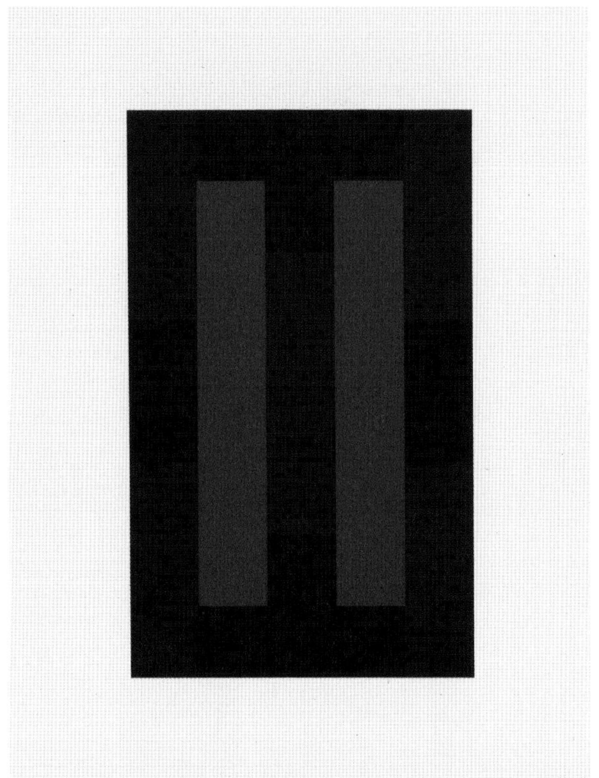

262 Ad Reinhardt
Blätter aus: 10 Screenprints, 1966
Serigraphien, 56 x 44 cm. Auflage: 250, nicht signiert
Two silkscreens, 22 x 17 in. Edition: 250, unsigned

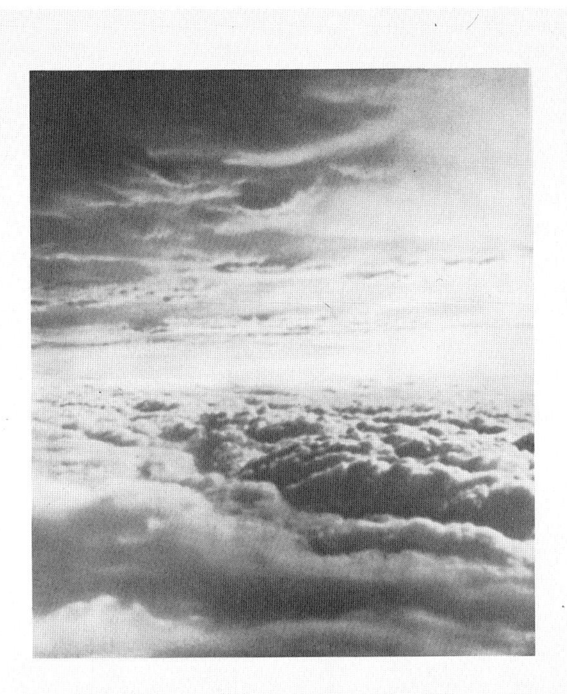

263 Gerhard Richter
Wolken, 1969
Offset, 55 x 50 cm.
Auflage: 300
Offset lithograph,
21½ x 19½ in.
Edition: 300

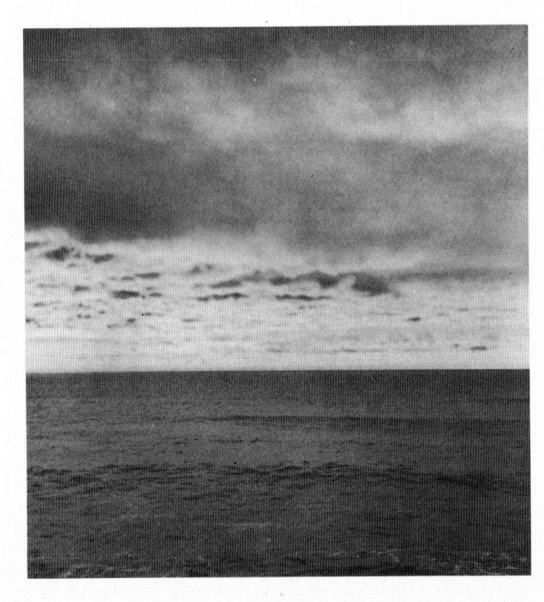

264 Gerhard Richter
Seestück, 1969
Offset, 51 x 49 cm.
Auflage: 150
Offset lithograph,
20 x 19 in.
Edition: 150

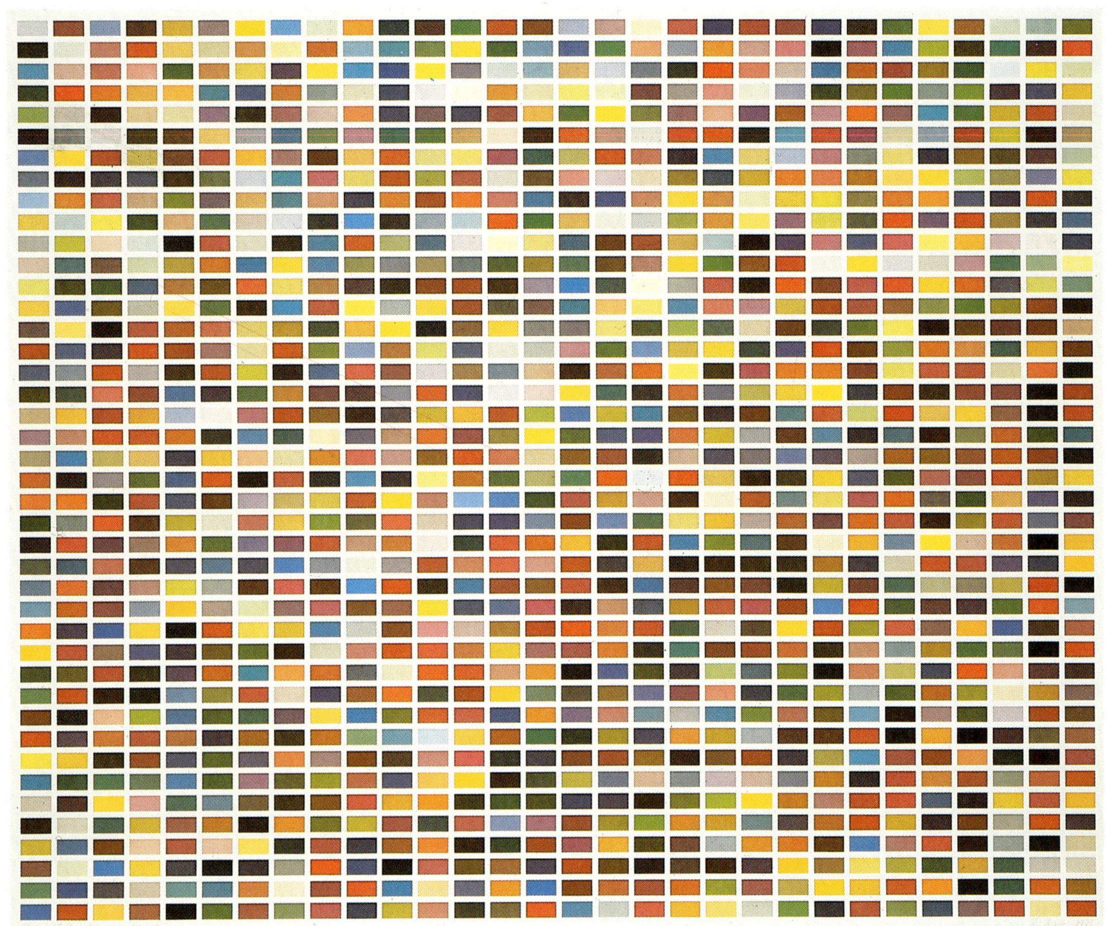

265 Gerhard Richter
6 Anordnungen von 1260 Farben, 1974
Mappe mit 6 Blättern Offset (Tangiertechnik), 64,5 x 79,5 cm. Auflage: 32
Portfolio with 6 offset prints, 25½ x 31¼ in. Edition: 32

266 Gerhard Richter →
Kanarische Landschaften, 1971
Mappe mit 6 Heliogravüren, gedruckt graugrün, auf Bütten, 40 x 50 cm. Auflage: 50
Portfolio with 6 photo etchings, printed on rag paper in greenish grey ink, 15¾ x 19¾ in. Edition: 50

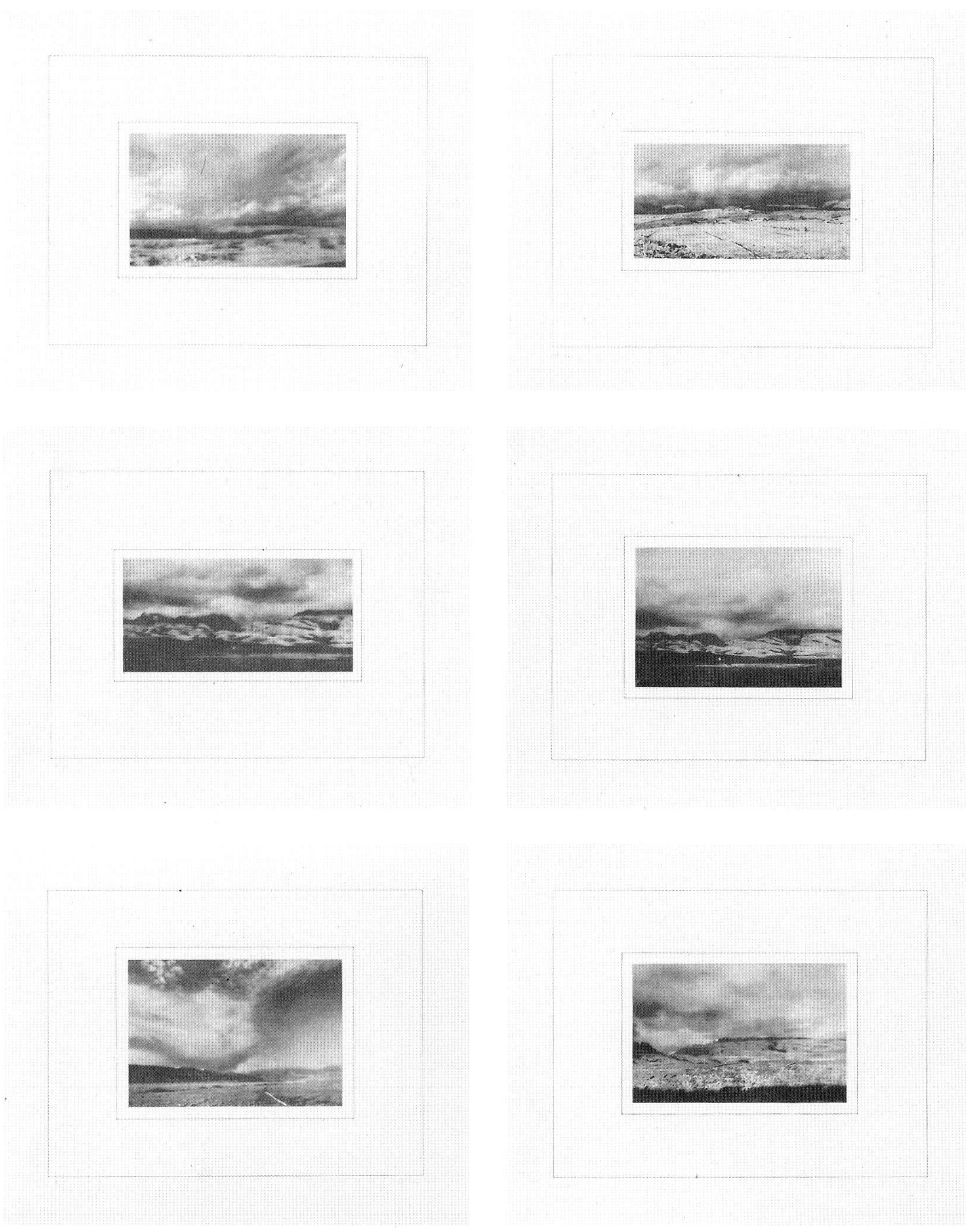

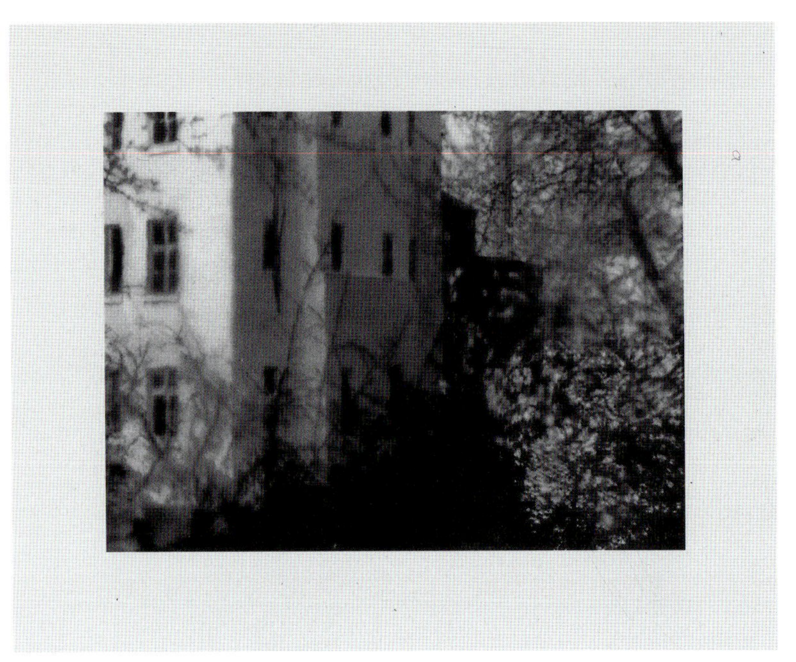

267 Gerhard Richter
Besetztes Haus, 1990
Offsetdruck (Duotone),
62,5 x 80 cm. Auflage: 100
Offset print (duotone),
24½ x 31½ in. Edition: 100

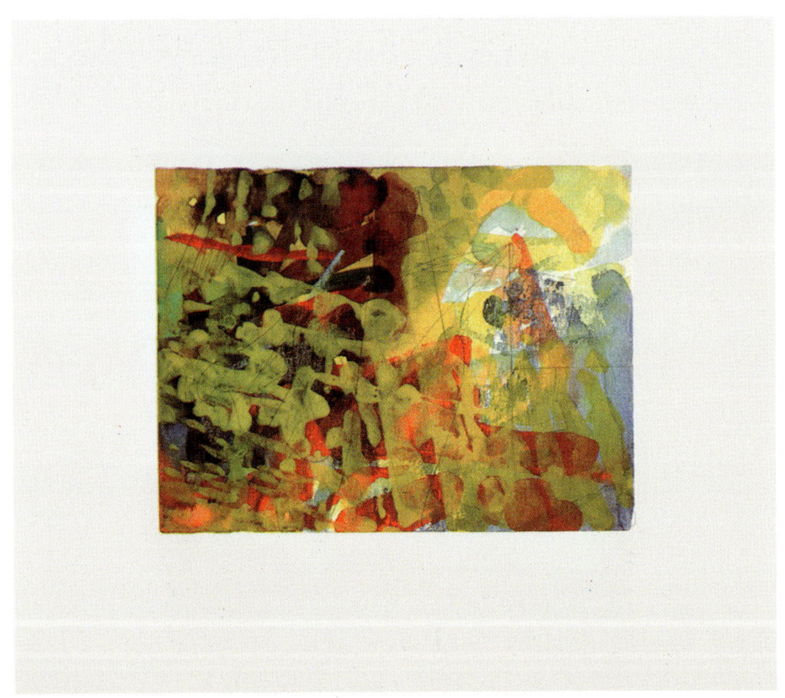

268 Gerhard Richter
Ohne Titel, 1988
Farboffset mit Bleistiftzeichnung,
50 x 58 cm. Auflage: 75
Color offset with pencil drawing,
19½ x 23 in. Edition: 75

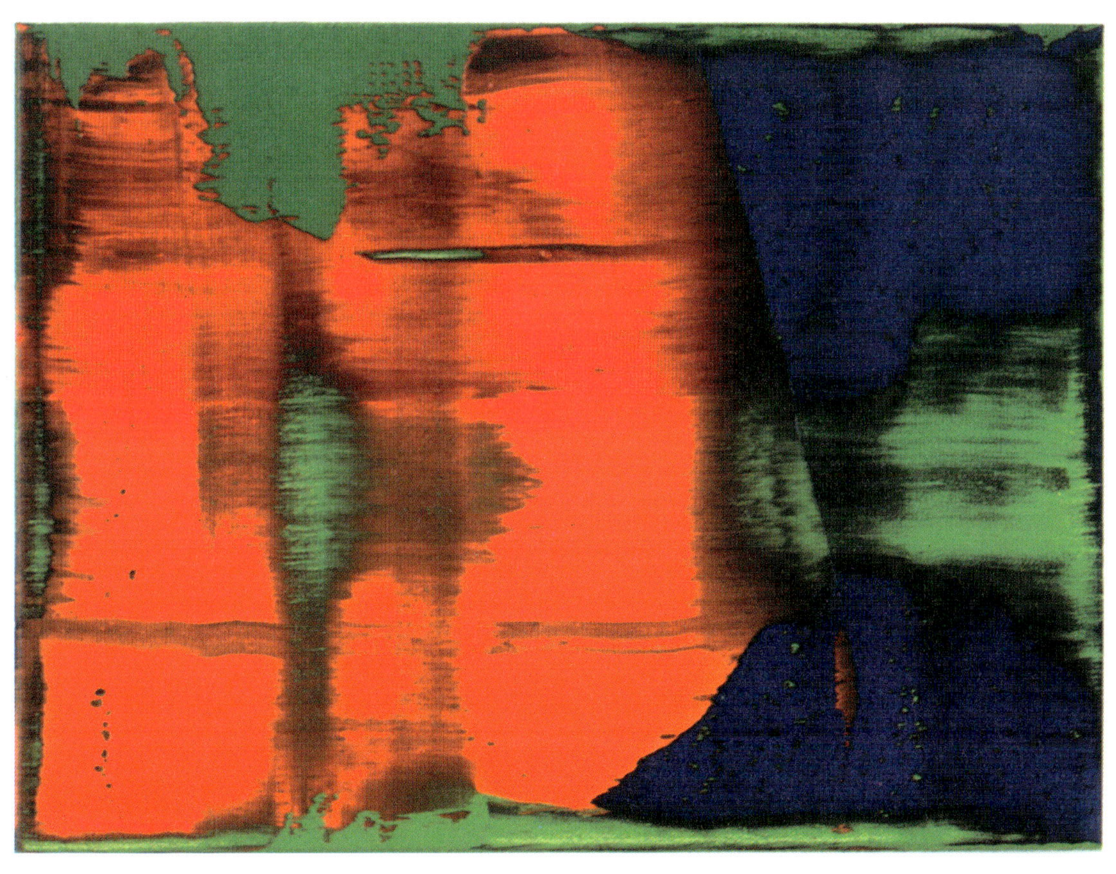

269 Gerhard Richter
Grün - Blau - Rot, 1993
Ölfarbe auf Leinwand, auf Keilrahmen aufgespannt, 40 x 40 cm. Auflage: 115
Oil on canvas, mounted on stretcher, 11¾ x 15¾ in. Edition: 115

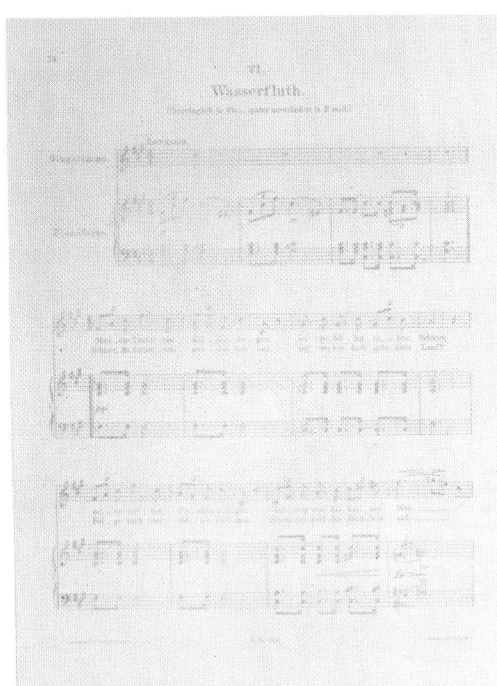

270 Tim Rollins & KOS
Winterreise-Wasserfluth, 1989
Notenblatt, mit weisser Grundierung übermalt,
auf Karton 30 x 23 cm. Auflage: 80
Sheet of music, handpainted with gesso,
on cardboard 12 x 9 in. Edition: 80

271 Tim Rollins & KOS ■
Black Alice, White Alice, 1989
a. weiß [abgebildet] *white [illustrated]*
b. schwarz [nicht abgebildet] *black [not illustrated]*
2 Offsetlithographien, Serigraphie und Collage,
mit Grundierung handübermalt, 84 x 132 cm. Auflage: 50
2 offset lithographs with silkscreen and collage,
handpainted with gesso, 33 x 52 in. Edition: 50

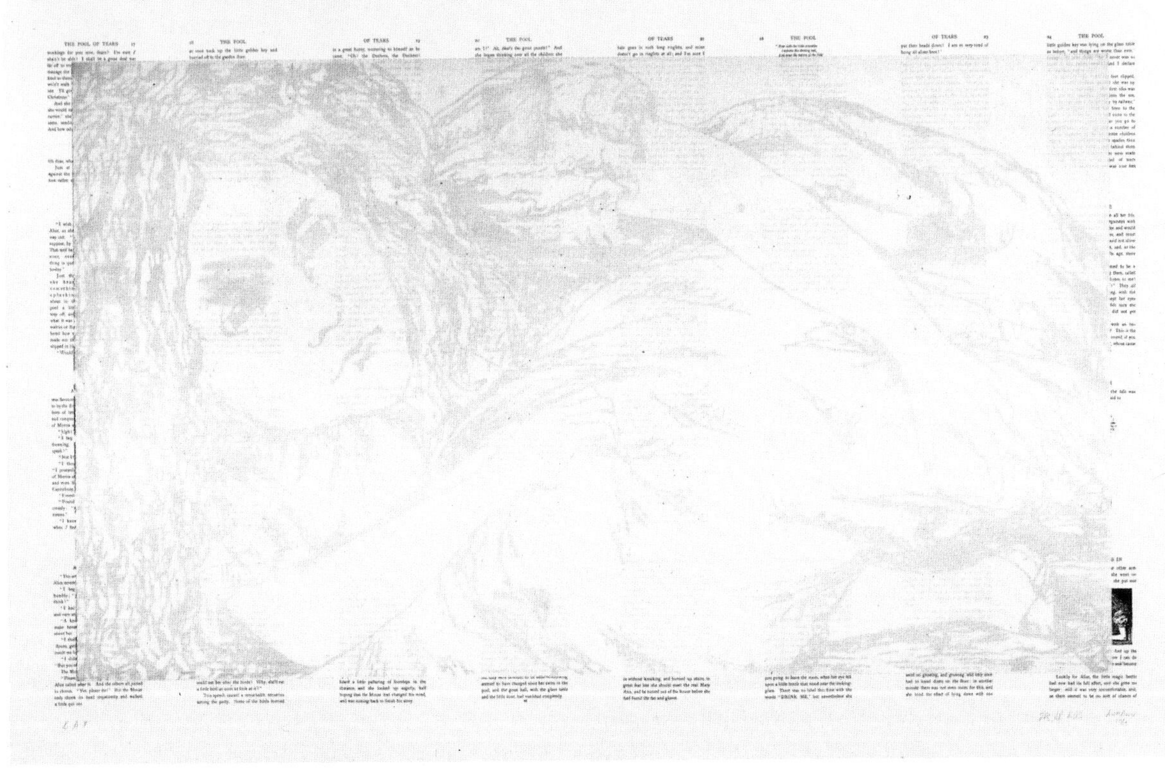

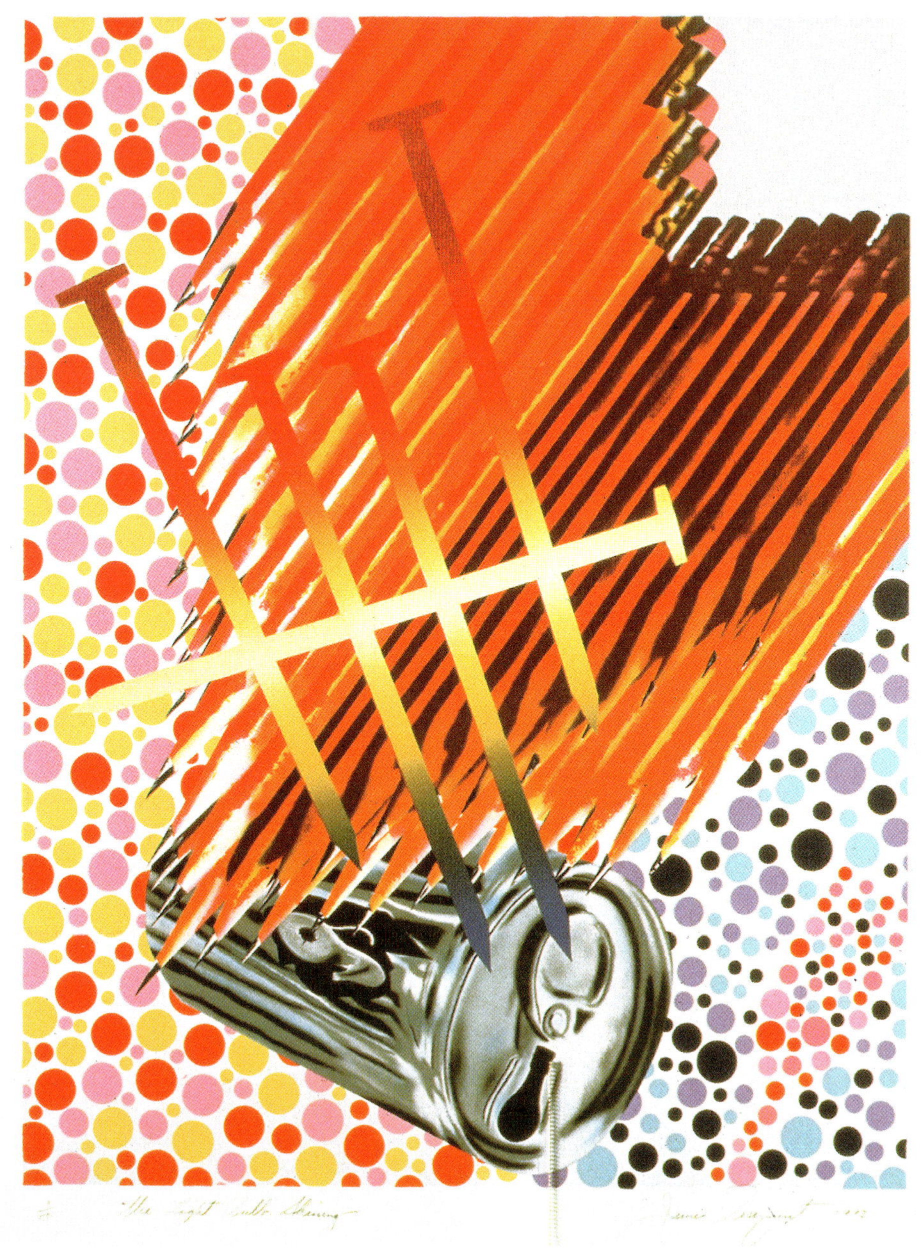

272 James Rosenquist
The Light Bulb Shining, 1992
Farblithographie (21 Farben), mit Metallkette, 133 x 105,5 cm. Auflage: 50
Color lithograph (21 colors), with attached metal chain, 52½ x 41½ in. Edition: 50

The Man Who Would
Be King
The Man Who Would
Be B.B. King
The Man Who Would
Be Queen Bee
The Man Who Would
Be Aunt Bea
The Man Who Would
Be Bea Arthur
The Man Who Would
Be King Arthur
The Man Who Would
Be Art King

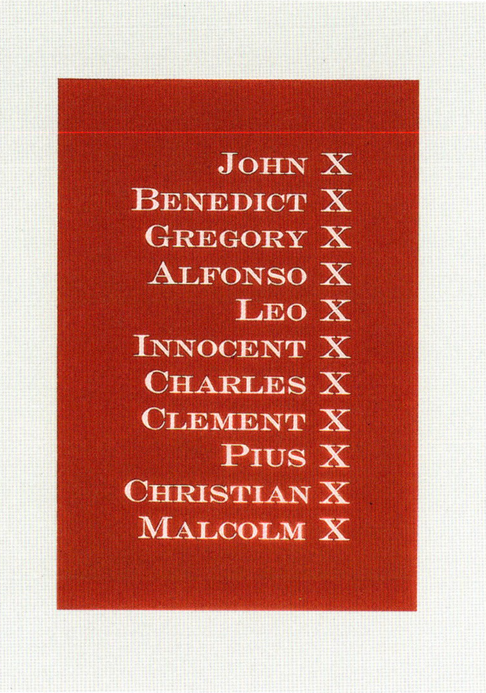

273 Kay Rosen
The Man, 1991
Radierung auf Bütten, 65 x 49,5 cm. Auflage: 32
Etching on rag paper, 25½ x 19½ in. Edition: 32

274 Kay Rosen
Palimpsest, 1990
Prägeradierung auf Bütten, 65 x 49,5 cm. Auflage: 27
Relief etching on rag paper, 25½ x 19½ in. Edition: 27

275 Ulrich Rückriem ■ →
Ohne Titel (Granit bleu de Vire), 1992
Granit, gespalten, gesägt, poliert, 120 x 60 x 30 cm. Siehe Appendix. Auflage: 10
Granite, split, sawn, and polished, 47¼ x 23½ x 11¾ in. See appendix. Edition: 10

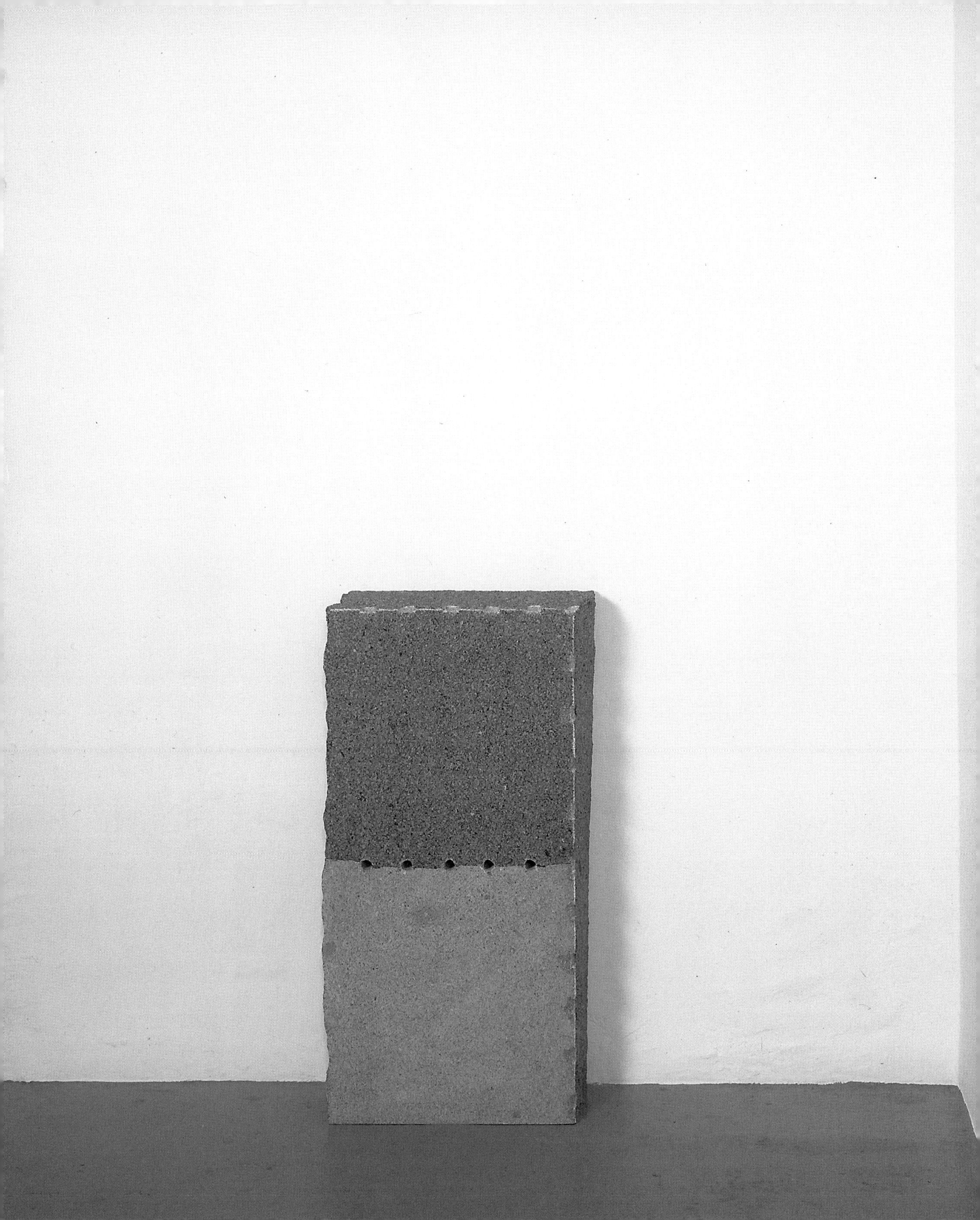

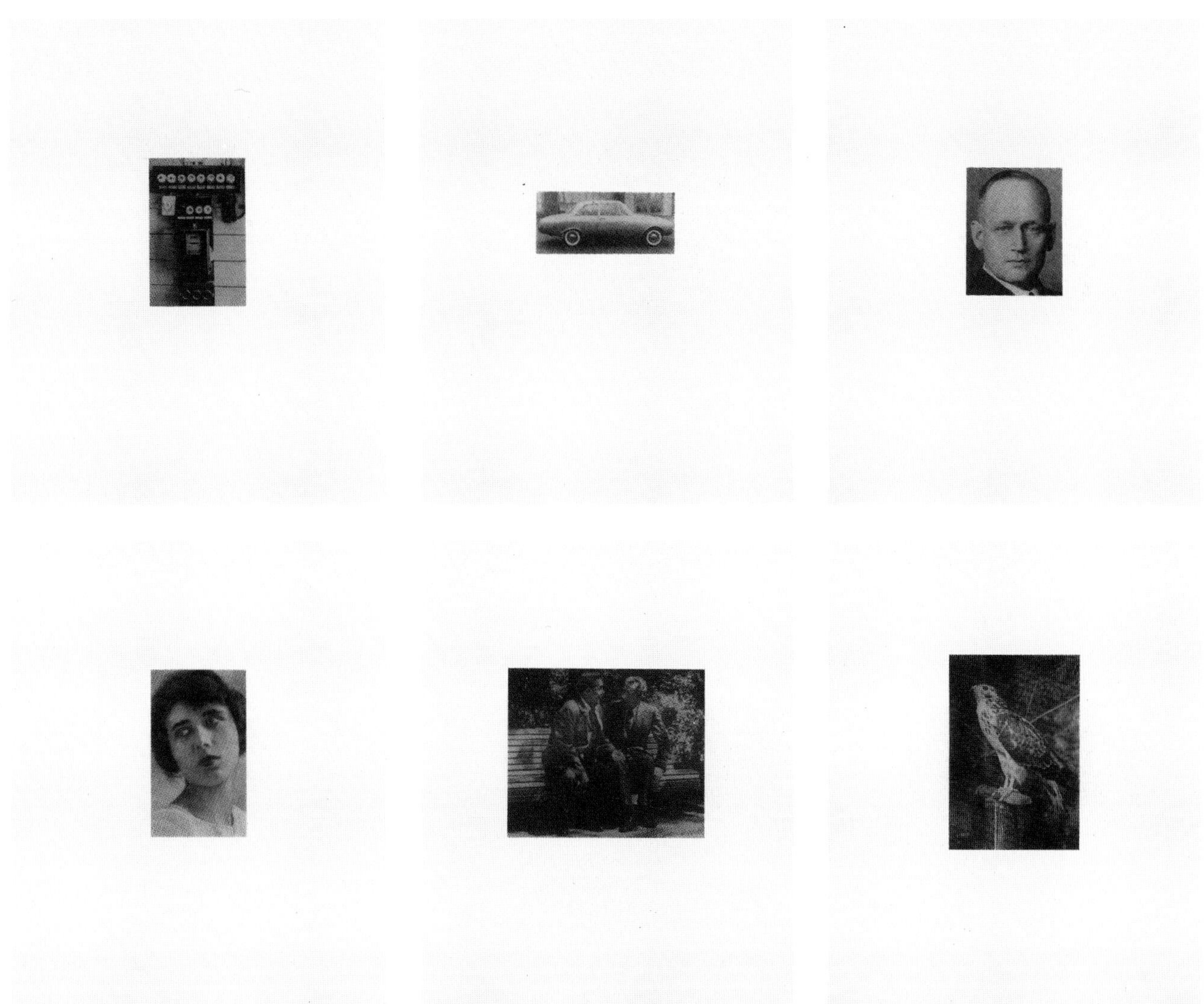

276 Thomas Ruff ■
Zeitungsphotos, 1991
Kassette mit 24 Offsetlithographien, 50 x 40 cm. Auflage: 35
Portfolio box with 24 offset lithographs, 19½ x 16¾ in. Edition: 35

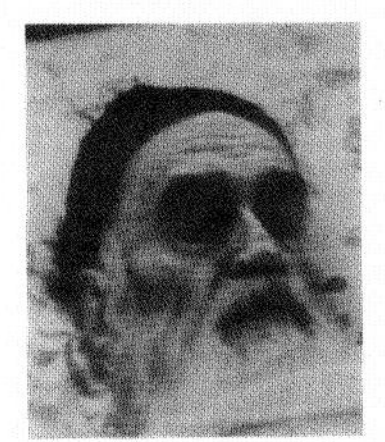

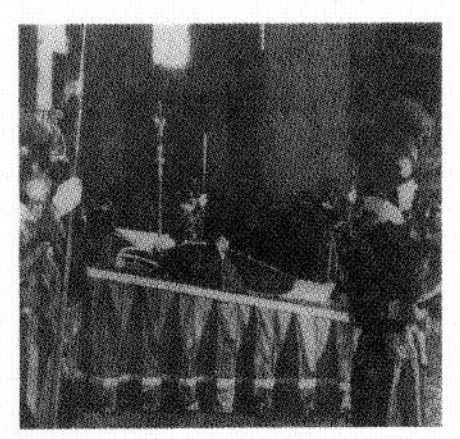

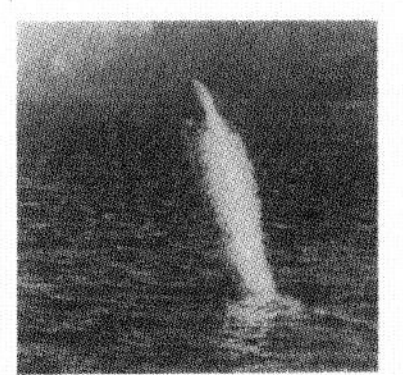

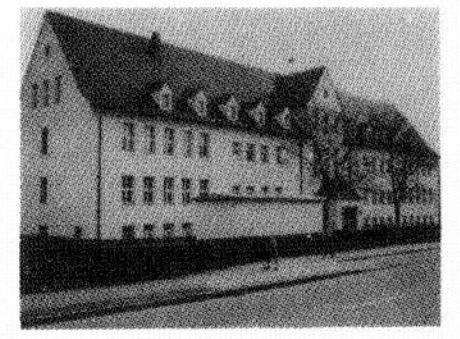

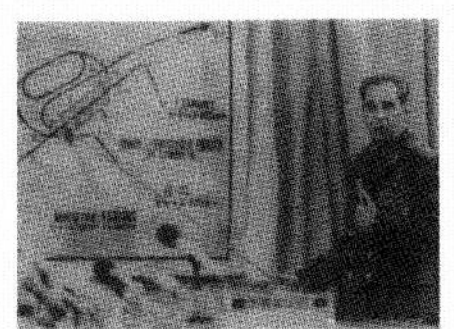

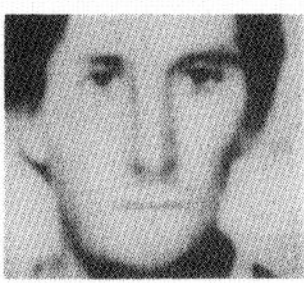

277 Thomas Ruff ■
Sterne, 1990
Mappe mit 8 Granolithographien, drucklackiert, 89 x 65 cm. Auflage: 40
Portfolio with 8 granolithographs, varnished, 35 x 25½ in. Edition: 40

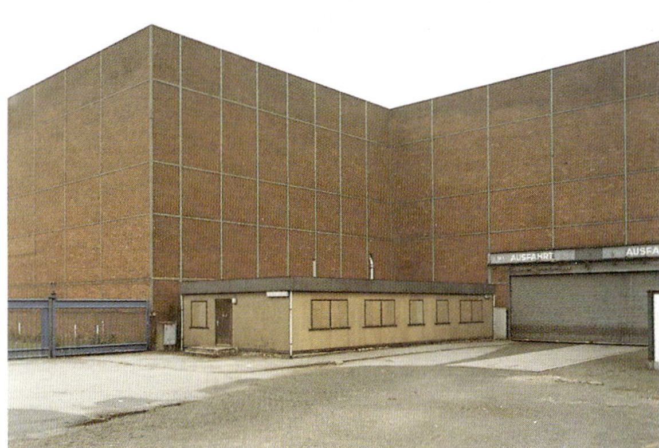

278 Thomas Ruff ■
Häuser, 1989
Mappe mit 5 Photographien (dye transfer), 45 x 55 cm. Auflage: 12
Portfolio with 5 dye-transfer photographs, 17¾ x 21¾ in. Edition: 12

279 Thomas Ruff → →
Nachtphotos, 1993

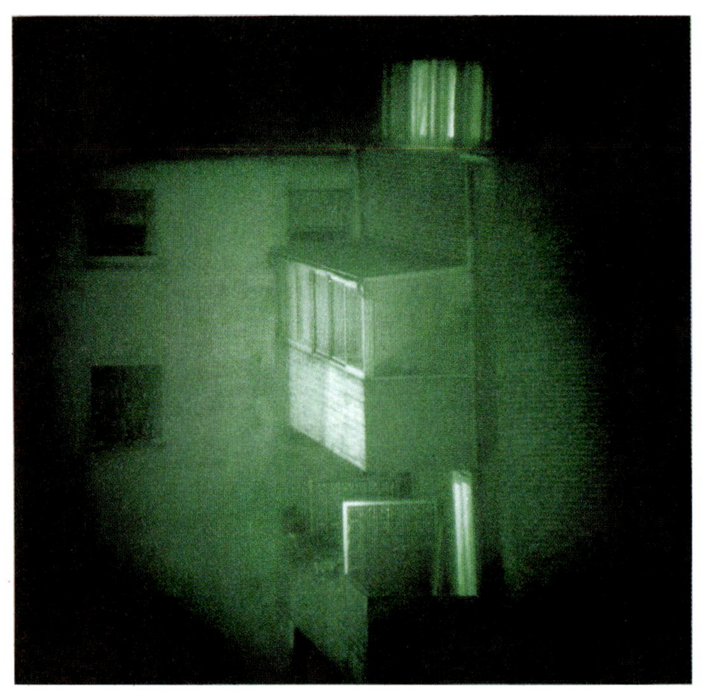

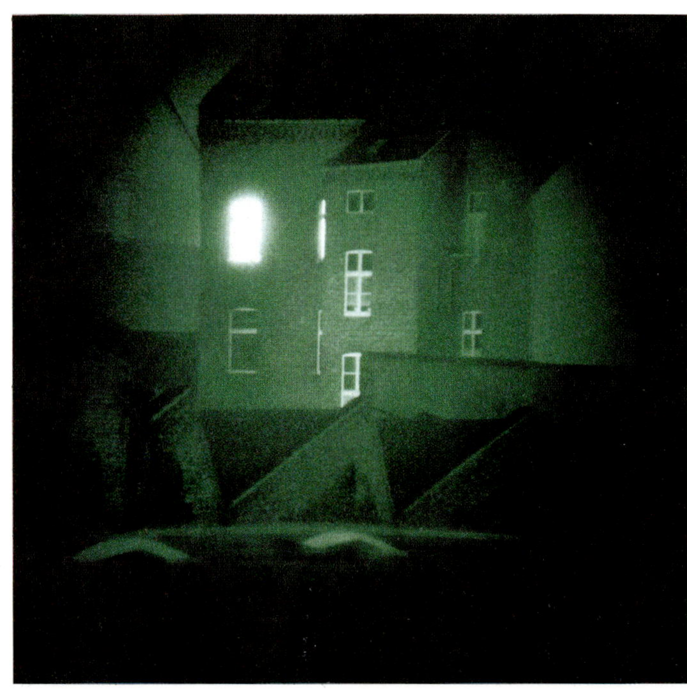

279 Thomas Ruff ■
Nachtphotos, 1993
Mappe mit 5 Granolithographien,
71 x 74 cm. Auflage: 45
Portfolio with 5 grano lithographs,
28 x 29 in. Edition: 45

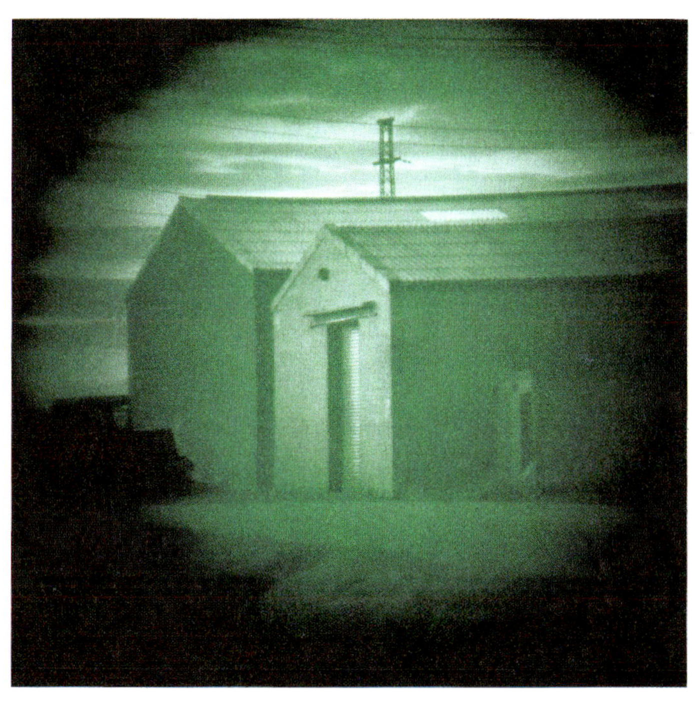

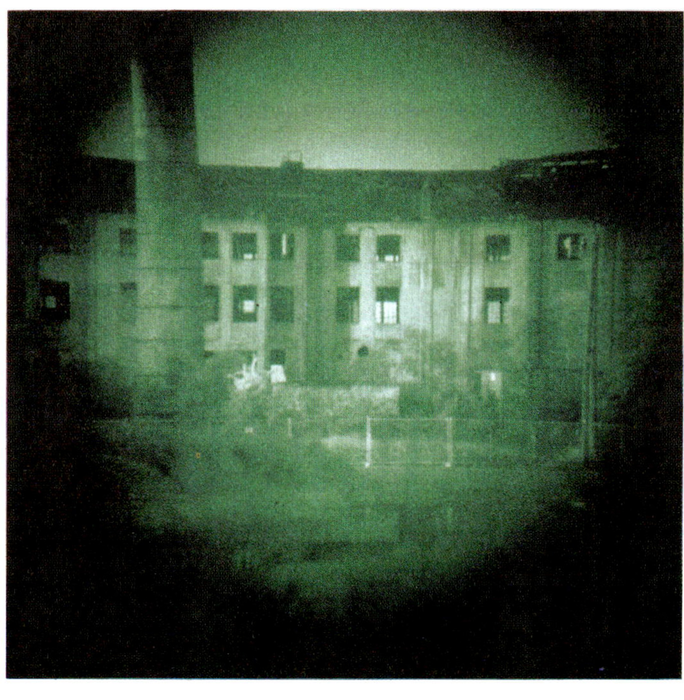

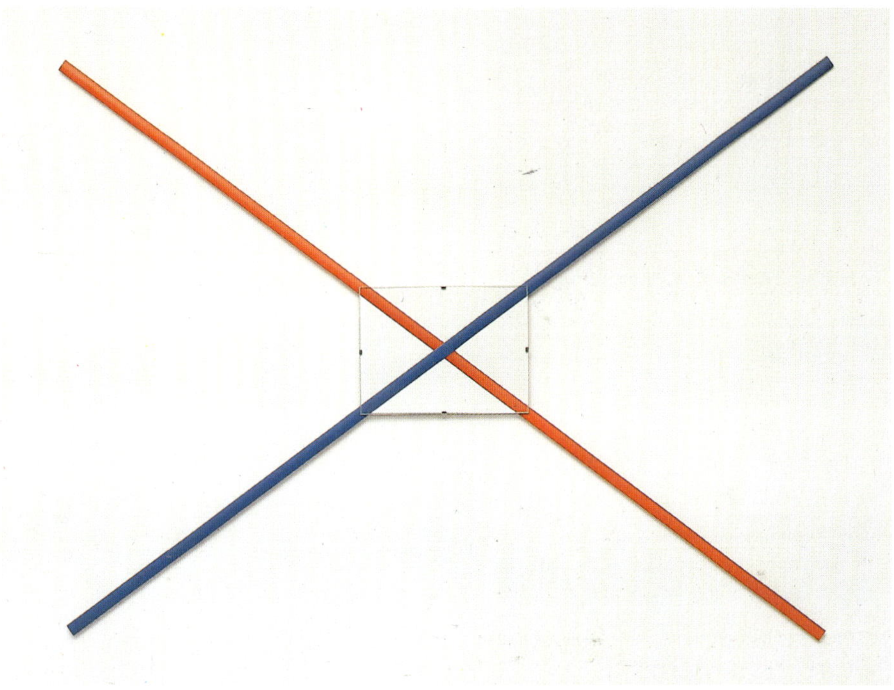

280 Rainer Ruthenbeck
Blau/Rote Überkreuzung in Rahmen, 1988
Objekt, 58 x 80 cm. Auflage: 10
Mixed media object, 23 x 31½ in. Edition: 10

281 Rainer Ruthenbeck ■ →
Verdecktes Zentrum, 1992
Schwarze Stabüberkreuzung mit zentraler Gipsfixierung, nach den Anweisungen des Künstlers an einer Wand zu installieren, siehe Appendix, 185 x 300 x 4 cm. Auflage: 10, mit sign. und num. Zertifikat.
Crossed aluminum bars, painted black, fixed in plaster at the center, to be installed on a wall according to the artist's instructions, see appendix, 73 x 118 x 1½ in. Edition: 10, with a signed and numbered certificate.

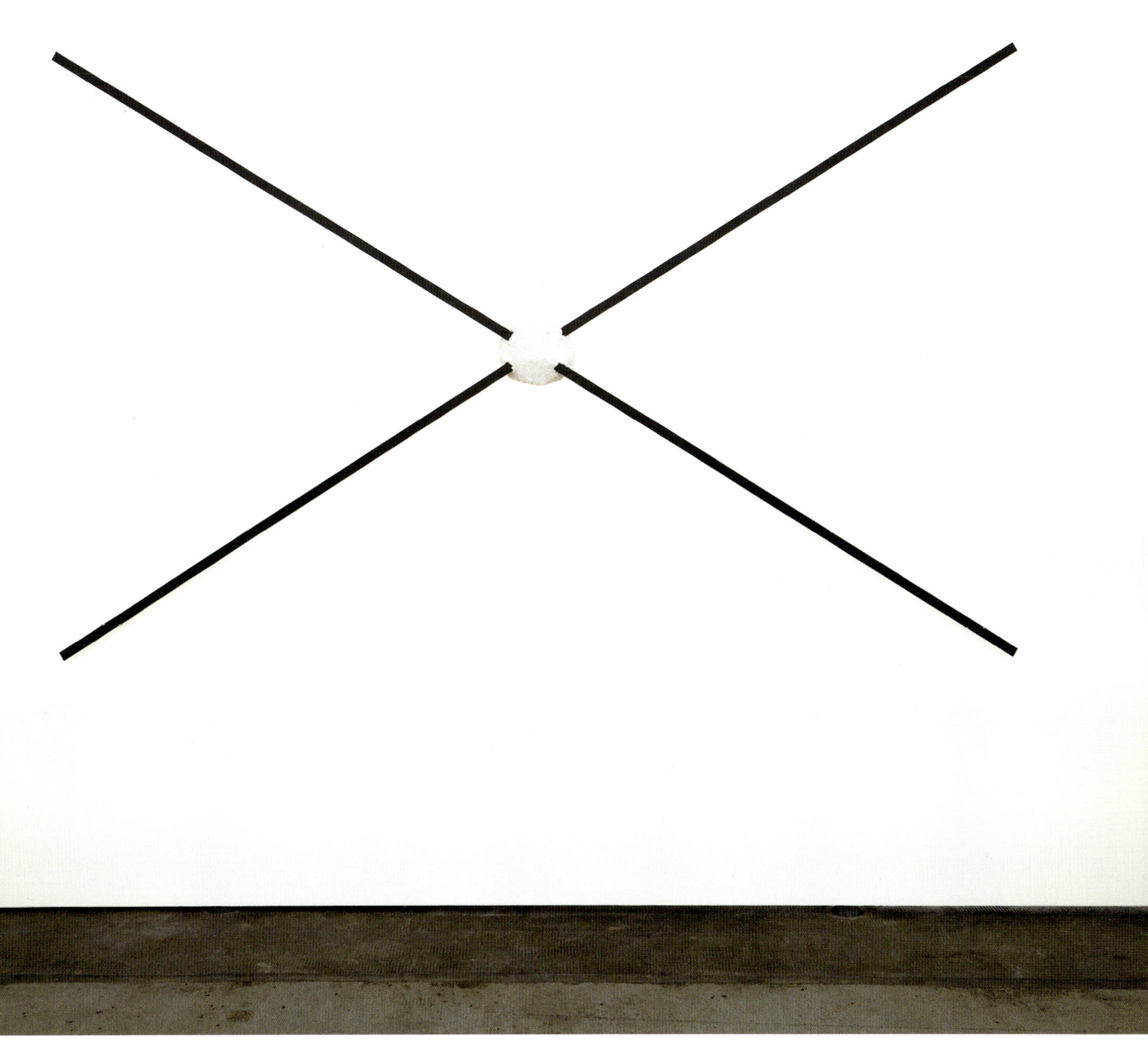

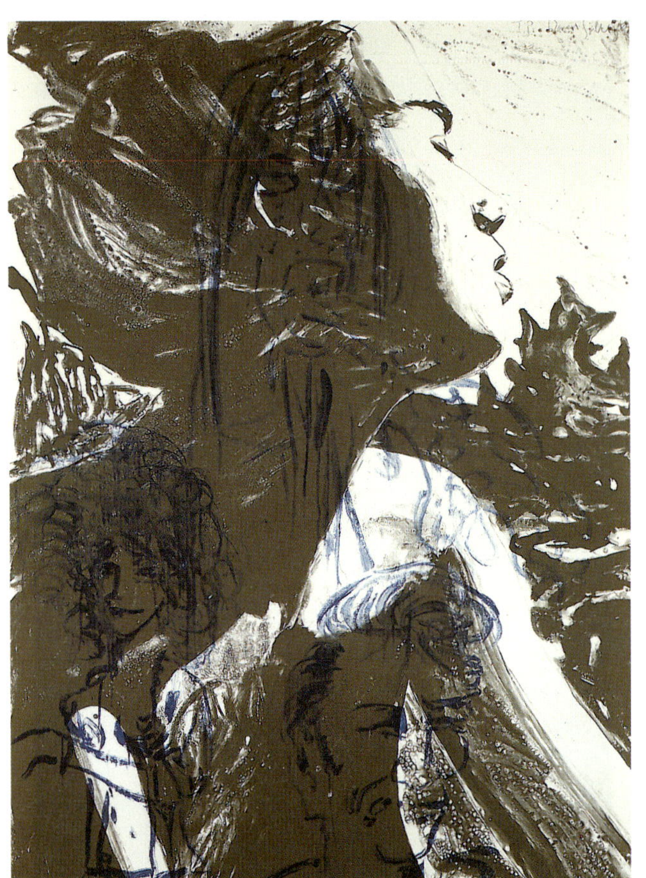

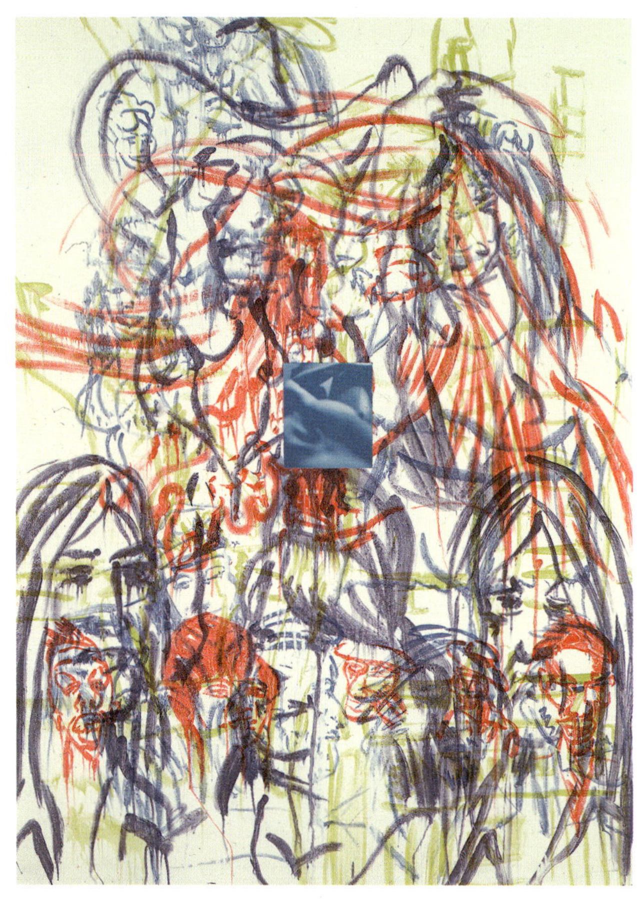

282 David Salle ■
Probedruck aus "Theme for an Aztec Moralist", 1983
Lithographie, 117 x 86 cm, eins von 6 Trial Proofs
Trial proof from "Theme for an Aztec Moralist", lithograph, 46 x 34 in., one of 6 trial proofs

283 David Salle ■
Theme for an Aztec Moralist, 1983
Folge von 6 Farblithographien, 117 x 86 cm. Auflage: 40
Set of 6 lithographs in colors, 46 x 34 in. Edition: 40

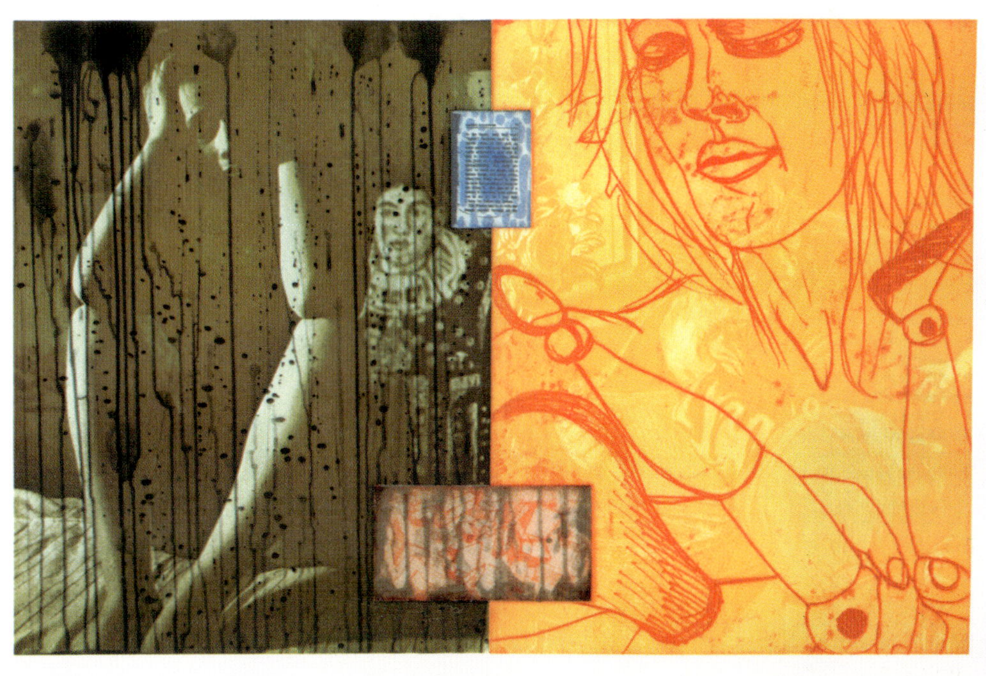

284 David Salle
Canfield Hatfield (9), 1990
Radierung (Weichgrund, Aquatinta und Heliogravur) auf Bütten, 77 x 111 cm. Auflage: 60
Etching (softground, aquatint, spit-bite and photo etching) on rag paper, 30 x 44 in. Edition: 60

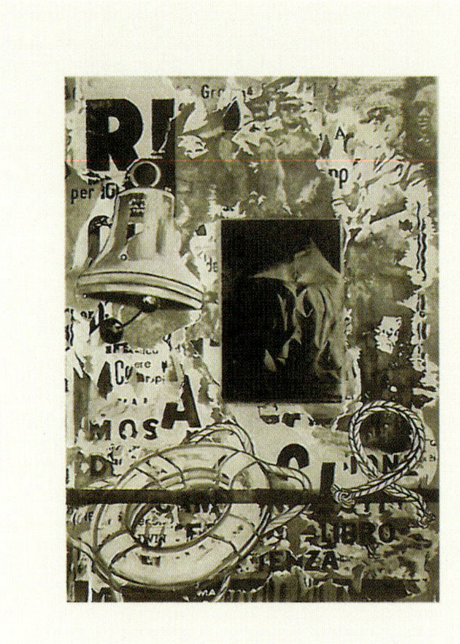

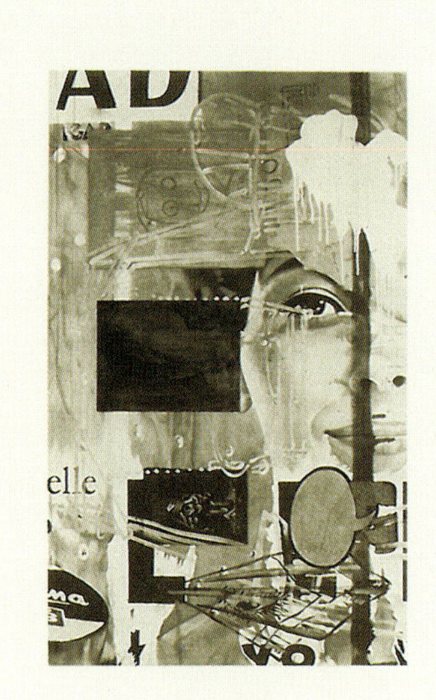

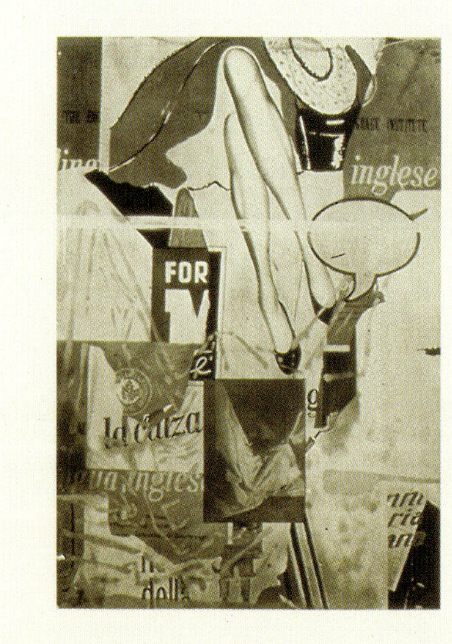

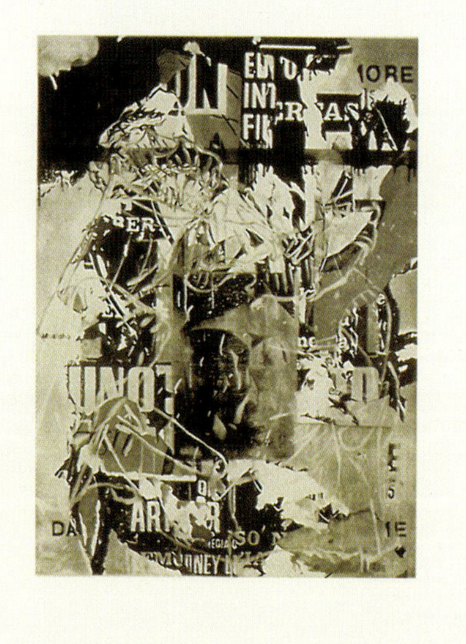

285 David Salle
Lucky I-VI, 1992
Folge von 6 Heliogravuren auf Bütten, 76 x 56 cm. Auflage: 35
Suite of 6 heliogravures on Lana rag paper, 30 x 22 in. Edition: 35

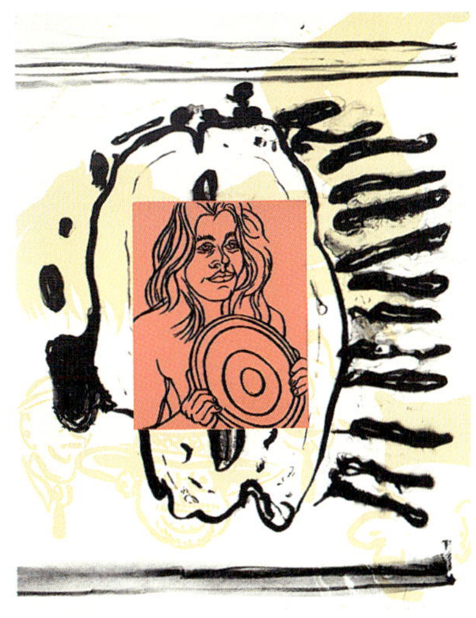
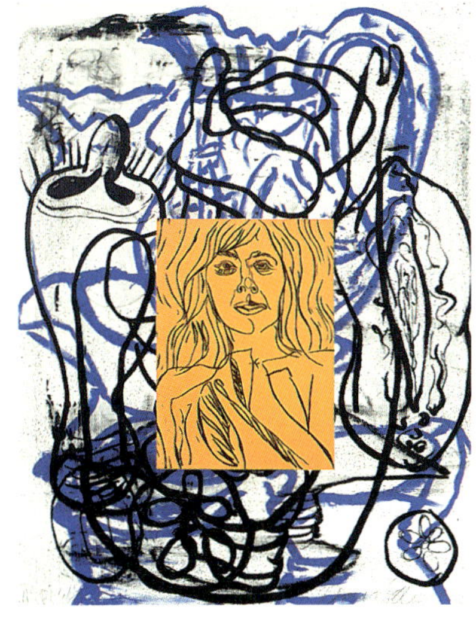
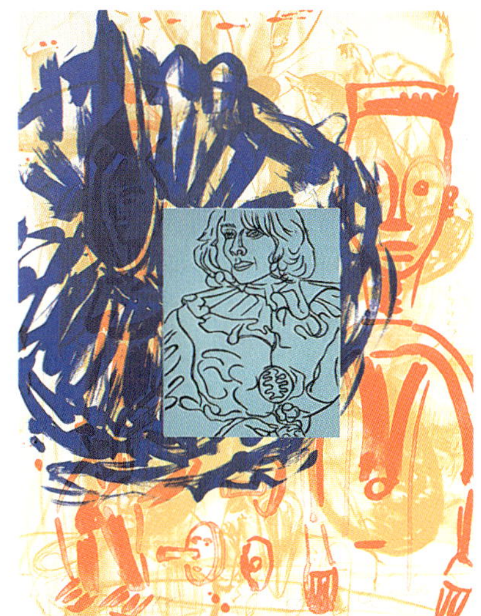
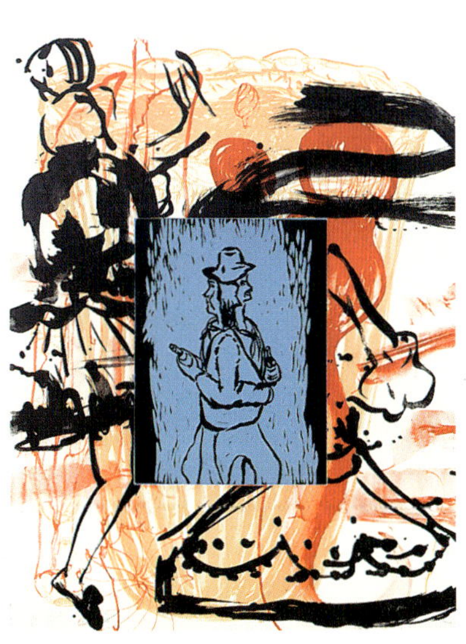
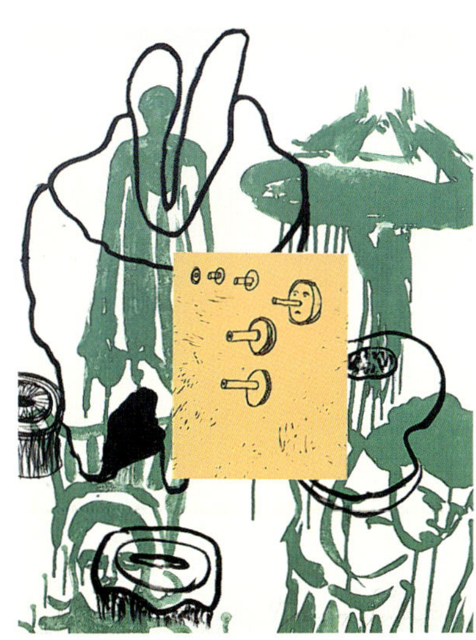
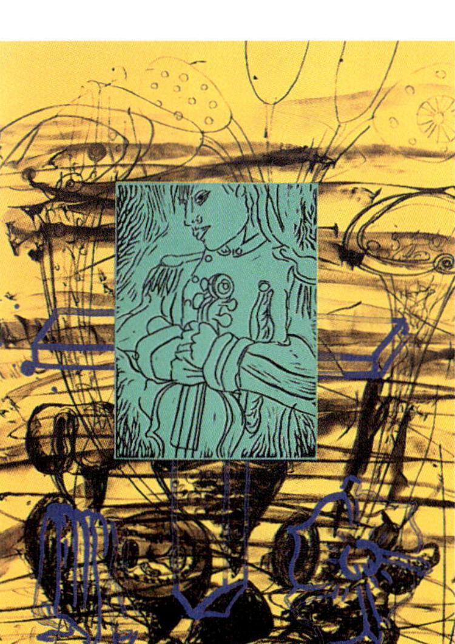

286 David Salle
Lively Iris, 1992
6 Lithographien/Linolschnitte, 69 x 54 cm. Auflage: 40
6 lithographs/linocuts, 27 x 21¼ in. Edition: 40

287-289 Julian Schnabel

287 Pandora + The Flying Dutchman, 1991 →
Radierung und Aquatinta über Collage, 198 x 137 cm. Auflage: 48
Etching and aquatint, printed over collage, 78 x 54 in. Edition: 48

288 Le Tango I, 1991 → →
Radierung und Aquatinta über Collage, 198 x 137 cm. Auflage: 48
Etching and aquatint, printed over collage, 78 x 54 in. Edition: 48

289 Flamingo I, 1991 → → →
Radierung und Aquatinta über Collage, 198 x 137 cm. Auflage: 48
Etching and aquatint, printed over collage, 78 x 54 in. Edition: 48

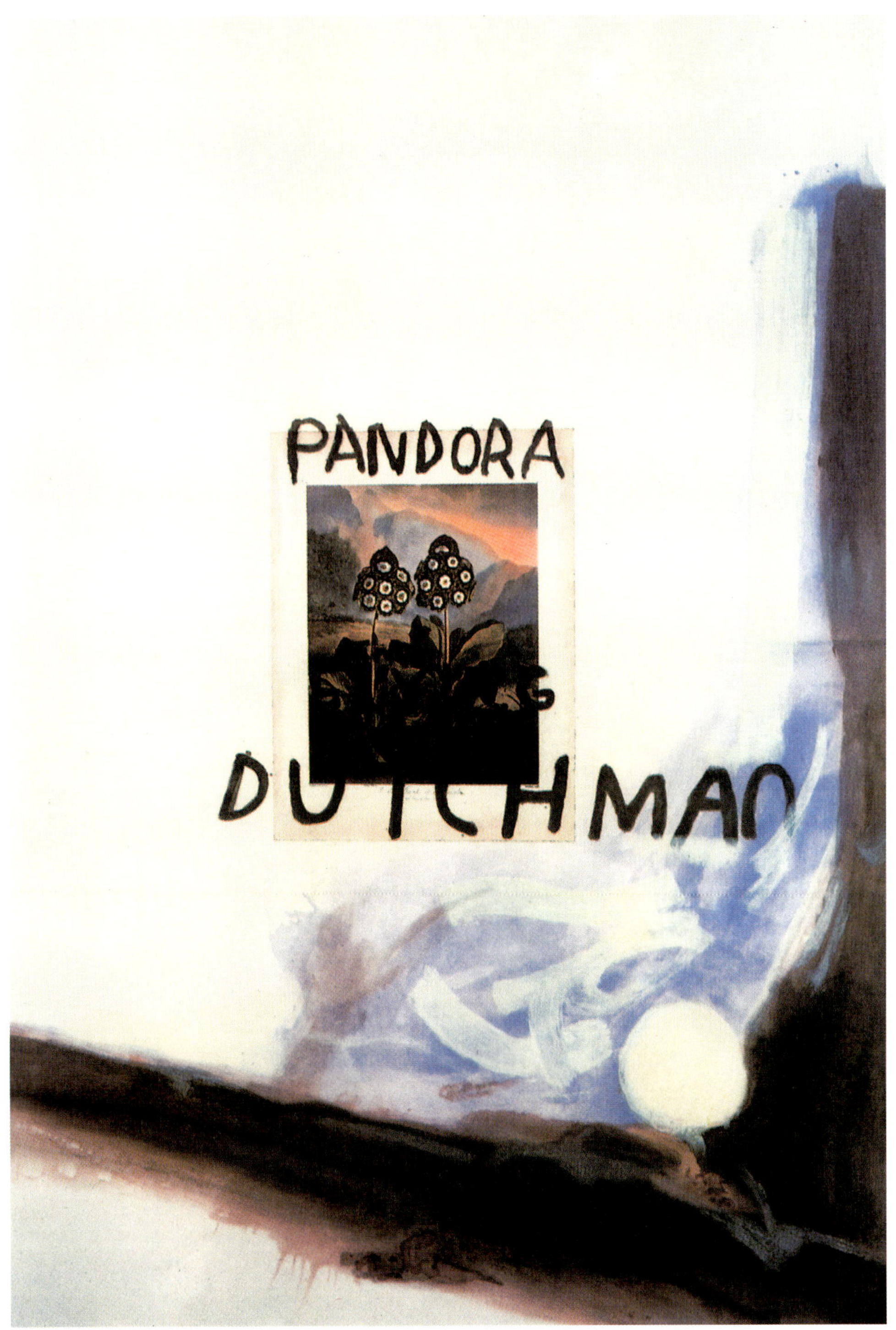
PANDORA
G
DUTCHMAN

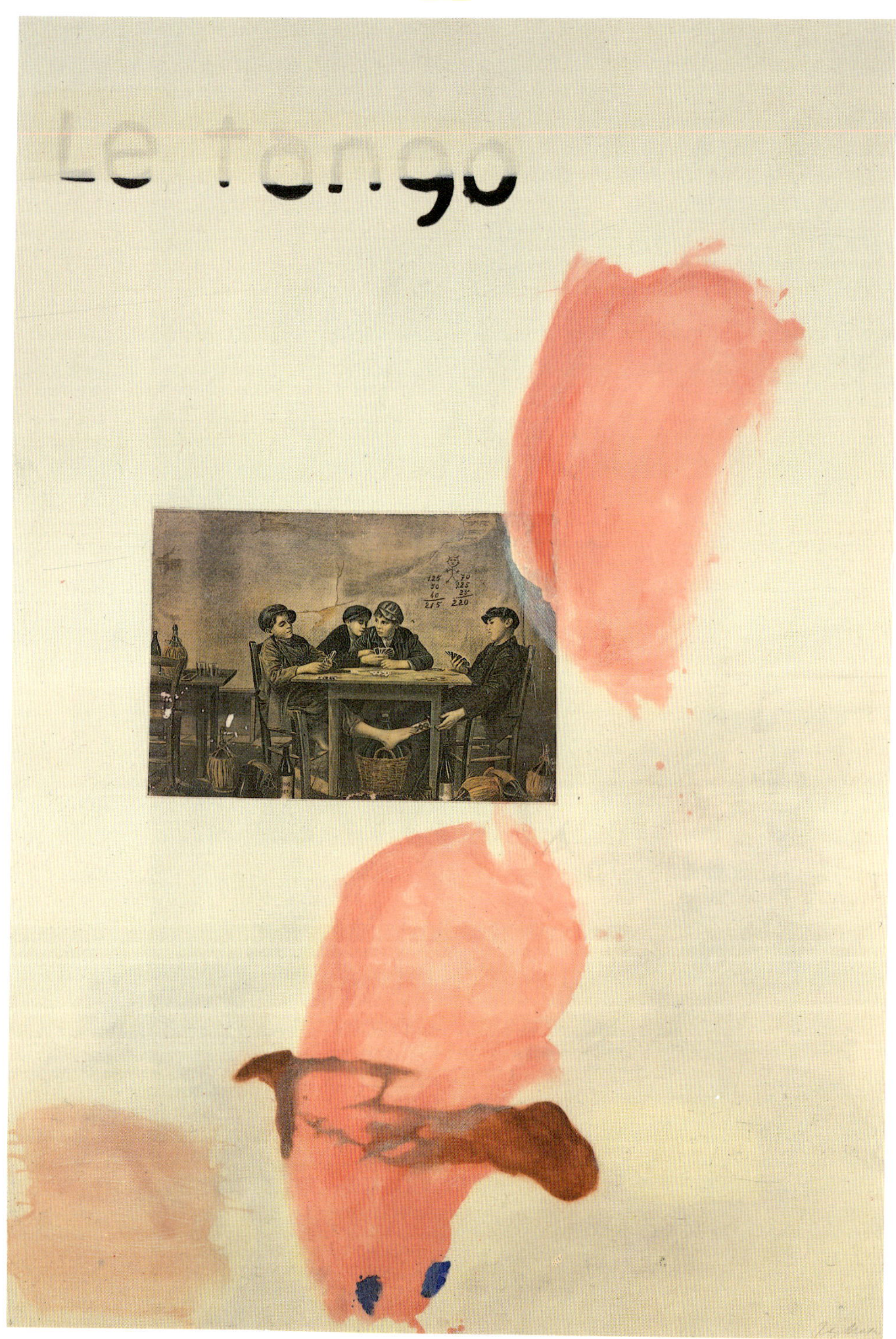
Le Tango

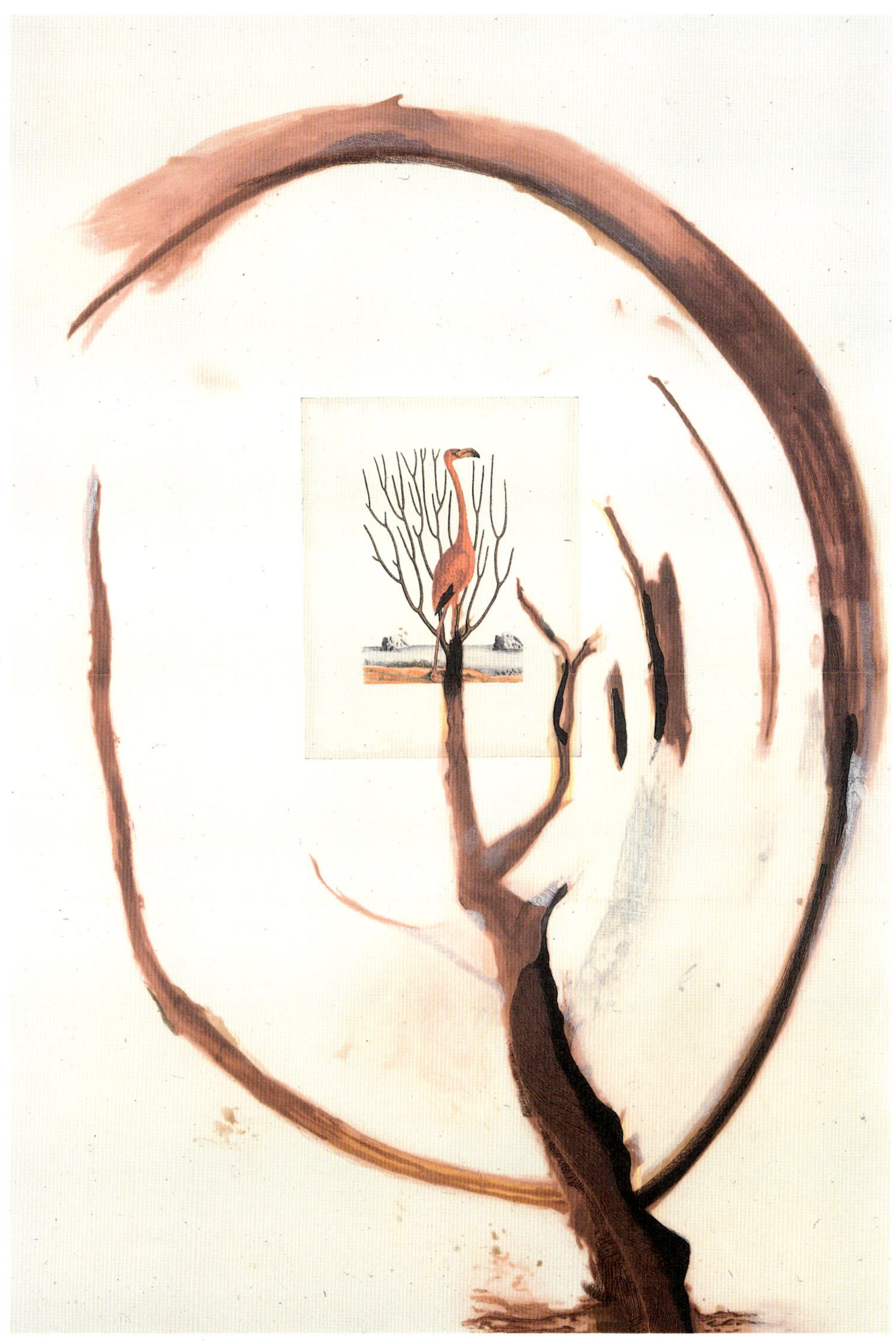

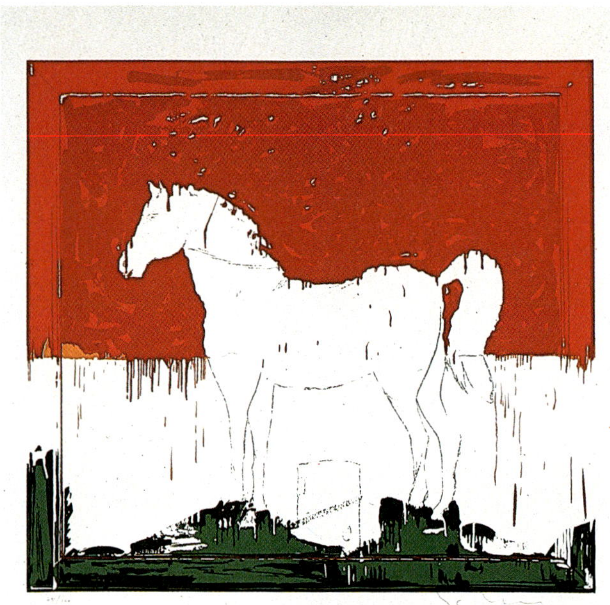

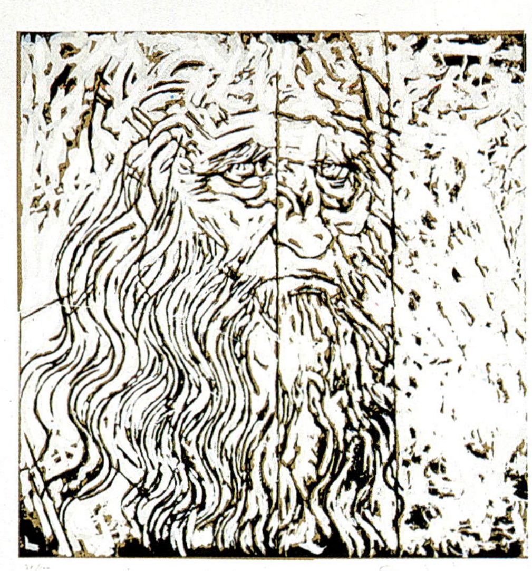

290 Mario Schifano
Cavallo, Leonardo da Vinci, 1982
Zwei Farbserigraphien auf Collage, 95 x 95 cm. Auflage: 100
Two silkscreens on collage, 37 x 37 cm. Edition: 100

291 Richard Serra →
Spike, 1991
Ölkreide und Siebdruck auf schwerem Karton, 350 x 244 cm. Auflage: 10
Paintstick and screenprint on coated paper, 138 x 96 cm. Edition: 10

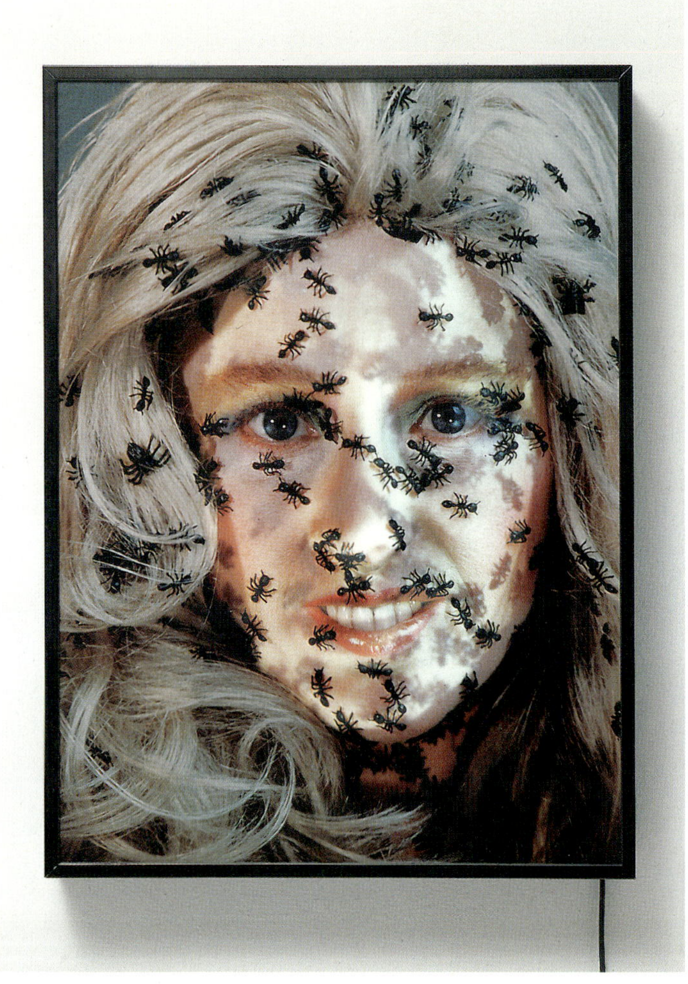

292 Cindy Sherman ■
Untitled, 1989
Lichtkasten mit zwei übereinander liegenden Dias,
80 x 60 x 8,5 cm. Auflage: 24
Light box with two transparencies superimposed,
31½ x 23½ x 3½ in. Edition: 24

293 Cindy Sherman ■ →
Untitled, 1993
Lichtkasten (schwarz) mit Farbdia, 155 x 100 x 8,5 cm. Siehe Appendix. Auflage: 15
Light box with color transparency, 61 x 39½ x 3¼ in. See appendix. Edition: 15

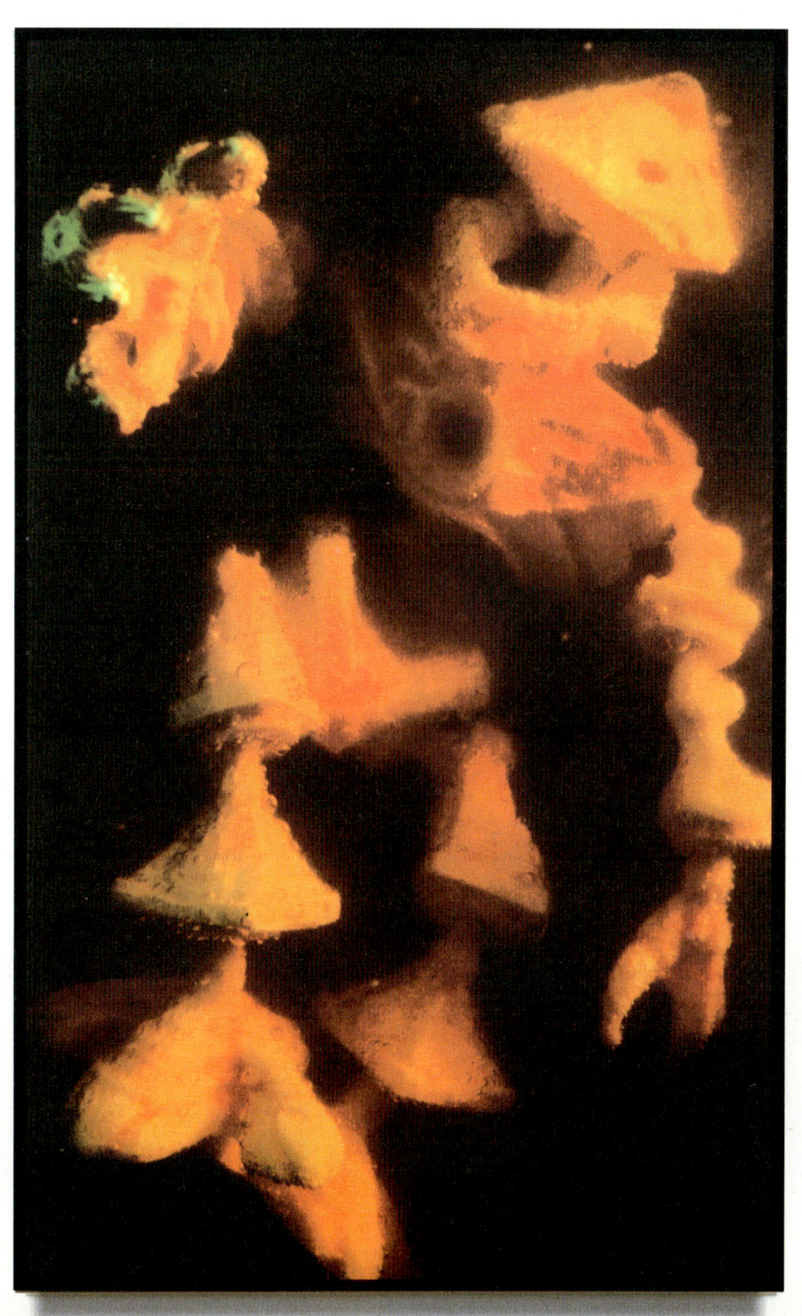

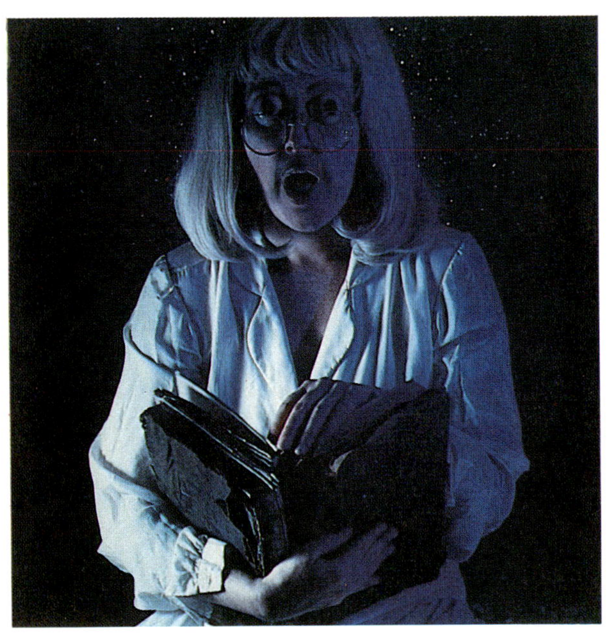

294 Cindy Sherman
Untitled, 1986/93
Farbphotograhie, 28 x 35,5 cm. Auflage: 200
Color photograph, 11 x 14 in. Edition: 200

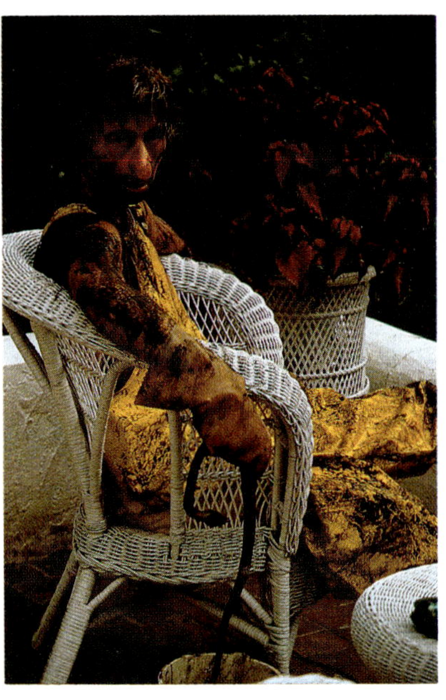

295 Cindy Sherman
Untitled, 1987
Farbphotographie, 35,5, x 28 cm. Auflage: 125
Color photograph, 14 x 11 in. Edition: 125

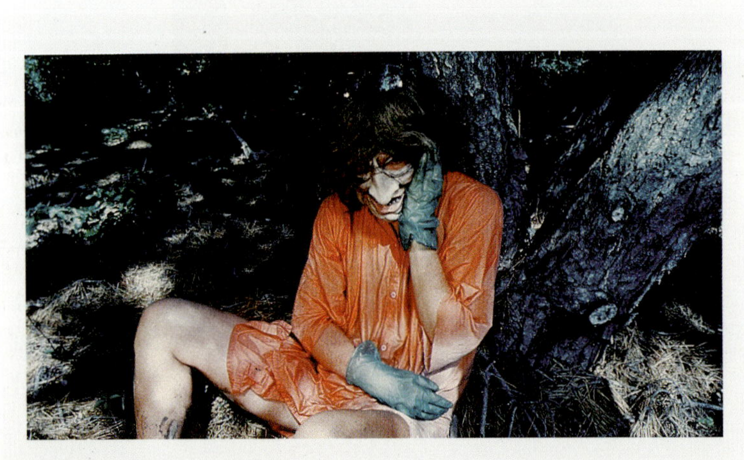

296 Cindy Sherman
Untitled, 1986
Farbphotographie, 51 x 61 cm. Auflage: 75
Color photograph, 20 x 24 in. Edition: 75

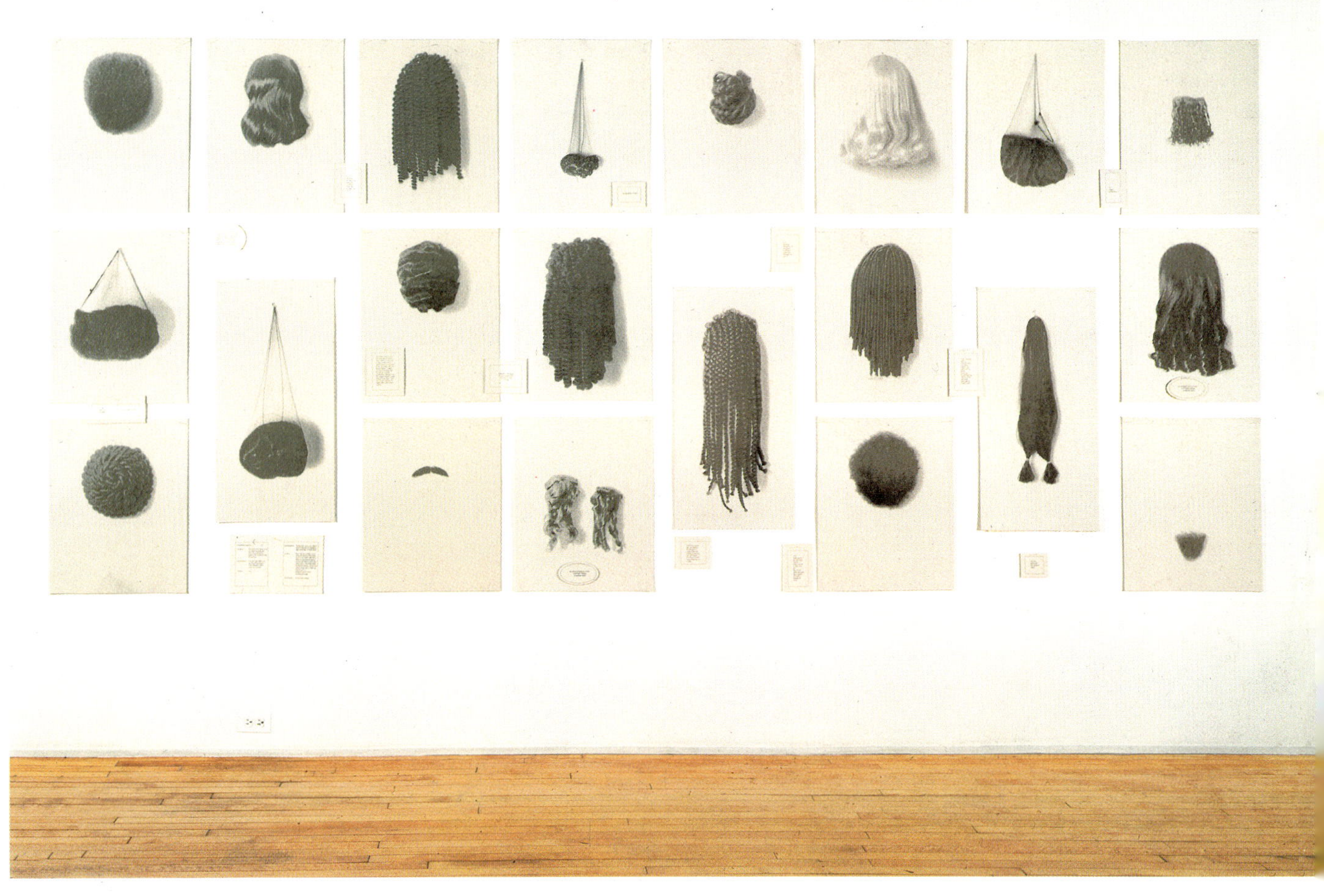

297 Lorna Simpson
Wigs, 1994
Mappe mit 39 Lithographien, auf Filz gedruckt, insgesamt 183 x 413 cm. Auflage: 15
Portfolio with 39 waterless lithographs on felt, overall 72 x 162½ in. Edition: 15

298 Katharina Sieverding
Waerme, 1993
Farbphoto, 108,5 x 52,5 cm. Auflage: 9 unikate Variationen.
Color photograph, 42¾ x 20¾ in. Edition: 9 unique variations.

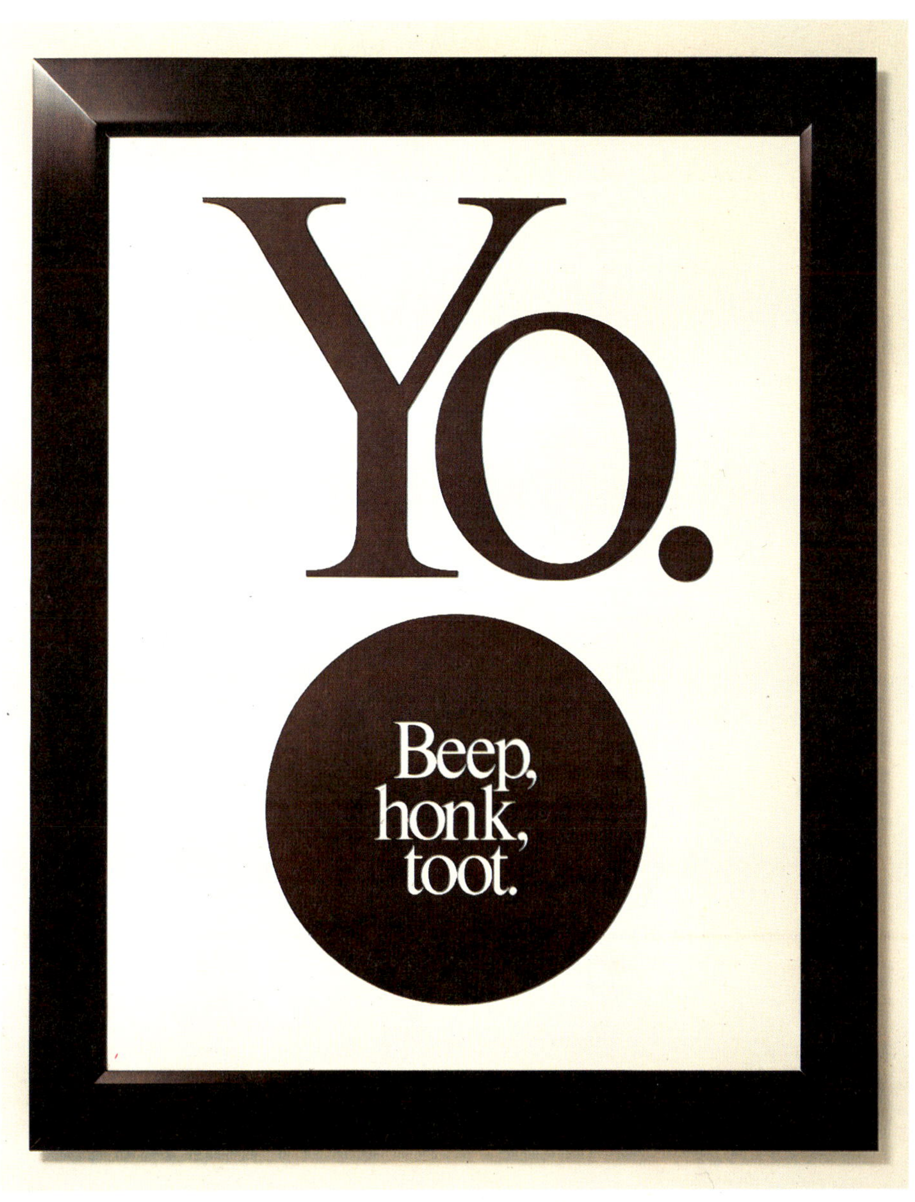

299 Haim Steinbach ■
yo. beep, honk, toot, 1993
Lithographie in eloxiertem Aluminiumrahmen, 137 x 108,5 x 5 cm. Auflage: 20
Lithograph in anodized aluminum frame, 54 x 42¾ x 2 in. Edition: 20

300 Haim Steinbach ■

big brown bag, 1992

Schrifzug (Wandfarbe schwarz) auf einer Wand, Behälter aus Edelstahl; nach den Anweisungen des Künstlers zu installieren, siehe Appendix. Gesamtmaße: 262 x 221 x 56 cm. Auflage: 15, mit sign. und num. Zeichnung

Slogan stencilled on a wall in black paint, with trash can, to be installed according to the artist's instructions, see appendix. Overall size: 103 x 87 x 22 in. Edition: 15, with a signed and numbered certificate drawing

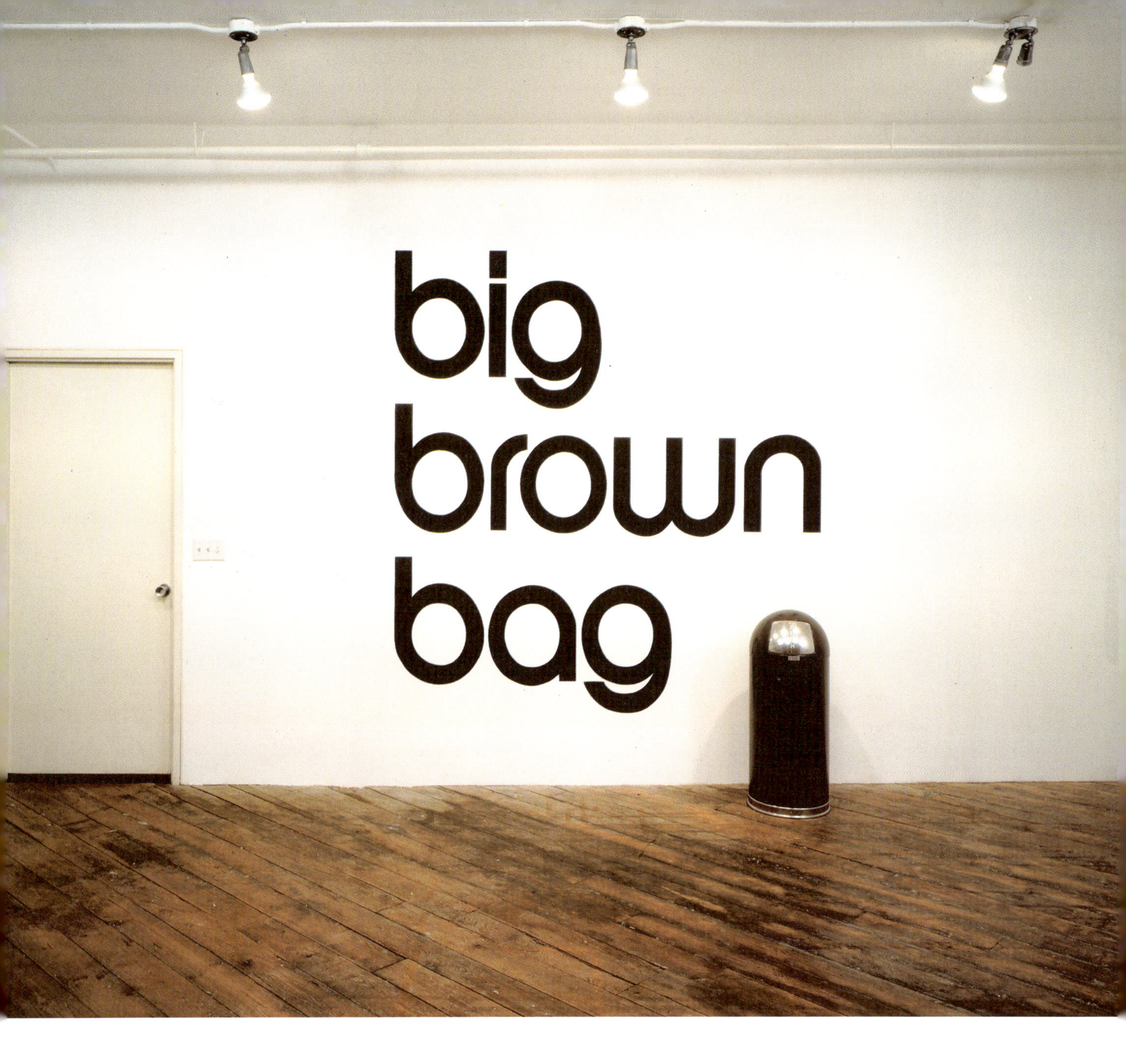
big
brown
bag

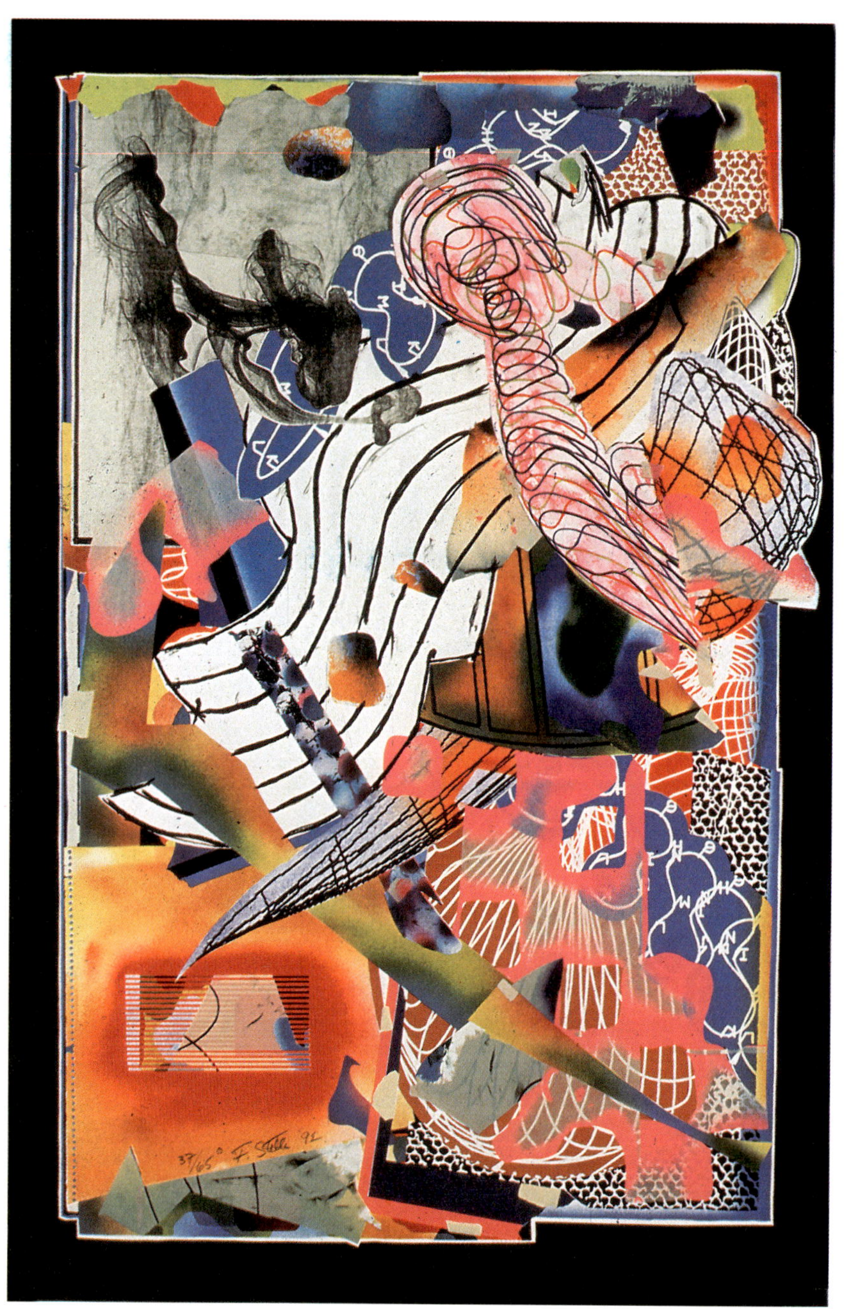

301 Frank Stella
The Candles, 1992
Lithographie, Siebdruck und Collage (25 Farben), 148 x 99 cm. Auflage: 65
Lithograph, screenprint, collage (25 colors), 58¼ x 39 in. Edition: 65

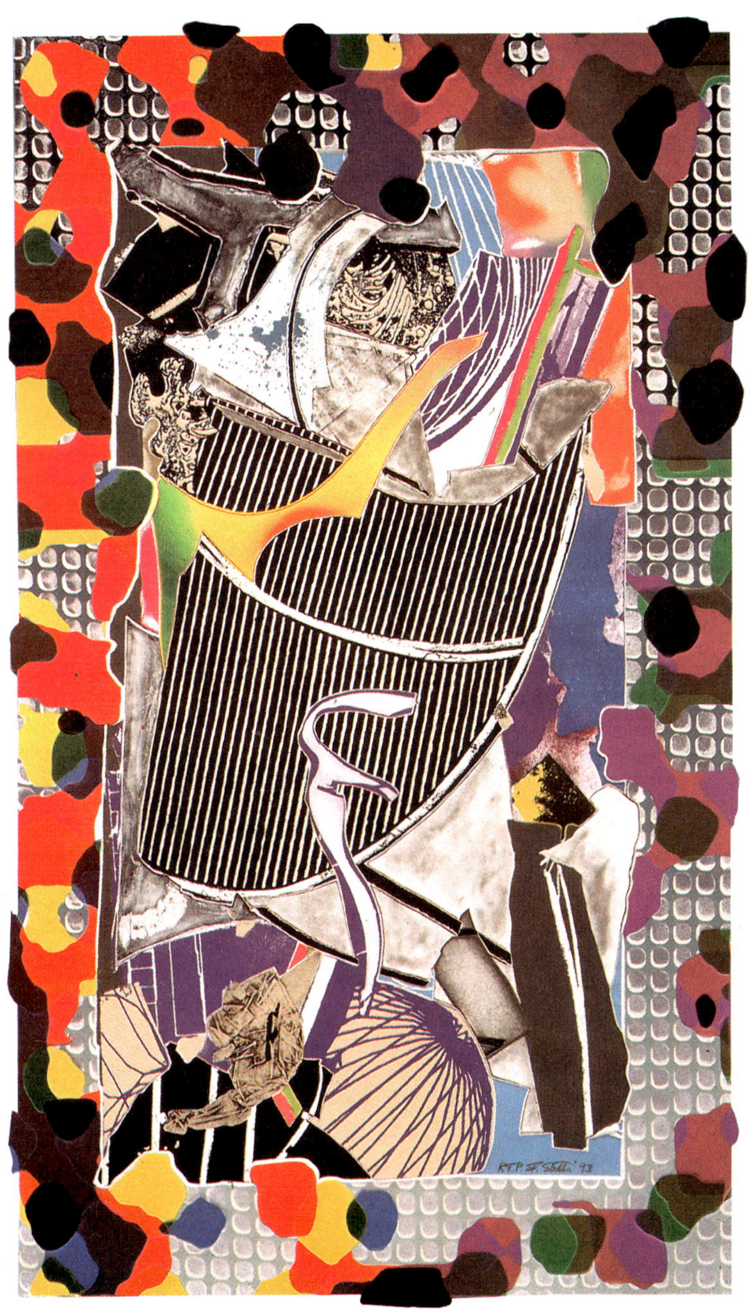

302 Frank Stella
The Battering Ram, 1993
Lithographie, Radierung, Aquatinta, Relief und Siebdruck (insges. 48 Farben), 151 x 90 cm. Auflage: 30
Lithograph, etching, aquatint, relief, engraving, silkscreen (altogether 48 colors), 59½ x 35½ in. Edition: 30

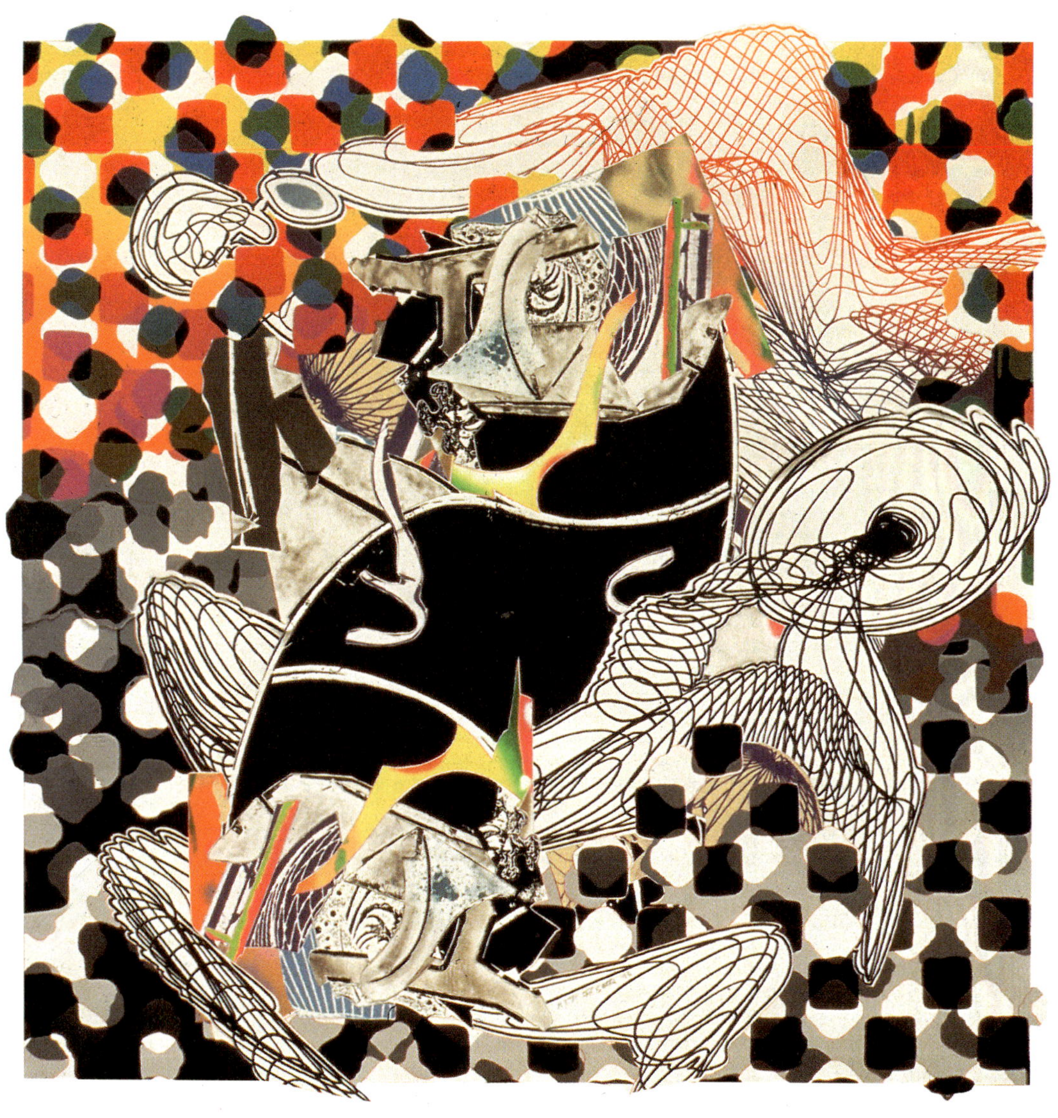

303 Frank Stella
The Whale-Watch, 1993
Lithographie, Radierung, Aquatinta, Relief (insges. 35 Farben), 184 x 185 cm. Auflage: 26
Lithograph, etching, aquatint, relief (altogether 35 colors), 72½ x 73 in. Edition: 26

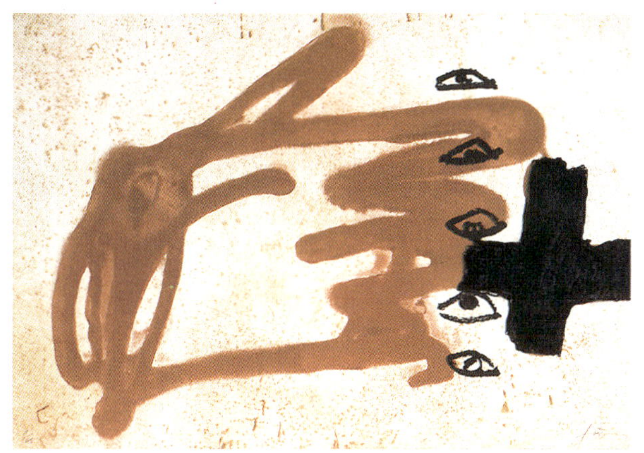
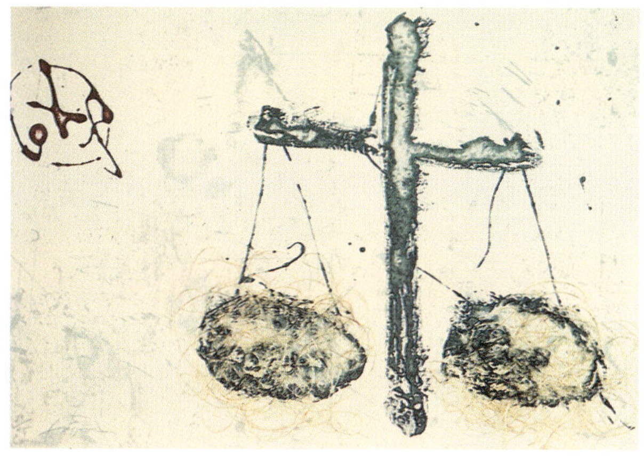
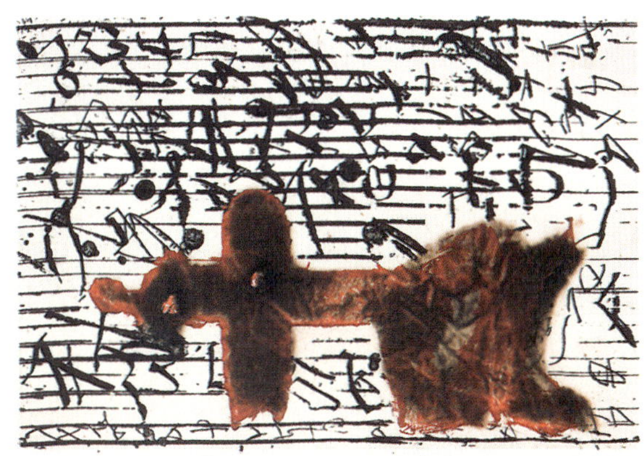
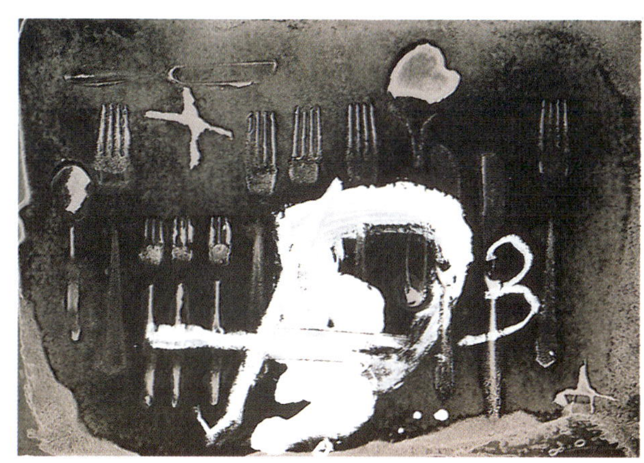
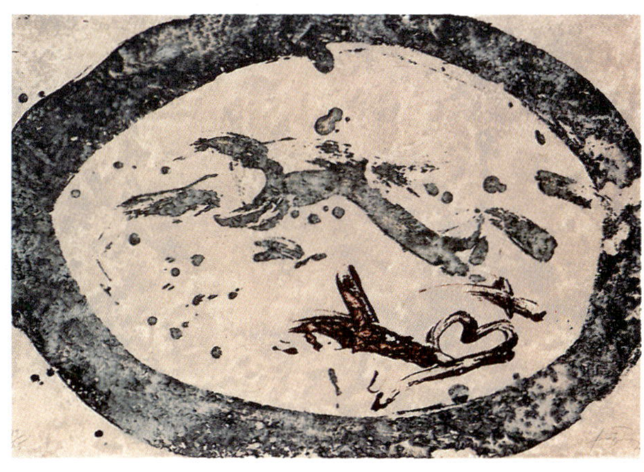
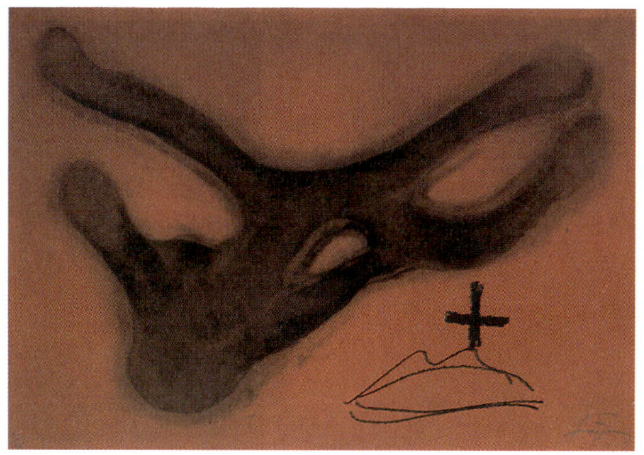

304 Antoni Tàpies
Grabados, 1994
Folge von 10 Aquatintaradierungen, 33 x 50 cm. Auflage 45. *Suite of 10 etchings, 13 x 19¾ in. Edition: 45*

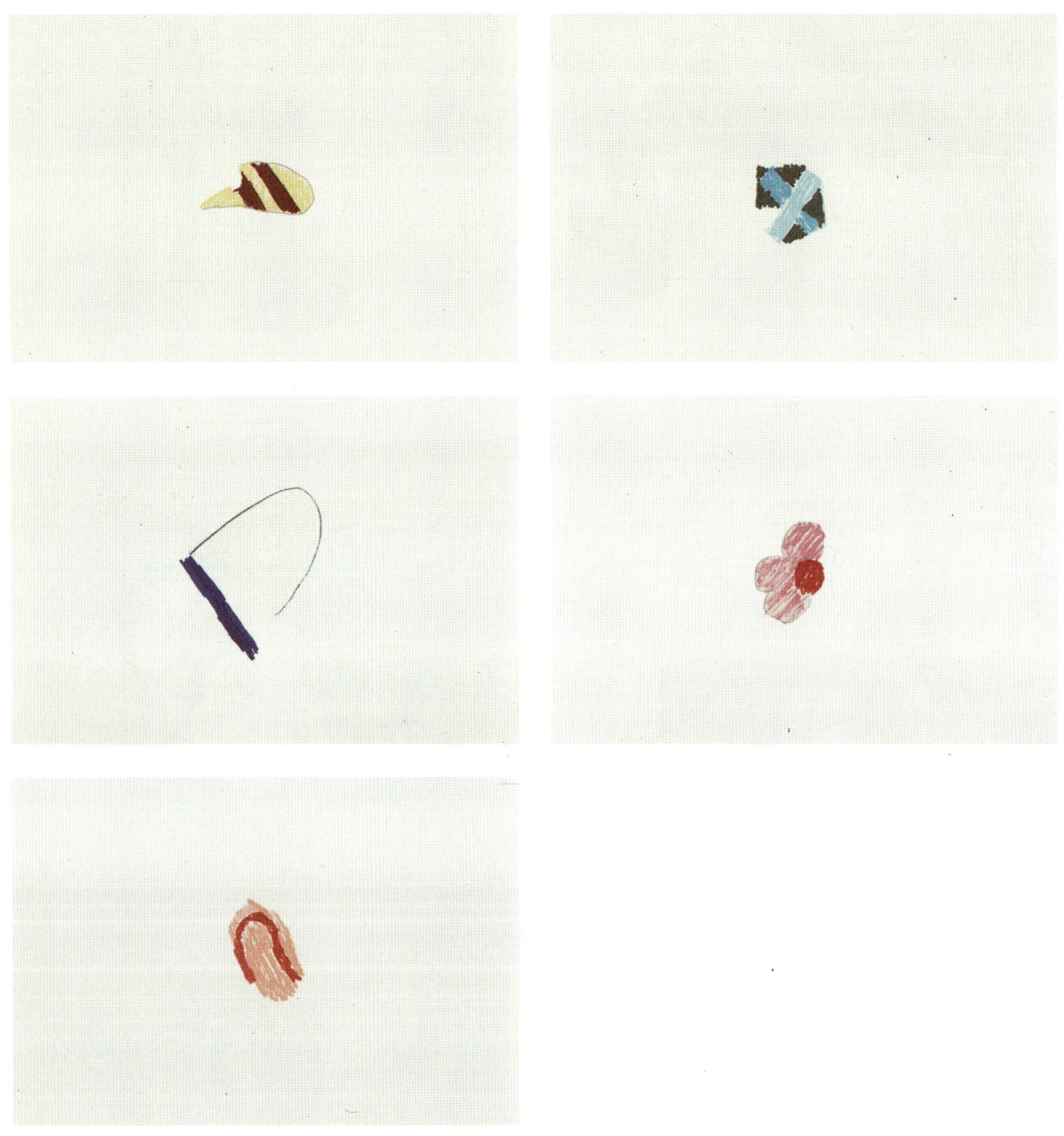

305 Richard Tuttle
Perceived Obstacle, 1991
Folge von 5 Lithographien, 30,5 x 92 cm. Auflage: 45. *Set of 5 lithographs, 12½ x 36½ in. Edition: 45*

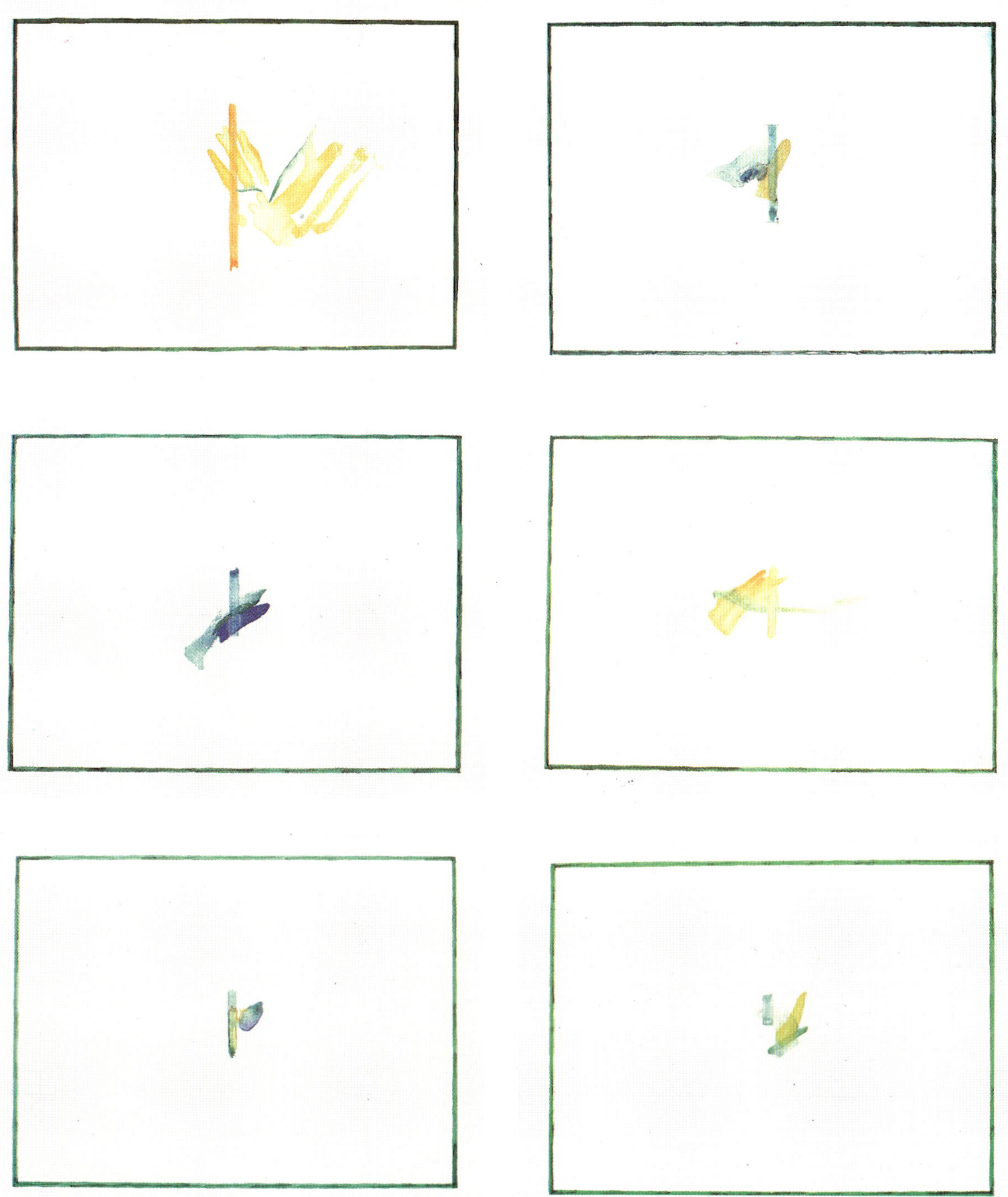

306 Richard Tuttle
Galisteo Paintings, 1993
Mappe mit 7 Holzschnitten, 30,5 x 40,5 cm. Auflage: 30. *Portfolio of 7 woodcuts, 12 x 16 in. Edition: 30*

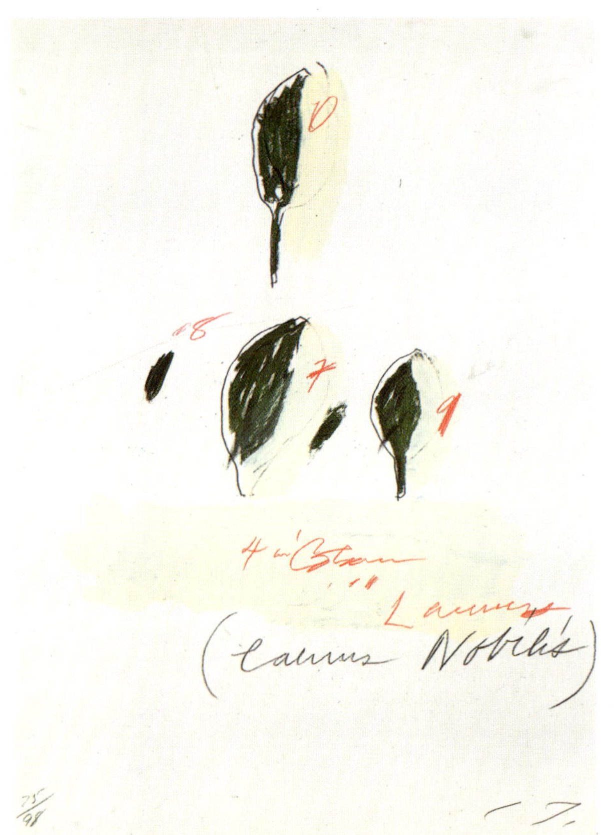

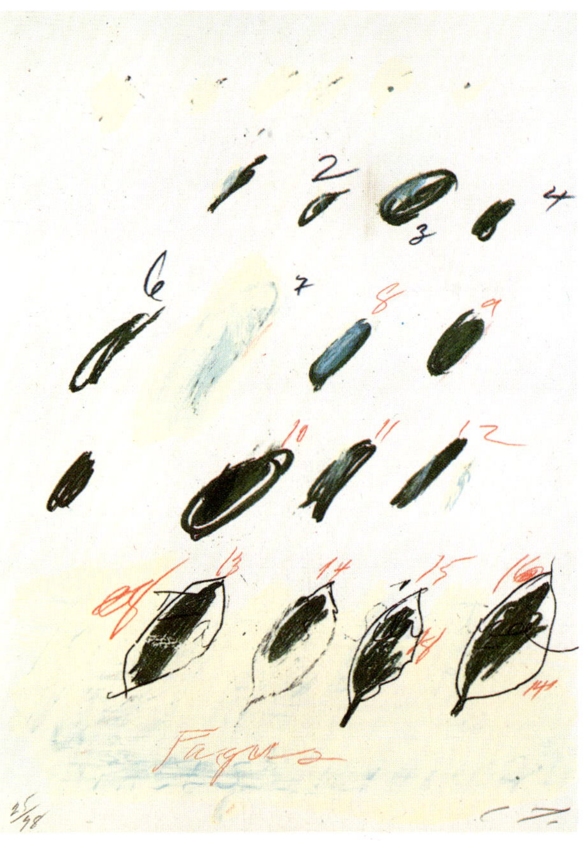

307 Cy Twombly
Natural History II (Some Trees of Italy), 1976
Mappe mit 8 Farblithograhien, 76 x 56 cm. Auflage: 98
Portfolio with 8 lithographs, 30 x 22 in. Edition: 98

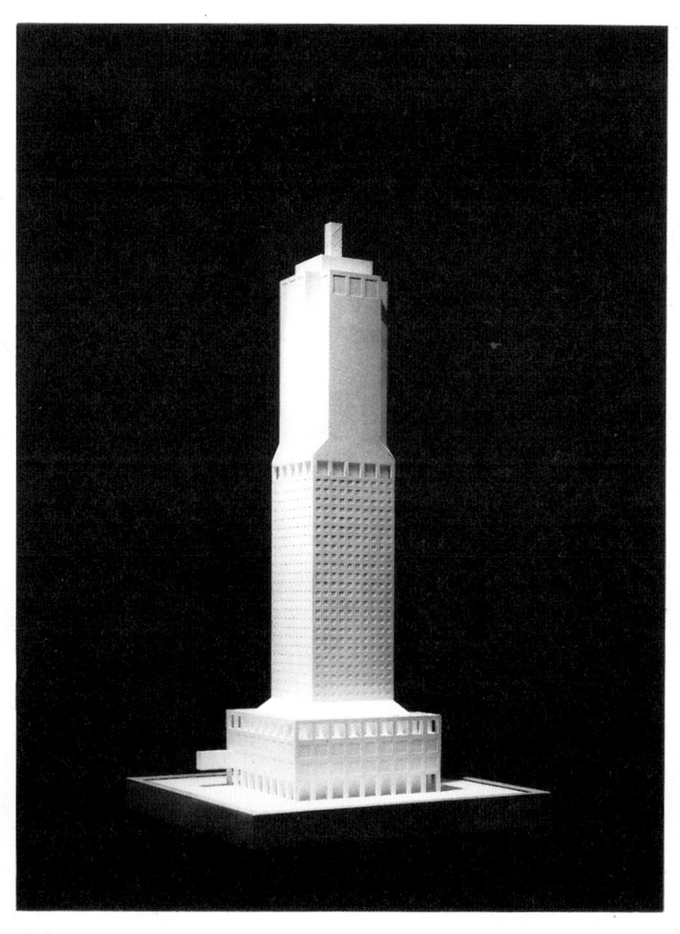

308 Oswald Matthias Ungers
O.M. Ungers, 1994
Mappe mit 12 Heliogravuren, 80 x 60 cm. Auflage: 15 + V
Portfolio of 12 photo etchings, 80 x 60 cm. Edition: 15 + V

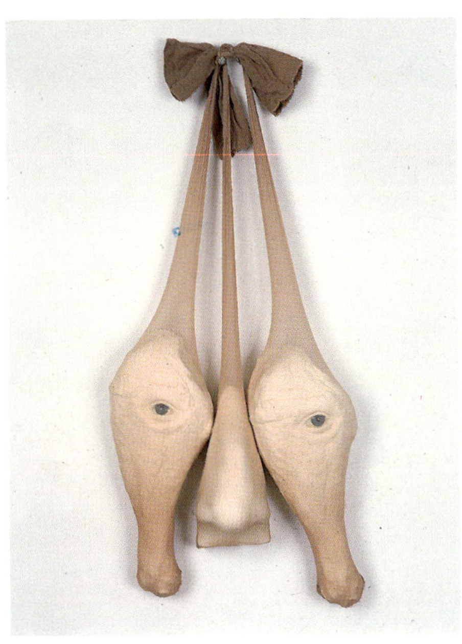

309 Meyer Vaisman
Turkey Parts (Blue Eyes), 1993
Verschiedene Materialien,
44,5 x 32 x 11,5 cm. Auflage: 3
Mixed media object,
17½ x 12½ x 4½ in. Edition: 3

310 Meyer Vaisman
Summer Suite, 1989
Mappe mit 6 Serigraphien, 126 x 86 cm.
Auflage: 75
Portfolio of 6 serigraphs, 49½ x 34 in.
Edition: 75

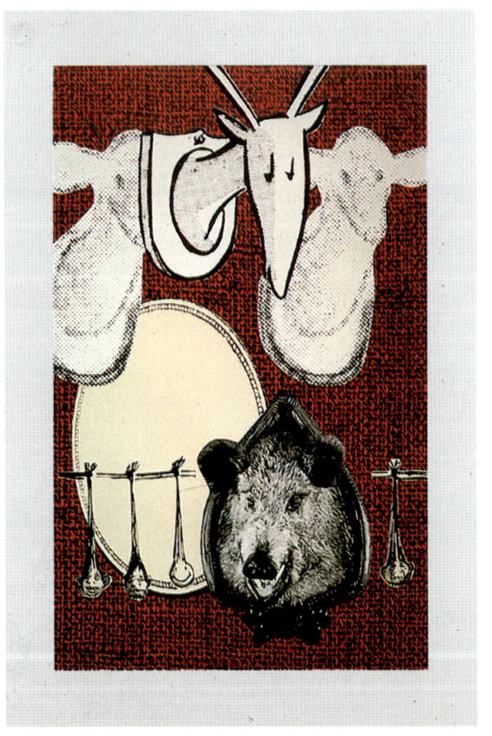

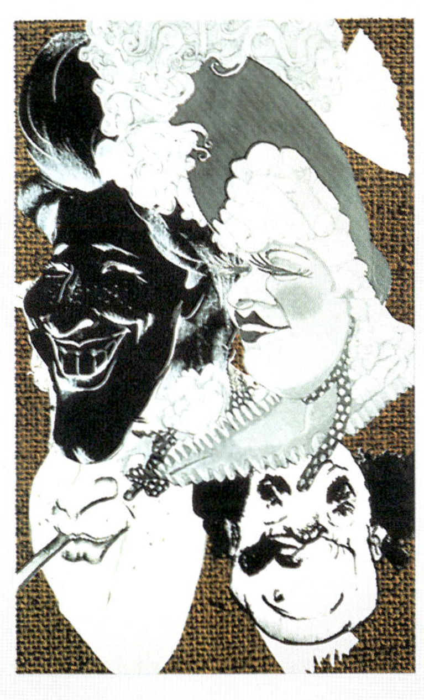

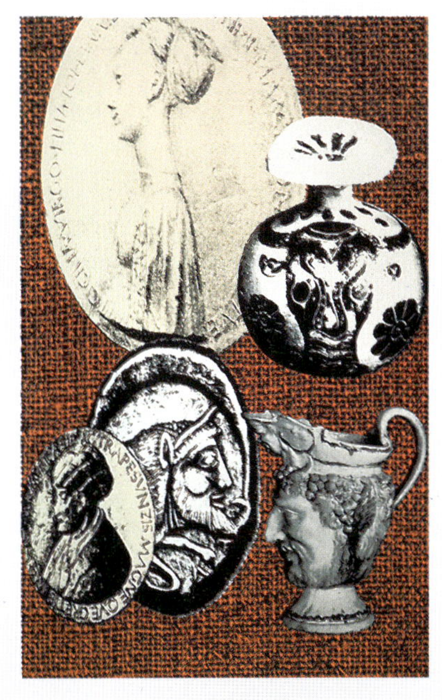

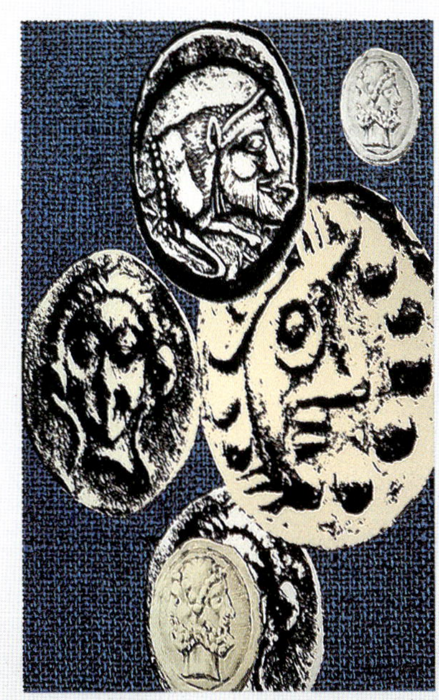

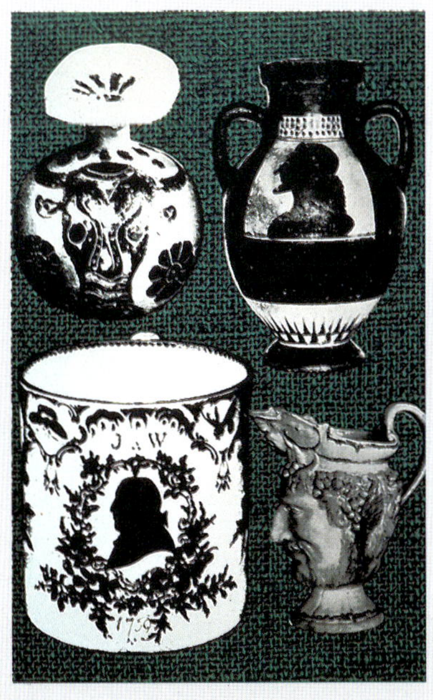
J A W

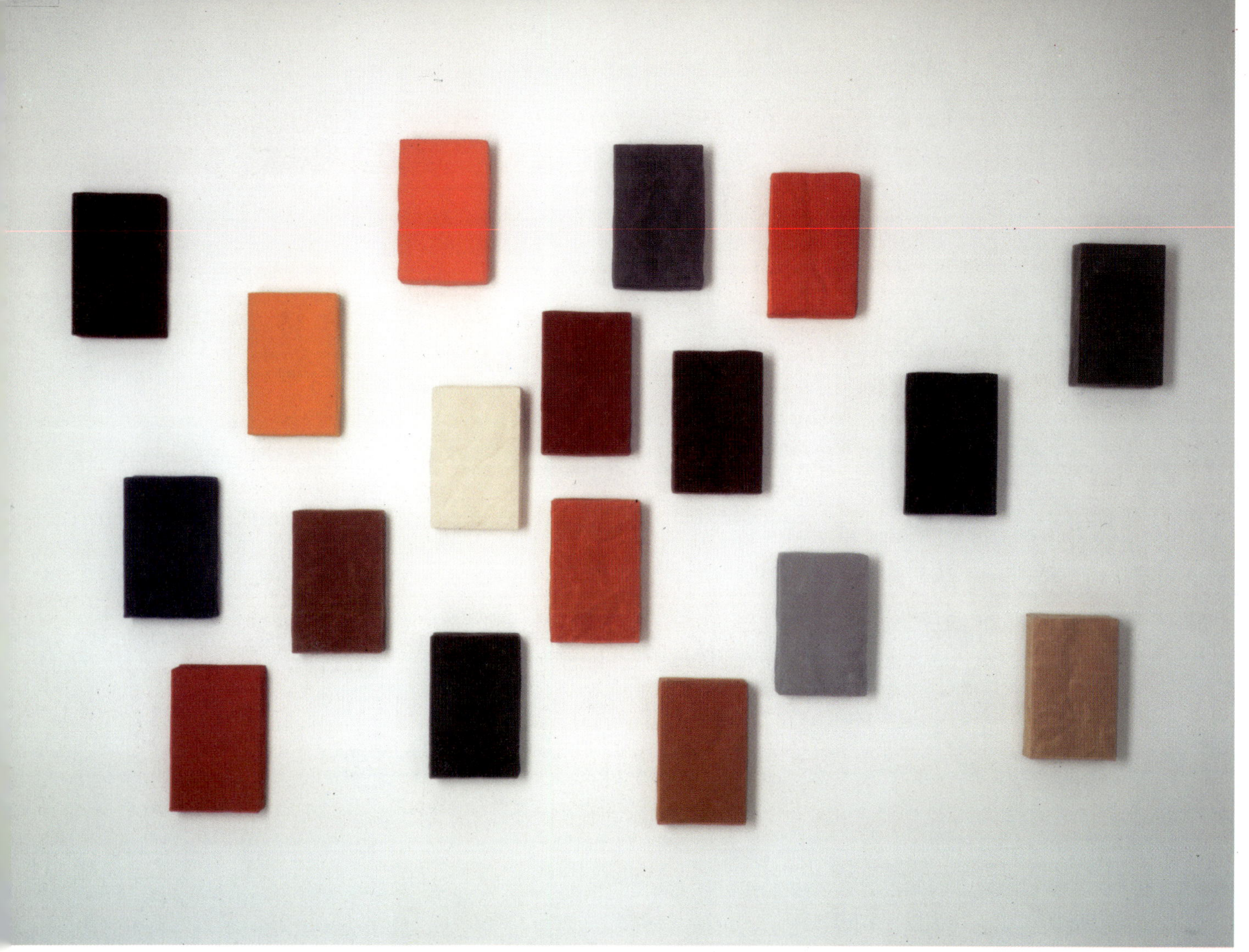

311 Franz-Ehrhard Walther
Wandgesang, 1990
18 Stoffobjekte, je 28 x 18 x 6,5 cm, in Holzbox 151,5 x 22,5 x 31 cm. Auflage: 40
18 objects (cotton), 11 x 7 x 2½ in. ea., in wooden box, 59½ x 9 x 12 in. Edition: 40

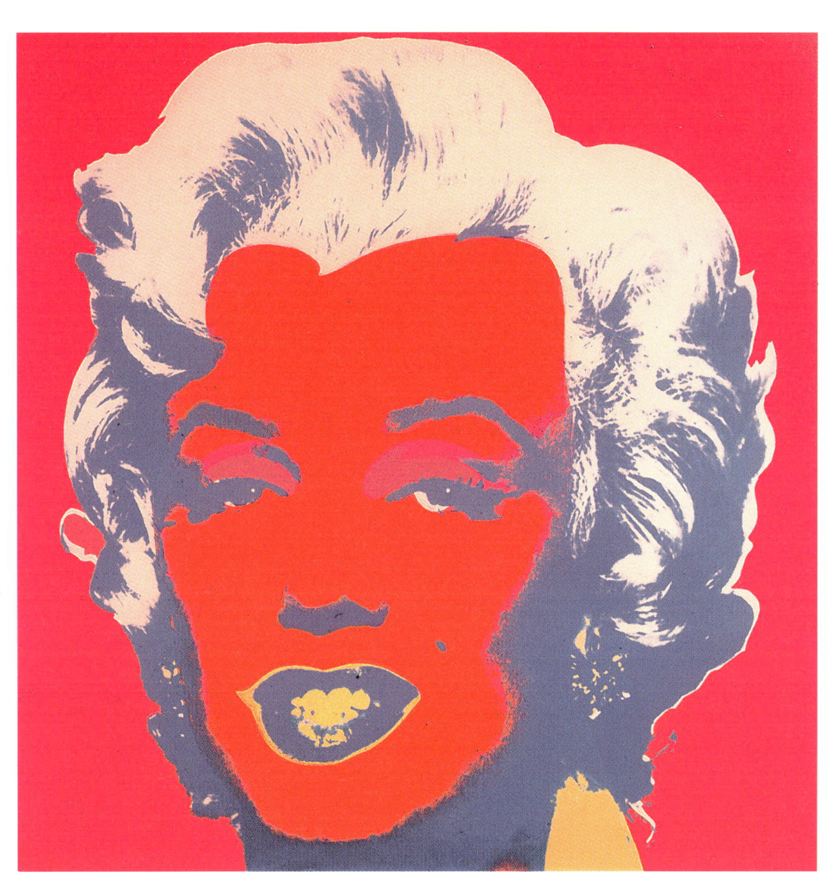

312 Andy Warhol
Marilyn Monroe, 1967
Serigraphie, 91 x 91 cm. Auflage: 250
Silkscreen, 36 x 36 in. Edition: 250

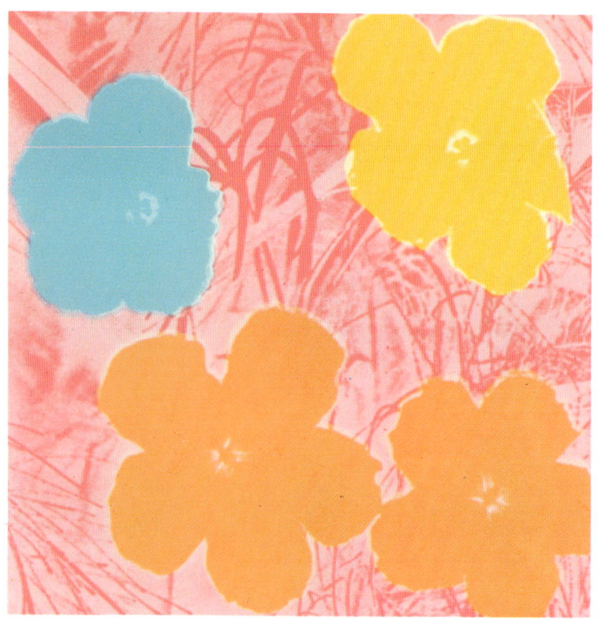
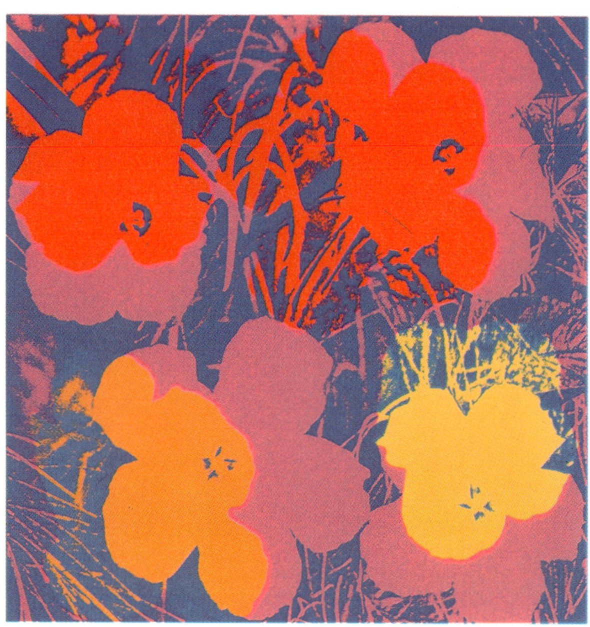

313 Andy Warhol
Flowers, 1970
Serigraphien, 91,5 x 91,5 cm. Auflage: 250
Silkscreens, 36 x 36 in. Edition: 250

314 Andy Warhol
Electric Chair, 1971
Serigraphie, 90 x 122 cm.
Auflage: 250
Silkscreen, 35½ x 48 in.
Edition: 250

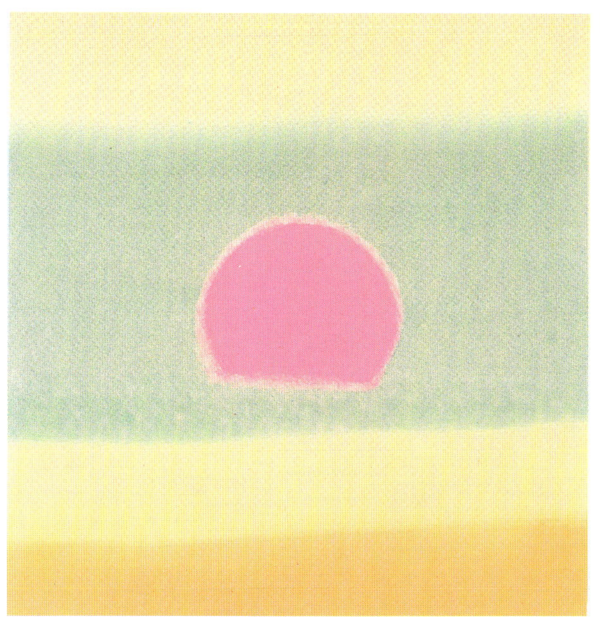

315 Andy Warhol
Sunset, 1972
Serigraphien, 86,5 x 86,5 cm. Auflage: 632 unterschiedliche Farbversionen
Silkscreens, 34 x 34 in. Edition: 632 prints unique in color

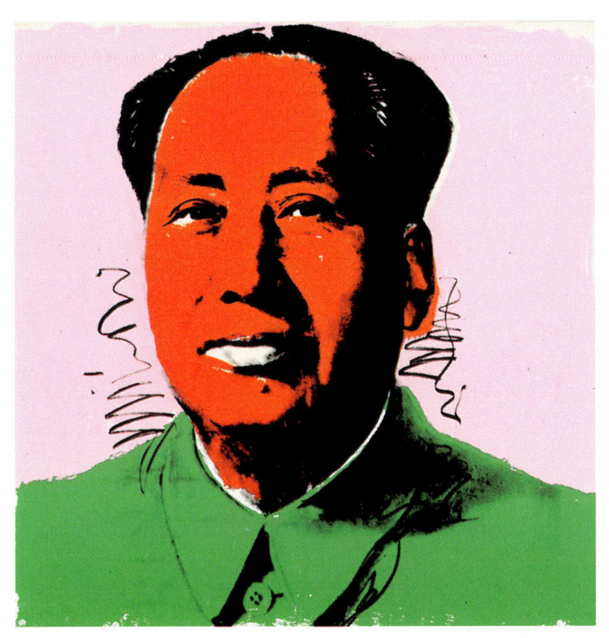

316 Andy Warhol
Mao Tse-Tung, 1972
Serigraphien, 91 x 91 cm. Auflage: 250
Silkscreens, 36 x 36 in. Edition: 250

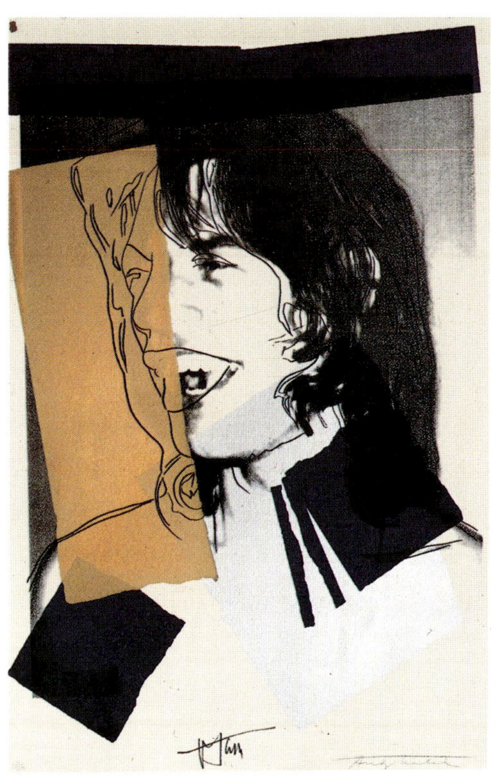

317 Andy Warhol
Mick Jagger, 1975
Serigraphie, 110 x 74 cm. Auflage: 250
Silkscreen, 43½ x 29 in. Edition: 250

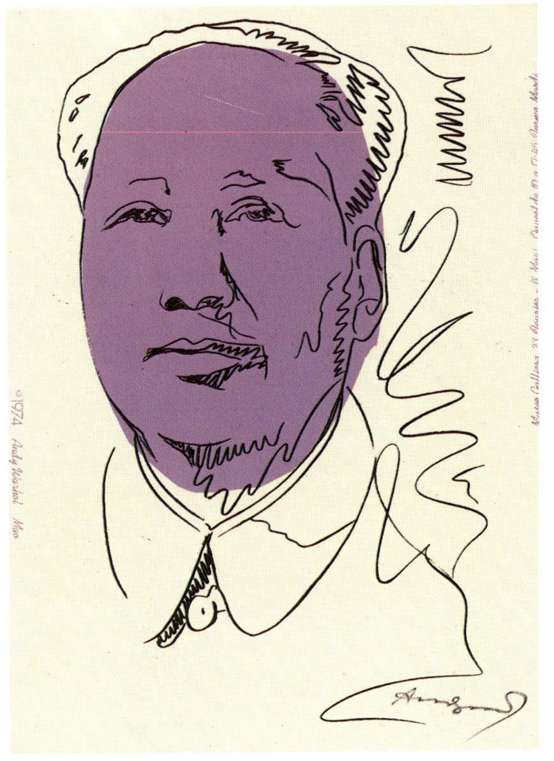

318 Andy Warhol
Mao, 1974
Serigraphie auf Tapetenpapier, 102 x 75 cm. Auflage: 100
Silkscreen on wall paper, 40 x 29½ in. Edition: 100

319 Andy Warhol →
Shadows II, 1979
Mappe mit 6 Serigraphien mit Diamantstaub, 110 x 77,5 cm. Auflage: 10, Farben der Hintergründe variieren innerhalb der Auflage
Portfolio with 6 silkscreens with diamond dust, 43 x 30½ in. Edition: 10, backgrounds vary in color within the edition

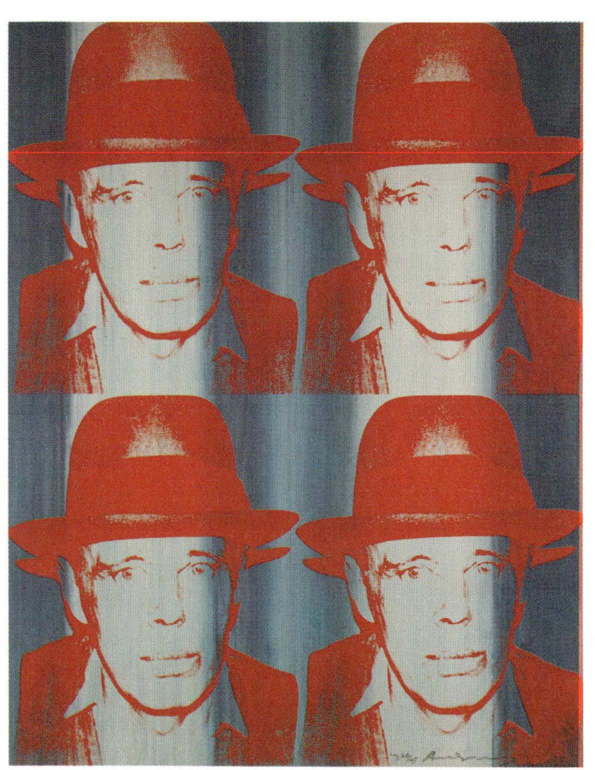

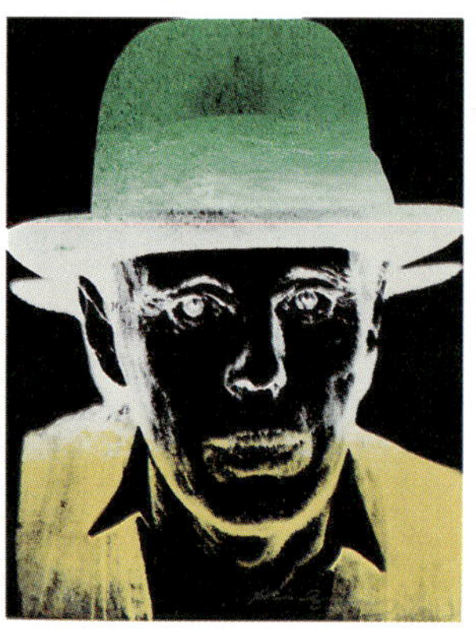

320 Andy Warhol ■
Joseph Beuys, 1980/83
↑ **a.** Serigraphie, Probedruck (Trial proof),
51 x 40 cm. Unikat
Silkscreen trial proof, 20 x 15¾ in. Unique print
← **b.** Serigraphie, Probedruck (Trial proof),
102 x 81 cm. Unikat
Silkscreen trial proof, 40 x 32 in. Unique print

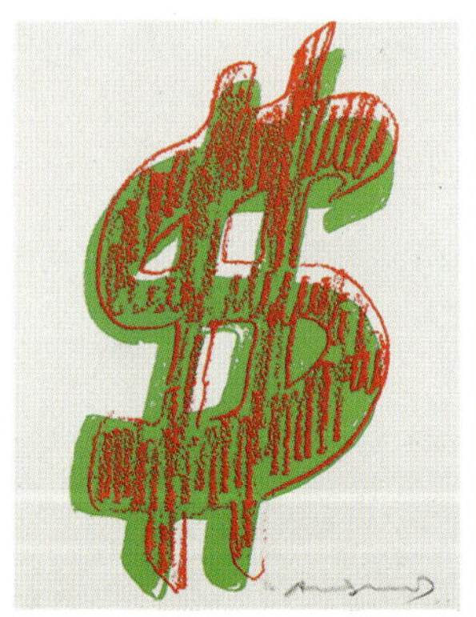

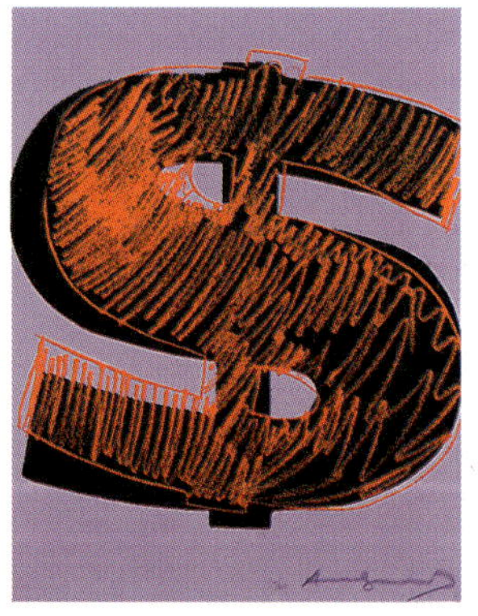

321 Andy Warhol
$1, 1982
Mappe mit 6 Serigraphien, 50 x 40 cm.
Auflage: 60, alle Blätter unterschiedlich in den Farben
Portfolio of 6 silkscreens, 19¾ x 15¾ in.
Edition of 60, each print unique in colors

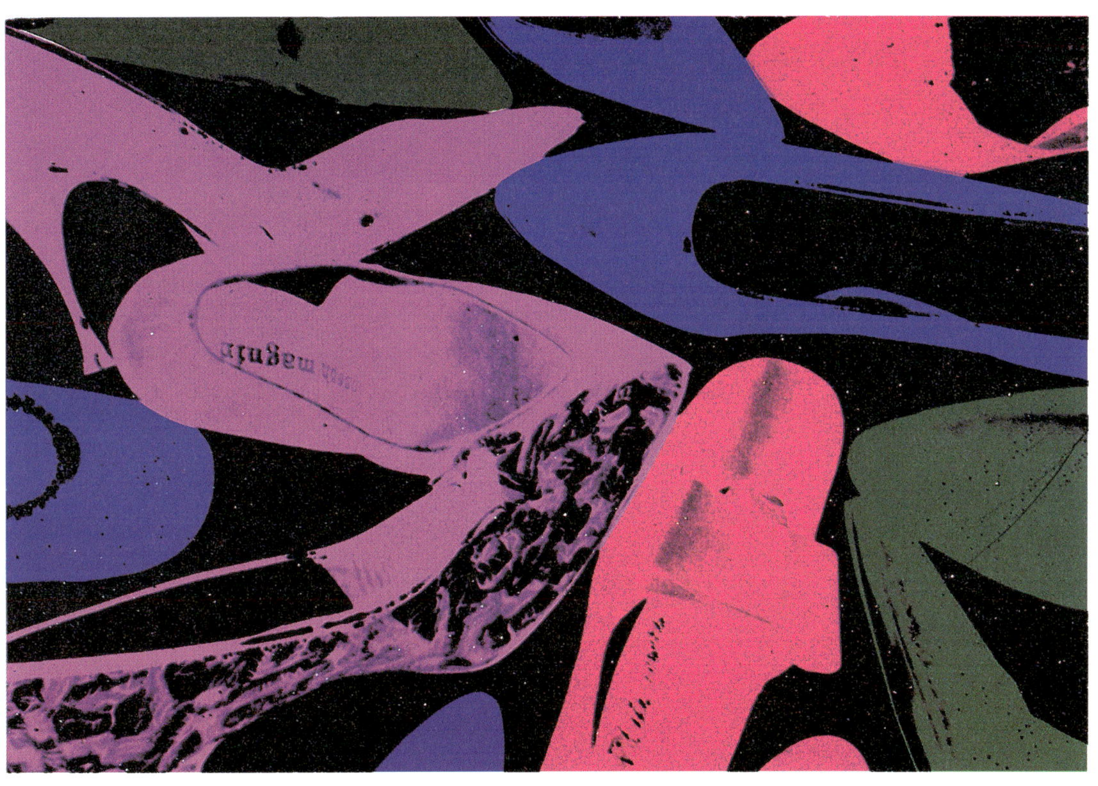

322 Andy Warhol
Shoes, 1980
Serigraphie mit Diamantstaub,
102 x 151 cm. Auflage: 60
Silkscreen with diamond dust,
40 x 59½ in. Edition: 60

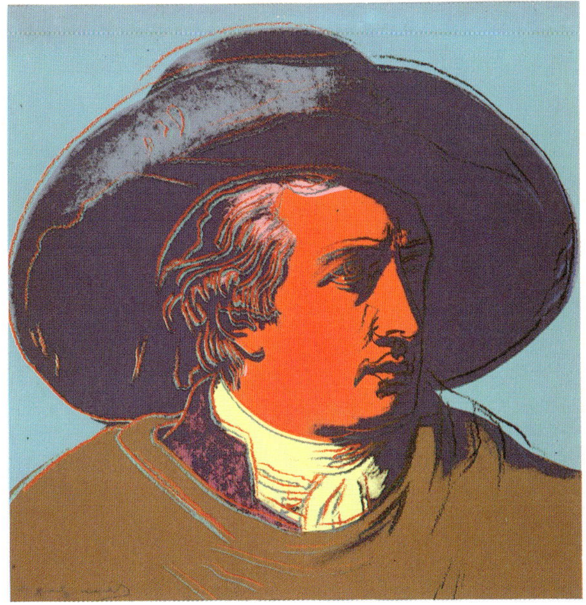

323 Andy Warhol ■
Goethe, 1982
Serigraphie, Probedruck (Trial proof),
97 x 97 cm. Unikat
Silkscreen trial proof, 38 x 38 in.
Unique print

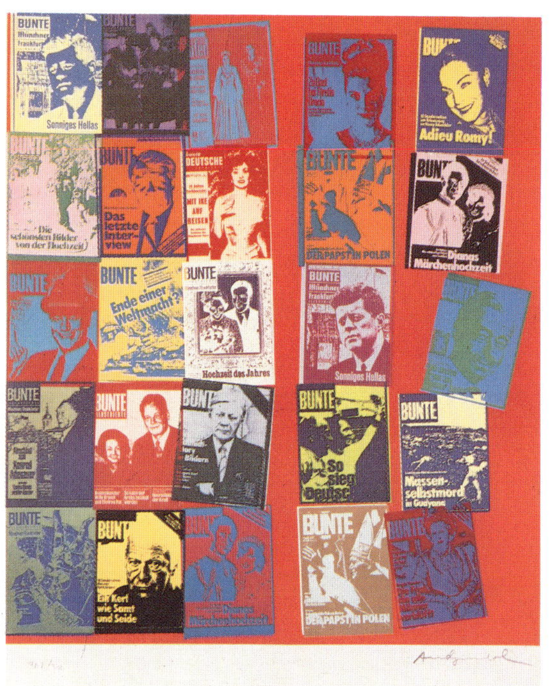

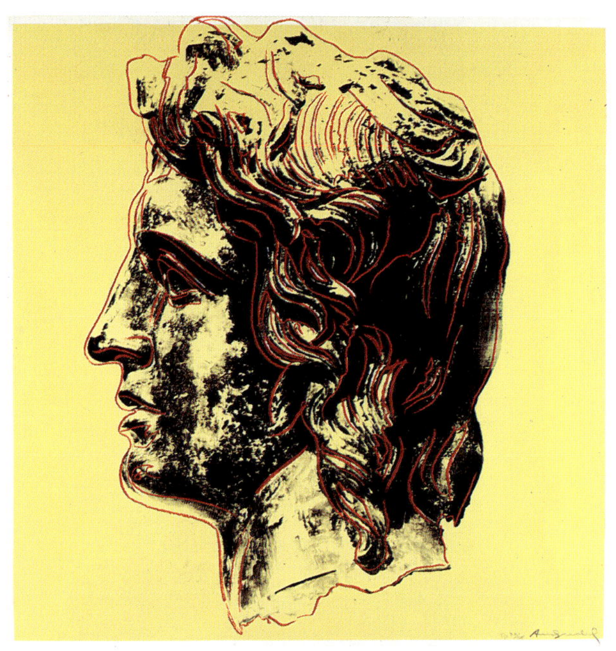

↖ 324 Andy Warhol
Magazine and History, 1983
Serigraphie und Offsetlitho, 85 x 70 cm. Auflage: 500
Silkscreen and offset litho, 33½ x 27½ in. Edition: 500

325 Andy Warhol
Alexander the Great, 1982
Serigraphie, Probedruck (Trial proof), 100 x 100 cm. Unikat
Silkscreen trial proof, 39½ x 39½ in. Unique print

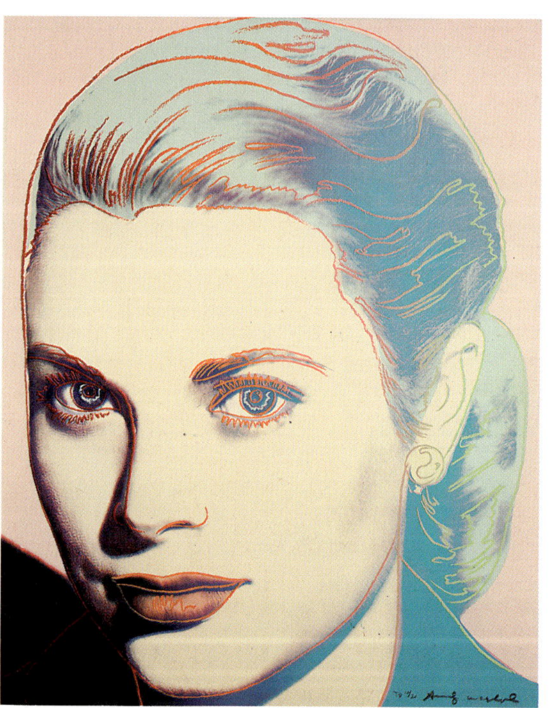

326 Andy Warhol
Grace Kelly, 1984
Serigraphie, Probedruck (Trial proof), 101,6 x 81 cm. Unikat
Silkscreen trial proof, 40 x 32 in. Unique print

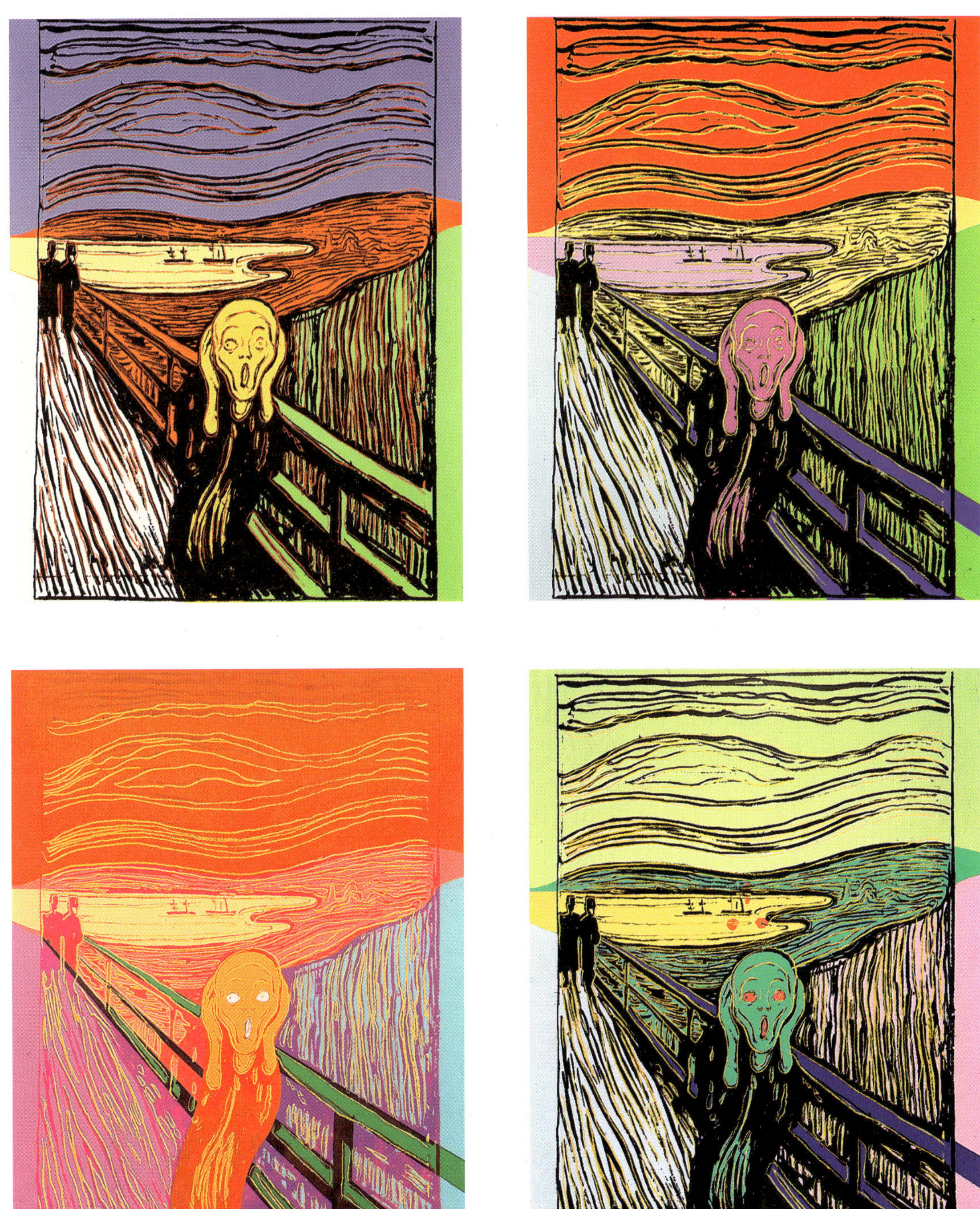

327 Andy Warhol
The Scream (after Munch), 1983
Serigraphien, Probedrucke (Trial proofs), 101,5 x 81,5 cm. Unikate. *Silkscreen trial proofs, 40 x 32 in. Unique prints*

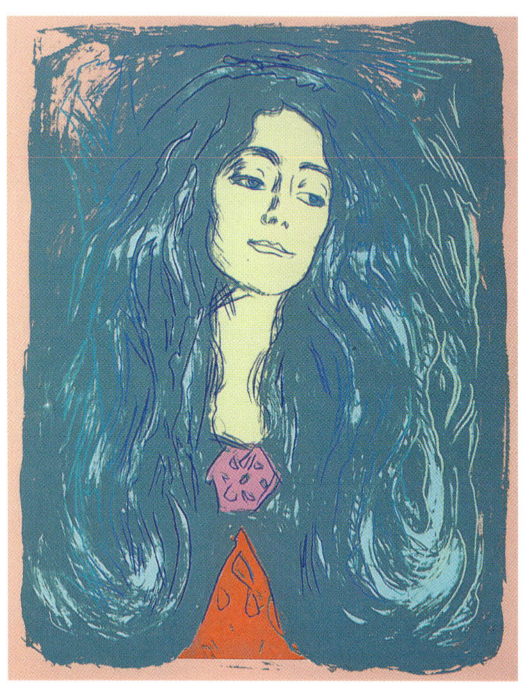
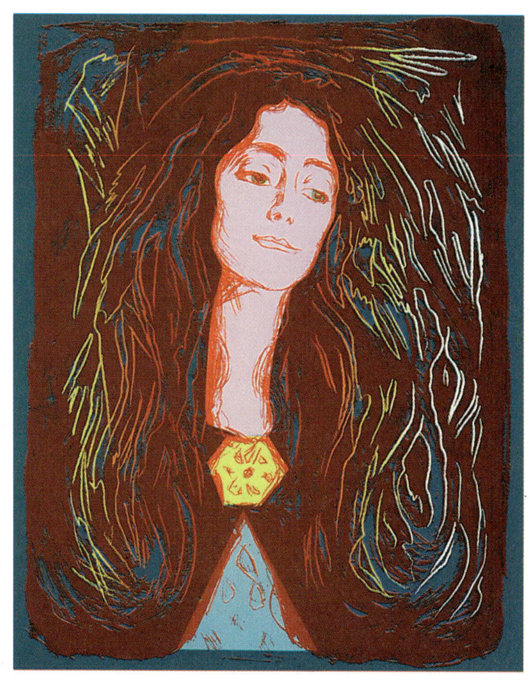

328 Andy Warhol
Eva Mudocci (after Munch), 1983
Serigraphien, Probedrucke (Trial proofs), 101,5 x 81,5 cm. Unikate
Silkscreen trial proofs, 40 x 32 in. Unique prints

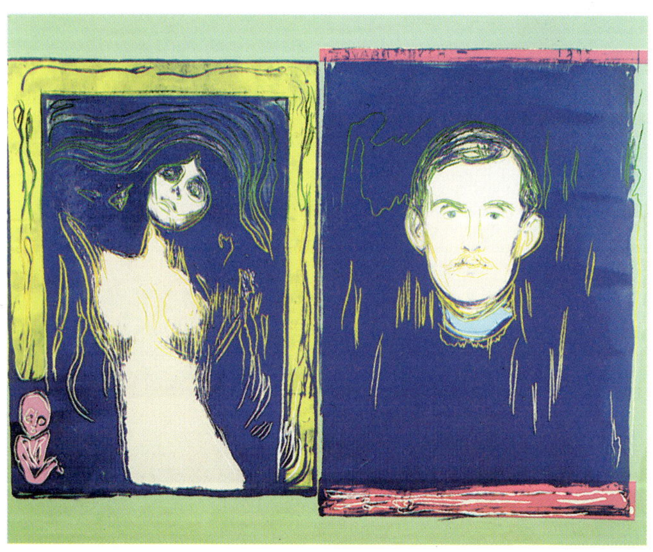

329 Andy Warhol
Madonna and Self-portrait with Skeleton Arm (after Munch), 1983
Serigraphien, Probedrucke (Trial proofs), 81,5 x 101,5 cm. Unikate
Silkscreen trial proofs, 32 x 40 in. Unique prints

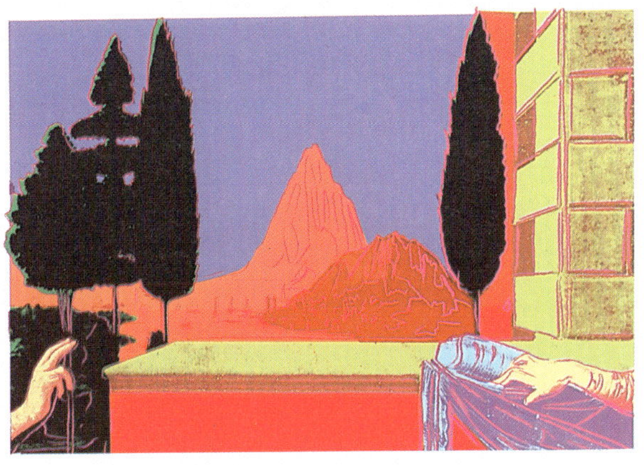

330 Andy Warhol ■
Details of Renaissance Paintings
(Leonardo da Vinci 'The Annunciation'), 1984
Mappe mit 4 Serigraphien, 81 x 112 cm. Auflage: 60
Portfolio of 4 silkscreens, 32 x 44 in. Edition: 60

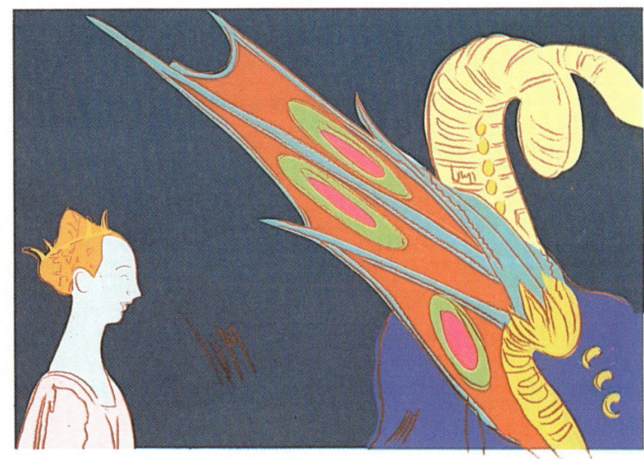

331 Andy Warhol ■
Details of Renaissance Paintings
(Paolo Uccello 'St. George and the Dragon'), 1984
Mappe mit 4 Serigraphien, 81 x 112 cm. Auflage: 50
Portfolio of 4 silkscreens, 32 x 44 in. Edition: 50

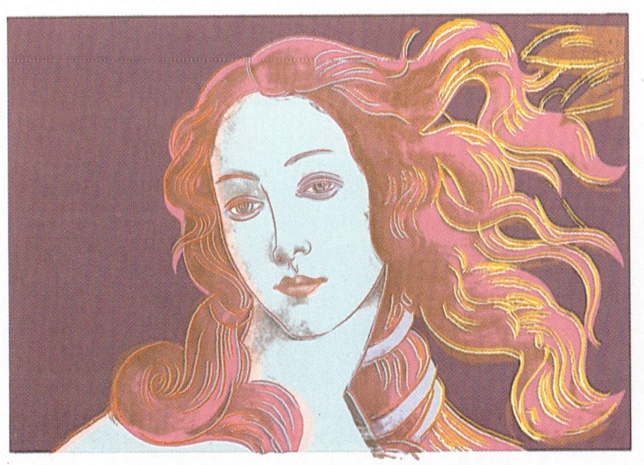

332 Andy Warhol ■
Details of Renaissance Paintings
(Sandro Botticelli 'Birth of Venus'), 1984
Mappe mit 4 Serigraphien, 81 x 112 cm. Auflage: 70
Portfolio of 4 silkscreens, 32 x 44 in. Edition: 70

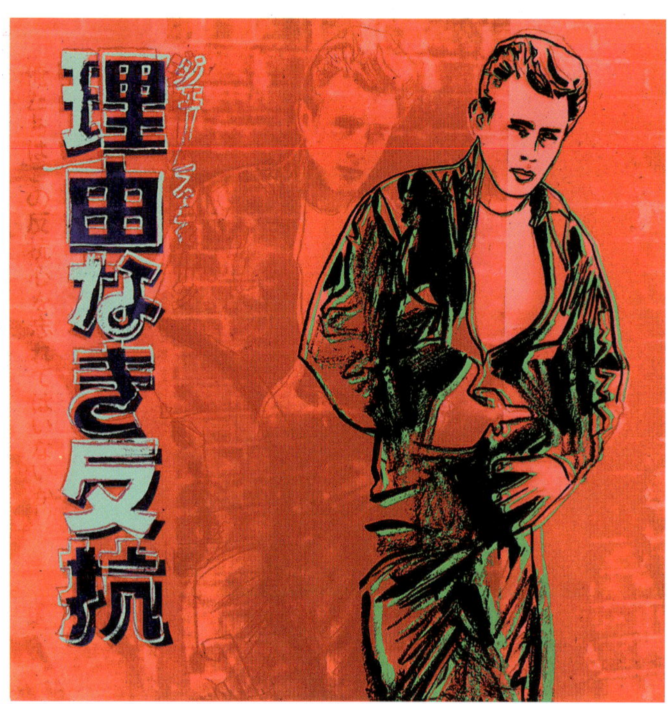

333 Andy Warhol
James Dean (aus Mappe: Ads), 1985
Serigraphie, 96,5 x 96,5 cm. Auflage: 190
Silkscreen, 38 x 38 in. Edition: 190

334 Andy Warhol
Three Portraits of Ingrid Bergman, 1983
Mappe mit 3 Serigraphien, 96 x 96 cm. Auflage: 250
Portfolio with 3 silkscreens, 38 x 38 in. Edition: 250

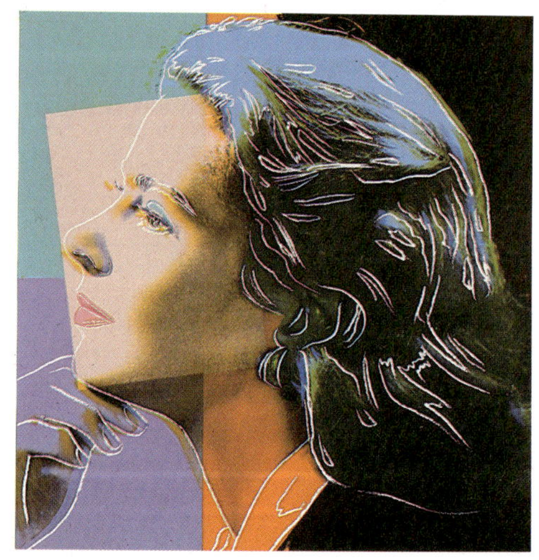

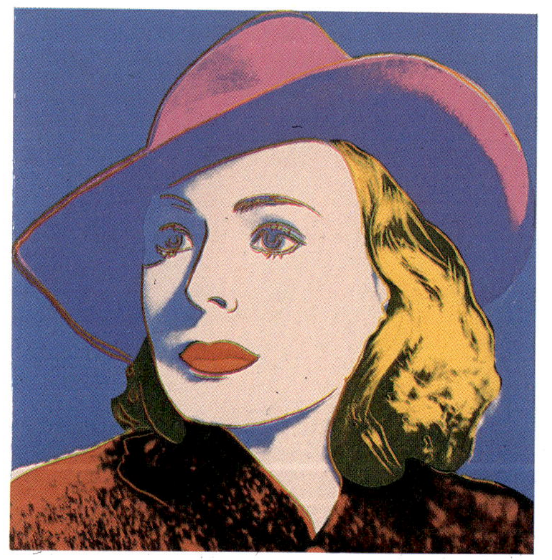

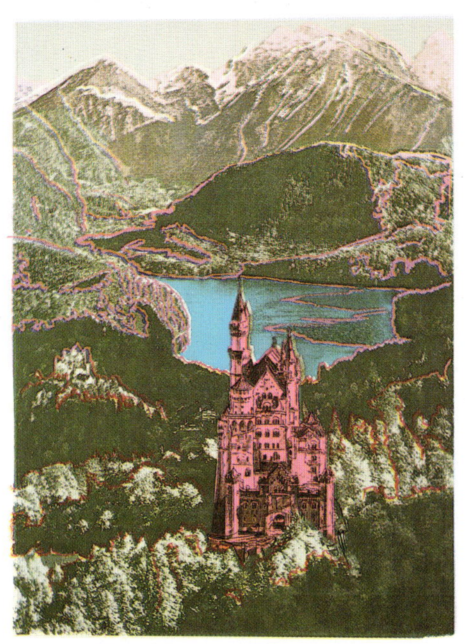

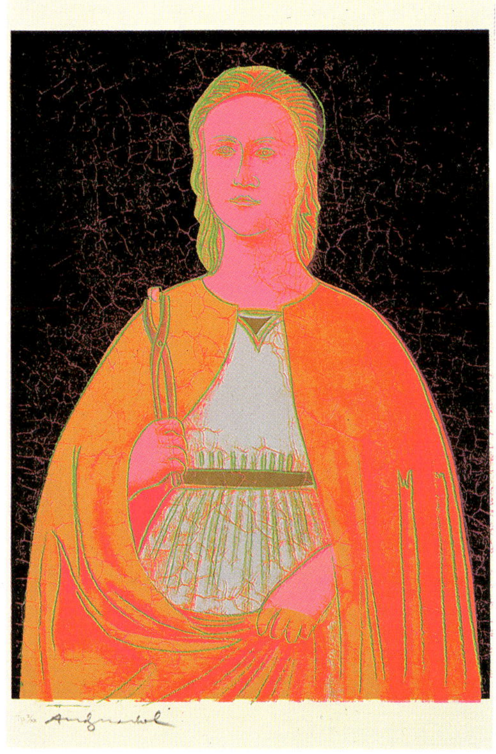

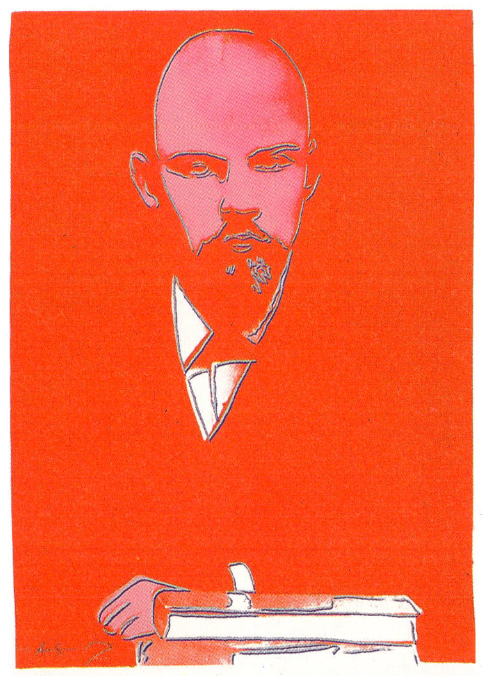

↖ 335 Andy Warhol ■
Neuschwanstein, 1987
Serigraphie, Probedruck (Trial proof), 110 x 77 cm.
Unikat
Silkscreen trial proof, 43 x 30 in. Unique print

336 Andy Warhol ↑
Saint Apollonia, 1984
Serigraphie, Probedruck (Trial proof), 88 x 59 cm.
Unikat
Silkscreen trial proof, 34½ x 23 in. Unique print

← 337 Andy Warhol
Lenin, 1986/87
Serigraphie, Probedruck (Trial proof), 100 x 75 cm.
Unikat, nachlaßsigniert
Silkscreen trial proof, 39¼ x 29½ in. Unique print, estate signed

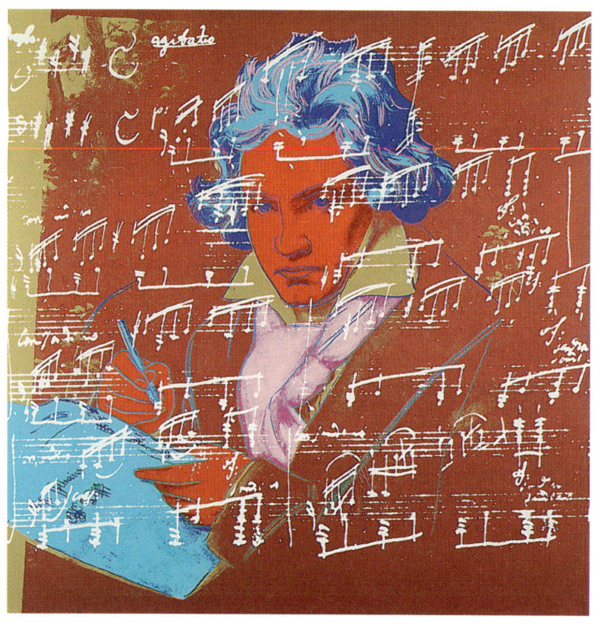

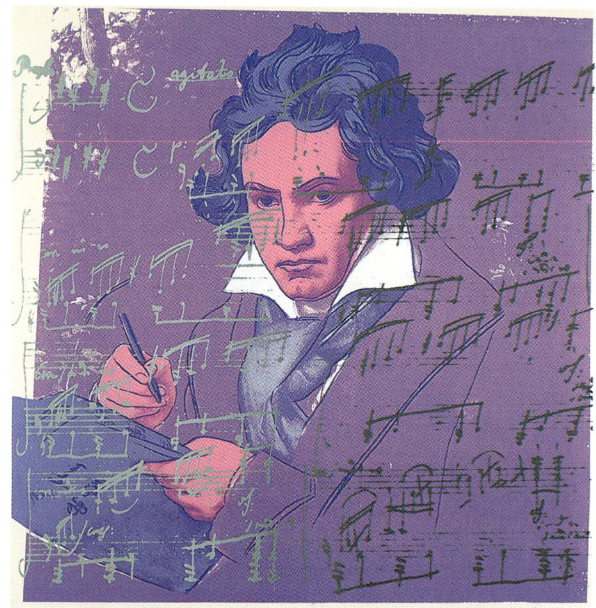

338 Andy Warhol
Beethoven, 1987
Serigraphien, Probedrucke (Trial proofs),
102 x 102 cm. Unikate, nachlaßsigniert
Silkscreen trial proofs, 40 x 40 in.
Unique prints, estate signed

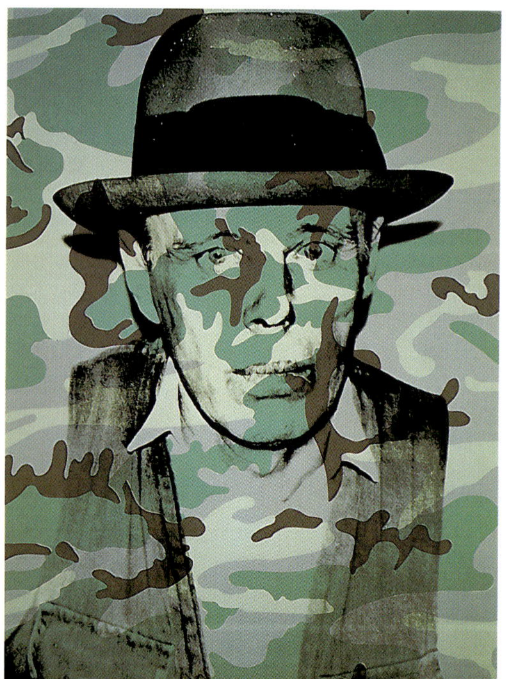

339 Andy Warhol ■
Joseph Beuys, aus Mappe: Für Joseph Beuys, 1986
Serigraphie, 81,3 x 61 cm. Auflage: 90
Silkscreen, 32 x 24 in. Edition: 90

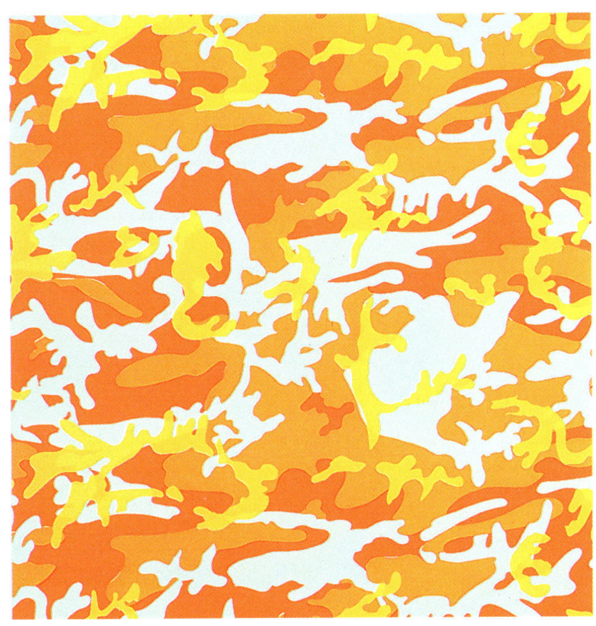
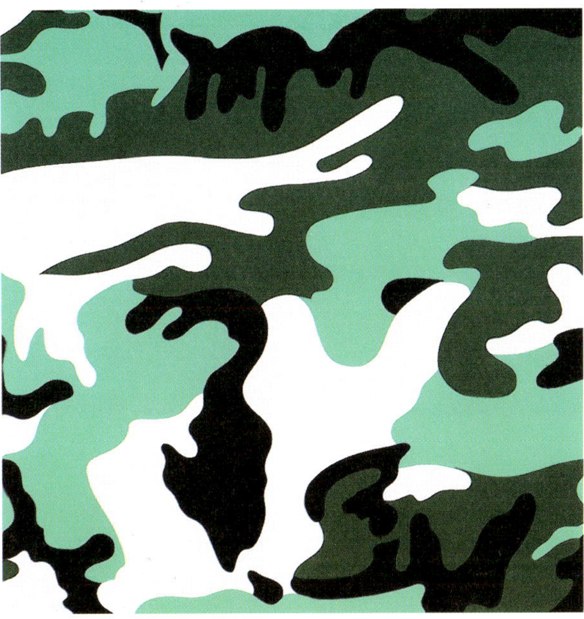
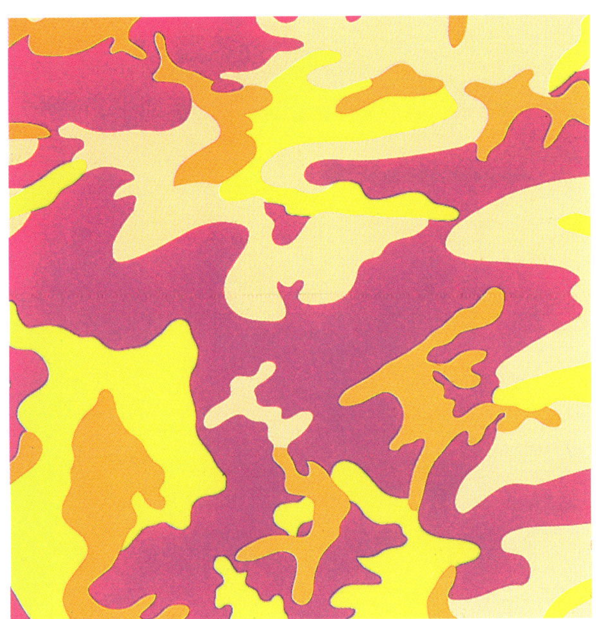
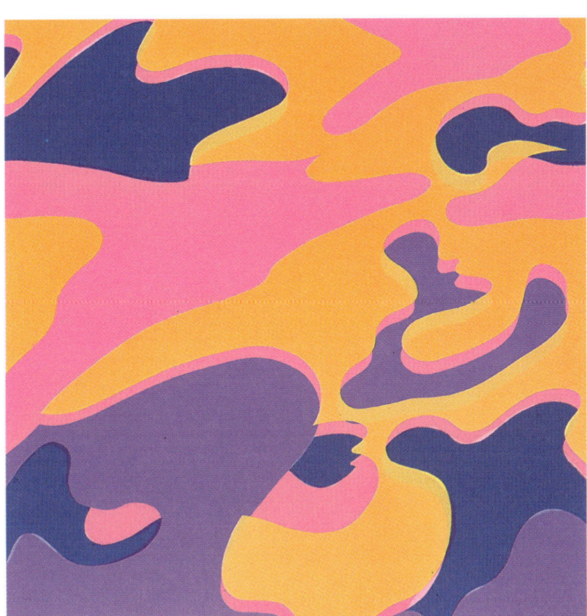

340 Andy Warhol
Camouflage, 1987
Mappe mit 8 Serigraphien, 96,5 x 96,5 cm. Auflage: 80, nachlaßsigniert
Portfolio with 8 silkscreens, 38 x 38 in. Edition: 80, estate signed

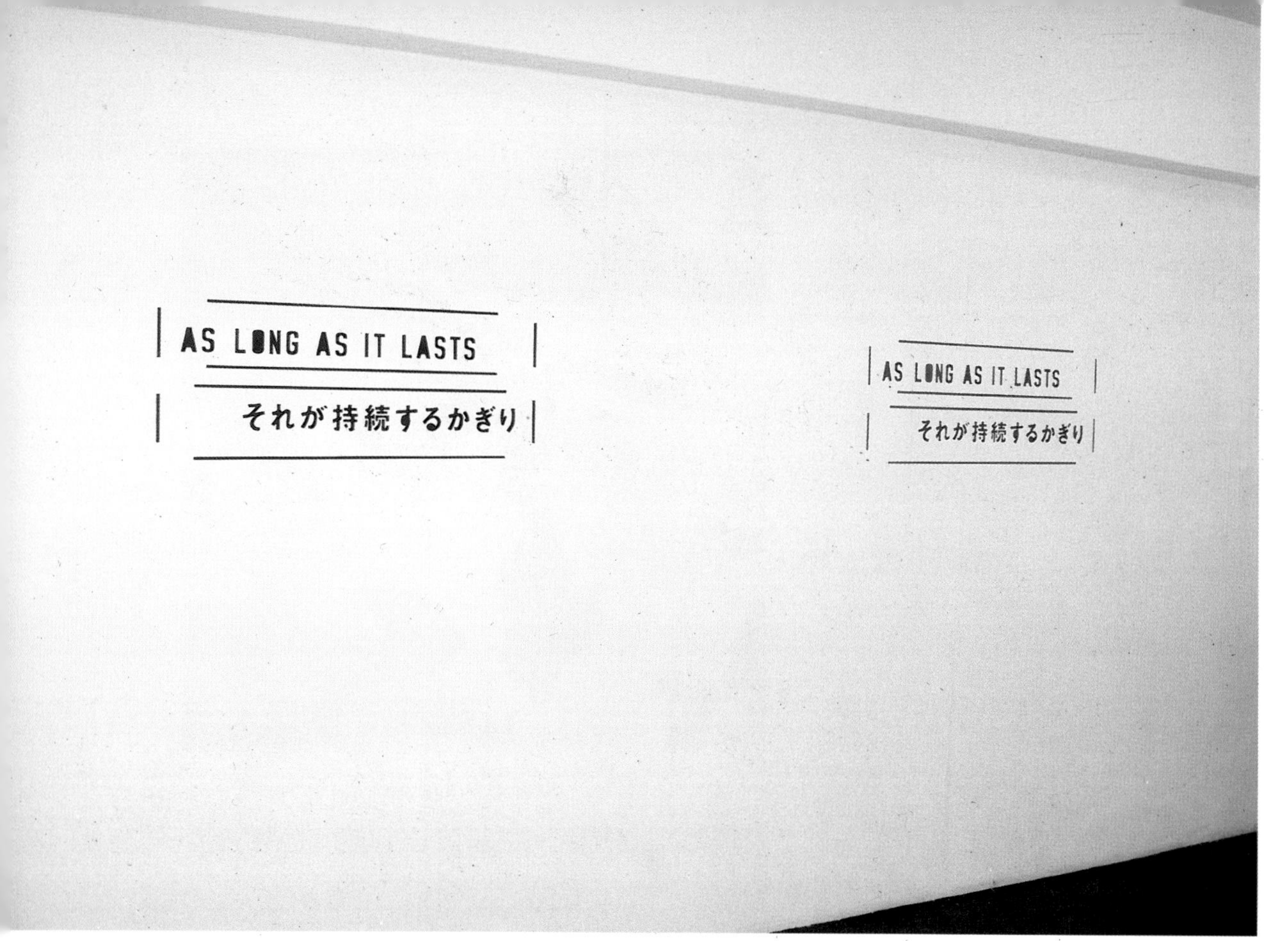

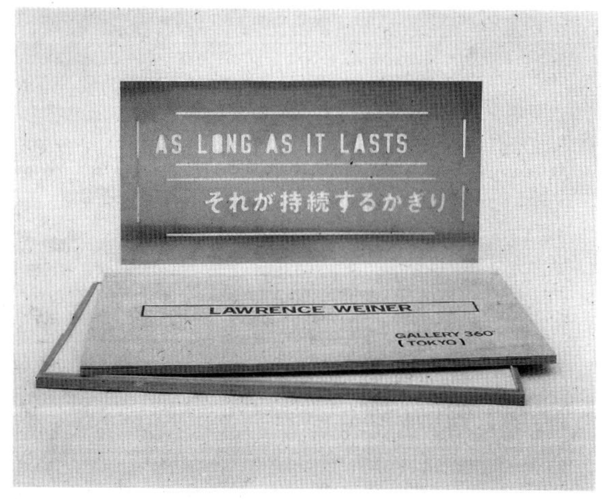

341 Lawrence Weiner
As Long As it Lasts, 1992
Wandarbeit. Schablone aus Edelstahl, 50 x 100 cm, in Holzkasten. Auflage: 28
Wall work. Stainless steel, cut-out, 19¾ x 39½ in., in wooden box. Edition: 28

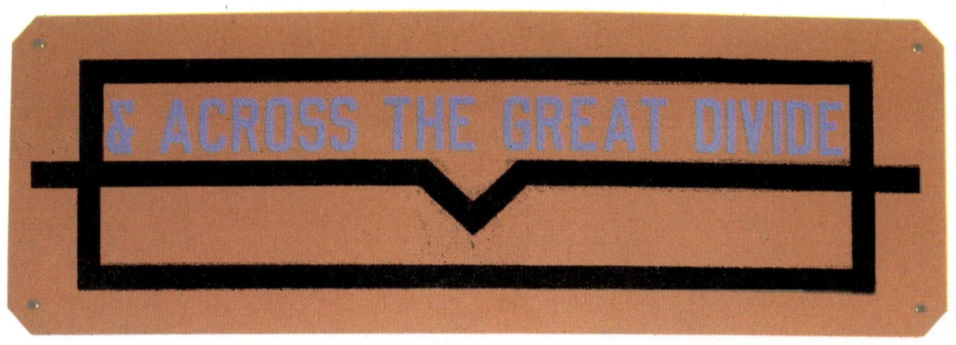

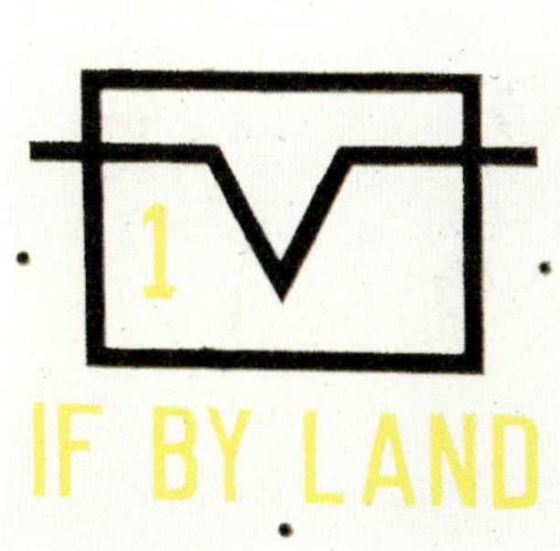

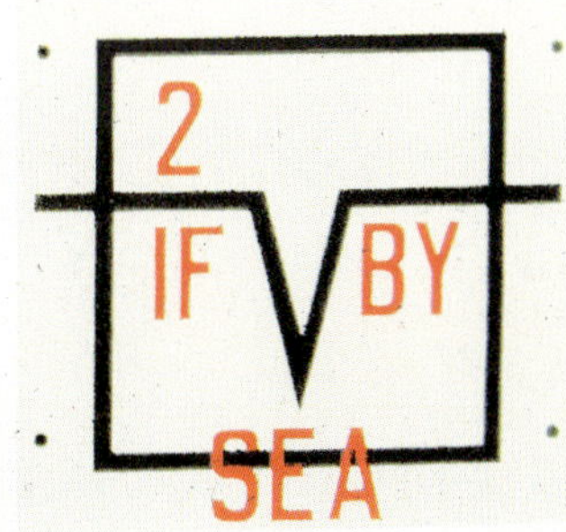

342 Lawrence Weiner
& Across the Great Divide, 1991
3 emaillierte Metallschilder, 30,5 x 91,5 bzw. 30,5 x 30,5 cm. Auflage: 45
3 baked enamel signs, 12 x 36 and 12 x 12 in. Edition: 45

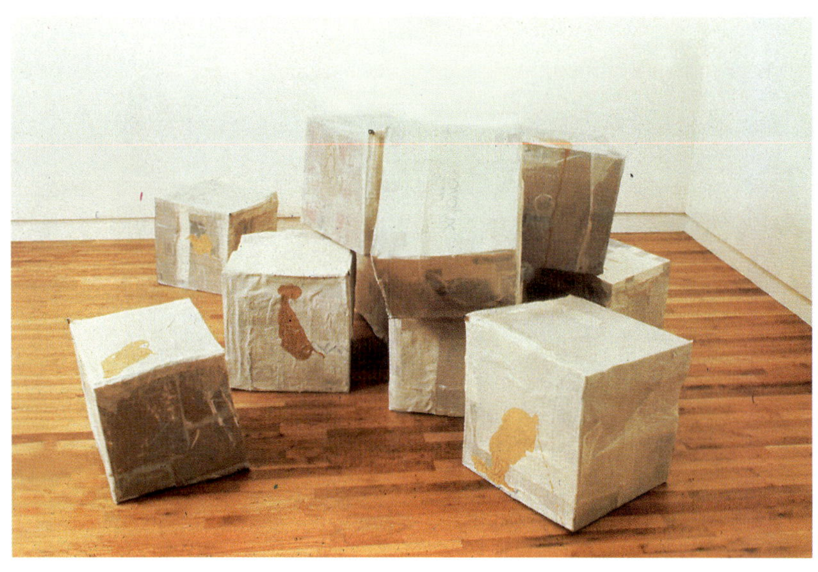

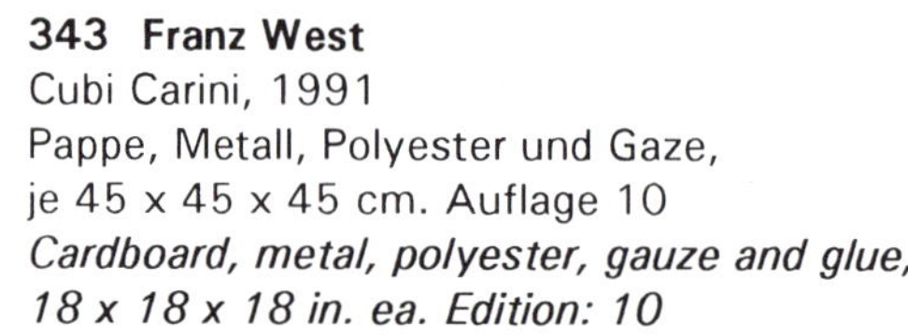

343 Franz West
Cubi Carini, 1991
Pappe, Metall, Polyester und Gaze,
je 45 x 45 x 45 cm. Auflage 10
Cardboard, metal, polyester, gauze and glue,
18 x 18 x 18 in. ea. Edition: 10

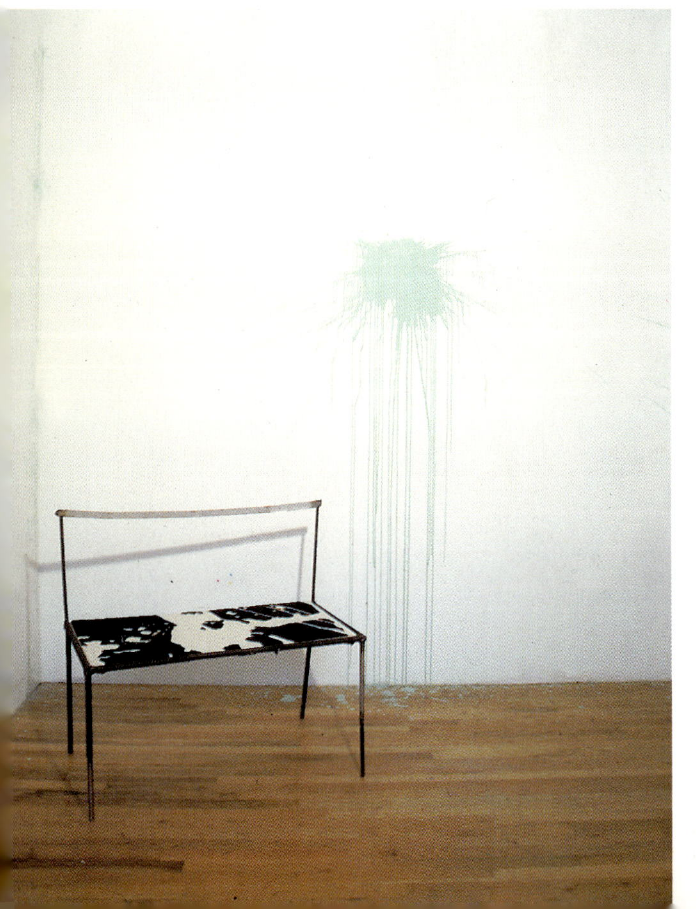

344 Franz West
Green (The Description of this Color), 1993
Truthahneier gefüllt mit Farbe, Sägemehl, Karton
mit Videokassette, 11 x 11 x 9 cm. Auflage: 30
Paint filled turkey eggs, sawdust, cardboard with
instructional video cassette, 4½ x 4½ x 3½ in.
Edition: 30

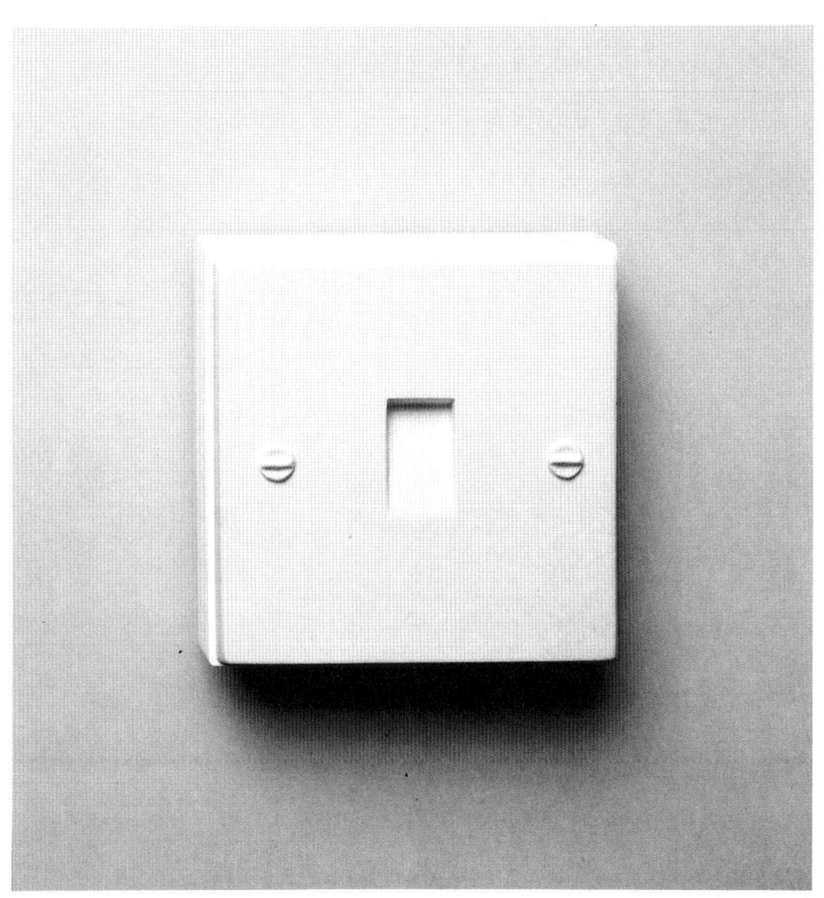

345 Rachel Whiteread
Switch, 1994
Gips und Messing, 9 x 9 x 3 cm. Auflage: 60
Plaster and brass, 3½ x 3½ x 1¼ in. Edition: 60

346 Terry Winters
Glyphs, 1995
Suite von 6 Indigo-colorierten Linolschnitten, 62 x 44,5 cm. Auflage: 27
Suite of 6 Indigo-dyed linoleum cuts, 24½ x 17½ in. Edition: 27

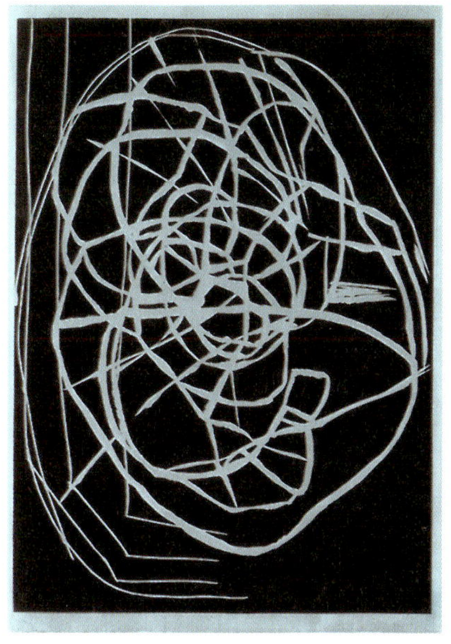
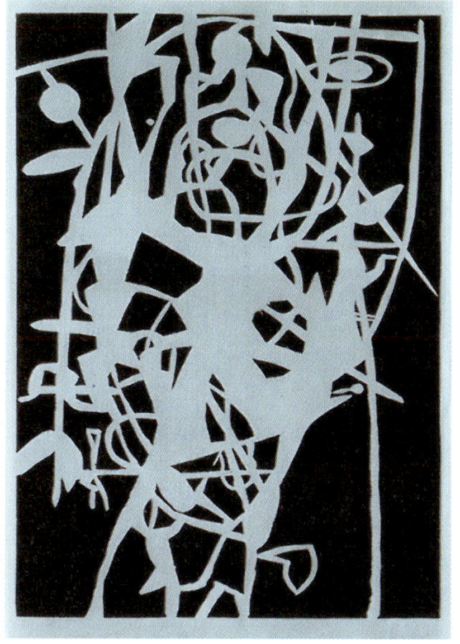
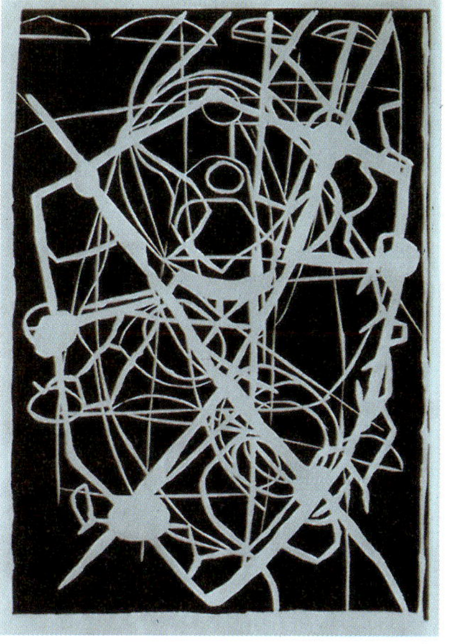
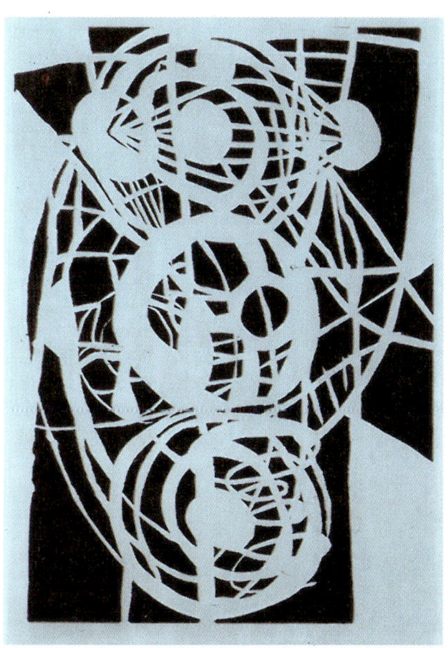
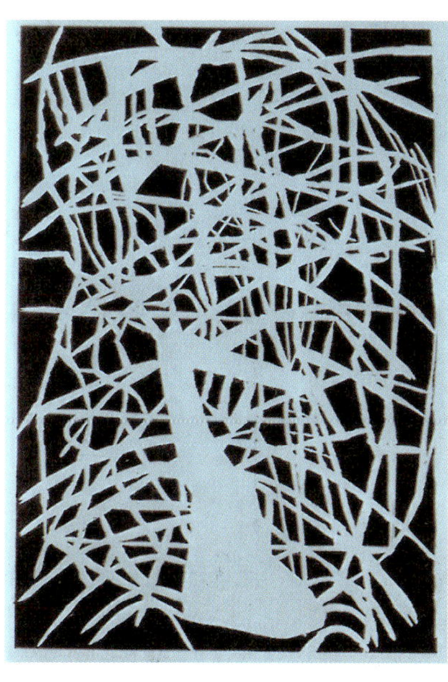
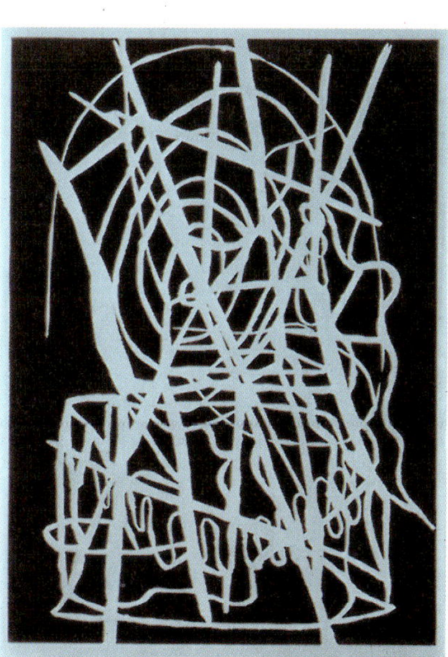

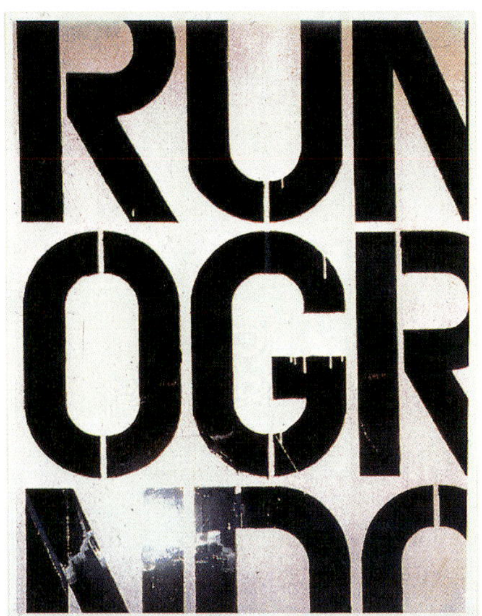

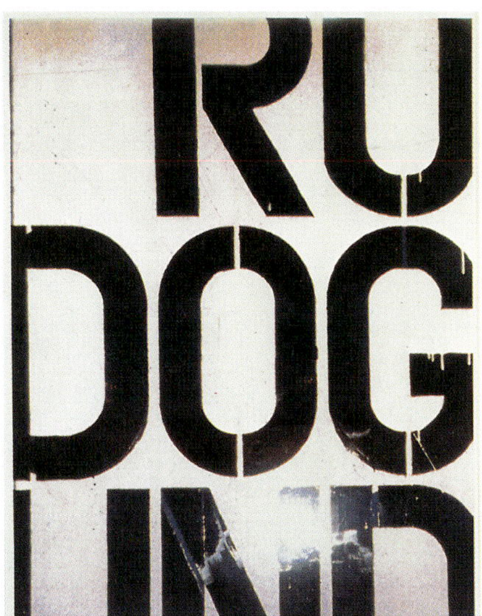

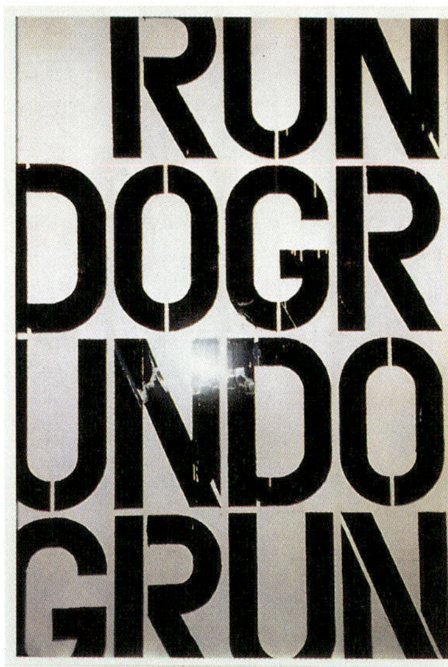

347 Christopher Wool
Untitled, 1991
Mappe mit 3 Offsetdrucken, 88,5 x 70 bzw. 88,5 x 64,5 cm. Auflage: 25
Portfolio of 3 offset prints, 34¾ x 27½ and 34¾ x 25½ in. Edition: 25

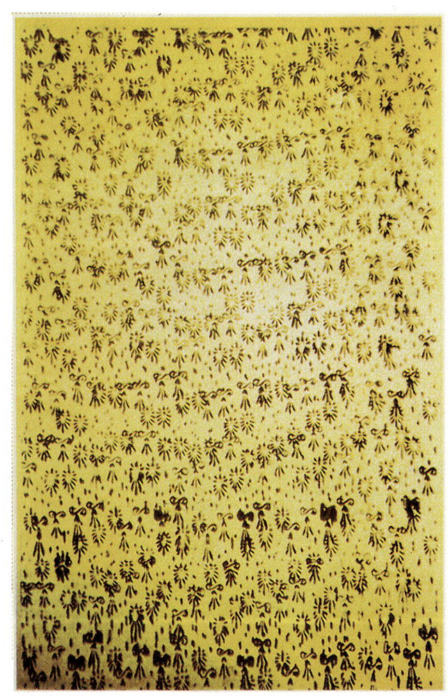

348 Christopher Wool
Untitled, 1991
Offset, 98,5 x 65 cm. Auflage: 40
Offset print, 38¾ x 25½ in. Edition: 40

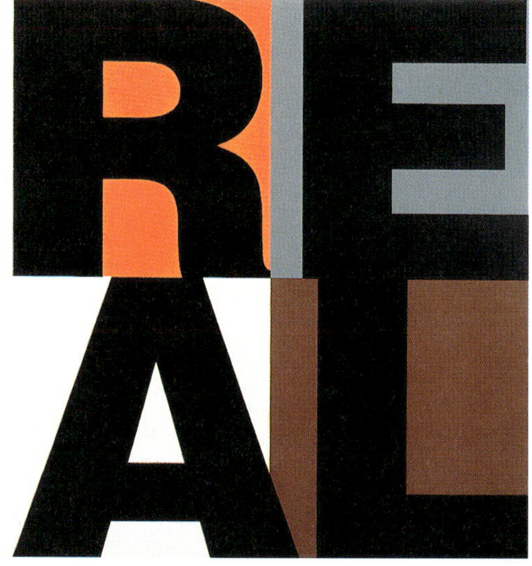

349 Heimo Zobernig
REAL, 1993/94
Siebdruck auf Leinwand/Keilrahmen, 124 x 118 cm. Auflage: 6
Silkscreen on canvas/stretcher, 49 x 26½ in. Edition: 6

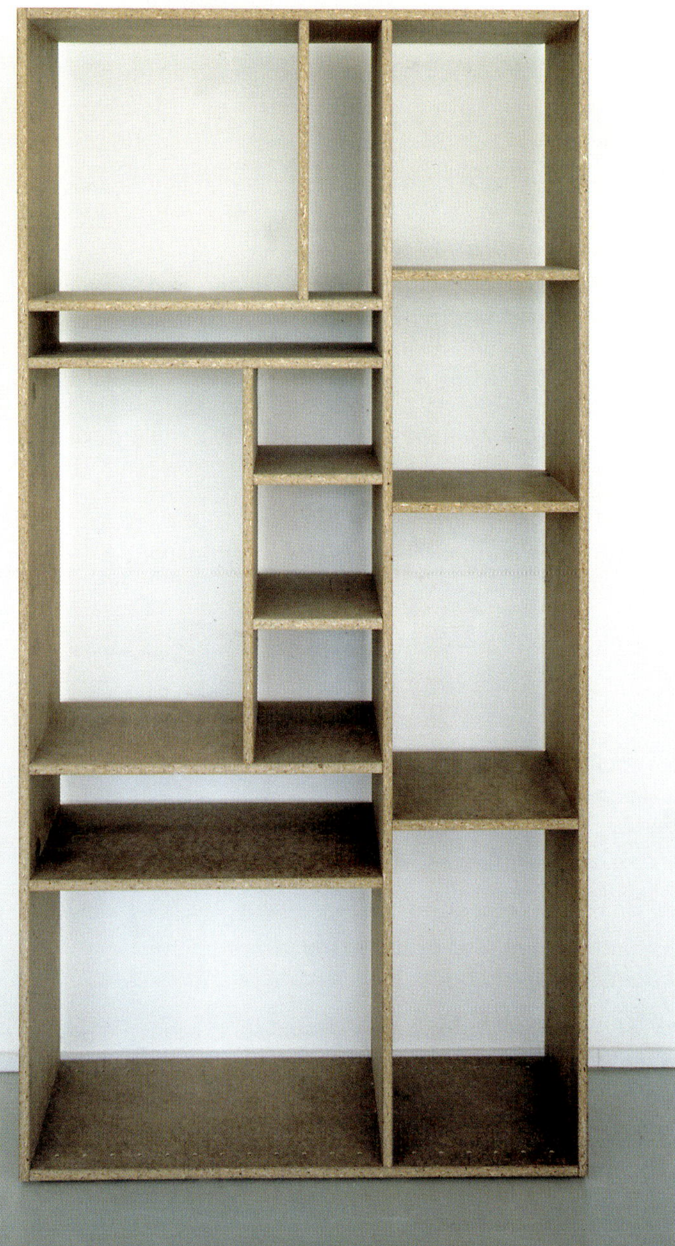

350 Heimo Zobernig
o.T., 1994
Holzspanplattenregal mit variabler Einteilung, 202 x 102 x 30 cm. Auflage: 10
Chipboard shelf with variable divisions, 80 x 40 in. Edition: 10

APPENDIX: WALL WORKS

Technische Informationen zur Ausführung der Wall Works in diesem Katalog.
Technical information for the execution of the Wall Works shown in this catalog.

*

Die Wandarbeiten sind entsprechend den Anweisungen der Künstler, wie sie in den Zertifikaten zu den Arbeiten und in diesem Katalog festgelegt sind, zu installieren. Die Edition Schellmann bietet Beratung und Mithilfe bei der Ausführung an.
Einige Künstler sind bereit, die spezielle Situation der Installation zu berücksichtigen und evtl. zusätzliche Variationen in Anordnung, Farbe oder Größe auf Anfrage vorzuschlagen.

Die Edition erhält von jeder realisierten Arbeit ein professionelles Dia, das der Kontrolle der richtigen Ausführung und zu Archivzwecken dient.

Alle Wandarbeiten (mit Ausnahme der von Don Judd) können, z.B. wenn der Besitzer umzieht, erneut ausgeführt werden. In diesem Falle muß die alte Arbeit zerstört werden. Das Zertifikat autorisiert nur **eine** existierende Arbeit.

*

The Wall Works are to be installed according to the specifications given in the artists' certification and in the additional notes below. Edition Schellmann will give advice and further assistance to the execution of the works upon request.
Some artists have indicated that they may allow for further variations in configuration, color or size if the specific site of execution is presented to them.

For each piece installed the artist and the publisher require a professional transparency to be shot and sent to the publisher, Edition Schellmann, Cologne, for approval and for archival purposes.

All works (with the exception of Don Judd's work) can be re-installed if the buyer moves. With a re-installation the prior installation must be destroyed and the work then can be redone in the new place. Each certificate authenticated ***one*** *realized work only.*

1 Arakawa

Abgebildete Installation: Privatwohnung, München, Wandzeichnung 240 x 345 cm, Bodenteil 180 x 270 cm.
Anweisungen zur Ausführung laut Zertifikat: Die Arbeit ist in Graphit (Bleistift) auf einer weiß oder gebrochen weiß gestrichenen Wand zwischen 200 und 400 cm Höhe auszuführen. Zusätzlich sind sechs Rechtecke auf den Boden zu malen, eines, oben rechts, ist in Siebdruck zu drucken. Die Größe der Arbeit variiert mit der Größe der Wand.
Gelieferte Hilfsmittel: Vorlage für die Wandzeichnung, Film für den Siebdruck; Farbmuster.
Zertifikat: Siebdruck auf Bütten, 84 x 69 cm, signiert und numeriert.

***Installation illustrated**: Private house, Munich, wall drawing 95 x 136 in., floor segment 71 x 106 in.*
***Installation instructions** as given in the certificate: "This work is to be executed in graphite on a white or off-white wall (height 200 - 400 cm). In addition to this, six squares are to be painted on the floor; the sixth square, the one in the upper right corner, is to be done as a silkscreen." The size of execution varies with the size of the wall.*
***Components provided**: Photostat for wall drawing, acetate for silkscreen; color samples.*
***Certificate**: Screenprint on rag paper, 33 x 27¼ in., signed and numbered.*

4 Artschwager

Abgebildete Installation: Atelier des Künstlers, New York, Malerei 140 x 76 cm.
Anweisungen zur Montage: In oder auf einer Wandecke anzubringen.
Gelieferte Arbeit: Malerei auf Folie, Form ausgeschnitten.
Zertifikat: Skizze auf Papier, 28 x 22 cm, signiert und numeriert.

***Installation illustrated**: The artist's studio, New York, painting 55 x 30 in.*
***Installation instructions**: To be mounted in or at a corner.*
***Work provided**: Shaped painting on mylar.*
***Certificate**: Schematic drawing on paper, 11 x 8½ in., signed and numbered.*

47 Buren

Abgebildete Installationen: Nr. 47 links oben: Edition Schellmann, New York, Wand 335 x 300 cm; Nr. 47 links unten : University Art Museum, California State University, Long Beach, Wand 366 x 701 cm; Nr. 47 rechts: Edition Schellmann, München, Wand 305 x 560 cm.
Anweisungen zur Ausführung: Die emaillierten Tafeln werden so an einer Wand montiert, daß 5 Tafeln übereinander und 5 nebeneinander angeordnet sind. Die Wand muß mindestens 217,5 cm hoch sein, was dem Maß von 5 Tafeln mit je 43,5 cm Höhe, ohne Abstand übereinander plaziert, entspricht. Die Wand muß mindestens 252,3 cm breit sein, was dem Maß von 5 Tafeln mit je 43,5 cm Breite mit je einem Abstand von einer Streifenbreite (8,7 cm) entspricht.
Die Arbeit kann nicht realisiert werden, wenn die Wand kleiner ist; jede größere Wand ist geeignet. Farbe und Beschaffenheit der Wand sind unerheblich. Hat die Wand eine Tür und/oder ein Fenster an der Stelle, wo Tafeln plaziert wären, sind diese Tafeln wegzulassen. Müßten mehr als 10 Tafeln weggelassen werden, kann die Arbeit nicht ausgeführt werden.
Ist die Wand höher als das erforderliche Mindestmaß von 217,5 cm, müssen die senkrecht übereinander angeordneten Tafeln mit gleichen Abständen auf die Wand verteilt werden, wobei die oberste an der Kante zur Decke, die unterste an der Fußbodenkante installiert werden muß.
Ist die Wand breiter als das erforderliche Minimalmaß von 217,3 cm, müssen die waagerecht nebeneinander angeordneten Tafeln gleichen Distanz untereinander haben, wobei die Abstände anstatt **1** x 8,7 cm dann **3** x 8,7 cm (26,1 cm) oder **5** x 8,7 cm (43,5 cm) oder **7** x 8,7 cm (60,9 cm) usw. betragen müssen, um einen theoretisch kontinuierlichen Wechsel von weißen und farbigen Streifen zu erreichen. Die horizontale Anordnung der Tafeln beginnt an der linken Wandecke, sie endet entweder an der rechten Wandecke oder mit einem freien Abstand von max. 69,6 cm (das sind 4 Abstände von 2 Streifen) zur rechten Wandecke. Wäre der freie Abstand zur rechten Wandecke größer als 69,6 cm, müßten die horizontalen Abstände der fünf Tafeln untereinander in Schritten von je zwei Streifen vergrößert werden.

Gelieferte Bestandteile: 25 emaillierte Stahlplatten 43, 5 x 43,5 cm; Schrauben.
Zertifikat: Text auf Papier, 21 x 29,7 cm, signiert und numeriert.

***Installations illustrated**: no. 47 top left: Edition Schellmann, Cologne, wall 157 x 346 in.; no. 47 bottom left: University Art Museum, California State University, Long Beach; wall 144 x 276 in.; no. 47 right: Edition Schellmann, Munich, wall 120 x 220 in.*
***Installation instructions**: "The enamelled elements are to be mounted an a wall, five elements in vertical, and five elements in horizontal order. The wall must be at least 217,5 cm high, which is equivalent to five of the elements, 43,5 cm high ea., stacked on top of each other with no space in between. The wall must be at least 252,3 cm wide, which is equivalent to five elements 43,5 cm ea. wide, plus four spaces of one stripe, 8,7 cm ea., between each element.*
The piece cannot be installed on a wall of a smaller size. Any larger size will work. The color and texture of the wall don't matter. If a wall has a door or a window at a place where elements are supposed to be installed, these elements must be left out. A maximum of 10 elements can be left out without changing the spirit of the work. If more elements must be left out, the piece cannot be installed.
If the wall is higher than the minimum required, the vertically installed elements must have equal spacing between them, the uppermost element touching the ceiling, the bottom element touching the floor.
*If the wall is wider than the minimum required, the horizontally installed elements will have equal spacing between them, the distances instead of being **1** x 8,7 cm must be **3** x 8,7 cm (26,1 cm) or **5** x 8,7 cm (43,5 cm) or **7** x 8,7 cm (60,9 cm), etc. This way there is virtually a continuous alternation of white and color stripes. The horizontal installation of the elements must begin at the left edge of the wall, it must end with either no space or an empty space not wider than 69,6 cm, the horizontal spacing of the five elements must be expanded in paths of two stripes each."*
***Components provided**: 25 pieces of enamelled steel, 43,5 x 43,5 cm, and screws for installation.*
***Certificate**: Printing on paper, 8 x 11¾ in., signed and numbered.*

96-97 Flavin

Abgebildete Installationen: Atelier des Künstlers, New York.
Anweisungen zur Ausführung: In Augenhöhe auf eine Wand zu montieren, Kabel sichtbar, links.
Gelieferte Bestandteile: Montierte Leuchtstoffröhrenkörper mit 2 Sätzen Röhren, in spezieller Transportkiste.
Zertifikat: Schreibmaschinentext und Skizze auf Papier, 28 x 21,6 cm, signiert und numeriert.

***Installations illustrated**: The artist's studio, New York.*
***Installation instructions**: Light fixtures to be installed on a wall at eye level, electric cord hanging to the left.*
***Components provided**: Electrical fixtures with 2 sets of bulbs, in a special wooden crate.*
***Certificate**: Typewriter text with diagram on paper, 11 x 8½ in., signed and numbered.*

105 Förg

Abgebildete Installation: Edition Schellmann, München, Wand 305 x 525 cm.
Anweisungen zur Ausführung laut Zertifikat: Auszuführen auf einer Wand, deren Proportionen etwa der auf der Gouache abgebildeten Wand entsprechen. Die Wand ist vertikal von der Decke bis zum Fußboden in zwei gleiche Teile zu unterteilen. Die ganze Wand ist weiß zu streichen, dann die rechte Hälfte gelb. Befindet sich auf der Wand eine Tür [oder ein Fenster], ist diese weiß zu streichen.
Gelieferte Bestandteile: Temperafarbe Pelikan Plaka II, gelb, auf Anfrage.
Zertifikat: Gouache und Bleistift auf Büttenpapier, rückseitig Text, 57 x 76 cm, signiert und numeriert.

***Installation illustrated**: Edition Schellmann, Munich, wall 120 x 207 in.*
***Installation instructions** as given in the certificate: "To be installed on a wall with proportions similar*

to the gouache diagram. The wall is devided vertically from floor to ceiling into two equal parts. The whole wall is painted white, then the right half is painted yellow. If there is a door [or window] in the wall, it must be painted white."
***Components provided**: Paint Pelikan Plaka II, yellow, upon request.*
***Certificate**: Gouache and pencil on rag paper, with text printed on verso, 22½ x 30 in., signed and numbered.*

112 Gilbert & George

Abgebildete Installationen: Nr. 112 links: University Art Museum, California State University, Long Beach; Nr. 112 rechts: Edition Schellmann, Köln.
Anweisungen zur Ausführung: Direkt auf die Wand zu kleben.
Gelieferte Bestandteile: Vierteiliges Plakat, gedruckt auf Citychrom Plakatpapier 135g, je 108 x 135 cm. Für eventuell erforderliche Neuinstallierungen können weitere Exemplare des Plakates angefordert werden.
Zertifikat: 1 zusätzliches signiertes und numeriertes Exemplar des Plakats.

***Installations illustrated**: no. 112 left: University Art Museum, California State University, Long Beach; no. 112 right: Edition Schellmann, Cologne.*
***Installation instructions**: To be posted on a wall.*
***Components provided**: Four-part offset poster, printed on Citychrom billboard paper 135 g, 42½ x 53 in. each part. In case of re-installation, extra unsigned poster copies are available upon request.*
***Certificate**: 1 additional signed and numbered set of the posters.*

118 Grünfeld

Abgebildete Installation: Atelier des Künstlers, Köln, Wand 360 x 392 cm.
Anweisungen zur Ausführung: "Unterkante Objekt 100 cm vom Boden. Mittig auf durchgehende Wand. Bei Unterbrechung (Tür, Fenster) mittig auf verbleibende durchgehende Wand. Wandfarbe jeweils auf komplette Wand."
Gelieferte Bestandteile: Objekt, 97,5 x 210 x 35 cm; vier verschiedene Wandfarben.
Zertifikat: Computerausdruck mit Skizze und Text, aufmontierte Ledermuster, 30 x 42 cm, signiert und numeriert.

***Installation illustrated**: The artist's studio, Cologne, wall 142 x 154 in.*
***Installation instructions** as given in the certificate: "Base line object 100 cm from floor, Centered on continuous wall. With interruption (door, window) centered on remaining continuous wall. Wall paint in any case on complete wall."*
***Components provided**: Wooden object, 38½ x 82 ¾ x 13 ¾ in.; four different colors of wall paint.*
***Certificate**: Computer printout diagram and text, with collage of leather samples, 12 x 16½ in., signed and numbered.*

120 Halley

Abgebildete Installation: Edition Schellmann, Köln, Wand (graue bemalte Fläche) 400 x 440 cm.
Anweisungen zur Ausführung der Wandzeichnung: Nach den gelieferten schematischen Skizzen und Farbmustern in Siebdruck (Flächen gemalt) auf eine Wand aufzubringen. Die Wand soll mindestens 275 cm hoch und 485 cm lang sein; ist sie größer oder kleiner, kann die Zeichnung mit individueller Zustimmung des Künstlers anders angeordnet werden.
Gelieferte Bestandteile: Keine. Hilfsmittel: Filme oder Siebe, 5 Farbproben.
Zertifikat: 4 Computer-Farbausdrucke, 21,5 x 28 cm, auf einem signiert und numeriert.

***Installation illustrated**: Edition Schellmann, Cologne, wall (grey painted part) 158 x 173 in.*

__Installation instructions__ for wall drawing: To be silkscreened and painted on a wall according to the artist's diagrams and color samples. Wall should be at least 9 feet wide. If the chosen wall is smaller or larger, a layout variation can be made, subject to the artist's approval.
***Components provided**: None. Tools provided: Acetates or screens, 5 color samples.*
***Certificate**: Four laser prints, 8½ x 11 in., signed and numbered on one of them.*

139 Hirst

Abgebildete Installationen: Nr. 139 links: University Art Museum, California State University, Long Beach, Malerei 254 x 381 cm.; Nr. 139 rechts: Atelier des Künstlers, London, Malerei 193 x 294,5 cm.
Anweisungen zur Ausführung laut Zertifikat: Größe variabel entsprechend der vorhandenen Wand. Anordnung: 15 Kreise horizontal, 10 Kreise vertikal. Alle Kreise gleich groß. Der Abstand der Kreise untereinander ist gleich der Größe der Kreise. Die Farbe jedes einzelnen Punktes wird nach dem Zufallsprinzip aus den 150 gelieferten Farben bestimmt.
Gelieferte Bestandteile bzw. Hilfsmittel: Holzkasten mit 150 Dosen verschiedener (Ausnahme: fünf mal schwarz) Lackfarben, 150 Pinsel, Zirkel.
Zertifikat: Druck auf Papier, 30 x 21 cm, signiert und numeriert.

***Installations illustrated**: no. 139 left: University Art Museum, California State University, Long Beach, wall painting 100 x 150 in.; no. 139 right: The artist's studio, London, wall painting 76 x 116 in.*
__Installation instruction__ as given in the certificate: "Dimensions variable, depending on the wall. 15 spots to be placed horizontally and 10 spots vertically. All the spots must be of equal size. The size of the spots is equal to the size of the gaps in between them. The spots are to be applied randomly using one of the 150 colors for each spot."
***Components and tools provided**: Wooden box containing 150 tins of enamel paint, each color different (except that there are 5 tin of black), 150 brushes, and a compass.*
***Certificate**: Printing on paper, 11¾ x 8 in., signed and numbered.*

159 Judd

Abgebildete Installation: Edition Schellmann, Köln, Wand 300 x 588 cm.
Anweisungen zur Ausführung laut Zertifikat: Nur eine Ausführung, nicht zu verändern. Nur unter der Kontrolle des Nachlasses von Donald Judd auszuführen. Zwei Vertiefungen, mittig auf einer Wand auf den Linien, die die Wand in drei gleiche Teile unterteilt. [Ist die Wand kleiner als 500 cm breit, liegen die Vertiefungen nicht auf den Drittellinien, sondern haben links, in der Mitte und rechts gleiche Abstände.] Jede Vertiefung ist 75 cm breit, 50 cm hoch, 25 cm tief. Die Wand und die Laibungen der Vertiefungen sind in Putz oder Gipskarton auszuführen und weiß zu streichen. Die Rückseite der Vertiefungen bestehen aus rotem, blauem oder grünem Plexiglas oder aus verzinktem Eisenblech. Die Oberkante der Vertiefungen ist 165 cm vom Boden.
Gelieferte Bestandteile: Je zwei Platten rotes, blaues oder grünes Plexiglas oder verzinktes Eisenblech.
Zertifikat: Text auf Papier, 29,7 x 21 cm, nachlaßsigniert und numeriert.

***Installation illustrated**: Edition Schellmann, Cologne, wall 118 x 232 in.*
__Installation instructions__ as given in the certificate: "One work only, not to be altered. To be made only under the supervision of the Donald Judd Estate. Two recesses centered, on one wall, on the lines dividing a wall into thirds [unless the wall is smaller than 500 cm (16 feet) wide, in which case the recesses must be placed equidistant]. Each recess is 75 cm long and 50 cm high x 25 cm deep. The wall and the sides of the recesses are to be made of white plaster or white plaster board. The back of the recesses are to be red or blue or green plexiglas or galvanized iron. The tops of the recesses are at 165 cm from the floor."
***Components provided**: Two sheets of red, blue or green plexiglas or galvanized iron.*
***Certificate**: Printing on paper, 11¾ x 8¼ in., signed by the estate and numbered.*

172 Knoebel

Abgebildete Installation: Atelier des Künstlers, Düsseldorf.
Anweisungen zur Ausführung: Nach geliefertem Schema an eine Wand zu malen.
Zertifikat: Malerei (Mennige) auf Karton, in gestanzter Schablone, 102 x 73 cm, sign. und num.

***Installation illustrated**: The artist's studio, Düsseldorf.*
***Installation instructions**: To be painted on a wall according to the artist's diagram.*
***Certificate**: Painting in red lead on board, in window mat, 40 x 29 in., signed and numbered.*

177 Kosuth

Abgebildete Installation: Privatwohnung, München.
Anweisungen zur Ausführung laut Zertifikat: Die Arbeit kann unter Benutzung der auf dem Photo abgebildeten Vorlage in einer der folgenden Techniken ausgeführt werden: 1. Siebdruck direkt auf die Wand, 2. Ausführung per Hand durch einen Schriftmaler genau nach der Vorlage. Das große "T" soll 10 cm Höhe haben, woraus sich eine Gesamtlänge des Textblocks von 275 cm ergibt. Die Arbeit kann in schwarz, weiß oder grau ausgeführt werden. Diese genauen Anweisungen können nicht ohne schriftliche Erlaubnis des Künstlers geändert werden.
Hilfsmittel: Film oder Sieb auf Anfrage.
Zertifikat: Photo, rückseitig Text, mit Prägestempel, 21 x 29,5 cm, signiert und numeriert.

***Installation illustrated**: Private house, Munich.*
***Installation instructions** as given in the certificate: "Using the production model depicted on the certificate photograph, the work can be produced in either of the following ways: 1. It can be silkscreened directly on the wall; 2. It can be copied by a sign painter by hand, with instructions to follow closely the example. The capital letter "T" should measure 10 cm high. This will make the length of the work 275 cm. The work can be produced in black, white or grey. These specific production instructions cannot be altered without the written permission of the artist."*
***Tools provided** upon request: Acetate or screen.*
***Certificate**: Photostat, with text on the verso, embossed, 8½ x 11½ in., signed and numbered.*

183 Kounellis

Abgebildete Installation: Edition Schellmann, Köln, Wand 400 x 440 cm.
Anweisungen zur Ausführung: Zwei Doppel-T-Träger aus Stahl, Querschnitt 12 x 6 cm, entsprechend der Länge der Wand zuschneiden, sodaß die beiden äußeren Schuhe 8 cm Abstand von den Wandecken, die beiden inneren 4 cm Abstand voneinander haben. Die Träger sind auf 160 cm Unterkante vom Boden zu montieren. Die Schuhe stecken etwa zur Hälfte verdeckt in den Trägern.
Gelieferte Bestandteile: Zwei Paar schwarze Schuhe; die Träger sind vor Ort zu besorgen und auf Maß zu schneiden.
Zertifikat: Druck auf Papier, 29,7 x 42 cm, signiert und numeriert.

***Installation illustrated**: Edition Schellmann, Cologne, wall 158 x 173 in.*
***Installation instructions**: Two steel I -Beams (cross section 5 x 2½ in.) cut to size according to a given wall: When installed, the very left and the very right shoes are to be 3 in. distant from the edges of the wall, the two inner shoes are to be 1½ in. distant from each other. The height of the beams is 63 in. from the floor to the bottom of the beam. Half of each shoe is to be hidden in the beam.*
***Components provided**: Two pairs of black shoes; I-Beams to be purchased and cut to size at the site of installation.*
***Certificate**: Printing on paper, 11¾ x 16½ in., signed and numbered.*

194 LeWitt

Abgebildete Installationen: Nr. 194 links: Ausstellungsraum Edition Schellmann, München, Wand 350 x 260 cm; Nr. 194 rechts: Edition Schellmann, Köln, Wand 300 x 400 cm.
Anweisungen zur Ausführung laut Künstler: Der Besitzer schreibt die Worte "Wall Drawing" eigenhändig in Technik und Größe seiner Wahl auf eine Wand seiner Wahl.
Zertifikat: Der Besitzer schickt ein Photo (schwarz/weiß, ca. 18 x 24 cm) seiner Wandzeichnung an den Künstler, der das Photo signiert und numeriert zurückschickt.

Installations illustrated: *no. 194 left: Exhibition space, Edition Schellmann, Munich, wall 138 x 102 in.; no. 194 right: Edition Schellmann, Cologne, wall 118 x 158 in.*
Installation instructions *as given by the artist: "The owner will write the words 'Wall Drawing' in his own hand on any wall of choice, in any medium of his choice, in any size of his choice."*
Certificate: *An 8 x 10 in. black white photograph of the installation must be sent by the owner to the artist, who will sign, number and return it.*

224 Merz

Abgebildete Installation: Edition Schellmann, Köln, Wandmalerei 150 x 440 cm.
Anweisungen zur Ausführung laut Zertifikat: "Wandmalerei (Pigment kobaltgrün), Höhe: 150 cm, Breite: gesamte Länge der vorhandenen Wand, Position: Mitte Wand. Edelstahl horizontal und vertikal auf Mitte Wandmalerei."
Gelieferte Bestandteile: Edelstahlstab mit Halterungen, 250 x 10 x 10 cm. Farbmuster kobaltgrün.
Zertifikat: Photokopie mit Text, 21 x 29,7 cm, signiert und numeriert.

Installation illustrated: *Edition Schellmann, Cologne, wall painting 59 x 173 in.*
Installation instructions *as given in the certificate: Wall painting to be executed in pigment cobalt green, height 59 in., width to the length of the wall, centered on the wall. Stainless steel element vertically and horizontally centered on the wall painting.*
Components provided: *Stainless steel piece with hanging brackets, 98½ x 4 x 4 in.; color sample of paint.*
Certificate: *Photocopy with instructions, 8 x 11¾ in., signed and numbered.*

245 Paolini

Abgebildete Installation: Edition Schellmann, Köln.
Anweisungen zur Ausführung: Beide Teile sind mit einem Abstand von 35 cm gegen eine Wand aufzustellen.
Gelieferte Bestandteile: Zwei halbe Gipsbüsten, je 40 x 20 x 10 cm; zwei halbe Podeste aus weiß gestrichenem Holz, je 130 x 27 x 15 cm.
Zertifikat: Bleistiftzeichnung mit aufmontiertem Photo, 50 x 65 cm, signiert und numeriert.

Installation illustrated: *Edition Schellmann, Cologne.*
Installation instructions: *Pieces to be placed against a wall with a 13¾ in. space between them.*
Components provided: *Two halves of a plaster bust, 15¾ x 8 x 4 in. ea.; two halves of a wooden pedestal, painted white, 51 x 10½ x 6 cm. ea.*
Certificate: *Drawing in pencil with collaged photograph, 19¾ x 25½ in., signed and numbered.*

275 Rückriem

Abgebildete Installation: Ausstellungsraum Edition Schellmann, München.
Anweisungen zur Ausführung: Stein gegen eine Wand aufzustellen.
Gelieferte Arbeit: Granit, zweiteilig, 120 x 60 x 30 cm.
Zertifikat: Photokopie, 21 x 29,7 cm, signiert und numeriert.